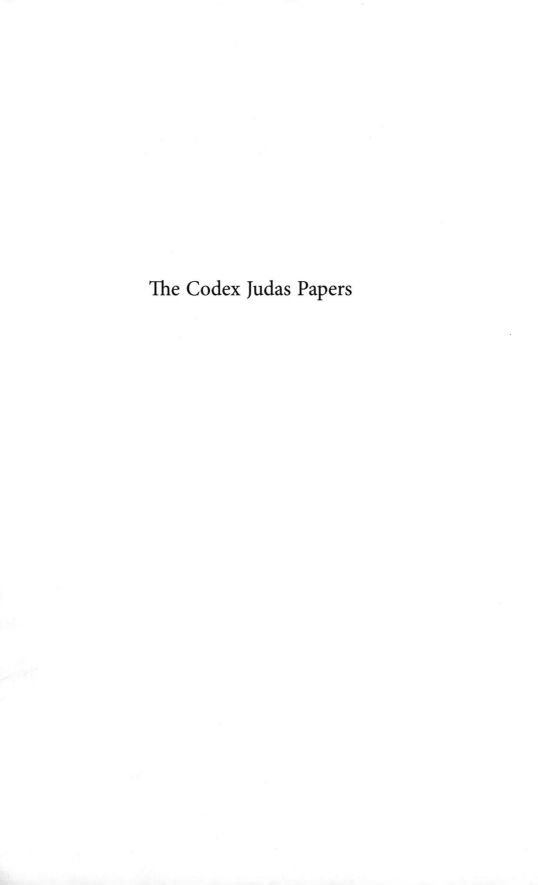

The Codex Judas Papers

Nag Hammadi and Manichaean Studies

VOLUME 71

The Codex Judas Papers

Proceedings of the International Congress on
the Tchacos Codex held at Rice University,
Houston, Texas, March 13–16, 2008

Edited by

April D. DeConick

BRILL

LEIDEN • BOSTON
2009

This book is printed on acid-free paper.

Library of Congress Cataloging-in-Publication Data

International Congress on the Tchacos Codex (2008 : Houston, Tex.)
   The Codex Judas papers : proceedings of the International Congress on
the Tchacos Codex held at Rice University, Houston, Texas, March 13–16,
2008 / edited by April D. DeConick.
     p. cm. — (Nag Hammadi and Manichaean studies, ISSN 0929-2470 ;
v. 71)
   Includes bibliographical references and index.
   ISBN 978-90-04-18141-0 (hardback : alk. paper) 1. Gospel of Judas—Criticism,
interpretation, etc.—Congresses. 2. Codex Tchacos—Criticism, interpretation, etc.—
Congresses. I. De Conick, April D. II. Title.

   BS2860.J832I59 2008
   229'.8—dc22

                                                            2009043367

ISSN 0929-2470
ISBN 978 90 04 18141 0

Copyright 2009 by Koninklijke Brill NV, Leiden, The Netherlands.
Koninklijke Brill NV incorporates the imprints Brill, Hotei Publishing,
IDC Publishers, Martinus Nijhoff Publishers and VSP.

PRINTED IN THE NETHERLANDS

in memoriam

Antoine Guillaumont (1915–2000)
Hans-Martin Schenke (1929–2002)
Gilles Quispel (1916–2006)
Jean Doresse (1917–2007)
David M. Scholer (1938–2008)
Søren Giversen (1928–2009)

CONTENTS

IDENTITY AND COMMUNITY

PORTRAITS OF JUDAS

ASTROLOGICAL LORE

SALVATION AND PRAXIS

TEXT AND INTERTEXT

MANUSCRIPT MATTERS

THE CODEX JUDAS CONGRESS AND ITS PROCEEDINGS

April D. DeConick

The Codex Judas Papers contains the proceedings from the first international conference held to discuss the newly-restored Tchacos Codex. The *Codex Judas Congress* was convened on March 13–16, 2008, on the campus of Rice University in Houston, Texas. The Congress was sponsored by a generous grant from the Faculty Initiative Fund established by the President's Office at Rice University. This fund supports adventurous faculty projects which promise to result in research breakthroughs and innovations. Given that the Tchacos Codex is a newly-conserved ancient book of Christian manuscripts which had yet to be discussed collaboratively by a body of scholars, the research conducted and published within this book by the members of the *Codex Judas Congress* is nothing less than a landmark in Gnostic studies.

The Restoration and Initial Interpretations of the Tchacos Codex

The Tchacos Codex is a fourth-century Coptic book that contains several early Christian texts similar to those from the Nag Hammadi collection. At this time, sixty-six pages and 293 tiny unplaced fragments of the original book have been conserved by Rudolphe Kasser, Gregor Wurst, and François Gaudard.[1] A large portion of this Codex is outstanding, some of which is housed in Ohio and inaccessible to the academic community at present. Fifty of the Ohio fragments have been photographed, although these have not been released to the scholarly community yet. Among these fragments is one that shows page number 108, evidence that this Codex contained additional pages, more than what have been recovered and conserved so far.[2] The texts that have been conserved include the *Letter of Peter to Philip* (TC 1–9), *James* (TC 10–30), the *Gospel of Judas* (TC 33–58), and a revelation

---

[1] Kasser et al. 2007.
[2] Kasser et al. 2007, 28.

to *Allogenes* (TC 59–66). The first two texts are variant copies of two texts found in the Nag Hammadi collection: the *Letter of Peter to Philip* NHC VIII,2 and the *First Apocalypse of James* NHC V,3. *Allogenes* TC does not appear to be the same text as *Allogenes* NHC XI,3, thus I am suggesting that we designate it the *Revelation of Allogenes* to distinguish it from the book of *Allogenes* from Nag Hammadi. Jean-Pierre Mahé has identified Ohio fragment 4578 as deriving from *Corpus Hermeticum* 13.2, and this has made the identification of Ohio fragment 4579 possible. It derives from *Corpus Hermeticum* 13.1.[3] Based on these identifications, it is likely that the Tchacos Codex contained at least one Hermetic tractate.

The Tchacos Codex has a difficult history to uncover, and much of it remains mysterious as the journalist Herbert Krosney relates in his book.[4] The recovery of this Codex first was announced by Rodolphe Kasser to the academic community on July 1, 2004, during a session at the Eighth Congress of the International Association for Coptic Studies which was held in Paris. Access to the Codex, however, was restricted to a small team of scholars that the National Geographic Society had put into place to restore the manuscript. It was two years later on April 6, 2006, that a provisional Coptic transcription of the most famous text in the Tchacos Codex, the *Gospel of Judas* was released on National Geographic's website.[5] The same day, the first English translation and popular commentary, which was authored by Rodolphe Kasser, Marvin Meyer, and Gregor Wurst, was published by the National Geographic Society.[6] Photographs of the Codex (reduced by more than 50% in size) and transcriptions of the other books in the Codex were published in the summer of 2007 by the National Geographic Society.[7]

The idea to hold an international conference to discuss the Tchacos Codex came to me at the end of April, 2006, soon after the initial release of the *Gospel of Judas* to the public. The knowledge that we actually possessed a copy of the notorious *Gospel of Judas* mentioned by Irenaeus and Epiphanius, and that other Coptic texts in the Codex were promised to be released in due time, was so thrilling that I could

---

[3] Kasser et al. 2007, 29–30.
[4] Krosney 2006.
[5] Kasser-Wurst 2006.
[6] Kasser et al. 2006a.
[7] Kasser et al. 2007.

hardly contain my excitement. So I began a series of correspondences with a number of Coptic and Gnostic experts around the world to see if they would be interested in participating in an international conference devoted to the Tchacos Codex. My top priority was to create a "gnostic think-tank" in which a significant number of the world's experts could meet face-to-face to work through these newly-restored texts together, exchanging ideas, collaborating, and constructing academic opinions about them. The response was overwhelming. The original twenty scholars whom I invited wanted to come. Because the contents of the entire restored Codex had yet to be released, I set the date for the conference two years off, hoping that this would give enough time for scholars to prepare presentations once the photographs and the rest of the contents were released to us.

What I didn't know in these initial stages of planning was how important this Congress would become to our academic community, which soon found itself in turmoil over the *Gospel of Judas*. The first indication that controversy was on the horizon struck me when I attended the international conference on the *Gospel of Judas* convened at the Sorbonne by Madeleine Scopello on October 26–27, 2006. The proceedings have been edited and published by Madeleine Scopello.[8] Louis Painchaud, John Turner, and I delivered papers in which we raised serious questions about the transcription, translation and interpretation of the *Gospel of Judas* that had been released by National Geographic and that was taken up by a number of books initially published.[9] Working independently of each other, we all had come to very similar conclusions that Judas was not a hero, but a villain associated with the creator god whose sacrifice of Jesus was being used by the author as a polemic against conventional Christianity. Stephen Emmel's paper had a similar orientation: "I agree with those who interpret the *Gospel of Judas* 56,17–21 in this way, namely that when Jesus says to Judas, 'You will surpass them all, for you will sacrifice the man that bears me,' he is predicting that Judas will do the *worst* thing of all (not something best of all), namely that he will betray Jesus

---

[8] Scopello 2008.
[9] Painchaud in Scopello 2008, 171–186; Turner in Scopello 2008, 187–237; DeConick in Scopello 2008, 239–264. Regarding some of these initial publications, see Wright 2006a; Ehrman 2006b. For slightly later publications, see Pagels-King 2007; Gathercole 2007a.

and thus bring about his (sacrificial) death."[10] During that meeting, I learned that Louis Painchaud had just spoken publicly about this issue at the University of Ottawa on September 30, 2006, at the colloquium "Christian Apocryphal Texts for the New Millenium." That paper was later published in *Laval Théologique et Philosophique*.[11] I also learned that Einar Thomassen had delivered a paper on November 10, 2006, at the University of Illinois in Chicago in which he seriously questioned whether the *Gospel of Judas* rehabilitated Judas. His paper was included in the Sorbonne volume published by Madeleine Scopello.[12]

The following year I published a trade book that discussed the problem and offered an alternative English translation and interpretation of the *Gospel of Judas*.[13] During the 2007 Society of Biblical Literature Annual Convention held in November, Birger Pearson came out with his own analysis of the Gospel in which he also argued that the text had been misunderstood by those of his colleagues who had initially published on it: Judas was not hero but a demon.[14] It was at this meeting that I learned of Gesine Schenke Robinson's analysis of the Gospel which was along the same order and which has since been published in the *Journal of Coptic Studies*.[15] I also became aware of the German commentary of the Tchacos Codex edited by Johanna Brankaer and Hans-Gebhard Bethge, a book also released at the convention.[16] These scholars too had called into question the initial interpretation of the Gospel made by the National Geographic team and understood the Gospel in terms of its polemic and Judas in terms of his connections to Saklas.

Since the National Geographic Society had made the *Gospel of Judas* and its hero a topic of household conversation through a strong media campaign the year before, I decided to publish a short Op. Ed. in the *New York Times* on December 1, 2007 to raise public awareness about the emerging critique and questions that were being generated by a number of scholars, and to highlight the need for the distribution of

---

[10] Emmel in Scopello 2008, 36.
[11] Painchaud 2006.
[12] Scopello 2008, 157–170.
[13] DeConick 2007.
[14] Pearson 2007a.
[15] Schenke Robinson 2008a.
[16] Brankaer-Bethge 2007.

high-resolution photographs to help resolve some of these issues.[17] The National Geographic Society responded with a press release of its own.[18] Marvin Meyer posted a web paper nuancing his position.[19] Amidst this controversy in January 2008, the National Geographic Society uploaded to its website a set of high-resolution photographs of each of the sixty-six pages of the Tchacos Codex for use within the scholarly community.[20] We are very grateful to Society for these photographs, since they provide us with the means to examine the manuscript.

THE CODEX JUDAS CONGRESS

Two months later, the *Codex Judas Congress* convened. Given the turmoil and questions of the previous months, the Congress served as a positive platform for all of us to gather together around a single table and talk through the textual and hermeneutical issues facing us with this new Codex. The members of the Congress covered a great deal of territory.

Identity and Community

The self-identity and communal affiliation of the Tchacos texts as a collection was taken up by two scholars. ALASTAIR LOGAN (Senior Lecturer, University of Exeter) examined the Tchacos Codex as a book, pursuing the question, "Whose book was it?" He thinks that this book is the product of a persecuted third century Sethian Gnostic community living in the vicinity of Oxyrhynchus. This suggests that there was a Gnostic community in Middle Egypt at this time which began to translate its Greek texts into Coptic late in the third century. This community self-identified as Christian and was struggling with problems of suffering and persecution. He thinks that such an identity predates the growth of coenobitic monasticism, so the book was not collected or copied by monks (a point, he thinks, substantially weakens

---

[17] Available from < http://www.nytimes.com/2007/12/01/opinion/01deconink.html? ex=1354251600&en=91c478a2d5fb0116&ei=5124&partner=permalink&exprod=perm alink>.

[18] Available from <http://press.nationalgeographic.com/pressroom/index.jsp?page ID=pressReleases_detail&siteID=1&cid=1196944434958>.

[19] Meyer 2008a.

[20] Available at <ftp://ftp10.nationalgeographic.com/>.

such a claim for the Nag Hammadi Codices). He closes by suggesting that the Tchacos Codex may have been known to the group that was responsible for collecting and copying the core collection of the Nag Hammadi Codices. KAREN KING (Professor, Harvard University) found that the extant works of the Tchacos Codex showcase alternative ways in which Christians were struggling with violence and assigning meaning to the deaths of Jesus and themselves. The three extant texts of the Codex are concerned with violence, persecution and death. The authors of these texts appear to have been frightened and enraged at the Romans and at each other. The stories they tell in this book served to help them overcome their fear and face the uncertainty of future violence and death. Thus the Tchacos Codex offered its readers what King calls "preparation for martyrdom," showing believers how they ought to prepare for suffering and death in the face of persecution through different strategies.

Issues of identity and community with regard to the *Gospel of Judas* were addressed by a number of Congress members. Two scholars argued that the Gospel was produced in the second century. JOHANNES VAN OORT (Professor, Universities of Utrecht, Nijmegen, and Pretoria) focused his attention on Irenaeus' testimony of the *Gospel of Judas*, offering a detailed linguistic analysis and retranslation of *Against the Heresies* 1.31.1. His philological commentary and textual analysis has led him to conclude that Irenaeus, in all probability, had first-hand knowledge of the Gospel and its contents. Irenaeus appears to have read the text and he summarizes it in his treatise. The Gospel was produced by a group of second-century Gnostics who venerated Judas as a fellow Gnostic in the same way that they positively venerated Cain. They taught a myth that discussed the redeeming activity of Sophia as well as the negative characteristics of the creator god in contrast to the superior God. This group became known as the Cainites in later tradition. MARVIN MEYER (Professor, Chapman University) argued that the *Gospel of Judas* likely represents a second-century form of Sethian Gnosis whose basic mythological foundation was Hellenistic Jewish material. This material was marginally Christianized in ways very similar to other Sethian texts like the *Apocryphon of John* and the *Sophia of Jesus Christ*. The Hellenistic Jewish material was set in a framework of Gnostic spirituality. This group identified itself with the exalted generation of Seth, and is extremely critical of all forms of Christianity that have anything to do with sacrifice, whether it be Jesus' death, the eucharist celebration, or martyrdom. Meyer concludes by comparing the mythological figure, (Pistis) Sophia with Judas and suggests that Judas is neither a totally positive figure nor a demonic figure in the *Gospel of Judas*. Rather he is caught like (Pistis) Sophia in this world of mortality, while striving for gnosis and enlightenment.

A third century date was posited by two other scholars. GESINE SCHENKE ROBINSON (Professor, Episcopal School of Theology and Claremont School of Theology) discussed the relationship between the *Gospel of Judas* and its implied audience by making an analysis of the text's composition history. From this analysis, she concludes that the Gospel in its present form is a late and distant offshoot of Sethianism. The Gospel we have is likely a later neo-Sethian version of whatever Irenaeus knew in the second century, revised as a polemic against the conventional Christian churches and their leaders in order to deal with the violence the community was experiencing at their hands. JOHN D. TURNER (Professor, University of Nebraska) made a detailed comparison between the myth in the Gospel and other Sethian narratives. He highlights the oddities of the Gospel's system, including the point that the Gospel has no soteriological narrative. He argues that the purpose of the cosmological section is not soteriological but demonological, serving to explain Judas' role as the thirteenth daemon until the apocalyptic end. Furthermore, his comparison leads him to conclude that the composition of the Gospel took place in the early third century at a time with the Sethians were making a break from Christian tradition and were becoming immersed in pagan Platonism.

Portraits of Judas

Several scholars examined the character of Judas in the *Gospel of Judas*, offering alternative views about the meaning of his elevation above the other disciples. BIRGER PEARSON (Professor, University of California, Santa Barbara) approached Judas as the thirteenth demon, a number which associates him with the world-creator. Pearson makes a distinction between the immortal generation and the kingdom, arguing forcefully that the kingdom in this Gospel refers to the cosmic kingdom and cannot be equated with the eternal generation without a king. He points out that the act of sacrifice according to this Gospel is a negative action, including Judas' sacrifice of Jesus. Likewise, his star is errant. This leads Pearson to conclude that the *Judas* is "an ironic literary caricature of a gospel." FERNANDO BERMEJO RUBIO (Lecturer, University of Barcelona) found that the text represents the kind of irony implicit in

a *reductio ad absurdum* argument. He comes to this position by analyzing Jesus' laughter. Bermejo Rubio finds that Jesus' laughter occurs
in ominous contexts, linking it with damnation and destruction. This
disparaging laughter is mockery deriving from Jesus' awareness that it
is not possible for those who belong to the demiurge and his sphere to
reach the ontological level of Jesus himself. This laughter reflects the
type of laughter attributed to God (in certain biblical psalms and proverbs), a laughter which is the result of God's defeat of his adversaries
and their damnation. In order to explain the text's ambiguous characterization of Judas as the damned but still the one singled out to receive
a revelation, Bermejo Rubio wonders whether or not *Judas* ought to be
read as a *reductio ad absurdum*. He concludes that the author of *Judas*
was arguing that the sacrificial theory of the conventional Church was
logically inconsistent with Judas' own canonical story.

KEVIN SULLIVAN (Assistant Professor, Illinois Wesleyan University)
approached the text from a narratological perspective, inquiring when
Judas becomes the thirteenth demon. The Gospel is about Judas coming to grips with his true dark identity as the thirteenth demon and the
role that comes with this identity, namely that Judas will sacrifice Jesus.
When Judas "becomes" the thirteenth, he will be cursed and he will
rule over his cursers. Sullivan identifies this moment with a transfigu-
ration-like event, when Judas (not Jesus) enters the cloud at the end of
the Gospel. The author chose to parody the canonical Transfiguration
story in this way because he was criticizing the orthodox tradition
which directly links Jesus with the god the Gnostics knew to be the
lesser one. It is Judas who is connected to this god, not Jesus.

Two scholars provided analyses of Judas' character that emphasized a medial position. ISMO DUNDERBERG (Professor, University
of Helsinki) wanted to know how Judas could be described as "the
perfect human" while also being characterized as irascible. The solution for him lies in ancient moral philosophy where the concept of
"the perfect human" was widely discussed as the ultimate (but rarely
achieved) goal of moral progress. Certain philosophers recognized
several lower steps on the morality ladder. Judas' anger disqualifies
him from belonging to the uppermost group of perfect humans. So he
is likely positioned among those who have taken some initial steps in
virtue training but who still succumb to grave passions like anger. This
analysis, Dunderberg says, suggests that the character of Judas ought
not to be framed in either-or categories such as "good" or "bad." In
fact, Judas' elevation to the highest cosmic level as ruler over the gen-

erations that cursed him, plays with the theme found in Jewish tradition that the vindication of the righteous amounts to a reversal in their present suffering. At the end of times, they will become the judges of their oppressors. PIERLUIGI PIOVANELLI (Professor, University of Ottawa) was interested in making a comparative analysis between *Judas* and apocryphal stories that circulated in late antiquity about Judas' role in the Passion. Piovanelli argues that sympathetic versions of the Passion were circulating in Jewish circles as early as the second century where Judas was considered a wise man who knew the name of God and unmasked the evil magician Jesus, the illegitimate son of Miriam and Joseph Panderi. The Christians built their own, heavily demonized stories of Judas in response to the heroic Jewish ones as part of the ongoing controversy between the Jewish and Christian communities. The Sethian Christians who wrote the Gospel appear to be part of this controversy, arguing with other Christian communities. Their ability to cast Judas as a knowledgeable even heroic character in the narrative has more to do with their awareness of this controversy than with their identity with the hypothetical Cainites. This makes for a Judas who is not as horrible as we find in other Christian texts, a tragic victim rather than a hangman.

Astrological Lore

There was keen interest among members of the Codex Judas Congress to study astrological phenomena as they were depicted in the Tchacos texts. My own contribution (APRIL D. DECONICK, Rice University) set out to map broadly the relationship between the twelve apostles and the cosmic archons in the Tchacos Codex texts and other early Christian literature. I find that these relationships rely on a brand of Greco-Egyptian astrology known to the Hermetics that had combined Hellenistic speculations with the Egyptian decanal system. The consequential astrological correspondences between the apostles and the archons were mapped as counterpoints (positively perceived apostles replace negative stars in an opposing relationship) and counterparts (the negatively perceived apostles stand in for the negative stars in a sympathetic relationship) depending upon the text, its tradition, and its age. After mapping these relationships in the *Gospel of Judas*, Valentinian texts including the *First Apocalypse of James*, and Pistis Sophia, I conclude that individual Gnostic movements began as lodge movements supplementing the conventional synagogue and church.

Over time, the individual lodges began to define themselves as reform movements within the conventional tradition and as separatist movements opposing the conventional tradition and persecuted by them. By the late third century, with the rise of Manichaeism and Mandaeism and the creation of Gnostic handbooks such as the Books of Jeu and Pistis Sophia, a new eclectic religious movement (which we can rightly call "Gnosticism") had emerged through an intentional process of consolidation of the various individual Gnostic systems and mimicry of orthodox success.

Several scholars investigated the astrological nature of certain aspects of the *Gospel of Judas*. NICOLA DENZEY LEWIS (Lecturer, Harvard University) approached the Gospel from the perspective of Jewish apocalypticism and Jewish teachings about the nature and influence of the stars. In her contribution, she reviews the references to stars in *Judas* and compares these with similar references to stars in Jewish apocalyptic literature, concluding that the astrology in the Gospel derives from sectarian Jewish apocalyptic teachings. Denzey Lewis draws attention to the visions of the heavenly temple in Jewish apocalyptic writings, and the visions of the Temple shown to the disciples and Judas. Building from these Second Temple traditions (which in some cases include a kind of "demonizing" of the heavenly temple), the Gospel author creates a narrative in which the disciples' vision represents a corrupted "demonic" temple in the heavens, while Judas' vision corresponds with an incorrupt Temple beyond, where the immortal generation dwells. This picture serves as a scathing indictment of Judaism and conventional Christianity which the author of *Judas* sees as corrupt. GRANT ADAMSON (Doctoral Student, Rice University) made a study of the Gospel of Judas 57.15–20, examining the statement "the leading star is your star" within the perspective of ancient Greco-Egyptian and Hermetic astrology and the practice of horoscopy. His examination (which includes a comparative analysis of a horoscopic spell from *PGM* 13) leads him to see Jesus' speech as that of an ancient astrologer. Jesus teaches familiar Greco-Egyptian astrological doctrines and employs technical astrological language when he predicts the fate of Judas and the disciples. Although Judas is the recipient of private revelation, his horoscope is not good news. Jesus predicts from the stars that Judas will betray him and become the thirteenth, being replaced by another disciple after dying violently. NICLAS FÖRSTER (Research Fellow, University of Münster) focused his attention on identifying Judas' star (the star that goes ahead while ruling over the others) with a particular astrological body. Upon consideration of popular astrology in antiquity, Förster argues that Judas' star is the sun. This symbolism was used by pagan kings and Jewish rulers as a sign of royal power to legitimize their dynasty. Even Jewish messianism relied on this imagery to bolster the messianic claims of certain leaders and their disciples. In the case of *Judas*, the symbolism of the sun star was used to create a special Gnostic doctrine that placed Judas as ruler over the twelve cosmic aeons, and by association, the twelve disciples and even humanity as a whole.

The Tchacos Codex version of *James* and its association with ancient astrology was studied by FRANKLIN TRAMMELL (Doctoral Student, Rice University). He chose to explore the astrological meaning of the reference to the *polos* on p. 13 of *James,* a reference not found in the Nag Hammadi version. He argues that the author relied on an assumed relationship between the *polos* and the Zodiac, negatively identifying the twelve apostles with the twelve zodiacal powers. Implicit in this doctrine is a mythology that has equated the Hebrew god with the cosmic pole dragon whose powers were thought to make up the cosmos. The author understands Jesus' crucifixion as the binding of the dragon to the cosmic axis, while the suffering of his followers function to continually restrain the dragon's archons. This negative correlation between the apostles and the cosmic powers serves to attack the representatives of apostolic Christianity, identifying the author's apostolic opponents who appear to be persecuting his community with the ruling powers who killed Jesus and James.

Salvation and Praxis

Issues of salvation and praxis were investigated by a number of scholars. Baptism is mentioned in several of these papers, but it was the focus of the work of two scholars. ELAINE PAGELS (Professor, Princeton University) offered a holistic interpretation of the *Gospel of Judas* that considers the text's nuances, its positive and negative features, including its opening remark that Jesus came for the salvation of humanity. She thinks that the previous discussions of the *Gospel of Judas* have missed the underlying theme of the transformative power of baptism, which offered Christians the promise of rescue from damnation. She compares the teaching within the *Gospel of Judas* to baptismal teaching in other Sethian texts, suggesting that the *Gospel of Judas* is a catechistical instruction book meant to prepare initiates for baptism and polemicize against forms of baptism and eucharist that the author(s) thought inadequate. Bas van Os (Research Scholar, Amsterdam Free University) examined *Judas'* relationship to apostolic Christian sacramental practices, especially baptism. He argued against reading the text as a metaphor condemning martyrdom for several reasons, including that the text does not speak of persecution by Roman authorities. Rather the sacrifices are being offered by the disciples who represent priests within the apostolic churches. This leads Os to think that the sacrifices which are opposed by the author are the eucharist and baptism as performed within the conventional churches. Baptism, however, is the sacrament most likely being referenced in the Temple vision because humans are being sacrificed. Baptism was understood by early Christians as a form of death where their bodies were being presented as living sacrifices in Jesus' name. Van Os suggests that Judas represents Gnostic Christians who were crossing the boundaries between the Gnostic and apostolic communities. They were continuing to sacrifice while knowing the truth, so the author was accusing them of following Judas rather than Jesus.

Two papers investigated the possibility that the *Gospel of Judas* is not utterly bleak, that salvation is the point of the Gospel. Johanna Brankaer (Research Fellow, University of Jena) started her exploration with the question "whose savior?" is Jesus in a Gospel that sees no profit to Jesus' death yet states that Jesus came to save humanity. Furthermore, what are we to make of the fact that the text in other passages designates the human race as the damned? Brankaer questions the apparent determinism in the Gospel, suggesting that there are more groups than the holy ones (the Gnostics) and the human race(s) (the apostolic Christians). There is a middle group, the race of Adam, who will not be destroyed. The door of conversion and redemption has been left open to them. But they remain a "virtual" race because of the strong polemical nature of this Gospel, harshly treating conventional Christian practices like the eucharist and baptism. The persuaded readers of the Gospel belong to this virtual race. They are the ones who find themselves persuaded by the narrative to condemn a form of Christianity that they now see as a travesty of the sacrificial Temple cult. Tage Petersen (Postdoctoral Fellow, University of Copenhagen) explored the Gospel as an example of ancient philosophical dialogue. These dialogues have an epistemology which casts the interlocutor as a someone who must get rid of his false assumptions (*doxa*) through a mental collapse (*aporia*) in order to achieve a spiritual breakthrough.

Judas functions as a *religio mentis*, a text in which the reader encounters the interlocutor's *doxa*, not to confirm it, but to confront and reject it. What is the *doxa* to be rejected? The doctrines of the conventional Church including its rituals and doctrines about Jesus. Whether or not Judas ever becomes a gnostic himself by abandoning the eucharist and rejecting what the other disciples did not, Petersen thinks, cannot be known due to the fragmentary nature of the extant manuscript. The text is a gospel, however, in the sense that it would have been used by people to identify false *doxa* and reject it in favor of the real *doxa* which would lead them to salvation.

Text and Intertext

The tradition history of the *Gospel of Judas* was the subject of four Congress papers. Three of these papers focused on assessing the meaning of difficult Coptic passages in the *Gospel of Judas* through comparative intertextual analyses. LOUIS PAINCHAUD (Professor, Laval University) and SERGE CAZELAIS (Doctoral Student, Laval University) offered an alternative way to read and understand p. 46.16–17, "What is the profit?" They argue that the author of *Judas* was alluding to Ecclesiastes 6:11b–12 (LXX) since the author not only uses the same phraseology, but reflects the wider context as well, linking the concepts of human life and number of days with the question of profit. To have these words come from Judas' lips twice in the Gospel (cf. 53.8–9) is suggestive that the author intended to link Judas with Solomon, connecting him with the king and master of demons who built the Temple and its sacrificial cult with the aid of the demons. MATTEO GROSSO (Research Fellow, University of Torino) examined the opening lines p. 33.3–6, "during eight days, three days before he celebrated Passover." What is meant by this puzzling expression? Convinced that chronological references have literary and ideological functions with gospel narratives, Grosso demonstrates how the canonical gospels rely on different temporal arrangements and, through these chronologies, foster different theological agendas. He reviews the recent opinions in scholarship about how the chronological arrangement of the *Gospel of Judas* is to be conceived. Finally he offers his own reading of *Judas'* chronology. He thinks that the expression is a reference to Mark's chronology which is the only gospel that arranges the time between Jesus' entry into Jerusalem until his resurrection in an eight-day sequence. The three-days refers to a period within this eight-day sequence during which time the revelation recorded in the Gospel was thought to have taken place. Based on an exhaustive comparison with Mark, Grosso concludes that the precise time of this revelation is three days before the Passover feast, which corresponds to the fourth, fifth and sixth days in the Markan series. LANCE JENOTT (Doctoral Student, Princeton University) made a close reading of p. 45.3–9, "and that house had a roof of greenery." He thinks that the Coptic ογοτε should be understood as a variant or corrupted spelling of the feminine noun ογητε which would mean "lightning" or "fire" instead of "greenery." Such a reading would have the advantage of fitting the literary context of descriptions of the heavenly Temple in Jewish apocalyptic literature. This reading would also make contextual sense since the author of *Judas* is contrasting the corrupt earthly Temple officiated by the Twelve with the transcendent heavenly Temple seen by Judas. This contrast is employed by the author in order to criticize the glorification of martyrdom as a eucharist sacrifice which was taught by some leaders of the apostolic church.

SIMON GATHERCOLE (Lecturer, University of Cambridge) was interested in determining the whereabouts of Paradise in the *Gospel of Judas*. Relying on intertexual data, he explains that the Paradise tradition in *Judas* reads Genesis 1–2 in a "misanthropic" manner because it bifurcates the Genesis story in such a way that the non-human elements are viewed positively while the human are not. The inhabitants of Paradise are those from the enduring generation mentioned on p. 43. The house with the herb roof mentioned on p. 45 is inhabited by holy ones who are not subjects of the sun and moon. This house also is located in Paradise according to Gathercole. Since Paradise was created on the third day according to some Jewish traditions, it is not subject to the rule of the sun and the moon which were formed on the fourth day. Developing Painchaud's suggestion that the kingdom in Judas refers to the archonic world, Gathercole argues that Judas does not enter the kingdom because it is located spatially below him and is the domain of the twelve apostles and the apostolic church. He concludes that the thirteenth aeon in which Judas will come to reside is not Paradise, but a region between Paradise and the twelve, an intermediate realm between paradise and the damned.

Manuscript Matters

Issues concerning the physical manuscripts (and their variant versions) were addressed by three scholars. GREGOR WURST (Professor, University of Augsburg) provided the Congress members with several corrections to the *Critical Edition* of the Tchacos Codex. These corrections are based on his sustained study of the manuscript located at the Bodmer Library in Geneva, the published fragments and a set of older unpublished photographs which show some of the pages in better physical condition. In addition, some corrections are the result of suggestions that have been made by different colleagues. Wurst also announces in his paper the placement of four smaller fragments which he has puzzled together. On p. 55.9, the phrase "servants of Saklas" have been restored to their context. On the opposite side p. 56.11, has been reconstructed so that the saying of Jesus beginning in line 9 ought to read: "[I say] to you, '[No] hand of (a) mortal man [will...] against me.'" WOLF-PETER FUNK (Research Fellow, Laval University) made a thorough textual and philological comparison of the two extant versions of the *First Apocalypse of James*. The NH version is not as well-preserved as the TC version. So the result of Funk's analyses is a more complete understanding and restoration of the NH version (since what could be learned from the NH version had already been taken into account in the *Critical Edition* of the TC). He offers several new restorations of the NH version based on parallels in the TC *James*. He evaluates whether commonly accepted restorations of the NH version are confirmed or disconfirmed by the TC manuscript. While most are confirmed, one that has far-reaching implications is for the lacunae on V 36.3 which ought to read "seventy-two" instead of "twelve." New emendations of NHC V,3 are suggested based on the TC parallels. Finally Funk suggests solutions for four items that have caused scholars difficulty previously, including a resolution for the syntactic problem on p. 24.16–19, a correction of the meaning of ϣⲁϣⲟⲩ, an explanation of the grammatically difficult expression ⲁϥϣⲛ̄ⲧ̄ϥ̄ ⲭⲉ ⲡⲭⲟⲉⲓⲥ, and a new understanding of the word ϣⲉⲥⲓ (which, in the past, has been improperly translated "be bitter" from ϣⲓⲥⲉ). ANTTI MARJANEN (Research Fellow, University of Helsinki) also worked on the two versions of *James,* which he thinks had no direct literary connections to each other. His observations leads him to conclude that their Greek *Vorlage* was different. He reexamines the conclusions previously drawn from the NH version about the seven women. With a better preserved version of the passages about the seven women in the TC, Marjanen confirms and disconfirms various reconstructions of NHC V and their interpretations. It is confirmed that Arsinoe is one of the women. Marjanen supports the solution of Brankaer-Bethge that the third woman is "the other Mary." The TC version, however, does not help to resolve the ambiguity about the three women Sapphira, Susanna, and Joanna, although both versions appear to regard them as positive prophetic figures, suggesting at least the possibility that the Christians behind this text were battling with apostolic Christianity and relying on a form of Christianity in which women had more visible roles.

This section concludes with the presentation of JAMES M. ROBINSON (Professor, Claremont Graduate University). He highlights issues that he thinks ought to be resolved or investigated by scholars who are working on the Tchacos Codex. He wants to know where the Codex will be permanently housed and when this transfer to Egypt will be made. He asks for more information about the leather cover and the cartonnage since this analysis has not been completed yet, and so much could be learned from it. He would like to know what the original length of the book was and how many tractates it contained. He suggests that an examination of the extant quires and kollemata would give us more knowledge of the lost half of the Codex. This would also aid in the placement of some of the 293 fragments and the yet-to-be-released Ohio fragments because this can be done by the examination of the fibers. He ends his inquires with a significant question that the academic community will have to address in the future: what should we agree to name the Tchacos Codex? His questions are cautionary and advisory, pointing out how many questions remain regarding the physical Codex, and how much more work there is ahead of us.

Afterward

The *Codex Judas Congress* was a very special academic gathering that fostered a collaborative constructive examination of the Tchacos Codex. Although a variety of opinions were expressed during the conference, by the end several points of general agreement appear to me to have emerged as they are reflected in this volume of papers. First, it is most likely that the texts within the Codex were composed in Greek sometime between the mid-second century and the mid-third century. Second, the Christians who composed these texts appear to be in conflict with other Christians, conflict that they identify as persecution and/or violence. Third, the *Gospel of Judas* is a text highly critical of the apostolic Christians and the conventional church, opposing its sacrificial doctrines and related practices. Fourth, the *Gospel of Judas* does not present us with information about the historical Judas. Fifth, the characterization of Judas remains contested (positive, negative, ambiguous, and "I don't know"), although he appears to be treated less heroically than tragically in the presentations and papers of the Congress members. Sixth, as for the stars, they are not considered positive forces by the author of the *Gospel of Judas*. But how deterministic they are has yet to be determined. Seventh, the *Gospel of Judas* is connected to a movement that has classic Gnostic or Sethian affinities.

Although I cannot speak for other scholars present, the experience of collectively "think-tanking" about these Gnostic documents was nothing less than transfiguring for me. Listening to others' arguments, examining alternative solutions, and hearing new knowledge brought to the table, impacted my own opinions and, in some cases, opened up new platforms of interpretation for me. Although none of the discussions altered my own opinion that Judas is the Ialdabaoth demon in the *Gospel of Judas* and that the narrative tells the story of his tragic fate, the nuances and subtleties of the text became more focused for me. This is particularly the case regarding the use of the word "kingdom" in the *Gospel of Judas*. My previous understanding had to be modified. Over the course of the conference as I considered the arguments that were being put forth especially by Louis Painchaud, Birger Pearson, John Turner, and Simon Gathercole, I came to realize that the employment of this word, like almost everything else in this text, is not straightforward. The reason for this is that the *Gospel of Judas* is a highly polemical text. Its author employs terms customarily used by his opponents, but then turns them inside-out by way of critique. So the term "kingdom" is employed ironically by the author, implying that the apostolic Christian understanding of the term is deficient. The kingdom is not the fabulous place of spiritual habitation where Christians expect to go. The kingdom is the cosmos, and Judas the demon rules it together with the twelve apostles. What Christians think is the kingdom is really chaos and hell, and as long as they continue to unknowingly worship the lesser god sponsored by the Church, they will remain in his kingdom until their final destruction. The ultimate place of spiritual habitation and bliss, in fact, is a dwelling place that transcends the cosmos, an abode that has no kings, no rulers, no planets, and no stars.

Acknowledgments

I wish to extend my warmest gratitude to all those who made this conference a reality. Each of you helped to provide thirty scholars and ten graduate students with the opportunity to "think-tank" for three and a half days about an ancient book that may be one of the most significant early Christian manuscript "finds" of my generation.

This conference would not have been possible without the generous monetary support of Rice University in the form of a Faculty Initiative Grant; the Department of Religious Studies at Rice University; the Houston Society Archaeological Institute of America; the Boniuk Center for the Study and Advancement of Religious Tolerance; the Peachtree Planning Corporation, Rome, Georgia.

Those who worked behind the scenes to help organize the conference were Ata Anzali, Chad Day, Sylvia Louie, and Franklin Trammell. A number of people assisted as moderators for the sessions: Elias Bongmba (Rice University); David Capes (Houston Baptist University); Kelley N. Coblentz Bautch (St. Edward's University); David Cook (Rice University); Matthias Henze (Rice University); Werner Kelber (Rice University); Jeffrey Kripal (Rice University); George Nickelsburg (University of Iowa); William Parsons (Rice University); and Paula Sanders (Rice University). Several people made possible "Gnosis in Song," an afternoon of Gnostic liturgies performed at the Rothko Chapel: Becky Baxter (harpist); Sonja Bruzauskas (soloist); Alison Pruitt (operations coordinator). My graduate students assisted me in building the main bibliography of this book, creating the indices and putting the footnotes into proper style: Grant Adamson, Michael Heyes, and Franklin Trammell.

I am extremely grateful to Johannes van Oort (Universities of Utrecht, Nijmegen and Pretoria) who participated in the conference and encouraged me to bring the conference papers together into a book for the Brill series, Nag Hammadi and Manichaean Studies. He has supported the production of this book (quite literally) from the beginning, and has kindly advised me all along the way in his capacity as Editor for the series. It was a delight to work with Wilma de Weert who labored patiently and carefully in the expedient production of this volume.

This conference was a wonderful expression of collegiality and academic rigor. Its proceedings represent an inaugural study of the Tchacos Codex and ancient Gnostic writings. The wisdom and knowledge found in these chapters in many ways is accumulated wisdom and knowledge, dependent on the work of our predecessors. Because of this, *The Codex Judas Papers* is dedicated to the memory of a number of scholars who devoted significant portions of their careers to the study of the Nag Hammadi literature, but who departed this life just as the Tchacos Codex was coming to light.

April D. DeConick
Good Friday, April 10, 2009

Codex Judas Congress
March 13-16, 2008
Rice University, Houston, Texas

ABBREVIATIONS

AGJU	Arbeiten zur Geschichte des antiken Judentums und des Urchristentums
ANRW	*Aufstieg und Niedergang der römischen Welt.* Edited by H. Temporini and W. Haase. Berlin, 1972–
ANF	*Ante-Nicene Fathers*
ARC	The Journal of the Faculty of Religious Studies, McGill University
BCNH	Bibliothèque Copte de Nag Hammadi
BIFAO	*Bulletin de l'Institut français d'archéologie orientale*
BZNW	Beihefte zur Zeitschrift für die neutestamentliche Wissenschaft
CCL	Corpus Christianorum: Series Latina. Turnhout, 1953–
DACL	*Dictionnaire d'archéologie chrétienne et de liturgie.* Edited by F. Cabrol. 15 vols. Paris, 1907–1953
EdF	Erträge der Forschung
EPRO	Etudes préliminaries aux religions orientales dans l'empire romain
ExpTim	*Expository Times*
GCS	Die griechischen christlichen Schriftsteller der ersten [drei] Jahrhunderte
HTR	*Harvard Theological Review*
JAC	*Journal of Ancient Civilizations*
JAOS	*Journal of the American Oriental Society*
JBL	*Journal of Biblical Literature*
JRAS	*Journal of Royal Asiatic Society*
JSJ	*Journal for the Study of Judaism in the Persian, Hellenistic, and Roman Periods*
JSNT	*Journal for the Study of the New Testament*
JSP	*Journal for the Study of the Pseudepigrapha*
JTS	*Journal of Theological Studies*
KEK	Kritisch-exegetischer Kommentar über das Neue Testament
LCL	Loeb Classical Library
LNTS	Library of New Testament Studies
LSTS	Library of Second Temple Studies

MBPF	Münchener Beiträge zur Papyrusforschung und antiken Rechtsgeschichte
MdB	Le Monde de la Bible
NEAEHL	*The New Encyclopedia of Archaeological Excavations in the Holy Land.* Edited by E. Stern. 4 vols. Jerusalem, 1993.
NHMS	Nag Hammadi and Manichaean Studies
NHS	Nag Hammadi Studies
NIGTC	New International Greek Testament Commentary
NovT	*Novum Testamentum*
NTOA	Novum Testamentum et Orbis Antiquus
NTS	*New Testament Studies*
RAC	*Reallexikon für Antike und Christentum.* Edited by T. Klauser et al. Stuttgart, 1950–
RSém	*Revue de sémitique*
RSR	*Recherches de science religieuse*
SC	Sources chrétiennes. Paris: Cerf, 1943–
StPat	*Studia patavina*
TC	Tchacos Codex
TLZ	*Theologische Literaturzeitung*
TSAJ	Texte und Studien zum antiken Judentum
TU	Texte und Untersuchungen
VC	*Vigiliae christianae*
WUNT	Wissenschaftliche Untersuchungen zum Neuen Testament
ZAC	*Zeitschrift für Antikes Christentum*
ZDMG	Zeitschrift der deutschen morgenländischen Gesellschaft
ZNW	*Zeitschrift für die neutestamentliche Wissenschaft und die Kunde der älteren Kirche*
ZTK	*Zeitschrift für Theologie und Kirche*

IDENTITY AND COMMUNITY

THE TCHACOS CODEX

Another Document of the Gnostics?

Alastair Logan*

The Tchacos Codex is a late third or early fourth century papyrus codex discovered in the late 1970s in the Al Minya province of Middle Egypt near Maghagha, and finally published in 2007. It contains in Coptic as the work of a single scribe (1) *The Letter of Peter to Philip*,[1] (2) *The (First) Apocalypse of James*,[2] (3) *The Gospel of Judas*,[3] (4) a *Book of Allogenes*,[4] and possibly (5) a Hermetic treatise.[5] I would argue that it is best understood as a document of the Gnostic cult movement I have sought to identify in previous books and articles.[6] In this paper, I will first make my case for this view. I will consider the rationale behind the choice of texts in the Tchacos Codex, its context, concerns and date, and the light it can cast on the development of the 'classic' Gnostic myth of Irenaeus, *Adversus Haereses* 1.29–30, the *Apocryphon of John*, the *Gospel of the Egyptians*, *Trimorphic Protennoia* and related texts.

THE SELECTION OF TEXTS FOR THE TCHACOS CODEX

My claim that the Tchacos Codex is a further document of the Gnostics is based primarily on its contents. Thus the *Gospel of Judas* undoubtedly presents a version of the 'classic' Gnostic myth, focusing on the

* I would like to express my grateful thanks to April DeConick for her kind invitation to participate in the Codex Judas Congress and for her inspiration and unfailing helpfulness in the preparation and submission of this paper.
[1] TC 1.1–9.15//NHC VIII,2.
[2] TC 10.1–30.27//NHC V,3. In TC, the title is simply 'James' (30.27).
[3] TC 33.1–58.28.
[4] TC 59.1–66+, not//NHC XI,3.
[5] Ohio fragments 4578 and 4579//CH XIII,1–2.
[6] Cf. Logan 1996; Logan 1997, 188–206; Logan 2006. I prefer 'Gnostic' to 'Sethian', as the more original designation, unlike e.g. Meyer in Kasser et al. 2006a, 6–7, 139–43, and DeConick 2007, 4, 20, 22–24, and passim. See below.

figures of Autogenes, Adamas and Saklas,[7] and may bear some relation to the book of that title attributed by Irenaeus in around 180 C.E.
to a group that he links with the Gnostics of 1.29–30.[8] What is more,
Jesus in the *Gospel of Judas* warns against the practice of the Catholic
eucharist, a sacrament I have suggested the Gnostics tended to ignore
or dispense with.[9] Then again the *Book of Allogenes* has the figure of
Christ as Seth, 'the alien (*Allogenēs*),' as its protagonist, recalling books
of that name possessed by the Sethians, Archontics and Gnostics of
Epiphanius.[10]

If the other two treatises are not overtly 'Sethian,' nevertheless, as
one commentator notes, *The Letter of Peter to Philip* does seem to
reflect the 'classic' myth of Irenaeus and the *Apocryphon*,[11] and both
works occur in what I have argued is the core collection of the Nag
Hammadi library. This I suggest consisted of codices IV and VIII as
a double volume, the heart of the collection, containing the original
myth and rite of initiation (*Apoc. John, Gos. Eg.*) and ancient testimony (*Zost.*), as well as supporting material (codices V, VI, and IX).[12]
What is more, the inclusion of the so-called *First Apocalypse of James*
further bears out my appeal to a particular interest on the part of
the Gnostics, including the Roman Naassenes, in James, the Lord's
brother, as source of secret tradition.[13] Indeed in both the *Apocalypse*

---

[7] Cf. TC 47.1–54.12.

[8] *Adv. Haer.* 1.31.1. He does not name them; the title 'Cainites' is given by later
heresiologists such as Ps.-Tert. (*Adv. haer.* 2), Clem. Alex. (*Strom.* 7.17.17), and Epiph.
(*Pan.* 38). Nagel 2007, 213–76 (221–7), argues on various grounds for the likelihood that
our version is not identical, but closely related to the work which Irenaeus mentions.

[9] Cf. TC 40.18–41.4; 56.11–13; Logan 2006, 80–82. Conversely, Jesus's apparent
criticism of the practice of baptism in his name (TC 55.21–56.1) may, as DeConick
suggests (2007, 132–3), imply his promotion instead of Gnostic baptism in the name
of their Trinity (cf. the Archontic condemnation of Catholic baptism in the name
of Sabaoth (Epiph. *Pan.* 40.2.6–8)). See on this Logan 2006, 77–80. In addition the
concern with healing shown by the Gnostics (see Logan 2006, index s. v. 'healing') is
reflected in *Ep. Pet. Phil.* NHC VIII,2 139.8–9; 140.4–11.

[10] Cf. *Pan.* 39.5.1 (Sethian library including seven books attributed to Seth, others
to *Allogeneis*); 40.2.2 (Archontics using *Allogeneis*); 26.8.1 (Gnostics with books in the
name of Seth).

[11] Meyer, in his introduction to *Ep. Pet. Phil.* in Robinson 1990a, 432, notes that
Jesus's first answer to his disciples (NHC VIII,2 135.8–136.15//TC 3.16–4.21) "reflects
a rather simple version of the myth, and is similar to the Sophia myth of *Apoc. John*
and the Barbelognostics of Iren. (*Adv. Haer.* 1.29.1–4) in terminology and general
presentation."

[12] See Logan 2006, 18–23. Note that in this core collection (Group B), as with TC
(and III), each codex is the work of a single scribe.

[13] See Logan 2006, index s. v. 'James.'

and the Naassene *Preaching* we find a significant link between James and Mary, heroine of the *Gospel of Mary* in the Berlin Gnostic Codex (BG 8502) from Achmim. Thus the latter referred to a great number of discourses delivered by James, the Lord's brother, to Mariamne (i.e. Mary),[14] while in the former Mariamme is one whom Jesus commends to James as worthy of the supreme One Who Is and as having recognised who Jesus is.[15]

Finally the likely inclusion in the Tchacos Codex of Corpus Hermeticum XIII, the Secret Sermon on the Mountain on rebirth,[16] in many ways the culmination of the Corpus, reflects the considerable interest of the Gnostics in this very similar pagan literature, as attested by the Hermetic documents and revealing scribal note in NHC VI.[17] Intriguingly the latter, which is part of the core, if a miscellaneous collection of texts on the fate of the soul, a fundamental concern of the community and a key theme uniting the various collections, like the Tchacos Codex begins with a Petrine text involving the apostles, *The Acts of Peter and the Twelve Apostles*, and ends with Hermetic texts. Moreover if the Tchacos Codex indeed is to be dated to the late third century, this would represent one of the earliest external testimonies to the Hermetic corpus and tend to support its claimed Egyptian provenance.[18]

Although we do not know for certain where exactly the codex was found, whether east of the Nile in a cave among the cliffs of Jebel Qarara,[19] or west of it and a little further south near Beni Mazar, a village five miles south of Oxyrhynchus,[20] and what was found with it,[21]

---

[14] Ps.-Hipp. *Haer.* 5.7.1.

[15] Cf. *1 Apoc. Jas.* TC 27.24–28.5.

[16] CH XIII includes the same terms in its title (*Logos Apokryphos*) as *Gos. Jud.* (TC 33.1).

[17] See Kasser et al. 2007, 29–30. Dirkse, Brashler and Parrott (in Parrott 1979, 343, 345) note the similarities of NHC VI,6 to CH XIII. Similarities in the latter to TC themes include 'intellectual Wisdom/Sophia' as the womb of man (*anthrōpos*) (XIII,1–2), the son of God, the one Man (*Anthrōpos*) as producer of regeneration (XIII,4), and the human body as formed by the twelve powers of the Zodiac (XIII,12).

[18] It would also attest the earliest version in Coptic.

[19] So Krosney 2006, 9–27.

[20] As in Emmel's 1983 report in Robinson 2006, 120. Emmel counsels caution about such information.

[21] According to Emmel in Robinson 2006, 117f., there were three other texts, a Coptic codex of letters of Paul, including certainly Hebrews, Colossians and 1 Thessalonians, a Greek biblical text (Exodus) and a Greek mathematical textbook on weights and measures. On p. 128 Robinson gives the list of Martin Schøyen indicating dates and

the contents would suggest that, as with the Nag Hammadi and Berlin codices, we are dealing with a community product. More light on this issue and that of its general provenance may be supplied by analysis of the cartonnage of the single surviving leather cover.

In the meantime we must be content with the evidence we have. Here, even if we believe the account transmitted by Krosney of its burial in a limestone box in the sarcophagus of a wealthy man,[22] that would not preclude the possibility that it was produced and used by a community. The variety of views represented in the codex (Gnostic Peter traditions echoing Acts, Jewish-Christian James material of Syrian provenance, a version of the 'classic' Gnostic myth, a Sethian *Allogenes* text, a Hermetic treatise) makes it unlikely to be a work which simply reflects the interests of an individual.[23]

Thus it is very comparable to NHC III, another singleton with its own distinct hand, codicology and history, whose similarity in contents and themes I have noted to yet another, the Berlin Gnostic Codex, suggesting that both belong to and attest the existence of further Gnostic cult communities.[24] Both NHC III and BG contain the 'classic' Gnostic myth as set out in the *Apocryphon of John*, which the former puts first, followed by the *Gospel of the Egyptians* as constituting accounts of primordial origins and an overview, including allusion to the five seals initiation rite, followed by ancient testimony (*Eugnostos*) and Christ's revelation to his disciples (*Sophia of Jesus Christ* and *Dialogue of the Saviour*), in what Michael Williams has described as a 'History of Revelation' arrangement, an arrangement he also finds in what he calls the 'two-volume set,' codices IV (*Apocryphon of John* and *Gospel of the Egyptians*) and VIII (*Zostrianos* and *Letter of Peter to Philip*).[25]

---

length: 1. Exodus, 4th century, 50 ff. Greek; 2. 3 Gnostic texts, Coptic 25 ff. + 10? in fragments, 4th (incl. 1 cover); 3. Letters of Paul ca. 400, 30 ff. (incl. 1 cover & spine); 4. Mathematical, 5th c. 12 ff.? However, *pace* DeConick 2007, 64–65, the discrepancy in dates, the very varied character and the two languages involved suggest they were not originally part of a single collection. Certainly TC betrays very little trace of Pauline influence, another characteristic of Gnostic texts. See Logan 2006, 64.

[22] Krosney 2006, 10. Note the recent admission that the Nag Hammadi collection was buried near a skeleton (Ehrman 2003, 52).

[23] The fact that the scribe in NHC VI 65.8–14, who copied Hermetic treatises, refers to his addressees in the plural, implies a Gnostic community, keen on collecting Hermetica and similar material, as is well reflected in the very varied contents of NHC VI.

[24] See Logan 2006, 18–21; Robinson 1975a, 184–90.

[25] Williams 1996, 249–51, table 5.

As we shall see, the *Gospel of Judas* seems to have assembled its version of the 'classic' myth from earlier versions of the *Apocryphon* and the *Gospel of the Egyptians*, as well as from *Eugnostos*. The Berlin Codex may have put the *Gospel of Mary* first in what I have argued represents a concern with and attempt to vindicate the feminine,[26] but it follows it with the 'classic' myth of the *Apocryphon* and the *Sophia* as Christ's revelation to his disciples. The *Gospel of Mary* sets the scene and lays down the parameters for interpreting the following tractates.

What then is the rationale behind the selection of texts in the Tchacos Codex, if one can assume a rationale, as Michael Williams has plausibly argued in the case of the Nag Hammadi codices.[27] First it is worth noting that all the tractates seem to share an apocalyptic genre, the revelations of the Saviour (or a similar figure) in dialogue with his disciples or disciple on a mountain,[28] involving a reassuring message about ultimate salvation from this physical world of deficiency despite persecution and suffering at the hands of its ruling powers. Here one could profitably compare NHC V which begins with *Eugnostos* as ancient testimony, and then contains a series of apocalypses (of Paul, James and Adam), which include a common text (*James*) and share similar traditional features and a similar message of salvation. As NHC V begins with ancient testimony (Eugnostos), so the Tchacos Codex ends with ancient testimony (Hermes). Williams suggests an ascent followed by eschatology scheme for NHC V,[29] but he has to bracket out *Eugnostos*. Furthermore, such a scheme would not fit the Tchacos Codex very well.[30]

However the Tchacos Codex may also reflect a Gnostic imitation and alternative version of Catholic New Testament scripture by its order Peter, James, Judas (the proper title of the NT book),[31] and Revelation (i.e. Apocalypse).[32] The marked Jewish-Christian character

---

[26] Logan 2006, 21.

[27] Williams 1996, 241–62.

[28] Cf. *Ep. Pet. Phil.* NHC VIII,2 133.12–15 (Mount of Olives); *1 Apoc. Jas.* TC 17.7–20//NHC V,3 30.18–31.2 (Mount Galgela/Gaugela); *Allog.* TC 59.13–15 (Mount Tabor); CH XIII,1 (the Mount). Only *Gos. Jud.* lacks this traditional feature.

[29] Williams 1996, 254, table 8.

[30] Thus neither *Ep. Pet. Phil.* nor CH XIII apparently involve an ascent scheme or eschatology, if the other texts appear to, to some extent.

[31] Cf. Robinson 2006, 35, referring to Matt 13:55.

[32] Cf. Williams 1996, 254, table 6, arrangements imitating the order of collections of Christian Scripture. Peter here may come before James because of the greater interest in him at this period as shown by Petrine pseudepigrapha and his developing cult.

of the Tchacos Codex may also explain why texts in the name of Peter
and James were chosen as the first two tractates in the codex: they
were heroes of the Jewish Christians and their Gnostic successors, not
only figures close to Jesus and recipients of his secrets, as is attested in
the *Apocryphon of James* in NHC I, and hence authoritative,[33] but also
victims, like Jesus, of persecution and martyrdom. Thus the *Letter of
Peter to Philip*, perhaps originally composed in Alexandria in the early
third century,[34] sets out a Gnostic version of the Peter of the first part
(chs 1–12) of the Acts of the Apostles,[35] perhaps building on the developing interest in the second century onwards in the figure of Peter,
and presenting him not, as in the 'Great Church', as the origin of the
episcopate, but rather as a source of revelation and of authority, as well
as of healing and miraculous power.[36] Its treatment of classic Gnostic
themes, the questions of their origin and destiny, of the nature of this
'deficiency' and the heavenly 'fullness' (*plērōma*), and particularly its
graphic depiction of the Saviour's passion while denying that he really
suffered, form a suitable opening work to the codex, of which a pervasive theme is suffering, physical and spiritual, and the overcoming
of it.[37] The context would thus seem to be one of persecution by opponents, particularly the 'Great Church,' whose ministers are attacked in
Judas in the guise of the twelve disciples.[38]

The concern with persecution and the meaning of suffering in the
case of Christ and of his followers, coupled with the predilection for
the pseudepigraphical genre, might cast light both on the period of

---

Although the NT order may not yet have been fixed, Athanasius's canon list for Egypt
of 367 C.E. (*Ep. fest.* 39.2: PG 26 1437B) has the catholic epistles directly after Acts in
the 'traditional' order; James, Peter, John, Jude.

[33] Cf. Clem. Alex., who notes in book 7 of his *Hypotyposes*, as quoted by Eus., *Hist.
eccl.* 2.1.4: "After his resurrection the Lord imparted knowledge to James the Just and
John, and Peter, they imparted it to the remaining apostles." Cf. *Strom.* 1.11.3 etc.

[34] Cf. Pearson 2004, 11–81 (73).

[35] Cf. the introduction by Meyer to *Ep. Pet. Phil.* in Robinson 1990, 431–3.

[36] Cf. Bienert 1992, 21, referring to Koschorke 1978, 32f. Peter's healing power (cf.
Acts 3:1–10) is stressed in NHC VI,1 *Acts Pet. 12 Apos.* and in BG 8502,4, an excerpt
from the *Acts of Peter* (see Schneemelcher 1992b, 278–9, 285–6).

[37] Thus there is not only the physical suffering of the Saviour and his disciples of
Ep. Pet. Phil., *1 Apoc. Jas.* and *Gos. Jud.*, but also the spiritual temptation of Christ/
Allogenes by Satan in *Allog.* TC and of the Hermetic initiate by the twelve tormenting
passions of CH XIII.

[38] TC 37.20–40.26. The twelve disciples of *1 Apoc. Jas.* are negatively presented
as types of the twelve rulers of the lower heavenly realm (i.e. Zodiac signs?) (cf. TC
12.12–13.8; 22.23–23.2). It may be significant that the disciples/apostles are not numbered in *Ep. Pet. Phil.* or *Allog.* TC.

composition of the individual treatises of the Tchacos Codex and on the dating of and rationale for their selection and incorporation in the Tchacos Codex. Thus the original dates of composition would seem to cover the second to early third century when the Gnostics were battling with Catholics over how to understand the figure of Christ and how to deal with pagan persecution, whether to seek it, suffer it or avoid it by flight or denial.[39]

That same period witnessed the growth of pseudepigraphical gospels, acts, letters, apocalypses, particularly favoured by the Gnostics as the most persuasive vehicles for their propaganda.[40] The chain of transmission in the *First Apocalypse of James*,[41] from James via Addai, founder of Syrian Christianity, through at least four generations, which we can now reconstruct more fully from the Tchacos Codex version, would suggest a date of writing well into the second century.[42] The link with Irenaeus's *Gospel of Judas*, if genuine, would suggest that the original version of it must have been written around the middle of that same century,[43] while the emergence and growth of Petrine pseudepigrapha such as the *Kerygma Petri* and *Gospel of Peter* through the course of the second century might suggest, as we noted above, a second or early third century date for the *Letter of Peter to Philip*.[44] The growing interest in the figure of Seth, 'the alien (*Allogenēs*),' as an increasingly elevated figure attested by Christian and Manichaean sources of the early third century onwards,[45] would also suggest that the *Book of Allogenes* was written around the same time.

All four of these works of course would have been originally composed in Greek and translated into Coptic from the late third century onwards when such a practice became common.[46] That such transla-

---

[39] Cf. Pagels-King 2007, chs 2–3; Frend 1965, chs 10–12, esp. 12. See also King's paper in this volume.

[40] Cf. Logan 2006, 69–70.

[41] Cf. TC 23.10–25.14//NHC V,3 36.13–38.11.

[42] Cf. Funk 1991, 314–15, suggesting a date "at the earliest towards the end of the 2nd century," noting a likely East Syrian provenance.

[43] Nagel 2007, 225, suggests around 160.

[44] On the *KP* see Schneemelcher 1992a, 34–41. On the *Gos. Peter* see Maurer-Schneemelcher 1991, 216–22. A possible fragment (P. Oxy. 2949), dating from the late second to early third century, was discovered at Oxyrhynchus.

[45] Cf. Logan 1996, 47–49; Pearson 2004, 268–82, esp. 276–81.

[46] Cf. Nagel 2007, 217–19, on translation into Coptic and the likely Greek original of *Gos. Jud.* He suggests around 300 as the likely date of the Coptic translation (225), but does not consider it the first, rather a copy of an unknown original of the last decades of the third century (217).

tion was now called for would further strengthen the hypothesis that the Tchacos Codex was a community product: wealthier, more educated individuals would be happy with Greek originals, but local, less wealthy, less educated groups would require a Coptic translation.

A final strand that seems to run through the varied treatises of the Tchacos Codex and may help to explain the logic behind their selection is a keen interest in uranology and astrology and in the number twelve and multiples of it, in particular. Thus in the *First Apocalypse of James* an important question raised by James is over the number of the rulers (*archōn*) and of the hebdomads over which they preside, which turns out to be twelve rather than the seven of scripture.[47] The text seems to be moving from a focus on the number seven related to the week and to the seven planetary rulers,[48] to an interest in the twelve signs of the Zodiac associated with the twelve rulers, the prototypes of the twelve disciples.[49] Related to these are seventy-two inferior heavens, existing under the authority of the twelve rulers.[50]

The *Gospel of Judas* develops this material to a far greater degree, clearly borrowing from the heavenly arithmetic of *Eugnostos*. Thus the Autogenes makes seventy-two luminaries appear in the incorruptible generation, and they in turn make 360 luminaries appear in it, five for each.[51] Mention is then made of twelve aeons of the twelve luminaries with six heavens for each aeon, making up seventy-two heavens for the seventy-two luminaries, as in the *First Apocalypse of James*. Each of the heavens has five firmaments, making a total of 360 firmaments.[52] They are given authority and countless serving angels and spirits.[53] What is rather garbled here is rather clearer in the source, *Eugnostos*. As emerges later, the twelve luminaries and aeons seem to serve as

---

[47] TC 12.8–13.1//NHC V,3. 'Hebdomads' appear to refer to the heavenly spheres ruled by the archons. The scripture involved is probably Daniel 9:25 LXX (seven hebdomads).

[48] Cf. Iren. *Adv. Haer.* 1.30.4, 8–10 (the hebdomad as the planets and the week); *Apoc. John* NHC II,1 11,34–35 and par (the seven planetary rulers as the week); *Orig. World* NHC II,5 101.25–26 (female name of Ialdabaoth) etc.

[49] Cf. TC 12.10–13.6; 22.23–23.4.

[50] TC 13.1–9//NHC V,3 26.13–24.

[51] TC 49.9–17. Cf. *Eugn.* NHC III 83.10–19//NHC V 11.20–12.1 (12/6/72/5/360 powers). The source is clearly *Eugn.* as the parallel passages are missing from the *Soph. Jes. Chr.*

[52] TC 49.18–50.3. Cf. *Eugn.* NHC III,3 84.12–85.7//NHC V,1 12.21–13.6 (12/6/ 72/5/360 heavens).

[53] TC 50.3–12. Cf. *Eugn.* NHC III,3 88.21–89.3.

archetypes for the twelve lower rulers of the Zodiac circle and their assisting angels who preside over this visible universe.[54] Thus Judas is counted as a thirteenth spirit (*daimōn*), superior to the latter.[55]

The author of the *Gospel of Judas* also has an interest in the stars that seems lacking in other Gnostic treatises.[56] Thus, perhaps influenced by Plato's idea, he or she asserts that everyone has a star,[57] that the stars bring everything to completion,[58] but are in error and will finally be destroyed.[59] At one point Judas's star is said to have led him astray.[60] The author's view of the stars seems predominantly negative, as with Gnostic texts in general.[61] In this light the later passages where Jesus affirms that Judas's star will rule over the thirteenth aeon,[62] that it has ascended and that among the stars it is the one that leads the way,[63] are perhaps best interpreted as relating him ultimately to a ruling role in this lower 'cosmic' world.[64] Finally although we cannot be sure whether or not the *Book of Allogenes* included revelations about the heavenly world and the stars, as it well might, certainly CH XIII

---

[54] Cf. TC 51.4–52.13.

[55] TC 44.21. Cf. 46.19–20. DeConick 2007, 48–51, rightly stresses the negative connotations of the term. See n. 62.

[56] However *Testim. Truth* seems to share a similar view of the errant stars completing their courses (NHC IX,3 29.15–19; 34.8–15), and *Mars.* seems to refer to the Zodiac (NHC X 21.14; 39.28), which is coupled with references to stars, the seven planets and thirty six decans (41.25–42.6). Finally *PS* is much concerned with how the Saviour affected the behaviour and influence of the stars (cf. Schmidt-MacDermot 1978b, 25–28, 30–32).

[57] TC 42.5–8. Cf. *Tim.* 41d–42b.

[58] TC 40.17–18; 54.15–24. Cf. *Testim. Truth* NHC IX,3 34.8–11.

[59] TC 46.1–2; 55.15–20. Here the six stars mentioned seem to be the moon and planets. The five combatants would appear to be the five rulers of the underworld (cf. TC 52.4–14). See Logan 1996, 130–34.

[60] TC 45.12–14.

[61] The 'classic' myth of *Apoc. John* and related texts interprets the realm of *heimarmenē*, of the seven planets and twelve Zodiac signs, negatively (cf. BG 38.19–44.9 and par; NHC II,1 28.12–32 and par). On the astrology of *Gos. Jud.* see the papers in this volume by DeConick, Denzey Lewis, Adamson and Förster.

[62] TC 55.10–12. See DeConick 2007, 110–13, on the negative connotations of 'thirteen' in Sethian texts. To her list one could add *PS* (cf. Book 1.19 (Schmidt-MacDermot 1978b, 19.6f.), 29 (Schmidt-MacDermot 1978b, 41.26, 42.18, 43.14f.), 30 (Schmidt-MacDermot 1978b, 43.12, 44.6f., 10f., 45.9), 31 (Schmidt-MacDermot 1978b, 46.3), 55 (Schmidt-MacDermot 1978b, 104.8f.); Book 2.84 (Schmidt-MacDermot 1978b, 188.10–13)) on the thirteenth aeon as the sphere of Pistis Sophia and the great Authades, producer of the lion-faced Ialdabaoth. However in the *Sec. Bk. Jeu* 52 (Schmidt-MacDermot 1978a, 134.3), the thirteenth aeon is a heavenly realm of the great invisible spirit, if with an aeon or more beyond it.

[63] TC 56.23; 57.16–20.

[64] So DeConick 2007, ch. 6. See also the papers in the volume by DeConick, Förster, and Gathercole.

refers to the twelve signs of the Zodiac in a negative way as involved in the creation of the human body.[65]

As regards the date of the Tchacos Codex, it would seem likely from the carbon dating of the fibres and leather cover of the Tchacos Codex, and from analysis of the ink,[66] that the Tchacos Codex was written by a single scribe sometime towards the end of the third and beginning of the fourth century.[67] This would put it into the era of imperial persecutions, between those of Decius (249–52 C.E.) and Valerian (257–8 C.E.) and the Great Persecution under Diocletian (303–12 C.E.). Living in such a period in which they felt threatened both by pagan authorities and by Catholics, it is not surprising that Gnostics in Middle Egypt might have put together just such a collection of texts as we now have in the Tchacos Codex, honouring their suffering martyr heroes and saviour, Peter, James, Judas, Christ/Seth. As Eusebius of Caesarea attests in his detailed excerpts from Dionysius of Alexandria (247–65),[68] the persecutions under Decius and Valerian had a powerful and wide-ranging effect on Christians in Egypt. The 'Great Persecution' under Diocletian went one further in requiring Christians to surrender their scriptures and holy books.[69]

In such circumstances the concealment or burial of the Tchacos Codex in a rich man's grave might not be so surprising. The grave itself may not have been far from Oxyrhynchus where there was a bishop and thus at least one Catholic church,[70] and where Greek fragments of the *Gospel of Mary*, of the *Gospel of Thomas* and of the *Sophia of Jesus Christ* were discovered.[71] This might suggest the existence of a Gnostic community in Middle Egypt from the third century on, which began to translate their Greek texts into Coptic later in that century. Such a community was clearly, and considered itself to be, Christian,

---

[65] CH XIII,11–12. The twelve evil tormentors are identified with the signs of the Zodiac, responsible for the human body. See Grese 1979, 110–112, 139–41, 199.

[66] On the dating of fibres and ink see Krosney 2006, 270–5, 302–4.

[67] The mean year of all the carbon dating measurements was 280 C.E. (Krosney 2006, 274).

[68] Cf. *Hist. eccl.* 6.39–42.5; 7.10–11.25; 21.1–23.

[69] Cf. Eus. *Hist. eccl.* 8.2.4–5; *Gesta apud Zenophilum* (CSEL 26 186–8). See Frend 1965, ch. 15.

[70] Cf. Harnack 1905, 313f., referring to the *Passio* of Peter of Alexandria. Harnack notes (317) that there was also a Meletian bishop there in 325.

[71] *Gos. Mary*: P. Oxy. 3525 and PRyl 463, probably also from there (see Tuckett 2007, 4, 7–9, 80–85 etc.); *Gos. Thom.*: P. Oxy. 1, 654, 655; *Soph. Jes. Chr.*: P. Oxy. 1081.

wrestling with the problems of identity, of suffering, physical and spiritual, and of persecution.[72]

THE DEVELOPMENT OF THE "CLASSIC" GNOSTIC MYTH

Such a community evidently predated the growth of coenobitic monasticism, unlike those responsible for the Nag Hammadi collection or collections, even if only one group (A: I, VII, XI) seems to have had some association with a monastic milieu.[73] The close similarities in content and logic of composition demonstrated above between the Tchacos Codex and the Nag Hammadi core texts would thus seem to further weaken the claim that the Nag Hammadi texts were collected and copied by monks.[74] But, on the other hand, in what sense can the group responsible for the Tchacos Codex be classed as 'Gnostic' in that, unlike the Nag Hammadi collections, three of which have the 'classic' myth as the first in their codices (II, III, IV), it only contains a brief summary of that myth in its third treatise?

What kind of Gnostics would not have, and give pride of place to, a version of their 'classic' myth? We have already suggested why those responsible for BG 8502 might have decided to relegate the *Apocryphon* to second place. Conversely, what are we to make of the fact that the authors of the Nag Hammadi core collection selected the first two (*Ep. Pet. Phil.* and *1 Apoc. Jas.*) for inclusion and not the third? As Nagel has noted, we have multiple copies of a number of the Nag Hammadi and related texts, including no less than four of the *Apocryphon of John*,[75] and even the *Book of Allogenes* seems multiply attested,[76] while

---

[72] The Manichees of Egypt supply a revealing parallel, spreading in Middle Egypt (Lycopolis) in the later third century, seeing themselves as Christians, concealing themselves among the Catholic population, especially when persecuted, translating their holy books into Coptic. See Stroumsa 1986, 307–19.

[73] Cf. Logan 2006, 18.

[74] The striking absence in both of biblical and patristic works and allusions also serves to confirm the significant differences between them and the Dishna Papers, which do seem to represent a Pachomian monastic library (see Déroche et al. 1990/91, 26–39).

[75] Nagel 2007, 225–6 (two versions of *Gos. Eg., 1 Apoc. Jas., Ep. Pet. Phil., Eugn., Gos. Truth, Soph. Jes. Chr., Orig. World*, three versions or fragments of *Gos. Mary, Gos. Thom.*). He fails to include P. Oxy. 1081 as containing a third version of *Soph. Jes. Chr.*

[76] See n. 8 on the evidence of Epiph. The NH tractate *Allog.* also refers to 'Books of Allogenēs' (NHC XI,3 69.17–19).

we only have one (or two?) of the *Gospel of Judas*. Could it be that it was considered rather idiosyncratic,[77] not properly reflecting or harmonizing with the 'classic' myth of the *Apocryphon*,[78] at the heart of no less than three separate library collections? We may compare the way Irenaeus writes about the group of Gnostics responsible for the Gospel of Judas, a group that Epiphanius later associates with the Cainites. Irenaeus does not appear to have any direct knowledge of them or their texts, supplying no summary as with the earlier Gnostic groups whose texts he clearly knows directly. As Harry Gamble has pointed out, heterodox texts disappeared not because they were suppressed by Catholics, a popular misconception, but because they were not copied enough.[79]

So how exactly does the *Gospel of Judas* treat the 'classic' myth? What is striking is how much it leaves out of that myth, how far it seems to depart from or misunderstand it, and what it chooses to develop instead. Certainly the entire text revolves round a standard Gnostic theme, the proper understanding of the great, holy, kingless, incorruptible generation of Jesus and the Gnostics, beyond the grasp of everyone, humans and even angels of this world.[80] However when Jesus finally comes to instruct Judas, who alone knows where he, Jesus, is from, namely the aeon of Barbelo,[81] about the nature and origin of the great incorruptible generation, we get a very truncated version of the 'classic' myth. This does begin in familiar style with the great and boundless aeon of the great invisible Spirit,[82] but the author does not mention Barbelo and her emanations directly again, nor the Son, Christ, and his,[83] but proceeds immediately to the origin

---

[77] As the last of a series of possibilities Nagel 2007, 228 suggests it might be "ein singulärer Nebenzweig"!

[78] Its promotion of Judas and denigration of the rest of the disciples would hardly fit the *Apocryphon*'s presentation of John as recipient of the Saviour's revelation (NHC II,1 1.1–4), and as transmitting it to the rest at the end (NHC II,1 32.1–5 and par).

[79] Gamble 1995, 127.

[80] TC 34.11–17; 36.13–37.16; 44.8–13; 45.14–24; 46.11–18, 24–47.4; 53.22–25; 57.9–14. Cf. *Apoc. John* BG 22.15 and par; 63.14f. and par; 65.2 and par; 71.11–14 and par; 75.20 and par; *Gos. Eg.* NHC III,2 51.8–9 and par; 54.8f. and par; 59.13–15 and par; 61.12f., 19f. and par; 62.17–19 and par; *Hyp. Arch.* NHC II,4 97.4f. etc.

[81] TC 35.14–21.

[82] TC 47.5–13. Cf. Iren., *Adv. Haer.* 1.29.1; *Apoc. John* NHC II,1 5.6; *Zost.* NHC VIII,1 2.26; 14.6; *Steles Seth* NHC VII,5 121.20f. (boundless aeon); *Apoc. John* NHC II,1 2.29–33; 4.34–5; *Gos. Eg.* NHC III,2 40.13 and par; *Zost.* NHC VIII,1 24.9–15 (great invisible Spirit).

[83] Cf. Iren., *Adv. Haer.* 1.29.1; *Apoc. John* NHC II,1 4.26–7.4 and par.

of the Autogenes figure as an angel who is attended, not as in the 'classic' myth by four named luminaries, who play a key role, but by four unnamed angels.[84]

Unfortunately the first few lines of the next page are very damaged. The Autogenes has a male figure come into being[85] and creates a luminary to rule over him, along with myriad serving angels, followed by a luminous aeon who is not named, with the second luminary to rule over him and a similar angelic train.[86] The text then refers to "the rest of the luminous aeons of light" as reigning over them with their angelic train.[87] Is this a garbled version of the emanation of heavenly Adamas and his son Seth, or of the four luminaries and their attendants of the 'classic' myth?[88] The editors assume the former by their proposed restoration, and certainly we hear immediately in what follows of Adamas as in the first cloud of light,[89] then a few lines later of the incorruptible generation of Seth being made to appear.[90] But there is no evident sign of the clear pattern and hierarchical and temporal structuring of the 'classic' myth, which has the four luminaries with distinctive names which occur in many Gnostic texts[91] emanated before Adamas (and Seth), and the latter's offspring assigned to their aeons, as in the *Apocryphon*.[92] Indeed the text seems to downplay or obscure the four luminaries and their major role. What is more, if Adamas is a valid conjecture, the text conspicuously fails to identify the second luminous aeon as Seth.

Then follows the extended passage about the multitude of luminaries based on the number twelve which we described above, and the lower realm of an equal number of heavens, which is dubbed "cosmos, that

---

[84] TC 47.16–26. Cf. Iren., *Adv. Haer.* 1.29.2; *Apoc. John* NHC II,1 7.30–8.25 and par; *Gos. Eg.* NHC III,2 51.17–19 and par (Harmozel, Oroiael, Daueithe, Eleleth).

[85] Only the first letter, A, survives. The editors of the critical edition (215) conjecture 'Adamas,' which Gathercole (2007a, 90) accepts with a question mark, while Nagel (2007, 251) and DeConick (2007, 81), leave dots.

[86] TC 48.1–15. See on this Pearson's paper in this volume.

[87] TC 48.15–21.

[88] Cf. Iren., *Adv. Haer.* 1.29.2; *Apoc. John* NHC II,1 7.30–8.21 and par.

[89] TC 48.21–26.

[90] TC 49.5–6.

[91] Cf. Iren., *Adv. Haer.* 1.29.2; *Apoc. John* NHC II,1 7.30–8.18 and par; *Gos. Eg.* NHC III,2 51.17–18 and par; *Zost.* NHC VIII,1 51.17–18; 127.19–128.6; *Trim. Prot.* NHC XIII,1 38.34–39.5; *Melch.* NHC IX,1 6.4f.; Untitled Text of Bruce Codex ch. 20 (Schmidt-MacDermot 1978a, 264.5–6).

[92] Cf. NHC II,1 7.30–9.23 and par.

is perdition."[93] But again, instead of this leading into the appearance of Sophia and her role in producing the demiurge Ialdabaoth, as in the 'classic' myth,[94] a heavenly voice calls for twelve angels to rule over chaos and the underworld, resulting in the emergence from a cloud of a fiery, bloody angel, Nebro (= Nimrod?), interpreted as 'rebel' and also called 'Ialdabaoth.'[95] This is followed by a further angelic emanation from the cloud, Saklas, who with Nebro/Ialdabaoth produces twelve rulers and their angels,[96] and later with his six angels creates Adam and Eve.[97] This seems a very modified version of the 'classic' myth, excluding Sophia, splitting Ialdabaoth and Saklas, and reflecting, if not entirely accurately, the versions of these events found particularly in the *Gospel of the Egyptians* but also in *Trimorphic Protennoia*.[98] In both it is the fourth luminary, Eleleth,[99] who makes the proclamation which leads in the former to the appearance of a cloud, 'hylic Sophia,'[100] which, at the request of an angelic minister for a ruler, emanates two monads, the great angel Saklas and the great demon Nebruel. They in turn produce twelve angels to rule their worlds. In the latter the angelic utterance is a statement and question about who belongs to chaos and the underworld, and only one figure appears, the great demon called 'Saklas,' 'Samael,' 'Ialtabaoth.'[101] Here too the Sophia of the 'classic' myth occurs as the guileless victim robbed by the great demon of her power.[102]

The following passage in the Tchacos Codex in which only the first five of the twelve angels who rule over chaos and the underworld

---

[93] TC 49.8–50.14.

[94] Cf. Iren., *Adv. Haer.* 1.29.4; *Apoc. John* NHC II,1 9.25–10.19 and par.

[95] TC 51.3–15.

[96] TC 51.16–23.

[97] TC 52.14–25. DeConick (2007, 97–100, 115, 132, 140–141) persistently identifies Ialdabaoth as the creator god, worshipped by the apostles, rather than Saklas, as in the text. Ialdabaoth seems rather redundant in *Gos. Jud.*

[98] Cf. *Gos. Eg.* NHC III,2 56.22–57.7; *Trim. Prot.* NHC XIII,1 39.13–32.

[99] There is a lacuna in TC 51.4 which seems too short for Eleleth, but may have contained El, which occurs in l.1 as the name of the aeon containing the cloud and angel (cf. 50.22–51.1). See the editorial comment in the critical edition ad loc. (221). DeConick (2007, 84 n. 10) supports Turner in reading 'Eleleth.'

[100] There may be a hint of this figure in the 'corruptible Sophia' of TC 44.4.

[101] Cf. *Apoc. John* NHC II,1 11.15–18 (Ialtabaoth, Saklas, Samael); *Hyp. Arch.* NHC II,4 95.7–8 (Saklas, Ialdabaoth = Samael at 87.3).

[102] Cf. Iren., *Adv. Haer.* 1.29.4; *Apoc. John* NHC II,1 10.19–21 and par.

according to the 'classic' myth are named,[103] seems to mark a further misunderstanding of the latter, in that, in it, it is the last five, not the first, who rule over chaos and the underworld. What is more, the name of the first ["S]eth, who is called 'the Christ,'"[104] instead of the Athoth/Aoth/Iaoth of the *Apocryphon*,[105] also seems to represent a misunderstanding. Seth and Christ are surely beings of the supreme world, not angels of Saklas. Athoth may have been misunderstood in an Egyptian context and replaced by the Egyptian god of the under-world, Set, which, in turn was understood as heavenly Seth or Christ.[106] In a further modification of the 'classic' myth, the *Gospel of Judas* has Saklas and his (six?) angels create both Adam and Eve,[107] despite quot-ing Genesis 1:26 "Let us make a human being," and with no allusion to the appearance of the image of heavenly Man (Adamas) which sparks this off in the 'classic' myth.[108]

The author of the *Gospel of Judas* has clearly used material both from the 'classic' myth, as found in Irenaeus's summary and earlier versions of the *Apocryphon* and the *Gospel of the Egyptians*, and from *Eugnostos*, itself a favourite text of the Gnostics and Gnosticized by them as the *Sophia of Jesus Christ*. What is striking is how often and how much material seems to derive from the versions of these texts in NHC III. An example is the term *parastasis* used of divine enti-ties assisting others.[109] But there are clear differences and a differ-ent agenda. The *Gospel of Judas* has focused on a few key figures and events (Autogenes, Adamas, Saklas), on the one hand, while expanding

---

[103] TC 52.3–14. Cf. *Apoc. John* NHC III,1 16.15–17.5 and par; *Gos. Eg.* NHC III,2 58.7–22.

[104] TC 52.5. The editors of the critical edition ad loc. (223) exclude the reading Athoth.

[105] *Apoc. John* NHC II,1 11.26//III,1 17.22//BG 41.18. *Gos. Eg.* NHC III,2 58.8 seems to read Ath[oth].

[106] The Harmathoth of TC 52.7 may be an attempt to conserve an original Athoth. Epiphanius's libertine Gnostics list Seth as third ruler (*Pan.* 26.10.1). However Turner's proposed reading "[Ath]eth, who is called the good one" (interpreting *chs* as an abbreviation of *chrēstos*, not *Christos*: see DeConick 2007, 112), may offer a more plausible solution.

[107] TC 52.14–19 (*plassein*).

[108] Cf. *Apoc. John* BG 48.6–49.6 (*plassein*). Note however an allusion to heavenly Eve/Zoe in TC 52.19–21 (Eve is called 'Zoe' in the cloud).

[109] Cf. TC 47.16–21 and *Apoc. John* NHC III,1 11.3–6; Iren. *Adv. Haer.* 1.29.2 (*ad repraesentationem*); TC 47.21–25 and *Apoc. John* NHC III,1 11.15–19; Iren., *Adv. Haer.* 1.29.2 (*ad circumstantiam Autogeni*)—the Latin translator has used two differ-ent terms for the same Greek word.

certain themes (i.e. uranography, astrology), on the other, the whole account culminating in the generation of Adam and Eve.

The author's main aim after all, as indicated in Jesus's words to Judas initiating the exposition of the myth, was to explain the origin of the great generation of Adam(as). However in pursuing this the author has effectively written the female figures (Barbelo, Sophia, Pro(ten)noia) who play such a central role in the *Apocryphon*, the *Gospel of the Egyptians* and *Trimorphic Protennoia*, out of the script. Perhaps significantly the somewhat biologically coloured processes of production involving the union of male and female aeons in Irenaeus, still evident in the *Apocryphon*,[110] have been replaced by purely spiritual processes (entities produced by clouds of light),[111] a development we also see at work in the *Gospel of the Egyptians*.[112] However there is no lack of generative female spiritual entities in the latter (Barbelo, Mirothoe, Prophaneia, Plesithea), whereas there are no females, including disciples, apart from the unavoidable Eve/Zoe (and perhaps corruptible Sophia), in the *Gospel of Judas*.

Conversely, the author seems to be using earlier, less developed forms of the 'classic' myth. This even seems to be the case with the central Gnostic theme of the great, incorruptible, kingless race (*genea*), usually interpreted to apply to Seth, as based on the cumulative evidence of several Nag Hammadi treatises.[113] In fact, as we have seen, Seth occurs only once, if in connection with the incorruptible race,[114] and the main subject of the treatise seems to be the heavenly first man, i.e. Adamas.[115] Thus Jesus calls on the disciples to bring out the perfect human, which they cannot do,[116] Adamas appears in the first cloud of light with his incorruptible powers,[117] earthly Adam appears to be

---

[110] Cf. Iren., *Adv. Haer.* 1.29.1–2; *Apoc. John* NHC II,1 6.10–8.28 and par.

[111] Cf. TC 47.14–26; 51.8–17.

[112] Cf. *Gos. Eg.* NHC III,2 49.1–12 (Adamas from a cloud, Mirothoe); 57.1–18 (a cloud producing Saklas and Nebruel). This seems a later toning down rather than an alternative tradition as Pearson has suggested in his paper.

[113] Cf. *Apoc. John* NHC III,1 32.7–9; *Gos. Eg.* NHC III,2 59.13–15 and par; *Zost.* NHC VIII,1 7.25–27; *Steles Seth* NHC VII,5 118.12–13; *Apoc. Adam* NHC V,5 65.5–9.

[114] TC 49.5–6. I discount 52.5 (see above).

[115] In CH XIII,4, the producer of regeneration is the one Man, the son of God.

[116] TC 35.2–14. Not even Judas can do so as not perfectly informed or in the image, thus not a member of or eventually ascending to the great, holy generation, as DeConick (2007, 54–57, 117–19) persuasively argues.

[117] TC 48.21–26; 50.18–21.

formed after the image and likeness of heavenly Adamas,[118] and in the consummation the image of the great generation of Adam (not Seth!) will be exalted, as representing the first, pre-existent generation from the heavenly aeons.[119] This would seem to fit in with my argument that the 'classic' myth of Irenaeus originally only involved Adamas, undominated and kingless, and that the myth was Sethianized in the early third century with the introduction of heavenly Seth, reflecting the interest in Seth of mainstream Christians and as a way of defending the Gnostics from the charge of novelty. They could claim to be the children of heavenly Seth.[120]

We have noted the lack of interest of the text in the four luminaries, key figures in the Seth material of the *Apocryphon* and the *Gospel of the Egyptians*. We might explain this in terms of the author's drastic abbreviation of the myth because of his or her interest in other matters, but yet we have the clear focus on Adamas and the mention of Seth and his incorruptible race. We seem therefore to be at a stage of development of the myth between the *Trimorphic Protennoia* and the *Hypostasis of the Archons*, neither of which features heavenly Seth and Sethian material,[121] and the *Apocalypse of Adam*, where the figure of heavenly Seth, son of Adamas and father of the incorruptible race, is beginning to appear.[122]

This earlier stage would also seem to be reflected in the *Book of Allogenes*, in which the hero is Christ as Seth, the *Allogenēs*, from another, higher, race, who undergoes spiritual temptation by Satan in a combination of the temptations and transfiguration of Jesus of the gospels,[123] and receives a saving revelation from the supreme God in a luminous cloud.[124] This understanding of Christ as an incarnation of Seth, the original human rather than the divine progenitor of the elect race, is much closer to the views of Epiphanius's Sethians, whom he thinks he may have met in Egypt, and who insisted that Seth, the son of Adam, was Christ and Jesus.[125]

---

[118] TC 52.14–19.
[119] TC 57.9–14.
[120] Cf. Logan 1996, 45–46.
[121] Cf. Logan 1996, 44–47.
[122] Cf. *Apoc. Adam* NHC V,5 64.5–65.9 and Logan 1996, 47–48.
[123] Cf. Matt 4:1–11//Mark 1:12–13//Luke 4:1–13 (temptation) and Matt 17:1–13//Mark 9:2–13//Luke 9:28–36 (transfiguration).
[124] TC 59.12–62.24.
[125] *Pan.* 39.1.2–3.

Another Gnostic Codex

In the light of all this I would conclude that the Tchacos Codex is indeed a further document of the Gnostic cult movement, containing texts which both reflect (*Ep. Pet. Phil., Allog.*?) and modify for distinctive theological purposes (*Gos. Jud.*) an earlier version of the 'classic' myth found in more developed form in the mid-fourth century copies of the *Apocryphon*, the *Gospel of the Egyptians* and *Trimorphic Protennoia*. Its texts reflect the Gnostic interest in Jewish-Christian themes and figures like Peter and James as authorities and martyrs (*Ep. Pet. Phil., 1 Apoc. Jas.*), and the Gnostic interest in Judas as antihero, as in Irenaeus's account of the 'Cainites,' or as villain in a subtle parody of the beliefs and practices of Catholic clergy as descendents of the apostles and reassuring exposition of the true nature of the Gnostic elect, the great holy generation, as in *Judas*.[126] The latter also echoes the Gnostic rejection of the eucharist, and perhaps criticism of over eager Catholic acceptance of martyrdom.

The Tchacos Codex also shows a typical Gnostic interest in Hermetism (CH XIII), but clearly predates Pachomian monasticism. It reveals no sign of the later more philosophical developments in the Gnostic movement, in dialogue with Neoplatonism, which are found not only in Nag Hammadi texts such as *Zostrianos, Allogenes, Marsanes*, and the *Three Steles of Seth*, and in the Untitled Text of the Bruce Codex, but have also begun to make their mark on our present versions of the *Apocryphon*[127] and the *Gospel of the Egyptians*.[128]

The Tchacos Codex would appear to be the work of a third century Gnostic community in Middle Egypt, perhaps in the vicinity of Oxyrhynchus, conscious of the threat of persecution by outsiders, seeking to confirm its own identity, and reflecting the process, beginning later in the century, of translating Greek original texts into Coptic. The preferred self-identification of the community, at least in the *Gospel of Judas*, seems to have been 'the great, kingless, incorrupt-

---

[126] On Judas as villain and the *Gos. Jud.* as a subtle Gnostic parody see DeConick 2007, esp. ch. 8.

[127] E.g. the triple power, triple-male figure (cf. *Apoc. John* NHC II,1 5.8–9, *Zost.* NHC VIII,1 128.20–21; *Steles Seth* NHC VII,5 120.29–30; 121.30–33 etc.).

[128] E.g. figures like Moirothoe (cf. *Gos. Egy.* NHC III,2 49.4 and *Zost.* NHC VIII,1 6.30; 30.14; *Steles Seth* NHC VII,5 119.12), the child of the child Ephesech/Esephech (cf. *Gos. Egy.* NHC III,2 50.2; 53.25; 55.22; 62.6, and *Zost.* NHC VIII,1 13.8; 45.2, 11) etc.

ible generation (or race) of Seth,' i.e. 'Sethians,' although its choice of the *Book of Allogenes* reflects a focus on the earthly Seth or Christ as with Epiphanius's Sethians, and there is a noted paucity of reference in the Tchacos Codex to heavenly Seth and his luminaries/aeons. On the other hand, like the groups represented in the Nag Hammadi collections and Epiphanius's Sethians, Archontics and Gnostics, it may very well have had more than one manuscript in its library, perhaps even an earlier version of NHC III, although, as with our NHC III and BG 8502, only one has survived.

If the *Gospel of Judas* were indeed dependent on an earlier version of NHC III, this might suggest a later date for the version we have than the second century of the text Irenaeus alludes to (and perhaps a different text). In any case the fact that the *Gospel of Judas* did not make it into the Nag Hammadi collections, unlike the *Letter of Peter to Philip* and the *First Apocalypse of James* (and NHC III!), might suggest that, if undoubtedly Gnostic, it was a rather idiosyncratic and peripheral text. Its interest in Judas and in astrological speculations did not find much of an echo among later Gnostics (apart from the community responsible for *Pistis Sophia* as regards the latter), although its critique of Catholic belief and practice does have a counterpart in the *Testimony of Truth* (NHC IX,3), part of the core collection. Finally the Tchacos Codex, or a version of it, may have been known to the group who was responsible for the core collection of Nag Hammadi texts, who copied two of its treatises,[129] and also incorporated NHC III, on an earlier version of which a third, the *Gospel of Judas*, may have been dependent.

---

[129] However, there are differences between the two Coptic versions of each text (see Funk's paper in this volume), which would actually imply two different prior versions and thus even more copies in circulation.

MARTYRDOM AND ITS DISCONTENTS IN THE TCHACOS CODEX

Karen L. King

In *Reading Judas*, Elaine Pagels and I argued that the bitter anger of the *Gospel of Judas*'s author and his violent denunciations of other Christians belong to the situation in which Christians were in danger of arrest and execution at the hands of the Romans.[1] Christian leaders, who were apparently claiming authority as heirs of Jesus's twelve disciples, were saying that God desired these deaths as sacrifices pleasing to Him, but the *Gospel of Judas* opposes this kind of theology, and instead offers an alternative way to understand Jesus's death and hence the death of believers.[2] Jesus's revelation to Judas portrays such deaths as idolatrous worship of false gods, thereby putting worship in the Jewish Temple on a par with other Greco-Roman sacrificial practices—or even worse, portraying them as human sacrifice, a practice uniformly denounced throughout the Mediterranean world as something of which only the worst peoples are capable. To expose this idolatry, Jesus reveals his Father, the true God above, and admonishes people to turn their souls toward the realms which are on high. The *Gospel of Judas* thus engages in a sharp polemic aimed not at Romans or even Jews—though it is certainly anti-Jewish in its rhetoric[3]—but against other Christians.

Not only the *Gospel of Judas*, however, but also the first two texts inscribed in the Tchacos Codex, the *Letter of Peter to Philip*[4] and the *First Apocalypse of James*,[5] are concerned with persecution and

---

[1] Following the lead of Iricinschi et al. 2006, 32–37.

[2] See Pagels-King 2007, especially pp. xvi–xviii, 43–57, 71–74.

[3] See Pagels-King 2007, 165.

[4] *Ep. Pet. Phil.* survives in two manuscripts, both Coptic translations from Greek. One copy is inscribed in the fourth century Nag Hammadi Codex (NHC VIII,2); the other in the fourth century Tchacos Codex (TC). Citations of the NHC VIII,2 are from the critical edition and translation by Wisse in Sieber 1991; citations of the TC are from Kasser et al. 2007.

[5] *1 Apoc. Jas.* is extant in two fourth century Coptic manuscripts, NHC V,3 and the TC. Citations of the NHC V,3 are from the critical edition and translation by William Schoedel in Parrott 1979; citations of the TC are from Kasser et al.

death.[6] Here I want to offer some first thoughts about the possibility
of reading these three works as offering what we might call "preparation for martyrdom." My suggestion is that these works illumine some
aspects of early Christian debates not only over how to understand
the violent death of Jesus, but also over how believers should prepare
themselves to face suffering and death, especially in the face of persecution. Moreover, although these works were composed independently in Greek in the 2nd or 3rd centuries C.E.,[7] their survival in a 4th
century C.E. Coptic manuscript[8] also leads us to ask how they might
have been read alongside each other by Coptic-speaking Christians.

Before proceeding, however, it is necessary to address the question
of whether these works in the Tchacos Codex can, properly speaking, be said to belong to the phenomena of "martyrdom." How one
addresses this problem depends of course upon how "martyrdom" is
defined. At present, a considerable debate is going on concerning the
meaning and origin of Christian martyrdom. At issue are the technical meaning of the term "martyr" within Christian literature, and
also the origin and historical development of martyr ideology within
ancient Mediterranean culture.[9] The problem is partially one of circular reasoning: whether or not a text is addressing martyrdom depends
upon how martyrdom is defined, as well as whether the presence
of the terminology of "martyr" is strictly necessary. Certainly some
ancient Christian notions of martyrdom would preclude discussing
the Tchacos texts under that rubric, for example, that martyrs attest
to Christ's death as atoning sacrifice—a notion nowhere found (positively) in these works. It is, however, precisely how Christians were
variously (and polemically) engaging situations of persecution and
violent death that is the question here, whether the term "martyr"

---

[6] Although the fourth work inscribed in the TC, *Allog.*, also shows points of topical congruence, such as the notion of two races, the manuscript is too fragmentary to
conclude whether or not it deals with issues of Jesus's death or the violent deaths of
Christians. Moreover, the extant text does not appear to present a context of persecution directly, although Allogenes does pray that he may be saved from everything
evil, but the reference is too general to assume it refers to persecution as such (see
Allog. 61.20–22).

[7] I am persuaded by Wurst 2008 that this *Gos. Jud.* is a version of what was known
by Irenaeus, and therefore it can in some form be dated to the second century C.E.
The composition of *Ep. Pet. Phil.* and *1Apoc. Jas.* can be dated to the late second or
early third century C.E. (see Meyer 1981, 194; Funk 2007, 322–323).

[8] For this dating of the TC, I rely on Wurst in Kasser et al. 2006a, 133–134.

[9] See especially Bowersock 1995 over against the position of Frend 1965.

is used or not. Methodologically, then, I propose a capacious under-standing of the category of martyrdom for our purposes here, one that does not presume any particular predetermination of the meaning of Jesus's death or the deaths of his followers—for that is precisely what was at issue.

Preparation for Martyrdom

What is meant by "preparation for martyrdom"? I would apply this des-ignation to a rather broad variety of the literature written by Christians in the second to third centuries, a time when the issue of persecution and martyrdom had become increasingly prominent in Christian writ-ing. A variety of new genre appear, especially martyr acts and exhor-tations to martyrdom, such as those by Origen and Ps. Tertullian.[10] These texts arguably articulated a set of practices aimed at training potential martyrs. Although historically relatively few Christians died as martyrs, most may have recognized persecution as a possibility for which they needed to be prepared. Indeed, scholars have already been looking at some of this literature in terms of Michel Foucault's notion of the "formation of the self,"[11] notably Judith Perkins and Elizabeth Castelli.[12]

I want to focus here on four commonly deployed strategies. Works aimed at "preparation for martyrdom" frequently set out models for imitation (and avoidance),[13] as well as offered exhortations to prayer and mastery of one's passions, especially fear and grief.[14] They encour-age believers to focus on the joys of eternal life, rather than on the ephemeral pain and suffering of the flesh. The martyrs' deaths are often represented as imitations of the suffering and death of Christ,

---

[10] See e.g., the collection of Musurillo 1972, Orig., *Mart.*; Ps.-Tert., *Mart.*

[11] See esp. Foucault, "The Hermeneutic of the Subject," "Self-Writing," "Technologies of the Self" in Rabinow 1997.

[12] The best treatment of such strategies to date is Castelli 2004 who theorizes the history of martyrdom as ideology in terms of the development of collective memory. See also Kelly 2006, on philosophical formation. Regarding strategies of counternarra-tive and "self-writing," see esp. chapters 3 and 4. See also Perkins 1995, esp. 104–123. In the past, similar dynamics have been treated, but within a very different theoretical framework in terms of social control (see esp. Riddle 1931).

[13] They sometimes offer counter examples of "failed martyrs"; for example, Quintus in *Mart. Pol.* 4.

[14] For a discussion of fighting the fear of death as a common trope in Roman notions of dying nobly, see Edwards 2007, esp. pp. 78–112.

heroic apostles, or Biblical heroes, and martyrs are ensured of an
eternal place in God's realm. "Preparation for martyrdom" texts also
frequently offer counter-narratives that (re)frame and (re)signify the
meaning of these deaths, challenging implicit Roman claims that the
bodies they shame, torture, and kill demonstrate the just punishment
of criminals; instead Christian literature represents them as witnesses
to the true God, evidence of heroism in the battle against false gods
and idolatry. Their spectacular tortured and humiliated bodies do not
attest to the greatness of Roman law and order, but to the courage and
endurance of those who love God.[15]

In short, despite the considerable diversity of genre, four elements
can be identified that are commonly offered in terms of "preparation
for martyrdom" (although not all are always present and others may
be identified as well). Its strategies presuppose that people had to be
trained well in the true teaching, learn to overcome fear, imitate laud-
able models from the past, and keep their eyes firmly fixed on the goal
of salvation.

These common strategies, however, show considerable diversity
in deployment. Significant differences appear not only in matters of
genre, but also in who is offered as a model for imitation and what is
to be imitated; what is the correct teaching about the nature of God,
the world, Jesus, and the self; how is one to overcome the passions;
and what is the ultimate end toward which one is admonished to
strive. Much therefore was at stake, including foundational theological beliefs, ethical practice, human relationship to God (salvation), and
indeed the meaning of life and death.

The first three works in the Tchacos Codex do not belong to the
genre of martyr acts or exhortations to martyrdom, but rather are narratives with substantial revelation dialogue featuring Jesus and one or
more of his disciples. This genre should not be surprising. How believers understood the deaths of their fellow Christians often depended
very much upon how they understood Jesus's death—and that was
itself an issue of enormous contention. Already in the first century
gospels, we can see Christians telling and retelling the passion story
as a way to grasp why Jesus was killed and what that might mean for

---

[15] Much recent work is being done on the issue of martyrdom and spectacle; see
e.g., Coleman 1990; Frilingos 2004; Gleason 1999; Castelli 2004, 104–133; Bowersock
1995, 41–57. On honor and shame, see esp. C. Barton 1994.

them. It is entirely plausible that Christians in the second and third centuries continued this narrative exploration, and indeed the widespread possibility of persecution may have been one reason that the letters of Paul and the four ultimately canonized gospels, with their theological and/or narrative focus on Jesus's passion and resurrection, became so prominent in Christian communities at this time. So, too, the first three works of the Tchacos Codex provide narratives in which Jesus speaks with one or more of his disciples, instructing them about how to understand his suffering in order to face their own. All are directed at Christian readers. Especially the *Letter of Peter to Philip* and the *First Apocalypse of James* employ all four of the strategies described above, and may be considered among the Christian literature of "preparation for martyrdom." The *Gospel of Judas* offers a more difficult case, as we will see, but it, too, is deeply interested in how the death of Jesus and his followers is understood, and therefore in how believers should prepare for their own deaths.

THE *LETTER OF PETER TO PHILIP* AND THE *FIRST APOCALYPSE OF JAMES*

The *Letter of Peter to Philip* and the *First Apocalypse of James* both present narratives in which readers are asked to follow prominent disciples of Jesus as they journey toward understanding suffering and death from persecution. Both emphasize accepting true teaching from Jesus as the way to overcome their fear. At the opening of the *Letter of Peter to Philip*, the apostles petition the Son to "give us power, for they seek to kill us"—perhaps hoping that such power will save them from violent deaths.[16] But by the end, they respond with joy when Jesus

---

[16] *Ep. Pet. Phil.* NHC VIII,2 134.8–9. For the question of the historical situation of persecution, see, for example, the discussion of Meyer 1981, 196–197, which describes suffering and death in terms of the mythic framework taught by Jesus in the work. He suggests very interestingly that Jesus calling the apostles "witnesses" sets them polemically against "the Great Church": "Other Christian literature can also refer to the unbelief of the followers of Jesus while he was still alive, before Easter faith came alive in their hearts. Here in the *Ep. Pet. Phil.*, however, the unbelief of the apostles may be interpreted more precisely. For it is these apostles who are the witnesses, the bearers of the tradition, the guarantors of the authenticity of the tradition since primitive times. It is these apostles who establish the oral and the written traditions, and to them the church looks for guidance. And their unbelief may be taken as the unbelief of the Great Church, which has not acknowledged the spiritual truths of Christian Gnosis" (119). There are a number of problems here, but that *Ep. Pet. Phil.* seeks

tells them that they will suffer.[17] They have accepted that the mission to preach the gospel and to heal will necessarily lead to suffering, and they go out with power in peace.[18] In this way, the text affirms that overcoming the passion of fear is an essential aspect of preparing to preach the gospel.

Similarly at the beginning of the *First Apocalypse of James*, James shows his fear of violence when he asks Jesus: "Rabbi, what are you saying? If they arrest you, what shall I do then?"[19] And again, when Jesus is in fact condemned, James responds only with grief. But by the end, James's reactions have been transformed. He goes to his death not with fear or grief, but only with words of compassion for those who kill him in ignorance: "My Father, you [who are in the] heavens, forgive them, for they do <not> know what they are doing."[20] What has led to these changes of heart? The disciples overcome their fear and grief by accepting the truth Jesus teaches.[21]

In the *Letter of Peter to Philip*, Jesus Christ appears as a great Light and instructs the apostles about the origin of the world and humanity's place in it. Readers are given a rather condensed version of the "Sophia myth" to explain all this. Jesus tells them that deficiency arose because the Mother acted to create aeons without the Father's per-

---

to appeal to apostolic authority—against other Christians—is intriguing. Koschorke argues, however, that Peter's citation of the "kirchlichen Credos" is not simply denied or declared false in *Ep. Pet. Phil.*, but rather it is interpreted as the starting point for a higher, spiritual understanding (Koschorke 1977, 330, 333–334). Thus he does not see polemics, but rather the fashioning of a gnostic hermeneutics within the church (Koschorke 1977, 334–343). It is therefore possible to accept Meyer's proposal that the apostles are meant as guarantors of the authority of the text's teaching, without necessarily seeing in it a strong polemic against other Christians—and yet we know from Irenaeus and others that tensions would indeed arise, if they had not already. The repeated call "to come together," in order to come to a common understanding as the basis of apostolic preaching, could itself be seen as a call for unity around a uniform message—a message that also resonates with the text's intertextual reading of *Acts*.

[17] *Ep. Pet. Phil.* NHC VIII,2 139.4–5.

[18] *Ep. Pet. Phil.* NHC VIII,2 140.23–26.

[19] *1 Apoc. Jas.* TC 11.17–19.

[20] *1 Apoc. Jas.* TC 30.21–26. The ignorance of the people who demand his death is not merely a case of mistaken identity—indeed the judges recognize that he is innocent (perhaps a trope from Luke-Acts?)—but more crucially they are ignorant regarding the truth of the situation (e.g. the cosmological drama in which they are involved). Ironically, they claim that "James is not worthy of life," meaning this life of the flesh, but of course the reader now understands that James is indeed worthy of life—immortal life.

[21] For a discussion of the philosophical strategy of overcoming the passions by proper instruction, see Nussbaum 1987.

mission. When she spoke, this audacity took on its own existence as the Arrogant One, and after she left, he grasped the (spiritual) part of her that had been left behind. He sowed it and subordinated it to his own powers and authorities, enclosing it within the mortal aeons. All of these lower powers were ignorant of the pre-existent Father and were strangers to Him. Out of pride and envy, the Arrogant One then commanded his powers to form mortal bodies, leading to lawlessness (TC) or malformation (NHC). Jesus was sent down in the mortal body to speak to those who had gone astray and to give them authority to become heirs of the Father.

Thus according to the *Letter of Peter to Philip*, Christ descends not to save the world, but to help free the part of the Mother that had been left behind and enclosed in the mortal body.[22] He teaches the apostles that when "(you) strip off from yourselves what is corrupted, then you will become illuminators in the midst of mortal humans"—that is, they will become missionary teachers.[23] This is a task of joy. The problem of suffering arises because the world's ruling powers don't want humanity to learn the truth, and so they fight against the inner man.[24] The only way to oppose them, Jesus urges, is to teach salvation in the world. He assures them that they can rely on the power sent by

---

[22] See Koschorke 1979. As Koschorke notes, this self-revelation constitutes a kind of "paraphrase" of the Johannine prologue, but one which gives it quite a new meaning by reading it intertextually with the narrative of the Mother's deficiency.

[23] *Ep. Pet. Phil.* NHC VIII,2 137.6–9.

[24] *Ep. Pet. Phil.* NHC VIII,2 137.21–22; TC 6.2–3. That suffering is one of the major themes of the *Letter of Peter to Philip* has been widely recognized, and some scholars have suggested it indicates that either the author or his community were suffering and perhaps being persecuted (see Scholten 1987, 65–68; Bethge 1991, 345–346; Meyer 1981, esp. 196–197; Ménard 1977, 9). Scholten suggests that this persecution might be considered explicitly in terms of Christian martyrdom, but ultimately he rejects this notion due to "the lack of a perspective of succession, especially imitation (of Jesus by the apostles) and other martyrological terminology" (65–66). The definitive point for Scholten is the lack of a historically transmitted witness. While it is true that Jesus calls the apostles "witnesses," they witness not to his suffering, death, and resurrection, but rather to the fact that the teaching contained in the text is the same as what he had told them before (*Ep. Pet. Phil.* NHC VIII,2 135.4–6), presumably during his earthly ministry. For Jesus says to his disciples, "It is you yourselves who witness that I spoke all these things to you before" (NHC VIII,2 135.4–6). Here the witness they give is that the teaching Jesus gave before his death is the same teaching he is now giving to them in a luminous revelation. Such an understanding of what it means to witness is not surprising here since the main task of the disciples in this text is missionary—to teach salvation in the world—but teaching in this text requires suffering and death, for they are opposed by the rulers of the world. As Jesus died (TC) or suffered (NHC), so will they.

the Father and by his own continuing presence—just as he had told them when he was in the body.

The *First Apocalypse of James* focuses on James's initial ignorance and his steady progress in coming to understanding. So although at the beginning Jesus had told James "you are ignorant concerning yourself," in the end James can claim: "Rabbi, I have come to believe all these things and they are well (established) within my soul."[25] Moreover, as James grows in understanding, he is able to overcome the fear and grief that had been overwhelming him.[26] What does Jesus teach him? Initially, he does not present an extended treatment of cosmology, but only a brief explanation that originally "Nothing existed except the One Who Is."[27] Jesus himself is second, deriving from It. Femaleness also exists, and she created powers and deities. This is practically all we learn initially of the transcendent Deity and the origin of the world, but Jesus tells James more later, offering again a condensed version of the "Sophia myth," describing *in nuce* that the powers that try to entrap the soul were created by the ignorant female Achmoth who acted without a male.[28] It seems that Jesus is concerned to help James understand about those powers who are ruling the world now and who oppose him, as well as about those beings (like Sophia) whom he can look to as models or call upon for help.

After the brief description at the beginning of his revelation, Jesus immediately moves to describe his purpose: to reveal the One Who Is, and to show people the "image of the powers" so that people can distinguish between what is theirs and what is not.[29] This is the "mystery" he has come to reveal. It is followed by a prediction of his arrest and condemnation. Jesus calls these events "my [deliverance]" and he specifically denies that he died.[30] So, too, Jesus teaches James (and the reader) that James's own death is also "his deliverance."[31] He tells James to "throw off the blindness that is in your heart, [and] the very body that is in the flesh. Then you will attain to the One Who Is, and you will no longer be James, but someone who in every respect is in

---

[25] *1 Apoc. Jas.* TC 10.5–6; 25.15–17.
[26] See *inter alia 1 Apoc. Jas.* TC 14.18; 17.1, 23–25; 19.6–8. Note the list of terms Scholten amasses concerning suffering (Scholten 1987, 73–74).
[27] *1 Apoc. Jas.* TC 10.8–9.
[28] *1 Apoc. Jas.* TC 22.1–15.
[29] *1 Apoc. Jas.* TC 11.1–7.
[30] *1 Apoc. Jas.* TC 11.14–15; cp. 10.1; 18.9.
[31] *1 Apoc. Jas.* TC 11.20–23.

the One Who Is."[32] Jesus's own death is part of this revelation: He says, "I shall [appear] in order to rebuke the rulers, [and I shall] reveal to them that there is one who cannot be grasped."[33]

In contrast to the *Letter of Peter to Philip*, the *First Apocalypse of James* is not interested in James becoming a missionary teacher or healer. "Do not be concerned about anything except your deliverance," Jesus urges him.[34] Although the text itself serves, if you will, as a kind of "missionary document" (with its own prophetic story of its inscription and fate), neither James (nor readers) are urged to spread the gospel; indeed he is to be quiet about all this, except to tell one person who will pass the teaching on. While it is true that James is portrayed as "a second master" to "his disciples," his role to them is as "a comforter."[35]

And in the end, James is not killed because of preaching the gospel or anything else he did—it was a case of mistaken identity![36] Or perhaps not. We are told that "the just God" is angry with James because James used to serve him—that, readers are told, was how he got his epithet "James the *Just*."[37] Other powers, too, will oppose James, notably the toll collectors who carry off souls; but Jesus equips him with the necessary knowledge ("the word of your power") to escape them when he is arrested.[38] That escape consists primarily in understanding both his own nature (that he is not subject to mortal suffering and death) and in understanding the nature of the powers who oppose him (that they belong to ignorance and flesh).[39] The people who kill James thus appear as ignorant dupes of "the just God," who is the real power

---

[32] *1 Apoc. Jas.* TC 13.20–14.2.

[33] *1 Apoc. Jas.* TC 16.16–20.

[34] *1 Apoc. Jas.* TC 15.20–22.

[35] *1 Apoc. Jas.* TC 23.10–25.14; 17:11–15.

[36] See n. 20 above.

[37] *1 Apoc. Jas.* TC 18.16–20.

[38] *1 Apoc. Jas.* TC 19.21–22.23.

[39] In his excellent study, Clemens Scholten argues that "The lack of questioning about the necessity especially of the suffering of the Savior underscores the separation of salvation from suffering, between which no bridge exists," (Scholten 1987, 80, my translation). But I would formulate this a bit differently—rather the connection between the two is different, as he notes. Rather than see Jesus's suffering as atonement, etc., Scholten argues persuasively that suffering is defined rather as a function of the text's metaphysics (76), with the result that "suffering is not intentionally accepted as a way to preserve faith but rather is accepted as an occurrence which cannot be changed" (78). Given this situation, however, if Jesus is to teach humanity, he too has to undergo suffering; it comes with the territory, so to speak.

behind the violence. Given the correspondence between James's death and that of Jesus, it is likely that the author of the *First Apocalypse of James* interprets Jesus's words in the *Gospel of Luke* 23:24 ("Father forgive them for they know not what they do") as having the same import: the real power behind Jesus's death is not the Romans nor the Jews, but "the just God." Those who believe otherwise are ignorant.

Jesus not only teaches James in revelatory speech, he also demonstrates the truth in his own suffering and death. He tells James explicitly that he did not die; it was "the *tupos* of the archons" who suffered and died.[40] The "weak flesh," he insists, will get what is coming to it—but that is no cause for distress.[41] So, too, will it be with James. The rulers will oppose him. He will be arrested and stoned to death—but this is nothing to be concerned about. James understands, and in the end, his only concern is for those who are still in ignorance.

This treatment of suffering articulates two perspectives to believers. On the one hand, human beings who come to know their true spiritual nature realize, like Jesus, that because their nature is not flesh, they do not suffer and the powers cannot harm them. On the other hand, suffering is requisite to living in the world, in a body of flesh under the domination of ignorant and malicious world rulers. In this situation evil has two aspects that the believer must strive to overcome: the passions of the flesh and the malice of the rulers. Using James—apparently well-known to have died as a martyr—the *First Apocalypse of James* illustrates exactly how this is to be done. James receives knowledge to challenge the rulers' ignorance and rebuke their forgetfulness.[42]

In the *First Apocalypse of James*, Jesus is clearly a model for imitation by James. So, too, the *Letter of Peter to Philip* offers a close correspondence between Jesus and the apostles. Both heal and teach in order to save others; both are persecuted by the world's powers because of this; their bodies suffer and die, but their true selves are untouched by this suffering and death. If we consider this as a "preparatory" work, it is first of all preparation for boldly preaching the good news taught by Jesus.[43] But it is precisely that activity which brings persecution. Preaching the gospel, therefore, requires the willingness to suffer and die. The text offers an example to imitate (Jesus' suffering and death),

---

[40] *1 Apoc. Jas.* TC 18.8–15.
[41] *1 Apoc. Jas.* TC 19.13–16.
[42] *1 Apoc. Jas.* TC 14.21–25.
[43] *Ep. Pet. Phil.* VIII,2 134.6–135.1; TC 3.5–9.

correct teaching to counter unbelief, and an admonition to overcome
the passion of fear. By receiving the Savior's revelation with joy and
by being willing to go forth to preach and heal, the apostles themselves
thereby become models for the readers of the text to imitate.

The ultimate end for all is immortality. In the *First Apocalypse of
James*, they are taught that their fate is not tied to the flesh; its suffering and death are not theirs. Like Christ, they too are strangers to this
suffering. Focus, Jesus tells James, on your deliverance: "(T)hrow off
the blindness that is in your heart, [and] the very body that is in the
flesh. Then you will attain to the One Who Is, and you will no longer
be James, but someone who in every respect is in the One Who Is."[44]
For the apostles in *Letter of Peter to Philip*, the ultimate end is not so
different, as Peter tells the others:

> 'Did our Lord Jesus, when he was in the body, show us everything? For
> he came down. My brothers, listen to my voice.' And he (Peter) was
> filled with a Holy Spirit. He spoke thus: 'Our illuminator, Jesus, [came]
> down and was crucified. And he bore a crown of thorns. And he put on
> a purple garment. And he was [crucified] on a tree and he was buried in
> a tomb. And he rose from the dead. My brothers, Jesus is a stranger to
> this suffering. But we are the ones who suffered through the transgres-
> sion of the Mother. And because of this he did everything according to
> a likeness for us.'[45]

Jesus demonstrated that suffering is not the ultimate reality, but merely
a consequence of the Mother's ignorant transgression. It is Jesus who
is the originator of their true life. The text ends with the message it
wants most to convey: "Be not afraid; behold, I am with you forever."[46]
This presence is one of power, peace, and joy.

Thus both the *Letter of Peter to Philip* and the *First Apocalypse of
James* demonstrate strategies that would prepare Christians to face
persecution: Each offers models for imitation, both in the figure of
Jesus and in his disciples. Jesus provides teaching, especially about the
nature of God and the world, that corrects erroneous views and allows
the disciples to see Jesus's death—and their own—in a very specific

---

[44] *1 Apoc. Jas.* TC 13.20–14.2.

[45] *Ep. Pet. Phil.* NHC VIII,2 139.9–28. The TC version reads "in a likeness" (*Ep.
Pet. Phil.* 8:6). The language of "likeness" here (TC: ϩⲛ ⲟⲩⲉⲓⲛⲉ or NHC: ⲕⲁⲧⲁ ⲟⲩⲉⲓⲛⲉ
suggests the theme of imitation). The translation of the TC critical edition is "symbolically" which I think does not as clearly communicate this theme.

[46] *Ep. Pet. Phil.* NHC VIII,2 140.21–23.

cosmological drama. Much as other Christians are resignifying the
Roman perspective that Christians are criminals deserving of death by
portraying those who are killed as martyrs battling against the forces
of Satan, so, too, the *Letter of Peter to Philip* and the *First Apocalypse
of James* cast Christians' battle as one against the wicked cosmological forces who rule the world and their (ignorant?) followers. Jesus's
teaching also helps the disciples to overcome the passions of fear and
grief by affirming that the world's powers can do nothing to harm
their true spiritual natures. Free of ignorance and fear, they are able
to go forth in truth and joy to follow the path that Jesus had already
modeled for them. And in this sense, the disciples themselves become
models for Christian readers.

THE *GOSPEL OF JUDAS*

When we turn to the *Gospel of Judas*, several important features distinguish it from these other two works in the Tchacos Codex regarding the question of "preparation for martyrdom." While it, too, is
very likely aimed at Christian readers in a situation of persecution,
its polemics are aimed not at Romans or even rhetorical Jews but
against other Christians, people who also claim to be living—and
dying—according to Jesus's teaching.[47] Moreover, while it is true that
the *Gospel of Judas* offers a retelling of Jesus's death, its resignification
is directed against a sacrificial theology and eucharistic practice promoted by other Christians—not Romans or other "pagan" idolaters.
Indeed, its rhetoric requires that readers already recognize Roman
sacrifice as idolatrous worship of false gods; the "new" message is that
Jesus's death and the death of his followers are no different—they too
are idolatrous offerings to lower angels. The *Gospel of Judas* also lacks
a characteristic focus on overcoming the passions, especially fear, a
central feature in other literature I am calling "preparation for martyrdom." Rather anger is the over-riding passion—a passion that fits
well with the context of heightened inner-Christian polemics.[48] And

---

[47] To call Christians who suffered at the hands of other Christians "martyrs" might
appear to be a radical deployment of the term, but the terminology of persecution at
the hands of other Christians is found already in the *Sec. Treat. Seth*. There Christians
describe their "persecution" at the hands of ignorant people "who (wrongly) think
they are advancing the name of Christ" (*Sec. Treat. Seth* NHC VII,2 59.19–60.3).
[48] For further discussion, see the contribution of Dunderberg in this volume.

finally, one has to ask whether Jesus or Judas serves as a model for anyone else to imitate.

In the *Gospel of Judas*, Jesus was sent from the immortal realm above to perform signs and wonders "for the salvation of humanity." He comes to teach his twelve disciples "about the mysteries which are beyond the world and about the things which will occur at the end."[49] He aims to expose the nature of the world rulers, their blood-thirsty violence and their impotence, and to demonstrate the reality of the immortal spirit and the heavenly world beyond this mortal sphere. However, all of them—except Judas—fail to comprehend who Jesus is and indeed they react angrily at his attempts to correct them. Judas alone is drawn aside and given advanced instruction. Then, near the end of the gospel, Jesus tells Judas, "As for you, you will surpass them all. For you will sacrifice the human being who bears me."[50]

What does Jesus's death accomplish, according to this gospel? The goal is not to free Jesus from being trapped in the flesh—he has shown at other times that he can come and go as he likes to the transcendent world.[51] Then what does his death mean? We can start to answer this question by noting that the *Gospel of Judas* ends when Judas hands Jesus over. No account of his arrest, trial, death or resurrection is given—and none is needed. While it is possible to think that Christian readers of the second century didn't need the rest of the story because they already knew it well, I think it is rather the case that everything necessary for salvation had already been said. The death of Jesus has already been predicted, so the reader knows what will happen, just as the *Gospel of Mark* leaves no doubt about the reality of Jesus's resurrection even when the author ends the story with the empty tomb. Moreover, Jesus's death is not central to salvation for the *Gospel of Judas*. It is Jesus's revelations to Judas that lead readers to understand the nature of the world, its rulers, and their place in it; it is his instruction that leads them to turn their souls toward worship of the true God so as to escape the final destruction. The sacrifice of "the human who bears Jesus" does not bring salvation, except insofar as it demonstrates a core teaching: that the true spiritual nature of humanity is not fleshly, nor can the spirit-filled soul be constrained by death. It

---

[49] *Gos. Jud.* 33.6–18.
[50] *Gos. Jud.* 56.15–21.
[51] See Pagels-King 2007, 135.

is Jesus's teachings that brings eternal life, not his death or even his resurrection.

It is this teaching that has the clearest resonance with the *Letter of Peter to Philip* and *1 Apocalypse of James*. Jesus took on a body in order to show the nature of human reality, that the mortality of the material flesh need not be the ultimate fate of human beings who were created in the image of the heavenly Adam. By turning to worship of the true God, their souls can become permanently tied to the spirits God has given them.[52] The sacrifice of Jesus's mortal body ("the human who bears him") is an attestation to his teaching, a demonstration of its truth.

Is Jesus, then, a model for the disciples in the text or for readers? He is certainly no model for the Twelve. Not only does the *Gospel of Judas* represent Jesus railing against the Twelve,[53] but it claims that Judas will be stoned to death by the Twelve. Far from being models for the reader, the disciples (except for Judas) do not repent and improve, they react with anger and blaspheme Jesus. Jesus tells the Twelve that they are the ones who are leading people astray like domestic animals brought to the altar for sacrifice.[54] These disciples, then, are not presented as models for the readers such as we find with the disciples in the *Letter of Peter to Philip*, or James in the *First Apocalypse of James*. We see no progression from ignorance to knowledge, from anger to joyous acceptance.

Is Judas, then, the model disciple? Certainly he shows more promise than the rest, and Jesus sets him apart from the others to give him special revelation. As with the disciples in the *Letter of Peter to Philip* and the *First Apocalypse of James*, we see Judas come slowly to greater understanding.[55] The author of the text clearly portrays him as the recipient of Jesus's highest teaching, and through him offers instruction to the reader about the nature of God, the origin of the world and humanity, the nature of the powers who rule over it, and human salvation. Such theological and cosmological teachings are not secondary additions to the gospel, but its core message. Those who understand

---

[52] For discussion of the *Gos. Judas'* teaching on the two spirits, see Pagels-King 2007.

[53] In the context of second and third century persecution, this invective was presumably aimed against those who rely upon apostolic succession from the Twelve for their authority (see Pagels-King 2007, 59–75).

[54] *Gos. Jud.* 39.18–40.2.

[55] So, also Marjanen forthcoming.

the truth will be able to join with the immortal spirits sent by God and ascend to the heavenly temple. Revelation to Judas is the device used by the author to convey these teachings.

Yet none of the disciples—even Judas—is charged to pass on this teaching. It is the literary work of the *Gospel of Judas* itself that plays this role. Rather, as Antti Marjanen has argued, Judas "is pictured as Jesus' special disciple because, through him, the text can criticize the other disciples and the form of Christianity they represent."[56] The *Gospel of Judas* exploits the well-known opposition between Judas and the other disciples to attack the kind of Christianity being authorized in the name of the Twelve in the second and third centuries.

Yet the gospel's portrait of Judas is also exegetically tied to a wide-spread Christian portrait of him as the betrayer, the vilified other, and the ultimate heretic, for at the end of the gospel it reproduces the story of Judas handing Jesus over and taking money for doing so. Does the *Gospel of Judas* really expect readers to see this act in an unambiguously positive light? How are readers expected to understand Judas's action in view of the teaching he received and Jesus's statement that Judas will surpass all the others? In handing Jesus over—and thereby acceding to the demands of the false gods—is Judas displaying the knowledge he has learned from Jesus that the body is not the self? In handing over "the human who bears" Jesus, is Judas not actually betraying the true God at all, but only giving over to the angelic rulers what already belongs to them? After all, Judas knows that he will himself suffer a violent death at the hands of the Twelve.[57] If he has understood Jesus's message, then readers must assume that Judas has accepted that fate and knows that all mortal bodies are destined for destruction and the other disciples can do no harm to his soul—and certainly the scribes can do no harm to the divine Jesus.

Yet precisely here, where Judas hands Jesus over, knowing that other Christians will persecute him, the logic of the *Gospel of Judas*'s narrative retelling starts to fail. Judas can be no model for other Christians suffering persecution by the Romans. The *Gospel of Judas* is surely not asking believers to turn over Christians—heretics or not—to the authorities. It is surely not furthering the expectation that more

---

[56] Marjanen forthcoming.
[57] *Gos. Judas* 44.23–45.1.

betrayals will lead to more intra-Christian reprisals.[58] Whether Judas himself attains the highest level of salvation in the gospel—a point currently being hotly debated among scholars[59]—the author cannot portray Judas's act as lacking all ambivalence, and he cannot therefore offer Judas as a model that the reader should imitate.

In what sense, then, can the *Gospel of Judas* be regarded under the rubric of "preparation for martyrdom"? Certainly it exhibits two of the common strategies: like other Christian gospels, it offers correct teaching that resignifies Jesus's death, and it asks readers to focus on the immortal realm above as their final goal. On the other hand, it offers no real models for imitation, nor does it teach readers to overcome fear and grief. The central aim is polemical—to combat the false views of other Christians.[60] In that, it is hardly unique. "Preparation for martyrdom" required correct teaching, but since Christians did not agree about what that teaching was, polemics were directed against other Christians who were believed to be recommending false views and practices—witness Tertullian's *Scorpiace* and the *Testimony of Truth* discussed below. We should place the *Gospel of Judas* among this literature of intra-Christian polemics, aimed at inculcating the true teaching in part by attacking the false. In that sense, it is preparing Christians to face opposition from the powers who rule the world, opposition that might mean their own violent deaths.

---

[58] For another case of polemic regarding Christians persecuting other Christians, see *Treat. Seth* NHC VII,2 59:19–60.3. Precisely what this 'persecution' involved is not clear.

[59] For differing views of how Judas is characterized in the *Gospel of Judas*, see esp. Kasser et al. 2006a; Ehrman 2006b; Pagels-King 2007; Painchaud 2006; DeConick 2007; Marjanen forthcoming; Pearson in this volume.

[60] In particular, the "anti-sacrificial" motif is strong and probably connected to the Savior's criticism of the Eucharist (*Gos. Jud.* 33.26–34.11; see Pagels-King 2007, 59–75). That the rejection of the fleshly, mortal body as the self does not require polemic against sacrifice is demonstrated by *1 Apoc. Jas.*, where it is treated allegorically. There Jesus tells James that the Father has sent him "as a priest. And everywhere one has to give me the first fruits and the firstborn. The [priest of] this [wo]rld receives the first fruits and assigns sacrifices and offerings. But I am not like this. Rather, I receive the first fruits of those who are defiled, so that I may send them up [un]defiled, that the true power may be revealed" (*1 Apoc. Jas.* TC 28.8–18). In context, we can read Jesus's self-description as a resignification of sacrifice: a true priest (Jesus) receives what is defiled (by the flesh) and cleanses it, revealing its true nature and power. This is quite different, however, from the *Gospel of Judas*.

Oppositional Polemics

What is gained by considering the first three works of the Tchacos Codex in terms of "preparation for martyrdom"? First of all, it lets us place these works in the broader context of early Christianity, a context in which Christians are not only concerned with facing possible torture and death but in which they are in bitter dispute with one another about how to understand why they are being persecuted. As Hadot has argued, philosophy was not merely about abstract ideas of truth or virtue, it was about practicing a way of life.[61] So, too, Christian theological treatises, dialogues, or gospel narratives, no matter how diverse, were always about how to live in preparation for eternal life. The literature we're calling "preparation for martyrdom" took as its particular challenge to teach believers how to maintain their confession to be Christian even under torture and threat of death. Disputes over the nature of the world and differences in narratives about Jesus and his followers were therefore never mere fanciful cosmology nor simply contested historical reconstructions.

Placing the writings of the Tchacos Codex within the context of orthodoxy and heresy debates thus only begs the question: Why are Christians disputing these particular issues? What was at stake? What difference did it make for how people faced suffering and death? How Christians conceived of God and the universe, how they narrated the foundational story of their "remembered" past—these were practices basic to their formation as Christians. And indeed it is important to see these texts not as ancient artifacts, but to imagine them in action. Imagine people composing them, probably out loud; imagine scribes writing them down, copying, and correcting ("editing") them; imagine people studying them, teaching them, and arguing about their contents; imagine people shaping and being shaped by these stories, and putting them into practice in a myriad of unpredictable and improvised ways in their lives—and at their deaths.

Although presumably the Roman persecutions of the second and third centuries provided the central impetus for Christians composing, reading, and studying these works, the fact that the Tchacos Codex was inscribed in the fourth century indicates that the texts in it, like martyr acts and exhortations, continued to be alive in practice even after the

---

[61] See Hadot 1995.

persecutions ended. Whether they were read for general spiritual self-
formation and theological education or some other aim is hard to say.
We may, however, speculate that the fact that all three were inscribed
in the same codex led to them being read together, such that the codex
as a whole may have enlarged upon or clarified difficult and disputed
points, as well as challenged the views of other Christians in its own
day, such as the development of atonement theology.

Reading these works as "preparation for martyrdom" also helps dis-
pel the blanket claims of polemicists like Irenaeus and Tertullian that
"heretics," who held views like those represented in the Tchacos Codex,
denounced martyrdom or fled out of cowardice.[62] Some no doubt did
flee, and at least one text from Nag Hammadi, the *Testimony of Truth*,[63]
confirms that others certainly directed virulent invective against "the
foolish" who think that confessing to being a Christian and suffering
a human death actually bring them salvation. Such people not only
destroy themselves, it claims, but they depict the Father as a vainglo-
rious deity who desires human sacrifice. Rather "the true witness," it
claims, is this: "When a person comes to know himself and God who
is over the truth, he will be saved, and he will crown himself with
the crown unfading."[64] Like Clement of Alexandria, who argued that
heretics could not rightly be numbered as martyrs because *as heretics*,
they could by definition not witness to the truth, so too the author of
Testimony of Truth argues that "the true witness" can be given only by
someone who understands that God requires not human sacrifice, but
renunciation of the world. Such a text offers an exemplary confirmation of Irenaeus's claim, as scholars have frequently noted.[65]

Yet scholars in our field today widely recognize that the Nag
Hammadi literature also offers evidence that questions the polemical claims of church fathers like Irenaeus and Tertullian.[66] Some
works suggest instead that at least some of the Christians who were
denounced as heretics actually insisted upon the necessity of suffer-

---

[62] See Tertullian, *Scorpiace*; Irenaeus, *Adv. Haer.* 4.33.9. This position has often been
reproduced in histories of early Christianity; see, for example, Chadwick 1976, 31.

[63] *Testim. Truth* NHC IX,3 31.21–32.21; 34.1–26.

[64] *Testim. Truth* NHC IX,3 45.1–6.

[65] See *Stromateis* IV.4 and *inter alia* Koschorke 1978, 127–137; Scholten 1987,
105–109; Middleton 2006, 21–23, 28. Scholten notes, insightfully, that the *Testimony
of Truth*'s critique does not foreclose the behavior of Gnostics in practice (Scholten
1987, 117–118).

[66] See especially the monograph of Scholten 1987, esp. 13–119.

ing and dying as Jesus had—and even Irenaeus concedes that some of the heretics had in fact suffered death for being Christian: "borne the reproach of the name."[67] Indeed, as I have shown above, such Christians actually wrote treatises preparing people to die as a consequence of their Christian beliefs. What sets these Christians apart is not that they sought to avoid martyrdom nor were not put to death as Christians, but rather that the meaning they gave to their suffering and deaths was distinctive. Indeed, the first three works in the Tchacos Codex exemplify attitudes which challenge the meanings that other Christians were (themselves variously) assigning to the deaths of Jesus and believers.[68] They demonstrate new ways in which Christians were struggling with the violence—and the potential of violence—in their midst. Clearly some were very frightened, and some were very angry. They wrote stories of encounters with Jesus to address their fears and their rage, rage not only at Romans but at each other. The *Letter of Peter to Philip* and *First Apocalypse of James* offer two examples of works aimed at least in part at preparing believers to overcome their fear and to face both the uncertainty of violence and the certainty of death. The *Gospel of Judas*, while sharing some of their views, offers something quite different. It lets us see, perhaps more clearly than we had before, how violence aimed at Christians from the outside took full root within the community itself, where we hear Christians raging against each other and can imagine communities torn apart.

Yet despite the heat of oppositional polemics and the very important differences among Christians, the more significant lesson in viewing these works as "preparation for martyrdom" lies in their similarities to other Christian works of this kind. Not only were they generated in comparable contexts where persecution was an on-going possibility, they were using very similar strategies to prepare themselves and were engaging very similar sites for theology-making and self-formation, notably the deaths of Jesus and his immediate followers. Before we move too quickly to acknowledge the historical winners and losers, we need to linger and observe quietly and carefully what it meant for people to be persecuted so violently for their religious beliefs. The heroized portraits of martyrs—whether the "orthodox" *Martyrdom of Polycarp*

---

[67] *Adv. Haer.* IV.33.9.

[68] It is important to note that it is not possible to sketch a single "orthodox" position over against which a single "heretical" position can be placed. Rather this period saw Christians articulating a variety of meanings to suffering and death.

or the "heretical" *First Apocalypse of James*—aim less at historical portraits of the complex reality than at instruction and encouragement to
fellow Christians. Narratives of heroic models shaped a "usable past"
for Christian aims, but at the same time Christianity was shaped in
decisive ways by entrenching narratives of violence and oppositional
polemics at the heart of the Christian story. Damaged and partial as
they are, the pages of the Tchacos Codex offer an important contribution to charting the theological and literary creativity of Christians in
the face of violence and disagreement.

In putting Christians to death in the second and third centuries,
Roman officials may have aimed to remove obstinate subjects and
atheistic criminals, but their actions had unanticipated effects on how
Christianity was constructed. A new emphasis upon forming oneself
spiritually to face violent death may have led to a particular kind of
interest in the death of Jesus and his earliest disciples. The rich literature of gospel passion narratives, martyr acts, exhortations to martyrdom, and works focusing on inner-Christian polemics sharpened and
altered discussions about the meaning of Jesus's death by "reading"
it anew in the face of Christians' violent deaths. Not only "orthodox"
writers, but "heretics" as well were engaged in this important theological practice.

IRENAEUS ON THE *GOSPEL OF JUDAS*
AN ANALYSIS OF THE EVIDENCE IN CONTEXT

Johannes van Oort

As far as we can see, the first person in history bearing testimony to a *Gospel of Judas* is Irenaeus of Lyon (ca. 180–185 CE). Oftentimes in recent publications his testimony has been mentioned and sometimes it is even discussed at length. The passage in question, however, seems to be worth a close rereading, both in the context of Irenaeus' *Against Heresies* and in relation to other patristic testimonies.

Irenaeus speaks about a *Gospel of Judas* at the end of his first book *Against Heresies*, in a passage immediately following his description of the ancestors of the Valentinians.[1] After his overview of gnostic doctrines from the arch-heretic Simon Magus up to and including the Gnostics who usually are termed 'Ophites', he concludes in *Adv. haer.* 1,30,15: 'Such are the opinions current among those people, from which opinions, like the Lernaean hydra, a many-headed beast has been generated: the school of Valentinus (…)'.[2]

Irenaeus proceeds by speaking of *alii*, 'others', that is to say: other Gnostics.[3] The full passage in question, in the modern editions and translations rather misleadingly printed as the first paragraph of a new

---

[1] *Adv. haer.*, quoted here according to the critical edition (with French translation, introduction, notes, and appendices) of Rousseau-Doutreleau 1979. The older editions of Massuet 1710, Stieren 1848–1853 and, in particular, Harvey 1857, have been consulted as well.

[2] *Adv. haer.* 1,30,15 (Rousseau-Doutreleau 1979, 384): 'Tales quidem secundum eos sententiae sunt: a quibus, uelut Lernaea hydra, multiplex capitibus fera [de] Valentiniani scola generata est…'.

[3] Cf. the parallel introduction of the (in later tradition) so-called Ophites in *Adv. haer.* 1,30,1 (Rousseau-Doutreleau 1979, 364): 'Alii autem…'.

chapter,[4] runs in a fairly literal (if not clumsy) Latin rendering[5] of the lost Greek text as follows:

> Alii autem rursus Cain a superiore Principalitate dicunt, et Esau et Core et Sodomitas et omnes tales cognatos suos confitentur: et propter hoc a Factore impugnatos, neminem ex eis malum accepisse. Sophia enim illud quod proprium ex ea erat abripiebat ex eis ad semetipsam. Et haec Iudam proditorem diligenter cognouisse dicunt, et solum prae ceteris cognoscentem ueritatem, perfecisse proditionis mysterium: per quem et terrena et caelestia omnia dissoluta dicunt. Et confi(n)ctionem adferunt huiusmodi, Iudae Euangelium illud uocantes.[6]

An English translation that is as literal as possible may run as follows:

> And others again declare (that) Cain (was) from the superior Principle, and they confess that Esau and Korah and the Sodomites and all such people are their cognates: and for this reason attacked by the Creator, none of them has suffered harm. For Sophia snatched away that which belonged to her out of them to herself. And Judas, the betrayer, they say, had got a thorough knowledge of these things; and he alone, knowing the truth above all the others, accomplished the mystery of the betrayal. Through him all things, both earthly and heavenly, have been dissolved, as they say. And they adduce a composed work to this effect, which they call 'the Gospel of Judas'.

---

[4] The division in chapters and paragraphs with their (sub)headings does not stem from Irenaeus, but has been added later. On the so-called Latin 'argumenta', based on Greek manuscripts now lost, and their subsequent insertion as chapter headings in the Latin manuscripts, see the various remarks by Doutreleau in Rousseau-Doutreleau 1979, 30 ff., and, moreover, the corresponding expositions mainly pertinent to the edition of the other books of *Adv. haer.* in previous volumes of the *SC* (e.g. *SC* 100, 186–191; *SC* 210, 47–48). Still important is the seminal study by Loofs 1890.—Oftentimes in recent discussions the complicated question of the chapter headings has not been taken into account, with the result that some scholars maintain on the basis of Irenaeus' testimony (i.e., in actual fact, on the later added chapter heading) that the *Gos. Jud.* stems from the so-called Cainites while others argue that in this respect Irenaeus is wrong. But, strictly speaking, Irenaeus himself does not speak of 'Cainites' in the famous 'paragraph' in which he makes mention of the *Gos. Jud.* The link between this text and Cainite Gnostics is found in later antique testimonies (or may be inferred from them; see below) and, in particular, is suggested by the chapter headings in many modern editions and translations.

[5] In all likelihood the translation stems from a person who had little command of Latin but an excellent mastery of Greek. See e.g. Doutreleau's remarks—for an important part based upon the studies of Lundström—in the various *SC*-volumes. The literalness of the translation (which, moreover, rather easily can be retransferred into Greek) fully warrants for being the basis of our analysis.

[6] *Adv. haer.* 1,31,1 (Rousseau-Doutreleau 1979, 386).

In order to get a better understanding of the passage, first some words and phrases may be briefly annotated. In these annotations I take notice of a number of previous English translations of Irenaeus' text, in particular the recent ones published in books and other studies on the *Gospel of Judas*.[7] Moreover, special attention will be paid to other patristic testimonies to the *Gospel of Judas*: first the Greek testimony of Epiphanius, the bishop of Cyprus who ca. 375 wrote his *Panarion*, commonly known as the *Refutation of all heresies*;[8] secondly the Greek testimony of Theodoret, bishop of Cyrrhus in Syria, who sometime in the middle of the fifth century composed his *Compendium of Heretical Fables*.[9] It is generally assumed that Epiphanius in his testimony is dependent on Irenaeus on the one hand and probably on a second written source on the other, while Theodoret in his brief paragraph on the 'Cainites' appears to hand down an abstract of Irenaeus' passage based on its original Greek wording.

a superiore Principalitate...: from the superior Principle... This Principle, being the supreme Authority above all things, is elsewhere indicated as ἐξουσία or αὐθεντία. See the presumed original Greek text of Irenaeus reconstructed on the basis of Theodoretus, *Haer. fab.* 1,15 (αὐθεντία) in Rousseau & Doutreleau, I/1, 312. Cf. *Principalitas* in e.g. Irenaeus' account of Cerinthus (*Adu. Haer.* 1,26,1; Rousseau & Doutreleau I/1, 344) and its Greek equivalent ἐξουσία.

In recent English discussions of the passage (e.g. Wurst, 123 = *idem*, 170; Gathercole, 116; DeConick, 17; Turner, 190) *principalitas* is translated as 'power'. The noun 'power', however, seems best to be reserved for translating *uirtus* in Irenaeus' account of Gnostic systems like in *Adv. haer.* 1,30,1ff or 1,26,1 (cf. δύναμις in the Greek reports).

propter hoc...: for this reason... Namely for being *a superiore Principalitate*.

---

[7] Kasser et al. 2006, 121–135 and notes 171–173; Kasser et al. 2008, 169–179 and notes 193–195; Ehrman 2006b; Pagels-King 2007; Gathercole 2007; DeConick 2007; Turner 2008, esp. 190–191. Cf. for other English translations of *Adv. haer.* 1, 31 e.g. Irenaeus' *Against Heresies* in: Roberts-Donaldson 1994, 2:358; Foerster 1972, 41–42; Layton 1987, 181; Unger-Dillon 1992, 102–103. In contrast to its German original, the translation in Haardt 1971, 65–66 is of little value.

[8] *Pan.* 38 (Holl 1915, 62–71).

[9] *Haereticorum fabularum compendium* 1,15 (*MPG* 83, 368).

Sophia enim illud quod proprium ex ea erat abripiebat ex eis ad semetipsam: For Sophia snatched away that which belonged to her out of them to herself. One may translate the imperfecum *abripiebat* (cf. Theodoretus' aorist ἀνήρπασεν) also strictly as 'was in the habit of snatching away'. Moreover, *illud quod proprium ex ea erat* may be very literally rendered as 'that which was her own from herself' or 'that which was her own (and came) out of her'. Cf. Theodoretus, *Haer. fab.* 1,15, who transmits: 'For Sophia snatched away that which was her own in them out of them': ἡ γὰρ σοφία ὅπερ εἶχεν ἐν αὐτοῖς ἀνήρπασεν ἐξ αὐτῶν.

Iudam proditorem...: Judas, the betrayer... See below on *proditionis mysterium*: 'the mystery of the betrayal'.

haec...: these things... *Haec* refers to the immediately foregoing, namely (an essential part of) the myth of Sophia. The note of B. Layton (*Gnostic Scriptures*, 181): 'Perhaps referring to the union of the anointed (Christ) and Jesus as related in 1.30.12–13' is interesting and might specify an essential part of the message of the *Gospel of Judas*, but is highly problematic in view of the standard use of the Latin pronoun *haec*.

solum prae ceteris cognoscentem ueritatem...: he alone knowing the truth above all the others.... 'Above' or 'better than the others', *i.e.*, the other disciples or apostles. Cf. Theodoretus, *Haer. fab.* 1,15: μόνον ἐκ πάντων τῶν ἀποστόλων. The verb *cognoscere* (and not *scire*, for example) once again refers to a process: 'having become acquainted with', 'having learned'. Cf. Theodoretus: ἐσχηκέναι τὴν γνῶσίν. The subject of this initiation process is 'the truth' or, according to Theodoretus' apt wording, the *gnosis*, namely of (the essence of) the myth of Sophia.

proditionis mysterium...: the mystery of the betrayal... From Irenaeus' text it is not clear whether *proditio* in *perfecisse proditionis mysterium* has any negative connotation (cf. the New Testament παραδίδοναι), but from Theodoretus' rendering τὸ τῆς προδοσίας μυστήριον and, all the more, from the traditional expression τῆς προδοσίας μισθόν (cf. Acts 1:18: ἐκ μισθοῦ τῆς ἀδικίας) in his next sentence, one may conclude that here (like probably already by the Gnostics themselves?) the meantime current designation of Judas' deed

with προδοσία = *proditio* = 'betrayal' has been adopted. This traditionally negative meaning of *proditio*/προδοσία, however, is now reversely
evaluated in a very positive way (and thus fully coincides with the
positive meaning of *mysterium*).

per quem...: through him... The Latin *per quem* refers to Judas and
not to the preceding *mysterium*. In the latter case it should read 'per
quod', but neither Rousseau & Doutreleau, Harvey, Stieren nor Massuet
do indicate such a reading from any of the mss. This does not imply,
however, that 'by which' (so e.g. Foerster & Wilson, *Gnosis*, 42) is
completely beside the mark. 'By/through him' appears to imply here:
'through his deed', *i.e.*, the deed of the one who did get knowledge of
(and hence *knows*) the truth.

dissoluta...: dissolved... Curiously most of the English translations I
was able to consult either render *dissoluta* as 'thrown into confusion'
(e.g. *ANF*, 358; cf. Pagels & King, xii; DeConick, 174; Turner, 191) or
'thrown into dissolution' (e.g. Layton, 181; cf. Wurst, 123 and *idem*,
170). I do not see any reason for introducing the concept 'confusion'
into the text and the same goes for the verb 'throw' if taken literally.
Irenaeus' text says 'dissolved' (so rightly Foerster & Wilson, 42; cf.
Gathercole, 116). On the verb *dissoluere*, see below. This *dissoluere*
may also be translated as 'destroy' (so Unger & Dillon, 103, followed
by Ehrman, 63): probably the original Greek read καταλύειν (cf. e.g.
Adv. haer. 1,24,2 and also 1,21,4, like so many passages in the New
Testament).

confi(n)ctionem...: a composed work... From the existing editions
(see in particular the *apparatus criticus* in Rousseau & Doutreleau,
I/2, 386) it is clear that only Erasmus in his *editio princeps* of 1526
reads 'confinctionem'. The principal manuscripts C (= Claromontanus
from the 9th c.) and V (= Vossianus from the year 1494) read 'con-
fictionem', however. Moreover, the ms. A (= Arundelianus, 12th c.)
reads 'confinetionem' and the ms. Q (= Vaticanus, c. 1429) reads
'confinnectionem'. On the possible implications of these *variae lectio-
nes*, see below.—In point of fact the Latin word *confi(n)ctio* can be
translated as 'fabrication', 'invention', or even 'fiction'. The consulted
English renderings have 'a fictitious history' (*ANF*, 1, 358; Pagels &
King, xii; DeConick, 174); 'a fabrication' (Foerster & Wilson, 42); 'a

fabricated work' (Layton, 181; Wurst, 123; *idem*, 170; Turner, 191); 'a fabricated book' (Gathercole, 116); and even straightforwardly 'fiction' (Unger & Dillon, 103; Ehrman, 63). However, it is doubtful whether here the word *confinctio* (so Harvey) or *confictio* (the most likely reading, rightly followed by Massuet and Stieren; cf. above on the mss.) first and foremost has a negative connotation (Haardt & Hendry, 65 even 'translate': 'a second-rate work'). Literally 'con-fictio' (*fictio* like *fi(n)ctio* being derived from *fingere* and originally denoting the act of forming) may indicate a 'com-posite' (cf. *Thesaurus Linguae Latinae*, V, 205 s.v. *confictio* and 213-214 s.v. *confingere*, the second meaning of *confingere* being *componere, conficere*), a work that has been conflated from several components (and, in the case at issue, even from several Gnostic traditions). Therefore my translation: 'a composed work'. Cf. Theodoretus (a Gospel 'which they have composed': ὅπερ ἐκεῖνοι συντεθείκασιν) and Epiphanius (συνταγμάτιον), all of which evidence seem to justify the translation given here.—On the basis of a parallel text like *Adv. haer.* 1,20,1 (see below) one may suppose that Irenaeus' original Greek read something like σύμπλασις,[10] which word in the first place indicates a writing moulded or fashioned together and then, in a transferred sense, also may have the predominantly negative overtones of 'fabrication' or even the completely negative meaning of 'fiction' or 'feigned work'.—It is important to note that in regard to the writings of the Marcosians—which he mentions as one of his sources of information—Irenaeus also speaks of writings 'they *adduce*' and 'have *composed/fabricated*'. See *Adv. haer.* 1,20,1 (Rousseau & Doutreleau, I/2, 288): *Super haec autem inenarrabilem multitudinem apocryphorum et perperum scripturarum, quas ipsi finxerunt, adferunt...*, which text runs according to the Greek rendering of Epiphanius: Πρὸς δὲ τούτοις ἀμύθητον πλῆθος ἀποκρύφων καὶ νόθων γραφῶν, ἅς αὐτοι ἔπλασαν, παραφέρουσιν....—In their translation of *confinctio* in 1,31,1, Rousseau & Doutreleau (I/2, 387) steer a middle course: 'un écrit de leur fabrication'.

adferunt....: adduce... *Adferunt* has several meanings (so rightly Wurst, 127 and *idem*, 172). Accordingly one may translate 'they bring

---

[10] If not, perhaps, like Epiph., συνταγμάτιον! Cf. Reynders 1954, 62. But see also Loewe 1888, 442 (σύμπλασις-*confictio*) and 446 (σύνθεσις-*confictio, compositio*). Lundström (1943, 1948) does not discuss the problem.

forth', 'they adduce', 'they produce', 'they put forward', 'they present', etc. Cf. Epiphanius, *Pan.* 38,1,5 Holl 63,14: φέρειν. Ehrman, 64
concludes: 'Irenaeus never says that the Gospel of Judas was actualluy
written by the Cainites, only that they used is'. In my view, however,
the use of the verb *adferre* or φέρειν in no way excludes that this Gospel is their own product. First, one may compare Irenaeus' reference
to the writings *of* the Marcosians and their παραφέρειν in the preceding annotation. Secondly, one may closely read Irenaeus' subsequent
remark about the (other) writings of the Gnostics he is dealing with
(see below). Thirdly, we have the testimony of Theodoretus, who may
be considered to abstract Irenaeus' lost Greek text word for word or,
in any case, nearly verbatim. Theodoretus explicitly says: Προφέρουσι
δὲ αὐτοῦ καὶ Εὐαγγέλιον, ὅπερ ἐκεῖνοι συντεθείκασιν: 'And they also/
even bring forth a Gospel of him [sc. Judas], which they themselves
have composed'.

Before expanding upon Irenaeus' rather brief but essential passage, I
quote the immediately following line as well. Here Irenaeus states:

> *Iam autem et collegi eorum conscriptiones(,) in quibus dissoluere opera
> Hysterae adhortantur: Hysteran autem Fabricatorem caeli et terrae
> uocant.*[11]

> And,[12] further, I have also made a collection of their writings(,)[13] in which
> they exhort to dissolve the works of the Hystera (Womb): Hystera they
> call the Creator of heaven and earth.

The sentence is quite clear about one thing that is of prime interest in
this context. Irenaeus explicitly states that he made a collection of the

---

[11] *Adv. haer.* 1,31,2 (Rousseau-Doutreleau 1979, 386).

[12] Here and in the previous Latin quotation, we may render *autem* either by 'and'
or 'but' or leave it untranslated. *Autem* here and elsewhere in Iren. apparently seems
to render the original Greek δέ.

[13] Or, perhaps, 'compositions' as well? The word *conscriptiones*, however, in the Latin
Iren. seems to denote writings in general; cf. e.g. *Adv. haer.* 1,25,5, where the Greek
original reads συγγράμματα (Rousseau-Doutreleau 1979, 342).—It is interesting to
speculate about the comma here. As far as I can see on the basis of the editions available to me, the said punctuation mark seems (or better, in view of its likely absence
in the mss, is *supposed*) to be necessary. Theod. does not have the passage and Epiph.
writes: καὶ ἄλλα τινὰ συγγράμματα (some other written compositions!) ὡσαύτως
πλάττονται κατὰ τῆς Ὑστέρας, ἣν Ὑστέραν κ.τ.λ., which passage does not provide a
clue to our problem. However, in case the comma is rightly supposed to be absent,
Iren. states he has collected the other writings of these Gnostics in which they spoke
of (the theme of) *dissoluere*.

writings of the Gnostic sect he is dealing with. However, what does his statement actually imply? As I indicated in my translation already, the Latin *iam*[14] appears to make the connection between this sentence and the preceding lines: 'Further/Moreover, I have also made a collection of their (other)[15] writings'. One may infer from this explicit statement that Irenaeus himself[16] succeeded in collecting these scriptures and that, moreover, the provided information does stem from these books. In their books the Gnostics under discussion 'exhort to dissolve the works of the Hystera', *i.e.*, the works of 'the Creator of heaven and earth'.

In recent publications in which Irenaeus' testimony relating to the *Gospel of Judas* has been discussed,[17] an antithesis is discerned between the just quoted sentence and the preceding information. With regard to the *Gospel of Judas*, so it is inferred, Irenaeus does not indicate any first-hand knowledge. His reference to personally collecting some gnostic writings seems to be in sharp contrast with the preceding lines. The conclusion then is that—in all probability—Irenaeus did not have any direct knowledge of the *Gospel of Judas*.

One may express doubts about this view. Reading the report as we have it—and without being influenced by any subdivision of the text that does not emanate from Irenaeus[18]—another conclusion turns out to be the most likely one. Irenaeus makes mention of the *Gospel of Judas* and, immediately after that, he states that he has even made a collection of the (other) writings of the Gnostics who 'adduced' it. The first and, apparently, main characteristic of these writings is that they exhort to

---

[14] See the use of *iam* in widely-read (and imitated) writers like Cicero and Vergil, which word—apart from 'already'—in these writers also denotes 'moreover' or 'indeed'.

[15] Although 'other' is not literally present in the text by means of, for instance, the adjective *aliae*, a translation like the one given here is quite naturally justified by the context (and, perhaps, also by the rather emphatic *et*). Cf. the French translation in Rousseau-Doutreleau 1979, 387: 'J'ai pu rassembler d'*autres* écrits émanant d'eux'.

[16] Cf. below the discussion of the possible sources from which the passage might have been taken, leading to the conclusion that we are dealing here with first-hand knowledge of Iren. himself.

[17] E.g. Wurst 2008, 127–128, 173–174; cf. Gathercole 2007, 119.

[18] In the edition of Rousseau-Doutreleau 1979, 386, the sentence *Iam autem et collegi* etc. is the beginning of the new paragraph 1,31,2, like e.g. in the influential translation in *ANF* 1, 358 and the rendering by Foerster-Wilson 1972, 42. In many recent references to and discussions of Irenaeus' testimony (e.g. Ehrman; Pagels-King; DeConick), the information from this sentence is not mentioned at all. It is also conspicuously absent in Layton 1987, 181.

dissolve the works of the Creator.[19] This activity of *dissoluere* is just described as a central tenet of the *Gospel of Judas* as well: 'through him (= Judas) all things, both earthly and heavenly, have been dissolved'.

Hence this *dissoluere*[20] appears to indicate an essential relation between the contents of the various writings. It is clear that, according to Irenaeus, the *Gospel of Judas* and the other writings stem from one and the same Gnostic group. Their same subject matter (most prominent in the case of the central concepts *Hystera* and *dissoluere*, but also in the equivalent *Factor* and *Fabricator* and the closely parallel *diligenter cognouisse* and *scientia perfecta*, among others) entitles to conclude that the writings are closely akin.

And did Irenaeus personally read them? Few will doubt any actual reading in regard to the writings of which he so emphatically states that he collected them. A person who has intentionally collected some writings and, moreover, is able to communicate central tenets from their contents, will be supposed to have read them.

But does the same go for the *Gospel of Judas*? I do not see any compelling reason to cast doubts on this feasible possibility either. As in his references to the doctrines of the various 'Valentinians' and other Gnostics of whom Irenaeus explicitly states that he had copies of their works available,[21] here his procedure of communicating their contents is in the same vein. In *Adv. haer.* 1,31 he relates some essentials

---

[19] The remainder of Irenaeus' notice is nothing else than a further explication of this principal duty to which the writings exhort: *Nec enim aliter saluare eos nisi per omnia eant, quemadmodum et Carpocrates dixit. Et in unoquoque peccatorum et turpium operationum Angelum adsistere, et operantem audere audaciam et immunditiam inferre, id quod inest ei operationi, Angeli nomine dicere: O tu, Angele, abutor opere tuo; o tu, illa Potestas, perficio tuam operationem. Et hoc esse scientiam perfectam, sine timore in tales abire operationes, quas ne nominare quidem fas est* (*Adv. haer.* 1,31,2; Rousseau-Doutreleau 1979, 386).

[20] Which has a remarkable parallel in the *Gos. Mary* (*BG* 8502, 15,20–16,1). See the recent edition and translation by Tuckett 2007, 94–97: 'I have recognized that the All is being dissolved, both the earthly (things) and the heavenly things'; and his subsequent commentary.

[21] E.g. *Adv. haer.* 1, *praef.* 2 (Rousseau-Doutreleau 1979, 22): *cum legerim commentarios ipsorum... Valentini discipulorum*; *Adv. haer.* 1,20,1 (Rousseau-Doutreleau 1979, 228) with regard to the 'Marcosians' (after having given samples from their 'exegesis', obviously from their own writings as well): *Super haec autem inenarrabilem multitudinem apocryphorum et perperum scripturarum, quas ipsi finxerunt, adferunt...* (with subsequent discussion of their contents); *Adv. haer.* 1,25,4 (Rousseau-Doutreleau 1979, 338) with regard to the followers of Carpocrates: *secundum quod scripta eorum dicunt*; cf. 1,25,5 (Rousseau-Doutreleau 1979, 342): *In conscriptionibus autem illorum sic conscriptum est et ipsi ita exponunt.*

of the doctrines of the Gnostic group he is discussing. Moreover, he rather emphatically (while repeatedly) states: *dicunt*: 'they declare', 'they say', 'as they say' and also *uocant*: 'they call'. The same *dicunt*[22] or *uocant*—and, significantly, the same procedure of detailing essentials of the doctrinal contents of their writings—time and again are found in those descriptions of the Gnostics and their doctrines the first-hand knowledge of which no one will doubt. It may suffice here to refer to the very first sentence of Irenaeus' first report: '*Dicunt* esse quendam in inuisibilibus et inenarrabilibus altitudinibus perfectum Aeonem, qui ante fuit; hunc autem et Proarchen et Propatora et Bython *uocant*'.[23] Further proof one may easily gain from a glance at the ensuing reports[24] like, for example, from his discussion—apparently based on their writings—of other Valentinians,[25] of the Gnostic Marcus and the Marcosians,[26] and of the followers of Carpocrates.[27]

Although brief according to our standards (and eagerness to know), but actually not markedly brief (or conspiciously vague) in the context of an appendix to his overview of the ascendants of the 'Valentinians', Irenaeus' information about the tenets of the Gnostic group under discussion and about their view of Judas appears to be rather detailed.

Before discussing some of the details relevant to our topic further, we have to enter a vexed and still much disputed issue. Oftentimes in previous research it has been stated that Irenaeus, either for his entire overview of the ascendants of 'the Valentinian school' (*Adv. haer.* 1,23–30/31) or in any case for his description of the ancient and more remote ancestors of the 'Valentinians' (*Adv. haer.* 1,23–28) is dependent on a source. This source is supposed to be the *Syntagma* of Justin Martyr[28] or some updated version of this—unfortunately lost—heresiological

---

[22] And not e.g. *dicuntur*: 'They are said...'. Cf. e.g. *dicitur* in *Adv. haer.* 1,23,1, indicating some second-hand story.

[23] *Adv. haer.* 1,1,1 (Rousseau-Doutreleau 1979, 28).

[24] *Adv. haer.* 1,1,2 ff. (Rousseau-Doutreleau 1979, 32 ff.).

[25] *Adv. haer.* 1,11–12, in particular 12,1 ff (Rousseau-Doutreleau 1979, 180 ff.).

[26] *Adv. haer.* 1,13 ff. (Rousseau-Doutreleau 1979, 188 ff.).

[27] *Adv. haer.* 1,25 ff., in particular 1,25,4 (Rousseau-Doutreleau 1979, 338 f., e.g.: *secundum quod scripta eorum dicunt*).

[28] Lipsius 1865. On pp. 181–188, Lipsius, starting from Epiphanius' *Pan.* 38 discusses most of Irenaeus' *Adv. haer.* 1,31 as well. For Justin's *Syn.*, see the earliest reference in his *Apol.* 1,26,8.

work.[29] Indeed one may discern a marked difference between the long
sections in *Adv. haer.* 1,1–21 in which Irenaeus purports to have as his
resources—apart from his personal contacts with them—works of the
Gnostics he is refuting and the separate section (*Adv. haer.* 1,23–28) in
which he briefly discusses their obviously more remote ancestors. There
seems to be much reason to assign the main contents of *Adv. haer.*
1,23–28 to a source, be it Justin's *Syntagma* or some reworked version
of this writing.[30] However, already in regard to *Adv. haer.* 1,29–30 (on
the so-called 'Barbelo-Gnostics' and the Gnostics termed in later tradition 'Ophites'), one may side the opinion of those who argue that here,
once again, Irenaeus because of his style and rather detailed summary
is referring to sources current among these Gnostics, writings moreover
he was personally acquainted with.[31]

This very same impression one gets from the immediately following section *Adv. haer.* 1,31,1–2[32] as well. Like the preceding 'Ophites'
(1,30,1–14), being like the previously described 'Barbelo-Gnostics'
(1,29,1–4) a branch of the *multitudo Gnosticorum* Irenaeus is going to
discuss from 1,29,1 onwards, he introduces the Gnostics of the *Gospel of
Judas* in *Adv. haer.* 1,31,1 as some other *alii*: 'Others again declare…and
confess'. What exactly they 'declare' and 'confess' and 'say' and 'call'
is outlined briefly, even with the inclusion of what appears to be an
explicit quote from one of 'their other writings'.[33] But not only because
of its style and contents it seems to be difficult to assign this section
to an underlying heresiological source. If so, then Irenaeus would turn
out to be a very clumsy 'author' who even copied from his source: *Iam
autem et collegi eorum conscriptiones*: 'Moreover, I have also made a

---

[29] Thus the later view of Lipsius 1875. An excellent overview of the discussion in
which, among others, also Harnack played his part is provided by Hilgenfeld 1884, esp.
46–58. For a number of reasons, Hilgenfeld himself remained an adherent of Lipsius'
original theory. As regards the *Gos. Jud.* and the possible sources of Irenaeus' report in
1,31,1–2, neither Lipsius nor Hilgenfeld provide any specific clue. But it seems worth
to underline here Hilgenfeld's passing remark (Hilgenfeld 1884, 49) that Irenaeus 'auch
über die gnostischen Vorläufer der Valentinianer selbständige Forschungen angestellt
hat (1, 31, 2)'.

[30] See also Wisse 1971, esp. 214–215.

[31] Perkins 1976, esp. 197–200. Cf. Hilgenfeld 1884, n. 29.

[32] Or, perhaps more precise: 1,30,15–31,2. Cf. the division in Rousseau-Doutreleau
1979, 384–387 and the heading 'Sectes apparentées' preceding the French translation
of this section. One might also suppose, however, that in 1,30,15 Irenaeus is speaking
of a subgroup of the 'Ophites'; cf. Scholten 2001.

[33] *Adv. haer.* 1,31,2 (Rousseau-Doutreleau 1979, 386): *O tu, Angele, abutor opere
tuo; o tu, illa Potestas, perficio tuam operationem.*

collection of their writings'.[34] Since there is no reason to suppose that
Irenaeus' rhetorical skill (which is not absent from his writing)[35] would
not have prevented him from making such a blunder, or that his first
readers may have been unintelligent persons, or that, moreover, all of
the later manuscript writers would have been inattentive,[36] it may be
concluded that the concerted evidence points only in one direction:
Irenaeus himself communicates his personal collecting and reading of
the writings he discusses and even quotes. Likewise, there seems to be
no other conclusion in regard to the *Gospel of Judas*: Irenaeus will have
had first-hand knowledge of its existence and contents and, moreover,
he himself appears to have read the text.

On the basis of the preceding remarks, we may summarize the most
important particulars transmitted by Irenaeus as follows:

1. there is a *Gospel of Judas*;
2. this Gospel is linked to Gnostics who consider themselves in line
   with the (positively evaluated) Old Testament figure of Cain and
   persons related to him;
3. these Gnostics know of a superior Principle and they speak about
   the Creator in a negative way;
4. they speak of Sophia and her activity;
5. Judas is considered to be well acquainted with (parts of) a myth
   in which—in any case—Sophia is a redeemer figure;
6. it is for this reason that Judas is characterized as a person 'knowing the truth', in other words: as a real Gnostic, in contrast to 'the
   others' (*i.e.*, the other apostles);
7. because of this Judas 'accomplished the mystery of the betrayal';
8. 'through him', *i.e.*, because of his deed of 'betrayal', 'all things, both
   earthly and heavenly, have been dissolved';
9. a special group of Gnostics (being termed in later tradition as
   'Cainites') have forwarded a writing to this effect, which they call
   "the Gospel of Judas";
10. this writing is explicitly referred to as 'a composed work'.

---

[34] The sentence did not fit (part of) Wisse's theory about Irenaeus' sources and thus,
in a footnote, he curiously remarks: 'Since Irenaeus in the preface to *Adv. haer.* 1 refers
only to the "commentaries" of the disciples of Valentinus, the first person singular in
1,31,1 must have been copied from his source'. See Wisse 1971, 215 n. 44.

[35] See e.g. Reynders 1935; Schoedel 1959. And see in particular Perkins 1976.

[36] None of the current editions (Stieren 1853–1858, Harvey 1857, Rousseau-Doutreleau 1979) indicates another reading.

An essential crux in Irenaeus' report is the word *huiusmodi* that appears near the end of the passage: 'Et confi(n)ctionem adferunt *huiusmodi*, Iudae Euangelium illud uocantes'. I have translated: 'And they adduce a composed work *to this effect*, which they call "the Gospel of Judas"'. One may also translate: a composed work 'of that kind' or 'of/in that manner'. The question is: does '*huiusmodi*', being a further specification of the Gospel's contents, indicate that it only dealt with Judas, his particular gnosis, his 'betrayal', and its cosmic effects? Or does '*huiusmodi*' *also* refer to a comprehensive mythological story of which Irenaeus presents an outline? On the basis of the preceding *haec*[37] ('Et *haec* Iudam proditorem diligenter cognouisse dicunt': 'And they say that Judas the betrayer was thoroughly acquainted *with these things*') I deem the latter possibility to be the most likely one. According to Irenaeus the *Gospel of Judas* not only spoke about Judas, his gnosis, his performance of the mystery of the betrayal based on that knowledge, and its earthly and heavenly consequences. It also contained a myth in which—in any case—the redeeming activity of Sophia and, accordingly, the mythologically closely-related bad Creator and the superior Principle either explicitly or at least implicitly played an important part as well.

Strictly speaking, that is: preeminently on the basis of the just-mentioned *haec* as primarily referring to Sophia and her activity, one cannot deduce from Irenaeus' passage that the *Gospel of Judas* should have spoken about Cain and other Old Testament figures like Esau, Korah and the Sodomites. What is suggested by Irenaeus is that the person of Judas is venerated by these particular Gnostics in the same *positive* way as they venerate Cain and the others. As it is the case with Judas, 'they confess' that 'all such people are their cognates'. In other words, Judas is of the same race as Cain and the other people. All of these persons are considered to be the real Gnostics.

A final remark may be made here on Irenaeus' specifying the *Gospel of Judas* as a *confin(c)tio*. As I indicated already, Theodoretus states that the 'Cainites' have 'composed' (συντεθείκασιν) the Gospel and, moreover, Epiphanius speaks of a συνταγμάτιον. All these designations not only seem to have a negative connotation, but they also may indicate real characteristics of the literary structure of the writing. According to Epiphanius, then, it was a short work; and both Theodoretus and Epiphanius appear to confirm Irenaeus' specification of the writing

---

[37] See above, the annotation to: '*haec*...: *these things*...'.

as a composition. Once again considered in the context of Irenaeus'
testimony in *Adv. haer.*, this feature seems to have important consequences. The Gnostics who not only 'adduced', but in actual fact seem
to have 'produced' the Gospel, apparently did so by putting together
several (Gnostic) traditions. If this last inference is correct[38] and, moreover, if Irenaeus (and also Epiphanius and Theodoretus) speak of the
same *Gospel of Judas* recently discovered,[39] it may be inferred that a
downright interpretation of its contents from a 'Sethian' point of view
is beside the mark. Although the myth transmitted in the newly discovered text undoubtedly has 'Sethian' characteristics,[40] already from
Irenaeus' testimony read in context we may learn that the Gnostics of
the *Gospel of Judas* are others (*alii*) than, for instance, the previously
discussed '[Barbelo-]Gnostics'. The Gospel of Judas Gnostics—in later
tradition unequivocally termed as 'Cainites'—seem to have made use of
'Sethian' tenets.[41] But much in their system—if their diverse doctrines[42]
may be indicated as such—was already for Irenaeus a reason to discuss
them in a separate section of his *Adv. haer.*[43]

---

[38] A hint to this conclusion may also be Irenaeus' remark: *quemadmodum et Carpocrates dixit* (*Adv. haer.* 1,31,2; Rousseau-Doutreleau 1979, 386), which not only seems
to suggest that Irenaeus sees a parallel with the doctrines of the previously discussed
Carpocrates and his followers (*Adv. haer.* 1,25,1–6), but also might indicate that the
Gnostics under discussion were partly indebted to Carpocrates' teachings.

[39] By and then in recent discussions the idea is expressed that Irenaeus might have
been speaking of *another Gospel of Judas*. See e.g. Wurst 2008, 134, 178: 'But if the
Gospel of Judas published here is the one in Irenaeus...', and, in particular, Gathercole 2007, 119–123 (who concludes however: 'So there is, after all, a sporting chance
that Irenaeus is referring to what is to all intents and purposes our *Gospel of Judas*').
Indeed, there might be such a possibility (see below, n. 42), but nothing of this kind
is suggested let alone substantiated by the text of either Irenaeus or the *Gos. Jud.* as
we now have it.

[40] Even though, according to some readings, the name of Seth perhaps does not
appear in the text. Maybe we should read in stead of '[Se]th' on p. 52 of TC: '[Ath]eth'.
Cf. e.g. Kasser-Wurst 2007, 223 and, in particular, Kasser et al. 2008, 47 n. 125. But
the first editors—like e.g. Brankaer-Bethge 2007, 278–279; cf. 358—still prefer the
reading '[Se]th'.

[41] Cf. the conclusion of Scholten 2001, 981: 'Man wird daher das vermutete System der K. als eine Parellelbildung zum Entwurf der modern so genannten Sethianer
bezeichnen dürfen'.

[42] See e.g. the accounts of Ps.-Tert., *Adv. haer.* 2, 5–6 (*CCL* 2, 1404 Kroymann) and
Epiph., *Pan.* 38,3 (*GCS* 25, 65–66 Holl). If these discussions would have been based
upon or introduced into a *Gos. Jud.*, *then* there will have been one or more versions
of a *Gos. Jud.* It remains noteworthy, however, that in all these interpretations Judas
is always considered in a very *positive* way.

[43] More on Irenaeus and the Jewish-Christian background of the *Gos. Jud.* in van
Oort 2006 (2007[4]). Further on the *Gos. Jud.* as *confi(n)ctio* in van Oort 2009.

WHEN THE SETHIANS WERE YOUNG

The *Gospel of Judas* in the Second Century

Marvin Meyer

Doubtless one of the most significant features of the *Gospel of Judas* is the apparent date of its composition. The *Gospel of Judas* is a text, with a Sethian orientation, that derives from a time no later than around the middle of the second century. The *Gospel of Judas* is mentioned by Irenaeus of Lyon, who is writing around 180, and Irenaeus refers not only to the title of the text but also to its basic contents. As we might anticipate, the lines Irenaeus devotes to the *Gospel of Judas* in *Adversus haereses* 1.31.1 indicate that he doesn't like it much. He reports that the people behind the *Gospel of Judas* claim that Judas Iscariot knew the ways of God, and that Judas was the only one of the disciples who understood the truth. Judas consequently performed the mystery of the betrayal, the handing over of Jesus, Irenaeus continues in his report, and this act is linked to the dissolution of all that is earthly and heavenly. Irenaeus suggests that these are the very ideas to be found in the *Gospel of Judas*, and as Gregor Wurst shows,[1] his description fits rather well with the recovered text of the *Gospel of Judas* from the Tchacos Codex. Whether Irenaeus actually read all or part of the *Gospel of Judas* is uncertain, but he seems to have been familiar with its contents, in particular near the end of the recovered text, and when Irenaeus describes the extraordinary insight of Judas, the mystery of the betrayal, and the passing away of things earthly and heavenly, he rehearses themes reminiscent of the scenes in the last pages of the Coptic version of the *Gospel of Judas*—and in the same sequence. Irenaeus's comment about the dissolution of the cosmos in the *Gospel of Judas* may even help us understand a bit more precisely the essential point of the fragmentary passage on page 57 about the last days, the destruction of the archon of this world, and the glorious fate of "the great generation of Adam."

---

[1] Wurst 2008, 169–79.

A strong case can be made, then, for the *Gospel of Judas* in the Tchacos Codex as a later version, in Coptic translation, of the second-century text, most likely composed in Greek and referred to by Irenaeus in his *Adversus haereses*. Of course, we would assume that editorial modifications must have taken place between the second-century time of composition and the early fourth-century (or late third-century?) date of inclusion in the Tchacos Codex. The process of copying and recopying the text, and the task of translating the text from Greek to Coptic, would presumably introduce a number of changes, whether deliberate or inadvertent, into the version of the text that has survived. Nonetheless, Wurst offers this as his preliminary conclusion:

> In the case of this gospel, we have no reason to assume a complex history of editing, because it does not show the marks of subsequent reworking. This is not to say that textual alterations were not made while it was written. But there is no sign that extra parts, such as the revelation of the cosmology (*Gospel of Judas* 47–53), were written in as later additions. This kind of literary criticism would obviously destroy the original text.[2]

The place of the *Gospel of Judas* as a datable mid-second-century text in the Sethian tradition has obvious implications for our reconstruction and understanding of the history of Sethian gnosis, especially in the earlier period of the Sethian school of thought. The dating of ancient texts is an imperfect science at best, and firm dates for Sethian texts are not easy to determine. In his essay on "The Sethian School of Gnostic Thought," John Turner indicates four textual linkages with four suggestions of dates for Sethian texts, the first two quite certain and the last two more conjectural: 1) in about 175–180 Irenaeus discusses the *Gospel of Judas* and cosmogonic materials reminiscent of the opening of the *Apocryphon of John*; 2) in about 260 Porphyry recalls in his *Life of Plotinus* that versions of the texts *Zostrianos* and *Allogenes* were employed by members of Plotinus's philosophical seminar in Rome in the middle of the third century, and around the same time Plotinus seems to cite the ideas and perhaps the text of *Zostrianos* in his *Enneads*; 3) the author of *Zostrianos* and Marius Victorinus, in his work *Against Arius*, both make use of a Middle Platonic source that may well date from the time before Plotinus; and 4) the Nag Hammadi text *Trimorphic Protennoia* may echo Johannine discussions that are

---

[2] Wurst 2008, 179.

similar to what is reflected in *1 John*, which may have been composed in the first half of the second century (ca. 125–150).[3] Turner's discussion is helpful, but we may wish to qualify the presumed connection between *Adversus haereses* 1.29.1–4 and the *Apocryphon of John*, since the parallels in Irenaeus, close as they are, apply only to the cosmogonic section of the *Apocryphon of John* and hardly to the entire text as transmitted in the extant versions. That being noted, the place of the second-century *Gospel of Judas* becomes even more crucial as we attempt to understand the early development of Sethian thought.

In the balance of this paper I propose how the *Gospel of Judas* may be read as a mid-second-century text and how Judas Iscariot may be interpreted within a mid-second-century gnostic context—when, as we might put it, the Sethians were young.

The Gospel in the Second Century

The *Gospel of Judas* is a text that was known by its title from the comments of Irenaeus but has been made available only recently. The third text in the Tchacos Codex, a Coptic codex discovered in the 1970s and published in critical edition in 2007,[4] the *Gospel of Judas* presents a series of conversations between Jesus and his disciples, and especially Judas, conversations which are said to have taken place "during eight days, three days before he celebrated Passover (or, three days before his passion; 33)."[5] In much of early Christian literature Judas Iscariot is vilified and demonized, and he typically is considered to be the quintessential traitor, who turns in his master for money—the infamous thirty pieces of silver. I grant that the final fate of Judas according to the *Gospel of Judas* remains somewhat uncertain, largely on account of missing text at the conclusion of the narrative, and he may not be understood to attain ultimate bliss in the gospel. Elsewhere I also discuss possible indications of ambivalence about Judas in the *Gospel of Judas*,[6] and in the next section of this paper I suggest that a more nuanced, a more qualified Judas, portrayed with features of

---

[3] Turner 2008b, 788.
[4] Kasser et al. 2007.
[5] Here the translation of the *Gos. Jud.* is taken from Kasser et al. 2008, a consensus English translation based on the translation in the critical edition of Codex Tchacos, and the citations of the Coptic text are based on the critical edition.
[6] Cf. Meyer 2007b.

personified Wisdom and of any gnostic, is likely to be seen in the text. Still, the Judas of the *Gospel of Judas* essentially has a rather positive character—like Wisdom herself or like a person of gnosis. For this reason I consider the proposal of Birger Pearson that Judas may be taken to be a "tragic hero" in the *Gospel of Judas* to be of interest.[7] Now Gesine Schenke Robinson, in her essay in the second edition of *The Gospel of Judas*, draws a similar conclusion.[8]

What is clear is that within this remarkable gospel, as Irenaeus himself admits, Judas is the only one of the disciples who understands who Jesus actually is, and he is the recipient of a revelation from Jesus about the nature of the divine and the character of the universe. In the *Gospel of Judas*, Judas learns about the "mysteries of the kingdom."[9] In the end he is told by Jesus that he will hand over the mortal body Jesus has been using, and it seems to be implied that the inner, spiritual person of Jesus will be liberated, probably by entering the light in what might be termed a transfiguration or, perhaps better, an ascension account. The antecedent of the pronominal subject of ⲁϥϭⲱⲕ ⲉϩⲟⲩⲛ ⲉⲣⲟⲥ at 57,23 may be interpreted to be either Judas or Jesus, but Jesus seems to be the better choice.[10] Jesus says to Judas, "You will exceed all of them (probably the other disciples). For you will sacrifice the man who bears me."[11] That is just what Judas does at the end of the gospel.

The *Gospel of Judas* may be taken to represent what may be described as an early form of Sethian gnosis. How might it be read as a gnostic text from the middle of the second century? Like other Christian Sethian texts, the *Gospel of Judas* incorporates Jewish and Greek themes—most likely in Hellenistic Jewish form—in the context of Christian gnostic proclamation, but in the *Gospel of Judas* this appears to be accomplished in a fairly simple and unadorned fashion that may suggest a rather early stage of development. The specifically Jewish materials include one apparent instance in the Coptic text of the Hebrew title rabbi,[12] several names of divine and demiurgic figures

---

[7] Pearson 2007c, 14.

[8] Schenke Robinson 2008b.

[9] *Gos. Jud.* 35.

[10] Such an interpretation is preferred by Sasagu Arai and Gesine Schenke Robinson, and I tend to agree with them. Cf. Kasser et al. 2008, 52.

[11] *Gos. Jud.* 56.

[12] Largely restored, as [ϩⲣⲁⲃⲃ]ⲉⲓ, 43,12, but also attested elsewhere in TC.

derived from Hebrew and Aramaic,[13] a cosmological revelation that is representative of Jewish mystical gnosis (though it comes from the mouth of Jesus in the *Gospel of Judas*), and numerous examples of the authoritative declaration of Jesus, "I tell you the truth," with the word of Semitic derivation, ϩⲁⲙⲏⲛ. The reference to El, where we might anticipate Eleleth, as in the *Gospel of the Egyptians* and *Trimorphic Protennoia*, may reflect the preference in the codex in general to use proper names without honorific or other suffixes,[14] or the seemingly abbreviated reference may simply be due to uninscribed papyrus (as in the following lines of page 51 as well), so that the reference may conceivably be read as ⲏⲗ[ⲏⲗⲏⲑ].[15] Greek motifs emerge in the familiar Platonic concern for the world above as the pattern for the world below, perhaps in the use of the Greek word δαίμων addressed to Judas, and in a preoccupation with the role of the stars that reflects ancient astronomical and astrological interests, in general, as well as Platonic lore concerning people and their stars as found in the *Timaeus*.[16] If anything, the *Gospel of Judas* presents a Sethian message with a more overtly astronomical and astrological perspective than we typically see in Sethian texts, and this perspective gives a special astral emphasis to the message of the text.

All of this Hellenistic Jewish material in the *Gospel of Judas* is set in the framework of a Christian gnostic spirituality that proclaims the primacy of the exalted generation of Seth—"that generation" (ⲧⲅⲉⲛⲉⲁ ⲉⲧⲙ̄ⲙⲁⲩ)[17]—and is harshly critical of anything that smacks of sacrifice, whether that is the death of Jesus understood as sacrifice, or the celebration of the eucharist as a sacrificial meal, or, Elaine Pagels and Karen King suggest, participation in Christian martyrdom as an emulation of the sacrificial death of Jesus.[18] The death of Jesus, while only alluded to in the *Gospel of Judas*, is to be a sacrifice, to be sure, but only a sacrifice of the mortal body that the true, spiritual Jesus has been using—"the man who bears me," Jesus is made to declare in the

---

[13] Barbelo, El (cf. Eleleth, especially in later Sethian texts?), Nebro, Yaldabaoth, Sakla(s).

[14] For example, Addon rather than Ad(d)onaios in *James* 26, and Nebro rather than Nebroel in *Gos. Jud.* 51.

[15] *Gos. Jud.* 51,1.

[16] Cf. *Timaeus* 41d–42b.

[17] Cf. "those people," ⲛⲓⲣⲱⲙⲉ ⲉⲧⲙ̄ⲙⲁⲩ, particularly in the Sethian *Apoc. Adam*.

[18] Pagels-King 2007.

gospel.[19] This is presented in the *Gospel of Judas* in a tone much more reminiscent of the account of the death of the wise man Socrates at the conclusion of the *Phaedo*, Dennis MacDonald has suggested in a recent panel discussion, than anything like a violent sacrifice of Christ for the sins of the world.[20] As in the *Gospel of Judas*, there is also laughter in the *Phaedo*, in the middle of the dialogue about the soul separating from the body. In the end, the message of the *Gospel of Judas* is not darkness and death but light and life. This is the good news of the *Gospel of Judas*.

Several scenes in the *Gospel of Judas* may be particularly memorable as early Sethian expressions on the meaning of the divine, the savior, and life in the world. Near the opening of the gospel Jesus comes upon the disciples as they are gathered together for a sacred meal, portrayed as a Jewish meal or perhaps the Christian eucharist, and he laughs. Jesus laughs a great deal in the *Gospel of Judas*, as he laughs in other gnostic texts, apparently at the foibles and follies of human life in this world and the preoccupation of people with correct religious observance.[21] When the disciples take exception to this laughter of Jesus, Jesus explains that he is not laughing at them but instead at the scrupulous way in which they are trying to do the will of their God. The disciples respond by declaring, "Master, you [...] are the son of our God," but Jesus' rejoinder indicates that they are quite mistaken.[22] They think, wrongly, that Jesus is the offspring of the demiurge and thus a son of this world.

The disciples get angry at Jesus, so that Jesus invites them to step up and face him, but they all are unable to do so—except for Judas, who stands before Jesus but averts his eyes out of respect.[23] Then Judas utters his profession of who Jesus is and where Jesus is from: "I know who you are and where you have come from. You have come from the immortal aeon of Barbelo. And I am not worthy to utter the name of the one who has sent you." To make this profession is to acknowledge the transcendent origin of Jesus, who derives from the immortal

---

[19] *Gos. Jud.* 56.

[20] The panel discussion, on the theme "The Gospel of Judas: What the Scholars Are Saying" was held in Claremont, California, in September 2006 and was sponsored by the Institute for Antiquity and Christianity.

[21] Cf. *Apoc. John, Soph. Jes. Chr., Sec. Treat. Seth, Apoc. Peter,* Basilides in Iren., *Adv. Haer.* 1.24.4. Specific references may be found in Kasser et al. 2008, 30–31.

[22] *Gos. Jud.* 34.

[23] *Gos. Jud.* 35; cf. *Gos. Thom.* 46.

realm of Barbelo. Barbelo frequently is featured in Sethian texts as the divine mother, or the source of the divine offspring, or the exalted realm of the divine, especially in Platonizing Sethian texts. The word Barbelo itself most likely is from the Hebrew, and it may mean "God in four"—that is, God known from the tetragrammaton, the holy and ineffable name of God.[24] In Sethian terms, this confession of Judas is precisely the correct confession of faith.

In the central portion of the *Gospel of Judas*, Jesus invites Judas to come and attend to a cosmological revelation about things "that [no] human will (ever) see," and the result is a glorious Sethian vision of the world of light and the creation of the universe.[25] The origin of all that is, Jesus states, is the great invisible Spirit, "which no eye of an [angel] has ever seen, no thought of the heart has ever comprehended, and it was never called by any name." From this transcendent Spirit there emerge, as creations and emanations, a series of exalted beings that fill the realms above with light and glory—first the Self-Generated (Autogenes), the God of light, and thereafter Adamas (heavenly Adam), luminaries, angels, aeons, heavens, firmaments, and the exalted generation of Seth. Four unnamed angels in the *Gospel of Judas* (47) anticipate the figures of the four luminaries Harmozel, Oroiael, Daveithai, and Eleleth in other Sethian texts, for example the *Apocryphon of John*. The huge assembly of beings is termed the cosmos, or universe, and it is called "corruption."[26] In the evolution, or devolution, of the divine light, the light from above shines down into this world, and it may be seen progressively to lose some of its brilliance as the light grows dimmer here below. That light appears to be the light of God within people of gnosis. Demiurgic powers named Nebro,[27] Yaldabaoth, and Sakla eventually set up the cosmic bureaucracy in this gloomy world in which human beings live. Yet it is clear that the light within people is not forgotten in this world, for Jesus observes, "God caused knowledge

---

[24] Cf. Harvey 1857, 221–22.

[25] *Gos. Jud.* 47–53.

[26] *Gos. Jud.* 50.

[27] Cf. Nebruel or Nebroel in the *Gos. Eg.* and Manichaean texts; Nebrod is the Greek name of Nimrod in Gen and 1 Chron, and the meaning of the name, "rebel," suggested in *Gos. Jud.* 51, may reflect the meaning of Nimrod. Now Painchaud suggests that the Coptic word of Greek derivation for "rebel" (ⲁⲡⲟⲥⲧⲁⲧⲏⲥ) found in the *Gos. Jud.* may function as a part of a warning in the text against gnostic apostasy (cf. *Apoc. John* NHC II,1 27).

to be [given] to Adam and those with him, so that the kings of chaos and the underworld might not lord it over them."[28]

It is significant to note that while this cosmological revelation is put on the lips of Jesus in the *Gospel of Judas*, the only explicitly Christian element in the revelation is a single reference to "[Se]th, who is called 'the Christ.'"[29] This remains a peculiar and idiosyncratic reference, and it does not agree with the usual place of Seth and Christ in later Sethian texts. I recall that within a very short time after the preliminary Coptic transcription and English translation of the *Gospel of Judas* became available, Birger Pearson contacted me to underscore the fact that something must be wrong with the text here. From that moment other readings have been suggested for this problematic passage. Could there be an issue of orthography, so that we might read the abbreviation ⲭ(ⲟⲉⲓ)ⲥ rather than ⲭ(ⲡⲓⲥⲧⲟ)ⲥ—hence, "[Se]th, who is called 'the Lord'"? There is a supralinear stroke over the letters, and this may suggest a *nomen sacrum*—but now compare the reading, after Wolf-Peter Funk and Gesine Schenke Robinson, of 42,4–5 ("Lord [ⲭ(ⲟⲉⲓ)ⲥ], help us and save us").[30] Could ⲭ(ⲡⲓⲥⲧⲟ)ⲥ come from a copyist's mistaken reading of the original κριός, Greek for "ram"— hence, "[Se]th, who is called 'the Ram'", that is, Aries—so Jacques van der Vliet?[31] Attractive as this theory is, it must assume a scribal misunderstanding of the text, which is quite possible, but such a solution to a textual problem may say more about our inability to make sense of the Coptic text. Or could we read "[ⲁⲑ]ⲏⲑ" as a variation of "Athoth" and ⲭ(ⲡⲏⲥⲧⲟ)ⲥ instead of ⲭ(ⲡⲓⲥⲧⲟ)ⲥ—hence, "[Ath]eth, who is called 'the good one'", as April DeConick suggests, after John Turner?[32] But this assumes an equally odd variation of an angelic name, and it leaves the following name "Harmathoth" unexplained.

It remains most reasonable, I believe, to read this reference in the *Gospel of Judas* as an awkward attempt at Christianizing a Jewish cosmogonic text by inserting the name of Seth, who is commonly linked in Christian Sethian traditions with Christ. Athoth, who usually assumes first place in such lists of powers,[33] might then join forces with

---

[28] *Gos. Jud.* 54.
[29] *Gos. Jud.* 52,5–6.
[30] Cf. Kasser et al. 2008, 37.
[31] Van der Vliet 2006a, 137–52. Cf. *PS* 139.
[32] DeConick 2007, 112, 190. Cp. *Apoc. John* NHC II,1 12 in this regard: "First is goodness, with the first power, Athoth."
[33] Cf. *Apoc. John* NHC II,1/III,1/IV,1/BG,2 and *Gos. Eg.* NHC III,2/IV,2.

Harmas, who usually assumes second place in the lists, and in this way the composite name Harmathoth is created in order to make room for the Christian reference. This cumbersome process may be imagined as an early and ultimately unsuccessful way of introducing, secondarily, a Christian theme into a text of Jewish gnosis. Except for that allusion to Christ, the rest of the long cosmological revelation reflects Hellenistic Jewish thought, and this revelatory disclosure may be based upon a Jewish Sethian account of the place of the divine and the formation of the universe. In this regard the *Gospel of Judas* seems to include secondarily Christianized materials in a way somewhat like that of the *Apocryphon of John*; we may also think of the transformation of the Jewish text *Eugnostos the Blessed* into the Christian *Sophia of Jesus Christ* through the quill of a Christian editor. In several respects the account in the *Gospel of Judas* recalls Jewish mystical traditions, and a comparative study of the cosmogonic revelation in the *Gospel of Judas* with formulations of Jewish mysticism could prove fruitful.[34]

Furthermore, within the cosmological revelation in the *Gospel of Judas*, no mention is made of Sophia or wisdom herself (or itself) and there is no evidence for an account of the fall of Sophia or wisdom, or some other such jolt in the godhead, within the cosmogony. Perhaps El (or Eleleth) is thought to be responsible for the emergence of the demiurge and the creation of the world of corruption here below, as in the *Gospel of the Egyptians* and *Trimorphic Protennoia*, but there is not much wiggle room for El or Eleleth to act in the lacunae on the top of page 51. In contrast to the prominent place of Sophia in other gnostic texts, including some later Sethian texts, Sophia or wisdom— "corruptible wisdom"—is mentioned only once in the *Gospel of Judas*, in an earlier section with lacunae.[35] Nonetheless, Jesus teaches wisdom throughout the gospel, in a general sense of the term, and the *Gospel of Judas* is a gospel of wisdom rather than a gospel of the cross.

In short, the *Gospel of Judas* seems very much at home in the world of the second century, and it provides a set of perspectives that contrast strongly with those of Irenaeus and friends but show other contemporary Christian responses to the issues of the cross and sacrifice as they emerge in the faith and life of second-century Christians. With its potent anti-sacrificial message, the gospel proclaims that Jesus saves

---

[34] Cf. Scholem 1955, 1960a, 1960b, 1962, 1974b.
[35] *Gos. Jud.* 44,4.

not by dying to save people from their sins but by disclosing the light
of knowledge to bring people to the light and life of salvation. And
themes associated with wisdom, even personified Wisdom, may be
disclosed as well in the person of Judas Iscariot as a figure of wisdom
and a prototype of a person of knowledge in the *Gospel of Judas*.

JUDAS AND SOPHIA IN THE SECOND CENTURY

From the early days of work on the Coptic text of the *Gospel of Judas*,
the more positive ways in which Judas Iscariot is portrayed in the text
attracted scholarly attention, and those features of the gospel remain
impressive. After all, this text is entitled, in the titular subscript, the
Gospel—the Good News—*of Judas*, and the text opens with an incipit
in which the focus of the text is placed on conversations between Jesus
and Judas just before the time of the crucifixion. Judas is the chief
recipient of revelation from Jesus in the text, and after it is noted that
Judas and Judas alone has the proper profession of who Jesus actually is, Jesus recognizes that Judas is "reflecting upon the rest (of the
things) that are exalted (the other manifestations of heavenly things
above?)"[36] Near the end of the gospel Jesus says to Judas, "Look, you
have been told everything." and Judas does what Jesus says he will do:
he turns the mortal body of Jesus over to the authorities.[37] Beginning
in a formal way, however, in the autumn of 2006, in conferences at
the Sorbonne and in Washington, D.C.,[38] the response to the text on
the part of a number of scholars—April DeConick, Louis Painchaud,
Birger Pearson, Gesine Schenke Robinson, and John Turner, among
others—increasingly has emphasized the seemingly less favorable
statements about Judas in the *Gospel of Judas*, and these scholars have
advanced revised interpretations of Judas in the *Judas Gospel* according to which Judas is understood to be a tragic or even a demonic
figure. DeConick thus presents Judas in the gospel as a lackey of the
demiurge, the most evil of all the disciples, who is dubbed the thirteenth demon. Poor Judas turns out to be, in such an interpretation,

---

[36] *Gos. Jud.* 35.
[37] *Gos. Jud.* 57.
[38] The American Academy of Religion-Society of Biblical Literature Annual
Meeting.

in league with the devil, and he is on his way to spend his future with the megalomaniacal archon in the thirteenth aeon.[39]

Much of the ongoing discussion on Judas in the *Gospel of Judas* addresses the question of Judas as the thirteenth daimon heading, perhaps, for the thirteenth aeon. April DeConick, in *The Thirteenth Apostle*, recognizes that her thesis about Judas Iscariot in the *Gospel of Judas* hinges in large part on these statements about the daimon and the aeon. The word δαίμων occurs frequently in Plato and Platonic literature, including Middle Platonic and Neoplatonic literature, as well as Hermetic and magical texts, and in these instances the word may have a neutral or even a positive connotation. The term seems to be used to designate first and foremost intermediate beings at home between the divine and human realms. Within Jewish and Christian contexts, DeConick correctly observes, the word δαίμων often has an exclusively negative meaning, and commonly it may be translated as "demon." This word occurs only once in the extant pages of the *Gospel of Judas* and Codex Tchacos, and Antti Marjanen notes, in a review published on the National Geographic website, "Since the word 'daimon' appears only once in the entire text, some caution should be exercised in its interpretation. Even if it is taken as a negative reference, it does not necessarily mean that it is the final characterization of Judas in the text."[40] There obviously is no developed demonology in the *Gospel of Judas*; in fact, even the malevolent archons Nebro and Sakla are not called demons in the *Gospel of Judas*, but angels (ⲁⲅⲅⲉⲗⲟⲥ).

Judas is referred to as the thirteenth, the thirteenth daimon, with connections to the thirteenth aeon, in the *Gospel of Judas*. Initially Judas as the thirteenth calls to mind Judas as the disciple excluded from the circle of the twelve—the odd disciple out—and there are comments in the *Gospel of Judas* that would support such an interpretation. From the days of the conference at the Sorbonne to the present, however, DeConick and other scholars have explained the reference to the thirteenth, the thirteenth daimon, and the thirteenth aeon by noting references to the thirteen aeons and the god of the thirteen aeons—the demiurge, the creator of this mortal world below—in the *Gospel of the Egyptians* III 63 and *Zostrianos* 4. These scholars also have mentioned the thirteen kingdoms of the *Apocalypse of Adam*

---

[39] Cf. Scopello 2008; particularly note DeConick 2007.
[40] Lovgren 2007.

77–82, even though in this text the nature of the thirteenth kingdom is somewhat obscure.[41] On the basis of this evidence, DeConick draws her conclusions about wicked Judas and the unhappy fate that is in store for him in the *Gospel of Judas*.

Unfortunately, none of the parallels cited from these few sources make specific use of the phrase "thirteenth aeon," one of the key terms in the *Gospel of Judas*. This very term does occur elsewhere, though, in another gnostic text that has been known for a long time. The "thirteenth aeon" shows up more than forty times in the *Pistis Sophia* (and it also is to be found in the *Books of Jeu*), where it is "the place of righteousness" located above the twelve aeons and the heavenly home of the twenty-four luminaries—including Sophia, who calls the thirteenth aeon "my dwelling place."[42] In the literature of antiquity and late antiquity, the thirteenth realm can occupy a place just above the twelve (who are often considered to be the signs of the zodiac), on the border of the infinite—a place, it may be, between the world of mortality below and the world of the divine on high, and as such it is a place with a certain ambivalence. Sometimes, as in *Marsanes*, Elaine Pagels has pointed out, the thirteenth realm may be taken as the locale where the transcendent deity dwells (though the term is used in a different sense in *Marsanes* [2–4], in the context of the thirteenth seal).[43] According to the *Pistis Sophia*'s version of the myth, Sophia, straining to ascend to the light above, is deceived and comes down from the thirteenth aeon, descending through the twelve aeons to "chaos" below. Here in this world she is oppressed, and the powers of the world, including lion-faced Yaldabaoth, seek to rob her of the light within her. For a time, she is prevented from leaving the place of her oppression. In the words of Pistis Sophia, the cohorts of Authades, the arrogant one,

> have surrounded me, and have rejoiced over me, and they have oppressed me greatly, without my knowing; and they have run away, they have left me, and they have not been merciful to me. They turned again and tempted me, and they oppressed me with great oppression; they gnashed their teeth at me, wanting to take away my light from me completely.

---

[41] Cf., for instance, Stroumsa 1984.

[42] Schmidt-MacDermot 1978b; Schmidt-MacDermot 1978a.

[43] At the Society of Biblical Literature Annual Meeting, San Diego, California, November 2007.

In the midst of her suffering, Pistis Sophia—the wisdom of God weakened and languishing in this world, reflective of the soul of the gnostic trapped here below—cries for salvation, and eventually her cry is heard:

> Now at this time, save me, that I may rejoice, because I want (or, love) the thirteenth aeon, the place of righteousness. And I will say at all times, May the light of Jeu, your angel, give more light. And my tongue will sing praises to you in your knowledge, all my time in the thirteenth aeon.[44]

Throughout the *Pistis Sophia*, much of the language used to describe the words and deeds of Sophia recalls the *Gospel of Judas*. In her second repentance, for example, Pistis Sophia says:

> O Light of Lights, I have believed in you. Do not leave me in the darkness until the completion (ⲡⲭⲱⲕ, a term used in a similar fashion several times in the *Gos. Jud.*) of my time. Help me and save me (ⲃⲟⲏⲑⲓ ⲉⲣⲟⲓ ⲁⲩⲱ ⲛ̄ⲅⲛⲁϩⲙⲉⲧ: cf. *Gos. Jud.* 42,4–5 which has been restored by Wolf-Peter Funk, as noted above, to read ⲃⲟⲏⲑⲓ ⲉⲣⲟⲛ ⲁⲩⲱ ⲛ̄[ⲕⲧ]ⲟⲩⲭⲟⲛ) in your mysteries (ⲛⲉⲕⲙⲩⲥⲧⲏⲣⲓⲟⲛ, a term used several times in the *Gos. Jud.*). Incline your ear to me and save me. Let the power of your light save me and carry me to the aeons on high, for it is you who saves me and takes me to the height of your aeons. Save me, O Light, from the hand of this lion-faced power (Yaldabaoth), and from the hands of the emanations of the deity Authades. For you, O Light, are the one in whose light I have believed and in whose light I have trusted from the beginning. And I have believed in it from the hour that it emanated me forth (ⲉⲛⲧⲁϥⲡⲣⲟⲃⲁⲗⲉ ⲙ̄ⲙⲟⲓ ⲉⲃⲟⲗ: *Gos. Jud.* describes Judas separated from the generation above)…Now, O Light, do not leave me in the chaos (cf. *Gos. Jud.* 51, 52, 54) during the completion (ⲡⲭⲱⲕ ⲉⲃⲟⲗ) of my whole time. Do not abandon me, O Light (cf. *Gos. Jud.* 57, where Jesus says to Judas, "Lift up your eyes and look at the cloud and the light within it, ⲡⲟⲩⲟⲓⲛ ⲉⲧⲛ̄ϩⲏⲧⲥ̄").[45]

In other words, Sophia comes from the thirteenth realm above; she is separated from that realm, here below; and she is destined to return there again. While here below, moreover, she refers to herself in terms that resonate with Judas' portrayal in the *Gospel of Judas*, and one term she uses is particularly memorable: she refers to herself as a ⲇⲁⲓⲙⲱⲛ. In her fourth repentance, Sophia bemoans her fate, saying, "I have become like a peculiar demon (ⲇⲁⲓⲙⲱⲛ), which dwells in

---

[44] *PS* 1.50. Schmidt-MacDermot 1978b, 92–94 (184–89, slightly modified, here and below).

[45] *PS* 1.35. Schmidt-MacDermot 1978b, 56–57 (112–15).

matter, in whom is no light. And I have become like a spirit counter-part (ⲁⲛⲧⲓⲙⲓⲙⲟⲛ ⲙ̄ⲡ̄ⲛ̄ⲁ̄) which is in a material body, in which there is no light-power."[46] Again, in her twelfth repentance, Sophia laments that "they have taken away my light and my power, and my power is shaken within me, and I have not been able to stand upright in their midst, I have become like matter which has fallen; I have been cast on this side and that, like a demon which is in the air."[47] The word used for "demon" here is ⲣⲉϥϣⲟⲟⲣ, the Coptic equivalent of the Greek δαιμόνιον.

Hence, in a manner that closely parallels the portrayal of Judas Iscariot in the *Gospel of Judas*, Sophia in the *Pistis Sophia* is likened to a *daimon*, perhaps as an intermediary being; she is persecuted at the hands of the archons of the twelve aeons; and though long separated from it, she will return to her dwelling place in "the thirteenth aeon, the place of righteousness." That is the positive fate of Sophia in the *Pistis Sophia*.[48]

The *Pistis Sophia* thus raises fundamental issues about the under-standing of Judas in the *Gospel of Judas*. Rather than functioning as a close companion of Yaldabaoth, as some have proposed, Judas may be seen, in the light of the *Pistis Sophia*, to be a figure in the image of Sophia. Yet we might be inclined to dismiss this evidence, compel-ling as it is, as the somewhat later, "rambling revelations"[49] of a text that sometimes is considered as less than edifying and enlightening. If only such connections could be made in the literature of the second century!

It turns out that just this sort of link between Judas and Sophia was made by gnostics in the second century, as Irenaeus informs us.[50] According to Irenaeus, certain Valentinian Gnostics, who must have been enunciating their beliefs at almost exactly the same time in the mid-second century when the *Gospel of Judas* was being composed and read, established a close connection between the suffering of

---

[46] *PS* 1.39. Schmidt-MacDermot 1978b, 63 (126–26).

[47] *PS* 1.55. Schmidt-MacDermot 1978b, 107 (214–15).

[48] Note also Ps.-Tert., *Adv. Haer.* 1.2, in the context of the discussion of Simon Magus, who is said to have come into this world on behalf of an erring daimon (*dae-monem*), who is wisdom (*sapientia*).

[49] So Pearson 2004, 74.

[50] A similar argument about a "Judas-Achamoth typology" in the *Gos. Jud.* and elsewhere is made independently in the unpublished paper of Tage Petersen (Petersen 2007).

Sophia and the passion of Judas—both being linked, according to the interpretation of Irenaeus, to the number twelve, with Judas numbered as the twelfth and final disciple in the circle of the twelve and Sophia numbered as the twelfth aeon.

Irenaeus argues against the Valentinian gnostics as follows, from his proto-orthodox perspective:

> Then, again, as to their assertion that the passion of the twelfth aeon was proved through the conduct of Judas, how is it possible that Judas can be compared with this aeon as being an emblem of her—he who was expelled from the number of the twelve, and never restored to his place? For that aeon, whose type they declare Judas to be, after being separated from her Enthymesis (thought, reflection), was restored or recalled to her former position; but Judas was deprived of his office, and cast out, while Matthias was ordained in his place, according to what is written, "And his bishopric let another take" (*Acts* 1:20). They ought therefore to maintain that the twelfth aeon was cast out of the Pleroma, and that another was produced, or sent forth to fill her place; if, that is to say, she is pointed at in Judas. Moreover, they tell us that it was the aeon herself who suffered, but Judas was the betrayer, and not the sufferer. Even they themselves acknowledge that it was the suffering Christ, and not Judas, who came to the endurance of passion. How, then, could Judas, the betrayer of him who had to suffer for our salvation, be the type and image of that aeon who suffered?[51]

In some ways this statement on the part of Irenaeus is curious. Throughout his comments he is preoccupied with the number twelve—the twelfth aeon and the twelve disciples. If Judas was expelled from the twelve, he wonders, how can he also be compared to the twelfth? If Irenaeus had read and understood all of the *Gospel of Judas*, we might guess, he might have been able to gain some insight into the gnostic Judas, his place beyond the twelve, and the aeons. Irenaeus is also baffled by the fact that Sophia is separated and restored, whereas Judas is separated but Matthias takes his place. Again, if Irenaeus had been able to reflect upon the full text of the *Gospel of Judas*, he might have recognized that these issues of separation, replacement, and restoration are addressed there. Yet again, Irenaeus, who is committed to the proclamation of the reality of the suffering of Jesus, cannot comprehend how Judas, and not Jesus, could be said to be comparable to Sophia, the suffering aeon. Now we can observe that Judas is also

---

[51] Iren., *Adv. haer.* 2.20. Roberts-Donaldson 1994, 388, slightly modified.

opposed and oppressed according to passages within the *Gospel of Judas*, especially in passages occurring earlier in the text.

So Irenaeus—who at least knows of the existence of a text called the *Gospel of Judas* and the general contents of the last part of the text—admits that in the second century there were gnostics who compared Judas and Sophia and were convinced that Judas was "the type and image of that aeon who suffered." He also states, just prior to his reference to the *Gospel of Judas*, that some gnostics declared that after the resurrection, Christ, who himself was linked to Sophia, ascended to the right hand of Yaldabaoth for a thoroughly positive purpose—to aid in the salvation of souls.[52] This admission of Irenaeus, combined with the close similarities in theme and terminology in the presentations of Judas and Sophia in the *Gospel of Judas* and the *Pistis Sophia* (and the *Books of Jeu*), may suggest an important conclusion regarding the role of Judas Iscariot in the *Gospel of Judas*.

I suggest that among certain gnostics of the mid-second century, including some Irenaeus considered Valentinians and the folks who wrote and used the *Gospel of Judas*, the figure of Judas could be presented in terms that are reminiscent of the figure of Sophia, and that the account of Judas in the *Gospel of Judas* may be read with elements of the fall, passion, grief, and redemption of the wisdom of God in mind. Like Sophia in other texts and traditions, Judas in the *Gospel of Judas* is separated from the divine realms above, even though he knows and professes the mysteries of the divine and the origin of the savior; he goes through grief and persecution as a daimon confined to this world below; he is enlightened with revelations "that [no] human will (ever) see"; and at last he is said to be on his way, much like Sophia, to the thirteenth aeon of gnostic lore.[53]

The story of Judas, like the story of Sophia, recalls the story of the soul of any gnostic who is in this world and longs for transcendence.

---

[52] Iren., *Adv. Haer.* 1.30.14.

[53] The argument of Schenke Robinson that the figure of Sophia in the *PS* is only the lower Sophia in this world (compare the figures of a higher Wisdom and a lower Wisdom in Valentinian texts) presents no particular problem, since in my understanding Sophia in the *PS* and Judas in the *Gos. Jud.* may both represent the light of God trapped in this world below. Their state corresponds to the state of the gnostic in this world. The additional argument (of John Turner) that an appeal to the *PS* and the *Books of Jeu* in this regard is irrelevant, on account of the fact that the arrogant Authades is also identified with the thirteenth aeon, merely confirms the state of ambivalence that I suggest characterizes much of the gnostic experience of life and liberation in the world.

The *Gospel of Judas* may be understood to portray Judas as the type and image of Sophia and of the gnostic, and the text proclaims how salvation may be realized—not, it is emphasized, through a theology of the cross and the experience of sacrifice, but on the contrary through gnosis and insight into the nature of the divine and the presence of the divine in the inner lives of people of knowledge.

Without a doubt this interpretation of the *Gospel of Judas* calls into question many of the central tenets of an argument for the text to be viewed as a gospel parody or a gospel tragedy. Still, a number of uncertainties of interpretation will linger as long as the lacunae on the top portion of pages 55–58 of the *Gospel of Judas*, with the account of the conclusion of the story of Jesus and Judas, remain. Furthermore, there certainly is room for a more nuanced approach of the text, one which takes seriously the diverse features of this challenging document. I suspect that in the future the figure of Judas Iscariot in the *Gospel of Judas* may be interpreted, in the light of such parallel texts as those cited here, as neither a completely positive character nor a totally demonic being, but rather a figure, like Sophia, and like any gnostic, who is embroiled in this world of mortality yet is striving for gnosis and enlightenment.[54] To this extent aspects of a revised interpretation may be joined to the positive features of the *Gospel of Judas*, to give a balanced approach to the text. After all, Judas, like Sophia, is caught between the worlds of mortality and immortality, looking for liberation, and the *Gospel of Judas* shows how liberation may be achieved. Thus, the evidence of the *Gospel of Judas*, together with insights drawn from the *Pistis Sophia*, the *Books of Jeu*, and Irenaeus of Lyon, may provide a new set of perspectives on Judas and Sophia in second-century gnostic literature. What is clear, though, is that the mystical message of the *Gospel of Judas*, however it may be nuanced, remains supremely good news, from a gnostic point of view, some of the best news in the world. In the end, gnosis—and wisdom—triumph.

---

[54] Cf. the statement of Kasser on Judas in the *Gos. Jud.* near the conclusion of his essay (Kasser 2006a, 78): "We smile at the educational dialogues of the 'Master' (Rabbi) with his disciples of limited spiritual intelligence, and even with the most gifted among them, the human hero of this 'Gospel,' Judas the misunderstood—whatever his weaknesses."

THE *GOSPEL OF JUDAS*

Its Protagonist, its Composition, and its Community

Gesine Schenke Robinson

We have come a long way in our interpretation of Judas and the assessment of the manuscript in which he features so prominently. After the first overexcited view of Judas as a role model for all those who want to be Jesus' disciples,[1] and the provocative notion of the document turning Christianity on its head,[2] a more measured approach followed, sometimes along with amended translations and re-evaluations.[3] In recent publications however, Judas again is depicted in surprisingly extreme terms. He is either compared to Sophia, trapped in a mortal body and yearning to return to his celestial home,[4] or he is an evil demon and undercover agent of the arch-archon, with Jesus teaching him about his future so that he will suffer even more because he will step open-eyed into his demise.[5]

As a narrative character, Judas obviously can be all of this. Yet there is the nagging question: Does the text at hand support any of these interpretations?[6] The *Gospel of Judas* is full of irony and ciphers that the original audience would easily have understood, but that we have to unearth laboriously. Since it is a Gnostic text, everything has to be construed from a Gnostic point of view, not seen through a New Testament lens. This may seem self-evident, but the two kinds of representation are easily confused, resulting in statements still to be

---

[1] See e.g. Meyer's "Introduction" in Kasser et al. 2006a, 14–16, esp. 9, as well as his footnotes to the translation of the *Gos. Jud.* in that edition.

[2] See e.g. Ehrman 2006b; and Ehrman 2006a.

[3] Besides lectures at various scholarly conventions by Turner (unpublished manuscript) see e.g. Pearson 2007c; Nagel 2007; Van der Vliet 2006a; Painchaud 2006; and Schenke-Robinson 2008b.

[4] Cf. Meyer in Kasser et al. 2008, 155–168.

[5] Cf. DeConick 2007.

[6] Since the translation is essential for the understanding of the meaning of the text, I will quote from my own translation that often differs from the translation provided in Kasser et al. 2007. The Coptic wording of additional or diverging text reconstructions, as well as further explanations for dissimilar readings of the text, can be found in Schenke Robinson 2008a.

regretted, and keeping us occupied in trying to correct widely spread misconceptions. In the *Gospel of Judas*, the Gnostic Jesus is not the Jesus of the canonical Gospels, nor does Judas act according to a plan of salvation. In terms of salvation, Judas is simply irrelevant. A plan of salvation requiring the death of Jesus goes entirely against Gnostic thought. Hence Jesus is not dependent on Judas to be freed from his mortal coil, nor does Judas do Jesus a favor in assisting him on Jesus' request. The *Gospel of Judas* does not teach us anything about the historical Jesus or a historical Judas; likewise, the gospel is neither uttered *by* nor meant *for* Judas—not to speak of his fellow disciples. The ultimate recipient and beneficiary of the gospel, which apparently prefers to instruct by negative example and exclusion, is the audience beyond the text; the "Good News" inherent to the revelatory account is meant solely for the Christian-Gnostic community lying behind the *Gospel of Judas*.

In order to make the relationship between the text and its implied audience more transparent, a closer look at the structural arrangement of the composition may reveal a transmission history that reflects the community's place in the religious environment of the second century that the document presupposes. By reasoning backwards from what the text expresses to its function in the community that used it, we may be able to determine the specific role the figure of Judas plays in the unfolding account from a different—i.e. the community's—perspective.

The incipit

In its present compositional form, the *Gospel of Judas* appears to have two preambles, each stating different recipients of the message Jesus is about to convey. The first one declares Judas to be the receiver, but the subsequent introduction to the account mentions Jesus' disciples as the recipients of the revelation. As part of a brief summary of Jesus' ministry, the anonymous narrator states, "<He> called the twelve disciples, and began to speak with them about the mysteries that are upon the world, and the things that will happen at the end."[7] The difference

---

[7] *Gos. Jud.* 33,13–18. The translation "*beyond* the world" in Kasser et al. 2007 goes beyond the scope of the given Coptic preposition and thus presumably beyond the intent of the text. The prepositional phrase ϩιϫⲛ̄ ⲡⲕⲟⲥⲙⲟⲥ, here given as "*upon* the

in the designation of the addressees may already be an indication of editorial intervention. But the incipit also defines the message in a specific way. The initial phrase, "The secret declaration of judgment that Jesus communicated to Judas Iscariot,"[8] seems to express precisely what Jesus is about to deliver, at least in the present state of the *Gospel of Judas*: a final verdict on the orthodox church and its leaders. Thus the primary phrase provides the proper definition of the message to be rendered, and ties it to the overall eschatological theme prevalent in the entire composition.

The incipit continues with the peculiar chronological notation, that Jesus communicated his message "on eight days, three days before he suffered."[9] The phrase "before he suffered" alludes to the New Testament, but turns it on its head by hinting at what will only be revealed at the end: The Gnostic Jesus had already left *before* his mortal part was handed over. Thus the fallacy of the orthodox church, a topic that also will prevail throughout the text, is already exposed in the opening line: He suffered only according to the canonical Gospels; the communication during eight sequential days shortly before Passover ended with the departure of the spiritual Jesus, *three days before* the empty body that carried him during his earthly journey was crucified. In some Gnostic texts, the spiritual Jesus even stands by and laughs about the ignorance of those supposedly tormenting him.

Chronological entries are often simply literary devices intended to lend a text a certain historicity. However, since either the beginning or the end, or both, of the first four days are clearly marked, the remainder of the text could have been divided in a similar fashion.[10] Some sudden changes of topic or addressee within the text at least seem to

---

world," in the sense of *concerning the world*, appears to have a clear eschatological overtone: What happened to the world at the end is predetermined by how it came into being and what it entails, the mystery to be revealed.

[8] *Gos. Jud.* 33,1–3.

[9] *Gos. Jud.* 33,3–6. In the Kasser et al. 2007, the translation of the verbal expression ⲉⲘⲠⲀⲦⲉϥⲢ̄ ⲠⲀⲤⲬⲀ (*Gos. Jud.* 33,5–6) as "before *he* celebrated Passover" does not make any sense, since there would be no reason for Jesus to stop talking three days *before* he would have the last meal with his disciples. I believe the headline to read: *The secret word of judgment that Jesus communicated to Judas Iscariot on eight days, (ending) three days before he (allegedly) suffered.*

[10] If the other days also were specified by certain marks now lurking somewhere in the lacunae, this would, in any case, have to be understood as a purely literary devise, not reflecting but merely alluding to the "holy" week celebrated in mainstream Christianity, thereby correcting the false orthodox implications.

make a formal arrangement in accordance with the incipit feasible, though the fragmentary state of the text prevents ultimate certainty. However, we will now follow the story as it unfolds over the course of the presumed eight days.

THE FIRST DAY

After Jesus is summarily introduced, the *first day* commences.[11] Jesus encounters his disciples sitting together, worshipping and celebrating the agape meal, as the rite they perform could be assumed to mean. The first thing he does, when "he [looked] at his disciples, sitting assembled and giving thanks over the bread,"[12] is to laugh. He laughs at their naiveté with which they believe that this is what good Christians have to do. He also laughs about the irony, in that they worship *their* God, all the while believing it to be *his* Father, actually saying, "Teacher, you [yourself] are the son of our God."[13] They have no idea that they inadvertently only serve the God of the Hebrew Scriptures, who is an adverse deity, by far inferior to the true, supreme Father whom Jesus came to earth to reveal. When Jesus asks them how they think they know him, only Judas takes the bait and utters his now renowned confession. He admits to knowing that Jesus was sent to them from the transcendent realm. Yet since he had received no prior revelation, his knowledge of Jesus' true origin is somewhat surprising. In the canonical Gospels, especially the *Gospel of Mark*, it is initially only the demons that know who Jesus is.[14] Hence it looks as if Judas knows, because he also is a demon. However, throughout the entire gospel, he is portrayed as yet another clueless disciple, who needs enlightenment and receives it even to his own detriment. Thus the impression here could be misleading, and perhaps has to be solved rather by redaction criticism.[15] Even though Jesus laughingly will later call Judas the "thirteenth demon,"[16] the negative connotation of the term probably

---

[11] *Gos. Jud.* 33,22–36,10.

[12] *Gos. Jud.* 33,26–34,2.

[13] *Gos. Jud.* 34,11–13.

[14] Cf. e.g. Mark 3:11, 5:7.

[15] Judas' confession may originally have intended to counteract Peter's confession in the New Testament, and only consisted of the statement, "I know who you are and from where you have come," (*Gos. Jud.* 35,15–17), but was extended when the Sethian material was inserted (as I will be arguing below).

[16] *Gos. Jud.* 44,21.

alludes more to Judas' intended "betrayal" than to familiar demonology.[17] But for now Jesus takes Judas aside and mockingly promises to tell him about the "mystery of the kingdom"[18] to which Judas might go one day, but will be very aggrieved when he gets there.[19] Jesus knows that Judas will suffer when he realizes what the "kingdom" actually is. The irony here lies in the deception—a promise immediately followed by a put-down—as well as in a play on words, for the "kingdom" is not the exalted realm of the holy generation about which Judas hopes to hear, but the archontic world of the demonic demiurge whom Judas and the other disciples serve. When the confused Judas desires to learn more about it, Jesus departs.

THE SECOND AND THE THIRD DAY

Returning from precisely that holy generation on the *second day*,[20] Jesus laughs again at the inquiring disciples, because he knows that they will not understand. He teaches them that no person born mortal, nor any of the angels or stars for that matter, will ever see the holy generation. These unsettling predictions are voiced throughout the text, leaving the disciples troubled and speechless. On the *third day*,[21] the disciples tell Jesus their vision, which he then interprets. They saw a large house and *twelve* priests administering at a large altar, where "a crowd was waiting at that altar, [until] the priests [came out, bringing cattle as] offerings."[22] When Jesus interrupts, inquiring further about the people watching approvingly, and asks, "What kind of

---

[17] By comparison, the orthodox confession in Mark 8:29 is uttered by Peter; but some moments later Jesus calls Peter "Satan" (Mark 8:33). Nonetheless, it would never occur to us to assume that Peter is the devil in disguise; likewise, I cannot see Judas as an evil demon in disguise, as is suggested by DeConick 2007.

[18] *Gos. Jud.* 35,24–25.

[19] The new reading ⲟⲩⲭ ϩⲓⲛⲁ "Not so (that you will go there…)" (*Gos. Jud.* 35,26) in Kasser et al. 2007 is far less convincing than the earlier reading ⲟⲩⲛ ϭⲟⲙ "It is possible (that you may go there…)" that circulated among scholars before the publication. In my judgment, the remains of the Coptic text as available in Kasser et al. 2007 and on the Internet do not warrant the new reading.

[20] *Gos. Jud.* 36,11–37,20.

[21] *Gos. Jud.* 37,20–42,?. Only the beginning of the third day is clearly indicated. A line number replaced by a question mark indicates uncertainty about the exact place on a given page where the text is too fragmentary.

[22] *Gos. Jud.* 38,6–10. In Kasser et al. 2007, the mere reconstruction to "presenting the offerings" leaves the statement "the cattle brought in for sacrifice you have seen" in 39,25–27 without a precursor to refer back to.

[crowd]?,"[23] the disciples tell him that they perform all sorts of heinous deeds, namely "Some [abstain for] two weeks, [others] sacrifice their own children, others their wives, blessing [and] humbling each other, others lie with (other) men, others commit murder, and others carry out a great deal of (other) sins and crimes."[24] In his interpretation of the vision, Jesus bitterly complains about the receiver of the sacrifices, namely the God of the Hebrew Scriptures, charging, "[The lord of the world][25] will stand up, and this is the way he will invoke my name, and generations of faithful will abide in him,"[26] because the participants in these sacrificial rites are faithful to him; they will misguidedly continue their terrible sacrificial performances, since again and again "another man will join the [fornicators], and another [will] join the baby-killers, another the sleepers-with-men together with those who abstain, and the impure, lawless, and erroneous rest."[27] Jesus accuses his disciples of leading the way by stating bluntly, "It is you who lead the offerings to the altar you have seen: that one is the god you serve. The twelve men you have seen are you, and the cattle brought in for sacrifice you have seen, this is the multitude you lead astray at that altar."[28] They are the ones to blame. He sharply rejects this fruitless exploit, because the offerings only benefit this inferior God, the "servant of error," together with his cosmic powers. Thus Jesus commands unmistakably, "Stop [sacrificing cattle] that you have [brought] up to the altar, since they are for your stars and their angels."[29]

THE FOURTH DAY

An indication of the end of the third and the beginning of the following day could have been somewhere in the missing lines of page 42. After Jesus told his disciples that each of them has his own star, he was probably elaborating on the topic of the stars that destine humans' existence, but two-thirds of the page is missing. However, by

---

[23] *Gos. Jud.* 38,12–13.

[24] *Gos. Jud.* 38,14–23.

[25] My reconstruction to "The lord of the world," referring to the inferior demiurge Saklas, assumes a juxtaposition to the "Lord of the universe," the supreme God in the highest realm.

[26] *Gos. Jud.* 40,2–7.

[27] *Gos. Jud.* 40,8–15.

[28] *Gos. Jud.* 39,18–40,1.

[29] *Gos. Jud.* 41,1–6.

the beginning of page 43, the topic had clearly changed, and the end of that day is plainly marked by Jesus' departure.[30] On this *fourth day*,[31] Jesus explained what would happen to the human body and soul at death. When the spirit separates the body from the soul, the body will die, but the soul will be kept alive. Yet at the end, both body and soul will be destroyed in the cosmic annihilation, since "[this] is the way they [will perish] together with the [aeon] of the [defiled] race and the perishable Sophia, [and] the hand that created mortal people—their souls will <not> go up to the aeons on high".[32]

Here Sophia is mentioned on a par with the creator demiurge, not with Judas. Even though in the *Pistis Sophia*, a Gnostic text of the Askew Codex, the fallen Sophia is also likened to a demon and connected to the thirteenth aeon, Judas is certainly not her "spitting image," as has recently been argued.[33] Judas is not fallen from grace, bemoaning his fate of being separated from his transcendent home. Her plight does not "parallel that of Judas"; on the contrary, his existence could not be farther apart from Sophia's. Though Judas has a hunch about Jesus' provenance, he is still a dupe, just another deluded disciple who is misled by his star, as Jesus later explicitly tells him. Many other Gnostic texts shed light on the *Gospel of Judas*, and in certain ways the *Pistis Sophia* may be one of them, but there are simply no "elements of the fall, passion, grief, and redemption"[34] present in the *Gospel of Judas* that would have to be taken into account in assessing the figure of Judas. The condition and state of confusion in which the fallen Sophia finds herself in the *Pistis Sophia* neither compares with the portrayal of Judas in the document at hand, nor would a link

---

[30] *Gos. Jud.* 44,14; part of the line is even left empty, thus clearly denoting the break. Instead, Kasser et al. 2007 suggests an emendation of the text to "<they> departed" (i.e. the disciples), because the editors understand Jesus to render his revelation on three days rather than eight, with no other explanation for the eight days mentioned in the incipit than to state, "The exact meaning of the 'eight days' in relation to the 'three days' is unclear." However, nothing in the text indicates that the other disciples were not also present the entire time, even in the sections where Judas keeps asking the questions and Jesus talks mainly to him.

[31] *Gos. Jud.* 42,?–44,14.

[32] *Gos. Jud.* 44,2–7. Contrary to Kasser et al. 2007, I think an emendation to <not> is indispensable since the immediate context clearly suggests a negative outcome; otherwise it would imply that the demiurge ("the hand that has created mortal people") is going up to the highest realm, something nobody is seriously considering.

[33] Cf. Meyer 2008a and Meyer in Kasser et al. 2008, 125–154.

[34] Cf. Meyer, in Kasser et al. 2008, 151.

between the two add to the standing of Judas,[35] since according to the *Gospel of Judas*, neither of them will see the holy generation, given that Jesus adds, "[Truly,] I say to you, [neither humans], nor angels, [nor] powers will be able to see those [aeons] that [this great] and holy generation [will see]."[36] After having pronounced this distressing prediction, Jesus again departs—not the disciples.

THE FIFTH DAY

On the *fifth day*,[37] Judas is eager to recount also his own vision, telling Jesus, "I saw the twelve disciples throwing stones at me; they were [vehemently] running [after me]. And I came to the place [to which I followed] you. I saw [a house at this place], but my eyes could not [measure] its size. Venerable people were surrounding it. That house <had a> single room, and in the middle of the house was a [crowd of people who surrounded] you."[38] Then he seems to beg Jesus to take him along with the others into this house, if the reconstruction is correct and the text continues, "[Then he beseeched Jesus and said], 'Teacher, take me in together with these people.'"[39] Jesus had already teased Judas for his eagerness to get heard, when "he laughed and said to him, 'Why do you struggle so, you thirteenth demon?'",[40] thus reminding him of his earlier prediction, "For someone else will replace you, so that the twelve [stars] shall again be completed through their god."[41]

Yet his bleak prospect becomes even more obvious when Jesus flat out tells him that his star misled him into thinking he could follow

---

[35] To repeatedly refer to Sophia as the "Wisdom of God" (Meyer, in Kasser et al. 2008, 125–54 and Meyer 2008a) seems disingenuous, since this epithet is reserved for the divine consort of the supreme God, not for the renowned "fallen Sophia".

[36] *Gos. Jud.* 44,8–13.

[37] *Gos. Jud.* 44,15–47,1. The text does not explicitly state that the day had changed, but Jesus obviously came back as he has done before, each time on another day.

[38] *Gos. Jud.* 44,24–45,9.

[39] *Gos. Jud.* 45,10–12.

[40] *Gos. Jud.* 44,19–21.

[41] *Gos. Jud.* 36,1–4. Kasser et al. 2007 reconstructs "twelve [disciples]," but the Coptic word the editors chose (*Gos. Jud.* 36,3: ⲛ̄ⲥ[ⲃⲟⲩⲓ̈]) occurs nowhere else in the text; rather the Greek term ⲙ̄ⲙⲁⲑⲏⲧⲏⲥ is persistently used for the disciples. Moreover, Jesus already pointed out that each of the twelve disciples has his own star (cf. *Gos. Jud.* 42,7–9). These twelve stars are obviously connected to the Zodiac and thus must be complete for the world to go on.

Jesus and enter the upper realm, because "No person born mortal is worthy to enter the house you have seen. For that is the place reserved for the holy."[42] In yet another play on words Jesus again predicts, "You will become the thirteenth, you will be cursed by all the other generations, and you will be ruling over them. In the final days…you will not go on high to the holy [generation]."[43] The allusion to the future selection of another disciple as replacement for Judas is set over and against the "thirteenth aeon" that designates the highest place above the twelve aeons of the archontic kingdom. Destined by his star, Judas as the *thirteenth* demon will be stuck in the *thirteenth* aeon—and so will his star, since Jesus tells him later, "Your star will reign over the thirteenth aeon."[44]

This is too much for Judas, who now apparently realizes that his future hangs in the balance. Hence after Jesus concludes, "I have taught you [about] the error of the stars and [the] twelve [archons who rule] over the twelve aeons,"[45] he anxiously inquires about the prospect of his descendents, asking, "Teacher, could it be that my seed (only) controls the archons?"[46] At this point, Jesus apparently takes pity on Judas, saying "Come, and I [shall speak with you (again) about the mysteries of the kingdom. It is possible that you may go there], but you may be greatly groaning when you see the kingdom together with its entire generation."[47]

To be sure, the text here is very fragmentary, but Jesus again mockingly seems to reassure Judas that he will, indeed, rule over the kingdom, only to warn him another time, that he will not be too pleased when he realizes that this "kingdom" is not the place he aspires to go to. The promotion is not all that high compared to what he is denied. Thus it is not the disciples who will curse him out of jealousy, as has been maintained, but the inhabitants over which Judas will rule—though the disciples will ultimately be among them. Yet Judas obviously can still not fully grasp the implication of Jesus' words, thus asking Jesus

---

[42] *Gos. Jud.* 45,14–19.

[43] *Gos. Jud.* 46,19–47,1.

[44] *Gos. Jud.* 55,10–11.

[45] *Gos. Jud.* 46,1–4.

[46] *Gos. Jud.* 46,5–7. The Greek verb used in the text (*Gos. Jud.* 46,6–7: ϩⲩⲡⲟⲧⲁⲥⲥ[ⲉ]) has an active as well as a passive meaning, but the passive meaning "subjected, controlled" (Kasser et al. 2007 translates "under the control of") does not agree with Jesus' prediction that Judas will rule *over* the archons.

[47] *Gos. Jud.* 46,8–14.

in bewilderment, "What (then) is the benefit I have gained, since you have separated me *from* that (holy) generation?"[48] There is obviously no advantage in having received this revelation, since the errant stars control everyone's fate. No matter how hard Judas tries, the holy generation is out of his reach.

THE SIXTH DAY

A long discourse about the origin and establishment of the upper and lower world starts with 47,1. Since this unit, with no interaction between the revealer and his audience, deviates considerably from its surroundings, it is evidently an *inclusio*. Hence the communicated theogony, cosmogony and cosmology familiar from the Sethian system could have been assigned to the *sixth day*, ending in 53,4, even without literary elements specifically indicating a change of day. The disclosure of the origin of the universe begins with a brief introduction of the Great Invisible Spirit; it then shifts immediately to the Autogenes, without even mentioning Barbelo, the mother in the divine Sethian triad. The Autogenes brings forth the four great aeons of light and their illuminators, establishes the heavenly Adamas in the first light, and probably Seth in the second one—though only his generation is mentioned. After myriads of divine beings are generated, the pleroma is filled up and completed. The last of the four great lights, Eleleth, single-handedly establishes the lower world. Then Nebro—here surprisingly called Yaldabaoth—and Saklas appear and fill up their world. They create the traditional twelve archontic angels,[49] with whom Saklas in turn creates the primary human couple. However, the first in the familiar list of archontic angels, Athoth, is here replaced by "Seth,"

---

[48] *Gos. Jud.* 46,16–18. The misleading translation "set apart for" is still retained in Kasser et al. 2007, whereas the accurate meaning is only mentioned in the apparatus. Yet on every occasion Jesus makes clear that neither Judas nor the other disciples will reach "that generation" which is reserved for the "holy" (cf. e.g. *Gos. Jud.* 37,1–8; 44,8–13).

[49] Even though the text then goes on naming only the first five of the familiar list of angels, and summarizes, "These are the five who reigned over the underworld, and the first (five) over the chaos" (*Gos. Jud.* 52,11–14). The scribe obviously forgot to name also the five angels who rule over the underworld. In contrast, the translation "over the underworld and first of all over the chaos" (*Gos. Jud.* 52,3) in Kasser et al. 2007 appears to corrupt the text even further.

who is identified with Christ.[50] This epithet, amazingly not applied to the Autogenes in the typical way of christianizing originally non-Christian Sethian texts, but applied to an archontic angel, is the only Christian feature in the entire Sethian unit. More importantly, the epithet "Christ" itself occurs nowhere else in the *Gospel of Judas*. It seems strangely out of place, thus indicating that the entire section was in all probability secondarily inserted, and this obviously at a time when the section itself was already secondarily christianized.[51]

THE SEVENTH AND THE EIGHTH DAY

Shortly after the creation of the first couple, the topic changes again, although the fragmentary state of the papyrus prevents an unambiguous allocation of the new beginning. According to my reconstruction, the *sixth day* ends with the narrator's statement, "This [is the way Jesus spoke to Judas]," and the *seventh day*[52] starts with "The [Lord] said to him, 'Your life with your children will last (only) [a short] time.'"[53] The ensuing dialogue with Judas about the human generations and the souls apparently continues where it had been left off on the *fourth day*, now expanded to Jesus' teaching about the spirits. Then a change of the person(s) addressed (from the 2nd person singular to the 2nd person plural) could indicate that the dialogue with the other disciples about the holy generation and the errant stars in relation to humans is resumed on what probably constitutes the *eighth day*.[54] Here Jesus laughs at the erroneous stars because, albeit controlling all human generations, they will be destroyed together with the rest of the cosmos.

---

[50] The second angel, Harmas, is then conflated to Harmathoth, clearly a combination of Harmas and Athoth.

[51] The Christianization process can be clearly observed in the Nag Hammadi Library, where the non-Christian treatise *Eugnostos* NHC III,3; NHC V,1 can be found next to its secondarily Christianized version *Soph. Jes. Chr.* NHC III,4, now presented as a dialogue between Jesus and his disciples.

[52] *Gos. Jud.* 53,5–54,2.

[53] Although the narrator generally does not refer to Jesus as "Lord," Judas used this term in addressing Jesus (cf. *Gos. Jud.* 36,19). Since the article is extant, there are not many possibilities to fill the lacuna; Jesus is also addressed with "teacher" or "Rabbi," but it seems less likely that a narrator himself would use either term to talk about Jesus. However, it is not likely that Saklas is talking to Judas, as the translation in Kasser et al. 2007 would suggest (*Gos. Jud.* 53,5: "And the [ruler] said to him"), but that Jesus opens the dialogue anew after the end of the Sethian insert.

[54] *Gos. Jud.* 54,3–58,?.

He then returns to the discussion of the misguided sacrifices in listing again the evil deeds that will be performed just before the destruction. Though I partially reconstructed the text, it is evident from the extant remains that Jesus basically repeats what he alleged on the third day, namely that "they will fornicate in my name, and slay their children, and [lie with men, and commit (other) sins and lawless deeds in my name]."[55] He then directly ties Judas to these evildoers, charging, "Truly, [I] say to you, Judas, those [who] offer sacrifices to Saklas [who is called]…(they do)] everything wicked. Yet you will do more than all of them. For the man who carries me, you will sacrifice."[56] Jesus predicting that Judas will exceed all of them sounds like praise but becomes a mockery. Far from doing Jesus a favor, Judas is willing to offer Saklas the biggest crown: Jesus himself. Thus Judas will beat all others in doing something evil rather than beneficial. That he will not succeed but can merely deliver an empty body is not to his credit.[57] The context makes it abundantly clear that the concept of sacrifice has no positive connotation here.

JESUS' DEPARTURE

After having delivered his final revelation, Jesus once more turns to Judas, pointing to a cloud full of light surrounded by stars. Judas is told that the leading star is his star. This was supposed to confirm Judas' supreme role above and beyond the other disciples. Yet here again, Jesus deals with Judas in utter irony. After all we have learned about Judas' destiny and that of his errant star, it can only lead the way into the destruction of the entire cosmos.

The narrator tells us that Judas "looked up and saw the luminous cloud."[58] Then the sentence either continues, or a new sentence starts with "He entered it." Since there is no clear antecedent to the "he," this pronoun can refer back either to Judas or to Jesus. However, it is hardly conceivable that Judas ascends and then could immediately

---

[55] *Gos. Jud.* 54,24–55,3.

[56] *Gos. Jud.* 56,11–21.

[57] The prediction that Judas will only hand over "the man who carries" Jesus further proves that the separation of the spiritual and the corporeal part of Jesus happened already *before* Judas could execute his plan—and thus Jesus will disappear into the cloud, not Judas (see below).

[58] *Gos. Jud.* 57,21–22.

reappear in order to function in the next scene. The Gnostic Jesus, on the other hand, throughout the text freely ascends and descends like the canonical Jesus in his post-resurrection appearances, though here it would be his final ascent. The following sentence, "Those standing on the ground heard a voice coming from the cloud,"[59] clearly alludes to the voice from the cloud in the transfiguration of Jesus. Thus it is more feasible that Judas, like everybody else, hears the voice from the cloud, but it is *Jesus* who enters it.[60] This would be a further allusion to the New Testament, where the cloud lifts Jesus up and carries him into heaven[61]—though in the *Gospel of Judas*, of course, the ascent takes place before the "betrayal" and crucifixion. After Jesus fulfilled his task of delivering his message, a cloud from the world of light is ready to lift him up and take him home.[62] Judas cannot follow him, as Jesus told him before; Judas has to fulfill his own destiny.

Thereupon follows a very brief narrative scene where Judas willfully hands Jesus over to the Jewish authorities.[63] The scene is so abbreviated because it no longer has any real function. What happens between the spiritual Jesus' departure and the crucifixion of the corporeal body that carried him becomes irrelevant.

This eight-day configuration seems to have been a handy tool for giving the composition a final structure that binds together literary units conceivably inserted at various points in time. Several seams in

---

[59] *Gos. Jud.* 57,23–26.

[60] In order to strengthen the argument that it is Judas who ascends into the cloud, the scene here was on occasion compared to a similar scene in the *Allog.* 60–61 that follows the *Gos, Jud.* in the TC. Yet there Allogenes decidedly does not enter the cloud; he can barely look at it, but only hears the voice above him, "And I heard a word from the cloud and the light, and it shone upon me" (*Allog.* 62,15–18).

[61] Luke 24:5; Acts 1:9.

[62] The notion of a "transfiguration of Judas" has recently been modified by the idea of Judas obtaining a vision of the divine. Yet the initial interpretation still brought forth another novel idea: Judas did not enter a luminous cloud, but the cloud of Nebro and Saklas that brings him to his archontic place. A mention of his return is conveniently expected in the lacunae, and the "light" in the cloud is simply imagined away. See Brankaer-Bethge 2007, 370–371.

[63] Because in Kasser et al. 2007 the Greek loanword ⲕⲁⲧⲁⲗⲩⲙⲁ (*Gos. Jud.* 58,11) is translated as "guestroom," it was always assumed that the text alludes to a Passover celebration, but the term simply means "dwelling." There is no indication that a last meal was prepared or took place. The translation of the term as "guestroom" in the New Testament distinguishes the rented room from the rest of the house to which it belongs; this should not predetermine the meaning here. Connecting the scene of the betrayal to a last meal even with only the corporeal part of Jesus present is very unlikely, since the text is adamantly opposed to any rite performed in the orthodox church.

the textual flow, shifts in the topic, and abrupt transitions (between lines 44,14 and 15, and lines 53,4 and 53,5), as well as repetitions of the phrase "Jesus said" while he is still speaking (41,1 and within line 47,1) evidently betray an editorial hand. Furthermore, the long cosmological discourse with no interaction between revealer and recipients clearly interrupts the revelatory dialogue, which already seems to have been previously interrupted by the vision reports. Hence we should be open to the possibility that during the two hundred years that lie between the original Greek composition and the current copy of its Coptic translation, the *Gospel of Judas* was subjected to various editorial modifications and textual adaptations that reflect the social and religious experience of its users at different times in their history.

A SETHIAN *GOSPEL OF JUDAS*?

For the community using the *Gospel of Judas*, there could certainly have been a great need to adopt a version of the well-established Sethian system and incorporate it into their gospel in order to lend it more authority when competing with and fighting against the orthodox church. In terms of sectarian affiliation, however, the correlation between the *Gospel of Judas* and Sethianism seems merely to rest on the surface. There are hardly any Sethian features outside this unit. Moreover, the particular version of Sethianism at the redactor's disposal represents only a truncated form of the traditional material. It neither contains the Sophia myth nor the redeemer myth, both constitutive for Sethianism. Also any element of Sethian soteriology is notably absent; there is no mention of saving rituals, such as the Sethian baptism that reveals the knowledge of the five seals for safe passage during the ascent of the soul, nor of any anticipated or visionary ascent. The resemblance to other Sethian texts is limited to a mere outline of the main figures, lacking any description of their deployment and function.

Most of the features this unit employs are also prevalent in Gnostic texts other than Sethian. The familiar Sethian material is so substantially curtailed that it has already lost many of its distinctions from other non-Sethian Gnostic texts.[64] Even the way Barbelo is mentioned

---

[64] In its main characteristic, the laughing savior, the *Gos. Jud.* is much closer to the non-Sethian *Apoc. Peter* NHC VII,3 and the non-Sethian *Sec. Treat. Seth* NHC VII,2 than to any Sethian text.

earlier in Judas' confession hardly conforms to the Sethian standard. In Sethianism, Barbelo is the first manifestation of the supreme God, his divine consort; here Barbelo is just an aeon. The name Barbelo is also the only clear Sethian element *outside* the Sethian section; yet since it is affixed as a mere apposition to aeon, it could have been easily appended at the same time the Sethian unit was inserted. Without the name Barbelo, Judas' declaration would have no Sethian ring to it (and no demonic underpinning).[65]

Moreover, the *Gospel of Judas* is a distinctive Christian-Gnostic, albeit anti-orthodox, text, whereas Sethianism was basically a non-Christian, Jewish-Gnostic movement. Although Sethianism did come in contact with Christianity, and its texts were subjected to various degrees of Christianization, its focal point or main thrust never had a specifically Christian-Gnostic perspective; it was always more typified by an inner-Jewish tension. Sethian writings generally deal with notorious Old Testament figures by means of reinterpreting their purpose and function in the Hebrew Scriptures, and reassessing their reputation in Judaism; they do not employ New Testament characters.[66] Non-Sethian Christian-Gnostics, in contrast, favor personages who are marginalized in the orthodox church and give them a different role and meaning—as was, for instance, the case with Mary in the *Gospel of Mary*. Hence rather than being a document whose Sethian themes are not yet fully developed,[67] the *Gospel of Judas* in its present form appears to be a quite late and distant offshoot of Sethianism.[68]

---

[65] However, it is more likely that the entire second half of the current confession, "You came from the immortal aeon of Barbelo. He who sent you is the one whose name I am not worthy to utter" (*Gos. Jud.* 35,17–21) is a secondary addition.

[66] The *Apocryphon of John* seems to contradict this assertion, but John occurs only in the framework that secondarily christianizes the document.

[67] Christianizing the purely Jewish-Gnostic Sethian texts progressed from the most superficial identification of the Autogenes with Christ to an added Christian framework and the like; this renders an "*early* form of Christian *Sethian* thought" a contradiction in terms (Meyer, in Kasser et al. 2008,126), especially seen in the light of the overall claim that the *Gospel of Judas* would represent a form of Sethianism not yet fully developed.

[68] Perhaps having moved in the opposite direction than *Melchizedek*, a seemingly Sethian text, but one that is so Christianized and anti-docetic, that, in its essence, it is hardly Gnostic any longer.

Compositional Stages and the Community Behind It

A further indication that this unit is not original to the document at hand could lie in the way Irenaeus reports about a "fabrication" he knows as the *Gospel of Judas*. If he had the text in its present form available, he probably would have perceived it as Sethian and classified it accordingly—since he had just dealt with "Gnostics" (as he calls the Sethians) earlier—instead of assigning it to sub-groupings that have nothing to do with Sethianism. Hence Irenaeus may have had in mind a version of the *Gospel of Judas* quite different from the one we possess.[69]

This becomes even more apparent in light of the vision reports. Had those been part of the original *Gospel of Judas*, Irenaeus would certainly have ranted much harder against opponents who exhibit such callous and unforgiving language in their polemic against the orthodox church and its leaders. To be confronted with the kind of polemic that was usually employed against opponents of the church—and precisely by heresy hunters like Irenaeus—could not have left him mute on this subject. Instead he simply writes that Judas "alone was acquainted with the truth as no others were, and so accomplished the mystery of the betrayal. By him all things, both earthly and heavenly, were thrown into dissolution."

In both content and tone, this rather mild assessment seems to befit best the revelatory dialogue, which, thus, could be perceived as the primary composition. The dialogue was then embellished at beginning and end with the summaries of scenes familiar from the canonical Gospels during the course of the group using the text, separating itself from the orthodox environment. At that early stage, also the title may have been added in the unending quest for accreditation in competition with the canonical Gospels. This dialogue between Jesus and his disciples, with Judas being singled out as the favored dialogue partner, but also as the favored whipping-boy, may well have been the *Gospel of Judas* on which Irenaeus reported. Although the title was presum-

---

[69] Contrary to Wurst 2008, 135, we do not need Irenaeus' testimony to trace Sethianism back to the middle of the 2nd century, since it is already witnessed in the so called "Berlin Coptic Book" of the early second century; it quotes parts of a Sethian text and mentions after the citation that "this [is the doctrine] of the Sethians." Cf. Schenke Robinson 2004, esp. 256–257 as well as CSCO 611, 2004, xii–xv and 130.

ably applied to the document in order to accredit it over against the canonical Gospels, the selection of Judas as major dialogue partner may have been due to him being despised in the orthodox church. As a consequence, this notoriously disreputable figure was given a voice in the text. Yet although embraced by this group, and granted a leading role in the dialogue with their Jesus, he was still not seen as one of their own. He was utterly misguided in handing over Jesus, and will suffer for it eternally, but his action had no effect on the true Jesus, and thus he does not deserve the bad rap he was given in mainstream Christianity.

However, when at the end of the second century the Christological battles between orthodox and Gnostic Christianity were growing more violent, the combined text could have been augmented with the vitriolic vision reports. The dramatic change in tone suggests a fairly well-advanced state of mutual exclusivity. Severe disturbances, such as persecutions and excommunications from orthodox Christian communities, may also have brought about an enlargement of the incipit, now characterizing the gospel as a final judgment on the church and its leaders, who were apparently perceived as continuing the old ways of the failed Jewish religious practices in new clothes, as exemplified by the temple cult with its sacrificial rituals. The acts of piety attacked include fasting, the agape meal or eucharist, and baptism, but the polemic centers on the concept of sacrifice, especially rejecting the Christological interpretation of Jesus' death as a necessity for salvation. A further rationale for the schism becomes particularly discernible in the mention of sacrificing wives and children. This Christian-Gnostic community ostensibly despised and turned against the readiness for any kind of martyrdom as a pointless sacrifice to an inferior God who himself will perish at the end. There is no hope of salvation for anyone in this sacrificial approach.

The cosmological section, undoubtedly intended to accredit the sect with the long-since established and well-attested Sethian system, was certainly not inserted before the end of the second century. Its already corrupted and truncated version transformed the *Gospel of Judas* at best into a neo-Sethian document. Other revisions may also have been put in place at that juncture, such as extending the confession put in Judas' mouth in order to tie the Sethian discourse closer to the revelatory dialogue, or the repetition of the hideous deeds as signs of the apocalyptic end in the later section of the dialogue. Ultimately, the final redactor may once again have augmented the incipit, attaching to it the chronological notation that rationalizes his arrangement of the text into its present form of an eight-day revelatory discourse.

Taking this admittedly somewhat hypothetical development into account, the initial revelatory dialogue appears to have been composed in a chiastic form:

> Incipit (33,1–2)
>> Introductory narrative scene (33,6–22)
>>> Dialogue with disciples (33,22–37,20)
>>>> Dialogue with Judas (42,?–44,14; 53,5–54,2?)
>>> Dialogue with disciples resumed (54,3?–58,?)
>> Concluding narrative scene (58,?-26)
> Title (58,27–28)

The final redactor seems to have tried to retain this compositional form by reworking the material compiled at different times and for various reasons into an eight-day arrangement outlined above in more detail, although the vision reports clearly interrupt the initial literary structure:

> Incipit (33,1–6)
>> Introductory narrative scene (33,6–22)
>>> Dialogue with disciples (*day 1–2*: 33,22–37,20 [*day 3*: disciples' vision, 37,20–42,?])
>>> Dialogue with Judas (*day 4*: 42,?–44,14 [*day 5*: Judas' vision, 44,15–47,1])
>>> Discourse about Sethian cosmology (*day 6*: 47,1–53,4)
>>> Dialogue with Judas resumed (*day 7*: 53,5–54,2?)
>>> Dialogue with disciples resumed (*day 8*: 54,3?–58,?)
>> Concluding narrative scene (58,?-26)
> Title (58,27–28)

Even though the description given here is only one way of interpreting the clues the *Gospel of Judas* provides regarding the underlying social history of its audience, it is an attempt that accounts for the present form of the document in relation to what it may have been when it caught Irenaeus' eye or ear, and that tries to offer an understanding of the way the different literary forms compiled in this document relate to each other, as well as of the transmission history of the document we now possess.

The Gnostic's salvation

The *Gospel of Judas* evidently shows no interest in redemption and salvation of humankind, since everyone born mortal is under the control of the erroneous stars and thus destined for eternal doom. Toward the conclusion of the *Gospel of Judas*, Jesus talks about the things that will happen at the end, and predicts, "the stars come to an end over all these (things), and when Saklas completes his time that was allotted to him, their *first star* will come with the generations, and the things that have (just) been said will be completed."[70] The time of all humans is limited, given that "Adam together with his generation received his limited time at the (same) place where he (i.e. Saklas) has received his limited kingdom with its archon"[71]—Adam here merely representing all humans created by the demiurge Saklas.

Yet the prospect of the Gnostics is different, because Jesus also reveals, "God caused Gnosis to be [given] to Adam and to those with him, so that the kings of the chaos and the underworld may not lord it over them."[72] Hence the heavenly dwelling place of Adam and his seed is with the holy generation in the highest realm. In accepting the same Gnosis, this sect using the *Gospel of Judas* can be assured that they belong to the heavenly Adam and to those of whom Jesus says, "the Great One ordered Gabriel to give spirits to the great rulerless generation, the spirit along with the soul."[73] The acceptance of the redeeming knowledge guarantees them that their spirits and souls will not die; they will be exempt from the fateful catastrophe and therefore can confidently look forward to their rightful eternal dwelling place.

With a message like this, they were well equipped to compete in the diverse religious environment of the second century and beyond. By contrast, the apostles and their followers in the orthodox church belong to the doomed generation, since Jesus tells Judas, "God commanded Michael to give (only) spirits of humans to them, serving as a loan."[74] Their ignorance and devastating influence on believers by way

---

[70] *Gos. Jud.* 54,17–24. This first star is obviously the same star that Jesus, before his ascent, has pointed out to Judas as being his star that leads the way; this provides further proof that there is no positive connotation connected with Judas' star, but that it, indeed, will only lead into destruction.

[71] *Gos. Jud.* 53,11–16.

[72] *Gos. Jud.* 54,8–12.

[73] *Gos. Jud.* 53,22–25.

[74] *Gos. Jud.* 53,19–22.

of their misguided practices are callously exposed in the document. Judas is not better off, though; he is undone by his star. In terms of Christian-Gnostic soteriology, it is the knowledge that saves, brought down by the descending redeemer, who, after having fulfilled his task on earth, sheds his human body and ascends back home. As far as future converts are concerned, they also have to accept the offered knowledge—as Judas obviously did not—in order to be reunited one day with their true Father. There is no other salvation plan to be counted on.

Even though the *Gospel of Judas* does not provide us with any more reliable information about Judas than do the canonical Gospels, it plays a vital role in laying open the various traditions of early Christianity when the beliefs were still in flux, and lets us glance from a different perspective at the tensions between Christian-Gnostics and orthodox Christians in the raging battles of the second century.

THE SETHIAN MYTH IN THE *GOSPEL OF JUDAS*: SOTERIOLOGY OR DEMONOLOGY?

John D. Turner

As the original editors and virtually all other scholars note, the *Gospel of Judas* falls within the branch of Christian Gnosticism that claimed to be descended from Seth, the third son of Adam, commonly known as "Sethian" or "Classical" Gnosticism. Indeed, page 49 refers to "the incorruptible [generation] of Seth" that the divine Autogenes or Self-generated One revealed to the twelve luminaries occupying the divine luminous cloud that encompassed the divine Adamas and his son Seth.[1]

Beginning in the late the second century, the exaltation of the heavenly Seth and the holy generation descended from him becomes a prominent theme in gnostic literature, attested not only in Epiphanius' reports on the Sethians and Archontics, but also in six narrative revelations (the *Apocryphon of John*, the *Apocalypse of Adam*, the *Gospel of Egyptians*, *Melchizedek*, and *Zostrianos*) of the eleven Nag Hammadi titles included in the corpus of Nag Hammadi treatises conventionally called Classical or Sethian Gnostic.[2] As a Christian Sethian revelation dialogue between Jesus and Judas Iscariot, the *Gospel of Judas* has its closest formal affinity with the *Apocryphon of John*, while the content and outline of its mythical narrative is in many respects similar, not only to the mythology of the *Apocryphon* and the *Gospel of Egyptians*, but also to portions of the *Apocalypse of Adam*, and *Zostrianos*. In addition it also incorporates material very similar to the non-Sethian work *Eugnostos the Blessed* (possibly of 'Ophite' provenance).

On closer inspection, however, it turns out that the Sethian myth employed by the *Gospel of Judas* is of a very odd sort, containing a number of departures in content and sequence from its instances in

---

[1] *Gos. Jud.* TC [49] [1] "And [*in*] that [*cloud*] [2] [*Seth was begotten after*] [3] the image [*of his father Adamas*] [4] and after the likeness of [*these*] angels. [5] He revealed the incorruptible [6] [generation] of Seth [7] to the twelve [*luminaries*]."

[2] *Pan.* 39.3, 39.5, 40.7. Three Sethian treatises, *Norea*, *Allogenes*, *Steles Seth*, and *Marsanes* offer few if any traces of mythical narrative.

other Sethian works, and—unlike all other instances and testimonia of Sethian mythology—offers no soteriological narrative at all. In order to account for this phenomenon, I begin with a brief summary of the more broadly-attested features of Sethian mythology, and then continue with an examination of the content of the theogony, cosmogony, and anthropogony of the Sethian myth that Jesus reveals to Judas in this strange gospel, if indeed it can even be considered to be a "gospel" at all.

Sethian Mythology

As in the *Apocryphon of John*, many Sethian treatises locate at the summit of the hierarchy a supreme trinity of Father, Mother and Child comprising the supreme Invisible Spirit, his "first thought" Barbelo, and their child, the divine Autogenes. The Invisible Spirit seems to transcend even the realm of being itself, which properly begins with Barbelo as his projected self-reflection. The Autogenes Child is self-generated from Barbelo either spontaneously or from a spark of the Father's light, and is responsible for the creation and ordering of the remainder of the transcendent realm, which is structured around the Four Luminaries Harmozel, Oroiael, Daveithai, Eleleth and their associated transcendent aeons or eternal realms. The first three of these aeons become the heavenly dwellings of the archetypal Adam, Seth, and Seth's offspring, while the fourth aeon, Eleleth, is the dwelling of the last of the aeonic beings, Sophia.

Below this, the transitory realm of becoming originates either directly from the Luminary Eleleth's urging or from Sophia's own mistaken attempt to instantiate her own self-willed contemplation of the Invisible Spirit, but without its permission. This act brings into being the chief Archon or world ruler named variously Yaldabaoth, Saklas, Samael, Nebruel, etc. The Archon then steals from his mother Sophia a portion of the supreme Mother's divine essence, which he uses to create yet other archons as well as the phenomenal world. In response to the Archon's false boasting in his sole divinity, the mother Barbelo projects the true divine image, that is, the archetypal human, of which the Archon produces a defective earthly copy. He then attempts to capture the divine power stolen from Sophia by infusing it into the earthly protoplast. This projection constitutes the first of Barbelo's three major salvific initiatives, which mark three successive phases of the Sethian sacred history, the first two in primordial times, and the third and final in contemporary times.

The remainder of the myth narrates the steps by which the divine Mother Barbelo restores this dissipated divine essence to its original fullness and integrity. Appearing for the second time as her lower double, the spiritual Eve/Epinoia, she awakens Adam's dim knowledge of his divine origin and image, which is bequeathed to subsequent humanity through Adam's son Seth and his progeny, the seed of Seth. This ensures the preservation of future humanity's knowledge of its essential divinity despite the Archon's attempts to suppress it by various stratagems (the expulsion from paradise, the bringing of the flood, the inauguration of sexual lust through the fallen angels, and the conflagration of Sodom and Gomorrah). Finally, throughout subsequent history up to the present, the Mother continues to make salvific appearances in various guises (for example, in the form of a luminous cloud, or ethereal angels, or as Seth himself, or as Jesus). These appearances are mediated mainly through various rituals, especially baptism, to awaken subsequent humanity's potential self-awareness of its essential divinity to a full self-consciousness of being the elect seed of Seth. As far as I can see, the *Gospel of Judas*' version of the Sethian myth is unique in the almost total absence of this soteriological component.

The Sethian Myth in the *Gospel of Judas*

With the fundamental exception of its soteriological and ritual component, the basic outlines of this Sethian myth are certainly reflected in the *Gospel of Judas*. On pages 47–52 of the *Gospel*, Jesus teaches Judas about the composition of the divine world: the Great Invisible Spirit, the appearance of an unnamed luminous cloud—perhaps an Ersatz for Barbelo—from which emerges the angel Autogenes ("Self-Generated One"), who, from another luminous cloud, creates not only the four (unnamed) Luminaries (called "angels"), but also Adamas, Seth, and Seth's "generation," who dwell in that luminous cloud. Although up to this point there is no hint of rulership or control, the Self-generated One suddenly creates a hierarchy of luminous aeons consisting of two ruling luminaries with their associated aeons and myriads of angels, over which Adamas is to reign. Thereupon, the Autogenes reveals the generation of Seth to the twelve luminaries; although their origin is unaccounted for, these twelve luminaries suddenly multiply themselves into first seventy-two, and finally 360 luminaries and their associated "firmaments." Altogether, these beings apparently comprise a "cosmos" for the "holy generation" and the incorruptible powers of the "first human."

Thereupon follows an account of the lower world, which the *Gospel of Judas* generally designates as the "kingdom" (of the Archon of Saklas and eventually of Judas). From the aeonic cloud inhabited by the angel Eleleth—usually the fourth of the Sethian Four Luminaries—there arise another twelve angels to rule over the lower world. Their chief rulers are Saklas and Nebro, who is also called Yaldabaoth. Once they create five further angels to rule over the underworld, Saklas proposes to create a human being "after the likeness and after the image," which he and his angels then fashion as the earthly protoplasts Adam and Eve.

But the myth of the *Gospel of Judas* also contains a number of anomalies. There is first the complete absence of any traces of important traditional Sethian salvific motifs, such as the tripartition of sacred history marked by successive descents of the savior—be it Seth or Christ or the divine Mother in various guises. Nor does the myth contain traces of characteristic Sethian ritual elements, such as the baptism of the Five Seals featured in the *Apocryphon of John*, the *Trimorphic Protennoia*, and the *Gospel of the Egyptians*. Nor is there a trace of any practice of visionary ascent culminating in assimilation to the higher powers such as one finds in the Sethian Platonizing treatises the *Three Steles of Seth*, *Zostrianos*, *Allogenes*, or *Marsanes*.

So also this myth lacks elements of the Paradise narrative essential to the Gnostic theory of humankind's primordial enlightenment: there is no downward projection of the image of the archetypal human being, thus leaving unexplained the origin of the "image and likeness" in which the protoplasts are formed; there is no mention of the sundering of the primal androgyne into male and female whose primordial enlightenment is mentioned but not narrated;[3] and there is no mention of their expulsion from Paradise and subsequent rescue from flood and fire. Whereas it seems that the first half of the myth had applied the biblical hendiadys "image and likeness" of Gen 1:26 to both the Adamic and angelic nature of the *single* figure of the heavenly

---

[3] *Gos. Jud.* TC 54,5–12.

Seth,[4] the second half of the myth apparently interprets it as designating a *pair* of earthly protoplasts, Adam as the likeness and Eve as the
image of some unspecified entity, which other Sethian treatises identify as the divine image revealed by Barbelo.[5]

Another signature feature of Christianized Sethian treatises missing from the *Gospel of Judas* is the notion of the supreme trinity of
Father, Mother, and Child.[6] The great Invisible Spirit that all Sethian
treatises regard as hyperaeonic is identified merely as "a great and
boundless aeon."[7] Female protagonists like Barbelo and Sophia,
though mentioned,[8] play no role in this myth. Autogenes—who as the
Self-generated Child of Barbelo and the Invisible Spirit is the third
member of the Sethian trinity—is called merely a "great angel." While
most Christian Sethian treatises associate or identify the pre-existent
Christ with Autogenes, anointed with the Invisible Spirit's goodness
or Christhood (*chrēstia*),[9] the only occurrence of the epithet "Christ"
is applied to an *anti-divine* figure, the first of the angels over chaos
and the underworld, whom the text may even identify as Seth rather
than Athoth (as in the *Apocryphon of John* and the *Gospel of the
Egyptians*).[10] Nor does the myth mention other prominent salvific and

----

[4] *Gos. Jud.* TC 49,1–4. Cited in note 1 above; cf. *Apoc. John* NHC II,1, 15,2–4: "Let
us create a human after the image of God and after our likeness, so that its image
might be a light for us."

[5] *Gos. Jud.* TC 52,14–25.

[6] Cf. *Iren., Adv. Haer.* 1.29, *Apoc. John, Trim. Prot., Gos. Eg.*

[7] *Gos. Jud.* TC 47,5–9.

[8] Barbelo is named as an "aeon" only outside the bounds of the mythical narrative
in Judas' previous recognition of Jesus' identity and origin (TC 35,15–19) and Sophia
was perhaps used to identify the "cloud of knowledge" mentioned in 50,4 according to
my conjecture: *Gos. Jud.* [50] [22] "And in the aeon that appeared [23] with his generation
[24] is *located* the cloud of knowledge [25] and the angel [26] who is called [51] [1] Ele["leth.
And he dwells] [2] with [*the twelfth*] aeon [3] [*who is Sophia*]." *Pace* the original editors,
the "perishable wisdom (σοφία)" of 44,2–7 that will not enable the souls of the defiled
human generations to ascend into the aeons on high does not constitute a reference
to the Sophia of Sethian mythology.

[9] In *Apoc. John, Trim. Prot.,* and *Gos. Eg.*

[10] Despite the fact that Epiphanius, *Pan.* 26.10.1 lists Seth as the third archon, *Gos.
Jud.* TC 49,1–9 has already assigned Seth's incorruptible generation and perhaps Seth
himself to the realm of the divine luminaries, so the name of the first angel over
chaos in 52,5 can hardly be Seth (ⲥⲏⲑ), who clearly inhabits the divine realm, but
must be something like [Ath]ēth (ⲁⲑ]ⲏⲑ), whose epithet (ⲡⲉⲭⲥ̄) is not likely to be
'Lord' (ⲡⲭⲟⲉⲓⲥ) or 'Christ' (χριστός), but more likely "the Good One" (χρηστός), as in
Apoc. John NHC II,1, 12,16 ("goodness") and probably *Gos. Eg.* NHC III,2, 58,10. The
expected name for this first angel, Athoth, actually occurs as part of the bowdlerized
name for the second angel Harma{thoth}, normally Harmas.

revelatory figures featured in the *Gospel of the Egyptians, Zostrianos,* and *Allogenes,* such as the Triple Male Child, Youel, and Ephesech.

In the *Gospel of Judas,* the Self-generated Autogenes neither generates nor establishes the traditional Sethian Four Luminaries. Rather than "Luminaries," they are called merely "four other angels" that originate from "another (unidentified) cloud" to assist Autogenes. Like the *Hypostasis of the Archons,* the *Gospel of Judas* apparently knows only the name of the fourth of these Luminaries, Eleleth,[11] while the traditional names of the first three Luminaries[12] never appear. Nor does it know of the various ministers and baptismal powers (such as Gamaliel, Samblo, Abrasax, Micheus, Michar, Mnesinous, etc.) that populate these luminaries in a number of Sethian treatises (the *Apocryphon of John,* the *Gospel of Egyptians, Zostrianos, Melchizedek,* and even the Untitled Treatise of the Bruce Codex); of these, only the figure of Gabriel is mentioned, but not as the minister of the second Luminary Oroiael.

In fact, the *Gospel of Judas* displaces the prominence of these traditional four Luminaries even further by introducing a strikingly different set of luminaries completely unattested in any other Sethian work. After calling the divine Adamas into being, the Self-generated One then brings into being two unnamed ruling "luminaries" which can hardly be anything other than an allusion to the two properly *celestial* luminaries of Genesis 1:16, namely the sun and moon.[13] These two luminaries apparently generate twelve further luminaries which soon multiply into first 72, and then 360 luminaries, an astrological motif unattested in other Sethian works, but explicitly detailed in the treatises *Eugnostos the Blessed.* Unlike the *Apocryphon of John* and the *Gospel of Egyptians,* it is these twelve *nameless* luminaries rather than the traditional four *named* Luminaries that constitute the dwelling places of the heavenly Adam, Seth, and Seth's offspring.

Once the divine realm is completed, the *Gospel of Judas'* Sethian myth turns to the construction of the lower perceptible realms ruled by hostile powers. Sophia plays no role here; instead—as in the

---

[11] The initial letters ⲏⲗ in TC 51,1 should be restored as ⲏⲗ ᵛᵃᶜ ⲏ[ⲗⲏⲏⲑ, who is also the likely speaker in 51,3–4: "After these things, [*Eleleth*] said...."

[12] Harmozel, Oroiael/Raguel, and Daveithai as found in *Iren., Adv. Haer.* 1.29, *Apoc. John, Gos. Eg., Zost., Melch.,* and *Trim. Prot.*

[13] Gen 1:16: "And God made the two great lights, the greater light to rule the day, and the lesser light to rule the night; he made the stars also."

Trimorphic Protennoia and the *Gospel of Egyptians*—Eleleth generates the angelic governors of the lower world, twelve angels headed
by Nebro and Saklas, although exceptionally Nebro is identified as
Yaldabaoth while oddly Saklas is not. Of the traditional archontic
angels, only five are named, of whom the first, normally Athoth, is on
one possible reading named "Seth" and "Christ," which would constitute the sole Christian feature in the entire mythological section. These
peculiarities alone suggest that the entire Sethian mythical section is a
late and confused product, cobbled together from various sources, and
secondarily inserted into the *Gospel of Judas*.

TERMINOLOGICAL ISSUES

One of the challenges to a successful interpretation of the *Gospel of
Judas* is to assign the proper semantic valence to a number of key
terms throughout the text.

First of all, there is a fundamental contrast in reference between
the terms "kingdom" and "generation." Simply stated, it is important
to recognize that throughout the text, the term "kingdom," despite its
normally positive valence in the sayings of Jesus, consistently refers
only to the lower realm controlled by the evil rulers of the world.[14]
In fact, in the account of the Sethian myth, the term "kingdom" is
absent.[15] The only reference to "king" occurs at its end, in reference to
the "kings of chaos and the underworld."[16]

---

[14] See Painchaud forthcoming 2009. "Toutefois, il importe avant tout de constater
que l'expression de cette domination, qui fait appel à la royauté ou au royaume et aux
termes apparentés n'est jamais utilisée ni pour décrire le lieu réservé à la génération
sainte (45,3–11), ni le grand éon illimité (47,2–24), qui est également celui d'Adamas
(48,25–50,21) mais uniquement les éons créés par l'Autoengendré (47,25–48,21) et
ceux qui en découlent (50,22–53,16). Dans le contexte général de l'*Évangile de Judas*,
la fonction de cette « révélation séthienne » est donc de donner une explication théo-
cosmogonique au contenu de la première partie de l'écrit [i.e., the *inclusio* contained
between 36,24–25, "I shall tell you the *mysteries of the kingdom*" and 46,25–26, "I have
told you the *mysteries of the kingdom*"], c'est à dire de dévoiler l'origine du « règne
» révélé par Jésus à Judas" (ms. p. 10). Altogether, there are eight occurrences of the
verb "to rule" (Ⲣ̅Ⲣ̅ⲟ, Ⲣ̅ⲉⲢⲟ 37,5; 45,21; 48,5; 13.18; 51,6; 52,12; 55,10); two of the substantive "king" (Ⲣ̅Ⲣⲟ, ⲉⲣⲱⲩ 37,16; 54,11); five of the substantive "reign" or "dominion"
(ⲘⲚ̅ⲦⲉⲢⲟ 35,25; 43,18; 45,26; 46,13; 53,14); and one instance of the adjective "kingless"
ⲁⲧⲢ̅Ⲣⲟ 53,24).

[15] *Gos. Jud.* TC 47,1–54,12.

[16] *Gos. Jud.* TC 55,10–12.

By contrast, the valence and reference of the singular term "generation" is twofold.[17] Throughout, the text distinguishes between two generations, the one that is immortal and enlightened and the other that is mortal and misguided. The immortal generation, often called "*that* generation" (ⲧⲅⲉⲛⲉⲁ ⲉⲧⲙ̄ⲙⲁⲩ)[18] always occurs in the singular and is qualified by adjectives such as "great", "holy", "incorruptible", "strong", "kingless".[19] Or it is qualified by phrases such as "great generation of Adam," or the generation "of the first human" or the generation that is "superior" to the apostles.[20] On the other hand, the lower, mortal generation can be referred to sometimes in the singular in such phrases as "*this* generation" (ⲧⲉⲉⲓⲅⲉⲛⲉⲁ), the "human generation," the "generation of humans (or humanity)," the "generation of (the earthly) Adam," and the generation "of the stars."[21] It is sometimes found in the plural: the generations "of the angels," the "generations of the pious." the "other generations" that curse Judas, or "all the generations" of those who seek Adam.[22]

While the reference of the terms "kingdom" and "generation" is more or less unambiguous, a clear interpretation of the mythical section of the *Gospel of Judas* is greatly hampered by a rather ambiguous and even indiscriminate use of other key terms, especially "angel," "aeon," "cloud," and "luminary." The term "angel" is often ambiguous; it can designate angels that are i) good (the "holy" angels, 45,24; the highest Sethian divine beings, Autogenes, 47,15–21; the four Luminaries, 47,22–24; and the generations of angels in the fleshly realm, 54,7), ii) bad (the "angelic host of stars" that rule humanity, 37,5–6; lawless people equal to stellar angels, 40,1–16; 41,4–5; lower angels that cannot see the divine realm, 44,9–12; 47,7–11; 48,23–24; the 12 angels ruling the underworld, including Nebro/Yaldabaoth and Saklas 51,8–16; the five angels ruling mortals in the underworld, 52,1–14; Saklas

---

[17] The text distinguishes between two generations, the one immortal, the other mortal. The first is (A) the *great* generation ⲧⲛⲟϭ ⲛ̄ⲅⲉⲛⲉⲁ (36,16–17), ⲧⲅⲉⲛⲉⲁ ⲉⲧⲙ̄ⲙⲁⲩ, ⲧⲅⲉⲛⲉⲁ ⲉⲧⲟⲩⲁⲁⲃ, ⲅⲉⲛⲉⲁ ⲉⲥⲟⲩⲁⲁⲃ, ⲧⲅⲉⲛⲉⲁ ⲛⲁⲫⲑⲁⲣⲧⲟⲥ, ⲧⲅⲉⲛⲉⲁ ⲉⲧⲭⲟⲥⲉ ⲉⲣⲟⲛ, ⲧⲅⲉⲛⲉⲁ ⲉⲧⲭⲟⲟⲣ, ⲧⲅⲉⲛⲉⲁ ⲛⲁⲧⲣ̄ⲣⲟ, ⲧⲉⲉⲓⲅⲉⲛⲉⲁ, ⲧⲅⲉⲛⲉⲁ ⲙ̄ⲡⲣⲱⲙⲉ, ⲧⲅⲉⲛⲉⲁ ⲛ̄ⲧⲙⲛ̄ⲧⲣⲱⲙⲉ.

[18] *Gos. Jud.*TC 36,[8?]; 37,3.5.8; 43,9; 46,17; 54,14; 57,13.

[19] Cf. "great," *Gos. Jud.* TC 36,16–17; 53,24; "holy," 36,17; 44,12; 47,1; "incorruptible," 49,5.10.14; "strong," 36,26; "kingless," 53,24.

[20] *Gos. Jud.* TC 57,10–11; 50,23; 36,19.

[21] *Gos. Jud.* TC 43,14; 34,16; 37,10.12; 39,14; 40,19; 43,15.25; 53,12; 57,11; 39,13; cf. 54,22.

[22] *Gos. Jud.* TC 47,7; 54,7; 40,5–6; 46,22; 52,22.

and his assistants who create the earthly Adam and Eve, 52,15), or iii) angels of neutral or undecidable valence (angels of the two ruling luminaries, 48,3–20; the angelic likeness in which the divine Adamas is created, 49,4; the innumerable angelic host of the 360 firmaments, 50,4–6; the angel Eleleth, 50,25–51,4; and the angels subsequent to the holy generation, 57,12–14).

Likewise, aeons can be i) good (the great aeon inhabited by the Invisible Spirit and Barbelo, 36,17–18; 47,5–6; the aeons of the holy generation, 44,6–13; 45,23; 57,10–14; the 12 aeons of the 12 luminaries, 49,8–51,1), ii) bad (the aeon of mortals located in this world, 37,1–16; the 12 aeons of the archontic kingdom, 46,2; the thirteenth aeon over which Judas' star will rule, 55,10–11), or iii) of neutral or undecidable valence (the luminous aeons of the two luminaries, perhaps the sun and moon, 48,10–20).

Again, the valence of the term "cloud" can also be ambiguous; it can designate the realm of the holy generation (43,[1]; the luminous Barbelo, 47,15–19; the dwelling of the divine Adamas, 48,21–49,4; the "cloud of knowledge" where Autogenes, Adamas, the 72 luminaries, probably Eleleth, and perhaps even Sophia dwell, and the place where Saklas and Yaldabaoth originate, 50,11–51,17), but also apparently the realms associated with the errant stars, such as the luminous cloud surrounded by stars, including that of Judas.[23]

Moreover, certain technical terms in Sethian mythology seem to be misapplied, for example, the term "luminary" (φωστήρ), which in Sethian tradition normally refers only to the four Luminaries Harmozel, Oroiael, Davithe, and Eleleth, but whom the *Gospel of Judas* instead calls "angels." In the *Gospel of Judas* "luminary" refers instead to certain apparently distinct beings called respectively the "first" and "second" luminaries, and three further groups, consisting of 24, 72, and finally 360 "luminaries" who possess a corresponding number of aeons and heavens or firmaments.

Given these contrasts, ambiguities, and its similarities and differences from the general structure of Sethian mythology as reflected in other major Sethian works, I propose to examine in greater detail the Sethian myth narrated by Jesus in the *Gospel of Judas*, in terms of its theogony, cosmogony, and anthropogony, and then conclude with observations about its setting and function in the *Gospel* as a whole.

---

[23] *Gos. Jud.* TC 57,16–25.

The Theogony

The Supreme Trinity
Unlike the disciples' vision in the *Gospel of Judas'* theogony begins
with the supreme trinity of many Sethian treatises, which consists of
the supreme pre-existent Invisible Spirit, his First Thought Barbelo,
and their Child, the divine Autogenes or Self-generated One. Yet it is
clear that, unlike the main Sethian theogonies,[24] the *Gospel of Judas*
knows nothing of their trinitarian grouping as Father-Mother-Child.

The Invisible Spirit

> *Gos. Jud.* [47] [1] Jesus said, [2] "[Come], let me teach you [3] about [secrets
> that] [4] no person [has] seen.[5] For there exists a great and [6] boundless
> aeon, whose [7] extent no generation of angels [8] has seen, [in which] [9] is a
> great Invisible [Spirit] [10] that no eye of an angel [11] has seen, no reflection
> [12] has ever comprehended, nor was it called [13] by any name.[14]

Although the *Gospel of Judas* uses the traditional designation "Invisible
Spirit" for the supreme deity, and applies to it the traditional designations of incomprehensibility and unnameability,[25] it is odd that it
begins by first mentioning the great aeon he inhabits, even though
other Sethian literature specifies that he transcends and pre-exists any
aeon. In lieu of the extended negative theology of the supreme deity so
evident in Sethian (and other, e.g., *Eugnostos the Blessed*) treatises such
as the *Apocryphon of John*, *Allogenes*, and *Zostrianos*, the *Gospel of
Judas* prefers phrases modeled on Paul's characterization of the divine
wisdom ("What no eye has seen, nor ear hears, nor the heart of man
conceived," 1 Cor 2:9, derived from Isaiah 64:4), or "that no *generation* of angels has seen."[26] Indeed the context and placement of this
theogony suggests that it recalls and refers directly to Jesus' previous
statement to Judas:

---

[24] E.g., *Apoc. John* NHC II,1, 2,14; 9,10–11; *Trim. Prot.* NHC XIII,1, 37,22; *Gos. Eg.*
NHC III,2, 41,9; IV,2, 56,24; 58,3–4; 59,13; 55,9–10), and Codex Bruce, *Untitled* c. 1
(Schmidt-MacDermot 1978a).
[25] Unnameable: *Apoc. John* NHC II,1, 3,16; *Gos. Eg.* NHC III,2, 40,11; 55,20; 65,11;
Zost. NHC VIII,1, 74,7, 21. Incomprehensibility: the *Apoc. John* NHC II,1, 3,15, 26;
Trim. Prot. NHC XIII,1, 25,11; *Norea* NHC IX,2, 27,20.
[26] *Gos. Jud.* TC 47,5–13; 48,23–24.

> Gos. Jud. [44] [8] [Truly] I say to you, [9] [*no principality nor*] angel [10] [nor] power will be able to see [11] [those realms that] [12] [*this great*] holy genera-tion [13] [*shall see*]."

Barbelo

> Gos. Jud. [47] [14] And there appeared in that place [15] a luminous cloud (i.e., Barbelo) [16] and it said, "Let [17] an angel come into being *for* my [18] *assistance*."

While in most Sethian treatises the driving force behind the salva-tion of the Gnostics is the divine Mother Barbelo, the theogony of the *Gospel of Judas* only hints at her origin and existence by the rather non-descript phrase "there appeared in that place a luminous cloud (f.)," which may reflect her dominantly feminine gender or luminous origin but does not actually name her. Indeed, the figure of Barbelo is only named much earlier by Judas himself in recognition of Jesus' identity and origin:

> Gos. Jud. [35] [14] Judas [said] [15] to him, "I know [16] who you are and whence you have come. [17] You are from [18] the immortal aeon of Barbelo. [19] And the name of the one who has sent you [20] I am not worthy to utter." [21]

According to certain other Sethian treatises (the *Apocryphon of John*, the *Gospel of Egyptians*) and testimonia from Epiphanius, Barbelo is the merciful Mother who sends Jesus, often as a guise for the divine Seth.[27] It is also significant here that Barbelo is in effect masculinized as the "aeon (m.) of Barbelo (f.)," as is the custom in the third-century Sethian Platonizing treatises *Zostrianos*, *Allogenes*, the *Three Steles of Seth*, and *Marsanes*, where she is conceived as a masculine divine intel-lect (ὁ νοῦς) rather than a divine mother who descends to rescue her fallen members. This suggests that the *Gospel of Judas* as we have it is unlikely to be a second-century treatise, and has been influenced by comparatively later Sethian literature.

Autogenes, the Self-generated One

> Gos. Jud. [47] [18] And there emerged [19] from the cloud a great [20] angel, the Self-Generated One, the God [21] of the light.

---

[27] *Pan.* 39.2.4–3.5.

The initial part of the theogony concludes with the emergence of Autogenes the Self-generated One as the third member of the Sethian Father-Mother-Child trinity. It is odd, however, that he is designated merely as a "great angel" called "the God of the light," an identity and epithet of Autogenes that is completely unattested in other Sethian literature. On the other hand, the *Gospel of Judas* does attest the Sethian view that Autogenes serves for Barbelo's "assistance" (παράστασις; cf. παραστάτης, "royal attendant"), a term that the *Apocryphon of John* and Irenaeus also apply, not only to Autogenes, but also to the four Luminaries he brings into being.[28]

The Four Luminaries
In almost all Sethian theogonies, the aeonic realm is structured by the four Luminaries generated and established by the divine Autogenes.

> *Gos. Jud.* [47] [21] And [22] on his (Autogenes's) behalf, four other [23] angels came into being from another [24] cloud, and they became [25] *assistance* for the angelic Self-Generated [26] One.

There can be no doubt that these four unnamed "angels" are identical with the four Luminaries of Sethian theology. While their names Harmozel, Oroiael, Davithe, and Eleleth are richly attested throughout Sethian literature (the *Apocryphon of John*, the *Trimorphic Protennoia*, the *Gospel of Egyptians, Melchizedek, Zostrianos*, Codex Bruce, *Untitled*, and Irenaeus, *Adversus Haereses* I.29), of these four, only one, the fourth Luminary Eleleth, can be conjectured to have been present in the *Gospel of Judas*.[29] While almost all Sethian works call them "Luminaries" (φωστῆρες),[30] the *Gospel of Judas* identifies them by the generic but vague term "angels,"[31] suggesting that the author is not very familiar with the broad range of Sethian literature.

Adamas

> *Gos. Jud.* [47] [26] And [48] [1] the Self-Generated One said, 'Let [2] [Adamas] come into being,' and [3] [another *emanation* came into being].

---

[28] *Apoc. John* NHC III,1, 11,5, 19; *Adv. Haer.* 1.29.1.

[29] *Gos. Jud.* TC 51,1 with traces of El[...and perhaps in a lacuna at 51,4.

[30] While the longer version of *Apoc. John* consistently refer to them as the four "illuminators" (ⲛ̄ϥⲱⲥⲧⲏⲣ) aeons, while the shorter version calls them "lights" (ⲛ̄ⲟⲩⲟⲉⲓⲛ).

[31] In *Apoc. John* NHC II,1, 8,4–8 ("Grace exists with the aeon of the luminary Armozel, i.e., the first angel"), the gloss identifies Grace (Charis), not Harmozel, as the first angel.

In almost all Sethian theogonies, Autogenes gives rise to the divine archetypal Adamas, often named "Pigeradamas"[32] and establishes him in Harmozel, the first of the four Luminaries.

> *Ap. John* II, 8 [20] These are the four luminaries [21] who stand near the divine Self-originate. [22] These are the twelve aeons who stand near [23] the Child of the great One, the Self-originate, the Anointed, [24] through the will and gift of the Invisible [25] Spirit. They are the twelve aeons. They belong to [26] the Child, the Self-generated One. And all things were [27] firmly established by the will of the Holy Spirit [28] through the Self-gener-ated One. From [29] the [Foreknowledge] of the perfect Mind, [30] through the revelation of the will of the Invisible Spirit [31] and the will of the Self-generated One: [32] \<the\> perfect, First-appearing [33] and true Human, whom [34] the Virginal Spirit named Pigeradamas.

But the *Gospel of Judas* neither specifies the aeonic location of Adamas nor gives any notice of his mother, who in the *Apocryphon of John* is Barbelo's attribute Prognōsis, and in the *Three Steles of Seth, Zostrianos,* and the *Gospel of Egyptians,* is Barbelo's lower double Meirothea/Mirothoë. Together with Barbelo and Sophia, such maternal figures seem to have been excluded from the narrative development in favor of sexless luminaries, clouds, angels and their emanations.

Interlude: Two Reigning Luminaries (The Sun, Moon and Stars of Gen 1:14–18?)

Perhaps the most unusual feature of the *Gospel of Judas'* theogonical myth is the section 48,1–20, which seems to have no equivalent in other Sethian literature. Right after he creates the four "angels," i.e., the four Luminaries, exactly where one usually finds details concern-ing the deployment and contents of each Luminary, Autogenes goes on to create two unnamed Luminaries, a first one to be "ruled" by Adamas, and a second one—whose origin is unaccounted for—to rule over an unnamed "second aeon."

> *Gos. Jud.* [48] [3] And [4] he [established] the first Luminary [5] for him to reign over. [6] He said, 'Let angels come into being [7] to serve [him],' [8] and myriads without number came to be. [9]
> He said, [10] '[Let] a luminous aeon [11] come into being,' and it came into being.' [12] He established the second Luminary [13] [to] reign over it, [14] together with myriads of angels without [15] number for their service.

---

[32] Perhaps meaning something like "the stranger Adamas" (from Coptic *pi* + Heb. gēr + Adamas) or "the old Adamas" (from Greek τὸ γῆρας Ἀδάμας) or even "the holy Adamas" (from Greek ὁ ἱερὸς Ἀδάμας).

> And that is how [16] he created the rest [17] of the *luminous* aeons. He [18] made them reign over them, and [19] he created for them myriads of [20] angels without number for assistance.

If these two Luminaries are not Harmozel and Oroiael, then one must assume the reference is to the two luminaries of creation mentioned in Genesis 1:16–18 ("And God made the two great lights, the greater light to rule the day, and the lesser light to rule the night; he made the stars also. And God set them in the firmament of the heavens to give light upon the earth, to *rule* over the day and over the night, and to separate the light from the darkness").[33] While these two luminaries, apparently ruled by Adamas, rule in turn over their two respective aeons as well as over "the rest of the luminous aeons"—presumably the stars—they certainly do not rule over the transcendent aeons, who are normally structured under the four Luminaries and established by the Self-generated One as dwellings for the holy generation. Concerning that realm, Jesus has already explicitly informed Judas that "There, neither sun nor moon nor day shall rule, but the holy will abide there always, in the aeon with the holy angels" (45,20–24). If so, we have an anomaly: in comparison with other Sethian treatises, the *Gospel of Judas* interrupts the theogony by introducing a properly cosmogonical account of the origin of the changeable, perceptible world between the generation of the divine Adamas and the account of the generation of Seth, his seed, and the divine realm of the of the Self-generated One in which they reside. Unfortunately, this puzzling anomaly causes difficulties in interpreting the remainder of this *Gospel*'s theogony and cosmogony.

Seth and the Generation (Seed) of Seth

> *Gos. Jud.* [48] [21] Adamas was [22] in the first luminous [23] cloud that no angel [24] has seen [25] among all those called [26] *divine*. {And he} [49] [1] And [*in*] that [*cloud*] [2] [*Seth was begotten after*] [3] the image [*of his father Adamas*] [4] and after the likeness of [*these*] angels. [5] He revealed the incorruptible [6] [generation] of Seth [7] to the twelve [*androgynous luminaries*].

This passage, which seems to have narrated the origin of Seth and his seed that comprises the holy generation, is a continuation of the initial theogony interrupted by the inserted cosmogony, since it clearly describes events in the divine realm.[34] It seems to have been based first,

---

[33] A point also noted by Painchaud forthcoming 2009, ms. p. 9.

[34] *Gos. Jud.* TC [49] [1] ⲁⲩⲱ [ϩⲣⲁⲓ ϩⲛ ⲧϭⲏⲡⲉ ⲉ] [2] ⲧⲙ̄ⲙⲁⲩ [ⲁϥϫⲡⲟ ⲛ̄ⲥⲏⲑ ⲕⲁⲧⲁ] [3] ⲑⲓⲕⲱⲛ [ⲙ̄ⲡⲉϥⲉⲓⲱⲧ ⲁ̄ⲇ̄ⲁ̄ⲙ̄ⲁ̄ⲥ] [4] ⲁⲩⲱ ⲕⲁⲧⲁ ⲡⲓⲛⲉ ⲛ̄ⲛ[ⲉⲉⲓⲁⲅ] [5] ⲅⲉⲗⲟⲥ. This restora-

upon the *Gospel of Egyptians*, according to which the Autogenes Logos cooperates with Adamas and his consort Prophania to generate his son Seth as well as the four Luminaries that will serve as dwellings for himself, Seth, and his seed, and second, upon the equivalent account in the *Apocryphon of John*:[35]

> *Ap. John* II 9 [12] And he [13] established his son Seth over the second [14] aeon, in the presence of the second luminary Oroiael. And in the third aeon [15] was established the seed of Seth, [16] over the third luminary Daveithai. [17] And the souls of the holy ones were established.

Just as the Invisible Spirit inhabits an aeon that no angel has seen, so too the divine Adamas inhabits a luminous cloud that no angel has seen, which other Sethian theogonies consider to be the Luminary Harmozel.

The succeeding mention of "image" and "likeness" suggests that the text was intended as an allusion to the well-known Sethian interpretation of Gen 5:3, according to which Seth is generated in the image and likeness of Adam. Although it is likely that the entity in whose "image" Seth is created would be Adamas, the significance of his being also in the "likeness of [these] angels" is puzzling. On the one hand, the antecedent of "angels" could be the four Luminaries (whom this text calls "angels"), perhaps including even the higher "angel" Autogenes; since these are clearly divine beings, the likeness would refer to his divine nature. On the other hand, these angels could be lesser beings, either those that surround the first two "luminaries," which seem to be stellar (sun, moon, and stars) in nature, or again those angels that are unable to see the luminous cloud, in which case the likeness refers to a less-than-divine component. If the intended antecedent is the lesser angels, then the contrast inferred by various ancient authors between the terms "image" and "likeness" of Gen 1:26 and 5:2–3 suggests that Seth's "likeness" to these angels should be contrasted with his being also the "image" of something more noble, perhaps an aspect of his divine father Adam, and I have restored the text accordingly.

Be this as it may, either Adamas or perhaps Autogenes then proceeds to reveal Seth's seed, the "incorruptible [generation] of Seth," to a set of "twelve [luminaries]" whose origin is so far unaccounted for. Presumably these luminaries would be the twelve aeons that the *Apocryphon of John* II 8,20–34 (cited above) associates with the four

---

tion, one among several possibilities, is complicated by the apparent beginning of (an incomplete?) sentence at the end of 48,26 ("And he…").

[35] *Gos. Eg.* III,2, 50,5–56,22; *Apoc. John* NHC II,1, 9,12–27.

Luminaries generated and established by the Self-generated Child; there they are defined as four tetrads of three aeonic attributes assigned to each of the four Luminaries, the last of which is Wisdom (Sophia).

The Aeons of the Self-generated One

The *Gospel of Judas* goes on to describe the generation of the divine aeons below them, aeons that the Sethian treatise *Zostrianos* calls the "Self-generated Aeons." In particular, the traditional realm of the Four Luminaries is populated with increasingly large multiples of the twelve luminaries or aeons. In both *Eugnostos the Blessed*[36] and the *Gospel of Judas*, these aeons are generated in successive multiples of six and five (12 x 6 = 72; 72 x 5 = 360).[37]

Gospel of Judas 49,8–50,10	*Eugnostos* III 84,12–85,3	*Eugnostos* III 83,10–20; 88,21–89,3
[49] ⁸ The [*Afterwards*] ⁹ he revealed seventy-two ¹⁰ luminaries in the incorruptible generation, ¹¹ in accordance with the will of the ¹² Spirit. The seventy-two luminaries ¹³ *for their part* revealed ¹⁴ three hundred sixty luminaries in the ¹⁵ incorruptible generation, in accord with *the* ¹⁶ *will* of the Spirit, so that their number should ¹⁷ be five for each. ¹⁸	84 ¹³ All-Begetter, their father, very soon ¹⁴ created ¹⁵ twelve aeons ¹⁶ for assistance for the twelve ¹⁷ angels.	

---

³⁶ Called "luminaries" in *Eugnostos* NHC III,3, 84,12–85,3 and NHC V,1, 12,21–30 or "powers," in NHC III,3, 83,10–20; NHC V,1, 11,20–12,3 (cf. *Orig. World* NHC II,5, 104,31–106,3). The account in *Soph. Jes. Chr.* BG,3, 107,5–8 is greatly truncated

³⁷ No doubt these speculations involving groups of 12, 72, and 360 originally had to do with ancient Egyptian calendrical and astrological speculation on the decanal divisions of the Zodiac. Although they contain similar groupings, the numerical speculation on the deployment of the divine aeons in such Sethian works as *Apoc. John*, *Trim. Prot.*, *Gos. Eg.*, and *Zost.* seems to be based more on basic Neopythagorean triads and tetrads.

Gospel of Judas 49,8–50,10	*Eugnostos* III 84,12–85,3	*Eugnostos* III 83,10–20; 88,21–89,3
And the [19] twelve aeons of the [20] twelve luminaries constitute their father. And [21] for each aeon, (there are) six heavens, [22] so that there are [23] seventy-two heavens [24] for the seventy-two luminaries, [25] and for each [50] [1] [of them five] firmaments, [2] [*that there might be*] three hundred sixty [3] [firmaments in all].	And in [18] each aeon there were six (heavens), [19] so [20] there are seventy-two heavens of the seventy-two [21] powers who appeared [22] from him. And in each of the heavens [23] there were five firmaments, [24] so there are (in all) three hundred sixty **85** [1] [firmaments] of the three hundred sixty [2] powers that appeared [3] from them.	**83** [10] Then the twelve [11] powers, whom I have just discussed, [12] consented with each other. [13] <Six> males (each) (and) (six> females (each) were revealed, [13] so that there are seventy- [15] two powers. [16] Each one of the seventy-two revealed [17] five spiritual (powers), [18] which (together) are the three hundred sixty [19] powers. The union of them all is [20] *the will....*
They were given [4] authority and an [5] *innumerable* [*abundance*] *of angelic hosts* [6] for glory and adoration, [7] [*and in addition*] virgin spirits [8] for glory and [9] [adoration] of all the aeons and [10] the heavens and their firmaments.		**88** [21] They provided for themselves [22] hosts of angels, myriads [23] without number for retinue **89** [1] and glory, even virgin [2] spirits, the ineffable lights. They have no sickness [3] nor weakness, but it is only *will.*

The text then continues with a surprising characterization of these luminaries and their associated aeons and heavens by calling them both "immortal" and yet "cosmic."

> *Gos. Jud.* [50] [11] Now the multitude of those immortals [12] is called [13] a cosmos—the [14] {perishable (*phthora*)}<*celestial circuit* (*phora*)>—by the father (apparently the 12 aeons) [15] and the seventy-two luminaries [16] who are with the Self-Generated One [17] and his seventy-two [18] aeons, the *place* where the first human [19] appeared [20] with his [21] incorruptible powers. [22]

Clearly these are immortal beings, since they are revealed in the holy "incorruptible generation" and are "with" the Self-generated One, apparently in the luminous cloud where the first human Adamas and his incorruptible powers appeared. When the text goes on to characterize them as a "cosmos," one might think either of the transcendent intelligible cosmos or of the perceptible cosmos of Platonic metaphysics, but then the text apparently glosses the term "cosmos" as "perishable" or as "corruption," which is rather inapposite for the immortal product of the divine Autogenes. Thus I suggest that the Greek noun φθορά be emended to read φορά, "orbit," or "celestial circuit." But even so, either reading would normally connote a non-transcendent, changeable and perceptible realm that can hardly be called immortal. Perhaps the text is intending to inform the reader that even though these are incorruptible aeons, they nevertheless have a lower peripheral boundary where there resides the power—principally the figure of Eleleth—who is responsible for the origin of the corruptible cosmos and its hostile rulers.

The Cosmogony

Eleleth

The *Gospel of Judas* 50,22–52,25 shares with the *Gospel of Egyptians* III 56,22–59,9 a very similar cosmogonical account of the origin and activity of the creators of the lower world:

Gospel of Judas 50,22–52,25	Gos. Eg. III 56,22–59,9
[50] [22] And in the aeon that appeared [23] with his (Autogenes') generation [24] is *located* the cloud of knowledge [25] and the angel [26] who is called [51] [1] *Ele.*"[*leth. And he dwells*] [2] with [*the twelfth*] aeon [3] [*who is Sophia*].	56 [22] After five [23] thousand years the great [24] light Eleleth spoke: "Let someone [25] reign over the chaos and Hades." [26] And there appeared a cloud 57 [1] [whose name is] hylic Sophia [2] [...She] looked out on the parts [3] [of the chaos], her face being like [4] [... in] her form [...] [5] blood. And [6] [the great] angel Gamaliel spoke [7] [to the great Gabriel], the minister of [8] [the great light] Oroiael; [9] [he said, "Let an] angel come forth [10] [in order that he may] reign over the chaos [11] [and Hades].
After [4] these things, [*Eleleth*] said, [5] 'Let twelve angels [6] come into being [to] [7] rule over chaos and the [underworld].' [8]	"Then the cloud, being [12] [agreeable, came forth] in the two monads, [13] each one [of which had] light [14] [...the throne], which she (Sophia) had placed [15] in the cloud [above. [16]

Gospel of Judas 50,22–52,25

And behold, there appeared [9] from the cloud an [angel] [10] whose face flashed with fire [11] and his appearance was defiled with blood. [12] His name was Nebro, [13] which means [14] 'apostate'; [15] others call him Yaldabaoth. [16] Another angel, Saklas, also came [17] from the cloud.

So Nebro [18] created six angels— [19] so too Saklas—for assistance, [20] and these produced twelve [21] angels in the heavens, [22] with each one receiving a portion [23] in the heavens. The twelve rulers [24] spoke with [25] the twelve angels: [26] "Let each of you **[52]** [1] [*create five angels*] and let them [2] [*rule over the human*] generations. [3] [*And there came to be*] [4] [*five*] angels:

The first [5] [is *Ath*]*ēth*, who is called [6] the *good one*. The [second] [7] is Harma{thoth}, who [8] [*is the evil eye*]. The [third] [9] is Galila. The [10] fourth is Yobel. The [11] fifth [is] Adonaios.

These [12] are the five who ruled over [13] the underworld, and first [14] over chaos.

Gos. Eg. III 56,22–59,9

Then the cloud, being [12] [agreeable, came forth] in the two monads, [13] each one [of which had] light [14] [...the throne], which she (Sophia) had placed [15] in the cloud [above. [16] Then] Sakla, the great [17] [angel, saw] the great demon [18] [who is with him, Nebr]uel. And they became [19] [together a] spirit of reproduction to the earth. [20] [They begot] assisting angels. [21] Sakla [said] to the great [22] [demon Neb]ruel, "Let [23] [the] twelve aeons come into being in [24] [the...] aeon, worlds [25] [....] [26] [...] the great angel [27] [Sakla] said by the will of the Autogenes, **58** [1] "There shall [be] the [...] [2] of the number of seven [...]" [3] And he said to the [great angels], [4] "Go and [let each] [5] of you reign over his [world]" [6] Each one [of these] [7] twelve [angels] went [forth. The first [8] angel is Ath[oth. He is the one] [9] whom [the great] generations [10] of men call [the good one. The] [11] second is Harmas, [who] is [the eye of envy]. [12] The third [is Galila. The] [13] fourth is Yobel. [The fifth is] [14] Adonaios, who is [called] [15] Sabaoth. The sixth [is Cain, whom] [16] the [great generations of] [17] men call the sun. The [seventh is Abel]; [18] the eighth Akiressina, the [ninth Yubel]. [19] The tenth is Harm[upiael. The] [20] eleventh is Arch[ir-Adonin]. [21] The twelfth [is Belias. These [22] are] the ones who preside over the underworld [and chaos]. [23]

Gospel of Judas 50,22–52,25
Then Saklas [15] said to his angels, [16]

"Let us create a human being after [17] the likeness and after the image." [18] They fashioned Adam [19] and his wife Eve, who is [20] called Zoë *in* the cloud. [21] For by this [22] name all the generations seek [23] him, and each [24] of them calls her [25] these names.

Gos. Eg. III 56,22–59,9
And after the founding [of the world [24] Sakla said to his [angels], [25] "I, I am a [jealous] god, [26] and apart from me nothing has [come into being," since he] 59 [1] trusted in his nature. Then a Voice [2] came from on high, saying, [3] "The Man exists, and the Son of the Man." [4] Because of the descent of the image (of Barbelo) [5] above, which is like its voice in the height [6] of the image which has looked out, [7] through the looking out of the image [8] above, the first creature was [9] formed.

This cosmological parallel with the *Gospel of the Egyptians* allows the possibility that the *Gospel of Judas* may have mentioned the figure of Sophia in the context of its mythical cosmogony, as I have indeed conjectured.[38] While the *Gospel of the Egyptians* identifies the cloud associated with Eleleth as the "material Sophia," the *Gospel of Judas* identifies it as the "cloud of knowledge," which—if my conjecture is close to the mark—it may have associated with Sophia as the twelfth aeon.[39] But it seems to lack any traces of the myth of the fall of Sophia such as one finds in the *Apocryphon of John* and the *Hypostasis of the Archons*. Instead, the *Gospel of Judas* reflects a tendency that appears in both the *Trimorphic Protennoia* (XIII 39,13–17) and the *Gospel of the Egyptians*, namely, to exonerate Sophia from her responsibility for the origin of the world creator by assigning the initiative for the production of the angels ruling over chaos to the fourth Luminary Eleleth. In the *Gospel of Judas*, as in the *Trimorphic Protennoia*, it seems that

---

[38] In *Gos. Jud.* TC 44,2–7, the "perishable wisdom (σοφία)" that will not enable the souls of the defiled human generations to ascend into the aeons on high does not constitute a reference to the Sethian myth of Sophia.

[39] Cf. the cloud in which Sophia hides Yaldabaoth in *Apoc. John* NHC II,1, 10,14–18.

the command to do so is spoken by Eleleth himself, while in the *Gospel of the Egyptians*, the command is issued by Gamaliel and Gabriel at Eleleth's urging.

The Origin of the Rulers of the Lower World
In the *Gospel of Judas*, the chief archon Nebro/Yaldabaoth emerges first, followed by his companion Saklas, while in the *Gospel of the Egyptians*, both archons—of which Saklas appears to be the more dominant—come forth simultaneously, and are conceived as distinct "monads," perhaps even male and female, who function together as a "spirit of reproduction to the earth." The *Gospel of Judas* is also exceptional in equating Yaldabaoth with Nebro rather than Saklas.

Interestingly, the *Gospel of Judas* seems to know nothing of a strikingly prominent tradition well-attested, not only in Sethian texts like the *Apocryphon of John*, the *Gospel of the Egyptians*, and the *Hypostasis of the Archons*, but also in Irenaeus, *Haer.* I.29: namely, Saklas' boast in his sole divinity, and its immediate refutation by the divine voice announcing that "the Human exists, and the Child of the Human."

In both accounts, this pair of archons produce twelve angels or aeons that will control the lower world. Although they apparently distinguish seven[40] (the "day signs") of the twelve as planetary rulers of the Zodiacal houses, both the *Apocryphon of John* and the *Gospel of the Egyptians* enumerate the production of a sequence of twelve angels that rule over the underworld and chaos, while the *Gospel of Judas* describes the production of only the first five, perhaps regarded as the "night signs."

---

[40] Cf. the similar sequence of seven powers in *Apoc. John* NHC II,1, 11,22–35: 11 [22] "The rulers [23] created seven powers for themselves, and [24] the powers created for themselves six angels [25] apiece, until they totaled 365 angels. [26] Now <these> are the bodies belonging to the names: the first is Athoth; [27] he is sheep-faced; the second is Eloaiou; [28] he is donkey-faced; the third [29] is Astaphaios; he is hyena-faced; the [30] fourth is Yao; he is [serpent]-faced, with [31] seven heads; the fifth is Sabaoth; [32] <he> is serpent-faced; the sixth is Adonin; [33] he is ape-faced; the seventh is Sabbede; [34] he is a face of shining fire. This is the [35] seven of the week." And *Orig. World* NHC II,5, 101,25–102,2: 101 [25] "Seven appeared in chaos, androgynous. They have their masculine names [26] and their feminine names. The feminine name [27] is Pronoia Sambathas, which is 'week.' [28] And his son is called [29] Yao: his feminine name is Lordship. [30] Sabaoth: his feminine name is Divinity. [31] Adonaios: his feminine name is Kingship. [32] Elaios: his feminine name is Jealousy. [33] Oraios: his feminine name is Wealth. [34] And Astaphaios: his feminine name is 102 [1] Sophia. These are the seven powers [2] of the seven heavens of chaos."

Gos. Judas 52, 3–52,14	Gos. Eg. III 58,6–22	Ap. John II 10,26–11,4	Ap. John II,12,13–25
[52] [3] [*And there came to be*] [4] [*five*] angels: [4]	III 58 [6] Each one [of these] [7] twelve [angels] went [forth.	II 10 [27] And he (Yaldabaoth) begot [28] authorities for himself.	II 12 [13] And [14] he (Yaldabaoth) named each power, beginning from [15] above:
The first [5] [is **Ath**]*ēth*, who is called [6] the *good one*.	The first] [8] angel is **Ath**[**oth**. He is the one] [9] whom [the great] generations [10] of men call [the *good one*.	Now the first was named [29] **Athoth**, whom the generations call [30] [*their good one*];	The first is [16] Goodness, with the first one, **Athoth**; [17]
The [second] [7] is **Harma**{thoth}, who [8] [*is the evil eye*].	The] [11] second is **Harmas**, [who] is [the *eye* of envy]. [12]	the second is **Harmas**, [31] i.e., [the *eye*] of envy;	the second is Providence, with [18] the second one, **Eloaio**;
The [third] [9] is **Galila**.	The third [is **Galila**.	the third [32] is **Kalila-Oumbri**;	the third is Divinity, with the third one, [19] **Astraphaio**;
The [10] fourth is **Yobel**.	The] [13] fourth is **Yobel**.	the fourth is **Yabel**; [33]	the fourth is [20] Lordship, with the fourth one, **Iao**; [21]
The [11] fifth [is] **Adonaios**	[The fifth is] [14] **Adonaios**, who is [called] [15] **Sabaoth**.	the fifth is **Adonaiou**, who is called [34] **Sabaoth**;	the fifth is Kingship, with the fifth one, [22] **Sanbaoth**;
	The sixth [is **Cain**, whom] [16] the [great generations of] [17] men call the sun.	the sixth is **Cain**, [35] whom the generations of people call [36] the sun;	the sixth is Jealousy, with [23] the sixth one, **Adonein**;
	The [seventh is **Abel**]; [18]	the seventh is **Abel**;	the seventh [24] is Wisdom, with the seventh one, [25] **Sabbateon**.
	the eighth **Akiressina**,	the [37] eighth is **Abrisene**;	
	the [ninth **Yobel**]. [19]	the ninth is **Yobel**;	
	The tenth is **Harm**[**upiael**.	[11] [1] the tenth is **Armoupieel**;	
	The] [20] eleventh is Arch[ir-**Adonin**]. [21]	the eleventh [2] is Melcheir-**Adonein**;	
	The twelfth [is **Belias**.	the twelfth [3] is **Belias**;	
These [12] are the five who ruled over [13] the underworld, and first [14] over chaos.	These [22] are] the ones who preside over the underworld [and chaos].	it is this one who is over the depths [4] of the underworld.	

Despite the fact that Epiphanius, *Panarion* 26.10.1 lists Seth as the third archon, the *Gospel of Judas* 49,1–9 has already assigned Seth's incorruptible generation and perhaps Seth himself to the realm of the divine luminaries, so the name of the first angel over chaos in 52,5 can hardly be Seth (c]нѳ), who clearly inhabits the divine realm, but must be something like [Ath]ēth (ⲁⲑ]нѳ), whose epithet (ⲡⲉⲭⲥ̄) is not likely to be 'Lord' (ⲡⲭⲟⲉⲓⲥ) or 'Christ' (χριστός), but more likely "the Good One" (χρηστός), as in the *Apocryphon of John* II 12,16 ("goodness") and probably the *Gospel of the Egyptians* III 58,10.[41] The expected name for this first angel, Athoth, actually occurs as part of the bowdlerized name for the second angel Harma{thoth}, normally Harmas. While the *Gospel of Judas* terminates the list with the fifth angel Adonaios, the *Gospel of the Egyptians* and the *Apocryphon of John* II 10,34–11,4 go on to list seven more, probably to designate rulers for the seven planets.[42] Clearly, there seems to be a common tradition here, but confusion reigns in the extant sources over the precise names and number of these lower powers.

The Anthropogony

The Protoplasts and their Names

The anthropogony of the *Gospel of Judas* begins with a brief account of the creation of Adam and Eve at Saklas' behest, a motif well-attested in other Sethian treatises.[43] This is followed by a comment on the names of the protoplasts:

---

[41] Accordingly, the standard reconstruction of *Apoc. John* NHC II,1, 10,29–30 "Athoth, whom the generations call [the reaper]" (ⲡⲁⲓ̈ ⲉⲧⲟⲩⲙⲟⲩⲧⲉ ⲉⲣⲟϥ ⲛ̄ϭⲓ ⲛ̄ⲅⲉⲛⲉⲁ ϫⲉ ⲡ[ⲭⲁⲓ̈ⲟ]ϩ̄ⲥ̄ should rather be "Athoth, whom the generations call [their good one]": ⲡⲁⲓ̈ ⲉⲧⲟⲩⲙⲟⲩⲧⲉ ⲉⲣⲟϥ ⲛ̄ϭⲓ ⲛ̄ⲅⲉⲛⲉⲁ ϫⲉ ⲡ[ⲟⲩⲭ̄]ⲣ̄ⲥ̄ (cf. *Trim. Prot.* NHC XIII,1, 49,8); indeed, the character at the end of the lacuna is more likely a ⲣ than a ϩ. Epiphanius, *Pan.* 26.10.1 makes Seth an archon, and *Orig. World* NHC II,5, 117,15–18 implies his archontic status.

[42] Namely Cain, Abel, Abrisina, Harmoupiel, Melech-Adonin, and Belias. If *Gos. Jud.* were dependent on traditional lists of twelve powers as in *Gos. Eg.* and *Apoc. John*, its refusal to associate Cain with the powers over the underworld by truncating the list to five angels might be used as an argument to suggest its "Cainite" affinity, but the name Cain is not found in the extant text. Indeed, it is doubtful whether there ever was such a group as Irenaeus' Cainites (*Adv. Haer.* 1.31).

[43] E.g., *Hyp. Arch.* NHC II,4, 87,23–33; *Apoc. John* NHC II,1, 15,1–13; *Trim. Prot.* NHC XIII,1, 40,22–29.

Gos. Jud. [52] [14] Then Saklas [15] said to his angels, [16] 'Let us create a human being after [17] the likeness and after the image.' They fashioned Adam [19] and his wife Eve, who is [20] called Zoë *in* the cloud. [21] For by this [22] (single) name all the generations seek [23] him, and each [24] of them calls her [25] (by both) these names.

While I have conjectured that the text previously claimed in 49,2–4 that "[Seth was begotten after] the image [of his father Adamas] and after the likeness of [these] angels", here the earthly human being is created after an unnamed likeness and image, presumably in the image of Adamas, the archetypal human rather than of Barbelo as the "first human."[44]

The singular human being proposed by Saklas turns out to be two separate but simultaneously-created human beings, perhaps as an interpretation of the previously-mentioned likeness and image. Rather than conceiving the protoplastic Adam as a single androgynous human from whom the earthly woman is extracted as a vehicle for the spiritual woman Eve or Zoë hidden within Adam,[45] in the *Gospel of Judas* the protoplasts originate as a primal couple. This of course allows no soteriological speculation on restoring a lost primordial unity.

In the *Apocryphon of John*, this spiritual Zoë designates the luminous Epinoia, mother of the living and lower double of the divine mother Barbelo, whom the Archons unwittingly cause to appear out of Adam's side in paradise in order to bring him to life and enlightenment:

Ap. John II 20 [9] Now the blessed Mother-Father, [10] the Beneficent and Compassionate One, [11] had compassion on the power of the Mother (Sophia) [12] that had been brought out of the chief ruler. And [13] since they were going to overpower the [14] psychical and sensible body again, he sent, [15] through his beneficent [16] spirit and great mercy, a helper [17] for Adam, a luminous Epinoia [18] that is from him, named 'Life.' [19] It is she who serves the whole creature, [20] toiling with it, restoring [21] it to its Perfection, and [22] teaching it about the descent of the [23] seed, teaching it about the path of ascent, [24] the path by which it had descended. [25] And the Epinoia of the Light hides in Adam, [26] so that the rulers might not

---

[44] Lacking Saklas' boast in his sole divinity and the immediate response of Barbelo by projecting her own image as the archetypal human with the announcement that "the Human exists, and the Child of the Human," the protoplasts are created in the image of Adamas, perhaps himself considered to be androgynous.

[45] As in the *Apoc. John* NHC II,1, 20,12–28 and 22,28–23,26, and the *Hyp. Arch.* NHC II,4, 89,3–17.

know (her), [27] but so that the Epinoia might become a correction [28] of the deficiency of the Mother.

The same figure appears as the spiritual woman of the *Hypostasis of the Archons*:[46]

> *Hyp. Arch.* II 89 [11] And the spirit-endowed woman (taken from Adam's side) [12] came to him and spoke with him, saying, [13] "Arise, Adam." And when he saw her, [14] he said, "It is you who have given me life; [15] you will be called 'Mother of the living.' [16] For it is she who is my mother. It is she who is the physician, [17] and the woman, and she who has given birth."

While the author of the *Gospel of Judas* may consider that the earthly Adam and the divine archetypal Adamas share only a single name, apparently his earthly wife Eve is considered to have a second name, Zoë,[47] the Greek equivalent of the Semitic name Eve, apparently designating her spiritual aspect. But her second name is used only "in the cloud," that is, only by the holy generation stemming from Seth, who along with Adamas inhabit the luminous cloud, while presumably the mortal human generations know her only as Eve.[48]

The apparent restriction in the use of the name of Zoë serves as a somewhat ironic transition to the next section of the *Gospel of Judas*, which is devoted to humankind's mortality or limited span of life (*zōē*). For subsequent mortal generations to invoke the primordial Adam and Eve by the names Adamas and Zoë will not bring them unlimited life or enlightenment. Instead, Saklas sees to it that both the lifespan and earthly dominion of Adam and his generation will be limited as a result of violating Saklas' command not to eat of the tree of knowledge.

Adam's Loss of Immortality and the Brevity of Human Life
Rather than presenting a full-blown Sethian midrash on the events in paradise, the author apparently has Jesus conclude his initial revelation

---

[46] See also *Apoc. John* NHC II,1, 20,19; 23,23 and *Hyp. Arch.* NHC II,5, 95,5, 19, 32; 96,1.

[47] In Sethian tradition, the "Zoë in the cloud" (i.e., the divine realm) could also designate Meirothea, the mother of the divine Adamas, as in *Gos. Eg.* NHC IV,2, 60 [30] "Then there came forth [from] 61 [1] that [place] the cloud [2] [of the] great light, the living [3] power, the mother of the holy, incorruptible ones, [4] the great power [Mirothoe]. [5] And she gave birth to him whose name [6] I name, saying, IEN [7] IEN EA EA EA, three times. [8] For this one, [Adamas], [9] is [a light] that radiated [from [10] the light; he is] the eye of the [light]."

[48] *Gos. Jud.* TC 48,21–49,7.

with a comment concerning the unfortunate result of Adam's eating of the fruit of the tree of knowledge, which I conjecture to have read somewhat as follows:[49]

> *Gos. Jud.* [52] [25] Now, Sakla did not [53] [1] [command *him to fast*] [2] except [*from the fruit of the tree*] [3] of [*knowledge. And*] [4] this [*is how he limited his days*]. [5] And the [ruler] said to him (Adam), [6] 'Your and your children's lifespan will be [7] [*short*].'" [8]
>
> Judas said to Jesus, "[What] [9] is the is the advantage [10] of human life?"
>
> Jesus said, [11] "Why *are you surprised* that Adam [12] and his generation received his [13] limited time in the place [14] where he received his *limited dominion* [15] along with his ruler?"

If this restoration is near the mark, the passage does not narrate but merely alludes to Adam and Eve's loss of immortality spelled out in Gen 3:1–3 and 3:16–19, leaving the reader to infer from an assumed knowledge of the paradise story that the couple did in fact eat from the tree of knowledge and became mortal as the penalty for disobeying Saklas' command. Since this allusion to the eating from the tree appears to be the author's own secondary periphrasis of the paradise myth, he may well have used a term such as "fasting" (νηστεύειν) to recall his previous condemnation of evil practices of the twelve priests who "[fast] for two weeks."[50] It is a practice condemned even by their own god Saklas: "But the Lord who commands is the one who is Lord over the universe."[51]

While according to Gen 1:26–29, mankind is initially created with a limited dominion over the creatures of land, sea and air, the "place where he received his limited dominion along with his ruler"—evidently Saklas—is apparently paradise, the same place where his lifespan was limited and where he received dominion over Eve.[52] Despite his limitation of Adam's lifespan, it nevertheless turns out that "God"— possibly the Invisible Spirit or Self-generated One acting through the

---

[49] The original editors suggest that the saying of Saklas promised Adam a long life on the earth which they reconstruct as: "May your life be [*long* (ⲡⲟⲩⲛⲟϭ)] with your children," echoing Gen 1:28 and 5:3–5. But since this whole section deals with the brevity of human life, it is more likely the creator promised either a short (ⲡⲟⲩⲕⲟⲩⲓ̈) or a finite, numbered (ⲡⲟⲩⲏⲡⲉ; cf. ⲍ̄ⲛ̄ⲟⲩⲏⲡⲉ TC 53,13, 18) life along the lines of Gen 3:19–22, i.e., rather than blessing his creatures, his curse upon a disobedient Adam and Eve first limited their existence to some 900 years, which the creator limits even further in Gen 6:3.

[50] *Gos. Jud.* TC 38,14–15; cf. 40,12–13.

[51] *Gos. Jud.* TC 40,23–25.

[52] Gen 3:16.

unwitting Saklas—"caused knowledge to be [given] to Adam and those with him, so that the kings of chaos and the underworld might not rule over them."[53] Evidently, however, this gift becomes a boon only for Adam's descendents through Seth, the kingless generation, for in response to Judas' question about the mortality of the human spirit, Jesus replies:

> *Gos. Jud.* [53] [16] Judas said to Jesus, [17] "Does the human spirit die?"[18]
> Jesus said, "This is how [19] God commanded [20] Michael to give spirits to humans: [21] on loan while they render service. [22] But the Great One (the Invisible Spirit) commanded [23] Gabriel to grant spirits [24] to the great kingless generation: [25] spirit along with soul! Therefore, [26] the [rest] of the souls [54] [1] *[dwell with their kings. They]* [2] *[shall not ascend to the realm of]* light [3] *[since they dwell with the kings of]* Chaos[4] *[and the underworld so they might]* surround (or: seek out) [5] *[your] inner* spirits, [6] *[which] you have allowed to* dwell in this [7] [flesh] among the generations of angels. But God caused [9] knowledge to be [given] to Adam and [10] those with him, so that the kings [11] of chaos and the underworld [12] might not rule over them."

The great kingless generation, though also born mortal, was granted not only the same knowledge that the transcendent God ordered to be given to Adam, but also the same spirit and soul, whereas all the other humans received no soul, but only human spirits, i.e., the breath of life, as a loan until "their breath separates from them" at death.[54] Although ordinary humans attempt to preserve this spirit of life in fleshly bodies, perhaps through procreation, the kings of chaos and the underworld who rule the flesh will surround (or "seek out," ΚΩΤΕ ΝΟΑ-) such spirits so as to recapture them at the death of the body. While the spirit of ordinary mortals will live only as long as they serve the world creator and will perish at death, the holy generation has not only received both spirit and soul as a permanent possession, but also, since the time of Adam, has been protected from enthrallment to the rulers of the lower world by its primordial enlightenment.

Here Jesus' mythical revelation seems to end on a note of hope for the primordial members of Adam's generation; despite a limited lifetime, their knowledge will protect them from the kings of chaos. As

---

[53] *Gos. Jud.* TC 54,8–12. See the *Apoc. John* NHC II,1, 19,11–20,9, where Barbelo commissions Autogenes and the four Luminaries to enlighten the inert, merely psychic Adam by tricking Yaldabaoth into insufflating him with his mother Sophia's *pneuma* that Yaldabaoth had hoped to capture for himself.

[54] Cf. *Gos. Jud.* TC 43,14–22.

Jesus has previously made clear on page 43, though their bodies die, their souls will be taken up to the aeons.[55]

> *Gos. Jud.* [42] 26 [...It was] not [*to sate*] [43] 1 *that he came from* [*cloud*]; it was 2 not to [*give drink from the spring*] of the tree 3 [of *fruit*] that he came. *Although the time*] 4 of this age [*lasts*] 5 for a while, [*he did not remain above*], 6 but has come to water God's 7 paradise and the [*fruit*] 8 that will endure, because 9 the [*course of*] that 10 generation *will not be defiled*, but [*it will be*] 11 for all eternity." 12
>
> Judas said to [him, "*Tell*] *me*, 13 what kind of fruit does this generation 14 possess?"
>
> Jesus said, 15 "The souls of every human generation 16 will die. But when these 17 people have completed 18 the time of the (archontic) kingdom 19 and their breath *parts* from 20 them, their bodies 21 will die, but their souls 22 will be made alive, and they will be taken 23 up.

Although it is not part of the secrets of the Sethian myth that Jesus reveals to Judas on pages 47–54, apart from this *Gospel*'s initial statement that Jesus had appeared on earth for the salvation of humanity (33,5–9), this rather damaged passage, together with the passage on pages 53–54 that concludes the myth, appears to constitute the only positive reference to soteriological activity in the *Gospel of Judas*. But since the passage on pages 42–43 is not a part of the narrated Sethian myth, it is almost impossible to specify the context and identity of the anonymous figure that descends from the cloud to enlighten the holy generation. The occurrences of the past tense and the mention of a certain "tree" and of the watering of "God's paradise," as well as the prediction of the future endurance and purity of the holy generation suggest that this descent occurred in primordial times. Possible candidates for the descending figure might be the Self-generated One, Seth, or indeed the preexistent Jesus himself. Apparently, like all humans,

---

[55] Cf. *Dial. Sav.* NHC III,5, 139,22–140,13: "Matthew said, 'Tell me, Lord, how the dead die, and how the living live.' The Lord said, 'You have asked me about a saying [...] which eye has not seen, nor have I heard it, except from you. But I say to you that when what invigorates a man is removed, he will be called 'dead'. And when what is alive leaves what is dead, what is alive will be called upon.' Judas (perhaps Iscariot rather than Thomas) said, 'Why else, for the sake of truth, do they <die> and live?' The Lord said, 'Whatever is born of truth does not die. Whatever is born of woman dies.'" Brankaer-Bethge 2007, 280–81 suggest restoring *Gos. Jud.* TC 53,25–54,5: "[53] 25 "Therefore, 26 the [rest] of the souls [54] 1 [are under dominion. And] they 2 [will not enter the] light, 3 [but they will die in the world]. 4 [Stop talking and] seeking 5 [for] the spirit in you..." ([54] 1 [ϩⲁⲧⲛ̅ ⲟⲩⲙⲛ̅ⲧⲉⲣⲟ ⲛ̅]ⲧⲟⲟⲩ 2 [ⲁⲉ ⲛⲉⲩⲃⲱⲕ ⲉϩⲟⲩⲛ ⲉⲡ]ⲟⲩⲟï̈ⲛ 3 [ⲁⲗⲗⲁ ⲉⲩⲉⲙⲟⲩ ϩⲙ̅ ⲡⲕⲟ]ⲥ̣[ⲙ]ⲟ̣ⲥ̣ 4 [ϩⲱ ⲉ]ⲣ̣ⲱ̣ⲧ̣ⲛ̣ ⲉϫ]ⲱ ⲙⲛ̅ ⲉⲕ̣ⲱⲧⲉ 5 [ⲛⲥⲱϥ ⲙ̅]ⲡ̣ⲡ̅ⲛ̅ⲁ ⲛ̅ϩⲏⲧⲧⲏⲩⲧⲛ̅....

even the members of the holy generation on earth will experience a natural death, but unlike ordinary mortals—including members of the apostolic churches—their souls will be taken up.

At this point, the dialogue between Judas and Jesus that precedes this mythical revelation resumes with Judas' question about the destiny of the mortal generations that belong to the twelve aeons of the archontic kingdom—the very kingdom that Jesus had predicted would be ruled by Judas as the thirteenth demon.[56] Jesus responds that those mortal generations ruled by Saklas will be finished off by the stars. When their first star appears, which seems to be none other than the star of Judas reigning over the thirteenth aeon, those generations will resume their immoral and violent manner of life until the time when Saklas' dominion comes to an end; then all of them and their rulers and the stars themselves will perish.

> *Gos. Jud.* [54] [13] Judas said to Jesus, [14] "So what will those generations do?" [15]
>
> Jesus said, [16] "Truly I say to you, [17] the stars finish things off [18] for all of them. When [19] Saklas completes [20] the times allotted to him, [21] their first [22] star will come with the generations, [23] and what has (just) been said will be [24] completed. Then they will [25] fornicate in my name and [26] slay their children [55] [1] and [they will *sleep with men*] [2] and [*work at murdering one*] [3] [*another and commit a multitude*] [4] [*of sins and lawless deeds…*] [5] [...] [6] [...] [7] [...] [8] [...] [9] [...in] my name, [10] and your star will [reign] [11] over the [thirteenth] aeon." [12] After that Jesus [laughed]. [13]
>
> [Judas said], "Master, [14] [why are you laughing at me]?" [15]
>
> [Jesus] answered [and said], "I am [16] not laughing [at you] but at the error [17] of the stars, because these six stars [18] wander with these five [19] adversaries (the rulers of chaos), and they all [20] will perish along with their *creations*."

THE CHARACTER AND FUNCTION OF THE SETHIAN MYTH IN THE *GOSPEL OF JUDAS*

In terms of the *Gospel of Judas* as a whole, the purpose of the account of the Sethian myth ("[secrets that] no person has seen") in 47,1–54,12 is not soteriological, but demonological. It serves not so much to explain the salvation of the holy generation as to explain to Judas his actual role as the thirteenth daemon as it appears in the myth's apocalyptic

---

[56] *Gos. Jud.* TC 44,21; 45,24–47,1.

conclusion, where Jesus predicts the completion of Saklas' regime, marked by the ascent of Judas' star and the advent of his apostolic accomplices who will promulgate heinous crimes in Jesus' name.

The demonological focus of the myth is evident on two main grounds. First, in comparison with the Sethian theogonies that appear in Irenaeus, *Adversus Haereses* I.29, the *Apocryphon of John*, the *Trimorphic Protennoia*, and the *Gospel of Egyptians*, the *Gospel of Judas* interrupts its theogony of the divine realm by inserting 48,3–20, a properly cosmogonical account of the origin of the two ruling luminaries and the luminous aeons and angels over which they rule, between the account of the generation of the divine Adamas in 48,1–3 and the subsequent account of the generation of Seth, his seed, and the divine luminaries of the Self-generated One in which they reside in 48,21–49,7. Presumably these luminaries are the sun, moon, and stars of Genesis 1:19 that account for the origin of the deceitful stars that rule the human generations previously described on pages 37–46.

Second, the demonological focus of the myth is evident from its sandwiching between Jesus' declaration to Judas that he himself is the thirteenth daemon destined to become the ruler of the lower twelve aeons that control the lower twelve aeons and the mortal generations, and his concluding apocalyptic prediction of the elevation of Judas' star to the level of Saklas' own thirteenth aeon.[57] That is, Jesus uses a version of the Sethian myth to teach Judas, not so much about the nature of the transcendent world, but rather about the identity, origin and location of Saklas and his demonic kingdom of the stars and their twelve archons that control the "other" mortal generations whom Judas is destined to lead. All of them including Judas are set apart from the holy generation.

Except for Judas' brief exclamation of recognition that Jesus comes from the aeon of the immortal Barbelo and perhaps Jesus' statement about the mysterious figure who came to water God's paradise and the enduring fruit of the holy generation, the narration of the Sethian myth is an integral and self-contained unit.[58] It seems to have been inserted into an original dialogue between Jesus and Judas concerning the kingdom of stars and archontic powers that rule the lower world as

---

[57] *Gos. Jud.* TC 44,21; 46,7–25; 54,16–55,11. This sandwiching is graphically illustrated in DeConick 2007 ch.6.

[58] *Gos. Jud.* TC 35,17–18; 42,26–43,11.

an explanation of its origin and nature. It also appears that the passage in 45,24–47,8 that immediately precedes the myth and the passage in 54,13–55,13 that immediately follows it were originally a contiguous and integral dialogue concerning the character and destiny of the lower mortal generations excluded from the holy generation. This dialogue seems to have been split apart in order to create an *inclusio* into which the Sethian myth has been secondarily inserted as an explanation of the origin of this lower generation and its distinction from the higher and holy generation.

> *Gos. Jud.* [45] [24] Behold, [25] I have told you the **mysteries** [26] **of the** (archontic) **kingdom** [46] [1] and I have taught you about the *deceitfulness* [2] of the stars; and [*about the twelve*] [3] [*rulers who control*] [4] the twelve (lower) aeons." [5]
>
> Judas said, "Master, [6] *my seed would never control* [7] the rulers!"
>
> Jesus answered [8] and said to him, "Come, let me [9] [*advise*] you [*that not only*] [10] [*will you control and rule*] [11] [*them*], but that you will [12] *lament greatly* when you see [13] the **kingdom** and all **its generation**." [14]
>
> When he heard this, [15] Judas said to him, "What [16] advantage have I have gained, [17] since you have set me apart from [18] **that generation**?"
>
> Jesus answered [19] and said, "You will become [20] the thirteenth, and [21] you will be cursed by [22] the **other generations** and [23] you will come to **rule** over [24] them. In the last days they [24b] <will [*turn and be subjected*]> [25] to *you and you will not ascend on high* [47] [1] to the **holy** [**generation**]."
>
> > Jesus said, [2] "[Come], let me teach you [3] about [secrets that] [4] no person [has] seen, [5] for there exists a great and [6] boundless aeon, whose [7] extent no **generation of angels** [8] has seen....
> >
> > *The Content of the Sethian Myth: Gos. Jud. 47,1–54,12*
>
> **Gos. Jud.** [54] [13] Judas said to Jesus, [14] "So what will **those generations** do?" [15]
>
> Jesus said, [16] "Truly I say to you, [17] the stars finish things off [18] for all of them. When [19] Saklas completes [20] the times allotted to him, [21] their first [22] star will come with **the generations**, [23] and what has (just) been said will be [24] completed. Then they will [25] fornicate in my name and [26] slay their children [55] [1] and [*they will sleep with men*] [2] and [*work at murdering one*] [3] [*another and commit a multitude*] [4] [*of sins and lawless deeds...*] [5] [...] [6] [...] [7] [...] [8] [...] [9] [...in] my name [10] and your star will [reign] [11] over the [thirteenth] aeon." [12] After that Jesus [laughed]. [13]
>
> [Judas said], "Master, [14] [why are you laughing at me]?" [15]
>
> [Jesus] answered [and said], "I am [16] not laughing [at you] but at the error [17] of the stars, because these six stars [18] wander with these five [19] adversaries, and they all [20] will perish along with their *creations*."

Interestingly, the passage in 45,24–47,1 that precedes the Sethian myth is itself the concluding portion of an *inclusio* in 35,21–47,1 identified by Louis Painchaud[59] concerning the "mysteries of the kingdom" controlled by the stars and the archons that Judas will ultimately rule over as the thirteenth. It begins in 35,21–27 with Jesus' admonition to Judas: "Separate from the others and I shall tell you the mysteries of the *kingdom*, not in order that you will go there, but so that you will lament greatly" and concludes in 45,24–47,1 with the words: "Behold, I have told you the mysteries of the *kingdom* and I have taught you about the deceitfulness of the stars, and [about the <twelve> *rulers who control*] the twelve aeons.... You will become the thirteenth, and you will be cursed by the other generations and you will come to *rule over* them. In the last days they <will [turn and *be subjected*]> to you and you will not ascend on high to the holy [generation]." Of course, as another self-contained unit, the narrative of the Sethian myth itself constitutes a second such *inclusio*, whose purpose is to explain the origin of the two generations introduced in the first. Thus we seem to have two *inclusios*, one inserted toward the end of the other, that contain the fundamental teaching of the *Gospel of Judas*.

> First *inclusio*, 35,21–47,1: the mysteries of the archontic kingdom over which Judas will rule
> Second *inclusio*, 47,1–55,12: the Sethian theogony, cosmogony and anthropogony
> Concluding resumption of the first *inclusio*, 54,13–55,13: destiny of the lower mortal generations

The first *inclusio* contains the main thrust of the *Gospel of Judas*, which is a vicious polemic against the sacrificial theology of the so-called apostolic churches of the later second century; they have been defiled by perishable wisdom.[60] It portrays them as still mired in the fleshly ritual practices of the Jews that many Christians believed they had superseded with their so-called "spiritual" or "rational" sacrifices. In Jesus' interpretation of the disciples' initial dream vision, the priests they saw offering sacrifices in the earthly temple are the disciples themselves, the altar on which they present their offerings is their god, and the animals they brought to sacrifice are the multitude of their follow-

---

[59] Pointed out by Painchaud forthcoming 2009, ms. pp. 5–6.
[60] *Gos. Jud.* TC 43,26–44,5.

ers that they have led astray.[61] These priests engage in fasting, child sacrifice, sodomy, and murder in Jesus' name, a practice which Jesus' interpretation ascribes to the apostolic successors of the disciples, who in reality are ministers of error, doomed angelic lackies of the lord ruling the universe.[62]

Rather than creating a new spiritual race that has superceded the fleshly race of the Jews, their sacrificial practices only confirm their membership in a similarly worldly and material race. Markedly singled out are their ritual practices such as baptism in the name of Jesus by which one participates in his death and resurrection, the practice of fasting like angels who need no food, and especially their priestly offering of Eucharistic sacrifices at the altar in the name of Jesus, whether those offerings be personal acts of abstemious loyalty or material elements such as bread and wine or fish or other animals—and perhaps even humans whose martyrdom echoes that of Jesus—symbolizing the redemptive death either of Jesus or of the sinful nature of the communicants themselves. Since they do not know that there is a higher God, they betray the name of Jesus by offering sacrifices to the wrong god, the God of Israel, and thus cannot join the higher, holy generation. This polemical *inclusio*, which is resumed after the Sethian myth with Judas' question about the destiny of the mortal generations that constitute the archontic kingdom of the stars, also conditions the figure of Judas himself, who is likewise a victim of the stars.[63] Destined by the stars to hand over for execution the human figure that bears Jesus about, Judas will become the chief "priestly" facilitator of the worst possible form of animal sacrifice, the sacrifice of a human child as an act of devotion to an evil god who desires the sacrifice his own children, thus making possible the apostolic doctrine of sacrificial atonement. As the thirteenth demon, Judas will become co-ruler with this infanticidal god over a lower kingdom that will ritually repeat and actually celebrate that sacrifice in Jesus' name.

The second *inclusio*, containing the Sethian myth, was then inserted near the conclusion of the first as an explanation of the origin of the two generations introduced in the first *inclusio*: the kingless holy generation that Judas may envision but will not join is thereby identified

---

[61] *Gos. Jud.* TC 37,20–39,3; 39,18–25; cf. 40,20–26; 39,25–28.
[62] *Gos. Jud.* TC 38,14–39,3; 40,1–26; cf. 54,24–55,9 at the conclusion of the *inclusio*.
[63] *Gos. Jud.* TC 54,13–55,20.

as the kingless generation of Seth, as opposed to the mortal generations ruled by the stars. In addition, the unnamed god of the first
inclusio to whom the twelve apostles offer sacrifice is now identified
as Saklas.[64] The twelve apostles who think themselves to be "equal to
the angels" are now identified as the earthly counterparts of the twelve
angels created by Nebro and Saklas to rule over the lower kingdom of
the heavens, the underworld, and mortal humans.[65] And Judas, whose
earthly place among the twelve is taken by another in 36,1–4, leaving
him to become the "thirteenth demon" who is destined, not only to
rule over the other twelve in 46,7–47,1, but also—as chief sacrificer—
to hand Jesus over for execution in 56,17–24, is thereby identified in
cosmic terms as Saklas' future coregent in the thirteenth aeon presiding over the lower twelve aeons and their ruling powers, all of whom
shall eventually perish. These inter-identifications show that the object
of the *Gospel of Judas'* critique is to show that Christian sacrificial theology is a mere perpetuation of the Israelite temple cult.

Finally, the two *inclusios* are again tied together by placing within
the first *inclusio* Judas' exclamation in 35,15–17 that Jesus is "from
the immortal aeon of Barbelo", even though the myth of the second
inclusio only mentions an anonymous "luminous cloud" calling for the
emergence of Autogenes, but says nothing of Barbelo or her aeon.[66]
One suspects that the first *inclusio* originally had Judas merely recognizing the holy and immortal generation as the generic location to
and from which Jesus (periodically?) ascends and descends without
mentioning the Sethian figure of Barbelo.[67]

The relationship between these two *inclusios* and the frame narrative yields the following narrative structure of the *Gospel of Judas*:

---

[64] *Gos. Jud.* TC 53,24; 49,6. In 54,19–24 Saklas' name (ⲛϭⲓ ⲥⲁⲕⲗⲁⲥ) would have
been added as the subject of an hypothetically original "When the times allotted to
them (ⲉⲩϣⲁⲛϫⲱⲕ ⲉⲃⲟⲗ ⲛⲛⲉⲩⲟⲩⲟⲉⲓϣ ⲛⲧⲁⲩⲧⲟϣⲟⲩ ⲛⲁⲩ) are completed, their first
star will come with the generations, and what has (just) been said will be completed."
So also Saklas' name would have been added at 56,12–13 ("[those who] offer sacrifices
to Saklas") to supply a name for the anonymous god named in 34,10–13 ("your/our
god"), 34,25–26 ("your god who is within you"), 36,2–4 ("the twelve may again be
complete in the presence of their god"), 39,21–22 ("That one is the god you serve"),
40,20–21 ("god has received your sacrifice"), 43,6–7 ("god's paradise"), 50,19–20 ("god
ordered Michael to give spirits to humans"); cf. also 54,8; 56,13.
[65] *Gos. Jud.* TC 40,15–18.
[66] *Gos. Jud.* TC 47,14–18.
[67] *Gos. Jud.* TC 36,13–17.

33,1–6: Incipit: 'The hidden word of judgment…'
33,6–22: Introductory narrative: Jesus' ministry of salvific signs, wonders, otherworldly teaching and prophecies
33,22–57,14: The Dialogue:

a) 33,22–36,10 opening Eucharist scene; the question of Jesus' true identity and provenance

b) 36,11–37,20 the next morning, Jesus' account of his ascent to the other generation

First *inclusio*, 35,21–46,4: the mysteries of the archontic kingdom
35,21–37,20: Jesus and the holy generation versus the mortal human generation
c) 37,20–39,5: "Another day…," the twelve disciples' vision of immoral sacrificial practices 39,5–44,14: Jesus' eschatological interpretation: the disciples and their successors constitute the doomed kingdom of mortals who sacrifice to the stars
d) 44,15–45,11: Judas' vision of the place of the holy generation 45,12–46,4 Jesus' eschatological interpretation of Judas' vision; Judas is excluded 46,5–47,1: Jesus predicts Judas will not ascend to the holy generation but instead will rule the lower kingdom of the stars

e) Second *inclusio*, 47,1–54,12: the Sethian theogony, cosmogony and anthropogony
47,5–48,3: the Invisible Spirit, Barbelo, Autogenes, the four Luminaries and Adamas
48,3–20: the origin of the kingdom of the stars that rule the lower world
48,21–51,3: Adamas, Seth and his seed inhabit the 360 divine aeons and luminaries
51,3–52,14: Eleleth gives rise the rulers of the lower kingdom: Nebro, Saklas, the 12 archons, and 5 underworld kings 52,14–54,12: The creation of Adam and Eve, their limited lifespan, and provisional enlightenment

f) 54,13–56,?: resumption of first *inclusio*: Jesus predicts Saklas' and the stars' destruction

g) 56,?–57,14 Judas' destiny: to sacrifice Jesus
57.15–58,? Ascension scene: Jesus or Judas?
58,?–26 Concluding narrative: the arrest of Jesus and Judas' payment
58,27–28: Title

THE RESULTING DOCUMENT

The resulting document is a revelation dialogue that clearly trades on well-attested Sethian mythology, but a Sethian revelation without a Sethian soteriology or history of salvation. Aside from the revelation that the supreme deity commanded Gabriel to grant immortal souls to the holy generation in 53,22–25 and caused knowledge to be given to Adam and those with him according to 54,8–10, whatever traces of soteriological activity there are occur outside the limits of the myth narrated by Jesus on pages 47–55, such as the mysterious figure who came to water God's paradise and the enduring fruit of the holy generation on pages 42–43.[68] Apart from this figure, there is no named redeemer or revealer like Barbelo or Epinoia or Seth who descends for the enlightenment of the protoplasts in primordial times. In contemporary times, the dialogical framework into which the myth is incorporated indicates that Jesus makes multiple descents from and ascents to the immortal generation in the aeon of Barbelo in the capacity of a revealer or prophet. While on earth, Jesus is said to perform certain unnarrated signs and wonders for the salvation of humanity according to 33,6–10, but neither he nor any other figure seems to effect any final salvific act, such as conferring the baptismal ritual of the Five Seals or overthrowing the hostile powers.[69]

As already noted, the *Gospel of Judas* lacks certain fundamental constitutive elements of the Sethian myth, such as the roles of Barbelo, the four Luminaries, and Sophia, and instead offers details of what usually are considered secondary elaborations, such as the numerical multiplication of aeonic emanations, as well as an otherwise unattested cosmological account of the origin of the stellar powers misplaced even before the end of the divine theogony. The resemblance to other Sethian texts is limited to a mere outline of the main figures arranged in a similar descending hierarchy, but with virtually no interest in their deployment and function. While the *Gospel of Judas* certainly utilizes elements of Sethian mythology, it is radically different from all other known Sethian treatises by virtue of its irony and polemical pessimism, which remains unbalanced by any clear mechanism by which

---

[68] *Gos. Jud.* TC 42,26–43,11.

[69] In this respect, *Gos. Jud.* resembles *Apoc. Adam* NHC V,5, 76,8–85,31 minus the doctrines of baptism and the descents of the Illuminator combined with a summary version of the theogony and cosmogony of the sort found in *Apoc. John*.

ordinary mortals, Christian or otherwise, might attain an enlightenment sufficient to gain inclusion in the holy generation.

The preceding observations about the apparent Sethian character
of the *Gospel of Judas* lead me to doubt whether it can actually be
the same text mentioned in the patristic testimonies that refer to it
by name. Given the fact that neither Irenaeus nor his successors give
any hint of the *Gospel of Judas*' obvious Sethian features—features of
which other segments of their antiheretical testimony show more or
less intimate knowledge—one may well wonder whether the *Gospel
of Judas* they had in mind was a work other than the one found in
Codex Tchacos, or whether they only knew of a version which lacked
the Sethian myth it now contains. Although it appears that, in the last
quarter of the second century, Irenaeus and perhaps Hippolytus (his
lost *Syntagma*) knew of a work entitled "the *Gospel of Judas*," they
seem to have known nothing of its content beyond the fact that it featured the figure of Judas as a specially enlightened individual.

But their claim that all earthly and heavenly things were thrown into
confusion by Judas and that certain devotees of this gospel esteemed
Judas' betrayal of Jesus as contributing to the salvation of humankind seems to find little support in its actual portrayal of Judas as a
mere dupe of the stars, and a doomed one at that. Most importantly,
the Sethian myth of the *Gospel of Judas* makes no mention of Saklas'
rape of Eve to produce Cain and Abel (the *Apocryphon of John*, the
Hypostasis of the Archons, the *Apocalypse of Adam*) or of Sodom as
the place where the ancient seed of Seth sought refuge from Saklas
(the *Gospel of the Egyptians*, the *Apocalypse of Adam*), which would be
necessary for making sense of Irenaeus' confused testimony concerning the protological beliefs about Cain and the Sodomites he claims
were held by the users of the *Gospel of Judas*. Moreover, the vicious
polemic against the sacrificial practices and theology of the apostolic
church and its leaders that occupies the first half of the text certainly
could not have escaped Irenaeus' antiheretical commentary had he
read this text.

I would rather suggest that the *Gospel of Judas* we now possess is a
third-century rewriting of a yet earlier non-Sethian treatise in which
Judas's handing over of Jesus was portrayed not merely as a sacrifice unwittingly offered to a lower god, but also as an act that was
fated by the stars. What is unique about this text is not its Sethian
affiliation—which is at best secondary—but rather its vilification of
the fraudulent sacrificial practices of a proto-orthodox church that has

no knowledge of the nature and origin of the true Jesus. This vilification is only enhanced by the introduction of Judas, a figure already demonized by those apostolic churches, as in fact the only disciple who did have a presentiment of Jesus' true identity. But despite this ironic presentiment, it turns out that he too was unwittingly fated to be the demonic agent of a lower god whose wrath was believed to be appeased only through blood sacrifice as the requirement for gaining entrance into his "kingdom of the heavens" ruled by deceitful astral powers.[70]

Rather than counting the *Gospel of Judas* as an originally Sethian treatise, I tend to regard it as a polemical writing contrasting the enlightened holy generation[71] with the unenlightened and sinful generation of mortals enthralled to the earthly kingdom of an evil god who demands sacrifice as a token of devotion. This god, who rules over the stars, angels, and his earthly kingdom of mortals, is merely called "your/our/their god" (34,10.12.25; 36,4; 39,22), the "lord of the

---

[70] Recent attempts to ameliorate the demonic status of Judas as the "thirteenth (demon)" in this "gospel" by reference to late *fourth* century works like *Marsanes*, *PS*, *1–2 Jeu* and to *Iren., Adv. Haer.* 2.20 are unpersuasive. The thirteen "seals" of *Marsanes* have absolutely nothing to do with the thirteen aeons of Sethian mythology; while the Unknown Silent One may be characterized as the thirteenth Seal at the peak of the ontological hierarchy, this seal marks an entity that utterly transcends any aeon whatsoever. While Meyer 2007c (cf. his essay in Kasser et al. 2008, 125–15) takes DeConick 2007 (and implicitly my own reading) to task for interpreting the thirteenth aeon as the acme of the thirteen realms ruled by the ignorant creator Saklas on the basis of later *second* and early *third* century Sethian works like the *Apoc. Adam*, *Gos. Eg.*, and *Zost.*, his invocation of what he instead considers as the proper and more correct characterization of the thirteenth aeon as "'the place of righteousness' located above the twelve aeons and the heavenly home of the twenty-four luminaries including Sophia" in the clearly later and *non-Sethian* works of *PS* and *1–2 Jeu*, contravenes the very criticism he levels against DeConick: "Further, it is not clear that any of the answers based on later *Sethian* sources provide appropriate insights into the Gospel of Judas. The use of later—in some cases much later—texts [for Meyer, *PS* and the *1–2 Jeu*] to interpret such an early text as the Gospel of Judas raises fundamental methodological questions." Equally irrelevant is Meyer's subsequent discussion of *Irenaeus'* (*Adv. Haer.* 2.20) rejection of Judas as a type of the twelfth aeon Sophia's passion in Valentinian speculation (Meyer 2008a), since this concerns the twelfth, not the thirteenth aeon. In fact, one might conjecture that *Gos. Jud.* itself associates Sophia with the twelfth, not the thirteenth aeon, as I myself have done in TC 50,22–51,3: "And in the aeon that appeared with his (Adamas') generation is located the cloud of knowledge and the angel who is called Ele[leth. And he dwells] with [the twelfth] aeon [who is Sophia]."

[71] The concept of a specially enlightened holy generation is not unique to Sethian thought; one finds the concept of the kingless or unshakable generation, or the generation of Adam in non-Sethian texts as well, such as *Eugnostos*, *Soph. Jes. Chr.*, *Orig. World*, and even *Paraph. Shem*.

universe" (40,23–25) who is even identified with the sacrificial altar (39,18–24) and was worshiped by the disciples and their successors who baptize and offer sacrifices in Jesus' name. The true name, identity, and origin of this god was later explained by the secondary addition of a rather truncated and corrupt sketch of a typically Sethian myth of the sort found in the *Apocryphon of John*. The final author of the *Gospel of Judas* demonstrates only a secondhand knowledge of a Sethian mythology which is unaffiliated either with Christianity (Jesus is said to originate from the Barbelo Aeon but otherwise plays no salvific role other than revealer, and the only occurrence of the apparent epithet "Christ" in 52,6 is applied to a demon) or with a Platonism of the sort found in the Sethian Platonizing treatises.

While the addition of this sketchy outline of Sethian myth does serve to illustrate the contrast between the higher realm of the holy generation and the lower kingdom of mortals ruled by a lower god, it has also been clumsily altered to show that even this lower god, like the disciples and their apostolic successors as well as Judas himself, is himself controlled by astral powers that came into being before them all. "It's all in the stars"—stars that have come to surround the periphery of the luminous cloud of aeons reserved for the holy generation. Except for Judas, who ironically can envision but cannot enter that realm, the false light of the stars has obscured that generation from mortal sight.

In terms of my own theory of the development of the Sethian tradition, this is enough to locate the present *Gospel of Judas* no earlier than the second quarter of the third century, after the outbreak of the second century Sethian polemic against the Christology and baptismal practices of the so-called apostolic churches so evident in the *Apocalypse of Adam* and the *Trimorphic Protennoia*. This suggests a date of composition perhaps around or slightly after the time of the Sethians' early third century break with Christian tradition marked by the wholesale immersion into pagan Platonism so noticeable in the Platonizing Sethian treatises *Zostrianos*, *Allogenes*, the *Three Steles of Seth*, and even later in *Marsanes*.

PORTRAITS OF JUDAS

JUDAS ISCARIOT IN THE *GOSPEL OF JUDAS*

Birger A. Pearson

When the first translation of the *Gospel of Judas* was published with much fanfare in April, 2006, it was trumpeted in the press as a sensational document which rehabilitates the infamous traitor of Jesus, Judas Iscariot, and possibly even presents the real story of who he was and what he did. In Marvin Meyer's translation Judas is presented as the "hero" of the gospel, a "thoroughly positive figure" and a "role model."[1] In an essay contributed by Bart Ehrman in the same volume entitled "Christianity Turned on Its Head: The Alternative Vision of the Gospel of Judas,"[2] Judas is described as "Jesus' closest intimate and friend," "the ultimate follower of Jesus, one whose actions should be emulated rather than spurned." Judas is said to have "the spark of the divine within him" which puts him "in some sense as on a par with Jesus."[3]

Meyer's translation elicited a spate of hastily written books by prominent scholars such as Elaine Pagels, Karen King, Simon Gathercole, N.T. Wright, and others, including a full-scale book by Ehrman.[4] Meyer's and Ehrman's interpretation of the figure of Judas is followed and elaborated by the aforementioned scholars. Now, after considerable painstaking study of the text, first on the basis of the preliminary edition of the Coptic text by Rodolphe Kasser and Gregor Wurst published online by the National Geograpic Society, and more recently on the basis of the critical edition, I have come to the conclusion that the initial interpretation of the figure of Judas is fundamentally wrong.[5]

---

[1] Kasser et al. 2006a, 3, 9.

[2] Kasser et al. 2006a, 77–120.

[3] Kasser et al. 2006a, 80, 90, 97.

[4] Pagels-King 2007; Gathercole 2007a; Wright 2006a; Ehrman 2006b. Bishop Wright, while accepting the initial interpretation of *Gos. Jud.*, devotes the bulk of his book to a defense of traditional Christianity.

[5] Kasser-Wurst 2006. But now see Kasser et al. 2007. See now also the introduction to, and translation of, *Gos. Jud.* in Meyer 2007a, 755–69. I am not the only one to question this interpretation. Meyer reports that April DeConick and John Turner presented papers at a conference in Paris in October, 2006, in which they suggested

That case has meanwhile been forcefully made by April DeConick in her recent book, *The Thirteenth Apostle*.[6]

JUDAS ISCARIOT AS A DEMON

How does Judas know who Jesus is? The short answer to that question is: Judas knows who Jesus is because Judas is a demon.

At the beginning of the gospel Jesus is together with his disciples, and he laughs at their "prayer of thanksgiving over the bread."[7] When they protest at being so treated by one whom they take to be the son of their God, Jesus challenges them to stand before his face and "bring out the perfect human," presumably by confessing who Jesus really is.[8] Only Judas is able to stand up to Jesus, and he says, "I know who you are and where you have come from. You have come from the immortal aeon of Barbelo."[9] Since Judas has received no prior revelation from Jesus, how does he know who Jesus is? He knows because Judas is a demon, something that is explicitly stated later in the text, when Jesus addresses Judas with the words "you thirteenth demon."[10]

The word used here is *daimon* in Greek. Previous translators have preferred not to translate this word as "demon." Meyer's first translation reads "thirteenth spirit." In a note he argues that *daemon* here indicates that Judas' "true identity is spiritual," and compares the *daimon* (or *daimonion*) associated with Socrates in Plato's dialogues.[11] Meyer translates similarly in a more recent translation, and adds a note referring again to Socrates.[12] The Meyer-Gaudard translation in the *Critical Edition* is non-committal, "thirteenth daimon," and there

---

that Judas in this gospel should be taken as a tragic figure (2007b, 758). This is essentially the position I took in an earlier essay of mine (Pearson 2007c). Meyer cites other "revisionists" in his most recent book (2007b).

[6] DeConick 2007. That book came to me after I had prepared the first draft of this paper, which I presented at the Annual Meeting of the Society of Biblical Literature in November, 2007.

[7] *Gos. Jud.* TC 34,2–3. Translations of passages from the *Gospel of Judas* are usually taken from Kasser et al. 2007. Exceptions are indicated in footnotes.

[8] *Gos. Jud.* TC 35,3–5.

[9] *Gos. Jud.* TC 35,15–19.

[10] *Gos. Jud.* TC 44,21.

[11] Kasser et al. 2006a, 31.

[12] Meyer 2007a, 764. He persists with this rendering in Meyer 2007b, 59.

is no note.[13] Karen King commits herself to an extravagant view of Judas with her rendition, "thirteenth god."[14]

It is, of course, true that, from Homer on, the Greek word *daimon* was neutral, and could even be used for the lesser gods of the Greek pantheon. The substantivized adjective *daimonios* (*daimonion*) is a virtual synonym. Plato's definition of *daimones* as spiritual beings intermediate between gods and mortals became standard in the Hellenistic world.[15] So the question before us is this: Is "spirit" or "god" an appropriate translation of *daimon* in the *Gospel of Judas*?

To find the answer we shall have to search for parallels in the relevant literature. We begin with the other Sethian Gnostic tractates preserved in Coptic,[16] and we find that in every occurrence of the word ⲆⲀⲓⲘⲰⲚ the being or beings indicated are malevolent powers. In the *Apocryphon of John*, whose basic Gnostic myth comes closest to that of the *Gospel of Judas*, we read of the "origin of the demons" of the body, and there are four chief ones.[17] Then there are the "angels and demons" referred to later, including the "demons of chaos."[18] Similar uses of the word *daimon* appear in the *Hypostasis of the Archons* (NHC II,4), *Zostrianos* (NHC VIII), *Melchizedek* (NHC IX,1), and *Trimorphic Protennoia* (NHC XIII,1). Reference is made in the *Gospel of the Egyptians* to Saklas and "the great demon Nebruel," who is with him, and reference is made to other demons as well in that tractate.[19] In *Trimorphic Protennoia* the world creator is referred to as "the great demon."[20] Reference is made in the *Apocalypse of Adam* to Solomon's "army of demons," picking up a Jewish tradition about Solomon and his power over the demons.[21] The word *daimon* does not occur in the other Sethian tractates known to us.[22]

While we have noted that *daimones* and *daimonia* can be positive or at least neutral beings in Greek literature, that is not at all the case with the Hebrew Bible and the Jewish Pseudepigrapha. After surveying the

---

[13] Kasser et al. 2007, 207.
[14] Pagels-King 2007, 115.
[15] Plato, *Symposium* 202e. See Foerster 1964, 2:1–20.
[16] Meyer rightly refers to *Gos. Jud.* as a "Sethian gospel" (2007b, 759).
[17] *Apoc. John* NHC II,1, 18,2; 18,15.20.
[18] *Apoc. John* NHC II,1, 19,11; 28,19; 31,18.
[19] *Gos. Eg.* NHC III,2, 59,17.22.
[20] *Trim. Prot.* NHC XIII,1, 40,5.
[21] *Apoc. Adam* NHC V,5, 79,5.
[22] These are *Norea* NHC IX,2, *Steles Seth* NHC VII,5, *Marsanes* NHC X,1, *Allogenes* NHC XI,3, the Untitled Text in the Bruce Codex, and the *Book of Allogenes* TC,4.

evidence Werner Foerster could state categorically, "we may conclude that the decisive feature in Jewish demonology is that the demons are evil spirits," and "there is no bridge between evil spirits and good."[23] The same can be said of the use of the terms *daimon* and *daimonion* in the New Testament.[24]

Indeed, the New Testament gospels provide the closest parallels to the portrayal of Judas in the *Gospel of Judas*. In the only occurrence of the term *daimon* in the New Testament, Matthew 8:31, the demons in that passage recognize Jesus as "the Son of God." In Luke 4:41 the demons (*daimonia*) exorcized by Jesus recognize him as "the Son of God." In Mark 1:34 we are told that Jesus would not let the demons (*daimonia*) speak, "because they knew him." In like manner, Judas in the *Gospel of Judas* knows who Jesus is because he is a demon.[25]

THE NUMBER THIRTEEN

Is the number thirteen Judas' "lucky number?" In his essay in *The Gospel of Judas*,[26] Bart Ehrman refers to the contrast between the picture given in the gospel of the twelve disciples of Jesus and that given of Judas. The twelve disciples never understand the truth; only Judas "both knows and understands Jesus and the secrets he has revealed.... Judas is outside their number, and so Jesus calls him 'the thirteenth.' Here, thirteen is the lucky number."[27]

How lucky is the number thirteen, really? At the beginning of the gospel Judas is included in the number of the twelve disciples. After Judas recognizes Jesus and his origin, Jesus says to him, "someone else will replace you, in order that the twelve [disciples] may again come to completion with their god."[28] This obviously reflects the post-Easter

---

[23] Foerster 1964, 2:15.

[24] Foerster 1964, 2:16–19. There is one exception in the New Testament that proves the rule: In Acts 17:18 some (pagan) Athenians accuse Paul of introducing new *daimonia* into the city (just as the Athenians had accused Socrates four and a half centuries earlier).

[25] This had completely escaped my notice in my earlier essay (Pearson 2007c). The gospel author's depiction of Judas as a demon may reflect influence from John 6:70: "one of you is a devil (*diabolos*)." On Judas as a demon see now also DeConick 2007, 109–24.

[26] Kasser et al. 2006a, 77–120.

[27] Kasser et al. 2006a, 113. Meyer concurs in his essay in the same volume (Kasser et al. 2006a, 165): "thirteen turns out to be a lucky number for Judas."

[28] *Gos. Jud.* TC 36,1–4.

choice of Matthias as Judas' replacement in Acts 1:15–26, but in the *Gospel of Judas* no names are given to the members of the twelve disciples. "The twelve" simply become a cipher of the institutional church of the gospel author's own time. Judas stands apart from the twelve in what follows in the gospel and becomes, in effect, "the thirteenth." But the "thirteenth" what? We have already noted that Jesus later refers to him as the "thirteenth demon."[29] What the adjective "thirteenth" implies is made clear in what follows in the text.

Judas reports a vision that he had had of the twelve disciples stoning him, after which he comes to a beautiful house that he cannot enter because it is "reserved for the holy."[30] Judas is told that he will grieve much when he sees "the kingdom and all its generation."[31] What is meant by "the kingdom" here poses a problem to which we shall return.[32] Judas then says, plaintively, "What is the advantage that I have received? For you have separated me from that generation,"[33] i.e. the immortal, kingless generation.[34]

Jesus' reply is unequivocal: "'You will become the thirteenth, and you will be cursed by the other generations, and you will come to rule over them. In the last days they <will...> to you, and[35] you shall not ascend on high to the holy [generation].'"[36] What this reflects is the widespread demonization of Judas "the betrayer" by the institutional church of the second century.

In the sequel to this interchange (interrupted by the lengthy revelation expounding the Sethian Gnostic myth), unfortunately obscured by a lacuna of several lines, Jesus says to Judas, "[...in] my name, and your star will ru[le] over the [thir]teenth aeon.'" Then he laughs.[37]

---

[29] *Gos. Jud.* TC 44,21.

[30] *Gos. Jud.* TC 44,23–45,19.

[31] *Gos. Jud.* TC 46,11–13.

[32] See discussion below.

[33] That sentence is mistranslated in Kasser et al. 2007 as "For you have set me apart for that generation," following Meyer's earlier translation. The result is that the sentence is given the meaning opposite to what the text really says. ⲡⲱⲣⲁ ⲉ- must be translated "separate from" (Crum 1939, 271b). The translation in Kasser et al. 2007 simply follows Meyer's earlier translation.

[34] *Gos. Jud.* TC 46,15–18. See discussion below.

[35] Omitting "(that?)" in Kasser et al. 2007, and translating "shall" instead of "will" (Future III, neg.).

[36] *Gos. Jud.* TC 46,18–47,1.

[37] *Gos. Jud.* TC 55,9–12. On Jesus' laughter see Fernando Bermejo's essay in this volume.

The "thirteenth aeon" does not appear to be a happy place to wind up. That can be seen clearly when we compare what is said about the "thirteenth aeon" in other Gnostic texts. In *Pistis Sophia*, reference is made to a demonic being called "Authades...who is in the thirteenth aeon, who had been disobedient."[38] Closer to home, the "thirteenth aeon" occurs in Sethian tractates as well. In the *Gospel of the Egyptians* we find the Great Seth renouncing the world and the "god of the thirteen aeons."[39] In the tractate *Zostrianos*, Zostrianos recounts how he was "rescued from the whole world and the thirteen aeons in it and their angelic beings."[40] The thirteenth of the thirteen aeons is obviously at the highest cosmic level, associated with the world-creator.[41] We see here a statement as to Judas' ultimate destiny. It is clear that the number thirteen is not at all "lucky" for Judas.[42]

THE IMMORTAL GENERATION

Can Judas be seen as a member of the "immortal generation"? In order to answer that question satisfactorily, we shall have to explore the relevant passages in the gospel in order to determine what this "immortal generation" is.

The term "generation" (Greek, *genea*) occurs very often in the *Gospel of Judas*, and often appears in contexts where different generations are contrasted. The first occurrence of the term is used to refer to an inferior generation associated with the twelve disciples. Jesus says to them, "no generation of the people that are among you will know me."[43] Jesus departs, and when he is later asked where he went he says, I went to another generation, one that is great and holy."[44] When the disciples ask what this generation is that is superior to them he says, "'No one born [of] this aeon will see that [generation], and no host

---

[38] *PS* 30 (Schmidt-MacDermot 1978b, 89).

[39] *Gos. Eg.* III,2, 63,17–18.

[40] *Zost.* VIII,1, 4,25–28.

[41] We shall have more to say of the "thirteenth aeon" later in this chapter. In my earlier essay, I cited these references to the "thirteenth aeon" to support my conclusion that Judas turns out to be a "tragic hero" in the gospel that bears his name (Pearson 2007c, 14).

[42] On the number thirteen see now also DeConick 2007, 110–19.

[43] *Gos. Jud.* TC 34,16–18.

[44] *Gos. Jud.* TC 36,16–17. My translation. Kasser et al. 2007 reads, "I went to another great and holy generation."

of angels of the stars will rule over that generation, and no person of mortal birth will be able to associate with it.'"[45]

Later in the text the great and holy generation is referred to as "the incorruptible [generation] of Seth," and "the great generation with no ruler over it."[46] There are several other references in the text to that immortal generation, but there is no indication at all that Judas is included in it. Indeed, in a passage we have already encountered, he is explicitly excluded from it. Judas says, "you have separated me from that generation."[47] And Jesus concurs, "you shall not ascend on high to the holy [generation]."[48]

"THE KINGDOM"

What is "the kingdom" whose mysteries are revealed to Judas? At the beginning of the gospel, after Judas has recognized who Jesus is, Jesus takes him aside and says to him, "I shall tell you the mysteries of the kingdom, not (simply) that you might go there, but (also) that you might grieve greatly (when you get there)."[49] Later on Jesus says, in answer to a question posed by Judas as to the fate of human souls, "When these people, however, have completed the time of the kingdom and the spirit leaves them, their bodies will die, but their souls will be alive, and they will be taken up."[50] "These people" refer to the members of "the race (*genos*) that will last," i.e. the immortal generation of Seth.[51] The "kingdom" has a limited time, and will come to an end.

Later, after further dialog, Jesus says to Judas, "I have explained to you the mysteries of the kingdom, and I have taught you about the error of the stars."[52] Then Jesus adds a prediction, "You will grieve much when you see the kingdom and all its generation."[53] I take these statements to mean that the "kingdom" is a cosmic entity associated

---

[45] *Gos. Jud.* TC 37,2–8.
[46] *Gos. Jud.* TC 49,5–6; 53,25.
[47] *Gos. Jud.* TC 46,16–17.
[48] *Gos. Jud.* TC 46,25–47,1.
[49] *Gos. Jud.* TC 35,24–27. My translation.
[50] *Gos. Jud.* TC 43,16–23.
[51] *Gos. Jud.* TC 43,7–8.
[52] *Gos. Jud.* TC 45,25–46,3.
[53] *Gos. Jud.* TC 46,11–13.

with the "error of the stars."[54] That is the kingdom whose mysteries are revealed to Judas. No wonder that Judas will "grieve much" when he sees it![55]

It must be concluded from the aforementioned passages that "the kingdom" in the *Gospel of Judas* cannot in any way be equated with "the eternal generation." That generation is one "without a king."[56]

JUDAS' SACRIFICE

To whom does Judas offer his sacrifice? A key passage in the *Gospel of Judas* has to do with a sacrifice offered by Judas: "But you will exceed all of them. For you will sacrifice the man who bears me."[57] In Meyer's first translation, which is here essentially followed by the *Critical Edition*,[58] he adds a footnote: "Judas is instructed by Jesus to help him by sacrificing the fleshly body ("the man") that clothes or bears the true spiritual self of Jesus. The death of Jesus, with the assistance of Judas, is taken to be the liberation of the spiritual person within."[59] In Meyer's discussion of this passage in his Introduction, he writes, "He (Judas) does nothing Jesus himself does not ask him to do, and he listens to Jesus and remains faithful to him. In the Gospel of Judas, Judas Iscariot turns out to be Jesus' beloved disciple and dear friend."[60] Other interpreters have followed this interpretation of the passage, but it is clearly wrong. Jesus does not instruct or request Judas to do anything. He simply prophesies what Judas will do.

In order to ascertain what is involved in Judas' sacrifice, we must back up to an earlier passage in the text dealing with sacrifices. One day the disciples tell Jesus of a vision that they had seen of a large house (the Temple) with twelve priests offering sacrifices on an altar. They also commit a "multitude of sins and deeds of lawlessness." While they are doing this they are invoking Jesus' name.[61] Jesus pro-

---

[54] On the role of stars in the *Gospel of Judas* see below. See also Denzey Lewis' essay in this volume.

[55] *Gos. Jud.* TC 46,12; cf. 35,27.

[56] *Gos. Jud.* TC 53,25. DeConick 2007 has missed that point.

[57] *Gos. Jud.* TC 56,17–20.

[58] Meyer's first translation reads "the man that clothes me." There is no note to this passage in Kasser et al. 2007.

[59] Kasser et al. 2006a, 43 n. 137.

[60] Kasser et al. 2006a, 10.

[61] *Gos. Jud.* TC 37,20–39,3.

vides an interpretation of the disciples' vision of the Temple and the sacrifices: "It is you who are presenting the offerings on the altar you have seen. That one is the god you serve, and you are the twelve men you have seen. And the cattle that are brought in are the sacrifices you have seen—that is, the many people you lead astray before that altar."[62] Jesus tells them that people who follow their teachings and misuse his name will be "put to shame" on the last day.[63]

The same themes appear again toward the end of the gospel, this time also with references to baptism in Jesus' name.[64] Unfortunately this part of the text is riddled with lacunae. After one long lacuna, Jesus is saying to Judas, "Truly [I] say to you, Judas, those [who] offer sacrifices to Saklas…"[65] Then, after four unreadable lines, Jesus statement to Judas resumes, "…everything that is evil. But you will exceed all of them. For you will sacrifice the man who bears me."[66]

It is important to note that the disciples' sacrifices are offerings to Saklas, and are altogether evil. When Jesus says to Judas, "you will exceed all of them," he is certainly not at all setting up a contrast between the disciples' evil sacrifices and Judas' good one. Judas' sacrifice is also an offering to Saklas, and is also evil. The only difference between Judas' sacrifice and those of the disciples is the victim: "the man who bears me." Ironically, the result of that sacrifice will be the liberation of Jesus' spiritual self, of which Judas is given a preview in his vision of Jesus' (not Judas'!) transfiguration in a luminous cloud.[67]

Jesus' prophecy of Judas' coming sacrifice is immediately followed by four psalm-like verses:

> Already your horn has been raised,
> And your wrath has been kindled,
> And your star has passed by,
> And your heart has [become strong].[68]

Jesus sees that Judas has already steeled himself for the final act of the story.[69]

---

[62] *Gos. Jud.* TC 39,18–40,2.
[63] *Gos. Jud.* TC 40,2–26.
[64] *Gos. Jud.* TC 54,24; 55,21+.
[65] *Gos. Jud.* TC 56,11–13.
[66] *Gos. Jud.* TC 56,17–21.
[67] *Gos. Jud.* TC 57,16–26+.
[68] *Gos. Jud.* TC 56,21–24. Cf. Psalm 74(75):4–5; 2:12; 26(27):14. The meaning is that Judas' star has ascended to the right position. On his star, see below.
[69] On Judas' sacrifice, see now DeConick 2007, 124–39.

Judas' Star

What is Judas' star, and where does it lead him? In order to answer this question, we must first take a look at what the *Gospel of Judas* tells us about stars in general.

The first occurrence of the word "star" is found in a passage we have already encountered in another context: "No host of angels of the stars will rule over that generation," i.e. the immortal generation of Seth.[70] We then read about "the generations of the stars," and "the stars that bring everything to completion," and again in a later context, "the stars that bring matters to completion."[71] These stars are obviously associated with the destiny (*heimarmene*) that controls the cosmic order and what goes on in it.[72] They are by no means positive entities, for they are themselves characterized by error, "the error of the stars."[73] At one point, when Jesus laughs at Judas and the other disciples, he says that he is not really laughing at them but at "the error of the stars."[74] In short, stars are uniformly given a negative evaluation in the *Gospel of Judas*. They are part of the lower cosmic order, and govern the affairs of the human generations.

We are also told that each person has his or her own star. Jesus says to his disciples, "Each of you has his own star."[75] In Marvin Meyer's comments on this passage, he quotes at length a passage from Plato's *Timaeus* in which Plato says that the creator,[76] as part of his creative activity, "assigned each soul to a star."[77] While the reference to Plato's discussion is apposite, Meyer overlooks that fact that, for Plato, the created order is good. While the Gnostics certainly adopted Platonist ideas in creating their systems, they also adapted them by giving them a new interpretation. That each person has his/her own star is, for the author of the *Gospel of Judas*, not a good thing.

---

[70] *Gos. Jud.* TC 37,4–6.

[71] *Gos. Jud.* TC 39,13–14; 40,17–18; 54,17–18.

[72] The Greek word εἱμαρμένη does not occur in the *Gospel of Judas*. But see *Apoc. John* II,1, 28,11–32 for the Sethian interpretation of *heimarmene*.

[73] *Gos. Jud.* TC 46,1–2.

[74] *Gos. Jud.* TC 55,16–17.

[75] *Gos. Jud.* TC 42,7–8.

[76] Plato's word for the creator is "Demiurge (*demiourgos*)," a term widely used by Gnostics, but with a different connotation.

[77] *Timaeus* 41d–42d, quoted in Kasser et al. 2006a, 164.

What about Judas' own star? Meyer argues that "the native star of Judas is blessed," but is that really the case?[78]

There are four references to Judas' star in the *Gospel of Judas*. The first one occurs in the context of Judas' report to Jesus of a vision that he had seen of a large, beautiful house, with great people surrounding it. Judas says, "Master, take me in along with these people."[79] Jesus replies, "Your star has led you astray, Judas."[80] Jesus then continues, "No person of mortal birth is worthy to enter the house you have seen, for that place is reserved for the holy."[81] "The holy" are the people of the "[great], holy generation" referred to previously.[82] Judas' star has led him to think that he might have a place in that generation, but he is clearly mistaken.[83]

The second reference to Judas' star is found in a passage that has already been discussed in another context.[84] Jesus says to Judas, "your star will ru[le] over the [thir]teenth aeon."[85] Then he laughs. Not that Jesus necessarily thinks that this is funny; his laughter is more sardonic. In any case, we have in this passage a statement referring to Judas' ultimate destiny.

The third reference to Judas' star is found in the quaternion of psalm-like verses we quoted above: "Your star has passed by."[86] I take this to mean that Judas' star has aligned itself so as to influence his pending action, i.e., the handing-over of Jesus.

The fourth and final reference to Judas' star is found in a passage toward the end of the gospel in which Jesus says to Judas, "Lift up your eyes and look at the cloud and the light within it and the stars surrounding it. And the star that leads the way is your star."[87] What happens immediately after that is a matter of some controversy: "So Judas lifted up his eyes and saw the luminous cloud, and he entered it. Those standing on the ground heard a voice coming from the cloud,

---

[78] Kasser et al. 2006a,101; cf. Ehrman's discussion in Kasser et al. 2006a, 101. Also see, Pagels-King 2007, 98.
[79] *Gos. Jud.* TC 45,11–12.
[80] *Gos. Jud.* TC 45,13–14.
[81] *Gos. Jud.* TC 45,14–19.
[82] *Gos. Jud.* TC 44,12.
[83] Cf. discussion above.
[84] See discussion above.
[85] *Gos. Jud.* TC 55,10–11.
[86] *Gos. Jud.* TC 56,23.
[87] *Gos. Jud.* TC 57,16–20.

saying...".[88] What the voice says is unfortunately lost in a highly damaged section at the top of the next page, which is also the last page of the tractate.[89] But the main question here is: Who is the "he" who enters the luminous cloud? Judas? Or Jesus?

In a note to his first translation, Meyer refers to this passage as "the transfiguration of Judas." "He is vindicated by being glorified in the luminous cloud, and a voice speaks from the cloud." We are invited to compare the accounts of the transfiguration of Jesus in the canonical gospels.[90] In his more recent translation in the *Nag Hammadi Scriptures*, Meyer refers in a note to a suggestion made by Sasagu Arai and Gesine Schenke Robinson that "he" here refers to Jesus, not to Judas.[91] I think they are right.

Two arguments can be adduced in support of the interpretation of the passage according to which it is Jesus who enters the luminous cloud, one from a consideration of Coptic grammar, and the other from a consideration of the context.

The first argument revolves around the presence or absence of the Coptic conjunction ⲁⲩⲱ, "and." In the Coptic Perfect I conjugation (past tense) two or more clauses can be strung together without the use of ⲁⲩⲱ, where in English we would translate "and." This is called asyndeton.[92] The use of asyndeton binds the respective clauses closely together, e.g. clauses with the same subject. In our passage asyndeton is found in the first two clauses: "Judas lifted up his eyes, he saw the luminous cloud." The third clause is introduced with ⲁⲩⲱ, "and he entered it." Had this clause also been introduced without ⲁⲩⲱ, we would naturally take "he" to refer to the same subject as the previous two clauses, i.e. Judas. The use of ⲁⲩⲱ allows us (though it does not compel us) to treat this "he" as a different subject, i.e. Jesus.

The second argument is based on context. In a previous passage, Judas is told that he will sacrifice the "man" who "bears" Jesus, i.e. Jesus' body. This is clearly a reference to the handing over of Judas with which the gospel concludes. I take the stars that surround the luminous cloud in Judas' vision and the star that leads the way as an

---

[88] *Gos. Jud.* TC 57,21–26.

[89] *Gos. Jud.* TC 58.

[90] Kasser et al. 2006a, 44, n. 143.

[91] Meyer 2007a, 769, n. 123. Schenke Robinson 2008a makes this point very convincingly. I am grateful to her for giving me an advance copy.

[92] See Layton 2000, 182–183, section 237.

allusion to the story of the arrest of Jesus in the New Testament passion narratives. Jesus is surrounded by an armed crowd with Judas "leading them."[93] In the *Gospel of Judas* Jesus, i.e. his real self, enters a luminous cloud and disappears. The corporeal Jesus remains to be handed over by Judas in the narrative that follows.

At the end of the gospel Jesus is said to be in the "guest room" at prayer, presumably with his disciples. I see here a reference to the last supper. Judas pointedly remains outside, where he is approached by "scribes" who are watching what is going on. They ask him what he is doing out there (and not inside with the others), since he is also a disciple of Jesus.[94] The gospel concludes, rather enigmatically, "And he answered them as they wished. And Judas received money and handed him over to them."[95] In doing this Judas has been led by his star.

What happens after that? In the Gospel of Matthew and the Book of Acts there are two accounts of what happens to Judas, both of them reporting his gruesome death (Matt 27:3–5; Acts 1:17–18). What happens to Judas in the gospel that bears his name after he has handed the corporeal Jesus over to the scribes for execution? The answer to that has already been given: He takes his place with Saklas in the thirteenth aeon.[96]

JUDAS' IDENTITY AND DESTINY

In the foregoing discussion we have found that earlier interpretations of the *Gospel of Judas* and Judas Iscariot's role in it must be called into question, and new interpretations of key passages in the text have been provided. As to Judas' person and role in the gospel, we have suggested answers to three key questions.

First, how does Judas know who Jesus is? Judas knows who Jesus is because he is a demon. Noting the meaning given to the Greek word *daimon* used in Jesus' address to Judas ("thirteenth demon") in Sethian Gnostic, biblical, early Jewish, and early Christian literature, we came to the conclusion that the word used in the *Gospel of Judas* cannot be

---

[93] Luke 22:47.
[94] *Gos. Jud.* TC 58,9–22.
[95] *Gos. Jud.* TC 58,22–26.
[96] Cf. 55,10–11, discussed above.

translated "spirit" or "god."[97] Like the demons in the New Testament gospels who recognize Jesus as "Son of God," Judas is a demon who instinctively knows who Jesus is and where he has come from.

Second, is the number thirteen Judas' "lucky number"? Noting the meaning given to the number thirteen in such phrases as "thirteenth demon," Judas as "the thirteenth," and the "thirteenth aeon," we have concluded that the number thirteen is not at all "lucky" for Judas.[98]

Third, can Judas be seen as a member of the "immortal generation"? Noting what is said in the *Gospel of Judas* about the immortal, holy generation of Seth, and how Judas is portrayed in these contexts, we had to conclude that Judas is in no way included in that generation. Indeed, at one point in the text he is explicitly excluded from it.[99]

As to Judas' destiny as depicted in the *Gospel of Judas*, we considered three additional questions. First, what is the "kingdom" whose mysteries are revealed to Judas? When Jesus takes Judas aside and tells him that "the mysteries of the kingdom" will be revealed to him, the reader will probably think that "the kingdom" is something special. Judas is told that it is possible for him to go there, but he will "grieve a great deal."[100] We understand the reasons for Judas' grief when we look at what is said later in Jesus' revelation about "the kingdom". It turns out that "the kingdom" is a cosmic entity associated with "the error of the stars."[101]

Second, to whom does Judas offer his "sacrifice"? In considering the contexts in which "sacrifices" are offered, we noted that the sacrifices offered by the twelve are evil sacrifices offered to Saklas. Jesus is told that he will exceed all of them because he will sacrifice the "man" who "bears" him, i.e. Jesus' physical body. The only difference between Jesus' sacrifice and those of the disciples is the victim offered. It is a supreme irony that Judas' evil act leads to the liberation of Jesus' spirit from his body.

Third, what is Judas' "star" and where does it lead him? Considering what is said in the gospel about "stars" in general, we noted that "stars" are malevolent entities associated with human fate. We noted, too, that every person has his/her own star. Judas' star is in no way a positive thing. It is said to lead him astray, and will ultimately rule over the

---

[97] *Gos. Jud.* TC 44,21.
[98] *Gos. Jud.* TC 46,20; 55,11.
[99] *Gos. Jud.* TC 46,25–47,1.
[100] *Gos. Jud.* TC 35,24–27.
[101] *Gos. Jud.* TC 45,25–46,3.

thirteenth aeon.[102] His star ultimately leads Judas to hand Jesus, i.e. his physical body, over to the scribes for execution.

In our discussion of Judas' star "leading the way" in Judas' vision of the luminous cloud, we had to consider the question as to who it is who is said to "enter" that cloud. On grammatical and contextual grounds, we concluded that it is Jesus, and not Judas, who enters the cloud.[103] Jesus' inner self disappears into the cloud, leaving behind the mortal body to be handed over by Judas to the scribes.

I cannot refrain here from calling attention to an entirely different interpretation of this passage given by Elaine Pagels and Karen King in their book: "Gazing upward and entering into the luminous cloud, Judas is but the first-fruits of those who follow Jesus. His star leads the way."[104] Following Judas and his star is certainly not tantamount to following Jesus!

In concluding this essay, I want to raise a question about the *Gospel of Judas* in general and the earliest published interpretations of it. How can seasoned and distinguished scholars so thoroughly misread this gospel? In attempting to answer this question we must note that the *Gospel of Judas* is a very unusual and complicated text. Its difficulties are compounded by the physical condition of the manuscript, with extensive lacunae occurring in crucial passages. Then, too, there are glaring ambiguities in the text that lend themselves to misinterpretations. One example is what is said about "the kingdom" and its "mysteries." The most crucial example is the passage about the luminous cloud and the question as to who the "he" is who enters it (Jesus, and not Judas as is so often assumed).

It may also be the case that the first interpreters of the *Gospel of Judas* were "primed" to see Judas as its hero by what is said about that gospel by St. Irenaeus. He reports that certain Gnostics have a *Gospel of Judas* in which Judas is honored for accomplishing the "mystery of the betrayal."[105] Indeed, I must confess that this prevented me from reading critically the earliest translation when, in the last minute, I was able to include a brief discussion of the *Gospel of Judas* in my book, *Ancient Gnosticism*.[106]

---

[102] *Gos. Jud.* TC 45,13; 55,10–11.
[103] *Gos. Jud.* TC 57,22–23.
[104] Pagels-King 2007, 98.
[105] *Haer.* 1.31.1.
[106] Pearson 2007b, 96–97.

In the Introduction to his translation of the *Gospel of Judas* in *The Nag Hammadi Scriptures*, Marvin Meyer rejects the "revisionist" interpretations of Judas suggested in a colloquium by John Turner and April DeConick.[107] He raises the question, "In that understanding of the text, what is the gospel, or good news, of the *Gospel of Judas*."[108] My answer to that is: There is none. The *Gospel of Judas* (and I assign the title to its author and not to a later scribe) is a text featuring two gospel genres: story (as in the canonical gospels) and revelation dialogue (as in so many Gnostic writings). But the product is unique. The interlocutors in the dialogue are not heroes but villains! I would look upon the *Gospel of Judas* as an ironic literary caricature of a gospel.[109] The only thing that makes it a "Sethian" gospel is the Sethian myth embedded in it. It is a supreme irony that that myth is addressed to Judas, and not explicitly to potential members of the generation of Seth. (They are, of course, the implied readers). What would motivate its clever author to produce such a work is, of course, a question I can't answer.

The publication of such a sensational text such as the *Gospel of Judas*, with its ambiguous presentation of Jesus' infamous "betrayer," poses a great temptation to enterprising scholars to rush into print with their own books about it. Perhaps it had been better to resist that temptation.

---

[107] Cf. n. 5, above.

[108] Meyer 2007a, 759

[109] On *Gos. Jud.* as a "parody," see DeConick 2007, 140–47.

LAUGHING AT JUDAS

Conflicting Interpretations of a New Gnostic Gospel

Fernando Bermejo Rubio

Paraphrasing Irenaeus, we could say that through Judas a lot of things have been thrown into confusion.[1] Against the view championed by the National Geographic team, according to which we have in the new gospel a rehabilitated Judas and even a Gnostic hero[2]—and thereby something like a Copernican revolution in the view of this disciple, if not a turnabout in the study of Christian origins[3]—, several dissenting voices have been raised, arguing that a gross misinterpretation has taken place, and that Judas is not to be fairly described in such a way.[4] This alternative vision has been labelled 'revisionist' by Marvin Meyer.[5] Although some scholars have defiantly accepted the term— Birger Pearson has said, "I am happy to count myself as one of the group that Meyer calls 'revisionists'"[6]—I think that this label should be carefully avoided. First, because it presupposes that the former view is a consolidated and normative approach, which is obviously not the case here. Not only was the alternative approach proposed very early (only some months after the first publication of the text), but it is striking to speak about a one-and-a-half year old interpretation as if it were a well-established tradition. Second, from a certain perspective, 'revisionism' is a label which could be used (and, in fact, has been used) to describe the positive view of Judas held by the editors because it diverges widely from the view of Judas held secularly in

---

[1] See Iren., *Adv. Haer.* 1.31, 1. I am deeply grateful to Barc, Painchaud, and Turner for letting me read some of their articles, not yet published.

[2] See Ehrman 2006b, 69, 98, 136. 'Hero' is also the term used in Kasser et al. 2007, 24.

[3] "This gospel […] will open up new vistas for understanding Jesus and the religious movement he founded" (Ehrman 2006a, 80). This claim is, of course, completely unwarranted.

[4] See Painchaud 2006, 553–568; Pearson 2007c; Turner 2008a; DeConick 2007; Barc forthcoming. Judas would be "im Grunde eine geradezu unüberbietbar negative Gestalt" (Brankaer-Bethge 2007, 260); among a growing trend.

[5] Meyer 2007b, 50.

[6] Pearson 2008, 52–57, esp. 54.

the Christian tradition. Third, in some contexts such as the European one, this term has unmistakably pejorative overtones, inasmuch as it is associated with historical negationism such as Holocaust denial. For all these reasons the label 'revisionism' should be jettisoned.

We are facing at least two interpretive paradigms, with the result that scholars are remarking what they see as anomalies in a paradigm, often while struggling to defend their own position by turning to immunization strategies. In this deeply contested but stimulating context, it is our challenge and responsibility to weigh up which of these competing paradigms is the most convincing one—unless we discover the possibility of something like a *tertium quid*.[7]

Among the many ambiguous elements in the text, there is Jesus' laughter.[8] This element has indeed a conspicuous presence in the new gospel, where Jesus laughs four times.[9] Some scholars think that this laughter shows Jesus' benevolence and friendliness towards his disciples,[10] while others hold an opposing view.[11] Given that these references are little more than *obiter dicta*, my aim is to take a closer look at the passages where Jesus laughs, in order to shed some more light on this topic.[12]

---

[7] We are of course only beginning to understand this fragmentary text. What would we think today of a scholar who, writing in 1960, would claim to be expressing the last word on *Gos. Thom.*? We all should remind ourselves that future generations will laugh at our hasty judgments, and we should be accordingly cautious.

[8] Other ambiguities included Judas' nature (is he a spirit or a devil?), the meaning of the expression "mysteries of the kingdom" (does it refer to the demiurgical or to the transcendent realm?), the character entering the cloud at the end of the Gospel (does Judas or Jesus enter it?), and so forth.

[9] *Gos. Jud.* TC 34,2 ff.; 36,22 ff.; 44,19 ff.; 55,12 ff. On this issue, see Bermejo 2008, 331–359 (see also the contributions by Most and Robinson in Scopello 2008).

[10] "Se trata siempre de una ironía amistosa" (Bazán 2006, 42 n. 22). Other scholars think that laughter has a positive meaning, insofar as through it Jesus urges his disciples to higher spiritual vision. See Pagels-King 2007, 126–8: "Whenever Jesus laughs in the Gospel of Judas, he is about to correct errors in someone's thinking. In this instance, Jesus' laughter is a kind of ridicule or mockery intended to shock the disciples out of their complacency and false pride;" also Krosney 2006, 286: "Jesus [...] is a friendly and benevolent teacher with a sense of humor."

[11] "His laughter is actually the scornful laughter often evident in Gnostic literature—the laughter of one who is actually *detached* from the world, who stands above it in supercilious and mocking contempt" (Gathercole 2007a, 167). Scholars holding the view of a non-Gnostic Judas have also referred to laughter as disparaging and ironic; see Painchaud 2006, 566; DeConick 2007, 140.

[12] When I tackled the issue of laughter for the Paris Conference (2006) I knew the editors' interpretation, but I had not put it into question, nor was I aware of the existence of an alternative view. I remarked and stressed, however, the extent to which Jesus' laughter did not seem to have a positive and joyful meaning. Here I will tackle

LAUGHTER IN GNOSTIC TEXTS

The discovery of the Nag Hammadi Library confirmed the reliability of some heresiological testimonies concerning the presence of a laughing Jesus in so-called Gnostic trends, all the more shocking due to the absence of a laughing Jesus in Christian canonical texts. Unlike other religious traditions in which laughter is closely linked to the divine realm, in the prevailing trends of Christianity laughter has played an insignificant role: the canonical image of a Jesus ἀγέλαστος[13] matches, and serves to justify, a certain hostility towards laughter in Patristic thought.[14] In these circumstances (and in the modern context, in which the critical potential of laughter has been re-evaluated) Gnostic laughter has understandably attracted the attention of several scholars. It has been interpreted by them as an expression of "metaphysical revolt" visible in the idea that there is a God beyond god, in the notion that the inner human self is a stranger to this world, in the concept that questions the need for a mediating hierarchy.[15] The use of the image of laughter seems to confirm the view of the so-called Gnostics as *enfants terribles* of Late Antiquity, and to raise the sympathetic approach of many modern scholars to this religious phenomenon.

Before the discovery of the new codex, and leaving aside some references to laughter in Valentinian circles such as in the cases of Ptolomaeus and the *Gospel according to Philip*, its presence is most conspicuous in Basilides, in the so-called 'Sethian' tradition and in some other tractates of difficult adscription.[16] In these cases, laughter appears in three different situations, but always in an inter-subjective context.[17]

---

this issue again, now taking into account the existence of two competing interpretive paradigms.

[13] Besides the *argumentum ex silentio* (Jesus cries in Luke 19:41 and John 11:35, but he never laughs), Luke 6:21, 25 and Eph 5:4 are cited. See Sarrazin 1994, 217–222; Le Brun 1997, 431–437.

[14] See Adkin 1985, 149–152. See now several nuanced articles in Mazzucco 2007.

[15] Dart 1976, 107 f., 131 f.; Dart 1988, 93 f. See Orbe 1976, 229–234; Bröker 1979, 111–125; Gilhus 1997, 73–77; Stroumsa 2004, 267–288; Bermejo 2007, 177–202.

[16] Iren. asserts that, according to the Valentinian Ptolomeus—perhaps inspired in Orphic theology—it is Sophia's laughter which produced the spiritual substance (*Adv. Haer.* 1.4.3: ἐκ δὲ τοῦ γέλωτος αὐτῆς); see *Gos. Phil.* NHC II,3, 74,22–35, where the Gnostic laughs at the world in a damaged passage.

[17] For a more detailed treatment of the contents exposed in the following paragraphs, see Bermejo 2007, 179–187.

The Dialogue of the Saviour with His Disciple(s)

In a text such as the *Apocryphon of John*, Jesus laughs while speaking with his disciple, and answering the disciple's questions. In this work, the disciple to whom the mysteries are revealed is designated explicitly as originating from "[the unwavering race] of the perfect [Man] (†ⲅⲉⲛⲉⲁ ⲉⲧⲉ ⲙⲁⲥⲕⲓⲙ ⲛ̅ⲧⲉⲡⲓⲧⲉⲗⲓⲟⲥ ⲛ̅ⲣⲱⲙⲉ)".[18] Thus, the smile accompanying Jesus' answers does not seem to have a disparaging or mocking sense, but seems rather to express the serene joy of the Revealer, who has a spiritual comprehension higher than that transmitted by both Judaism and the 'Great Church'.[19] Jesus' laughter in *The Apocryphon of John* seems always to be a smile which shows the complicity between a master and his disciple, deriving from the inner, spiritual kinship between them. Jesus has indeed a superior knowledge, which remains provisionally hidden from the disciple, but this state of things is overcome through the revelation transmitted by Jesus to John.

The Mocking Reaction to the Demiurge's Presumption

The Demiurge, unaware of the existence of a transcendent reality, publicly introduces himself as the only godhead, using typical Old Testament formulae. Nevertheless, the irruption of a higher reality creates a new perspective, which unveils the Demiurge's presumption as nonsensical and a sign of ridiculous arrogance. The laughing figures—either a spiritual instance or the powers which can make out a different reality—laugh precisely because they have a superior knowledge.[20] The Demiurge ignores an elementary principle, which commands lucidity regarding one's own limitations. So he becomes more a jester than a true god. Plato had already identified any object of ridicule (τὸ γελοῖον) with ignorance, and more specifically self-ignorance, the

---

[18] See *Apoc. John* NHC II,1, 2,24–25; BG,2, 22,14–16. Cf. "Signo de alegría serena y aun de natura divina" (Orbe 1976, 231).

[19] See *Apoc. John* NHC II,1, 13,19; 22,11; 26,25. In 27,15 Jesus rejoices when his disciple puts a question to him.

[20] "And then a voice—of the Cosmocrator—came to the angels: 'I am a God and there is no other beside me'. But I laughed joyfully when I examined his empty glory (ⲁⲛⲟⲕ ⲇⲉ ⲁⲉⲓⲥⲱⲃⲉ ϩⲛ̅ ⲟⲩⲣⲁϣⲉ ⲛ̅ⲧⲉⲣⲓⲙⲟⲩϣⲧ̅ ⲛ̅ⲡⲉϥⲉⲟⲟⲩ ⲉⲧϣⲟⲩⲉⲓⲧ)": *Treat. Seth* NHC VII,2, 53,28–33; cf. 64,18–65,1. In *Orig. World* NHC II,5, 112,27 ff., the powers, after having seen Light-Adam, laugh at the Creator "because he lied, saying, 'I am god. No one else exists before me'".

phenomenon opposed to the command given by the Delphi's oracle (γνῶθι σαυτόν).[21] As Henri Bergson wrote in his essay on laughter, a character is all the more comical when he does not know himself.[22]

A Spiritual Being Laughs at Figures Who Fail to Understand

The vanity which provokes this kind of laughter does not originate because an inferior being aspires to be superior. Rather it lies specifically in an (collective) attempt to control a higher figure in a violent way. This violence centers on the crucifixion of Jesus as a bloody act with homicidal purposes.[23] It is also revealed in stories of sexual aggression, and in cosmogonies which portray the creation of the human being as the attempt by lower powers to trap the Light.[24] In all instances, the lesser figures fail to attain their purpose, because their malignant action is counteracted by a salvific action undertaken by the spiritual realm. Sometimes, the potential victim is replaced by another one, as happens with Jesus on the cross, or with Eve becoming a tree.[25] Laughter breaks out in the face of such a failure.

This cursory review shows that laughter has different meanings in Gnostic texts. Sometimes, it has a rather luminous sense, as the joyful expression of a deeper and higher understanding (γνῶσις).[26] Or it is

---

[21] Plato, *Phileb.* 48c–49c.

[22] "Un personnage comique est généralement comique dans l'exacte mesure où il s'ignore lui-même. Le comique est *inconscient*" (Bergson 1969, 13). "Comedy is especially effective when power is its subject, and the ludicrous effect is strengthened when that power does not understand that it is fooled, as was the case with Jahweh/Ialdabaoth" (Gilhus 1997, 73).

[23] Iren., *Adv. Haer.* 1.24.4; *Treat. Seth* NHC VII,2, 56,19 ff.; *Apoc. Pet.* NHC VII,3, 81,11–82,8; 82,31–83,1 ff. See *Acts John* 102 (the disciple laughs at the ignorant crowd after having received the revelation).

[24] *Hyp. Arch.* NHC II,4, 89,20–29; *Orig. World* NHC II,5, 113,11–17: "Then the authorities received knowledge to create Man. Sophia Zoe [...] anticipated them, and she laughed at their decision because they were blind—(ⲁⲩⲱ ⲁⲥⲥⲱⲃⲉ ⲛ̄ⲥⲁ ⲧⲟⲩⲅⲛⲱⲙⲏ ⲗⲉ ϩⲛ̄ⲃ̄ⲗⲗⲉⲉⲩⲉ ⲛⲉ), in ignorance they created him against themselves—and they do not know what they will do. Because of this she anticipated them. She created her man first."

[25] *Adv. Haer.* 1.24.4; *Treat. Seth* NHC VII,2, 56,6–13; *Apoc. Pet.* NHC VII,3, 81,12–23. *Hyp. Arch.* NHC II,4, 89,23–26; *Orig. World* NHC II,5, 116,26: "She laughed at them for their witlessness and their blindness (ⲁⲥⲥⲱⲃⲉ ⲛ̄ⲥⲱⲟⲩ ⲉⲃⲟⲗ ϩⲛ̄ ⲧⲟⲩⲙⲛ̄ⲧⲁⲧϩⲏⲧ ⲙⲛ̄ ⲧⲟⲩⲙⲛ̄ⲧⲃⲗⲗⲉ); and in their clutches, he became a tree (ⲁϥⲣ̄ ⲟⲩϣⲏⲛ ⲛ̄ⲧⲟⲟⲧⲟⲩ), and left before them her shadowy reflection resembling herself." On the possible meanings of this transformation, see Pearson 1976, 413–415; Gilhus 1985, 69–72.

[26] "La sonrisa del Salvador anuncia la exégesis espiritual, superior a la corriente (psíquica) del Testamento Antiguo" (Orbe 1976, 231); "The Gnostics' laughter was closely connected with seeing through, understanding a point, acquiring new knowledge. The

used as an incentive for the disciple to deepen his knowledge beyond a simple πίστις. In this context, laughter has a transgressive nature, which unmasks the cognitive limitations of the supposed superior realm (predicated by the religious tradition) by unveiling the existence of a higher reality. Thus, it represents an instrument of liberation and a sign of transcendence. Nevertheless, laughter has also often ominous dimensions. Sometimes, it assumes the destruction of the Other.[27] Mockery and cruelty arise in unexpected contexts, because they do not match a view of a godhead "auquel la bonté est plus essentielle que la puissance", to put it in the words of Simone Pétrement.[28] In fact, the disturbing nature of this laughter has been pointed out by several scholars.[29]

Laughter in the Gospel of Judas

We have already pointed out that Jesus' laughter in the *Apocryphon of John* seems to have a positive meaning and to show the complicity between the master and his disciple. Since the laughter in both the *Apocryphon of John* and the *Gospel of Judas* occurs in a dialogue between Jesus and his disciples that takes place independently of the crucifixion, one could be tempted to interpret the laughter similarly. Several scholars, whether or not they take into account the placid atmosphere of the *Apocryphon of John*, have interpreted laughter in the new Gospel *in bonam partem*, considering the disciples as individuals who have not yet obtained a full understanding, but who are incited to reach such a comprehension precisely through Jesus' laughter.[30] This laughter would have a meaning similar to that found in Zen Buddhist texts, where the challenging attitude of the master serves as a

---

comic conveyed knowledge, an exploitation of the universal connection between wit and learning, 'ha-ha' and 'a-ha'" (Gilhus 1985, 75); "The entertaining potential of the myths is exploited [...] to wake up sleeping souls to see their spiritual origin" (Gilhus 1985, 76). For passages showing the Gnostic joy, see Bröker 1979, 123.

[27] This is very clear where laughter is linked to the idea of a substitution of characters.

[28] Pétrement 1960, 385–421, 400.

[29] "Tampoco denota siempre pura serenidad o complacencia" (Orbe 1976, 231); "Their laughter myths [...] revealed a complex and sometimes sinister mentality [...] The laughter of Gnostic mythology has a certain aggressive edge to it" (Gilhus 1985, 76); "The cosmic cruelty of this laughter seems to evoke Siva's mythic destruction of the demon's cities rather than Christ's traditional compassion" (Stroumsa 2004, 271).

[30] See above, n. 10.

stimulus for disciples to gain insight and prepare to reach the *satori* or illumination. However, should we consider this approach correct?

Ominous Contexts

There are indeed serious objections against a positive view of laughter in the *Gospel of Judas*. As several scholars have remarked, the text lacks an elaborate soteriological perspective. We do not find any hint that the disciples will be saved. Rather Jesus seems to say that they have no chance of going to the heavenly realm. He seems to discourage them in every possible way.[31] Laughter in this gospel is not expressed in a context of luminous joy, rather it is unmistakably linked with damnation. Admittedly, in this text laughter arises in a dialogue, not in a bloody context of crucifixion. But is this enough to consider this laughter truly placid?

Jesus' laughter appears for the first time in the *Gospel of Judas* 34,2–5. In 34,16–17, after the disciples call Jesus 'the son of our god', we see Jesus' reaction:

> In what way do [you] know me? Truly I say to you, no generation of the people that are among you will know me.[32]

This is the first of a series of statements where Jesus underlines the seriousness of his speeches through the use of 'amen' or 'truly'.[33] This is also the first of a whole series of statements in which Jesus speaks about the impossibility for many people to obtain knowledge and salvation. The message delivered by him is indeed unambiguous, as evidenced by the disciples' furious reaction, described by the narrative voice through three verbs (ⲁⲅⲁⲛⲁⲕⲧⲉⲓ, [ⲣ̄]ⲟⲣⲅⲏ, ϫⲓ ⲟⲩⲁ) and by Jesus as an 'angry agitation'. Later, a strong and holy generation (ⲧⲅⲉⲛⲉⲁ ⲉⲧⲭⲟⲟⲣ ⲁⲩⲱ ⲉⲧⲟⲩⲁⲁⲃ) will be opposed to the disciples, who are neither strong nor belong to the holy generation.[34]

The second occurrence of laughter is found in the *Gospel of Judas* 36,22–37,8.

---

[31] "Der Erkenntnisfortschritt, der aus den Dialogen hervorgeht, betrifft eher die Leserchaft als die intra-diegetischen Personen" (Brankaer-Bethge 2007, 258).

[32] ϩⲛ̄ ⲟⲩ[ϩ]ⲁⲙⲏⲛ [ϯ]ϫⲉ ⲙⲙⲟⲥ ⲛⲏⲧⲛ̄ ϫ[ⲉ] ⲙⲛ ⲗⲁⲟ[ⲩ]ⲉ ⲛⲅⲉⲛⲉⲁ ⲛⲁⲥⲟⲩⲱⲛⲧ ϩⲛ̄ ⲛ̄ⲣⲱⲙⲉ ⲉⲧⲛϩⲏⲧⲧⲏⲩⲧⲛ̄ (*Gos. Jud.* TC 34,15–17).

[33] ϩⲁⲙⲏⲛ, ϩⲛ̄ ⲟⲩ ϩⲁⲙⲏⲛ, ⲁⲗⲏⲑⲱⲥ. For a complete list of passages, see *infra*, n. 97.

[34] Note the opposition between *Gos. Jud.* TC 35,6 f. and 36,25–26.

And when Jesus heard this, he laughed. He said to them: 'Why are you thinking in your hearts about the strong and holy generation? Truly I say to you, no one born of this aeon will see that [generation], and no host of angels of the stars will rule over that generation, and no person of mortal birth will be able to associate with it' (ⲙⲛ̄ ⲗⲁⲟⲩⲉ ⲛ̄ⲭⲡⲟ ⲛ̄ⲣⲱⲙⲉ ⲛ̄ⲑⲛⲏⲧⲟⲥ ⲛⲁϣⲉⲓ ⲛⲙ̄ⲙⲁⲥ).

Once more, Jesus' words are eloquent enough. To think about (ⲙⲉⲟⲩⲉ ... ⲉⲧⲃⲉ) a holy thing does not mean to grasp it or to be able to associate with it.[35] In fact, this very thinking is unveiled by Jesus as useless. It aims seemingly at identifying a holy generation, supposedly in order to participate in it. But every possibility at obtaining such a goal is categorically precluded by Jesus, who indirectly categorizes the disciples as beings belonging to the mortal people or the angels of the stars.[36] Any contact of the disciples with the holy generation is repeatedly precluded through a triple statement: to see, to rule or to associate with it are impossible actions for them. In fact, later in the text the holy generation will be described as "the great generation with no ruler over it" (ⲧⲛⲟϭ ⲛ̄ⲅⲉⲛⲉⲁ ⲛⲁⲧⲣ̄ⲣⲟ),[37] while the disciples are said to have a ruler (Judas) over them.[38] Jesus' speech is discouraging to such an extent that the only possible reaction for the disciples is astonishment and silence: "When his disciples heard this, they were troubled in their spirits, each one (of them). They could not say a thing".[39]

While in the former passages Jesus had laughed in the context of a dialogue with all his disciples, in 44,18–20, Jesus laughs after listening to Judas. Later we will take a closer look at this passage. Let us now consider Jesus' answer to Judas' description of his vision in 45,13–19. Jesus says, "Your star has led you astray, Judas." And he continues, "No person of mortal birth is worthy to enter the house you have

---

[35] This should make us more cautious about interpreting TC 35,21 f. in a positive way. Jesus knows that Judas thinks of higher things (ϥⲙⲉⲟⲩⲉ ⲉⲡⲕⲉⲥⲉⲉⲡⲉ ⲉⲧϫⲟⲥⲉ), but this does not need to mean that Judas is a superior being. Note also that the disciples described the "great generation" as superior (ⲉⲧⲁⲟⲥⲉ: 36,20).

[36] Some lines later, in a lacunous text, the disciples seem to be identified with the generation of humanity (Gos. Jud. TC 37,12–13).

[37] Gos. Jud. TC 53,24.

[38] Gos. Jud. TC 46,19–24. Some scholars, however, seem to think that the disciples—who are depicted as blaspheming Jesus and committing the most horrible crimes—will finally be saved: "the others are not *yet* ready to hear" (Pagels-King 2007, 62, emphasis mine).

[39] ⲛ̄ⲧⲉⲣⲟⲩⲥⲱⲧⲙ̄ ⲉⲛⲁⲓ̈ ⲛ̄ϭⲓ ⲛ[ⲉϥ]ⲙⲁⲑⲏⲧⲏⲥ ⲁⲩϣⲧⲟⲣⲧⲣ̄ ϩ̅[ⲛ ⲡⲉⲩ]ⲡⲛ̄ⲁ ⲟⲩⲁ ⲟⲩⲁ ⲙ̄ⲡⲟⲩϭⲛ̄ ⲑ[ⲉ ⲉ]ϫⲟⲟⲥ ϫⲉ ⲟⲩ (Gos. Jud. TC 37,17–20). The term ϣⲧⲟⲣⲧⲣ̄ appears also in 34,24, to describe the disciples' former reaction.

seen, for that place is reserved for the holy."[40] This statement agrees
with other passages in which Jesus seems to tell Judas that he will
not ascend to the holy generation.[41] Judas, a person of mortal birth, is
excluded. These words reiterate what Jesus had said before about the
holy generation to all disciples: "No person of mortal birth will be able
to associate with it."[42] Judas has been misled by his star in thinking he
could enter the transcendent realm. Once more, laughter appears in a
context where the exclusion of the Other is announced. The image of
the house as a safe place (for the saints) and that of the crowd which
cannot enter has obviously a sharply negative sense, because everyone
who remains outside is to be damned in the eschatological judgment.

This disturbing message is even more explicit in the following text in
the *Gospel of Judas* 55,12–20:

> And after that Jesus [laughed]. [Judas said], 'Master, [why are you laugh-
> ing at us]?' [Jesus] answered [and said], 'I am not laughing [at] you but
> at the error of the stars, because these six stars wander about with these
> five combatants, and they all will be destroyed along with their creatures'
> (ⲛⲁⲓ ⲧⲏⲣⲟⲩ ⲥⲉⲛⲁⲧⲁⲕⲟ ⲙⲛ ⲛⲉⲩⲕⲧⲓⲥⲙⲁ).

Unfortunately, the top of the page is too damaged to let us know the
immediate context of this scene, but Jesus explains the target of his
laughter (the error of the stars, ⲧⲉⲡⲗⲁⲛⲏ ⲛⲛⲥⲓⲟⲩ) and its meaning
(the stars wander about and are to be destroyed). If previously laughter had been linked to the rejection of other beings, it is now explicitly
connected with damnation and total destruction. In this passage, Jesus
laughs at the prospect of the destruction of certain entities, insofar as
he foresees the eschatological time and their ill fate. Just as Tertullian,
at the end of his treatise *De spectaculis*, imagines a cruel spectacle in
which the persecutors of Christians will groan in the dark,[43] so in the

---

[40] ⲛϥⲙⲡϣⲁ ⲁⲛ ⲛϭⲓ ⲡⲉⲭⲡⲟ ⲛⲣⲱⲙⲉ ⲛⲓⲙ ⲛⲑⲛⲏⲧⲟⲛ ⲉⲃⲱⲕ ⲉϩⲟⲩⲛ ⲉⲡⲏⲉⲓ ⲛⲧⲁⲕⲛⲁⲩ
ⲉⲣⲟϥ ϫⲉ ⲡⲧⲟⲡⲟⲥ ⲅⲁⲣ ⲉⲧⲙⲙⲁⲩ ⲛⲧⲟϥ ⲛⲡⲉⲧⲟⲩⲁⲣⲉϩ ⲉⲣⲟϥ ⲛⲛⲉⲧⲟⲩⲁⲁⲃ (*Gos. Jud.*
TC 45,15–19). We can perceive here an intra-textual reference. In 35,19 Judas says: "I
am not worthy (ⲛϯⲙⲡϣⲁ) to utter the name of the one who has sent you". Of course,
the issues of worthiness are different, but there seems to be an indirect inclusion of
Judas in the "non-being worthy people". These are the only two occurrences of the
terminology of dignity in the text.

[41] See *Gos. Jud.* TC 35,26; 46,25—47,1 (although this last text is admittedly a difficult one).

[42] *Gos. Jud.* TC 37,6–8.

[43] *Spect.* 30.2–5.

Gospel of Judas, the combatants, whose creatures have been formerly designed as persecutors,[44] are envisaged *sub specie destructionis.*

Every time Jesus laughs, it follows a dialogue in which he speaks in an explicit and wounding way about the impossibility of obtaining salvation for many people, including his interlocutors. A number of verbs denoting a salvific possibility—to know, to see, (to be worthy) to associate with, to enter—are used in a negative form. The last passage states it in the clearest way: those excluded from the transcendent realm not only will not know, see, or enter, but they will also be destroyed. This constant association of laughter and pronouncements on damnation does not appear to be sheer coincidence, and I rather think that this link has been purposely intended. It seems that we should not read the resulting laughter *in bonam partem,* as a majestic and benevolent expression of calm joy, or as an invitation to obtain a deeper insight.

The relevance of this laughter for understanding the whole Gospel becomes more apparent when attention is paid to the places where references to this issue occur. The fact that Jesus' laughter happens in key moments of the narrative hints at its function as a literary device. For instance, the first occurrence of laughter is also the first gesture of the master towards his disciples, thus defining Jesus' attitude to them. Passages where laughter appears seem to play a role in the literary construction of the text, creating a framework which allows us to interpret, apparently in an ironic way, the contents of the whole Gospel.[45]

Admittedly, we could put forward the following objection.[46] In two cases—the first and the last time Jesus laughs—Jesus explicitly states that he does not laugh at the disciples, so his gesture does not seem to be disparaging towards them.[47] I do not consider, however, this objection very compelling for the following reasons. First, not only is there an occasion when Jesus clearly laughs at the disciples in a derisive way,[48] but the context where laughter occurs in this gospel always has

---

[44] *Gos. Jud.* TC 45,1–2.

[45] Painchaud has kindly suggested to me that the first and last references to laughter (TC 34,4–9; 55,12–16) could function as a kind of general *inclusio,* to be added to other instances of *inclusio* detected by him.

[46] This objection was in fact put forward by Dunderberg at the Codex Judas Congress, Houston.

[47] *Gos. Jud.* TC 34,7 f.; 55, 5 f.

[48] This is implied for instance in *Gos. Jud.* TC 36,22 f., where Jesus goes on to ask the disciples why they are even bothering to think about the holy generation.

the same ominous overtones. Second, Jesus states that he does not laugh at the disciples only after he was asked by them: "Why are you laughing at [our] prayer of thanksgiving?" and "Master, [why are you laughing at us]?"[49] In a polemical context to answer someone, 'I am not laughing at you…', is a very common device of irony to say exactly the opposite of the apparent meaning. If the *Gospel of Judas* is not a propaganda work, but rather a text intended for internal consumption, this is most likely the meaning of Jesus' answer. Ancient readers would have perceived the irony. Third, when Jesus says he does not laugh at the disciples, but rather at the error of the stars, it is hard to see where the difference lies. The Gospel states in several passages that there is a very close link between disciples and the deceiving stars.[50]

The meaning of some intra-textual references

In the *Gospel of Judas*, laughter has a sinister and ominous nature. Yet several scholars have argued that Judas is the hero of the Gospel insofar as he is the paradigm of the Gnostic. Therefore, it will be worthwhile to take a closer look at the passages where Jesus laughs in his dialogue with Judas.

The first passage in which Jesus laughs while speaking to Judas is included in a literary unit where Jesus reveals "the mysteries of the kingdom".[51] Here we have two visions, one of the twelve disciples (apparently including Judas), another one of Judas alone. These two visions have many elements in common.[52] In both cases Jesus uses these visions to correct the false beliefs of his disciples. Jesus understands the visions that the disciples and Judas have in negative terms. The disciples are unmasked as sacrificers who are no better than the priests in Jerusalem Temple. Judas is led astray by his star, and told he cannot enter the house he has seen, "for that place is reserved for the holy".

---

[49] *Gos. Jud.* TC 34,4–5; 55,13–14.

[50] *Gos. Jud.* TC 42,5–9; 45,12–14; 46,1–2. 39,13–14 speaks about 'the generations of the stars'.

[51] *Gos. Jud.* TC 35,22—46,4. As Painchaud points out (2009), the boundaries of this literary unit are marked through the rhetorical tactic of the *inclusio*, with the references to ⲙ̄ⲙⲩⲥⲧⲏⲣⲓⲟⲛ ⲛ̄ⲧⲙⲛ̄ⲧⲉⲣⲟ in *Gos. Jud.* TC 35,24–25 and 45,25–26.

[52] Compare *Gos. Jud.* TC 37,22–39,3 with 44,24–45,12. In both cases 1) Visions are described as 'great'; 2) A big house appears; 3) The twelve appear; 4) There is a crowd; 5) Violence takes place.

At first glance, Jesus' reaction to Judas in 44,20–23 ("You thirteenth daimon, why do you try so hard? But speak up, and I shall bear with you") seems to betray a certain indulgence towards his interlocutor. But the very manner of addressing him by asking him why he is trying so hard shows that Jesus is aware of the fruitless nature of Judas' efforts.[53] In fact, some scholars have argued that this way of designating Judas (ⲡⲙⲉϩⲙⲛ̄ⲧⲓϥ̄ ⲛ̄ⲇⲁⲓⲙⲱⲛ) must be translated "thirteenth demon", not 'thirteenth spirit' as the editors and many translators after them have done. And these same scholars have argued that the designation "thirteenth demon" has a radically negative meaning. I think the several reasons brought forward to support this view are quite convincing.[54] In any case, we should make up our minds on the precise meaning of this appellation. Calling Judas a devil is perhaps not to be taken literally, because it could have more to do with which side Judas is on than with him actually being a devil.[55]

A minor detail could support this interpretation of Judas as a negative character. The verb used by Jesus to describe the vain efforts of Judas is ⲣ̄ ⲅⲩⲙⲛⲁⲍⲉ. The verb γυμνάζειν means to 'exercise', 'practise' or 'train'.[56] However, this is the same verb used before by the omniscient narrative voice to describe the liturgical action performed by the ignorant disciples (ⲉⲩⲣ̄ ⲅⲩⲙⲛⲁⲍⲉ ⲉⲧⲙⲛ̄ⲧⲛⲟⲩⲧⲉ).[57] We can observe that in that first case it is crystal clear that the piety of the disciples is wrongly-oriented, and, in fact, is ridiculed by Jesus. He has made plain that the action of the disciples is meaningless. They are offering thanks

---

[53] ⲧⲁⲁⲛⲉⲭⲉ ⲙ̄ⲙⲟⲕ (Greek ἀνέχειν) has been translated by King as "I will hold you up" (Pagels-King 2007, 115), as if Jesus were supporting Judas (see Pagels-King 2007, 140: "The metaphor indicates that Jesus' teaching supports Judas, helping him to stand firm and gain the stability he needs in order to develop spiritually;" also 77: "rather than dismissing Judas, Jesus promises to support him"). This section has been translated otherwise by other scholars: "I shall bear with you" (Kasser et al. 2006a; DeConick 2007); "I will be patient with you" (Gathercole 2007a); "ich ertrage (auch) dich" (Nagel 2007); "(dann) will ich dich ertragen" (Brankaer-Bethge 2007). The meaning seems not to be that Jesus supports Judas, but only that Jesus is tolerant with him, albeit somewhat reluctantly. This reluctance would be very difficult to understand if Jesus thinks that Judas is really a disciple making progress (although it could make sense, for instance, as a narrative device to drive the story forward).

[54] See e.g. Painchaud 2006, 558–559; DeConick 2007, 109–113.

[55] Jesus calls Judas a devil in John, and Simon Peter is called "Satan" in Mark and Matt.

[56] On the problem of translating this verb in the *Gos. Jud.*, see Nagel 2007, 213–276, esp. 260–262.

[57] *Gos. Jud.* TC 33,25.

over the bread, thinking they are performing an act of piety, and they
explicitly say that they are doing what is right (ⲡⲉⲧⲉⲥϣⲉ).[58] When
Jesus approaches his disciples, he laughs and unmasks their actions
as caused by the lesser god, "your god."[59] While they think they are
cultivating a true devotion, they are unveiled as idolatrous people.

In my opinion, the occurrence of the same verb here and nowhere
else in the text is an intended intra-textual reference.[60] The ridiculous
nature of the disciples, unveiled by Jesus in the former text, hints at
the ridiculous nature of Judas in the latter.[61] Judas is not being stimu-
lated to advance, rather Jesus seems to imply that Judas' efforts are
thoroughly fruitless.

The last text in which laughter occurs unfortunately is quite damaged.[62] In the last sentences of the preceding lacunae-filled text, Jesus
addresses Judas. Afterwards he laughs. The reconstruction of the editors is as follows: "[Judas said]: 'Master, [why are you laughing at us?'.
[Jesus] answered [and said], 'I am not laughing [at] you but at the
error of the stars...'".[63] If this reconstruction is correct, then it means
that Judas is included again in the group of the disciples, from which
he would seem to have been separated. This would be a further sign

---

[58] *Gos. Jud.* TC 34,6.

[59] *Gos. Jud.* TC 34,10. In *1 Apoc. Jas.* TC,2, Addōn—the ruler equated with the God
of the Hebrew Scriptures—is featured in an explicit way as wholly ignorant: 26,14–15:
ⲁⲩⲱ ⲛⲧⲟϥ ⲉϥⲟ ⲛⲁⲧⲥ[ⲟ]ⲟⲩⲛⲉ. One of the signs of this ignorance is that he considers
Jesus to be his son, and so he is well-disposed towards him (26,14–19). Interestingly,
the ruler's gross mistake reflects that committed in *Gos. Jud.* by Jesus' disciples, unambiguously depicted as ignorant, who consider Jesus to be the son of their God: ⲡⲥⲁ̄ϩ
ⲛⲧⲟⲕ [...] ⲡⲉ ⲡϣⲏⲣⲉ ⲙ̄ⲡⲉⲛⲛⲟⲩⲧⲉ (*Gos. Jud.* TC 34,12–13). In both cases, with an
air of detachment Jesus underlines the ignorance involved in such confusion of the
transcendent God with the lesser deity. Jesus speaks about "your God (ⲡⲉⲧⲛ̄ⲛⲟⲩⲧⲉ)"
(*Gos. Jud.* TC 34,10–11). In a later dialogue with Judas, Jesus speaks of "their God
(ⲡⲉⲩⲛⲟⲧⲉ)" (*Gos. Jud.* TC 36,4).

[60] This intra-textual reference is usually lost in translations. An exception is Nagel
2007, 240, 248, who translates the verb as 'disputieren' in both occurrences.

[61] There are two other passages where Jesus asks his disciples: 'Why...?'. In all cases
it seems that he is unveiling the uselessness of the questions posed by them.

[62] *Gos. Jud.* TC 55,12 ff.

[63] The text structure is the same as that found in the first occurrence of laughter: a)
Jesus laughs; b) He is asked by the disciple(s) why he is laughing; c) Jesus answers by
saying 'I am not laughing at you...' and adds an explanation.

that Judas has not really abandoned the group of the ignorant and idolatrous disciples.[64]

If we go on reading the text, we can detect another possible intra-textual reference in the words addressed by Jesus to Judas: "Already your horn has been raised, and your wrath has been kindled, and your star has passed by, and your heart has [become strong].»[65] This passage should be interpreted in light of the preceding lines: "But you will exceed all of them. For you will sacrifice the man who bears me."[66] These lines have been read in a positive sense, as if Judas' betrayal of Jesus were a great exploit.[67] They have been interpreted as praise of Judas, who, in some readings, would be even a proclaimer and prophet of the end time.[68]

Several scholars, however, have remarked that the sentence ⲚⲦⲞⲔ ⲆⲈ ⲔⲚⲀⲢ ϨⲞⲨⲞ ⲈⲢⲞⲞⲨ ⲦⲎⲢⲞⲨ should be read in a negative sense: Judas' iniquity will surpass all others, because he will commit the worst sacrifice.[69] I consider this approach reasonable, not only because it takes context into account, but also because it seems to make sense of the text as a whole. In my opinion, it would be truly odd that a work in which sacrifice is everywhere negatively portrayed, and where we find a clear injunction of Jesus reacting against the sacrificial theology that was establishing itself in the Christianity of the second century,[70] had suddenly praised sacrifice.[71] Although we should not apply contempo-

---

[64] It is also significant that in *Gos. Jud.* TC 55,21–23 Judas seems to adopt the perspective of the majority Church, in so far as he asks Jesus about "those who have been baptized in your name". Therefore, Judas holds the view formerly held by the other disciples. Let us remark that the former references to people invoking Jesus' name (38,24–39,17; 40,4 ff.; 54,25) appear in a thoroughly negative context; see Brankaer-Bethge 2007, 367.

[65] *Gos. Jud.* TC 56,21–23.

[66] *Gos. Jud.* TC 56,17–20.

[67] "There is little doubt that this is pictured as a positive thing for Judas to accomplish [...] Judas is perhaps a kind of true Gnostic priest here [...] Judas is the ideal priest who acts, if not under Jesus' instructions, then at least in his service, presumably by releasing Jesus' spirit from its bodily imprisonment" (Gathercole 2007a, 106, 157). But, as some scholars have perceptively pointed out, Jesus does not need Judas' help at all to be 'liberated'; see e.g. Turner 2008a.

[68] See Pagels-King 2007, 163.

[69] See Painchaud 2006, 557–558; 2008. DeConick has proposed the following translation: "Yet you will do worse than all of them. For the man that clothes me, you will sacrifice him" (2007, 89, 125). Also Brankaer-Bethge hold this interpretation: "Das 'Übertreffen' kann in keinem Falle positiv interpretiert werden" (2007, 368).

[70] "Cease to sacrifice (Ϭⲱ ⲈⲢⲰⲦⲚ ⲚⲐⲨ[ⲤⲓⲀⲤⲈ])": *Gos. Jud.* TC 41,1–2.

[71] The verb used in *Gos. Jud.* TC 56,20 is the same as that used in 38,16: Ⲣ ⲐⲨⲤⲓⲀⲤⲈ.

rary standards of consistency to ancient groups, in order to accept that
these words are describing Judas in a positive way we would have to
assume that the author of this text was extremely tolerant of contradiction. I do not claim that there cannot be contradictions in Gnostic
texts,[72] but such a contradiction would be too flagrant, and it would
reveal the author as somewhat incompetent.

The idea of a negative Judas is strengthened, I think, if we consider
the content of the above-mentioned text, which contains many echoes
of the Psalms, where the bellicous and military resonances are evident. The horn (sophar) is the instrument to call the people to arms.[73]
Yahweh raises the horn of his Anointed and his people for war.[74] The
martial symbolism appearing through the text refers to the stars,[75] and
evokes the god of armies. But the most surprising thing is that the
wrath (ϭⲱⲛⲧ) is used to depict Judas. Wrath is a characteristic feature of the Old Testament God, so abhorred by Sethian Gnostics. In
Gnostic texts, it is usually attributed to the demiurgical sphere.[76] Of
course there is a positive meaning of anger, as a necessary tool against
wrongdoings.[77] We must note, however, that the same term had been
used before, in the first scene of the text, to feature the negative reaction of the ignorant disciples to the words pronounced by Jesus, precisely when they are told they will not be able to know him.[78] Neither
ⲟⲣⲅⲏ nor ϭⲱⲛⲧ are used elsewhere in the extant text of the *Gospel of*

---

[72] In fact, elsewhere I have proposed a systematic deconstruction of the Valentinian
myth; see Bermejo 1998.

[73] E.g. Ps 89:24; 92:10; 112:9; Judg 3:27–29; 6:34; 1 Sam 13:3; 2 Sam 20:1. But
Painchaud has recently suggested that this section of the text could recall Dan 8.

[74] See 1Sam 2:1; Luke 1:69.

[75] Host of angels of the stars (*Gos. Jud.* TC 37,4–5; 50,5); five combatants (55,18).

[76] See *Teach. Silv.* NHC VII,4, 84,25; *Great Pow.* NHC VI,4, 39,23; *Dial. Sav.* NHC
III,5, is framed by references to wrath: in 120,15–16 it might designate the chief of the
archons or the "first power of darkness" (122,4), and in 146,21 the disciple is warned
to conduct a constant effort to rid himself of wrath. In the *Tri. Trac.* NHC I,5, the
'choleric nature' (ⲙ̄ⲛ̄ⲧⲣⲉϥⲣ̄ⲟⲣⲅⲏ) is a feature of the bad people who will be judged. In
Orig. World NHC II,5, 106,30, Wrath (ϭⲱⲛⲧ) is the name of one of Death's offsprings;
it is also called 'irrational wrath' (ⲟⲩⲟⲣⲅⲏ ⲛ̄ⲙⲛ̄ⲧⲁⲑⲏⲧ) in 126,19.

[77] Plato, *Leg.* 731b. According to Aristotle, feeling less anger than the situation calls
for is as much a failure of moral perception as feeling more. On this issue, see the
article by Dunderberg in the present volume.

[78] *Gos. Jud.* TC 34,20–21. "When the disciples heard this, [they] began to be annoyed
and angry, and they cursed him in their hearts. When Jesus saw their ignorance, [he
said] to them, 'Why this angry uproar?'" (*Gos. Jud.* TC 34,18–24). Brankaer-Bethge
have also remarked the negative meaning of this passage, but without further references (2007, 369).

Judas,[79] so I am inclined to conclude that the occurrence of the second term on page 56 is a new intra-textual reference to the previous scene (in both cases the anger is directed against Jesus), where wrath has an unmistakably negative sense.[80] If this is correct, it is another sign that Judas is characterized as a being under the aegis of the Demiurge. It is not the 'holy anger' which moves a supposedly good Judas, but the wrath of the biblical God, denoting deficiency. Let us recall the fact that references to stars are always negative in this Gospel. In this way, Judas, the sacrificer *par excellence*, is depicted as an aggresive and violent man, whose impending action matches the bloody nature of the demiurgical realm.[81]

If the words addressed to Judas, who has been separated from the holy generation,[82] are at all a 'hymn', they should be conceived as utterly ironic. Again, it would be extremely odd that a work where wrath serves as a negative feature for the worshippers of the lesser god would later use the same image with a positive sense.

If the former reflections are on target, we should conclude that Jesus' laughter regarding Judas does not have a different meaning from the laughter addressed to other disciples. In every instance, laughter denotes not only the superiority of the laughing figure, but also the mockery deriving from the awareness that it is impossible for beings belonging to the demiurge's sphere to reach the level of knowledge and ontological completeness possessed by the laughing figure. Laughter is provoked by the perception of inconsistency between the inquirer's aspiration and his pathetically comical cosmic position. If this is correct, we should also conclude that laughter in the *Gospel of Judas* has

---

[79] There is no semantic difference between the Greco-coptic ⲟⲣⲅⲏ and ϭⲱⲛⲧ (which translates ὀργή in Rom 5:9 and ὀργίζειν in Matt 18:34). See Crum 1939, 822–823. Both terms are interchangeable, as shown not only in *Gos. Jud.* but also in another text of the same Codex: "He has stirred up his anger and his wrath against you (ⲁϥⲕⲓⲙ ⲛ̄ⲡⲉϥϭⲱⲛⲧ ⲉϩⲣⲏⲓ ⲉϫⲱⲕ ⲙ̄ⲛ ⲧⲉϥⲟⲣⲅⲏ)": *1 Apo. Jas.* TC,2, 19,3–5.

[80] The reference to 'your heart' (ⲡⲉⲕϩⲏⲧ: *Gos. Jud.* TC 56,24) might perhaps be a reference to 'their hearts' (ⲡⲉⲩϩⲏⲧ) in *Gos. Jud.* TC 34,22.

[81] ⲡⲉϥϭⲓⲛⲉ ⲭⲉ ⲉ[ϥ]ⲭⲟ[2]ⲙ ⲛ̄ⲥⲛⲟϥ (*Gos. Jud.* TC 51,11).

[82] As some scholars have convincingly argued, ⲁⲕⲡⲟⲣⲝⲧ̄ ⲉⲧⲧⲉⲛⲉⲁ ⲉⲧⲙ̄ⲙⲁⲩ (*Gos. Jud.* TC 46,17–18) must be translated as 'you separated me from that generation', and not 'you set me apart for that generation'. Cf. Painchaud 2006, 560 f.; DeConick 2007, 51–52; Brankaer-Bethge 2007, 347. In fact, Kasser's French translation is: "tu m'as séparé de cette generation-là". All Spanish translations made from the provisional edition translated in a correct way this passage. See García Bazán 2006, 52; Montserrat Torrents 2006, 74; Piñero-Torallas 2006, 47. However, the critical edition offers the correct translation only as an alternative one; see Kasser et al. 2007.

essentially the same meaning that Jesus' laughter has in texts such as the *Apocalypse of Peter* or the *Second Treatise of the Great Seth*, where its nature is unmistakably devastating and disparaging.[83] The fact that laughter appears in the *Gospel of Judas* in a dialogical context does not imply that we find ourselves in a calm atmosphere, such as that created between master and disciple in the *Apocryphon of John*. Insofar as this laughter is a gesture that focuses the disparaging attitude of the text's author(s) towards apostolic Christianity, it is not to be considered as a secondary or anecdotal element in the *Gospel of Judas*. Rather it could serve even as an hermeneutical clue, denoting the parodic nature of this deeply disturbing text.

The *Gospel of Judas* and the Literary Model of Gnostic Laughter

The contemptuous nature of laughter in several Gnostic texts, including the *Gospel of Judas*, should make us think about the possible literary model of this image. There have been only a few attempts to explain this issue. In an article written almost half a century ago, Robert Grant proposed to interpret Christ's laughter as a reflection on Psalm 2.4: "He who sits in the heavens laughs, the Lord has them in derision".[84] This perceptive proposal must be taken seriously due to the fact that, in absence of a laughing Jesus in the New Testament, the Jewish Tanakh is the natural place to search for precedents. Additionally it should be taken seriously because Psalm 2 was interpreted early in the tradition from a messianic perspective.

Recently, Guy Stroumsa has offered another interpretation. Given that in several texts the Saviour's laughter (or that of a heavenly figure seeking to imitate him) is related to his ability to avoid death at the hands of the archons, Stroumsa has pointed out that Gnostic laughter could be understood as a reflection on the Akedah. Since Isaac is a figure to be sacrificed but escaping death, in early Christianity he was thought to be a *typos* of Jesus.[85] Given that the etymological meaning

---

[83] In fact, that laughter is very much like that which Aristotle called ἐπιχαιρεκακία, the malignant joy felt in the face of another's unhappiness, and which is one of the genres of perversity (φαυλότης): *Eth. nic.* 1107a10.

[84] Grant 1959, 121–125, esp. 123–4.

[85] "If, as it seems, the first Christians were keenly aware of Isaac as a typos of Christ, there existed also, *prima facie*, another possibility for essentially exegetic minds:

of Isaac is connected with laughter, and that in Philo's works Isaac is described as a son of God and apparently even as born of a virgin,[86] these elements might have been known to some of the early Christians towards the end of the first century. They could have easily thought of Isaac and his Akedah when reflecting on the cruficixion of Jesus. Further reflection could have produced a docetic theology of Jesus' passion.[87]

The proposals of these scholars are extremely valuable, but I think they should be supplemented. In the case of Robert Grant, God's laughter at Psalm 2:4 by itself does not seem to explain the deeply ambiguous nature of laughter in many Gnostic texts. Guy Stroumsa's hypothesis does not explain every aspect of this issue either, for at least two reasons. First, in Gnostic texts the spiritual figure does not laugh only in crucifixion or docetic contexts.[88] In fact, in the *Apocryphon of John* and the *Gospel of Judas*, the context is the dialogue with disciples before or after the Passion. Laughter targeted at the Demiurge is also alien to such a context. Second, Isaac's laughter has been traditionally understood as an autonomous smile denoting a genuine joy,[89] while the laughter of the Gnostic Jesus often has an inter-subjective and

---

namely, that Jesus, just like Isaac, had not really died on the cross but had been saved *in extremis* by his father and replaced by a substitute sacrifice, just as Abraham had replaced his own son by a substitute sacrifice. While this suggestion, which strikes me as logically plausible, cannot be proven, it should be accepted at least as a working hypothesis. The obvious implication of this hypothesis is the existence of a docetic interpretation of Christ's passion at the very origins of the new faith" (Stroumsa 2004, 283–284).

[86] *Det.* 124 (Colson-Whitaker 1929b, 284–285); *Spec.* 3.219 (Colson-Whitaker 1929a, 450–451); *Cher.* 42–51 (Colson-Whitaker 1929b, 32 ff.); *Post.* 134 (Colson-Whitaker 1929b, 404–405).

[87] "If my analysis is convincing, Christ's laughter as it appears in some docetic traditions reflects the fact that very early on (in the first century) some (Jewish) believers in Jesus and in his redemptory role considered him to be, as it were, *Isaac redivivus*. In a second stage, when the docetic attitude became more or less identified with gnostic dualism and antinomianism, Christ's laughter received a new turn, as it came to reflect his sarcasm at the failed efforts of the forces of evil to kill him" (Stroumsa 2004, 287–288).

[88] Stroumsa himself avows that the laughter of the Saviour (or that of another transcendent character) only in some texts is linked to his ability to avoid death by the archons (2004, 275). He does not claim that his explanation exhausts this phenomenon (288).

[89] See Philo's etymological observations in *Deter.* 124, where he speaks about God as creator of the good laughter (σπουδαίου γέλωτος καὶ χαρᾶς); see also *Mut.* 131, with a reference to an Isaac whose name is that "of the best of good emotions, joy, inner laughter" (τῆς ἀρίστης τῶν εὐπαθειῶν, χαρᾶς, γέλως ὁ ἐνδιάθετος)".

ominous dimension. In these circumstances, the above-mentioned proposals are to be considered elements of the solution, but probably not the only clues.

Elsewhere I have advanced a hypothesis attempting a more complete interpretation than those previously put forward by Grant and Stroumsa.[90] In addition to Psalm 2, I have proposed to take into account three more passages in the Tanakh where Yahweh laughs:

> Psalm 37:13: "But the Lord laughs at the wicked, for he sees that his day is coming."
> Psalm 59:9: "But you, O Lord, laugh at them; you hold all the nations in derision."
> Proverbs 1:26–27: "I also will laugh at your calamity; I will mock when panic strikes you, when panic strikes you like a storm, and your calamity comes like a whirlwind, when distress and anguish come upon you."

The remarkable fact is that in all of these texts, God's laughter, far from denoting a joy caused by the divine blissful existence or by the proleptic vision of the salvation of the Righteous, is connected with God's defeat of his adversaries and their damnation.[91] The laughter of this kind of *deus ludens* is not at all compassionate, so it should not come as a surprise that Robert P. Carroll has described the laughter in Psalm 2 as "of the sadistic kind".[92]

It is obviously advantageous to consider all the texts where we find a laughing God and to understand them in their context. This allows us to account for the several types of laughter existing in Gnostic texts, including those passages where laughter has ominous overtones. Texts like the *Apocalypse of Peter* and the *Gospel of Judas* 55,17–20, where laughter is addressed against the (supposedly) bad people heading for damnation, might well have their literary model in a text such as Psalm 37:13, where God's adversaries are explicitly envisaged *sub specie destructionis*.[93] The mocking laughter of Gnostic texts is also to be

---

[90] See Bermejo 2007, 192–201. For a briefer presentation, see Bermejo 2008, 353–355.

[91] "The divine laughter of the Old Testament is more derisive than that of any other God" (Gilhus 1997, 22). In fact, this laughter has troubled many exegetes, who strive to discern in it something positive, usually a parenetical or pedagogical intention; see e.g. Voeltzel 1961, 47 f.

[92] See Carroll 1990, 169–189, esp. 170.

[93] Both in Ps 37 and *Gos. Jud.* TC 45,1–2, the impious people are described as having behaved formerly as persecutors. Mockery, seemingly funny but linked to destruction and death, has another close parallel in the Tanakh, in the episode of *Kulturkampf* on the Mount Carmel, where Elijah's mockery on the 450 Baal' priests

found in the laughter of God in the Jewish Scriptures. The existence of a reinterpretation of the religious tradition in Gnostic trends is not to be doubted, but the fact that a disparaging gesture has been transferred from the Old Testament God to the Gnostic Revealer betrays also some limitations of that reinterpretation. The violence contained in the biblical tradition is not utterly cancelled out, but survives in Gnostic world-views.[94]

SHOULD THE *GOSPEL OF JUDAS* BE READ AS A *REDUCTIO AD ABSURDUM*?

In my opinion, the *Gospel of Judas* is one of the works exemplifying the ominous nature of Gnostic laughter, which we find also in Nag Hammadi texts such as the *Apocalypse of Peter* and the *Second Treatise of the Great Seth*. Given that Jesus laughs in the new gospel at his disciples, and that Judas is also the target of this contemptuous laughter (which seems to have the same meaning in every occurrence of it), the presence of this image should be also used as an argument against the idea of Judas as a 'hero' of the Gospel or as a 'perfect Gnostic'. In this work, Jesus' laughter unveils the disciples as inferior beings, incapable of salvation.

The ominous context of laughter in the *Gospel of Judas* should be taken into account by all readers. There are many people, including scholars, who approach Gnostic texts with religious assumptions and interests. Some of them find texts such as the *Gospel of Judas* abhorrent. Others, with a different agenda, find this text stimulating for its alternative view of Christianity. Perhaps we all can learn something from this new text. The most orthodox among us might see that some ancient religious people had a genuine abhorrence for the beliefs of Christian communities which would later be envisaged as 'orthodox.' Those scholars prone to feel sympathetically towards the *Gospel of Judas* might find it thought-provoking that a text with a pronounced anti-sacrificial agenda and which separates a lesser demiurgic realm

---

ends in a massacre (1 Kgs 18:21–40). This mockery of Elijah matches that of God (1 Kgs 18:27 LXX uses μυκτηρίζω: καὶ ἐμυκτήρισεν αὐτοὺς Ηλιου; while Ps 2:4 LXX uses ἐκμυκτηρίζω).

[94] For an analysis of violence in the new gospel, see Bermejo 2008, 346–352. As Gathercole has rightly pointed out, we find here 'a loveless Jesus' (2007, 163 f.).

with bloody features from a transcendent realm with an apparently deeply loving and good God, insists so strongly upon the destruction of others, and with such a contemptuous gesture.[95] This tension, not to say contradiction, is to be found in another religious phenomenon partially linked to Gnostic trends, such as Manichaeism. This religion, which foremost was an extreme exercise in non-violence, could not help envisaging a final situation where a gigantic cosmic *ekpýrosis* will take place, a violent event which is hardly discernable from a sacrifice.[96] However, this very tension is also to be discerned in the mainstream Jewish and Christian traditions, where identity is also fashioned by constructing sharp and incompatible contrasts between the Self and the Other, whose destruction is envisaged in the eschatological vengeance.[97]

On the basis of the survey offered, it appears we must conclude that the interpretation which argues that Judas' destiny, as it is portrayed in the *Gospel of Judas,* is not blessed, has a higher degree of verisimilitude than the editors' reading. I plainly avow, however, that ambivalence is a disturbing feature of the picture of Judas we find in the new apocryphal text. It is undeniable that Judas is depicted as the only disciple who recognizes Jesus' true identity, who has the strength to stand before Jesus, who is taken aside by Jesus and singled out to receive a revelation, and who will be harassed by the other disciples.[98] Even where Judas' negative nature seems to be obvious, some ambivalence remains. Despite the fact that a contextualized reading shows that the sacrifice made (or propitiated) by Judas will be a violent and dark action, it is revealing that the author has not said this

---

[95] According to Pagels-King 2007 xxiii, *Gos. Jud.* restores to us "a call for religion to renounce violence as God's will", but the uncomfortable position of these scholars towards the text also emerges (xii–xiii).

[96] Burkert, who stated that Manichaeism "als radikalster Versuch der Gewaltlosigkeit gelten kann,—abgesehen vielleicht von der Lehre des Buddha", also wondered: "Ist die Aggression gebannt, wenn als Ende der Dinge ein Weltbrand ausgemalt wird, der vom Bösen nichts als einen toten globus horribilis—wir möchten sagen: ein schwarzes Loch—übrig lässt: Triumph der Vernichtungsphantasien?" (Burkert 1996, 184–199, esp. 189, 199].

[97] See Collins 1989, 729–749; Stendahl 1962, 343–355; Collins 2003, 3–21, esp. 16. We should note that Mark has Jesus declare: "Woe to that one by whom the Son of Man is betrayed! It would have been better for that one not to have been born" (Mark 14.21).

[98] Referring to *Gos. Jud.* TC 36,4, Gathercole remarks: "For now, Judas is being portrayed in a positive light: Jesus talks to Judas of the disciples and 'their' (i.e. not Jesus' or Judas's) god" (2007, 72).

in a straightforward manner. The author has only implied it through a comparison with the sacrifices made by other people. Immediately after this, Jesus addresses Judas in an almost poetic style, and, because of this at first sight it is possible to see the hymn as a praise of Judas and an indication of his strength of character. Hence it follows that there appears to be an odd (irreducible?) ambivalence in the new Gnostic Gospel. For this reason, interpreters have maintained a lively debate over the meaning of the text.

Despite the undeniable merit of interpretations that see in Judas a figure who is not the model of a Gnostic, I am not convinced that the considerable degree of ambiguity in Judas' portrayal has been satisfactorily explained thus far. So I have the impression that recent expositions of a negative Judas have not yet obtained a consensus in the guild. An increasing number of scholars, comfortable or not with some of the interpretations offered, are stressing the ambiguous elements in the new Gospel, yet, as far as I know, the presence of such an ambiguity has not been accounted for in a convincing way.

The fact that we are still in a preliminary stage of research in the interpretation of the *Gospel of Judas* encourages me to suggest another approach. Instead of focusing on the critical passages in the text, which have a dubious meaning or have provoked a harsh debate, it might be more enlightening to start by analyzing those elements in the text whose meaning is clear enough for every attentive reader, and which have already been explained in scholarly work.

Thus we might agree on the following points:[99]

1) In *The Gospel of Judas*, Judas Iscariot is a main character.[100]
2) The *Gospel of Judas* has a very aggressive and polemical tone.
3) It contains a harsh anti-sacrificial stance.[101]

---

[99] I leave aside the contents of the cosmological section (TC 47,2–54,14), since it is a self-contained unit which, according to several scholars, could have been secondarily inserted in the text. To the arguments advanced in favor of this hypothesis I would like to add a minor one: the expression "Truly I say to you" is used in the Gospel time and again, from the beginning to the end (eight times in the preserved text: 34,15–16; 37,1; 39,7–8; 44,8; 54,16; 55,24–25; 56,11; 57,1), but it is wholly absent (as also, for instance, are references to stars) from the specifically cosmological portion.

[100] This statement is not trivial; let us recall the role Thomas plays in *Gos. Thom.*

[101] This becomes evident in the concentration of sacrificial vocabulary: 'sacrifice' (*Gos. Jud.* TC 39,3.26; 40,21); 'to sacrifice' (38,16; 41,2; 55,18); 'altar' (38,2.8.25; 39,9.20; 40,1; 41,4); the term 'priest' (38,5.9.13; 39,8; 40,21) might be added.

4) Judas is (at least partially) distinguished from the rest of the disciples.

5) Judas' status is featured by an intriguing ambivalence.

6) Judas is promised he shall rule over the twelve disciples.[102]

7) The twelve disciples are consistently presented in a thoroughly negative light, and they are representative figures of the 'Great Church'.

8) References to Jesus' name (which, according to the Gospel's author, is used by the guides of the apostolic churches in an unfair and misleading way) have a conspicuous presence in the text.[103]

9) Jesus states that Judas will sacrifice 'the man who clothes' him, and this statement is an important one.[104]

10) Judas' suffering (and persecution) is referred to in several occasions.[105]

11) References to stars and astral determinism permeate the whole text.[106]

12) Jesus freely ascends to the divine realm, where the holy generation abides, whenever he wishes.[107]

---

[102] This teaching is important, since it is mentioned twice: one in *Gos. Jud.* TC 46,20–24, another one in 55,10–11. This insistence on Judas' ruling (which could also be alluded to in 56,19–20) is all the more significant because the holy generation is "the great generation with no ruler over it" (53,24).

[103] See *Gos. Jud.* TC 38,5, 26; 39,11, 12, 16; 40,4; 54,25; 55,9.

[104] This is so for several reasons: a) Jesus does not simply speak but testifies, introducing his words with the solemn and emphatic 'Truly'; b) The prophecy is followed by a kind of poetical composition which confers to it a greater solemnity; c) the text uses sacrificial language, which is so important throughout the gospel; d) the prophecy seems to be again alluded to precisely in the last lines of the Gospel: "And Judas received money and handed him over to them".

[105] See *Gos. Jud.* TC 35,27; 46,13–14 (the same verb—ⲁⲱ ⲁϫⲟⲙ—appears also in 57,6, but in a quite damaged passage). This aspect is relevant, since it is also stated that Judas will be cursed by the other generations (46,21), and in the first portion of his vision Judas sees that the twelve disciples stone him and persecute him (44,23–45,1). Judas is depicted here as a kind of victim.

[106] There are fifteen mentions to stars in the preserved text: *Gos. Jud.* TC 37,5; 39,14; 40,17; 41,5; 42,8; 45,13; 46,2 (reconstructed); 54,17.22; 55,10.17.18; 56,23; 57,18.19.20. On this issue, see the articles by Barc forthcoming; Kim 2008; and the contribution of Denzey Lewis in the present volume.

[107] *Gos. Jud.* TC 33,22–27; 36,10–16; 37,21–22; 44,13–14. Whatever translation of 33,18–21 is preferred, it shows Jesus' freedom regarding the material body. Jesus appears and goes away, much as in the accounts of his resurrection appearances in the canonical Gospels.

Could these issues become the platform on which to base a scholarly consensus on the Gospel? Each one of these points is essential for understanding the text, since no doubt every one of them is relevant from a quantitative point of view or a qualitative one. If we agree on this set of statements, is it possible to advance a hypothesis which can account for these features in a simple and unifying way? Is ambiguity simply the impression of readers faced with such a lacunous and (probably) interpolated text, or is it rather a purposely intended feature of the Gospel?

Towards this end, I venture to hypothesize that the *Gospel of Judas* be read as a *reductio ad absurdum* of the sacrificial view of Jesus' death held by the proto-orthodox Christians. This *reductio ad absurdum* may have been driven by the perception of the ambiguities which characterize the figure of Judas in the New Testament and which were later definitively confirmed by the ecclesiastical atonement theology.

The interpretation of Jesus' death by the 'Great Church' as atonement sacrifice, through which that death is conceived as the payment for the salvation of mankind, was viewed by some Gnostics as deeply wrong and hideous. Thus far, several scholars have argued that this was the case of the author of the *Gospel of Judas*, who seems to have assessed that interpretation of Jesus' death as spiritually disgusting and/or morally perverse.[108] This is no doubt correct, but I would add that the author of the new Gospel might have seen in that sacrificial theory something not only repellent from a theological and moral point of view, but also logically inconsistent, and that this interpretation may have been strengthened by taking into consideration the figure of Judas Iscariot in mainstream Christianity who in scripture and early Christian tradition is depicted as desperately ambiguous.

There are at least two factors showing this ambiguity. On the one hand, although Judas is usually viewed in a very negative way and the process of his vilification in the Christian tradition is well-known,

---

[108] "Tout se passe comme si l'auteur de l'Évangile de Judas faisait de ce même Judas le père d'un christianisme proto-orthodoxe qui, à ses yeux, trahissait le nom de Jésus en proposant une interprétation sacrificielle de sa mort, et perpétuait ainsi l'économie sacrificielle du judaïsme" (Painchaud 2006, 567); "The Gospel goes a long way toward criticizing and mocking apostolic interpretations of Jesus' death in sacrificial terms. This criticism condemns apostolic interpretations of the crucifixion, which held that Jesus' death atoned for sins. To the Gnostic Christians who wrote the *Gospel of Judas* this interpretation was hideous because it assumed child sacrifice" (DeConick 2007, 131).

Matthew 27:3-10 is a pericope which opens the door for a more favourable view of him.[109] It portrays Judas as someone who expresses knowledge of his wrongdoing. He declares Jesus to be wholly innocent, returning the money as an act of contrition and hanging himself in an apparent act of radical repentance.[110] On the other hand, although Judas is abhorred as the Lord's betrayer, the sacrificial view of Jesus' death makes Judas a key figure of the soteriological economy. Without him, Jesus' death and the consequent redemption would not have taken place. Judas' behaviour allowed the fulfilling of Scripture.[111] The aporetic nature of the sacrificial interpretation is also to be perceived in several New Testament texts which imply a twofold idea: Judas' treacherous behaviour is indispensable for redemption, but for having performed his acts he will have to face tragedy and damnation.[112] Judas' agency becomes somewhat of a puzzle. In these circumstances, it would be simplistic to consider Judas as merely evil in a univocal sense.

People prone to detect problems in the proto-orthodox view, as Gnostics were, are likely to have identified such ambivalence very early on. All the more so, since this ambivalence raises disturbing questions about Judas' responsibility and moral status, not to mention logical comprehensibility and divine justice. Is Judas really free? Is he impelled by Satan? Or rather is he controlled by God? Or is he manipulated by Jesus himself?[113] What kind of god would have allowed such a tragic fate? Does Judas' story make any sense at all?

---

[109] On the probable influence of Matt on the new Gospel, see Gathercole 2007a, 134–138.

[110] The possibility of a *in bonam partem* reading of this passage is proved by Origen, who held sometimes a relatively sympathetical view of Judas, as a person who was not wholly bad. See *Cels.* 2.11; cf. Laeuchli 1953, 253–268. Even more positive views of Judas may have been widespread in the 2nd century, as some later heresiological accounts (e.g. Pseudo-Tertullian, *Adv. omn. haer.* 2.5–6) suggest.

[111] John 13:18.

[112] Mark 14:21; John 17:12.

[113] See John 13:27. It is revealing that several contemporary exegetes have tried to vindicate Judas, sometimes recurring to retroversion of sections of NT texts into the original Aramaic. See H. Stein-Schneider 1985, 403–424, who concludes that "Judas est totalement innocent" (p. 421); "Es ergibt sich als unumgängliche Folgerung, dass Judas bei der Festnahme Jesu nicht aus eigenem Antrieb handelte, sondern tat, was er, der Weisung Jesu gehorchend, tun musste [...] Das Endergebnis der hiermit vorgelegten 'aramaistischen Untersuchungen [...]' besteht darin, dass Judas von dem Vorwurf, 'der Verräter Jesu' gewesen zu sein, freigesprochen werden muss: weil er, als er Jesus erst an die Häscher, danach an die jüdischen Oberpriester 'übergab', nicht aus eigenem Antrieb handelte, sondern im Auftrage Jesu" (Schwarz 1988, 231, 237). For other

In light of the intrinsic ambiguity of Judas' portrait and assessment, the mainstream Christian view of Jesus' death as due to God's will and as having a salvific effect—a death in which Judas would have played such an important role—might have been further judged by some Gnostics as unavoidably and unmistakably inconsistent. Thus those Gnostics could infer that a good way to deconstruct that sacrificial view would be to focus on Judas. More specifically, the task would have been to take the proto-orthodox view of this character to its (il)logical conclusions.

On the one hand, if Judas were the instrument of Providence, he ought to be presented as a special disciple, because, whereas the other disciples do not want to accept the idea of Jesus' death, Judas' behavior corresponds exactly to God's plan. Judas must have known something that the other disciples did not and might have had a close relationship to Jesus.[114] Judas ought to be presented as the ultimately leading figure of the disciples, since the sacrificial logic would prevail in Christian circles.

On the other hand, however, Judas is the perpetrator of Jesus' betrayal and the instrument of a blood sacrifice, and therefore he could not have been truly rehabilitated and saved. He must be denigrated and persecuted and grieve deeply. So, in the new apocryphal Gospel, Judas is the traitor harassed by the twelve disciples and cursed by the other generations, but simultaneously the figure which will rule over his persecutors![115] The stone rejected by the architects of the sacrificial interpretation becomes its cornerstone. By implying that Judas is as much the villain as the leading star of the disciples, the absurdity of the apostolic soteriology is exposed.

Interpreting the *Gospel of Judas* as a *reductio ad absurdum* of the sacrificial theory could make sense of several features of this work, beginning from the central role played in it by Judas. Although this figure seems to be utterly irrelevant in the soteriological perspective of the author, Judas is here a main character precisely because he is *nolens volens* so important in the proto-orthodox view, which the work

---

similar examples in the history of interpretation, see e.g. Meiser 2004, 167–169. For general problems involved in the assessment of Judas, see Klauck 1987; Klassen 1996; Cane 2005.

[114] See John 13:27.

[115] This paradoxical reversal is clearly expressed in *Gos. Jud.* TC 46,19–23.

aims at discrediting and subverting.[116] If Jesus is frequently depicted as freely ascending to the divine realm during his life, it is so because it clearly establishes the insignificance of his death. The frequent reference to the misuse of Jesus' name is found because a core message of the Gospel is that the apostolic churches have thoroughly misunderstood Jesus and—through the sacrificial cult, particularly baptism and Eucharist—betrayed his name. References to stars and astral determinism abound, probably because the author wants to remark that Judas hands Jesus over because he is determined by his star. His behaviour is to be understood only in the light of Saklas' blood nature, not in the light of the true God's will.

Through this lens one of the most disturbing features of the text could become more understandable. Judas' ambiguity might simultaneously reflect, highlight and deconstruct the ambiguous Judas of the New Testament and mainstream Christianity. Judas' ambivalence in the new apocryphal text may have been an intended feature. While certain Gnostics are not concerned with Jesus' death, Judas' ambivalence in the *Gospel of Judas* would aim to stress further the *aporetic* nature of the sacrificial theory that focused on Jesus' death in order to explain the salvation of humankind. According to the dualistic perspective of the author of the *Gospel of Judas*, not everyone is saved, and the holy generation is saved already and independently of Jesus' death.[117] So ambiguity in this Gospel might hint at the author's view of mainstream Christianity, at the untenable nature of the proto-orthodox view.[118]

If these reflections are plausible, the conspicuous presence of laughter in the *Gospel of Judas* could be understood even better. Whereas in the *Apocryphon of John* laughter seems always to be a smile which shows the complicity between a master and his (true) disciple, and

---

[116] This would mean that the image of Judas in the new apocryphal writing is not to be considered rigorously a truly 'Gnostic' view of Judas, but rather, so to say, the proto-orthodox (sacrificial) view of Judas taken—according to some Gnostics—to its logical conclusion.

[117] References to the impossibility of salvation for many pervade *Gos. Jud.*

[118] It is as though the author were saying to his adversaries: "You, who condemn Judas as a betrayer, are following him, inasmuch as you re-enact Jesus' death in your sacrificial cult and your atonement theology. So, Judas is your patron saint. You identify with Judas, you are the betrayer. And if you answer that this is absurd, I will tell you even more: absurd is your heritage. You, who make Jesus' death a necessary and salvific act, justify Judas as a key figure in the salvation of mankind. Whatever your reasoning, you are desperately misguided and wrong".

in *The Apocalypse of Peter* or *The Second Treatise of the Great Seth* Jesus laughs in a disparaging way at obviously alien people who are the powers responsible for crucifixion, in the *Gospel of Judas* Jesus has as interlocutors people apparently very close to him who are his own disciples(!), but at the same time deeply alienated from him because they are incapable of salvation, and even have a different god(!). In fact, his main interlocutor is Judas, who is his (favorite?) disciple. At the same time, he is the one who is ultimately responsible for the crucifixion. If the author's intention was to stress inconsistency in the figure of Judas as transmitted in Christian tradition (and thereby in the sacrificial view of Jesus' death) he could have chosen laughter (a gesture which can be interpreted as friendly or dismissive) as a further device allowing the display of ambivalence. But ambiguity does not mean undecidability. In the *Gospel of Judas*, an apparently friendly and joyful laughter is ultimately intended to make a mockery of the views held by the so-called apostolic churches.

"YOU WILL BECOME THE THIRTEENTH"

The Identity of Judas in the *Gospel of Judas*

Kevin Sullivan

In the *Gospel of Judas* 44:18–21 we read, "And when Jesus heard this, he [Jesus] laughed and said to him [Judas], 'You thirteenth *daimon*, why do you try so hard?'"[1] The translation of the Greek word, *daimon*, has been debated by scholars, and both "spirit" and "demon" have been suggested.[2] The difference between these two translations in modern English is clearly significant, because the choice of one over the other affects the interpretation of the gospel as a whole, i.e., choosing "spirit" supports a more positive portrayal of Judas, while choosing "demon," supports a more negative one.

In the initial publication, the National Geographic team opted to translate *daimon* as "spirit."[3] They note that this interpretation is largely based on Platonic thought about the nature of the *daimones*. As Marvin Meyer observes, "…it is evident that Sethian texts, including the *Gospel of Judas*, embraced themes derived from Plato, and in their own way they worked them into their own understanding of the divine and the universe."[4] Plato's description of the *daimones* in *The Symposium* 202e–203a is similar to the function of angels in Jewish and Christian literature of later centuries.

> "He's a great spirit, Socrates. Everything spiritual, you see, is in between god and mortal." "What is their function?" I asked. "They [*daimones*] are messengers who shuttle back and forth between the two, conveying

---

[1] Translations (and Coptic texts) taken from Kasser et al. 2007 unless there is a note showing my preference for the translation of DeConick 2007.

[2] Pagels-King 2007, 115, translate *daimon* as "god."

[3] Kasser 2006a, 31. In the n. 74, the translators offer "thirteenth demon" as an alternative and provide the Coptic via Greek, *daimon*. They then explain, "Judas is thirteenth because he is the disciple excluded from the circle of the twelve, and he is a demon (or daemon) because his true identity is spiritual. Compare tales of Socrates and his *daimon* or *daimonion* in Plato *Symposium* 202e–203a." In Kasser et al. 2007, the more neutral "*daimon*" was left in the text with no explanatory note (p. 207). In Kasser et al. 2008, "*daimon*" was again left in the text with an explanatory note (pp. 39–40, n. 76).

[4] Kasser et al. 2008, 146.

prayer and sacrifice from men to gods, while to men they bring commands from the gods and gifts in return for sacrifices. Being in the
middle of the two, they round out the whole and bind fast the all to all.
Through them all divination passes, through them the art of priests in
sacrifice and ritual, in enchantment, prophecy, and sorcery. Gods do not
mix with men; they mingle and converse with us through spirits instead,
whether we are awake or asleep. He who is wise in any of these ways is
a man of the spirit, but he who is wise in any other way, in a profession
or any manual work, is merely a mechanic. These spirits are many and
various, then, and one of them is Love."[5]

From this description, there seems little doubt that Platonic traditions
influenced Jewish, Christian and even Gnostic speculation about the
spiritual realm (e.g., angels and demons) for centuries, and insomuch
as it did, it represents an important background to the *Gospel of Judas*.
Nevertheless, it is important to recognize the significant chronological
gap between *The Symposium* and the *Gospel of Judas*—a period of no
less than 500 years. A great deal happened to the understanding of the
word *daimon* over that period, including its incorporation into the
New Testament writings, writings which, as we will see, clearly had
a significant and more direct impact upon the *Gospel of Judas*.[6] One
of the changes that occurred was that within in the early Christian
writings, *daimon* took on a decidedly negative connotation. Gone was
the neutrality found in Plato's description. Angels took on the role
of intermediaries between God and humans.[7] Demons (*daimon*) and
all its cognate words are seen as malevolent powers in early Christian
writings.[8] The more immediate and appropriate lens for interpreting
daimon would seem to be the canonical tradition, since the *Gospel of
Judas* is clearly aware of it.

   Summing up her analysis, DeConick states, "There is no doubt in
my mind whatsoever that for a Gnostic Christian text like the *Gospel
of Judas*, to call Judas "Thirteenth *Daimon*" is to identify him with a
demon and an Archon, not a benevolent spirit..."[9] Later she adds,
"So the question for me is not *whether* Judas is a demon, but *what*

---

   [5] Cooper-Hutchinson 1997, 485–486.
   [6] On the use of *daimon* in the NT, see Foerster 1964, 16–19. For detailed discussion
of the meaning of *daimon* in various contexts, see Foerster 1964, 1–20, and Toorn
et al. 1995, 445–455.
   [7] Sullivan 2004, 16–35.
   [8] DeConick 2007, 50.
   [9] DeConick 2007, 50–51.

demon he is."[10] She then convincingly makes the case for understanding Judas as being linked with Ialdabaoth, citing important parallels
in the Sethian texts: the *Holy Book of the Great Invisible Spirit*, the
Apocalypse of Adam, and *Zostrianos*, to outline how the "thirteenth"
is linked to Ialdabaoth.[11] The question then becomes: how can Judas
be both a disciple of Jesus and a demon?

It is not difficult to imagine Judas as evil or demonic. In the canonical tradition, Judas is vilified for his betrayal of Jesus.[12] In Luke and
John, Satan actually enters into or seems to control the actions of
Judas. Luke 22:3 says, "Then Satan entered into Judas called Iscariot,
who was of the number of the twelve," and John 13:2 states, "And during supper, when the devil had already put it into the heart of Judas
Iscariot, Simon's son, to betray him."[13] In these instances we have the
malevolent power actually entering into or taking over Judas. Again,
this is not surprising or difficult to suppose.

What is more difficult to grasp is how Judas, who is the main character of the gospel, and as some scholars have suggested, is even the
"hero" of the gospel, how can he be a demon?[14] A scene from the
Gospel of Mark involving an exchange between the preeminent disciple, Peter, and Jesus may be of some help to us in understanding
what is happening between Judas and Jesus in the *Gospel of Judas*. In
fact, Mark 8–9 is a particularly valuable heuristic tool for understanding the *Gospel of Judas* as a whole, and it may even have been a literary
source for the author of the *Gospel of Judas*.

Parallels with the Gospel of Mark

Scholars working on the *Gospel of Judas* immediately recognized the
affinity that it had with the Synoptic Tradition.[15] While the *Gospel of*

---

[10] DeConick 2007, 109.
[11] DeConick 2007, 110–113.
[12] E.g., Matt 27:3–10.
[13] Cf. also Acts 5:3.
[14] I believe that calling Judas a "hero" is inaccurate, but the title persists among
some scholars. See for example the review of DeConick 2007 by Witetschek (2008, 5).
[15] Robinson 2006, 208–210 has argued for the dependence of the *Gos. Jud.* upon
Luke-Acts. I agree with the observations that Robinson makes regarding the apparent relationship between the *Gos. Jud.* and Luke-Acts, so I reference his work here.
However, I want to stress two points. First, if the majority of scholars who support the
Two-Source Hypothesis are correct, then Luke is dependent upon Mark, and second,

Judas is very different from the gospels found in the canonical tradition, its main storyline is entirely and carefully framed to fit directly
into the traditional canonical storyline about Judas.[16] A close examination of the *Gospel of Judas* demonstrates significant parallels with the
narrative of Mark 8–9 in particular. To begin, there is a strong parallel
of one of the opening scenes of the *Gospel of Judas* with a passage in
the Gospel of Mark. The *Gospel of Judas* 35:2–20 states:

> "[Let] any one of you who is [strong enough] among human beings,
> bring out the perfect human, and stand before my face." And they all
> said, "We have the strength." But their spirits [*pneuma*] could not find
> the courage to stand before [him], except for Judas Iscariot. He was able
> to stand before him, but he could not look him in the eyes, and he turned
> his face away. Judas [said] to him, "I know who you are and where you
> have come from. You have come from the immortal aeon of Barbelo.
> And I am not worthy to utter the name of the one who has sent you."

We can compare this with a scene from Mark 8:27–33:

> And Jesus went on with his disciples, to the villages of Caesarea Philippi;
> and on the way he asked his disciples, "Who do people say that I am?"
> And they told him, "John the Baptist; and others say, Elijah; and others
> one of the prophets." And he asked them, "But who do you say that I
> am?" Peter answered him, "You are the Christ." And he charged them
> to tell no one about him. And he began to teach them that the Son of
> man must suffer many things, and be rejected by the elders and the chief
> priests and the scribes, and be killed, and after three days rise again. And
> he said this plainly. And Peter took him, and began to rebuke him. But
> turning and seeing his disciples, he rebuked Peter, and said, "Get behind
> me, Satan! For, you are not on the side of God, but of men."[17]

At first glance, there may not appear to be a strong parallel between
these two passages, but I have argued elsewhere that in the Gospel of
Mark, Peter's confession that Jesus is "the Christ"—which is followed
closely by Jesus' rebuke of Peter, "Get behind me, Satan"—is made
because Peter is himself inhabited by Satan.[18] Thus, the striking paral-

---

even if Judas is dependent upon Luke, that does not preclude Judas' use of Mark also.
So, while the author of the *Gos. Jud.* may have been reading and using Luke-Acts, it
is also clear that there is strong influence on his overall narrative from the Mark 8–9,
as I argue below.

[16] E.g. *Gos. Jud.* 33:1–18.

[17] Unless otherwise noted, all translations from the Bible come from the *RSV*. Cf.
Matt 16:13–23, Luke 9:18–22, and *Gos. Thom.* 13.

[18] Forthcoming in the journal, *Henoch*, under the title: "Spiritual Inhabitation in
the Gospel of Mark: A Reconsideration of Mark 8:33."

lel between these two passages is that both Peter and Judas have their knowledge, because they are closely affiliated with the spiritual world. Peter, because he is inhabited by Satan, and Judas, because he is in the process of becoming the thirteenth demon.

In my analysis of the Gospel of Mark, I argue that Mark understands human beings to be vessels in which spirits can reside. Because it seems that for Mark both benign and malevolent spirits can reside in a human being, I chose the term "spiritual inhabitation" to describe this phenomenon. Jesus too is such a being. The Holy Spirit enters Jesus at the baptism and stays with him throughout his career until the crucifixion.[19]

What first suggested this reading of Mark 8 to me was that Peter's confession, which is usually seen as a watershed moment in Mark, is followed so closely by Jesus' rebuke of Peter, "Get behind me, Satan."[20] The language of "rebuke," which is also a technical term used in exorcisms, also suggested that something was unusual about this pericope.[21] More importantly, though, this idea developed for me as an extension of the well-known observation that in the Gospel of Mark—except for Peter and the centurion at the end of the gospel—only demons and unclean spirits know Jesus' true identity.[22] Not even the disciples who are with Jesus really know who he is, and I argue that Peter too gets it wrong and only knows what he knows because he is "spiritually inhabited" by Satan. I also suggest that both Matthew and Luke, who are arguably the first interpreters of this Markan tradition, are rather uncomfortable with the "Satan" saying as it stands in Mark, so Matthew redacts it, adding the explanatory phrase, "you are a hindrance to me," and Luke omits it altogether.[23] If this is correct, then it would not be difficult for the author of the *Gospel of Judas* to exploit such a reading. That Matthew and Luke make significant changes to

---

[19] Mark 1:10, 12; 15:39. Cf. also Gal 2:20.

[20] Regarding Mark 8:27–33 as a crucial point in the gospel, see Dinkler 1971, 169–185. On p. 172, he goes as far as to say "It is no longer necessary to discuss the fact that for the evangelist a high point and a turning-point are intended in the structure of his book in the pericope Mark 8: 27–9:1..."

[21] Kee 1967, 232–246.

[22] In Mark's gospel the only entities besides the demons and unclean spirits who identify Jesus correctly are: the voice from heaven (chapter 1 and chapter 8), Peter (chapter 8), the centurion (chapter 15). I argue that except for the centurion, everyone who correctly identifies Jesus is strongly connected to the spiritual realm (either through the Holy Spirit or through demons). See also DeConick 2007, 106–108.

[23] Matt 16:13–23; Luke 9:18–22.

Mark's story only highlights the fact that such a misreading was at least possible, and they likely sought to avoid it in their own gospels.

Judas' words to Jesus in 35:15–18, "I know who you are and where you have come from. You have come from the immortal aeon of Barbelo. And I am not worthy to utter the name of the one who has sent you," are particularly striking in light of several parallels with Mark. In Mark 1:23–24 Jesus confronts an unclean spirit who says to him, "What have you to do with us, Jesus of Nazareth? Have you come to destroy us? I know who you are, the Holy One of God."[24] Similarly, in Mark 3:11, we see "And whenever the unclean spirits beheld him, they fell down before him and cried out, 'You are the Son of God.'" We should note especially the statement in Mark 5:7 when Jesus interacts with the demon, Legion, who, without introduction, says to Jesus, "What have you to do with me, Jesus, Son of the Most High God? I adjure you by God, do not torment me." All of these bear a striking resemblance to Judas' statement and are at least suggestive of similarities between the Gospels of Mark and Judas in their understanding of the way in which people come to know the identity of Jesus, i.e., through a close association with the spiritual realm, and in this case, the demonic.

Can we be confident the idea of spiritual inhabitation that we see in the Gospel of Mark exists in the mind of the author of the *Gospel of Judas*? It appears that we can. First, the overall Gnostic cosmology is one in which the divine 'spark' resides within each human being, so already there is some intermingling of the two kinds of substance, human and divine. Second, specific examples from the *Gospel of Judas* suggest it. Judas 34:24–26 says, "Why has this agitation led (you) to anger? Your god who is within you and [his---]." Again, in 37:18–19, "they [the disciples] each were troubled in [their] spirit [*pneuma*]." Also, in 53:17–20, "'Does the human spirit die?' Jesus said, 'In this way God ordered Michael to give spirits [*pneuma*] to them as a loan, so that they might offer service.'" More importantly, as we saw in the passage above, the disciples have spirits in them.

While the "spirits" of the other disciples are not able to stand before Jesus, Judas is able. How is Judas able to stand up and how does he know the identity of Jesus? Because Judas is the "thirteenth demon"? He is closely linked with a power that is privy to Jesus' true identity

---

[24] Cf. Luke 4:34.

as an aeon of the upper realm of heaven. The question then is not whether the followers of Jesus have a spirit in them but which spirit is in them and what that spirit empowers them to do.

The disciples (including Judas) also appear to have a correspondence with other heavenly bodies, namely the stars.[25] Jesus says to the disciples, "Stop struggling with me. Each of you has his own star…"[26] Pearson has studied the four passages in the *Gospel of Judas* that refer to Judas' star.[27] His analysis suggests that, "Judas' star is in no way a positive thing."[28] This is certainly implied in statements such as 45:13–14, "Your star has led you astray, Judas," and "I am not laughing [at] you but at the error of the stars."[29] The human-star correspondence only strengthens the idea of Judas' link to the divine realm, especially when Jesus says to Judas, "Your star will ru[le] over the [thir]teenth Aeon," "your star has ascended"—perhaps an indication that Judas' destiny is accomplished such that he can, "Lift up [his] eyes and look at the cloud and the light within it, and the stars surrounding it. And the star that leads the way is your star."[30] Judas clearly has a destiny that is closely linked with the spiritual realm and one that will eventually take him there to rule.

How can Judas, a disciple of Jesus who appears to have special knowledge about Jesus' identity also be a demon? It comes down to understanding the way in which ancient authors (and in particular that authors of the Gospels of Mark and Judas) conceived of the human person. The individual had both physical and spiritual components. The spiritual component could and did regularly impact individuals' thoughts and actions. In the case of Peter in the Gospel of Mark, his thoughts allowed Satan to control his words. With Judas in the *Gospel of Judas* it is different. He is already connected with the demonic realm,

---

[25] For a detailed discussion of this, see DeConick's contribution to this volume.

[26] *Gos. Jud.* 42:6–8. The idea of "struggling with Jesus" in 42:6–8 and 44:7 is similar to the canonical tradition of Jesus against Satan, but instead of direct confrontation (e.g., exorcisms) we have Jesus' knowledge of the cosmos pitted against Judas' misunderstanding as offered to him by his star, a star which Jesus knows has "led him astray" (45:13–14). This is strikingly similar to Peter's being "…not on the side of God, but of men' (Mark 8:33). On stars in the *Gospel of Judas*, see Denzey Lewis contribution to this volume.

[27] See Pearson's contribution to this volume.

[28] See Pearson's contribution to this volume.

[29] *Gos. Jud.* 45:13–14; 55:15–17, cf. 45:24–46:2.

[30] *Gos. Jud.* 55:10–11; 56:23 (here I prefer the translation by DeConick 2007 to Kasser et al. 2007: "your star has passed by"); 57:16–20.

but does not yet realize it. Jesus, recognizing that Judas is special, takes him aside, tells him special revelation, but also makes clear that Judas will not be pleased with what he learns, because he ultimately finds out that he only reason that he has this knowledge is because his true nature is that of the demon, Ialdabaoth.

BECOMING THE THIRTEENTH DEMON

When does Judas become the thirteenth demon? Is he a demon from the outset? Is he demon-possessed while he is speaking to Jesus (like Peter in the Gospel of Mark), and if so, why does Jesus not exorcise the demon? Or, does Judas become a demon sometime later?

About Judas DeConick states, "So Judas, with the nickname 'Thirteenth Demon,' is linked to Ialdabaoth and his realm. Judas is either a man operating under the influence of the demon Ialdabaoth, or Ialdabaoth's equivalent, perhaps understood to replace him or even merge with him one day."[31] I believe that both of these statements are correct. The *Gospel of Judas* presents us with Judas who throughout the Gospel comes to understand fully his true identity (as the thirteenth demon) and the earthly role that comes with that identity, namely, his sacrifice of Jesus. Thus, Judas is a man whose destiny of betrayal is predetermined, but he is also a man who, because of his demonic nature and dark destiny, possesses special insight into the identity of Jesus.

We have already considered an important passage above, "And when Jesus heard this, he laughed and said to him, 'You thirteenth daimon, why do you try so hard?'"[32] I suggest that we read that passage alongside the other passage that mentions Judas' identity as the thirteenth. When Judas asks Jesus in 46:16–18, "What is the advantage that I have received, since you have separated me from that generation?"[33] Jesus responds, "You will become [Coptic: ⲕⲛⲁϣⲱⲡⲉ] the thirteenth, and you will be cursed by the other generations, and you will come to rule over them."[34] I suggest that we place significant emphasis on this passage for the interpretation of the *Gospel of Judas*

---

[31] DeConick 2007, 113.
[32] *Gos. Jud.* 44:18–21.
[33] Here I prefer the translation by DeConick 2007 to Kasser et al. 2007: "set me apart for."
[34] *Gos. Jud.* 46:19–24.

as a whole. A great deal of information is divulged by Jesus in these few lines. First, and perhaps most importantly, Judas "will become" (Future I tense) the thirteenth.[35] When will Judas become the thirteenth and also what does that mean? Jesus offers further explanation as to what it will mean to become the thirteenth: (1) Judas will be cursed by other generations, and (2) he will rule over them. How is it that one can become both accursed and yet rule over those who curse him? The answer is that Judas will become the demon, Ialdabaoth who he will rule over the fallen world where the disciples are trapped in the failed worship of a lesser god.

My interpretation is that Jesus is telling Judas that he *will* become the thirteenth demon. It is a future event, but within the *Gospel of Judas*, Judas is literally in the process of "becoming" the thirteenth demon. So, I end this relatively brief section with the same question that I began it: when will Judas ultimately become the thirteenth demon? The answer, I believe, lies once again in another of the strong parallels between the Gospel of Mark and the *Gospel of Judas*.

THE TRANSFIGURATION OF JUDAS

In the Gospel of Mark, almost immediately after the discussion of Jesus identity, we find the Transfiguration story.[36] In another parallel between the gospels of Mark and Judas, we find what many scholars believe to be a Transfiguration scene near the end of the *Gospel of Judas*:

> "Look, you [Judas] have been told everything. Lift up your eyes and look at the cloud and the light within it, and the stars surrounding it. And the star that leads the way is your star." So Judas lifted up his eyes and saw the luminous cloud, and he entered it. Those standing on the ground heard a voice coming from the cloud saying [...].[37]

There are some significant similarities with the Gospel of Mark 9:2–8:[38]

> And after six days Jesus took with him Peter and James and John, and led them up a high mountain apart by themselves; and he was transfigured

---

[35] Crum 1939, 577–580.
[36] Mark 8:27–33; Mark 9:2–8. These stories are only separated by the teaching on discipleship (Mark 8:34–9:1).
[37] *Gos. Jud.* 57:15–26; cf. 47:14.
[38] Cf. 2 Cor 3:18; *1 En.* 14:8.

before them, and his garments became glistening, intensely white, as no fuller on earth could bleach them. And there appeared to them Elijah with Moses; and they were talking to Jesus. And Peter said to Jesus, "Master, it is well that we are here; let us make three booths, one for you and one for Moses and one for Elijah." He did not know what to say, for they were exceedingly afraid. And a cloud overshadowed them, and a voice came out of the cloud, "This is my beloved Son; listen to him." And suddenly looking around they no longer saw any one with them but Jesus only.

Both scenes contain a cloud and also a voice from the cloud. Unfortunately, though, the content of what the voice from heaven says is lost from the *Gospel of Judas*. In Mark, the voice is God's, confirming the identity of Jesus. We should note that in the Transfiguration story from the Synoptic Gospels, while Jesus is transformed by the experience (and he clearly seems to be in the presence of God), once it is over, Jesus remains in the same place and then returns to his ministry. The change to his countenance seems to be of limited duration. The event then was not primarily about ascent or transformation, but about *identity*. The voice from heaven confirms what was stated in Mark 1:11 that Jesus is God's son. This confirmation comes shortly after Peter's proclamation and the beginning of the three Son of Man predictions. Jesus does not depart from the disciples at this point. In fact, he has the disciples with him to witness the event.

Two Biblical scenes resonate with these scenes.[39] The first is Moses on Sinai in Exodus 24:18, "And Moses entered the cloud, and went up on the mountain. And Moses was on the mountain forty days and forty nights." Moses is brought into the presence of God, but what is not entirely clear is whether Moses ascended into heaven or merely ascended Sinai and met God there. What is clear is that after his experience, Moses was changed, "the people of Israel saw the face of Moses, that the skin of Moses' face shone; and Moses would put the veil upon his face again, until he went in to speak with him."[40] Moses, though, returns to live amongst the Israelites until his death. Moses is clearly transformed by the event and his identity as Lawgiver is girded by the

---

[39] There are obviously many more examples pertaining to luminous clouds in the literature (e.g., from the Hebrew Bible: Exod 13:21, 16:10, 19:9, 24:15–18, 33:9; 1 Kings 18:44–45, from the New Testament: Mark 14:62, 1 Thess 4:17, Rev 11:12, 14:14–16, and from the *NHL, Ep. Pet. Phil.* 134.9–16) that may be relevant, so for this discussion, I have limited the references to those where people enter the cloud.

[40] Exod 34:35.

fact that he shines from his interaction with God, but he otherwise remains on earth to carry on his role and leader and lawgiver.

The second passage is the Transfiguration story from Luke 9:29–36:

> And as he was praying, the appearance of his countenance was altered, and his raiment became dazzling white. And behold, two men talked with him, Moses and Elijah, who appeared in glory and spoke of his departure, which he was to accomplish at Jerusalem. Now Peter and those who were with him were heavy with sleep, and when they wakened they saw his glory and the two men who stood with him. And as the men were parting from him, Peter said to Jesus, "Master, it is well that we are here; let us make three booths, one for you and one for Moses and one for Elijah"—not knowing what he said. As he said this, a cloud came and overshadowed them; and they were afraid as they entered the cloud. And a voice came out of the cloud, saying, "This is my Son, my Chosen; listen to him!" And when the voice had spoken, Jesus was found alone. And they kept silence and told no one in those days anything of what they had seen.

What is intriguing here is v. 34. The text as it stands is ambiguous as to whether it is Jesus, Moses and Elijah who actually enter the cloud, or if it is Peter, John and James. Most interpreters believe that the ones entering the cloud can only refer to Jesus and his companions and not the disciples. That Jesus does enter the cloud is rather significant, however.[41] In this Transfiguration story Jesus does not disappear or leave the disciples. His appearance is transformed and his identity is confirmed by the voice, presumably for the benefit of those seeing him, so that they might come to accept his true identity, but Jesus then returns to the physical world and continues on his path to the cross. Conversely, the *Gospel of Judas* is explicit that Jesus comes and goes from the disciples.[42] From these two Biblical examples, entry into a luminous cloud does not transport the entrant and its effects, while obvious, are also limited.

Given the similarities with the Transfiguration story from the canonical gospels, as well as the links with the Gospel of Mark, I suggest that this scene in the *Gospel of Judas* is a Transfiguration, but not a Transfiguration of Jesus, because that would connect him with the lesser god. Instead, it is a Transfiguration of Judas.

---

[41] For an example of a standard interpretation of this passage, see Marshall 1978, 387.

[42] *Gos. Jud.* e.g., 33:19–20, 36:11–17.

WHO ENTERS THE CLOUD?

A number of scholars have argued that the one entering the cloud is Jesus. Birger Pearson has offered an intriguing interpretation of this scene.[43] Pearson's argument has two key considerations: a point of Coptic grammar and the context of the passage. Pearson notes that in this passage there are three clauses: (1) Judas lifted up his eyes, (2) he saw the luminous cloud, and (3) he entered it. He notes that the use of asyndeton binds clauses together. Since the third clause is not connected by a conjunction, he surmises that the subject is likely Jesus. From the context, Pearson notes that Judas has been told he will "sacrifice the man who bears Jesus," and also that Judas' star "leads the way" in 57:19–29, just as Judas leads the armed crowd who come to arrest Jesus (in Luke 22:47). These two observations combined lead Pearson to conclude that, "...Jesus, i.e., his real self, enters a luminous cloud and disappears. The corporeal Jesus remains to be handed over by Judas in the narrative that follows."[44]

As to his first consideration, the grammatical point regarding asyndeton is valid, but the more immediate referent is Judas. In the extant text, Jesus has not been mentioned by name for some time. An asyndeton expresses closer linkage than the use of the conjunction, but it does necessarily mean that the same subject cannot be meant, so this grammatical argument does not preclude the possibility that the referent is Judas.[45] As for the contextual argument, I am not entirely convinced by the idea that Jesus' spirit departs in the luminous cloud to heaven before Judas' sacrifice, while his body remains for the crucifixion. True, Jesus does come and go from the disciples, but when pressed where he has gone, Jesus says to other generations.[46] If Jesus can simply depart, this would not fit well with the overall Sethian Gnostic cosmology, wherein the spirit that resides in Judas is released upon his crucifixion.[47]

---

[43] See Pearson's contribution to this volume.

[44] See Pearson's contribution to this volume.

[45] On asyndeton, see Layton 2000, 182–183.

[46] Gos. Jud. 36:17–18.

[47] Kasser et al. 2008, note 151 regarding Gos. Jud. 56:17–20: "The man who bears Jesus is the fleshly body that bears the true spiritual self of Jesus. The inner, spiritual person of Jesus will not actually die, but will be liberated. See the Second Discourse of Great Seth, the Nag Hammadi Revelation of Peter, Basilides in Irenaeus of Lyon 1.24.4, etc."

About the luminous cloud passage, Gesine Schenke Robinson writes:

> Since there is no clear antecedent, this pronoun can refer back to either Judas or to Jesus. It is hardly conceivable; however, that Judas would ascend and then immediately reappear in order to betray Jesus in the next scene. The Gnostic Jesus, on the other hand, does freely ascend to his divine realm and reappears at will throughout the text. Moreover, the following sentence clearly alludes to the voice from the cloud in the transfiguration of Jesus (see Mark 9:7, Matthew 17:5, and Luke 9:34–35). In the same way Judas, like everybody else, hears the voice from the cloud, but it is Jesus who enters it. This is surely also an allusion to the New Testament, where the cloud lifts Jesus up an carries him into heaven (see Luke 24:5 and Acts 1:9), even though in the *Gospel of Judas* this event takes place before the betrayal and crucifixion.[48]

Earlier in the same paper, though, Robinson notes, "Since the *Gospel of Judas* is a Gnostic text, everything said and done by any character involved has to be interpreted in a Gnostic way, not seen through a New Testament lens." This makes her interpretation of the scene of the luminous cloud somewhat problematic, given that she is reading it entirely through a New Testament lens.[49] It is hard to have it both ways, choosing when to use a Gnostic lens and when to use a New Testament one.

Granted the Gnostic Jesus does "freely ascend to his divine realm and reappears at will," but is the luminous cloud a pre-requisite of Jesus' appearances to the disciples? When Jesus comes and goes throughout the rest of the Gospel, he seems to do so without mention of a luminous cloud. This may be something of an argument from silence, but this departure is not nearly as significant as it is in Acts 1:9, where Jesus ascends after his resurrection. Why the cloud only in the final departure if he can come and go freely?

Schenke Robinson offers *A Book of Allogenes* 62:9–63:1 in support of the idea that it is Jesus who enters the cloud. The passage says:

> And while I was saying this, look, a luminous cloud surrounded [me]. I could not stare at the light around it, the way it was shining. And I heard a word from the cloud and the light, and it shone over me, saying, "O Allogenes, the sound of your prayer has been heard, and I have been

---

[48] Schenke Robinson 2008b, 162–163.
[49] Schenke Robinson 2008b, 156.

sent here to you to tell you the good news, before you leave [this place], so that you may hear...[50]

About this passage Schenke Robinson writes, "Yet there Allogenes decidedly does not enter the cloud; he can barely look at it, but only hears the voice above him: 'And I heard a word from the cloud and the light, and it shone upon me' (*BookAllog* 62, 15–18)."[51] While she may be correct, the scenes are not altogether similar, since Allogenes states that he could not look at the cloud, but ironically, Jesus tells Judas to look into the cloud and he does! One wonders if this difference is significant in that Judas is indeed able to handle looking at the cloud and his star is in it. Is this because the cloud is indeed for or related directly to him and his fate? Additionally, while we have the words from the cloud in Allogenes, they are missing from the manuscript of Judas. I think that this parallel is somewhat ambiguous. So, while I agree that it is important to consider a parallel such as this from the same codex, I do not think that it necessarily precludes the possibility that Judas enters the cloud.

Both Pearson and Schenke Robinson make important observations, but they are not without doubt. I want to suggest alternatively that it is Judas who enters the cloud. I am neither first nor alone in suggesting that it is Judas who enters the luminous cloud. For example, speaking about the last tractate of Codex Tchacos, the so-called *Book of Allogenes*, Marvin Meyer says, "Jesus is Seth the Stranger incarnated as the Christ savior, and in the person of Allogenes he faces temptations by Satan and experiences transfiguration in a luminous cloud—just as Judas is transfigured in a luminous cloud in the *Gospel of Judas* (57–58)."[52]

WHY A TRANSFIGURATION OF JUDAS?

Why would the *Gospel of Judas* portray Judas as entering the cloud? His entry in the cloud and Transfiguration into his demonic self would represent the culmination of all Jesus' predictions as well as act as an identity marker for Judas. His entry would complete his identifica-

---

[50] Kasser et al. 2007, 267.
[51] See Schenke Robinson's contribution to this volume.
[52] Meyer, in Kasser et al. 2008, 140–141.

tion with the thirteenth demon, Ialdabaoth. This represents a turning point in the *Gospel of Judas* just as Jesus' Transfiguration does in the Gospel of Mark. After each one's identity is confirmed, they are ready to undertake the final steps in their respective destinies. In Mark, Jesus heads to Jerusalem for his Passion and crucifixion, while in the *Gospel of Judas*, Judas heads to the priests to betray Jesus in the gospel's final scene.

As DeConick has argued, the luminous cloud is strongly connected with Ialdabaoth.[53] This seems especially true given that Judas' star leads the way. As evidence for this connection, DeConick makes reference to an important parallel from another Sethian text, the *Apocryphon of John* 10:7–20:

> And when she [Sophia] saw (the consequences of) her desire, it changed into a form of a lion-faced serpent. And its eyes were like lightning fires which flash. She cast it away from her, outside that place, that no one of the immortal ones might see it, for she had created it in ignorance. And she surrounded it with a luminous cloud, and she placed a throne in the middle of the cloud that no one might see it except the Holy Spirit who is called the mother of the living. And she called his name Yaldabaoth.[54]

In this fundamental Sethian text, the cloud is created by Ialdabaoth's mother, Sophia, to hide him. Inside that cloud, she places a throne, from which he comes to rule over the Archons. Based on this parallel, we might even be able to go further and suppose that the scene in the Gospel of Judas is meant to be a reference to the enthronement of Judas as Ialdabaoth, but while intriguing, this is also somewhat speculative.

Of a possible Transfiguration of Judas, Schenke Robinson writes:

> The notion of a "transfiguration of Judas" touted with much fanfare is recently modified by the idea of Judas obtaining a vision of the divine. Yet the initial interpretation still brought forth another novel idea: Judas did not enter a luminous cloud, but the cloud of Nebro and Saklas that brings him to his archontic place. A mention of his return is conveniently

---

[53] DeConick 2007, 118–120.

[54] Trans.: Robinson 1990a, 110. Cf. the reference to Noah being put into a luminous cloud in the *Ap. John* II,1 28,34–29,15.

expected in the lacunae, and the "light" in the cloud is simply imagined away.[55]

Based on the gospel story a "Transfiguration" of Judas would not require a "return" as Schenke Robinson suggests. Jesus does not "return" from the Transfiguration, because he never leaves. The Transfiguration represents a fusion or boundary crossing, but it does not necessarily have to have a "return." This is especially clear in the example from the Gospel of Luke. All three enter the cloud, and presumably Moses and Elijah return, but Jesus remains. Thus, Judas too be could transfigured, allowing him to see his true identity as Ialdabaoth and yet could remain on earth to then move to the next and final scene where he betrays Jesus and the gospel ends.

Further, Schenke Robinson says, "The [final] scene is abbreviated because it no longer has any real function. What happens between Jesus' departure and the crucifixion of the corporeal body that carried him becomes extraneous."[56] This, I believe, is not entirely correct. The crucifixion is suggested in the *Gospel of Judas* 56:17, "Yet you will do worse than all of them. For the man that clothes me, you will sacrifice him."[57] However, the crucifixion is not actually mentioned in the *Gospel of Judas*, and I think that this is significant. The reason that the final scene is abbreviated is because it is Judas' betrayal that is most important. It is the fulfillment of his destiny. Schenke Robinson highlights "Jesus' departure" and the "Crucifixion" but neither of these is actually mentioned in the *Gospel of Judas*' narrative. I suggest instead that Judas is transfigured into the demon Ialdabaoth, so that he can see his destiny and carry out the betrayal of Jesus, a betrayal which is also the last line of the gospel, "And Judas received money and handed him over to them [the scribes/Jewish authorities]."[58] Judas' "sacrifice" is not the crucifixion, but his very handing over of Jesus.

In the Transfiguration story of Jesus in the Synoptic Gospels, Jesus does not disappear or leave the disciples. His appearance is transformed, presumably for the benefit of those seeing him, so that they might come to accept his true identity, but Jesus then returns to

---

[55] See Schenke Robinson's contribution to this volume. Therein she cites Brankaer-Bethge 2007, 370–371 as her referent.

[56] See Schenke Robinson's contribution to this volume.

[57] Here I prefer the translation by DeConick 2007 to Kasser et al. 2007: "you will exceed all of them."

[58] *Gos. Jud.* 58:24–26.

the world and continues on his path to the cross. This is significant, because those seeing Jesus enter the cloud either must bifurcate Jesus, such that his human body continues with the spirit gone (Pearson), or they must explain the cloud by reference to resurrection stories that are out of the chronological and narrative sequence of the gospels (Robinson). My interpretation instead suggests that Judas enters the cloud, is transfigured into his true identity, Ialdabaoth, so that "after being told everything," by Jesus, Judas comes to realize his true identity, and then fulfills his destiny in the final lines of the gospel by handing over Jesus. He then takes his place, the place (the throne?) created for him in the luminous cloud. This is a complete overturning of the Transfiguration story. Such an overturning fits well with the overall picture of the *Gospel of Judas* as parody of the canonical tradition that DeConick has offered. The author of the *Gospel of Judas* choose to parody the Transfiguration scene from the canonical tradition, because as part of the orthodox tradition it directly links Jesus with what, for the Gnostics, is the lesser god!

A TRANSFIGURATION PARODY?

It is striking that the main narrative of the *Gospel of Judas*, while chronologically set at the end of Jesus ministry, has such significant parallels with a crucial point in the Gospel of Mark.[59] It parallels both the question of Jesus identity, and the Transfiguration Story.[60] Certainly, the author of Judas knew well the canonical traditions, but I would go further to suggest that he was also aware of Mark in its literary form and that he used it in shaping his Gospel.

The majority of the "Gospel" of Judas is Judas' story—the story of his transformation from disciple of Jesus to betrayer of Jesus and ultimately into the demon Ialdabaoth. The gospel culminates in Judas being transfigured, where his true identity, and also his destiny, are thus revealed to him in the penultimate scene before his betrayal of Jesus in the final scene. Judas thus fulfills both of Jesus' key predictions:

---

[59] *Gos. Jud.* 33:3–6. On the chronology of the *Gos. Jud.*, see Grosso's contribution to this volume.

[60] Mark 8:27–32; 9:2–8.

(1) that Judas will do worse than all of them by sacrificing the man that clothes him, and (2) that he will become the thirteenth.[61]

Interestingly for a "gospel," there is little or no discussion about the identity of Jesus, nor does Jesus have a salvific role to play. Instead, as in many other Sethian texts, Jesus is a revealer, and he acts in many ways as an *angelus interpres*, appearing to the disciples when necessary and giving Judas special revelation. The *Gospel of Judas*, rather than being any type of "good news" about Judas (or Jesus, for that matter), is instead really about knowledge.[62] The two main questions that are answered in Jesus' revelations are: (1) who is Judas, and (2) what is the nature of the cosmos?

Who is Judas? Judas begins as a follower of Jesus like the other disciples. Each one of the disciples has a "spirit" but that spirit is not sufficiently strong to let the disciple stand before Jesus and identify him.[63] Judas, however, has special knowledge of Jesus' identity, and for this Jesus singles him out to receive further gnosis.[64] What is revealed to him, however, is not "good news" to Judas.[65] Judas is a demon, but not just any demon. He is the thirteenth demon, Ialdabaoth, and it seems likely that it was because of his *daimon*, as opposed to his spirit, that Judas was able to know who Jesus really is. Judas will also become the "thirteenth" disciple, who will ultimately be replaced, because of his betrayal of Jesus.[66] Judas resists this destiny throughout, but by the end of the gospel when Jesus says, "Look you have been told everything," I think Judas then enters the luminous cloud and is transfigured into his true demonic nature, so that he accepts his fate, carring out the betrayal of Jesus and assuming his place as ruler over the Archons.[67] He does not need to "return" from some ascent.

What is the nature of the cosmos? The Highest God is not the god worshipped by the disciples. He is the god from whom Judas knows that Jesus has come and to which Jesus ultimately returns. Jesus literally laughs at the worship of the twelve who fail to see that they worship a lesser god, not the higher God from whom he comes to them. The disciples are trapped in a generation who will never know

---

[61] *Gos. Jud.* 56:17–21; 46:19–24.
[62] E.g., *Gos. Jud.* 33:15–18.
[63] *Gos. Jud.* 35:2–10.
[64] *Gos. Jud.* 35:15–20; 35:23–36:4.
[65] *Gos. Jud.* 35:24–27.
[66] *Gos. Jud.* 44:20–21; 36:1–4.
[67] *Gos. Jud.* 46:5–6; 57:15; 58:25–26; 46:7.

the Higher God, and Judas will come to rule over them. His betrayal for "some money" shows how tragically rooted he still is in the fallen world of Saklas and Ialdabaoth.

Lastly, why was the *Gospel of Judas* written? As DeConick has correctly observed, the *Gospel of Judas* is a parody of the orthodoxy and its failed means of worship. Ironically, the worst of the orthodox disciples, Judas, is the one who is the closest to knowing the realities of the cosmos and Jesus' true identity. Judas, so vilified in the orthodox tradition is no hero for the Sethian Gnostics either.[68] Instead, he is a kind of tragic figure whose destiny is set from the beginning. His knowledge of Jesus' identity makes him unique among the disciples (just as it did Peter in the canonical gospels) and ultimately sets him apart as a "thirteenth" disciple, but the darker meaning of his identity as "thirteenth" is that he is linked with and fast-becoming the thirteenth demon, Ialdabaoth.[69] In their parody of the orthodox gospels, a demon sets in motion the sacrifice that the orthodoxy finds so important. The *Gospel of Judas* also parodies the Transfiguration story not by having Jesus transfigured, but instead by having Judas Transfigured into the same lesser god to whom the disciples sacrifice. Judas takes on his identity as the thirteenth demon to carry out the next action in the gospel, and also its last. It is the one foretold by Jesus—the betrayal and ultimate sacrifice of Jesus. It is that sacrifice, not Jesus' entry into the cloud that releases him to return to the immortal aeon.

---

[68] For more on Sethian Traditions, see Turner 2001. See also his contribution to this volume.

[69] *Gos. Jud.* 36:1–4.

JUDAS' ANGER AND THE PERFECT HUMAN

Ismo Dunderberg

Anger and "the perfect human" are prominent issues in the *Gospel of Judas*, although they have attracted relatively little attention in the quite numerous studies published on this text thus far.[1] The two topics are intertwined, as can already be seen at the beginning of the *Gospel of Judas*. Here it is told how the disciples become angry at Jesus because he scoffs at their Jewish customs, and how he, in response, challenges them to bring forth "the perfect human." Yet all of them fail miserably—except for Judas Iscariot, but even he is unable look Jesus in the eye.[2]

Because this passage implies that Judas, unlike the other disciples, did not succumb to anger, it strikes one as odd that also he is described later in the text as being filled with anger. After having revealed Judas' role as the traitor, Jesus says to him, "Your horn is already raised up, you are filled with rage (ⲁⲩⲱ ⲡⲉⲕϭⲱⲛⲧ ⲁϥⲙⲟⲩϩ), your star passed by, and your heart became [violent (?)]."[3] Notably, Judas is described here, not as *becoming* angry, but already *being* angry. This point in the story marks a remarkable shift in the role of Judas, who has been portrayed earlier in the *Gospel of Judas* as the only disciple who understood the true identity of Jesus and whom Jesus taught in private. While the other disciples lost their temper as soon as Jesus laughed at them, Judas did not show even the slightest irritation when Jesus laughed and heaped scorn at him by calling him as "the thirteenth *daimōn*."[4] Why then is

---

[1] While Pagels and King describe the *author* of Gos. Jud. as being angry, there is little discussion even in their book as to what this author says about anger; cf. Pagels-King 2007, xiii–xvi, 49–50, 99–100. For their analysis of "the perfect human," which is the most comprehensive one thus far, see ibid. 78–81, 131–132.

[2] Gos. Jud. TC 34–35.

[3] Gos. Jud. TC 56,21–24.

[4] Gos. Jud. TC 34,2, 18–22; 44,18–21. The latter is one of the key passages for the "revisionist interpretation" (for the proponents, see n. 5 below), which maintains that the word *daimōn* here means "demon." This interpretation is possible but not entirely certain; in any case, the Judas of Gos. Jud. is quite different from the demons described in the NT. It is true that, in the synoptic gospels, demons know who Jesus is (e.g., Mark 1:24; 3:11; 5:7), but it is hardly adequate to compare their "confessions" to that of Judas in Gos. Jud. TC 35,15–20. Jesus teaches none of the demons mentioned in

Judas now suddenly described as irascible,[5] and how does this description fit in with his role as the only disciple who was able to bring forth the perfect human and whom Jesus chose to teach in private?

In addressing this dilemma, I seek to strike a balance between the positive and negative features of the portrayal of Judas in the *Gospel of Judas*. I have not yet been able to fully convince myself of the validity of "the revisionist interpretation,"[6] according to which, even in his own gospel, Judas is portrayed as a negative, demonic being, or as "poor Judas."[7] This interpretation has corrected the initial interpretation of the text on a number of points, but the major problem with this reading is that its proponents have not yet seriously addressed any of the undeniably *positive* features attached to Judas in the *Gospel of Judas*. One of the questions the revisionists have thus far left unanswered is this: if Judas is *only* a demon according to this gospel, how is it possible that the text also implies that the perfect human resides in him?

What the present debate between the two conflicting interpretations of the *Gospel of Judas* has demonstrated is, rather, that the text's portrait of Judas is much more complex and ambiguous than was originally thought. One of the ambiguities in the gospel's picture of Judas is the tension between the perfect human residing in him and his assent to anger. The implicit ambiguity between these two features becomes increasingly visible, if we take a look at ancient moral philosophy. The use of the concept of "the perfect human" was widespread among phi-

---

the synoptic gospels in private, as he is said to have taught Judas in *Gos. Jud.* in consequence of the latter's confession, and nothing similar to the praise of Judas' intellectual capacity in *Gos. Jud.* ("since Jesus knew that Judas thought something else that was exalted…," *Gos. Jud.* TC 35,19–23) is said of any of the demons mentioned in the synoptic gospels.

[5] DeConick insists that Judas already protests against Jesus' teaching in *Gos. Jud.* TC 46,5–7. What she designates as "the corrected translation" of this passage runs as follows: "Teacher, enough! At no time may my seed control the Archons!"; cf. DeConick 2007, 53. This is one of the points where I think DeConick offers a plausible *alternative* to the editors' reading of the text, but I still fail to see convincing proof that the latter is based upon an entirely wrong or impossible interpretation of the text, as DeConick claims.

[6] This term was first used in this connection in Meyer 2008a which offers an extended response to DeConick's sweeping critique of the National Geographic editorial team's interpretation.

[7] This interpretation was first proposed by Painchaud 2006, 553–68. It has been now adopted by a number of other specialists; cf., e.g., DeConick 2007; Pearson in this volume; Robinson 2008a; Thomassen 2008b, 143–66, esp. 165–66; Turner 2008a.

losophers, but their prevalent view was that the perfect human is completely free of anger.[8] Judas, thus, would not qualify for the group of
perfect humans according to ancient philosophers. However, because
the perfect human was considered to be a very rare species, the philosophers also devised subtle categorizations for those on lower steps
of the morality ladder. My suggestion is that taking these theories into
account help us move beyond the polarized hero-or-villain debate
about the figure of Judas in the *Gospel of Judas*.

AN ARISTOTELIAN VIEW OF ANGER IN THE *GOSPEL OF JUDAS*?

Let me begin my analysis with briefly discussing one theory which I
initially considered a possible solution but which I finally discarded.
My initial working hypothesis was that the author of the *Gospel of Judas*
thought that anger can, in certain situations, be justified. Although this
position can already be found in Plato,[9] it was in antiquity usually
associated with Aristotle and his followers.[10] Cicero maintains that the
Peripatetics "have many words of praise for anger … and they say that
one who does not know how to become angry cannot be considered a
real man."[11] Seneca calls Aristotle "the defender of anger"[12] and attributes to him the teaching that "anger is necessary, and no battle can
be won without it."[13] In addition, in the light of Gerard Luttikhuizen's
recent attempt to trace Aristotelian ideas in the *Apocryphon of John*,[14]
with which the cosmogonic myth in the *Gospel of Judas* has much in

---

[8] Cf., e.g., Cicero, *Tusc.* 3.19: "The wise person never gets angry" (trans. Graves 2002, 11).

[9] Plato, *Leg.* 731b; cf. Harris 2001, 92. Harris points out that Plato speaks here of "*thumos*-anger" instead of "*orge*-anger." The former indicates "anger in appropri-ate form and quantity," (ibid.), while the latter usually denotes "rage," uncontrolled outbursts of anger.

[10] For Aristotle's position on anger, see Harris 2001, 94–98. Epicureans did not completely disapprove of anger, either; for the distinction between natural anger (ὀργή) and empty anger (θυμός) in Philodemus, see Tsouna 2007, 213–41, esp. 221–22, 226. Tsouna concludes (226) that, for Philodemus, "natural anger is the anger of the wise man, whereas rage is the anger of the fool."

[11] Cicero, *Tusc.* 4.43 (trans. Graves 2002).

[12] Seneca, *Ira* 3.3.1.

[13] Seneca, *Ira* 1.9.2; cf. 1.17.1. This position was also accepted for certain situa-tions by some early Christians, including the author of Mark, who did not hesitate to describe even Jesus as being angry (Mark 3:5), and Evagrius, who regarded anger as permissible in the battle against Satan and demons (cf. Louth 2007).

[14] Luttikhuizen 2006, 29–43.

common, it did not seem too far-fetched to assume that Aristotelian philosophy had some impact upon the *Gospel of Judas* as well.

My initial "Aristotelian" hypothesis was that while the other disciples got angry for the wrong reasons in the *Gospel of Judas*, Judas becomes angry for the right reason and for a purpose. The author of the gospel obviously took for granted that Jesus had to be sacrificed and that Judas had a part to play in the events leading to the death of Jesus. Consequently, if the author was familiar with the Aristotelian theory of anger, he might have thought that Judas *had to get angry* to be able to do what he was supposed to do, or that anger supplied Judas with the *courage* he needed to betray Jesus.[15]

However, it was for a number of reasons that I finally dismissed this explanation. First, both Plato and Aristotle consider anger acceptable only insofar as it is needed to prevent or correct *injustice*. This aspect does not seem to be present in the *Gospel of Judas*. It does not refer to any injustice Judas tried to prevent or correct by betraying Jesus, and it would be difficult to see what such injustice could be. Rather, the author of the gospel probably regarded what Judas did to Jesus as injustice. As the revisionists have pointed out, the sacrificial language used in this connection ("you will sacrifice the man carrying me") supports their interpretation since sacrifices, especially human sacrifices, are strictly condemned earlier in the *Gospel of Judas*.[16]

Second, I believe the revisionist interpretation is correct in maintaining that the role played by the stars in the *Gospel of Judas* is entirely negative. It can be thus inferred from the fact that Judas's anger is mentioned in connection with his star ("you are filled with rage, your star passed by," 56:23) that the author of this gospel disapproved of anger as well. Thirdly, and most importantly, Sethians, by whose views the author of the *Gospel of Judas* was obviously inspired,[17] preferred the Stoic ideal of *apatheia*, the complete freedom from emotions, to

---

[15] For the link Aristotle posited between anger ("*thumos*-anger") and courage, see *Eth. nic.* 3.8.1116b23–1117a9; cf. Harris 2001, 98.

[16] *Gos. Jud.* TC 38–41.

[17] Whereas most interpreters agree upon seeing *Gos. Jud.* as a Sethian text, John Turner, the leading expert on Sethianism, combats this view (cf. his article in this volume). There is, however, no denying a number of close affinities between the cosmic myth related in *Gos. Jud.* and those in Sethian texts. The question raised by Turner as to whether the author of *Gos. Jud.* truly understood Sethian thought (in the way Turner suggests it should be understood) or simply picked up some Sethian mythologoumena does not need to concern us here.

the Aristotelian ideal of *metriopatheia*, which allows for a moderate display of emotions in certain situations and for right purposes.[18] This general picture makes *metriopatheia* an unlikely option for the author of the *Gospel of Judas*. This all leaves little room for any positive value attached to anger in the *Gospel of Judas*.

THE PERFECT HUMAN AND "MORALITY LADDERS" IN ANTIQUITY

While the Aristotelian theory of anger does not seem to offer a credible solution to the ambiguity posed by the coexistence of the perfect human and anger in Judas, ancient theories of moral progress may help us understand this feature. The concept of "the perfect human" looms large in the works of ancient philosophers as indicating the ultimate goal of moral progress. The most prominent characteristic of the perfect human is freedom: this figure is free of emotions, of all worldly concerns, and, as Seneca summarizes, of the fear of humans and gods.[19] What is more, the perfect human no longer needs instruction because this person intuitively knows what to do in each particular situation.[20]

For ancient philosophers, "the perfect human" was first and foremost a pedagogical device. This concept lends an expression to the ideal human condition that set for those aiming at perfection a high standard, so high that it was in fact practically impossible to achieve. Nonetheless, we learn from Plutarch how this ideal served one's moral improvement. According to him, the progressing one should constantly compare himself "with the deeds and conduct of the good and perfect man (ἀνδρός ἀγαθοῦ καὶ τελείου)." One concrete way

---

[18] The ideal of *metriopatheia* was also shared by those who did not belong to the Peripatetics. Though not being an Aristotelian in a strict sense, Plutarch recommends *metriopatheia* as opposed to the Stoic *apatheia*, arguing that "when the vice of those who are making progress is transformed into more suitable emotions (εἰς ἐπιεικέστερα πάθη μεθισταμένη), it is being gradually plotted out" (Plutarch, *Virt. prof.* 84a [Babbitt 1927, 400–457]).

[19] Seneca, *Ep.* 75.

[20] This was obviously a matter of debate. The Epicurean philosopher Philodemus argued that even the sages should submit themselves to frank criticism, which clearly presupposes that "they too are fallible and feel the need to confess" (Tsouna 2007, 215).

of doing this, Plutarch says, is to pose to oneself the question, "what would have Plato done in this case?"[21]

It was universally agreed that the vast majority of humankind—in fact, all humans except for the very rare exceptions which can be counted with the fingers of one hand (Socrates, Diogenes, and, for Philo, Moses)—will never advance far enough to reach this goal. Early Christians made the ideal more accessible: Paul says that he discusses the wisdom of God "among the perfect" (ἐν τοῖς τελείοις, 1 Cor 2:6–7), thus claiming this elevated designation both for himself and for some of his fellow believers. The authors of Hebrews and the *Book of Thomas* (see below) bear witness to a similar tendency of making perfection available to a wider group of people than was traditionally assumed.

Since "the perfect human" was usually considered a rarity, moral philosophers also classified other humans into different moral categories, including those who have already come very close to perfection; those who are still further away from virtue; and those who show complete disdain for virtue. In what follows, I take examples of such divisions from Seneca, Philo, and the *Book of Thomas*, before I discuss more thoroughly the idea of the perfect human in the *Apocryphon of John*. In this way, I wish to demonstrate that the idea of the morality ladder, where reaching the level of the perfect human was the ultimate step, was well known and had impact on the views of Jewish and early Christian teachers, including Sethians. The list could be easily expanded; others have demonstrated the relevance of these distinctions to the interpretation of the Gospel of John, Paul, and Pastoral Epistles,[22] and I have suggested elsewhere that the Valentinian tripartite anthropology can be interpreted against the same background.[23]

---

[21] Plutarch, *Virt. prof.*, 85a; for the same advice in a different context, see Epictetus, *Gnom.* 33.12: "When you are about to meet somebody, in particular when it is one of those men who are held in very high esteem, propose to yourself the question, "What would Socrates or Zeno have done under these circumstances?" (trans. Oldfather 1925).

[22] For Paul, see Engberg-Pedersen 2000, 70–72; esp. 55; for Philo and John, see Buch-Hansen 2007, esp. 140–45. As for the Pastoral Epistles, I refer to the commentary by Saarinen 2008, in which their moral philosophical is thoroughly discussed from this perspective.

[23] Cf. Dunderberg 2008, 250n7.

The Stoics drew a strict distinction between the sage, that is, one who is truly wise, and all other humans, whom they considered to be merely "fools."[24] Nevertheless, there are different varieties of the fools according to the Stoic analysis; some fools have made more progress in virtue than others.[25] Seneca divides the progressing ones into three groups.[26] Closest to perfection are those "who have already laid aside all passions and vices, who have learned what things are to be embraced." These people are those who are already in the know; what is still lacking is that their endurance has not yet been tested in practice. Seneca, however, is confident that it is impossible for those who have reached this level to regress—even though they themselves do not yet know this. The second group consists of those who have already left behind the worst diseases and passions of the soul but who are, unlike the first group, still in danger of slipping back. Those in the third division have become free of the worst vices but not of all vices. One of the especially persistent vices is anger. Seneca says of those belonging to the third group: "For example, they have escaped avarice, but they still feel anger; they no longer are troubled by sensual desire, but they are still troubled by ambition; they have no desire any more, but they are still afraid…. They scorn death, but they are still in terror of pain." In addition to the three divisions among those who make progress described by Seneca, there are, by implication, two other groups at the opposite ends of the morality ladder: the truly wise at its uppermost end and, at its lowest level, those who are not at all concerned with progress in virtue.

In his treatise *On Anger*, Seneca offers numerous examples of the little things that drive people crazy; these include "manuscripts written in too small a script," and "a less honourable place at the table."[27] Yet Seneca is not only poking fun at petty people getting angry too easily,

---

[24] For a polemical (and therefore probably biased) description of the Stoic dichotomy, see Plutarch, *Virt. prof.*, 76a. Plutarch says that the absolute distinction the Stoics drew between the sage and all other humans "would assign all humankind to a general category of badness with the single exception of the absolutely perfect human." This description may be correct in principle, but in light of Seneca's more subtle analysis of this issue (see above), it offers a too rigid picture of the Stoics' teaching.

[25] Cf. Engberg-Pedersen 2004, 47–72.

[26] Seneca, *Ep.* 75.

[27] Seneca, *Ira* 2.26.2; 3.37.4. Descriptions of little irritating things were obviously stock materials for moral philosophers; for a similar account, see Plutarch, *Cohib. ira* 454a (Helmbold 1939, 92–159).

but his point is to argue that "anger is contrary to nature."[28] He reso-
lutely disapproves of all arguments seeking to justify anger and angry
behavior in some situations,[29] for example, in battle, after one's father
is murdered, and when people need to be punished.[30] Seneca even
maintains, chillingly, that when Romans fathers ("we") drown their
children with disabilities, "it is not anger but reason that separates
the harmful from the sound."[31] The only concession Seneca is ready
to make is that orators sometimes need to *pretend* to be angry when
delivering their speeches.[32] But, Seneca says, "anger in itself has nothing of the strong or the heroic, but shallow minds are affected by it."[33]
Hence it is a matter of course that the truly wise person neither feels
nor shows anger, not even towards sinners (*peccantibus*).[34] Seneca's
recipe for anger management is simple: "not to fall in anger, and in
anger to do no wrong."[35] He also recommends suspension of revenge
("the best cure for anger is waiting"), and withdrawal, instructing that
"if someone strikes you, step back."[36]

In his work *Allegorical Interpretation*, Philo coins a distinctly Jewish
version of the morality ladder. The fact that *all* groups in his classification are described as being obedient to the law, for one reason or
another, shows that this model applies to Jews only. Philo's model,
thus, leaves out at least one more group, that is, those who do not pay
heed to the law at all (either pagans or non-practicing Jews).

Philo divides the law-abiding Jews into three moral categories on
the basis of why they obey the law and of what kind of instruction
they need.[37] First, there is the perfect human who "possesses the virtue
instinctively," and, consequently, needs no instruction at all. The oppo-

---

[28] Seneca, *Ira* 1.6.5.
[29] Cf. also Cicero, *Tusc.* 4.48–54.
[30] Seneca, *Ira* 1.9.2; 1.12.1; 1.16.6.
[31] Seneca, *Ira* 1.15.2.
[32] Seneca, *Ira* 2.17.2. The same argument is made by Cicero in *Tusc.* 4.55. The usefulness of simulated anger was more widely accepted: the Epicurean Philodemus maintains that teachers can, for the purposes of philosophical therapy, feign anger (Philodemus, *Ir.* 34.18–20; cf. Tsouna 2007, 225).
[33] Seneca, *Ira* 2.10.6.
[34] Seneca, *Ira* 2.10.6.
[35] Seneca, *Ira* 2.18.1.
[36] Seneca, *Ira* 3.12.4; 2.34.5. These remedies were also common coin for representa-tives of different schools of thought; for similar advice to delay revenge, see Plutarch, *Control of Anger*, 455e.
[37] Philo, *Alleg. Interp.* 1.91–94. Buch-Hansen 2007 sees in the relevant passage of Philo's *Alleg. Interpr.* references to no less than five different groups of people.

site pole is represented by the bad human, who needs both injunction and prohibition. Between the two poles is the human being "in the middle," who is neither bad nor truly good. Those belonging to this group do not need prohibition or injunction, like the bad ones, but like children they need exhortation and teaching.[38]

Philo's division between the perfect human and those "in the middle" is linked with his allegorical interpretation of the Book of Genesis. He considers the perfect human to be identical with the original idea of the human being, who was created in the image of God. Philo identifies the human being in the middle, who is neither good nor bad, with the earthly Adam, who is knowledgeable (being able "to give names and to understand") but who remains ignorant of himself and his own nature. This is a noteworthy point since a very similar idea recurs in the *Apocryphon of John* (see below).

In another part of the *Allegorical Interpretation*, Philo distinguishes three different categories of human beings, which are the perfect one, the progressing one (ὁ προκόπτων), and the lover of delight (ὁ φιλήδονος).[39] The perfect human, represented by Moses, is one whose only concern is to achieve *apatheia*, the complete lack of harmful emotions. This person "has cut off all passions." The progressing one, represented by Aaron, aims at and is content with *metriopatheia*. This person is waging war against passions but not with the same devotion as the perfect one.[40] One more difference between the perfect human and the progressing one is that the former has received perfection as a gift from God and therefore practices it "free from toil," while the progressing one "acquires virtue by toil" and therefore lacks full perfection.[41]

Just as for Seneca, anger (θυμός) is for Philo a crucial point where the difference between the perfect human and the progressing one

---

[38] My reading of this passage in Philo is that "the good" (σπουδαῖος) is identical with "the perfect" and "the child" is identical with "the human being in the middle." Buch-Hansen 2007 regards both groups as separate categories; hence her division into five instead of three categories.

[39] Philo, *Alleg. Interp.* 3.159. The division forms the core of his lengthy explanation of Genesis 3:14 (3.114–181). Philo associates the "breast" and "belly" mentioned in this verse with the Platonic theory of the tripartite soul consisting of a reason-part, a *thumos*-part (which Philo identies with "breast") and a desiring (*epithumētikon*) part, which Philo identifies with "belly"—as denoting both the abdomen and the belly as the sources of desire.

[40] Philo, *Alleg. Interp.* 3.129, 131–34.

[41] Philo, *Alleg. Interp.* 3.135.

becomes visible. While the irascible element (θυμικόν) was a *necessary* part of Plato's tripartite soul, Philo maintains that Moses, the perfect human, was able to cut out this part of his soul, "loving not moderation (μετριοπαθεία) but only the complete lack of passion (ἀπαθεία)."[42] While the progressing one is unable to cut out the soul's irascible part completely, he or she can control it with reason.[43] It is "reason, the clarity of reason, and the truth of reason" that provides an antidote to the *thumos*-anger.[44]

What is striking here is that, in principle, Philo agrees with the Stoic ideal that the perfect human is completely free of emotions. He allots the Platonic virtue of controlling the lower parts of the soul with reason only to the progressing one, that is, to those on a lower step of the morality ladder. In practice, however, Philo is mainly concerned with these less virtuous people. Moses the perfect man, who has laid off passion entirely and practices virtue instinctively ("free from toil"), is an exceptional figure; most (or all) other people belong either to the progressing ones or to the lovers of pleasure. While the perfect human is able to renounce pleasures completely, "the progressing one" must be content with "welcoming simple and unavoidable delight, while declining what is excessive."[45] While the perfect human declines the pleasures of the belly "spontaneously and unbidden" and practices virtue instinctively, the progressing one "acts under orders" and needs guidance in practicing virtue.[46] The fact that Philo described the persons "in the middle" in the same way shows that those "in the middle" and the progressing ones are two different designations for the same, intermediate category between the truly good and evil persons.

Finally, according to Philo, even the perfect human is unable to get entirely free from the constraints of the body. Although the perfect sage has become completely free from *thumos*-anger, nature (φύσις)

---

[42] Philo, *Alleg. Interp.* 3.129, cf. 3.131. Philo supports his view of Moses by referring to Lev 8:29, according to which "Moses took away the breast part (τὸ στηθύνιον ἀφεῖλεν)" of a ram he sacrificed. Philo explains this verse as meaning that Moses seized "the breast, that is, *thumos*, and took it away and cut it off" (*Alleg. Interp.* 3.129–130).

[43] Philo, *Alleg. Interp.* 3.128. As evidence for this idea, Philo refers to the tablet put on Aaron's breast (Exod 28:30); this tablet contained "urim and tummim," which in the Greek translation used by Philo were understood as meaning "explanation and truth."

[44] Philo, *Alleg. Interp.* 3.124.

[45] Philo, *Alleg. Interp.* 3.140.

[46] Philo, *Alleg. Interp.* 3.144.

still requires necessary amounts of food and drink for the preservation of his or her body.[47] As will be seen below, a similar restricton appears in the *Apocryphon of John*'s description of the perfect ones.

The divisions of humankind in the *Book of Thomas* are basically similar to Seneca's and Philo's. This text presents itself as a teaching addressed to "the perfect" both in the main body of the text and in the full title given at the end of this document: "The Book of Thomas: The Contender Writing to the Perfect."[48] The teachings of Jesus in this text, however, are mostly addressed to those who have *not* yet reached "the greatness of perfection."[49] The author of this text makes a distinction between the perfect and an inferior group, the latter being called either "disciples" (ϩⲉⲛⲥⲃⲟⲩⲉⲓ) or "little children" (ϩⲉⲛⲕⲟⲩⲉⲓ).[50] It is striking that Thomas himself is placed in the *latter* group. Not only does he not understand visible and invisible things, but he also has difficulties in doing the right thing: "it is difficult," he admits, "to perform the truth before humans."[51]

Another related distinction in the *Book of Thomas* is that between the wise person (ⲣⲙⲛ̄ϩⲏⲧ) and the fool (ⲥⲟϭ).[52] The fools, who are also called "the blind" and "the ignorant," are utterly incapable of moral reasoning: they are unable to tell good from bad. The fire inside them supplies them with "an illusion of truth" and deceives them with beauty, pleasure and desire. The author of the *Book of Thomas* reckons thus with at least three kinds of people: the perfect, those who make progress ("the little children"), and the fools. While the "little children" show some inclination to progress and recognize their faults, the boundary between the wise person and the fool—also called "the ignorant" and "the blind"—is insurmountable: "…it is impossible for the wise person to dwell with a fool."[53]

---

[47] Philo, *Alleg. Interp.* 3.147. The pragmatic goal of Philo's argumentation becomes visible later in his treatise, where he teaches how it is possible to avoid excessive eating at banquets if one comes to these occasions well-prepared, that is, having reason as one's companion (*Alegl. Interp.* 3:155–159). This is meant as advice for the progressing ones, in which group Philo includes himself as well.

[48] *Thom. Cont.* NHC II,7, 140,10–11.

[49] *Thom. Cont.* NHC II,7, 138,35–36.

[50] *Thom. Cont.* NHC II,7, 138,35; 139,12.

[51] *Thom. Cont.* NHC II,7, 138,26–27.

[52] *Thom. Cont.* NHC II,7, 140,10–11.

[53] *Thom. Cont.* NHC II,7, 140,11. Turner has recently suggested that *Thom. Cont.* categorizes *four* groups of people, arguing that the text makes a further difference between benevolent fools (NHC II,7, 141,22–26) and those who scoff at the teachings

Although Thomas is Jesus' favorite disciple in the *Book of Thomas*,
Thomas is not placed in the group of the perfect ones but in the second group, consisting of those who still must be taught by Jesus. This
means that the idea in the *Gospel of Judas* that Judas does not belong
to the "holy generation," even though he is described as Jesus' closest
disciple, is not an entirely unique feature in early Christian revelation dialogues. Not only does Thomas fall outside the group of the
perfect in the *Book of Thomas*, but something similar also happens
to James in the *First Apocalypse of James*: Jesus accuses him of being
ignorant, and also points out that James, just like the other disciples
in the *Gospel of Judas*, has served the wrong god.[54] Like Thomas in the
Book of Thomas, James also readily confesses his lack of perfection:
"I am not perfect (ⲁⲛⲕ ⲟ[ⲩ]ⲧⲉⲗⲓⲟⲥ ⲁ[ⲛ]) in knowledge."[55] In fact,
it should not come as a surprise to us that the disciples in revelation
dialogues are often portrayed as being ignorant, confused, fearful and
anxious. A revelation dialogue between the Savior and a disciple who
is already perfect would be a contradiction in terms because the perfect one no longer needs instruction but knows the truth intuitively
and acts accordingly. Hence, it is only such imperfect disciples that are
in need of the instruction, encouragment and comfort Jesus offers in
these dialogues. What is more, Jesus is sometimes described as a harsh

---

of the Savior and his followers (143,21–23). Cf. Turner 2007, 599–633, esp. 605n8,
612–21. Turner further suggests that this division in *Thom. Cont.* roughly corresponds
to the Valentinian tripartite anthropology. The match, however, is not especially close
since the Valentinian distinction between "spiritual," "psychic" and "hylic" essences
and persons is absent in *Thom. Cont.* I would argue, rather, that the divisions used in
Thom. Cont. were borrowed from moral philosophy. As was mentioned above, "the
perfect" is customarily reserved for those very few persons (like Socrates and Diogenes
or Moses) who have reached the highest level on the morality ladder and no longer
need instruction but know and do the right thing instinctively. "Little children," and
related metaphors, like that of those who still need milk instead of solid food for their
nourishment, are used in the NT (1 Cor 3:2; Heb 5:12–14), in other early Christian
writings, and in other ancient texts for those who are at a less advanced stage in
their progress in virtue; cf. Denise Kimber Buell 1999, 127–129, with an informative
survey of Philo's views of education (with references to *Prob.* 160; *Prelim. Studies* 19;
Agriculture 9); and those of Clement of Alexandria (in *Strom.* 5.48.8–9). Finally, while
Turner points out a number of striking affinities between *Thom. Cont.* and Plato's
dialogues, a closer examination of the text's relationship to other Greco-Roman philosophical traditions would seem worthwhile. For example, the idea of "the winged soul"
(*Thom. Cont.* NHC II,7, 140) appears not only in Plato's *Phaedr.* (246c–249c), but
Plutarch also uses the metaphor of "the person provided with wings" for those whom
philosophy has helped advance in virtue (*Virt. prof.* 77b).

[54] *1 Apoc. Jas.* TC,2, 10,5–6; TC,2, 18.
[55] *1 Apoc. Jas.* TC,2, 15.12.

teacher in early Christian texts. Not only does he call Judas "the thir-teenth *daimōn*" in the *Gospel of Judas* and accuse Thomas and James of ignorance in the texts portraying these men as his favorite followers, but he also calls Peter "Satan" in the Gospel of Mark.[56] These texts take away some of the edge that has been seen in the designation of Judas as a "demon"—if this was really what the author of the *Gospel of Judas* intended by using the word *daimōn* for Judas.

THE SETHIAN PERFECT HUMAN: THE *APOCRYPHON OF JOHN*

The *Apocryphon of John* shows how crucial the concept of "the perfect human," which Jesus tries to tease out from his disciples in the *Gospel of Judas*, was in Sethian thought. In fact, the perfect human is one of the most dominant themes in the entire *Apocryphon of John*. At its outset, the perfect human is specified as one of the concepts that need to be taught to John by the Savior, and the implied audience of this text is defined as the offspring of the perfect human.[57] The creation myth told later in the text revolves largely around the question of what happens to the perfect human residing inside Adam, and the subse-quent exchange between Jesus and John about the fates of different groups of people begins with an account of the salvation of those who "will become perfect."

The perfect human is introduced in the *Apocryphon of John* as one of the eternal beings evolving in the divine realm and praising the invisible Spirit.[58] What lends a distinct characteristic to the perfect human being is the cognitive language used to describe it. The perfect human is said to have come into being by means of *revelation*, and this figure differs from other eternal beings insofar as only its praise of the invisible Spirit is fully described in the text. What is more, the perfect human is not only characterized by the right behavior—that of praise—in response to the divine revelation but also by the ability to formulate the right confession: "Because of you [the invisible Spirit] the All emerged and to you the All will return."

---

[56] Mark 8:33.
[57] *Apoc. John* BG,2, 22,8–10; 22,15–16.
[58] *Apoc. John* NHC II,1, 8–9.

The perfect human is called, variably in different versions of the *Apocryphon of John*, Adam, Adamas, and Pigera-Adamas.[59] All these names show an intrinsic link between this figure and the first human. After a story of how Yaldabaoth and his ilk came into being, the text in NHC II 14–15 relates how they were faced with a truly divine revelation, saw the image of the true God, created an essence (ϩⲩⲡⲟⲥⲧⲁⲥⲓⲥ)[60] imitating "the perfect first human," and gave to this creation the name "Adam." (The author of this story does not specify whether the lesser gods were instructed or knew instinctively that the perfect human being in the divine realm had a similar name.)

After this, a sequence of stories follow in which it is repeatedly described how the creators realize Adam's superior intelligence and either seek to destroy him in one way or another or to steal his divine essence. Yet he is time and again miraculously saved by the divine intervention and revelation. The creators first enwrap the image of the perfect human in a soul-body.[61] This body should probably be understood as consisting of a "fine" or "invisible matter" as distinct from the "heavy matter" (ϩⲩⲗⲏ) mentioned later in the text.[62]

In the long version of the *Apocryphon of John*, emotions form an essential part of the soul-body.[63] The author of this version literally demonizes the emotions by linking them with four primeval demons (Ephememphi, Yoko, Nenentophni and Blaomen). The underlying idea is certainly that it is demons who stir up humans' emotions, thus causing confusion and anxiety in them. At this point, the author offers a lengthy classification of emotions, which goes back to a Stoic source.[64] Notably, "anger" (ⲟⲣⲅⲏ) and "wrath" (ϭⲱⲛⲧ<— θυμός?) are mentioned in this passage as subcategories of desire.[65] This not only creates a connection with the theme of anger addressed in the *Gospel of Judas*, but it also paves the way for a subsequent discussion of differ-

---

[59] Adam (*Apoc. John* BG,2, 35,5), Adamas (*Apoc. John* NHC III,1, 13,4; Irenaeus, *Haer.* 1.29), and Pigera-Adamas (*Apoc. John* NHC II,1, 8,34–35).

[60] *Apoc. John* NHC II,1, 15,11–12.

[61] *Apoc. John* NHC II,1, 15–19.

[62] Cf. Schenke 1962, 65–66.

[63] *Apoc. John* NHC II,1, 18,14–31.

[64] The author of the long version not only follows the Stoic fourfold division of *pathos* (delight, desire, pain and fear), but also offers a detailed list of the subcategories of these four main emotions that is strikingly similar to that in Pseudo-Andronicus, *Pass.* 2–5 (for a similar list of definitions, see also Cicero, *Tusc.* 4.16–21); cf. Tardieu 1984, 313–316; Onuki 1989, 30–46.

[65] *Apoc. John* NHC II,1, 18,27.

ent groups of people and their salvation at the end of the *Apocryphon of John*.

As Yaldabaoth finally manages to make Adam alive by breathing the spirit of life into him, Adam proves to be both intelligent and virtuous. The long version of the *Apocryphon of John* plays with the idea of Adam's nakedness in paradise, explaining that he was "naked as regards evil" (ϥⲕⲏⲕ ⲁϩⲏⲩ ⲛ̄ⲧⲕⲁⲕⲓⲁ).[66] Adam's virtue, however, is now going to be tested in a number of different ways. The creators, jealous of his intelligence, first deport him to the region of "heavy matter" (ϩⲩⲗⲏ). Then they create for him the visible body, "the fetter of forgetfulness," and try to lull him into ignorance in the idleness of paradise.[67] Finally, by seducing Eve, the powers infect humankind with sexual desire.[68] This finally seems to do the trick: "Sexual intercourse has continued until now due to the head ruler."

The things in which the lesser gods enwrap the perfect human according to the *Apocryphon of John* are, thus, emotions, exile, body and sexual desire. It is probably no coincidence that the philosophers often discussed the same threats in connection with the perfect human. In their view, the ideal person neither yields to the tyranny of emotions, nor succumbs to bodily pain or pleasure, nor lets exile disturb her or his peace of mind,[69] nor is going to be "carried away" with or go mad because of sexual desire.[70] Instead, the perfect human remains constantly alert to all these threats, and controls his or her inner self in all situations by means of reason. In a similar manner, the *Apocryphon of John* describes how Adam is safeguarded in all his tribulations by his *cognitive capacity*: he has "the bright intelligence" (ⲧⲉⲡⲓⲛⲟⲓⲁ ⲙ̄ⲡⲟⲩⲟⲉⲓⲛ) inside him.[71] Despite their repeated attempts, the lesser gods prove unable to deprive Adam of this essence. His divine teacher instructs him about the descent and ascent of his offspring and awakens him from forgetfulness.[72]

---

[66] *Apoc. John* NHC II,1, 20,7. The reference to Genesis gets lost in Wisse and Waldstein's translation "he was free from wickedness." The allegory may be secondary because the short version affirms at this point (BG,2, 52,14–15; NHC III,1, 24,22–23) only that Adam "went to light."

[67] *Apoc. John* NHC II,1, 21.

[68] *Apoc. John* NHC II,1, 24.

[69] Cf. Epictetus, *Diatr.* 1.29.6–8; 3.22.22.

[70] Cf., e.g., Cicero, *Tusc.* 4.68–76.

[71] *Apoc. John* NHC II,1, 20,25.

[72] *Apoc. John* NHC II,1, 20 and 21, 23. The long version of *Apoc. John* identifies the divine teacher as Jesus; in the hymnic conclusion of this version, Jesus presents

The idea of the morality ladder appears in the *Apocryphon of John's* subsequent discussion of the different fates of humankind. No less than five divisions are outlined in this text. The uppermost group consists of those who "will…become perfect (ⲛⲥⲉϣⲱⲡⲉ ⲛ̄ⲧⲉⲗⲉⲓⲟⲥ)."[73] They are the ones who reclaim the lost innocence of Adam: just as he was naked as regards evil, they will be free from evil. Their state involves *apatheia* but this state is conditioned—just like in Philo—by their being in the body: the perfect ones are "not affected by anything, except for their being in the flesh, which they carry (ⲉⲓⲙⲏⲧⲓ ⲁⲧϩⲩⲡⲟⲥⲧⲁⲥⲓⲥ ⲟⲩⲁⲁⲧⲥ̄ ⲛ̄ⲧⲥⲁⲣⲝ ⲧⲁⲓ ⲉⲧⲟⲩϥⲟⲣⲉⲓ ⲙ̄ⲙⲟⲥ), waiting for the time when they will be met by the receivers. For they endure everything and bear everything."[74] Notably, still in the body, the perfect ones will already be "without rage and zeal."[75] This implies that one can in this life already become free from anger, which was given to the soul-prototype of the primeval human being along with other emotions before the creation of the visible body.

The second group in the *Apocryphon of John* consists of those who have received the Spirit but have not acted accordingly.[76] This group seems similar to Seneca's "second-best" group, which consisted of those who are almost there but whose endurance has not yet been truly tested, but the description of this group also recalls the way Thomas, in the *Book of Thomas*, was made to represent those who have not yet put their knowledge into practice. In the *Apocryphon of John*, Jesus generously promises that these underperformers will also "be completely saved" and "change," and promises that the Spirit saves them from being deceived. The idea seems to be here that once you have received the Spirit you *cannot* avoid making progress, though you may fall short of true perfection.

Thirdly, the *Apocryphon of John* reckons with the possibility of post-mortem improvement: the souls of those who have already "come away from their flesh" will gain strength and "flee from evil"—obvi-

---

himself as "the perfect providence," who awakens people from their deep sleep of ignorance (II,1, 30–31).

[73] *Apoc. John* NHC II,1, 25,23–26,7.

[74] The description of this group comes close to the way Jesus himself is described in the *Gos. Jud*—he keeps himself completely calm although he knows that "the man who carries" him is going to be sacrificed by Judas—and to the Stoic sage who has become completely free of emotions and other worldly concerns.

[75] *Apoc. John* NHC II 25:31.

[76] *Apoc. John* NHC II 26:2–22.

ously after their death. The subsequent fourth group consists of those who have been unable to resist the lures of the opposing spirit. The text promises post-mortem perfection even to these people. Thus, on the one hand, the *Apocryphon of John* insists that salvation is not possible without perfection, but, on the other, it grants the opportunity of becoming perfect to *all* humanity, either in this life or in the world to come.[77] There is one exception, though, and that is the apostates. The text gives no hope of salvation for "those who were in the know but turned away" but insists that they will receive eternal punishment.[78] It may emphasize the social threat posed by apostasy to a community that, even though the eschatological model cast in the *Apocryphon of John* is unusually inclusive, those in danger of falling away from the in-group are warned with the worst imaginable punishment.

The Picture of Judas in the *Gospel of Judas*

Concerning the picture drawn of Judas in the *Gospel of Judas*, the crucial facts are the following: (1) the perfect human resides in him; (2) he nonetheless belongs to the mortal humans who have no access to the holy generation; (3) he will be persecuted but finally vindicated as the ruler over the other disciples; (4) he succumbs to anger and is deceived by his star; and (5) Jesus calls him "the thirteenth *daimōn*."

The first conclusion from these facts seems quite clear to me: even if the term *daimōn* did mean "demon" in the *Gospel of Judas* (which is possible but not entirely clear), Judas cannot be *merely* a demon in this text since he also has access to the perfect human inside him. In Sethian theology, "the perfect human" stands for the divine essence deposited in all *humankind*—but not in demons! If the author of the *Gospel of Judas* wanted to claim that Judas was a demon, in whom the perfect human nevertheless could reside, the gospel would not be a "Sethian parody"[79] but a grave parody of Sethian theology itself.

---

[77] This is in keeping with *Apoc. John's* teaching that the divine power "will descend on every human being" (NHC II,1, 26,12–13par). This point is emphasized by Luttikhuizen 2006 (e.g. 30, 71, 91), who convincingly argues that the dwelling of the divine essene in all humans must be understood in terms of a potential which needs to be activated and which people realize to various degrees; cf. also Williams 1996, 196.

[78] *Apoc. John* NHC II,1 27:24–30.

[79] The designation "a Sethian parody" for *Gos. Jud.* does not seem particularly happy to me. I am in agreement with the interpretation, first suggested in the excellent short article by Iricinschi et al. 2006, 32–37, and now further elaborated by Pagels-King

A better explanation that, in my view, takes *all* the aforementioned facts into account would be that the perfect human and demons wage war against each other in Judas, just like they do in all other human beings. It remains unclear, however, how the story continues for Judas: does he overcome his anger or is it in the state of anger that he betrays Jesus? The puzzling account of the bright cloud, which Judas saw, does not help us resolve this problem in one way or another since it is far from clear *who* enters the cloud (Judas or Jesus?) and *which* luminous cloud is meant here.[80] Is it in the divine realm, or the place from which the lesser deities emerged?[81]

If we seek to place Judas on the morality ladders described above, it seems clear that his anger prevents him from qualifying for the uppermost group of the perfect humans. It is more difficult to say on which one of the lower steps he would belong. Following Seneca's classification, Judas could be placed in Group 3, consisting of those who have taken some initial steps in the direction of virtue but who still succumb to some grave passions, including anger. In Philo's three divisions (the perfect human, the progressing ones and the lovers of delight), Judas might belong to the second group, for those in this group are in need of instruction, just like Judas is, and have not yet cut off anger, which is obviously the case with Judas as well. If, however, Judas is thought of as betraying Jesus in the state of anger, which is possible but not certain, he falls short of the ideal of moderation, which Philo recommends to this group "in the middle."

As for early Christian revelation dialogues, Judas assumes the similar role of a man "in the middle" as do Thomas in the *Book of Thomas* and James in the *First Revelation of James*. Both texts assume, just like

---

2007, that the author of this gospel was seriously concerned about the eagerness with which some early Christians embraced the prospect of martyrdom. Antti Marjanen and I, independently of Pagels and King's work, argued for the same interpretation in our book, published in Finnish, on the Gos. Jud.; cf. Marjanen-Dunderberg 2006, 87–89. The label "parody" for Gos. Jud. is misleading because it blurs the seriousness of the author's tone throughout this text.

[80] *Gos. Jud.* 57:21–23.

[81] *Gos. Jud.* 47–48, 50; *Gos. Jud.* 51. The revisionist interpretation is alarmingly flexible at this point: if it is Judas who enters the cloud, then the cloud is that inhabitated by the inferior angels; if it is Jesus who enters, then the cloud is that in the divine realm; thus DeConick 2007, 119; Turner 2008a. Whoever enters the cloud and whichever cloud is intended, one thing is certain: the identification of the cloud cannot be decided on the basis of who is thought to enter it. Pagels-King 2007, 81, infer from this passage that "Judas finally understands Jesus's teaching," but this is not very clearly indicated in what is left of the text at this point either.

the *Gospel of Judas* seems to do, that there will be a more perceptive generation that will understand the teachings of Jesus better than his first followers.

Finally, one wonders where the authors of the *Apocryphon of John* would place Judas. (If the question ever occurred to any of them, of course, remains unknown.) Once again, it is clear that his anger disqualifies him from the perfect ones, who have rid themselves of this emotion. But would Judas be one of those who had the knowledge but did not put it into practice (Group 2)? Or does he rather belong to those who will gain perfection in the hereafter (Groups 3 & 4)? Or is he one of the apostates who were in the know but then turned away (Group 5)? The last option may be a tempting choice for a traitor, especially for the one to whom Jesus revealed "the secrets of the kingdom," but Judas's vindication promised in the *Gospel of Judas* seems to rule out this alternative.

While Judas's exact position on ancient morality ladders remains unclear, the most important aspect shown by the theories related to this theme is that, in the light of them, the bipolarized "either-a-good-guy-or-a-bad-guy" debate, which characterizes the present debate about the *Gospel of Judas*, seems too far too dualistic. The morality ladders described above allow for much more flexibility and nuances in estimating people's virtue and vice. This flexibility is needed if we want to account for all sides of the character of Judas in the *Gospel of Judas*, without turning a blind eye either to the negative or the positive aspects.

One possible explanation for a more nuanced assessment of Judas' role in the Gospel of Judas is, in fact, hinted at but not fully elaborated by April DeConick. Like other revisionists, she points out that "the thirteenth realm," to which Judas is connected, is usually Yaldabaoth's abode in the Sethian texts. Hence her conclusion that Judas *either* replaces *or* co-rules with Yaldabaoth.[82] While DeConick pays little attention to how these alternatives differ from each other, I think the difference is quite remarkable indeed. If Judas becomes a co-ruler with Yaldabaoth, he is certainly a negative figure in Sethian imagery. But if he is supposed to *replace* Yaldabaoth, then he is a much more positive figure. In the latter case, Judas would be a figure similar to Sabaoth, the son of Yaldabaoth, described in *On the Origin of the*

---

[82] DeConick 2007, 113.

World.[83] According to this text, Sabaoth repented, was provided "with great authority against all the forces of chaos," became "the Lord of the Forces," and was admitted to "dwell above the twelve gods of chaos."[84] The repentant Sabaoth, thus, is promoted to a place between the divine realm and that of Yaldabaoth.[85] A similar notion of repentance could be presupposed for the *Gospel of Judas*, especially if its author was familiar with Matthew's account of Judas' repentance.[86]

Although Judas will have no access to the divine realm in the *Gospel of Judas*, he will be promoted as high as is possible for those belonging to mortal humanity, and he will become the new ruler of the realm below the holy generation. This picture of the persecuted Judas, who will ultimately rule over his tormenters evokes a Jewish tradition of vindication of the righteous: the roles of the harrassing disciples and harrassed Judas will be reversed, just like it was promised in Jewish texts that the persecuted righteous will become judges of their persecutors at the end of times. By promising vindication to its suffering protagonist, the *Gospel of Judas*, in my view, offers good news to Judas after all;[87] perhaps "good news" in a limited sense, but definitely "good" rather than "bad."

---

[83] This interpretation has been proposed by Falkenberg in Petersen et al. 2008, 119–42, esp. 139–40.

[84] *Orig. World* NHC II,5 103–4.

[85] The storyline in this account makes it quite similar to that in the stories of Wisdom's repentance and restitution, which Meyer now links with the portrayal of Judas in *Gos. Jud.*; cf. Meyer 2008a and his article in this volume. In my view, however, the theme of ruling, to which the *Gos. Jud.* refers in describing Judas' future, is more dominantly present in the story of Sabaoth than in those of Wisdom.

[86] Matt 27:3–9. For the possibility that *Gos. Jud.* is dependent on Matt, see Gathercole 2007a, 134–38. Judas' repentance was emphasized by Origen, who gathered from Matthew's story that, despite his flaws, Judas was not entirely wicked. Origen took Judas's remorse as a sign of "what effect the teaching of Jesus could have on a sinner like Judas, the thief and traitor, who could not utterly despise what he had learnt from Jesus" (Origen, *Cels.* 2.11; trans. Chadwick 1953; for the same position attested in other works of Origen, see Chadwick's note to this passage). Strikingly, I have seen no references to this relatively sympathetic view of Judas, which challenges the neat dichotomy drawn between the "orthodox/hostile" and "heterodox/favorable" pictures of Judas, in any of the books published on *Gos. Jud.* thus far.

[87] It should be noted that the language of persecution makes Judas, not "poor Judas," but one of "us" (from the perspective of the implied audience of this gospel) for whenever early Christian texts speak about persecutions, they are referring to the *insiders'* sufferings, that is, what has happened to some of "us." Harrassment of the outsiders does not qualify as "persecution" in these texts. For example, Luke shows a complete lack of sympathy in describing how the Jewish archsynagogos Sosthenes fell victim to mob violence (Acts 18:17), and other early Christian authors pay no respect to the martyrs belonging to what these authors regarded as *wrong* Christian factions

This interpretation, obviously, raises the question of why Judas is then denied access to the divine realm. My suggestion (for now) is that this was the point where the author of the *Gospel of Judas* came to the "limits of maneuver." Although he felt free to considerably modify the more traditional picture of Judas, he accepted the tradition that Judas indeed betrayed Jesus. It may have seemed impossible to this author, who strictly condemned murder, that, having stained his hands with the blood of an innocent man, Judas could enter the divine realm.[88]

(such as Marcionites and Montanists); a good example of this attitude can be found in an early church history quoted by Eusebius, *Hist. eccl.* 5.16.20–21.

[88] Cf. Matt 27:4.

RABBI YEHUDA VERSUS JUDAS ISCARIOT

The *Gospel of Judas* and Apocryphal Passion Stories

Pierluigi Piovanelli*

The first announcement of the miraculous recovery, restoration, and imminent translation and publication of the *Gospel of Judas* from a Coptic codex found in the Al Minya region (Middle Egypt), around 1978, was made by Rodolphe Kasser at the Eighth Congress of the International Association for Coptic Studies, held in Paris, on July 1st, 2004. A preliminary translation of the text was subsequently released, on April 6th, 2006, by the team of specialists who were also responsible for the publication of the diplomatic edition of the entire codex a year later, on June 19th, 2007.[1] In the wake of the excitement stirred up by this sensational event an impressive number of short monographs have appeared.[2] In spite of their understandably different approaches and conclusions, all of the authors of this first wave of studies on the *Gospel of Judas* share the basic conviction that the text conveys a positive image of the wayward disciple and that, simply put, it serves to rehabilitate him. A closer analysis of the Coptic text, however, has led a few specialists to *independently* adopt a very different position which considers the protagonist of the *Gospel of Judas*, in April DeConick's words, to be "as evil as ever."[3] It is reasonable to assume that, because

* I would like to thank April DeConick, Louis Painchaud, Paul-Hubert Poirier, Gregor Wurst, and Claudio Zamagni, as well as my distinguished colleague Adele Reinhartz and my doctoral student Robert Edwards, for their insightful comments on different aspects of the present essay.

[1] Kasser and et al. 2006a; Kasser et al. 2007. Also see Meyer 2007a, 755–69; Meyer 2007b, 45–66 and 155–161. Krosney 2006, provided a popular and sometimes debatable reconstruction of the misadventures of the Al Minya codex, from its discovery to the intervention of the international team summoned by the National Geographic Society. Robinson 2006 immediately offered a strong criticism of the "commercializing" of the *Gospel of Judas* and what he considered to be a new scholarly "monopoly." On those and other issues, see Piovanelli 2007b.

[2] Among the most noteworthy are those of Ehrman 2006b; Pagels-King 2007; Gathercole 2007a. Also see Klauck 2006, 149–59; Simon Gathercole 2007b; Gounelle 2007; Nagel 2007.

[3] To the best of my knowledge, the first to advocate for such a "revisionist" (as Meyer calls it) interpretation was Painchaud 2006. He was followed by Pearson (see

of the poor condition of the Tchacos Codex it will be extremely difficult to reach a firm consensus and that the debate about the exact
nature of Judas's role in the text will go on for a very long time.[4]

Be that as it may, no matter what reading and interpretation we
choose to adopt, the *Gospel of Judas* is by no means the only "apocryphal" text to display a highly positive or extremely negative image of
the Iscariot. We do not even have to wait for the flourishing of modern
scholarship and literature to find characterizations of Judas as the arch-
villain or the misunderstood hero of the Jesus movement.[5] Actually,
this was already the case in late antique, fifth century Palestine, where
at least two opposing narrative cycles of Jesus' passion were circulating, each with its own specific set of heroes and villains. In what follows, (1) I will begin devoting some space to the figure of Judas in the
often overlooked Hebrew and Aramaic *Toledoth Yeshu* and in the little
known Ethiopic *Book of the Cock* and Coptic *Book of the Resurrection
of Jesus-Christ by Bartholomew the Apostle*; (2) then, I will show how
several traditions preserved in these relatively late "apocryphal" texts
are, in fact, much earlier and may even have some interesting connections with the *Gospel of Judas*; (3) finally, I will suggest some possibilities about the role of the Sethian (or "Sethianized") Judas on the
basis of the analogy offered by the presence of other New Testament
characters in Gnostic literature and the opportunities that an "association" with the Demiurge (similar to the one that is hinted at toward
the end of the *Gospel of Judas*) would eventually offer to them.[6]

---

his contribution to the present volume), Schenke Robinson, Turner, Brankaer-Bethge
2007, and especially DeConick 2007, 45–61 and 185–7.

[4] For Meyer's reaction, see Meyer 2007b, 50–2. He also replied to DeConick in his
contribution to this volume, and she responded to him in her own contribution.

[5] For the figure of the "historical" Judas—or at least, for the perception of his per-
sonage among contemporary theologians—see Klauck 1987; Maccoby 1992; Klassen
1996. On the different pictures of Judas in modern and contemporary culture, see
Paffenroth 2001; Dauzat 2006.

[6] *Gos. Jud.* 57:16–58:[8]. At least, according to the scholars mentioned above, n. 3.
See, e.g., DeConick 2007, 112–3, 116–20 and 191. Incidentally, the scribal error at
52:4–6 was also noticed by Van der Vliet 2006a, who proposed to reconstruct, "the
first is Athoth, he who is called the Aries (κριός)" (147–51).

RABBI YEHUDA AND MR. ISCARIOT: IMAGES OF JUDAS IN
LATE ANTIQUE APOCRYPHAL TEXTS

The most sympathetic picture of Judas—named here Rabbi Yehuda
'ish Bartōtā—is found in the medieval Jewish pamphlets known as the
Toledoth Yeshu, or "Stories about Jesus." It is generally agreed that
their original kernel may go back to the 4th–5th century, while the
texts themselves are certainly not earlier than the 9th–10th century.[7]
According to one of the latest and most developed versions,[8] Rabbi
Yehuda is the wise man who, thanks to his knowledge of the secret
name of God, unmasks the evil magician Yeshu the Nazarene, who is
the illegitimate son of Miriam and Joseph Panderi.[9] In a dramatic air
duel that is reminiscent of Simon Magus's fall from the sky and death
by stoning in the Vercelli version of the *Acts of Peter* 32, Yehuda brings
the flying Yeshu down by spilling his (?) sperm on him, thus making
him impure and unable to perform any other miracle.[10] Disguised as
one of Yeshu's disciples, Yehuda succeeds in identifying and delivering the Nazarene to the Jewish authorities, who condemn him to death
by stoning.[11] After the execution, Yehuda circumvents the adjuration
Yeshu had made to all the trees "that they were not to accept him for
hanging" by bringing an enormous cabbage stalk from his garden, on
which the corpse is successfully hung.[12] Finally, knowing that Yeshu

---

[7] Originally published by Krauss 1902. See Gero 1994; Thoma 1998; Newman
1999; Voorst 2000; Horbury 2003. Osier 1999 provides a useful anthology of texts
translated into French.

[8] Published by Schlichting 1982, and summarized by Klauck 2003, 211–20. Also
see Bammel, in Bammel 1997, 23–33; Klauck 1987, 18–21; Maccoby 1992, 96–100;
Paffenroth 2001, 92–5 and 167–8; Dauzat 2006, 104–8.

[9] *Toledoth Yeshu* § 150.

[10] *Toledoth Yeshu* §§ 158–61.

[11] *Toledoth Yeshu* §§ 212–3 and 225–30.

[12] *Toledoth Yeshu* § 250. This is the reversal of a well-known folkloric motif
(cf. Krauss 1902, 225–6): a wise man condemned to death by a lunatic king asks, as
his last wish, to choose the tree on which he will be hanged; after many hesitations,
he opts for a strawberry plant (or the like) and, as a result of his cleverness, he saves
his life. An echo of this theme can also be found in an interesting attempt to harmonize the different traditions about Judas's death (Matthew 27:3–8; Acts 1:16–19;
the sixth fragment of Papias's *Interpretations of the Sayings of the Lord*, quoted by
Apollinaris of Laodicea) made by the eleventh century archbishop Theophylactus of
Ochrida. According to Theophylactus, Judas "actually put his neck into the noose,
having hanged himself on a certain tree; *but the tree bent down and he continued to
live*, because it was God's will either to reserve him for repentance or for open dis-
grace and shame" (James Rendel Harris's translation, quoted by Paffenroth 2001, 120
[emphasis added]).

had announced his resurrection from the dead, Yehuda buries the body in his own garden and, after the discovery of the empty tomb, he hands it over to the authorities.[13]

An interesting variant of Jesus' capture and execution is preserved in an Aramaic fragment discovered in the Genizah of the Old Cairo Karaite synagogue.[14] In this earlier version "the wicked" Yeshu first transforms himself into a bird, and then into a rooster which flies on Mount Carmel; but Rabbi Yehuda Ganiba (גניבא) or Ginna'a (גנגא, sic), "the gardener," seizes him by the comb and brings him back to Rabbi Yehoshua ben Perahia in order to have him hung up and crucified on the usual cabbage stalk. As Jean-Pierre Osier aptly summarizes the global meaning of the "myth" told by the *Toledoth Yeshu*, "the one who would like to fly as an eagle, but who is not an eagle, will end his flight as a chicken."[15]

This reference to poultry leads us to our second example of a late antique "apocryphal" text in which Judas plays a major, albeit more traditional, role. The Ethiopic *Book of the Cock* is a passion gospel originally written in Greek, probably near to Jerusalem, during the years 451–479.[16] The episode of the rooster resurrected by Jesus that gives its title to the Ethiopic version was published in 1905, but it took eighty years to discover that the text is in fact much longer and contains a full description of the Holy Week from the day before the last supper to the burial of Jesus.[17] The first translation of the entire text into a modern language was recently published in the second volume of the *Écrits apocryphes chrétiens*, the French collection of "apocryphal" texts in translation edited by the "Association pour l'étude de la littérature apocryphe chrétienne" and released less than three years ago, on September 22nd, 2005.[18]

The passion story of the *Book of the Cock* begins on the Holy Wednesday, when Jesus and his disciples go out to the Mount of Olives.

---

[13] *Toledoth Yeshu* §§ 253–75.

[14] Originally published by Ginzberg 1928, 324–38, and partially reedited by Horbury 1970, 103–21 at 116–21; translated into French by Osier 1999, 121–8.

[15] Osier 1999, 21.

[16] See Piovanelli 2003a.

[17] By Chaîne 1905. On the defaults of this edition, see Piovanelli 2003a, 432–3, n. 14; Piovanelli 2003b. Credit for the discovery of the longer text goes to the late Roger W. Cowley (Cowley 1985).

[18] Piovanelli 1997–2005, 2:135–203, translated from the edition of Masqal 1990–91, together with four unpublished manuscripts.

There, a speaking "pillar of stone" miraculously reveals the betrayal of Judas.[19] The next morning Judas goes to Jerusalem to meet the Jewish religious leaders for the first time and returns to the Mount of Olives with a servant of the high priest.[20] Jesus then makes the decision to leave for Bethany and celebrate the Passover in the house of Simon the Pharisee and his wife Akrosennā. Jesus and his disciples arrive there in the afternoon, but Alexander the gatekeeper delays Judas because he is troubled by some ominous visions of the unfaithful disciple: "an enormous black serpent rolled up around (Judas's) neck, pulling his tongue out in order to kiss (him) on the mouth and harden thus (his) heart."[21] During the Passover meal in Simon's house, an unidentified sinful woman uses precious perfumes to anoint Jesus. What she does scandalizes Judas because "he was a thief and was accustomed to giving his wife what the Lord had entrusted him with for the offering box."[22] Jesus then washes the feet of the disciples, including Judas, foretells the denial of Peter, and announces for the second time the betrayal of the Iscariot, who nonetheless eats the bread and drinks the wine blessed by Jesus.[23] When Jesus expresses his wish to return to the Mount of Olives, Judas hurriedly leaves the assembly and runs to betray his master to the religious leaders of Jerusalem.[24] However, Jesus resurrects a rooster that was cooked by Akrosennā, and orders it to follow Judas.[25] Unbeknownst to Judas, the rooster spies on what he says and does in Jerusalem. The traitor then sleeps with his wife, who perfidiously counsels him as to the best way to betray Jesus to his enemies.[26] Next, he receives the reward for his betrayal, and agrees with Saul of Tarsus on the signal that will allow him to recognize and seize Jesus.[27] At this point, the rooster flies swiftly back to Bethany and reports all of these

---

[19] *Book of the Cock* 1:5–20.

[20] *Book of the Cock* 1:21–31.

[21] *Book of the Cock* 2:16–22. Cf. *Acts of Thomas* 32. On the motif of Judas's diabolical possession (*Book of the Cock* 1:19; 2:19; 4:3,5) in the Apocryphal Acts of the Apostles, see Klauck 1987, 142–4; Gathercole 2007a, 52–4.

[22] *Book of the Cock* 3:4–5. For John Chrysostom's anti-Semitic depiction of Judas as avaricious, see Paffenroth 2001, 37–9 and 154–5.

[23] *Book of the Cock* 3:13, 16–20, 24.

[24] *Book of the Cock* 4:1–5.

[25] *Book of the Cock* 4:6–8.

[26] *Book of the Cock* 4:9–10. Interestingly, the narrator declares that Judas "was the only among all the disciples to commit this kind of sin; because there is no one who, after having followed our Lord, has come back to the sin, with the only exception of Judas" (4:9).

[27] *Book of the Cock* 4:11–16.

events to Jesus and the disciples. In return for his services, the rooster is sent to heaven for a period of a thousand years.[28] At Gethsemane, in the Kidron valley, Jesus prays a last time to his Father. Judas and Saul then arrive at seven o'clock in the evening, and Judas delivers Jesus to Saul and his band of soldiers, who immediately and rudely lead him to Caiaphas the high priest.[29] Friday morning, Passover day, Paul of Tarsus (called here by his Roman name) comes to lead Jesus in chains to the court. The prisoner, however, manages to escape and hide within the Temple under the portico of Solomon, where he comes across "a woman belonging to the family of Judas Iscariot, who was suckling her son near to the first door." As she betrays him, Jesus punishes her by turning her into a rock.[30] Jesus is arrested again and led into the presence of Pilate, who decides to send him to Herod the tetrarch. In the meantime, having tried in vain to return the payment for his crime and obtain Jesus' freedom, Judas takes his own life.[31]

This is a short summary of Judas's tragic and negative role in the *Book of the Cock*. Some elements and features of such a *Leyenda Negra* were previously known from other related "apocryphal" texts. Thus, the resuscitation of a cooked rooster is also described in a Coptic fragment ascribed to the *Book of the Resurrection of Jesus-Christ by Bartholomew the Apostle*[32] and in the secondary forms M₂ and M₃ of the Greek Medieval ("M") recension of the *Gospel of Nicodemus*.[33] Other major agreements with the fragmentary beginning of the *Book of the Resurrection of Jesus-Christ* are represented by Judas's diabolical possession and the description of his wife as the wet nurse of Joseph of Arimathea's son.[34] While the sharp criticism expressed by the Jewish people—"It is he, his disciple, who was customary to eat and drink

---

[28] *Book of the Cock* 4:17–22.
[29] *Book of the Cock* 5:5–12.
[30] *Book of the Cock* 6:8–14.
[31] *Book of the Cock* 7:6–8.
[32] *Book of the Resurrection of Jesus-Christ* ms. A, 1:1–3. All the fragments ascribed to the *Book of the Resurrection of Jesus-Christ* known to date have been reedited by Westerhoff 1999, 48–197, and translated by Kaestli-Cherix, 1993, 143–241 and 249–52; Kaestli-Cherix 1997. Four new Coptic folios have subsequently been identified by Lucchesi (1997).
[33] *Gos. Nic.* 1:3. Originally published by Konstantin von Tischendorf (Tischendorf 1876, 287–322). We adopt here the classification proposed by Gounelle (1992; 2008). Accordingly, Tischendorf's ms. A belongs now to the M₁ family, ms. B to M₃, and ms. C to M₂. For a new translation of the M₁ recension, see Furrer-Gounelle 2005.
[34] See above, n. 21. *Book of the Resurrection of Jesus-Christ* ms. B, 2:1–2.

with him, and who has betrayed him and abandoned him to death"—
that makes Judas feel guilty is also shared by the *Gospel of Nicodemus*
M recension.[35] Some of these passages have found their way into
recent monographs or anthologies about Judas,[36] however one should
be aware of the possibility that the Coptic *Book of the Resurrection of
Jesus-Christ* actually recycled a part of the oral traditions that were used
independently by the *Book of the Cock*, while the *Gospel of Nicodemus*
M recension was probably created under the influence—direct or indirect—of the lost Greek original text of the *Book of the Cock*.[37] In other
words, in order to have access to the Judas traditions of late antiquity
the testimony of the *Book of the Cock* should now be given priority over the fragments of the more or less contemporary *Book of the
Resurrection of Jesus-Christ* and the secondary rewritings of the *Gospel
of Nicodemus* M recension.

This should lead us to the conclusion that some early versions of
the *Toledoth Yeshu*, the original texts of the *Book of the Cock*, and
perhaps, of the *Book of the Resurrection of Jesus-Christ*, together with
other "apocryphal" passion stories, were circulating and participating
in the same kind of Jewish-Christian controversy in the second half of
the fifth century.[38] The problem is now to see if some of the traditions
recycled by those late antique "apocryphal" texts are older than the
fourth, fifth, and/or the sixth century,[39] possibly as early as the second
century, or perhaps even contemporary with the *Gospel of Judas*.

---

[35] *Book of the Cock* 7:6; *Gos. Nic.* M₁ 11:2; M₂ 1:1–2; M₃ after 1:4.

[36] See Klauck 1987, 146–9; Paffenroth 2001, 102–3 and 169; Dauzat 2006, 72 (where
the exact reference should be to the *Gospel of Nicodemus* and not to the *Book of the
Cock*) and 83; Meyer 2007b, 122–4 and 169.

[37] *Pace* Gounelle 2008, 27–9. For a more in depth analysis, see Piovanelli 2003a,
437–42.

[38] This is especially evident in the polemical recycling, by all of these texts, of a
rooster motif that ultimately goes back to the Jewish legend about the gigantic Ziz
of Psalm 50:11, on which see Piovanelli 2003a, 442–4; Piovanelli 2006, 314. Gounelle
2003 and Nagy 2007 have examined the folkloric background of such a rooster legend.
Unfortunately, they both seem to have missed the point of the Jewish exegesis of Job
38:36, a verse that is traditionally repeated among the *Berakhoth* at the beginning of
the *Shaharith* morning service: "Blessed are you, O Lord, our God, King of the world,
who gives the cock intelligence to distinguish between day and night."

[39] For the dynamics of such a phenomenon, see Piovanelli 2007a; Piovanelli
2008a.

JUDAS ISCARIOT SUPERSTAR IN SECOND CENTURY JEWISH CHRISTIAN CONTROVERSIES?

The antiquity of some of the polemical motifs found in the *Toledoth Yeshu* is demonstrated by the allusions made to them by the famous second century authors Celsus and Tertullian. The pagan philosopher Celsus was, with the physician Galen, the first Greco-Roman intellectual to seriously engage in a well documented attack against Christianity.[40] In his *True Discourse* (or *Doctrine*), written in 177–180 and partially preserved in quotation by Origen's refutation *Against Celsus*, he demonstrated a good knowledge of Christian texts and traditions.[41] He clearly carried out personal research and interviewed at least one Jewish informant. Even if in the existing fragments of his work there is no explicit reference to Judas, Celsus knew of the rumors about Jesus' illegitimate birth;[42] his initiation, as Moses before him, into Egyptian magic;[43] his involvement with John the Baptist, described as "one of those who were executed with" Jesus (τινα ἕνα [...] τῶν μετὰ σοῦ κεκολασμένον), as well as the accusations of being a "charlatan"[44]—a series of elements shared with the *Toledoth Yeshu* (especially with the aforementioned Genizah fragment) that point to the existence and early circulation of some polemical proto-*Toledoth Yeshu* traditions.[45]

---

[40] See Wilken 1984, 68–125; MacDonald 1996, 82–120.

[41] Borret 1967–76. Hoffmann 1987, provides an easily accessible English translation of Celsus's fragments.

[42] Orig., *c. Cels.* I.28, 32: his mother "was pregnant by a Roman soldier named Panthera." See Schäfer 2007, 18–21 and 150–1. On Celsus's anti-Christian, rhetorical use of the episode of Jesus' betrayal, see below, n. 56.

[43] Orig., *c. Cels.* I.6, 28, 68, 71; II.49. See Stanton 1994.

[44] Orig., *c. Cels.* I.41. Bammel 1986 argued that such an ambiguous expression alludes to an episode of the Genizah fragment of the *Toledoth Yeshu*. In this version of the story, both John the Baptist and Jesus are brought before Pilate; in order to save their lives, Jesus predicts that the emperor's daughter will give birth to a male son; however, when she finally delivers but a stone, Jesus and John are condemned to be crucified together in Tiberias; John is executed first, while Jesus manages to escape. Orig., *c. Cels.* II.32. See Horbury 1998b, 162–75.

[45] This was already the opinion of Krauss and Ginzberg. More recently, the same position has been espoused by Bammel 1997a and Horbury (see below, nn. 48–49). According to Schäfer (2007, 151, n. 25), Celsus's "'Jew' is an important link between the Gospel traditions, the Talmud, and the later *Toledot Yeshu*, and the traditions that he presents are clearly older than the sixties and seventies of the second century C.E."

As for Tertullian, at the end of his *De Spectaculis* XXX.6, probably written shortly after his conversion to Christianity, in 197, the apologist from Carthage imagines that at the parousia of Christ, the day of the Last Judgment, he will be able to vehemently (as usual with him) rebuke those "who vented their rage and fury on the Lord" in the following manner.

> This is he, I shall say, the son of the carpenter or the harlot, the Sabbath-breaker, the Samaritan, who had a devil. This is he whom you bought from Judas; this is he, who was struck with reed and fist, defiled with spittle, given gall and vinegar to drink. This is he whom the disciples secretly stole away, that it might be said he had risen—unless it was the gardener who removed him, lest his lettuces should be trampled by the throng of visitors![46]

In such a passionate invective, traditions that Jewish contemporaries of Tertullian had borrowed from the gospels are interwoven with new legendary developments that would later become an integral part of the *Toledoth Yeshu*. This is not only the case of the defamatory treatment of Jesus' mother as a "prostitute" (*quaestuaria*), but also of the active role attributed to an anonymous "gardener" (*hortolanus*) in the removal of Jesus' body "lest his lettuces should be trampled by the throng of visitors." The latter reference is much more than a simple midrashic expansion based on the misunderstanding of Mary of Magdala in John 20:15 (NRSV: "Supposing him to be the gardener [ὁ κηπυρός], she said to him, 'Sir, if you have carried him away, tell me where you have laid him, and I will take him away.'"). Actually, such an incident is mentioned in a polemical context by the third century Latin poet Commodian in *Carmen Apologeticum* 440, as well as in much later Coptic apocryphal texts[47]—a constellation of allusions that seem to be a Christian response to the activities of Rabbi Yehuda "the gardener" in the *Toledoth Yeshu*.[48]

In conclusion, concerning the prehistory of some of the traditions found in the *Toledoth Yeshu* (including some elements of the Judas episodes) we cannot but subscribe to William Horbury's suggestion that "the outspoken Jewish polemic in the Toledoth Jeshu appears to

---

[46] Turcan 1986, 324 and 326; translated into English in Glover 1953, 299.

[47] *Book of the Resurrection of Jesus-Christ* 8; *Lament of Mary* (also known as *Gospel of Gamaliel*) 7:20. See Newman 1999, 71.

[48] See Horbury 1972, 455–459; Maier 1978, 69 and 258–9; Osier 1999, 154–5; Schäfer 2007, 111–2 and 181.

presuppose the importance gained by Tiberias under the Jewish patriarchs [i.e., in late Antiquity, from the third century onwards], but its
agreements with the speeches of the Jew of Celsus in Origen, with
Tertullian on Jewish claims, and with passages in the probably third-
century Commodian, indicate the currency of Jewish anti-Christian
traditions in the second century and later."[49]

Concerning the *Book of the Cock*, as I pointed out in a series of previous studies some of its traditions and/or sources are rooted in older
Jewish-Christian stories,[50] but these are not the only ancient features
that this apocryphal passion story has preserved. In this connection,
especially noteworthy is the fact that the text begins with a dialogue
between Jesus and his disciples on the Mount of Olives the day before
the celebration of the Passover in Bethany.[51] It is in that place, as I
mentioned before, that a rock miraculously reveals the betrayal of
Jesus by Judas. As a result, the latter, extremely shocked, denounces
the former as a magician: "The magic that you were used to practice,
O son of a blacksmith, was not enough? You succeeded in making a
stone speak! And the earth tolerates your ungodliness and what you
have done today declaring, 'The Lord Almighty, He is my truth!'"[52]
Thus, in the *Book of the Cock* as in the *Gospel of Judas*, the episode
describing Judas's new understanding of his master's role becomes the
necessary prelude to the subsequent story of Jesus' passion.[53]

Needless to say, this does not mean that in the fifth century the
author of the *Book of the Cock* used, or even replied to, the second century *Gospel of Judas*,[54] but at the very least it demonstrates that there

---

[49] Horbury 1992, 76–7.
[50] Particularly its anti-Paulinian tendency, on which see Piovanelli 2003a 445–6;
Piovanelli 2006, 311–3; Piovanelli, 2008b.
[51] *Book of the Cock* 1:3–20.
[52] *Book of the Cock* 1:19–20.
[53] In the case of *Gospel of Judas* 33:4–6, "three days before he celebrated Passover."
One should note that Judas's "initial confession" (as Gregor Wurst calls it) is not the
only episode that has been chronologically inserted at the same moment of the passion storyline of the *Gospel of Judas* and the *Book of the Cock*. This is also the case
of Judas's decisive meeting with the Jewish religious leaders that happens, in both
texts (*Gos. Jud.* 58:9–26; *Book of the Cock* 4:11–16), immediately after the last supper—an apocryphal scene that opportunely fills a blank (left between Mark 14:10–11
and 43–49 parr.) in the other gospel narratives. For the chronology of the *Gospel of
Judas*, see Matteo Grosso's contribution to the present volume.
[54] Painchaud and Cazelais have also noticed an intriguing intertextual link between
Judas's question to Jesus, "What is the advantage that I have received?," in *Gos. Jud.*
46:16–17, and Jesus' rebuke addressed to Judas's soul in the Amente, "What advan-

was an ancient tradition about a first disclosure of Judas's responsibility in Jesus' betrayal *before* the last supper. The goal of such a story was probably to provide a plausible explanation for the rather abrupt decision on the part of the disciple to hand over his master to the high priests in the synoptic gospels.[55] Apparently, the detail of the satanic possession added by Luke in 22:3 and John in 13:2 was insufficient, and as a consequence it was up to the omniscient Christ to reveal Judas's felony as part of the prophetic announcements of his death.[56] One author built a Gnostic (probably Sethian) dialogue on this tradition, while another one used it as the point of departure for an anti-Chalcedonian retelling of the passion.

In my opinion, it is likely that some elements of the Judas traditions embedded in apocryphal texts as late as the *Toledoth Yeshu* and the *Book of the Cock* are, in fact, much earlier, even datable to the second century. Their identification points to the existence of a strongly polemical debate between Jewish and Christian believers carried out through the medium of popular, oral retellings of the passion story. If this controversy was probably already going on before the end of the second century, possibly even before the 180s, we could envision the existence of two concomitant sets of antagonistic Judas traditions, a Jewish one, that later developed into the *Toledoth Yeshu* materials, and a Christian one, that was finally fixed into the *Book of the Cock* and other related apocryphal texts. In the latter case, the Judas traditions are deeply interwoven with passages, such as the episode of rooster, from unmistakably Jewish Christian origins that seem to have been crafted in response to Jewish criticisms.[57] Such a blending betrays a plausible Jewish Christian, possibly Ebionite, original setting for the ensemble of these traditions, including those pertaining to Judas. We can easily imagine that some Jewish Christians from Syria or Palestine, under the pressure of what they perceived as a threat from the emerging, mainstream, rabbinic Judaism, responded in an extremely vibrant manner and chose to demonize, among others, Judas Iscariot, the hero

---

tage, O Judas, have you derived from delivering me?," in *Book of the Resurrection of Jesus-Christ* 6. See their contribution to the present volume.

[55] Mark 14:10–11 // Matthew 26:14–16 // Luke 22:3–6.

[56] See Matt 26:1–2. This solution was also providing an apt reply to Celsus's objection (Orig., *c. Cels.* II.9, 12, 18–20) that the so-called Son of God had been unable to foresee the betrayal of one of his most intimate followers.

[57] See above, n. 38.

of the anti-gospel stories of their adversaries.[58] In doing so, they followed the same sectarian path already taken by their predecessors in
the marginalized Jewish Christian communities that had produced the
gospels of Matthew and John.[59] Tragically, when a couple of centuries later the heirs of the former minorities became the new majority,
those dissident voices and early stories gave birth to the first truly anti-
Jewish, not to say anti-Semitic passion narratives—beginning with the
Book of the Cock.[60]

Towards a Better Characterization of the Image of Judas in the *Gospel of Judas*

We can now proceed in our conclusions to make some suggestions for
drawing a more historically accurate picture of Judas and his *Gospel*
against the background of second century Jewish and Jewish Christian
polemical uses of the wayward disciple.

The first point to note is that earlier traditions preserved in the
Toledoth Yeshu and the *Book of the Cock* demonstrate that Judas was
a topical figure in second century Jewish and Christian apocryphal
stories. He was probably as popular as other illustrious "witnesses and
mediators of the teaching of Jesus" such as Peter, John, James, Thomas,
or Mary of Magdala.[61] Accordingly, it should not be so surprising to
find the Iscariot in the role of the hero of a Gnostic apocryphal gospel.
Traditions about him would have been easily accessible and usable in
order to introduce Christian readers to the mysteries of "the immovable race" in a narrative fashion. This should even represent a better
explanation than the customary answer of laying blame on a highly

---

[58] To the bibliography on Jewish Christianity quoted in Piovanelli 2006 we can now
add Mimouni 2004; Luomanen-Marjanen 2005; Jackson-McCabe 2007; Skarsaune-
Hvalvik 2007. The contours of the social and ideological modalities of such a late and
progressive "parting of the ways" have been dramatically reshaped by Boyarin 2004,
who convincingly argues that the construction of two differentiated identities—the
Christian religious one versus the Jewish ethnic one—was mainly the result of the
efforts of second century Christian heresiologists. For the fluidity, even in the long
term, of those artificially constructed boundaries, see Becker-Reed 2003. Concerning
the meaning of the name *Notzrim* and the date of its insertion into the twelfth "blessing" of the *Birkath ha-Minim*, Vana 2003 has demonstrated that it designates the
Christians in general and cannot be earlier than the end of the fourth century.
[59] See now Runesson 2008.
[60] See, for example, the well-documented survey of Cohen 2007.
[61] As Luttikhuizen 2006, 123–8, calls them.

hypothetical group of "Cainites" for the systematic rehabilitation of all of the worst villains of the Bible.[62]

The second point that deserves careful consideration is that a simple comparison between the pictures of Judas found in the traditions of the proto-*Toledoth Yeshu* and the proto-*Book of the Cock* reveals the specificity and originality of the portrayal of the Iscariot in the *Gospel of Judas*. There, the Iscariot is neither a kind of X-Man superhero, nor a corrupt individual obsessed with lust and money. On the contrary, in the *Gospel of Judas* we encounter a more sophisticated and humanized picture of the disciple, who dissociates himself from the rest of the Twelve and strives to obtain a deeper knowledge of Jesus' teachings. Judas is the only one brave enough to stand before Jesus and confess that the latter comes "from the immortal aeon of Barbelo."[63] And even if Judas won't ultimately be allowed to ascend to the holy generation,[64] Jesus actually proceeds to initiate him into the mysteries of the Kingdom—a revelation that enables Judas to fully understand and accept the terrible task of sacrificing "the man who bears" his master, that is, the corporeal and perishable envelope of the heavenly Christ. In this sense, the depiction of Judas in the *Gospel of Judas* is closer to the dramatic portrayal of him as the only disciple who is really aware of Jesus' special role and destiny in contemporary literature and popular culture such as in Nikos Kazantzakis's *The Last Temptation of Christ* or Tim Rice's *Jesus Christ Superstar*.[65]

A third point worth noting is that, no matter how negatively modern critics can (in my opinion, legitimately) perceive Judas's role in the *Gospel of Judas*, this might not necessarily have been the case for

---

[62] See, e.g., Gathercole 2007a, 118–9. Actually, it would be more accurate to say that in *Adv. haer.* I.31.1 Iraeneus is all but describing a Gnostic position. On the contrary, he is probably using the evidence of the *Gospel of Judas* to attribute to some Gnostics the belief that not only Judas, but also Cain, Esau, Korah, the Sodomites, and many other biblical felons were part of the spiritual race—a genealogy that, as DeConick 2007, 174–5, rightly argues, seems to be fictitious. In imagining such an improbable scenario on the basis of hearsays (*alii autem rursus* [...] *dicunt*), Irenaeus is but caricaturizing his adversaries.

[63] *Gos. Jud.* 35:6–21.

[64] On no ascension to holy generation, see *Gos. Jud.* 35:26; 45:12–19; 46:17–18; 46:25–47:1. On initiation into the mysteries of the Kingdom, see *Gos. Jud.* 35:23–25; 45:25–26; 47:1–4; 57:15. On Judas' sacrifice, see *Gos. Jud.* 56:17–24.

[65] On the cinematic treatment of Judas's figure, see Reinhartz 2007, 151–77 and 271–2. Concerning *Jesus Christ Superstar*, one should remember that, according to Staley-Walsh 2007, 196, n. 4, "[a] rumor, denied by the cast, claims the film was tentatively titled *The Gospel According to Judas*."

ancient Sethian readers.[66] One eloquent example is provided by Judas's eventual association with the demiurge Nebro-Yaldabaoth and/or his creature Saklas.[67] The possibility of such a connection depends on how one interprets the episode at the end of the revelatory dialogue between Jesus and Judas. Having told him "everything," Jesus invites the disciple to "lift up" his "eyes and look at the cloud and the light within it, and the stars surrounding it. The star which is leading (προηγούμενος) is" Judas's "star."[68] "So Judas—the text goes on—lifted up his eyes, he saw the luminous cloud and he entered it."[69] If it was Judas, and not Jesus, who ascended into the luminous cloud, then the disciple would probably not have experienced any kind of glorious "transfiguration" and vindication,[70] but he would rather have "join[ed] Ialdabaoth in his cloud becoming assimilated with Ialdabaoth in some way."[71] Nevertheless, even such a close encounter (of a special kind) with the creator of the material world could not have been so negatively perceived by an ancient Sethian audience. Actually, according to the "Ophite" (Sethian?) tractate summarized by Irenaeus in his Against the Heresies I.30.1–14, the resurrected Jesus himself was expected to have joined his father Yaldabaoth in order to work backstage, unknown to him, to retrieve the souls of Gnostic believers.[72]

---

[66] See above, n. 3.

[67] Generally, in Sethian cosmogonic traditions Yaldabaoth, Samael, and Saklas are but different names for the same demiurgical figure. In the Gospel of Judas, however, Nebro-Yaldabaoth and Saklas seems to be two distinct "angelic" entities. On one hand, Nebro-Yaldabaoth is the first who appears from the cloud (of the hylic Sophia?) and is responsible for the creation of the first six other angelic beings, including Saklas, to assist him (51:8–23). On the other hand, it is Saklas who makes the decision to make the first couple of human beings (52:14–19); who receives the sacrifices probably made by ordinary Christian believers (56:12–13); and whose domination will finally come to an end (54:18–21). This dualism is similar to the partnership between "the great [angel]" Saklas and "the great demon" Nebruel described in the Gos. Eg. (NHC III,2 57:17–58:2 // IV,2 69:1–5). Apparently, in the Gospel of Judas Nebro, and not Saklas, was secondarily and mistakenly identified with Yaldabaoth (51:15).

[68] Gos. Jud. 57:15–20.

[69] Gos. Jud. 57:21–23.

[70] As optimistically guessed by Kasser et al. 2006a, 44, n. 143. More prudently, Meyer, in Meyer 2007a, 769, n. 123, acknowledges that "it may be understood in the text that the spiritual person of Jesus returns through the transfiguration to the realm above and his fleshly body that is left behind in this world below is turned over to the authorities to be crucified." For an analogous scene of transfiguration in which the narrator (Jesus?) is surrounded by "a cloud of light," see now Allog. TC 62:9–63:1.

[71] DeConick 2007, 119.

[72] For a recent defense of its Sethian nature, see Rasimus 2005; Rasimus 2007.

And so he was taken up into heaven, where Jesus sits at the right hand of its parent Ialdabaōth, so that he (Jesus) might receive unto himself the souls of those who have become acquainted with him, once they have left behind their worldly flesh—thus enriching himself without his parent's knowing or even seeing him; so that to the extent that Jesus enriches himself with holy souls his parent is diminished and suffers loss, being emptied of the power that it has in the form of souls; for in consequence it does not have any more holy souls to send back into the world, except for those which derive from its essence, that is, those which come from its inbreathing. Moreover, the end will take place when the entire secretion or the spirit of light is gathered together and caught up into the realm of incorruptibility.[73]

If this kind of cohabitation with Yaldabaoth was acceptable for the "animate and spiritual" person of the resurrected Jesus, one wonders why it should not also have been the case for a Judas whose destiny was to remain suspended, so to speak, between heaven and earth.[74]

As a final point, the comparison with second century Jewish and Jewish Christian apocryphal traditions is particularly useful to emphasize the specificity of Sethian and Gnostic Christian perspectives. On one hand, in contrast to the derogatory Jewish stories about Jesus, we do not find any enthusiastic endorsement of Judas's role—not to mention the Jewish rabbis and leaders involved in Jesus' arrest and trial, in the Nag Hammadi and related texts, including the newly discovered *Gospel of Judas*. In this sense, despite its Jewish apocalyptic and mystical matrixes Sethian literature is firmly grounded in the Christian tradition. On the other hand, in contrast to Jewish Christian narratives, Gnostic texts, including the *Gospel of Judas*, display almost no animosity towards the wayward disciple and the other Jewish characters involved in Jesus' passion. It is easy to understand how such hatred would have been a paradox for Christian believers who belittled the theological relevance of the sufferings of a human Jesus left to die on the cross after the departure of the heavenly Christ. As the resurrected Valentinian Jesus says to his spiritual brother in the *First Revelation of James*, "James, do not be concerned about the people (λαός) or about

---

[73] The Latin version of the lost Greek original has been edited in Rousseau-Doutreleau 1979, 2:384; the English translation is taken from Layton 1987, 180–1 (I adopted the emendation proposed by the editors and restored the first occurrence of "Jesus," whereas Layton reads "the anointed [Christ]" with all the manuscripts and early editions).

[74] Iren., *Adv. haer.* I.30.13.

me. For I am the one who preexists in me. [For] I have not suffered at all and I did not die, and this people (λαός) has done no harm."[75] It also seems perfectly logical that the same Gnostic Christians who did not hold a sacrificial understanding of Jesus' death would have objected to the necessity of dying as martyrs for the cause of God.[76] Actually, from a sociological point of view this critical attitude towards martyrdom was part of a strategy to reduce political deviance and cultural distance from mainstream Greco-Roman society, a feature that betrays the non-sectarian and more accommodating nature of Gnostic groups in comparison with other more radical Jewish Christian and/or proto-orthodox movements.[77]

This less polemical attitude towards society at large is also confirmed by the absence of any specifically anti-Jewish trait among the *Erinnerungsfiguren*, or foundational narratives, of Gnostic cultural memory.[78] Contrary to the commonly held opinion that the transformation of the God of the Hebrew Bible into an arrogant and tyrannical lesser god was in the best case a heretical aberration, and in the worst case an anti-Jewish move, in proceeding to such a value reversal the Sethians, Valentinians, and other Christian Gnostics were simply placing the Jewish heritage of Christianity in an unusual and more distant perspective.[79] As a consequence, Gnostic Christianity was certainly not

---

[75] TC 18:4–11. The parallel text from Nag Hammadi is slightly different and reads, "James, do not be concerned about me or about the people (λαός). I am the one who existed in me. I have never suffered at all, and I was not distressed. This people (λαός) has done no harm to me" (*1 Apoc. Jas.* NHC V,3 31:15–22).

[76] As acknowledged by Pagels 1979, 70–101; Pagels 1980. Also see Pagels-King 2007, 44–57 and 175–8, who aptly comment at 51, "It is this kind of [sacrificial] thinking that horrified the author of the *Gospel of Judas*."

[77] See the insightful analysis of Williams 1996, 103–15 and 286–8, who used the Stark and Bainbridge's adaptation of Troeltsch's "sect" versus "church" typology.

[78] See Kirk 2007.

[79] As it is well known, Jonas was of the opinion that the "nature of the relation of Gnosticism to Judaism—in itself an undeniable fact—is defined by the *anti-Jewish animus* with which it is saturated" (quoted in King 2003, 126). Gathercole 2007a, 159 still believes that "to imagine that Christians could somehow get on better with Jews by downgrading the Old Testament is slightly peculiar. The fact is that *no Christianity worthy of the name* can abandon the Old Testament and its God, and yes this is precisely what the *Gospel of Judas* does" (emphasis added)—an appraisal that needs some qualifications. That a "Christianity worthy of the name" was able not to abandon, but to relativize the import of "the Old Testament [sic] and its God" is historically demonstrated by the very existence of second century Gnostic Christian groups. As for the worries about contemporary "downgrading" of the Hebrew Bible, advocated, for example, by Harnack (see King 2003, 66), such a concern is clearly a pastoral one dictated by a strong theological bias.

as aggressive and supersessionist as the other branches of second century Christianity. In fact, as the *Gospel of Judas* abundantly demonstrates, those who considered themselves as the seed of Seth were more prone to engage in polemical debates with their Christian colleagues than with their Jewish fellows. Since the Jews were not their main target, there was no need to make Judas more horrible than he finally and tragically is in the *Gospel of Judas*—a victim more than a hangman. When we compare the different pictures of Judas found in the proto-*Toledoth Yeshu*, the proto-*Book of the Cock*, and the *Gospel of Judas*, it is hard to escape the conclusion that (1) for some second century Jews (the few who had an interest in the question), Jesus was the problem and Judas its solution; (2) for a number of contemporaneous (Jewish) Christians, both Judas and (for different reasons) Paul were the problem—and sadly enough, late antique orthodox Christianity would soon inherit such a negative perception of Judas; while (3) for other (Sethian) Christians, the Twelve were the problem and Judas a part of its solution!

ASTROLOGICAL LORE

APOSTLES AS ARCHONS

The Fight for Authority and the Emergence of Gnosticism in the Tchacos Codex and Other Early Christian Literature

April D. DeConick

When I wrote *The Thirteenth Apostle: What the Gospel of Judas Really Says*, I highlighted two aspects of the *Gospel of Judas*.[1] The first—the concept of Judas as the thirteenth apostle and demon double of Ialdabaoth—I was able to explore more fully than the second—the concept of the twelve other apostles as the archons below him. Even as I was putting the finishing touches on the book manuscript, I realized that I had not plummeted the depths of this second concept. I had only barely scratched the surface.

In my book, I had concluded from Jesus' nightmarish interpretation of the disciples' dream, that the correspondence of the twelve apostles with the twelve archons below Ialdabaoth, was understood by the author of this text to be a negative correspondence. I postulated that this correspondence was made for polemical reasons since the Sethian Christians were criticizing the Apostolic Christians for basing their teaching on ignorant disciples who were unwitting assistants to the archons and worshipers of Ialdabaoth. But I was unable to penetrate these issues more fully at that time.

I had no idea that the significance of the correspondences between the apostles and the archons went far beyond the scope of the *Gospel of Judas*, that in fact, when fully mapped, understanding these correspondences would lead me to offer answers to questions whose answers have perplexed me and others for a very long time.[2] What I discovered by studying the correspondences between the apostles and the archons is that they not only reveal information about the relationships of

---

[1] DeConick 2007.
[2] For coverage of the recent debates over the category "Gnosticism," see Pearson 1994, 105–114; Layton 1995, 334–350; Williams 1996; King 2003; Marjanen 2005; Logan 2006.

Gnostic Christians to the Apostolic Church, but when set out chronologically with respect to the various Gnostic traditions, they also reveal
information about how Gnosticism comes to be. Since I have been an
advocate to severely restrict the use of the word "Gnosticism" in our
field, this was very much a surprise to me.

These correspondences show a progressive social demarcation over
four centuries that begins as a religious lodge movement, an esoteric
gathering for hierophantic teaching, attended by Jews and Christians
who were still affiliated with local synagogues and churches. Eventually
some of these lodge movements turn into reform movements which
continue to maintain their membership in the synagogue and church,
and allegiance to Judaism and Christianity, but understand their
movement as a protest and reform of those traditions. Other Gnostic
lodge movements become separatist movements that turn against the
synagogue and church, under the impression that the synagogue and
church are so corrupt as to be irredeemable. These Gnostics begin to
worship as completely separate groups from the synagogue and church.
It is their opinion that they alone know the road to salvation, and
non-Gnostic Jews and Christians should convert in order to be saved.
Ultimately, this progression culminates in the establishment of a new
religious movement that we can properly call Gnosticism, a movement that produces at least two great Gnostic religions, Manichaeism
and Mandaeism, but also the handbook compendia of *Jeu* and *Pistis
Sophia*.

Gnostic Astrology

The teaching that the twelve apostles are archons is a concept deeply
dependent on ancient astrology as it imploded within Gnostic environments. The baseline thought-form of astrology in antiquity is captured in the Hermetic maxim, "as above, so below," as well as Jesus'
prayer, "as in heaven, so on earth." It is properly characterized as the
reality of heaven-and-earth correspondences, that vertical, analogous,
symmetric vision of the world, where what happens in the heavens
happens also on the earth. This relationship of correspondences is not
always causal or mechanical as one might initially think. Instead, the
corresponding relationship between the heavenly event and the earthly
one was often viewed as simultaneous. The meaning of the dual events

needed to be probed in order to grasp what was *really* going on.[3] This concept is clearly expressed by the Valentinian Theodotus who taught that "the stars themselves do nothing except show the activity of the ruling powers, just as the flight of the birds it points out something, but does nothing (τὰ δὲ ἄστρα αὐτὰ μὲν οὐδὲν ποιεῖ, δείκνυσι δὲ τὴν ἐνέργειαν τῶν κυρίων δυνάμεων, ὥσπερ καὶ ἡ τῶν ὀρνίθων πτῆσις σημαίνει τι, οὐχὶ ποιεῖ)."[4] The ancient astrologers hoped to be able to grasp the meaning of these celestial occurrences and their earthly correspondences in order to discern the voices of the gods and figure out what was happening around them.[5]

The Gnostic literature, although not unique in its astrological underpinnings, is obsessed with mapping the correspondences between the heavens and the earth. The reason for this is that the Gnostic Christian systems of salvation depend upon altering the cosmic structures, physically changing the universe from a cage that traps the spirit to a portal that frees it. The universe before the advent of the Savior Jesus, is not only the creation of a lesser god—who is described as arrogant, jealous, ignorant, and in some cases, evil—but it functions as a prison for the spirit. The prison guards are the celestial beings, the rulers or archons, who reside in the planetary spheres above the earth and in the sublunar realm where the abyss or Hades was believed to be.

The various Gnostic systems play with the number of these archons, but all of them are built from astrological speculation about the numbers seven and twelve commonly assumed in the Greco-Egyptian and Hermetic environments in which these Gnostic systems originated. The number seven reflects the seven planets: Saturn, Jupiter, Mars, the Sun, Venus, Mercury, and the Moon. The Gnostics have even left us with enough evidence to reconstruct particular identifications of certain planets with certain named archons, although these identifications are not constant across the literature.[6] The number twelve is a correspondence with the twelve signs of the Zodiac: Leo, Virgo, Libra, Scorpio, Sagittarius, Capricorn, Aquarius, Pisces, Aries, Taurus,

---

[3] Von Stuckrad 2000b, 1–40; cf. Faivre 1994, 10–15; Hanegraaff 1995, 1–49; Hanegraaff 1996, 396–401.

[4] Clem. Alex., *Exc.* 70.2. Greek: Casey 1934, 84; translation mine.

[5] For recent treatments of astrology in ancient Judaism and Christianity, see Von Stuckrad 2000a; Popovic 2007; Hegedus 2007.

[6] Welburn 1978, 241–254.

Gemini, and Cancer. Exactly how the planetary archons relate to the
Zodiac signs has been discussed by scholars in the past, but has not
been worked out satisfactorily yet.[7]

By the time the Gnostic texts began to be authored, this Hellenistic
astrological system was combined with the old Egyptian decanal
system. Egyptian astrological speculation placed a very significant
emphasis on stars they called the "decans." Egyptian astrologers had
observed constellations that ascended with the sun every ten days. The
rising of the decans were used to divide time into hours.[8] The decans
were considered very powerful gods because, unlike the stationary
constellations, these stars, the astrologers thought, did not stand in
stations. Unlike the planets, they did not move backwards nor could
they be eclipsed by the sun.[9] Chapter six in Stobaeus' Hermetic handbook describes the decans as stars that rule from an area just above
the Zodiac signs in the sphere of the fixed stars, so that "they hold up
the circle of the universe and look down on the circle of the Zodiac."[10]
They exercise great power by slowing the circle of the universe and
hastening the movement of the planets. According to Stobaeus, one
of the decans, called the Bear, was thought to be centrally located
in the Zodiac, functioning like the spoke of a wheel making the
Zodiac revolve. The decans were the guardians of the cosmos, holding together everything and watching over the order of everything.[11]
In the Hellenistic period, the Egyptian astrologers parsed the thirty-
six decans into the Zodiac by allotting three decanal gods to each of
the Zodiac signs. This combination can be observed on the second-
century astrological boards recovered from an old well in Grand, a
village in Lorraine.[12]

In Egyptian speculation, these gods were doubled, so that seventy-
two rulers were apportioned to the Zodiac. This meant that thirty-
six decans and thirty-six horoscopes were each considered rulers of
every five-degrees of the Zodiac. Collectively they were identified as
seventy-two spirits.[13] Because they referenced every five-degrees of the

---

[7] Welburn 1978, 241–254; Pleše 2006, 183–191.
[8] Barton 1994, 20.
[9] Barton 1994, 28–29.
[10] Stob. Exc. 6.3–5. Festugière 1954a, 34–35.
[11] Cf. Firmicus Matermus, *Mathesis* 2.4, 4.22; Chadwick 1953, 496.
[12] Abry 1993; Evans 2004, 4–7.
[13] Von Stuckrad 2000a, 641–642.

Zodiac, they were considered to be special stars by the astrologers.[14] An important second-century astrological calendar based on this fifth-degree division of the Zodiac is published among the Oxyrhynchus Papyri. The year is divided into five-day weeks which are overseen by seventy-two deities who influence, for good or bad, what happens during their reign, including particular illnesses associated with them.[15]

So important were these stars, that some Egyptians singled out a favorite, a decan with a snake's body and a lion's face with sun rays radiating from his head. They called this decan, Chnoubis or Chnoumis. His image was reproduced on numerous green stone amulets.[16] This is the image that is eventually associated with Ialdabaoth, suggesting that the origins of the Ialdabaoth god are connected with a particular Egyptian decan.[17]

The identification of the archons with the planets, the Zodiacal signs, and various degrees of the Zodiac meant that powers opposing the supreme high God controlled not only what happened on earth, but what happened to the fallen spirit. Although there are many renditions in the Gnostic literature about how this happened in terms of agents, the baseline story is that the otherworldly spirit sinks into denser and denser cosmic materials, until it lodges within a human soul and body. This process was understood as a descent of the spirit through the cosmic realms through various Zodiac gates or along the cosmic pole, the *axis mundi*.[18] As the spirit sank, it literally passed through various constellations and planets, receiving along the way, the psychic or soul inclinations of each of these beings.

This speculation was assumed knowledge typical of Middle Platonic thought. Philosophers such as Numenius taught that as the *psyche* descended from the upper sphere of the fixed stars, it passed through certain star gates into the lower planetary spheres where certain faculties accumulated in the soul.[19] Some of these faculties were positive while others were negative. Macrobius says that the natural philosophers attribute to Saturn the rational powers of the soul, to Juptier the

---

[14] Quack, forthcoming.
[15] P. Oxy. 465. Grenfell-Hunt 1903, 126–137. I owe Adamson thanks for this reference.
[16] King 1887, 215–225; Mastrocinque 2005, 61–70.
[17] This is also the expressed opinion of Mastrocinque 2005, 78–79.
[18] For a discussion of the *axis mundi* in ancient religious literature, see Trammell's contribution to this volume.
[19] On this see Porphyry, *Antr. nymph.* 70.21–24.

active, to Mars the spirited, to the Sun the perceptive, to Venus the appetitive, to Mercy the linguistic, and to the Moon the nutritive.[20] Similar lists are attributed to Proclus and Servius.[21] The Hermetic traditions understood these accumulations to be largely negative. In the first book of the *Corpus Hermeticum* we find just such a negative list: falsehood, unlimited appetite, presumptuous audacity, arrogance, appetitive guile, evil devices, and nutritive.[22] Similarly we find negative equations in the Valentinian *Gospel of Mary* where "the wisdom of the wrathful person" is derived from Saturn the seventh planet, "the foolish understanding of the flesh" from Jupiter the sixth planet, "the rule of the flesh" from Mars the fifth planet, "the zeal for death" from the Sun the fourth planet, "ignorance" from Mercury the third planet, "desire" from Venus the second planet, and "darkness" from the Moon the first planet.[23] In Gnostic literature, these inclinations are largely negative ones, because they are derived from capricious or malicious archons.

In the *Apocryphon of John*, the psychic traits given to the descending soul are recounted in a slightly different fashion, since this text understands that each planetary archon is trying to fashion Adam's soul to imitate the image of the first perfect Man which had been revealed to them from above. Thus the writer of the *Apocryphon of John* states that the archons created the first man "by means of their respective powers in correspondence with the characteristics which were given. And each Authority supplied a characteristic in the form of the image which he had seen in its psychic form."[24] In this case, the planets appear to be described in ascending order by their powers, and each give one characteristic to Adam's soul. The Moon, associated with the archon Athoth, is called the "excellent" planet. He gives Adam his "bone-soul." The second planet, Mercury is the archon Eloaio(u). He is characterized by "foreknowledge" and creates for Adam his "sinew-soul." The third planet, Venus, is described as "divinity" and gives him "flesh-soul."

---

[20] Macrobius, *Comm. Scipio* 1.12.1–16.

[21] Proclus, *Comm. Timaeus* 1.148.1–6 and 3.335.12–15 (theoretical, political, spirited, linguistic, appetitive, perceptive, nutritive). Servius, *Comm. Aeneid* 6.127 (torpor, desire for absolute power, anger, passion, greed).

[22] *C.H.* 1.24–26.

[23] *Gos. Mary* BG,1 16.5–12. Coptic: Tuckett 2007, 96. Translation mine.

[24] *Apoc. John* NHC II,1 15.5–9.

Venus is the archon Astaphaio(s). The Sun, Iao, is the fourth planet. He is known by his "lordship" and creates Adam's "marrow-soul." Mars, the fifth planet is known as the "Kingdom." His archon name is Sabaoth. He gives the "blood-soul" to Adam. The sixth planet, Jupiter, is characterized by "envy." His archon name is Adonin or Adonein and he gives Adam "skin-soul." The seventh planet, Saturn, is called Sabbede or Sabbateon. His psychic characteristic is "understanding," so he makes Adam's "hair-soul."[25]

This text, as well as the teaching of Basilides, suggest that a large number of Gnostics even thought that different astrological powers—three-hundred and sixty(-five) to be exact—were responsible for creating each physical body part.[26] This means that each part of the human body was controlled by a different demon who was understood to be a stellar entity within the celestial realms, corresponding to the degrees of the Zodiac (plus five extra calendrical days). Basilides was known for his keen interest in *melothesia*, the exact correlation between the different parts of the human body with the different astrological entities that controlled them.[27] *Melothesia* is dependent on an astrological feature of the Zodiac called by astrologers the *monomoiriai* or single degrees of the Zodiac. Epiphanius, in fact, tells us about Phibionites, who, like the Basilidians, associated individual archons with every degree of the Zodiac. The ascending soul has to invoke each archon name in order to pass through the archons' territories and escape the hands of the authorities.[28]

The way that the universe and the human being were designed by the archons means that the spirit is entrapped in the material world. This continues to be so even after death. Upon the death of the body, the soul is seized by a particular archon who is the overseer and judge of souls. Since the soul, from the time of its incarnation until its release at death, is under the influence of the demonic archons, it cannot live piously. It is unable to transform its negative psychic aspects. So it remains impossible for it to gain its freedom and ascend back

---

[25] *Apoc. John* NHC II,1 11.23–12.25; 15.14–24. *Apoc. John* BC,2 48.11–50.5, supplies a different laundry list. Waldstein-Wisse 1995, 88–91. For the exact planetary associations, see Welburn 1978, 241–254.

[26] *Apoc. John* NHC II,1 15.30–19.6; Epiph., *Pan.* 24.7.6.

[27] On *melothesia*, see n. 28.

[28] Epiph., *Pan.* 26.9–10.

up the cosmic pole or through the star gates. Nor can it know about the existence of the supreme God, or how to worship that God since it is satiated or asleep, sedated by matter. Since the negative psychic aspects cannot be sloughed off, this also means that, upon the death of the body, the overseer archon is justified to put the soul back into another human body. Over the centuries, the spirit within the soul sinks deeper and deeper into matter. It becomes unconscious, buried alive in a tomb it can never leave.

It is only a divine action external to this cosmic system that can alter this situation. So Gnostic systems rely on the descent of redeemer gods into the universe to save the spirit. The most powerful redeemer god in the Gnostic Christian systems is Jesus, whose advent and death result in a physical restructuring of the cosmos. The story of his birth star allowed for the theory to take root that a new star was born which replaced the old *axis mundi*, a bright day star around which the cosmos now revolved. The death of Jesus was interpreted through Paul's teaching in 1 Corinthians 2:6–8, Ephesians 6:12, and Colossians 2:14–15, as the vanquishing of the cosmic powers. Jesus' crucifixion was their own. This meant, for Christians, that the cosmic archons and powers no longer controlled their fate, but Jesus did. After death, their souls would be able to ascend from Hades up through the cosmos along the *axis mundi*, unhindered by the archons. John 10:7, "I am the door," became a literal reality. The saved would enter the Pleroma through a new door that had opened up out of the heavens—Jesus himself.

This teaching had implications for Jesus' disciples, who numbered twelve and like the twelve tribes of Israel, were being mapped onto the twelve signs of the Zodiac. The ways in which these correspondences worked appear to have reflected some ways in which the ancient people thought that magic worked. For instance, in order to control demons and conquer them, to bid powers and harness them, magicians operated from the perspective that their actions on earth could and would affect the celestial gods, the stars and the planets. There seem to me to be at least two sorts of actions common to the magic arts. The first is foundational for the practice of exorcism. It is a concept based on a *counterpoint*. In this performance, the magician is able to subjugate the demon by invoking, through incantations or inscribing angel names, an angel opposite the demon. He might also use a sign of God or Christ to drive out the devil. In this case, the magician uses the principle of antipathy, an *opposite* power or counterpoint, to neutralize the demon.[29]

An early Christian application of the *counterpoint* correspondence is known from the *Pseudo-Clementine* literature.[30] What must have been a widely circulating tradition—that the twelve apostles stood in for the Zodiac—is preserved in the *Homilies*: "The Lord had twelve apostles, bearing the number of the twelve months of the sun."[31] This sort of speculation may be as early as the first century in Christianity, and occurred as well in Judaism.[32] The book of Revelation may be our earliest Christian reference to this correspondence when it describes Jerusalem as it descends down through the heavens. Upon the twelve "foundations" of the outer wall encircling the city are inscribed the twelve names of the apostles.[33] Although dated to the early fifth century, there is a Christian artifact housed in the Geneva Museum that visually depicts this *counterpoint* replacement of the apostles with the Zodiac. Stunningly, Jesus' image is in the center of a lamp. He is the new *axis mundi* around with the Zodiac whirls on the rim of the lamp. But the standard Zodiac signs are not present. Rather they have been replaced with the busts of the twelve apostles.[34] Behind each of these examples is an early teaching preserved by the fourth century bishop of Verona, Zeno, and, as we will see later, the second century teacher Theodotus the Valentinian—that converts when baptized are born again under a new set of Zodiac signs which destine them all to heaven.[35] It fits this pattern of belief then that we should have examples of early Christian sarcophagi picturing the twelve apostles with stars, one above each of the apostles' heads.[36]

---

[29] Cf. Mastrocinque 2005, 33–34 and n. 132.

[30] Cf. Daniélou 1959, 14–21.

[31] *Hom.* 2.23. Rehm-Irmscher 1969, 44.

[32] On the Zodiac in Judaism, see *Esth. Rabba* 7.11; *Num. Rabba* 14.18; *Pesiq. Rab.* 20, 27–28; Sukenik 1934, 33–35; Dothan 1962, 153–154; Kraeling 1956, 42; Charlesworth 1977, 183–200.

[33] Rev 21:10–14.

[34] Deonna 1920, 176–179.

[35] Zeno, *Teaching* 1.38; Clem. Alex., *Exc.* 25.2. For a complete analysis of the apostles and the Zodiac, see Hübner 1975, 120–137; Hübner 1983.

[36] Gundel 1972, 462–709; Leclercq 1907, 3014.

Christian zodiac on fifth-century red clay lamp
Inv. no. C 1478, The Geneva Museum of Art and History
© Musée d'art et d'histoire, Ville de Genève Reproduced with permission

The second practice is based on the concept of the *counterpart*. This is the idea that "like affects like," where the acts performed by a magician on a "double" were thought to be experienced in duplicate on the magician's subject. It is imitative by nature, or as Frazer long ago described, "homeopathic," a description that I still find *apropos*.[37] The *counterpart* concept relies behind the making of talismans, effigies, and certain types of amulets. It is believed to be effective because the magician's subject should experience the same fate as its double—a certain "sympathy" exists between the two.

---

[37] Frazer 1900.

If Orosius and Turibius fairly represent Priscillian's teaching on astrology, including Orosius' quotation of a letter fragment purported to be Priscillian's, the Priscillians in the fourth century provide us with a fine example of *counterpart* mapping of the Zodiac.[38] It follows from their reports that the Priscillians believed that souls were derived from a storehouse, and salvation depended upon their ability to conquer the bodies in which they had been bound by evil archons when they descended through the spheres. The bodies had been sealed with a written bond saying that they were the property of these evil powers, trapping the souls within. The Zodiac signs controlled the formation of the body, corresponding to twelve powers of Darkness and matter's domination. The soul's formation was controlled by the twelve heavenly spirits, who served as counterpoints to the twelve negative Zodiac powers. The twelve Jewish patriarchs, who represented the twelve virtues that strengthened the various parts of the soul, were mapped as the counterparts to these twelve spirits: Reuben the head-soul; Judah the breast-soul; Levi the heart-soul; Benjamin the thigh-soul; and so forth. In fact, Orosius says that they believed that each Patriarch ruled over a different aspect of the soul just as the signs of the Zodiac ruled over different parts of the body: Aries the head; Taurus the neck; Gemini the arms; Cancer the breast; and so forth.[39] When Jesus was nailed to the cross, the bond that trapped the soul in the body was nailed too, liberating the soul.[40]

In the Gnostic story, Jesus replaced the old cosmic pole, providing a restructuring of the cosmos which allowed for the escape of the trapped spirit. From this it followed, that his disciples must stand in

---

[38] Orosius, *Commonitorium de errore Priscillianistarum et Origenistarum* 2; Leo, *Ep.* 15, praef. 2, 15.16; Sigebertus Gemblacensis, *Chron.* a. 386.

[39] *Sefer Yezirah* parallels the Zodiac signs to the twelve parts of the human body. On this see Scholem 1955, 77–78. Simliar examples of *melothesia* can be found in Manichaean texts, especially *Kephalaia* 70, "On the body that is constructed according to the form of the cosmos," which has the same correspondences between the Zodiac signs and body parts: Aries (head); Taurus (neck and shoulders); Gemini (arms); Cancer (breast); Leo (stomach); Virgo (loins); Libra (vertebrae); Scorpio (sexual organs); Sagittarius (loins); Capricorn (knees); Aquarius (shinbones); Pisces (soles of the feet). This appears to be common knowledge, expressed also by Sextus Empiricus, *Adv. math.* 5.21–22; Manilius 2.456–65, 4.702–709; Vettius Valens 2.36; Porphyry, *Introductio in Tetrabiblum Ptolemaei* 44; Firmicus Maternus, *Mathesis* 2.24; P. Ryl. 63 (third century, Plato learns a *melothesia* from Peteësis an Egyptian prophet); P. Mich. Inv. 1, 1290 (second century, an extremely detailed mathematical *melothesia*).

[40] Hübner 1983, 18–24; Chadwick 1976, 190–202, 211–215; cf. Burrus 1995, 47–78.

for the Zodiacal signs, which were the archons. Whether this was a positive or negative correspondence, depends on both the peculiar Gnostic tradition engaging the correspondence and the date of the text in which this discussion is occurring. In the end, understanding these correspondences can help us resolve what Gnosticism is. It can help us see how Gnosticism is the culmination of a religio-social process that began as a lodge movement supplementing the synagogue and the church and ended as a new religious movement competing with them and persecuted by them.

GOSPEL OF JUDAS

The cosmic structures laid out in the mid-second century *Gospel of Judas*, from the beginning to the end of this gospel, mirror that of a group of Sethian Christians. The entire gospel is dependent upon a cosmos with the number thirteen as its ordering principle. In this volume and elsewhere, Marvin Meyer has suggested that the thirteenth realm in the *Gospel of Judas* is likely the same thirteenth realm from which Pistis Sophia is separated in a Gnostic text that bears her name.[41] Meyer no longer maintains his argument for a hero Judas who was Jesus' "soul-mate" as he envisioned Judas in his original essay published in National Geographic's first edition of *The Gospel of Judas*.[42] Meyer now suggests that Judas is something between a hero and a villain. Judas is a tragic figure similar to the repentant Sophia. "Like Sophia in other texts and traditions," Meyer writes in the second edition of his commentary in National Geographic's *The Gospel of Judas*, "Judas in the Gospel of Judas is separated from the divine realms above, even though he knows and professes the mysteries of the divine and the origin of the savior; he goes through grief and persecution as a *daimon* confined to this world below; he is enlightened with revelations that no human will ever see; and at last he is said to be on his way, much like Sophia, to the thirteenth aeon of gnostic lore."[43]

---

[41] Kasser et al. 2008, 125–154.
[42] In Kasser et al. 2006a, 137–169.
[43] Meyer in Kasser et al. 2008, 151.

Meyer's equation of the thirteenth Aeon, the residence of Pistis Sophia, with the residence of Judas is problematic and unconvincing. As we will see in the final section of this chapter, the *Pistis Sophia* is a very late Gnostic text, from the fourth century, written two hundred years after the *Gospel of Judas*. The text is dependent on the late third century Gnostic texts called the *Books of Jeu*. Together they comprise a compendium of Gnostic instructions about ascent and salvation. The teachings in these books do not represent a single school of Gnosis, but rather are an eclectic blend of Sethian, Valentinian, and Manichaean instructions, complete with diagrams and magical seals. The result is a totally unique form of Gnosticism that emerges in the late third century. It is not a representative of mid- to late second century Sethian Christianity. The thirteenth Aeon that Pistis Sophia flees is not the same place where Judas is going to go, as Meyer suggests. In the text *Pistis Sophia*, it is imagined as a place *beyond* this cosmos and its stars, ruled by the father of Ialdabaoth, Authades, rather than a realm *in* this cosmos with a star in it as the *Gospel of Judas* indicates. Judas does not follow Sophia's pattern as Meyer says. He does not start out in the thirteenth Aeon. He is not punished and driven out of it. He is not suffering here in the cosmos because he is in exile, or because he has been forced out of the thirteenth Aeon by the father of Ialdabaoth. Nor does he await redemption in top of the twelfth realm like Pistis Sophia. What and where is the thirteenth Aeon according to the *Gospel of Judas*?

Thirteen Realms and Their Archon

Although the top of p. 52 is fragmentary, it appears that the author of the *Gospel of Judas* knows a version of the Sethian myth in which Nebro-Ialdabaoth and his lieutenant Saklas live in a cloud in Chaos. The *Gospel of Judas* eventually drops references to Nebro-Ialdabaoth and consolidates these archons into one demiurge who emerges in the text by the name Saklas. For convenience and consistency, I have chosen to refer to this many-named demiurge by his well-known name Ialdabaoth, although I could have chosen to call him Saklas or Nebro just as easily.

Nebro-Ialdabaoth and Saklas each create six angels as their assistants. Another twelve angels are created to rule the heavens below them. Five of these are said to be the archons appointed to rule the Abyss, leaving the other seven, who are called collectively "the first," to rule Chaos. The five rulers of Hades are named [...]eth, Harmathoth, Galia, Yobel, and Adonaios.[44] The names of the seven celestial rulers are not preserved. But it appears that the Gospel of Judas is based on a system in which there are twelve cosmic realms with twelve apportioned rulers, seven of them planetary, five of them sublunar in the abyss.

Above these twelve archons and realms is the thirteenth cosmic realm, the abode of the "apostate" Archon, Nebro-Ialdabaoth, and Saklas. In astrological terms, it is to be identified with the realm of the fixed stars, called the eighth sphere since the seven planetary spheres were immediately below it. It may not be coincidental that this sphere, also known as *aplanes*, is where some Middle Platonic philosophers placed the Elysian fields.[45] This afterlife isle traditionally was ruled by Kronos, the baby-devouring Titan who had been imprisoned in Tartarus at the beginning of time. Eventually Zeus released him to take up the throne at Elysium.[46] When the afterlife fields were moved from Hades to the realm of the fixed stars in the Hellenistic period, it is quite possible that, in the popular imagination, Kronos was moved there as well. This may account for his confusion with Chronos who had been identified with the planet Saturn which resided in the seventh sphere immediately below the fixed stars.

Whatever is the case with Kronos, this cosmic structure is held in common with one of our earliest Sethian texts, the *Apocryphon of John* (ca. 100–125 CE). According to this text, the triple-named demiurge, Ialdabaoth-Saklas-Samael, left the regions where his mother Sophia lived in order to create twelve Archons to rule over the cosmic realms below him. Seven "kings (Ⲛ̄ⲢⲢⲞ)" he placed over the seven firmaments of the heavens, and five kings over the depth of the Abyss "so that they would reign (ϨⲰⲤⲦⲈ ⲀⲦⲢⲞⲨⲢ̄Ⲣ̄ⲢⲞ)."[47]

This is a fascinating way to align the Archons cosmologically. Does it represent some blending of the planetary seven with the Zodiacal twelve, somehow dependent on the astrological belief that each of the signs of the Zodiac is ruled by one of the planets as A.J. Welburn has

---

[44] *Gos. Jud.* 51.4–52.14.
[45] Cf. Macrobius, *Comm. Scipio* 1.11.8.
[46] Hesiod, *Op.* 156–158; Pindar, *Ol.* 2. 55–57; cf. Plato, *Gorg.* 525a–b.
[47] *Apoc. John* NHC II,1.9. Coptic: Waldstein-Wisse 1995, 68–69; translation mine.

argued?[48] Or is something else going on? However this came to be, in *John's* system as in *Judas'*, we now have twelve Archons below the demiurge, seven which are aligned with the planets, and five which rule Hades. These five likely correspond to the five gods traditionally found in the underworld palace both in the Greek tradition (Hades, Persephone, Minos, Rhadamanthus, and Aeacus) and in the Egyptian (Osiris, Isis, Horus, Thoth, and Anubis). This means that the demiurge resides in a thirteenth realm, which astrologically corresponds to the realm of the fixed stars just beyond the planets.

The *Gospel of the Egyptians* is another Sethian text. It is roughly contemporary to the *Gospel of Judas* (ca. 150–200 CE). In a cloud above Chaos and Hades, Saklas and Nebruel "the great demon (ⲡⲛⲟⳓ ⲛ̄ⲇⲁⲓⲙⲱⲛ)" dwell. The two become "the earth's spirit of conception ([ⲛ̄ⲟⲩ]ⲡ̄ⲛⲁ ⲛ̄ϫⲡⲟ ⲛ̄ⲧⲉ ⲡⲕⲁϩ)," which creates twelve realms below and twelve archons to rule over Chaos and Hades.[49] Jesus, in fact, conquered the archons when "he nailed the powers of the thirteen realms (ⲁϥⳉⲱϭⲧ ⲛ̄ⲛⲁⲩⲛⲁⲙⲓⲥ ⲙ̄ⲡⲙ̄ⲛ̄ⲧϣⲟⲙⲧⲉ ⲛ̄ⲁⲓⲱⲛ)" at his crucifixion. Indeed, like Jesus, the faithful are supposed to "renounce the world and the god of the thirteen realms (ⲡⲁⲡⲟⲧⲁⲥⲥⲉ ⲙ̄ⲡⲕⲟⲥⲙⲟⲥ ⲙ̄ⲛ̄ ⲡⲛⲟⲩⲧⲉ ⲙ̄ⲡⲙ̄ⲛ̄ⲧϣⲟⲙⲧⲉ ⲛ̄ⲁⲓⲱⲛ)."[50]

The other Sethian text that is aware of the importance of the number thirteen is the early fourth century non-Christian text *Marsanes*. This text was created by Sethian Gnostics who were involved in Neoplatonic metaphysical discussions and represents the latest in the group of Platonizing Sethian treatises, which includes *Zostrianos*, the *Three Steles of Seth*, and *Allogenes*.[51] The second half of the text divulges certain harmonies that are to be sung in order to enchant and overcome the celestial Powers of the universe, including those negative Powers *Marsanes* identifies as the planetary and Zodiac angels.[52] Marsanes instructions on these harmonies specifically says that they are effective in separating the initiate from these angels.[53] Thus the text tells us that the initiates were using wax tablets and emerald images in their

---

[48] Welburn 1978, 248.
[49] *Gos. Eg.* NHC III,2 57.11–58.23. Coptic: Böhlig-Wisse 1975, 120–125; translation mine.
[50] *Gos. Eg.* NHC III,2 63.19–64.9; cf. IV,2 75.5–20. Coptic: Böhlig-Wisse 1975, 144–147; translation mine.
[51] On this, see Turner 2001.
[52] *Mars.* NHC X 18.14–45.20.
[53] *Mars.* NHC X 32.1–5.

ceremonies.[54] These were amulets with *apotropaic* functions, warding off the evil angels with powerful words and images. The reward is that the soul will be transfigured, acquiring power and salvation.[55] In our fragmentary version, only the name Gamaliel survives, although the text probably contained many more names of powers and angels since it relates that the initiate should not cease "naming the angels."[56]

It is in the first half of *Marsanes* where we find the author reappropriating the number thirteen in a ritual sequence of thirteen seals. The performance of this series results in an ascent out of this cosmos and through the Pleromic aeons to the Unknown Silent God who is the foundation of the indistinguishable God. The first six seals work the soul through the cosmic realms, including the arenas where disembodied and repentant souls are kept, as well as the perfected souls. The seventh sealing begins the ascent through the Pleroma in the Aeon of Autogenes, ending with the thirteenth sealing in the Aeon of the Unknown Silent God.[57] The reappropriation of the number thirteen in this fashion likely was the result of the fact that in earlier Sethian texts, salvation and admittance to the Pleroma depended on the soul's ability to overcome thirteen archons. The thirteen sealings in Marsanes do not correspond to thirteen cosmic realms, and so are not equivalent to the thirteen cosmic realms in the *Gospel of Judas*.

The manuscripts of the *Apocryphon of John* and the *Gospel of the Egyptians* give alternative lists of the names of the twelve Archons:

NHC II 10.28–11.4	NHC IV 17.1–5	BG 40.5–18	NHC III 16.20–17.5	NHC III 58.6–23
Athoth		Yaoth	Haoth	Athoth
Harmas		Hermas	Harmas	Harmas
Kalioumbri		Galila	Galila	Galila
Yabel		Yobel	Yobel	Yobel
Adonaiu-Sabaoth		Adonaios	Adonaios	Adonaios-Sabaoth
Cain		Sabaoth	Sabaoth	Cain
Abel	Abel	Cainan, Cae, Cain	Cainan Kasin	Abel
Abrisene	Abrisene	Abiressine	Abiressia	Akiressina
Yobel	Yobel	Yobel	Yobel	Yubel
Arumpieel	Armoupiel	Harmoupiael	Armoupiael	Harmupiael
Melcheiradonein		Adonin	Adonin	Archir-Adonin
Belias		Belias	Belias	Belias

---

[54] *Mars.* NHC X 35.1–3.
[55] *Mars.* NHC X 39.18–40.3.
[56] *Mars.* NHC X 64.20; 39.5.
[57] *Mars.* NHC X 2.12–4.24.

These lists are not stable, especially when it comes to spelling and sequence, and sorting out possible Zodiacal correspondences with their planetary rulers is no easy task, although Welburn attempted this in a classic article on the subject.[58] The list of five Archons in the *Gospel of Judas* aligns with the first five Archons in these above lists, although the author has identified them as the five Abyss demons rather than the planetary ones. It may be that the author of the *Gospel of Judas* was reading the list in ascending order rather than descending, thus making a mistake in this identification.

NHC II 10.28–34	BG 40.5–10	NHC III 16.20–25	NHC III 58.6–15	TC 52.4–11
Athoth	Yaoth	Haoth	Athoth	[…]th
Harmas	Hermas	Harmas	Harmas	Harmathoth
Kalioumbri	Galila	Galila	Galila	Galia
Yabel	Yobel	Yobel	Yobel	Yobel
Adonaiu-Sabaoth	Adonaios	Adonaios	Adonaios-Sabaoth	Adonais

The first name preserved in the list in the *Gospel of Judas* must be reconstructed. My initial reading "Atheth" followed the *Critical Edition*'s reading, "eta".[59] Now that I can view a high-resolution photograph of this area, I observe that all that is left is a theta with a broken area preceding it. At the bottom of the broken area, one dot of ink is preserved. Whether this dot is enough to reconstruct eta, let alone "[S]eth," as the *Critical Edition* has it, is conjecture. The dot looks to me like it just as well could represent the bottom of the centerline of an omega, where the ink has eroded from the lower register as is the case with the omega at the beginning of line 11 on p. 50. The measurement between the centerline of this letter and the left edge of the theta appears identical to the distance between the centerline of the omega on 52.7 and the theta that follows it.

So there is no reason for us to think that the first archon in this list is any other than Athoth. In fact, the epithet of this archon, "Excellent (χρηστός)," and its placement in the list corresponds to Athoth elsewhere in Sethian literature. This archon is the who carries the title "Excellent (χρηστός)" identified by the standard abbreviation x̅c̅ or x̅p̅c̅ which is often confused with "χριστός."[60] In the *Apocryphon of*

John, Athoth is the first Power, "Excellence (χ$\overline{PC}$)."[61] Thus, in the same text, II.10–29–30 should be reconstructed: "the name of the first one is Athoth, whom the generations call [the excellent one (п[oүх̄]р̄c]." The same can be said for the reference to him in the *Gospel of the Egyptians*. It should read: "The first angel is Ath[oth. He is the one] whom [the great] generations of people call ["the excellent one (пoүх̄р̄c)"].[62] That the *Gospel of Judas* also has Athoth as the first archon in its list actually is confirmed in 52.7 where the scribe has made a copying error, perhaps due to *anablepsis*. He has accidentally repeated the archon's name following ϩλρμλ.

Judas as Ialdabaoth

The *Gospel of Judas* further plays on the correspondences between the archons and celestial beings by identifying the twelve planetary and abyss archons with the twelve disciples (including Matthias), while the thirteenth demon is said to be Judas. Jesus directly addresses Judas as the "Thirteenth Demon (ō пмеϩмнтīī λλιμων)."[63] He tells him that he will be the "Thirteenth" cursed by the generations that he will preside over.[64] Although he will dwell in the thirteenth cosmic realm where his star will rule, Judas will not ascend beyond this realm to the aeon where the Holy Generation resides.[65] In fact, Jesus has separated Judas from the Holy Generation when he interprets Judas' dream in such a way that Judas is locked out of the place reserved for the holy ones, the aeon above the cosmos where the planets do not rule.[66] Because the gospel attaches a star to the thirteenth realm, it locates Judas *within* this cosmos. Thus it is inappropriate to interpret Judas' connection with the thirteenth realm in the *Gospel of Judas* with traditions of the number thirteen in *Marsanes* where the thirteenth seal is performed in the highest aeon of the Pleroma or traditions of the thirteenth aeon in *Pistis Sophia* where it is a liminal realm outside of the cosmos proper, but below the divine world, the Treasury of Light.

---

[61] *Apoc. John* NHC II,1 12.16. Coptic: Böhlig-Wisse 1975, 75; translation mine.
[62] *Gos. Eg.* NHC III,2 58.10. For this interpretation and reconstructions, Turner 2008b, 204 and n. 12.
[63] *Gos. Jud.* 44.21. Coptic: Kasser et al. 2007, 207–208; translation mine.
[64] *Gos. Jud.* 46.19–24.
[65] *Gos. Jud.* 55.10–11; 46.25–47.1.
[66] *Gos. Jud.* 46.16–18; 45.13–19.

Jesus tells him that Judas will become the "Thirteenth," cursed by the generations that he will "rule over."⁶⁷ This "ruling" terminology is associated with the Archons. The Coptic text here uses ⲁⲣⲭⲓ, which is a Coptic variant of the Greek loanword, ἄρχω, "to rule." What the Archon (or Ruler!) does is "rule" over the cosmic realms and its generations.⁶⁸ This image is repeated a few pages later in the gospel when Jesus tells Judas that he will come to dwell in the thirteenth realm where Judas' star will rule. Here the Coptic does not rely on a Greek loanword for translation, but puts the word into good Coptic, ⲣ ⲉⲣⲟ, "to reign."⁶⁹ Judas' future is bound up with the thirteenth realm. Judas will not ascend beyond this realm to the Aeon where the planets do not rule but where the Holy Generation, the kingless generation, resides.⁷⁰ This separation is made clear when in Jesus' interpretation of Judas' dream. According to Jesus, Judas is locked out of the place reserved for the holy ones, the Aeon above the cosmos where the sun and moon do not rule.⁷¹

These associations make Judas the earthly *counterpart* of the Archon Nebro-Ialdabaoth. This heaven-earth correspondence was completely transparent to the Sethian Christians who wrote this text, and so they have left behind subtle references to the correspondence in their gospel. Nebro-Ialdabaoth was known to them as the "Apostate (ⲁⲡ[ⲟⲥ]ⲧⲁⲏⲥ)" Archon who was "corrupted with blood (ⲉ[ϥ]ⲭⲟ[ⲟ]ⲙ ⲛⲥⲛⲟϥ ⲉⲟⲩⲛ̄ⲧⲁϥ ⲙ̄ⲙⲁⲩ)."⁷² This image was traditionally linked to Judas in the Christian scriptures. He is the apostate, the rebel or traitor who had handed over "innocent blood," and whose thirty pieces of silver were used to purchase a cemetery for foreigners called the "Field of Blood."⁷³

These ideas may be connected to the widespread ancient belief that the places of demons are places filled with pain, blood, slaughter, weeping, mourning, and groaning.⁷⁴ But that Nebro-Ialdabaoth and Judas are being linked through this imagery is quite evident when it is realized that nowhere else in Gnostic literature do we find the

---

⁶⁷ *Gos. Jud.* 46.19–24. Coptic: Kasser et al. 2007, 211.
⁶⁸ *Gos. Jud.* 46.19–24.
⁶⁹ *Gos. Jud.* 55.10–11. Coptic: Kasser et al. 2007, 229.
⁷⁰ *Gos. Jud.* 46.25–47.1; 45.20–21; 37.1–6.
⁷¹ *Gos. Jud.* 45.13–19.
⁷² *Gos. Jud.* 51.11–15. Kasser et al. 2007, 220–221.
⁷³ Matt 27:4, 8; Acts 1:19.
⁷⁴ Cf. *Asc.* NHC VI,8 78. 25–31.

demiurge described as an apostate corrupted with blood.[75] He is, however, described as Sophia's "miscarriage of darkness" and his revolt is called an "*apostasis*" or "defection."[76] It is also fascinating that the Egyptians identified one of the presiding astral deities by the name "Nebu," a vulture-serpent faced ruler with the feet of a lion. Since he was the "Lord of wars," during his season when he reigned in the heavens there would be battle and destruction. Rebels (Greek: ἀποστάτης) would rise when he ruled the sky.[77] Could Nebu's portraiture have informed the Gnostic portrayal of Nebro/Nebruel and Judas's link to him?

In the *Gospel of Judas*, the "Lord over everything" is the one who commands that sacrifices be offered to him, sacrifices which are evil.[78] Judas will bring about the most evil of these sacrifices, because Judas will be the one responsible for Jesus' sacrifice.[79] Thus it is that Judas carries through on earth the will of his celestial star, Nebro-Ialdabaoth, who wants Jesus dead. His deed, in fact, is said to correspond to the moment when Judas' star moves through the heavens, which ascends above the other stars to Nebro-Ialdabaoth's realm, the thirteenth.[80] From this realm, Judas will rule over the twelve archons below him until the end of time, when the fate of the stars has been accomplished and the archons and their realms are destroyed.[81] Judas the demon will lament exceedingly, just as the Gnostics expected the archons to do when they were faced with the truth.[82]

Why is this *counterpart* correspondence between Judas and Nebro-Ialdabaoth so important to the Sethians? Because it turned on its head the teaching of the Apostolic Christians about the efficacy of Jesus' death as an atonement sacrifice made to God. The Sethian Christians were offended by this doctrine. For instance, in the *Second Treatise of the Great Seth*, the author calls the Apostolic atonement doctrine a "joke" (ογϲωβε) of the archons who "proclaim a doctrine of a dead

---

[75] The closest reference to "blood" corruption I have been able to locate, is to the fallen Sophia in the *Gos. Egy.* NHC III,2 57.1–5. But the passage is so fragmentary that it is impossible to know what the reference to blood actually means.

[76] *Apoc. John* BG,2 45.10–13. Coptic: Waldstein-Wisse 1995, 80.

[77] P. Oxy. 465 col. i.10–44. Grenfell-Hunt 1903, 128.

[78] *Gos. Jud.* 40.18–25; 56.11–17. Coptic: Kasser et al. 2007, 199, 231. Translation mine.

[79] *Gos. Jud.* 56.17–21.

[80] *Gos. Jud.* 56.23, 57.19–20, 46.19–24, 55.10–11.

[81] *Gos. Jud.* 55.15–20, 57.9.

[82] Cp. *Gos. Jud.* 46.11–47.1; *Orig. World* NHC XIII,2 125.32–35.

man and lies."[83] But it is only from the *Gospel of Judas* that we can puzzle out their reasoning. The Gnostics who wrote *Judas* take on the Apostolic Christians on their own turf, agreeing with them that Judas is a demon and that he is responsible for bringing about Jesus' sacrificial death. But then they ask the obvious. If Judas was a demon, and he brought about Jesus' sacrifice, was his sacrifice something that the demons desired? If so, sacrifice must be evil, and so must the doctrine of atonement. In fact, they concluded, this is all a trick by the demon who rules this world, Judas' celestial correspondence, Nebro-Ialdabaoth. It was brought about in order to deceive Christians and lead them astray. Whenever Christians perform a Eucharist ceremony in which the sacrifice of Jesus is reenacted, they are unwittingly worshiping Nebro-Ialdabaoth.[84]

Can Judas break this correspondence? Can he overcome his destiny as Ialdabaoth's servant? Some ancient people thought that it was possible to break these types of negative correspondences, and one of the ways in which they tried to do so was through the use of magical spells. The magical technique for changing an undesirable destiny involved invoking the aid of a powerful god by chanting his name according to a certain prescription. When the god appeared, the petitioner was instructed not to stare at the god's face, but look down and beseech him, "Master, what is fated for me?" The god then was supposed to tell the petitioner about his "star" and "what kind of daimon" he had. If the petitioner heard some terrible fate or correspondence, he was commanded not to cry or weep, but ask the god to "wash it off or circumvent it, for this god can do everything."

As Grant Adamson argues in his contribution to this volume, this particular spell resonates on many levels with the story about Judas Iscariot in his gospel, and may be an echo of shared popular

---

[83] *Treat. Seth* NHC VII,2 60.13–22. Coptic: Riley, 1996, 176. Translation mine. The *Treat. Seth* should be recognized as a Sethian Christian writing. It contains many of the mythic characters associated with the Sethian myth, including Sophia, Ialdabaoth, Adonaios, and Ennoia. So in my opinion, its connection to Sethianism is almost certain. It is an example, however, of a *Christian* Sethian text, as is the *Gospel of Judas*. Thus its focus is on the descent of Christ into Jesus, his crucifixion, and his victory over the archons. The crucifixion scene is similar to what we know about Basilides' teaching on the subject, and suggests a sharing of knowledge between the Sethian and Basilidian Christians, as there was between the Sethian and Valentinian Christians.

[84] *Gos. Jud.* 34.8–10.

knowledge in antiquity about ways in which fate could be conquered.[85] When Judas approaches Jesus for teaching, like the suppliant in the spell, Judas turns away his face. Throughout the gospel, Jesus provides Judas with the information about Judas' destiny, none of which Judas likes—neither his star, nor its movement in the skies, nor his identification with Ialdabaoth the thirteenth demon, nor his future reign as the archon in the thirteenth cosmic sphere. But when Judas tells Jesus that he does not want any of this, Jesus does not take it away. The god does not grant his request probably because the Sethians understood Judas to be an apostate, and as such his damnation was sure. So instead of granting Judas freedom from his cursed destiny, Jesus repeats the information as evident, even in process, and Judas is left to weep.

Twelve Apostles as Counterparts of the Archon

Who is responsible on earth for leading Christians astray, for teaching them the doctrine of atonement and the celebration of the Eucharist? The twelve disciples who are the earthly *counterparts* of the twelve archons residing below Judas.[86] Each one of them represents a human generation who will curse Judas, generations which will never know Jesus.[87] The twelve apostles represent the human generations that do not have connections to the holy generation beyond the cosmic realms.[88]

What is most fascinating here is the acknowledgement by the author of the *Gospel of Judas*, that Christians other than themselves understand this heaven-earth correspondence between the apostles and the stars in a positive sense. Thus the author of *Judas* mentions that some Christians say that the twelve apostles are "equal to the angels," by which these Christians mean that the apostles are "the stars which accomplish everything."[89] This is a *counterpoint* teaching about the apostles, that they, as positive entities, replace the stars and vanquish the stars' control over human Fate. These other Christians teach that

---

[85] *PGM* 13.705–715. Translated by Betz 1992, 189. Refer to Adamson's paper in this volume for a complete analysis of this important spell and its relationship to the *Gospel of Judas*.
[86] *Gos. Jud.* 46.5–24.
[87] *Gos. Jud.* 46.21–22; 34.15–18.
[88] *Gos. Jud.* 36.19–37.20.
[89] *Gos. Jud.* 40.15–18. Kasser et al. 2007, 199.

once initiated, the Christian's fate is no longer controlled by the stars, but by the apostles who have replaced these negative powers.

The author of the *Gospel of Judas*, however, goes on to insist that this *counterpoint* teaching is wrong. Instead the real teaching is that the apostles are twelve negative *counterparts* of the Archons. They are the twelve priests in the heavenly temple who make shameful sacrifices in the Name of Jesus. In so doing, they unknowingly make their offerings to the "Servant of Error," the "Lord over everything," leading countless of future generations astray. On the last day, they will be judged "guilty."[90]

This negative correspondence probably develops out of a standard Sethian Christian teaching as described by Irenaeus—that Jesus' disciples were ignorant and did not as a group receive his esoteric teachings. He states that the Sethians affirm that many of Jesus' disciples were not aware of the descent of Christ into him. Even when they saw him risen, they did not recognize him as the Christ. The disciples greatest error was their teaching about a physical resurrection, not being aware that flesh and blood do not possess the Kingdom. They remain unaware that Jesus was united to Christ, the incorruptible Aeon. Furthermore, during the eighteen months after his resurrection, Jesus was only able to teach a few disciples.[91]

Servant(s) of Saklas

Gregor Wurst of the University of Augsburg continues to piece together leftover fragments from the Tchacos Codex. At the Codex Judas Congress on March 14, 2008, held at Rice University, Professor Wurst revealed an important line that he has pieced together from four small fragments.[92] It reads [...ⲟ]ⲙ̄ϩⲁⲗ ⲛ̄ⲥⲁⲕⲗⲁⲥ, "servant(s?) of Saklas." Recently he has placed these fragments on page 55 of the Tchacos Codex, as words of Jesus spoken to Judas.[93] Jesus appears to be discussing the sins of the apostles who are servants of Saklas, telling Judas that he will rule over them.

Who is Saklas? In Sethianism, Saklas is understood to be both the demiurge's lieutenant living in the demiurge's cloud, and the

---

[90] *Gos. Jud.* 39.6–40.26.
[91] Iren., *Adv. haer.* 1.30.13–14.
[92] TC fragments I2, C29, H34, C4.
[93] Refer to Wurst's contribution to this volume.

demiurge himself. Sometimes he has both identities in a single text. In the *Apocryphon of John*, for instance, the demiurge is known as just "Ialdabaoth."[94] But it is also said in the same text that he goes by three names—Ialdabaoth, Saklas, and Samael.[95] In the *Apocalypse of Adam*, Sakla is the preferred name of the god of this world,[96] while in the *Gospel of the Egyptians*, the unnamed demiurge is created as a great angel with two monads, Sakla and Nebruel.[97] But later in the narrative, the god of this world goes by Sakla only, Nebruel vanishing along with the original unnamed demiurgic angel.[98]

The *Gospel of Judas* is just as ambiguous. The demiurge is described as an "angel" whose face "flashed with fire." He is "corrupted with blood." His name is "Nebro(el)" which means "Apostate." But he is also known as "Ialdabaoth." A second angel, Saklas, simultaneously comes into being.[99] After this brief accounting of the names, Nebro(el) and Ialdabaoth fall out of the narrative, and Saklas emerges as the name of the demiurge throughout the rest of the gospel.

As I mentioned previously, for the purposes of simplification, I have chosen to call this figure "Ialdabaoth," but I could just as simply have chosen "Saklas" or even "Nebro(el)." I imagine that the confusion over these names across the Sethian literature has to do with the likelihood that the demiurge had several descriptive names early on in the tradition, just as Jesus in early Christianity was known by a multitude of names including the Son, Logos, Angel, Yahweh, Captain, Glory, Holy Spirit, Wisdom, God, and Lord. The multiplicity of names for the single Gnostic demiurge became confused over time with the existence of independent beings, a confusion apparent in the Sethian corpus.

This new fragmentary reference to Saklas is fascinating. It appears to refer to the apostles as "servants of Saklas" as they make obeisance to the demiurge, the apostate archon with whom Judas corresponds. The fragment is additional evidence that the *Gospel of Judas* has a very specific understanding of the heaven-earth correspondences. The thirteen Archons correspond to Jesus' disciples including Judas who emerges as their cursed leader because he was the instrument in bringing about

---

[94] *Apoc. John* NHC II,1 10.20; 11.35; etc.
[95] *Apoc. John* NHC II,1 11.15–18.
[96] *Apoc. Adam* NHC V,5 74.3, 8.
[97] *Gos. Eg.* NHC IV,2 57.1–26.
[98] *Gos. Eg.* IV,2 58.24–59.1.
[99] *Gos. Jud.* 51.8–17. Coptic: Kasser et al. 2007, 221.

the demiurge's greatest trick on people—the doctrine of atonement and its institution in the performance of the Eucharist.

A Separatist Movement

Whoever wrote the *Gospel of Judas* is developing this standard Sethian teaching about the ignorance of the disciples of Jesus in order to attack the Apostolic Church. The author does this by identifying its apostolic authorities with ignorant and rebellious Archons, demons who curse the very demon who made possible their atonement. The reason that the author of the *Gospel of Judas* portrays the apostles so harshly is not because he hates Christianity. Rather, I think that he worried that many Christians were being led astray by the Apostolic Church, which claimed to rely on teachings derived from the Twelve. From his acquaintance with the Gospel of Mark, the author of *Judas* reasoned that the Twelve were so ignorant and faithless that even the demons—including Judas—were more knowledgeable than they were. So the author's purpose was to challenge the Apostolic Church's doctrines and practices, which were claimed by its leaders to be passed down as the authoritative teachings from the apostles to the current bishops in an unbroken chain of transmission.

For the author of the *Gospel of Judas*, the foundational link in this chain was corrupt. Because the disciples were ignorant and faithless, whatever information they passed on was bogus. Following their teachings leads Christians astray, and joining in their rituals tricks them into worshiping the wrong god! The consequence of this horrible situation was the annihilation rather than salvation of countless Christians. It was the weight of this hidden tragic knowledge that likely seeded the idea to retell Judas' story so that the Apostolic Christians would be critiqued, corrected, and hopefully brought into the Gnostic fold. The author clearly sees his Sethian community as a separatist movement, a non-conformist Christianity that alone knows the secrets of salvation.

Thus, the astrological correspondences in the *Gospel of Judas* connect Judas with the ruling archon, Ialdabaoth, while the other twelve disciples with the twelve subordinate archons who occupied the twelve realms below him. These correspondences were understood to be counterpart associations, where Judas and the twelve disciples function as the earthly doubles of these specific archons. A sympathy exists between them, so that they carry out on earth the brutal will of their ruling stars.

This negative correspondence works to severely critique the Apostolic Church whose doctrines and practices relied on the authenticity and authority of the twelve apostles and whose central feature was the sacrifice of Jesus brought about by Judas. If the Apostolic Church was ruled by Judas the apostate archon and the other disciples were subordinate archons, how much could the bishops and priests of the Apostolic Church really know? Evidently the Sethian Christians who wrote this gospel saw themselves as the only Christian church that possessed the Truth. As such, they identified themselves as a separate non-conformist church competing with the Apostolic Church, which they believed was defunct.

Identification of the apostles with archons is not a unique feature of the *Gospel of Judas*. In fact, this identification appears to be fairly standard in the early Christian literature. But, just because it is standard, it does not mean that the correspondences were consistently understood to be counterpart relationships as the *Gospel of Judas* has them. As we will see, in some cases, the correspondence was friendlier to the apostles. An examination of the correspondence maps across the Gnostic sources reveals a varied relationship between Apostolic Christians and Gnostic Christians within different communities and eras, revealing precious information about the origins, growth and development of Gnosticism.

THEODOTUS THE VALENTINIAN

The correspondence between the stars and the twelve Apostles was also known to Theodotus, a famous eastern Valentinian who taught in the mid- to late second century. He said that "the Apostles were substituted for the twelve signs of the Zodiac, for, just as birth is directed by them, so is rebirth by the Apostles (οἱ ἀπόστολοι μετετέθησαν τοῖς δεκαδύο ζῳδίοις, ὡς γὰρ ὑπ᾽ ἐκείνων ἡ γένεσις διοικεῖται, οὕτως ὑπὸ τῶν ἀποστόλων ἡ ἀναγέννησις)."[100] Here we encounter the exact teaching that the author of the *Gospel of Judas* was trying to eradicate. Each Apostle was a *counterpoint* for the stars that controlled Fate. Once baptized, the initiate was no longer dominated by the negative rule of the stars. Instead the positive Apostles controlled his or her fate.

---

[100] Clem. Alex., *Exc.* 25.2. Greek: Casey 1934, 58; translation mine.

A Restructured Universe

Theodotus expounds on this, noting that Fate is the coming together of many opposing forces, which cannot be seen. It guides the course of the stars and even governs through them. In this way, the Zodiac and the planets have power over human beings and direct human births. The twelve signs of the Zodiac and the seven wandering stars sometimes rise in conjunction and sometimes in opposition. The human being shares in the qualities of the stars wrestling with each other in the skies.[101] It is from this "battle of the Powers" that the Lord frees the newly converted Christian. The Lord gives the Christian peace from the Powers and Angels who are like "soldiers" and "brigands" fighting for and against God.[102]

How was this accomplished? A new strange star arose in the sky, which destroyed "the old astrological arrangement (τὴν παλαιὰν ἀστροθεσίαν)" of the stars and the planets. This new star "revolved on a new path of redemption (ὁ καινὰς ὁδοὺς καὶ σωτηρίους τρεπόμενος)" and corresponded to the Lord himself who "came down to earth to transfer from Fate to his providence those who believed in Christ."[103] This means that Fate through the stars continues to control unbelievers, but for those who realize that the birth of the Savior released them from Fate, baptism is in order.[104] Baptism is called "death" because Christians are no longer under the rule of "evil archons (πονηραῖς ἀρχαῖς)" and it is called "life" because Christ is now the sole Lord.[105] This is the context of the oft-quoted but misunderstood phrase: "Until baptism Fate is real, but after it the astrologists are no longer correct. It is not the washing alone that is liberating, but the knowledge of who we were, what we have become, where we were or where we have been put, where we hasten to go, from what we are redeemed, what birth is, what rebirth is."[106]

Such language is reminiscent of Ignatius of Antioch who writes to the Ephesians about this same cosmic restructuring. He states that at Jesus' birth "a star in the heaven shone more brightly than all the others." This new star is described as the cosmic pole. Thus Ignatius goes

---

[101] Clem. Alex., *Exc.* 69.1–71.2.
[102] Clem. Alex., *Exc.* 72.1–2. Greek: Casey 1934, 84; translation mine.
[103] Clem. Alex., *Exc.* 74.2. Greek: Casey 1934, 86; translation mine.
[104] Clem. Alex., *Exc.* 75.1.
[105] Clem. Alex., *Exc.* 76.1–77.1. Greek: Casey 1934, 86; translation mine.
[106] Clem. Alex., *Exc.* 78.1–2. Greek: Casey 1934, 88; translation mine.

on to say that "all the other stars with the sun and the moon gathered around that star in chorus." So bright was the star that it left astrologers bewildered. So great was their bewilderment that they asked, "Where could this newcomer have come from, so different from the others?" The old "empire of evil" was overthrown, for God was now appearing in human form to bring a new order, life eternal. All creation, Ignatius explains, was thrown into chaos over this restructuring, which God put into place in order to destroy death.[107]

What we have here is a commonly held Christian belief that the Christ event broke down the old cosmic structures and replaced them with new structures that allow for liberation. Quite literally, Jesus is a new star that the cosmos now revolves around. The Zodiacal signs are the twelve Apostles arrayed around him, replacing the evil Archons who have up until that time controlled human Fate. As such, Jesus replaces the old cosmic pole, becoming the new route for the soul and spirit to escape this world. The new pole corresponds to the Cross which Jesus uses to carry the saved "on his shoulders" into the Pleroma.[108] Once the initiate undergoes baptism, Christ becomes their new path of salvation, saving both the Elect (the Valentinians) and the Called (the members of the Apostolic Church) by bearing them aloft.[109] Christians literally are transferred from the lower regions of the earth up the cosmic pole to the Pleroma. Thus Ephesians 4:9–10 is quoted, "He who ascended also descended. That he ascended, what does it imply but that he descended? He it is who descended into the lower parts of the earth and ascended above the heavens."[110]

An Esoteric Lodge

Why did Theodotus make a *counterpoint* correspondence rather than a *counterpart* one such as we saw the Gnostic author of the *Gospel of Judas* make? Why did Theodotus teach that, for Christians at least, the evil Zodiacal Powers have been overcome and replaced with the good Apostles? The answer is simple. The Valentinians were not opposed to Apostolic Christianity, like the Sethian Christians appear to have been. In fact, the Valentinians attended Apostolic churches on Sundays,

---

[107] Ign., *Eph.* 19. Greek: Ehrman 2003, 238; translation mine.
[108] Clem. Alex., *Exc.* 42.1–3.
[109] Clem. Alex., *Exc.* 53.1–2.
[110] Clem. Alex., *Exc.* 43.5.

while also enjoying esoteric gatherings where they hoped to learn more about the mysteries of God and his Kingdom. As Zeno's writings in the fourth century reflect, Apostolic Christians likely thought as Theodotus had, that the apostles replaced the Zodiac signs at their own baptisms, birthing them under a new fate, with Christ as their cosmic savior.

In the east at this time the Valentinians appear to be an esoteric lodge movement on the verge of becoming a reform movement, teaching some alternative esoteric traditions while maintaining the exoteric teachings of the Apostolic Church. They held onto their membership in the Apostolic Church and their allegiance to it. Thus the early Valentinian systems reflect an acceptance of the Apostles and their doctrines, while additionally relying on esoteric traditions passed down along a separate line of transmission, perhaps through Theodas and his teacher Paul or through a figure outside the twelve, like James Jesus' brother or Mary of Magdala.[111]

PTOLEMAEUS AND MARCUS

When Irenaeus talks about the western Valentinians attached to Ptolemy's teaching, he does not present us with the same correspondences that Theodotus has. Instead of the good twelve Apostles replacing the evil cosmic Zodiac, Irenaeus says that he knows of Valentinians who follow both Ptolemaeus' and Marcus' systems. They all align the Apostles with the twelve last emanations in the Pleroma, the Duodecad.

Judas as the Twelfth Emanation

According to Irenaeus, the Valentinians say that the production of the Duodecad of aeons corresponds to the election of the twelve apostles.[112] The twelfth emanation, the suffering Sophia, corresponds with Judas the twelfth apostle, as does the woman who suffered from the twelve-year flow of blood, but for different reasons. That is, the correspondence with Judas has a different meaning from the correspondence with the hemorrhaging woman. The Valentinians used Judas

---

[111] Clem. Alex., *Misc.* 7.106; i.e., *1 Apoc. James* and the *Gos. Mary*.
[112] Iren., *Adv. haer.* 1.3.2.

specifically to indicate the correspondence between his "apostasy" and
that of the twelfth Aeon. Thus Irenaeus writes that they think that
Sophia's suffering points to Judas' apostasy because both were associated with the number twelve. He reiterates this by saying that the
Valentinians relate the suffering Sophia to the betrayal of Judas. Thus
her suffering was her error, when she did what was forbidden. It is
Sophia's betrayal that results in her suffering which the Valentinians
said corresponded to Judas' betrayal of Jesus, a correspondence which
Irenaeus cannot accept.[113]

Why does this correspondence bother him? Because, he explains, the
rest of stories about Sophia and Judas do not match. Sophia repents
while Judas does not. So, Irenaeus concludes, Judas cannot be a type
of Sophia. But the lack of correspondence on the issue of repentance
did not appear to bother the Valentinians who thought another story
corresponded to Sophia's repentance. It was the woman who suffered
with the flow of blood for twelve years, *not Judas*, who was used by
the Valentinians as a correspondence of repentance, a correspondence
that Origen confirms when he says that the Valentinians thought the
hemorrhaging woman symbolized Prounicos, while never mentioning Judas.[114] This point appears to have been well-known since Celsus
speaks of it as well.[115] The repentance of the wanton Sophia was correlated with the woman's turn to touch Jesus' garment and receive healing. Irenaeus explains that the Valentinians think that the woman who
was sick for twelve years corresponds with Sophia who was stretching
to touch the garment of the Son, the hem, to stay her dissolution. She
was stopped by Horos, the power that went forth from the Son, healed
by him and so she ceased to suffer any more.[116]

Irenaeus goes on to critique further the correspondence between
Judas and Sophia. His words put me in mind of the tradition about
Judas as the "thirteenth" apostle in the *Gospel of Judas*. In order to
argue against the Valentinian teaching, he says that Judas is not the
twelfth apostle, but was cast out of that seat and replaced by Matthias.
Because he was expelled from the twelfth number, he cannot correspond with the twelfth Aeon Sophia, but is an extra apostle outside
of the Pleroma. Although Irenaeus does not use the number thirteen

---

[113] Iren., *Adv. haer.* 2.20.2.
[114] Origen, *c. Cel.* 2.35.
[115] Origen, *c. Cel.* 2.35.
[116] Iren., *Adv. haer.* 1.3.3; 2.20.1–2.21.1.

to describe Judas, knowledge of this tradition appears to me to be the basis for his correction of this Valentinian doctrine. He goes on to argue that Sophia is the thirtieth aeon, not the twelfth, humoring himself further with the numbers game. He even goes so far as to suggest that Matthias and Judas might align with the upper and lower Sophias, but he disregards this idea because he says that Sophia is in actuality three: the restored aeon, her reasonable self, and her suffering self.[117]

The Twelve Apostles and the Body of Truth

The Marcosians appear to have had a peculiar form of the Valentinian teaching about these correspondences according to the records of Irenaeus. Their teaching shows an awareness of both Valentinian traditions about the twelve apostles that I have already discussed in this paper: Theodotus' catechism and the Ptolemaic catechism that Irenaeus knew. The Marcosians taught that the celestial Zodiac is the shadow of the Duodecad, that the twelve signs are images of the last twelve aeons produced in the Pleroma.[118] Furthermore, the Duodecad represents the twelve members of the Body of Truth. Each member consists of two letter sounds out of the twenty-four letters in the Greek alphabet. Their intonation is creative, resulting in the formation of the Pleromic world which is envisioned as a series of great angels of the Presence.[119]

Who do these twelve angels or aeons correspond to? The twelve apostles. Thus the Marcosians said that the Duodecad, as it is connected to the mystery of suffering, is found in many traditions of the twelve, but most importantly for us, in the selection of the twelve apostles.[120] The Marcosian teaching has the twelve apostles function as *counterparts* of the Aeons. They make up the Body of Truth or the Duodecad, which is to be associated with Sophia's suffering. In fact, they even call the Duodecad, "the suffering," because an error occurred in connection with the twelfth aeon. This Marcosian teaching

---

[117] Iren., *Adv. haer.* 2.20.4–5.

[118] Iren., *Adv. haer.* 1.17.1.

[119] Iren., *Adv. haer.* 1.14.1,4, 9; 1.18.1.

[120] Iren., *Adv. haer.* 1.18. 4. Also twelve sons of Jacob (Gen 35:22, 49:28), the twelve tribes of Israel, twelve stones on the breastplate of the High Priest and the twelve bells (Exod 28:2), twelve stones at the foot of Moses' mountain (Exod 24:4) and in Joshua's river (Josh 4:3), the twelve bearers of the ark of the covenant (Josh 3:12), and the number of stones set up by Elijah (1 Kg 18:31).

about the Duodecad is then connected to the Zodiac, where the twelve Zodical signs below the Pleroma are understood to be shadows of the aeons of the Duodecad. This means that the Zodical signs have an apostolic association. They are shadow reflections of the apostles as angels or aeons.

A Reform Movement

The Ptolemaic and Marcosian alignment of the twelve apostles with the Duodecad that Irenaeus recounts is more evidence of the positive regard for the Apostolic tradition within Valentinianism in the mid- to late second century. But Apostolic Christians like Irenaeus did not agree with the exegetical arguments that the western Valentinians were making in regard to the Duodecad, that Judas' earthly betrayal was an expression of Sophia's error when she was cast out of the Pleroma into suffering.

What might this mean in terms of the kind of social relationship that the western Valentinians had with the Apostolic Christians at this time? They still consider themselves to be part of the Apostolic church and heirs of its traditions, but have begun to move farther away from the Apostolic church in terms of exegesis. Thus Ptolemaeus writes to Flora in his letter about how he considers himself an heir of the apostles. He says, "You will learn in the future, if God grants it, about their origin and genesis, when you are worthy of the apostolic tradition which we have received through succession, because we can prove all our statements based on the teaching of the Savior."[121] Irenaeus confirms this, pointing out that the western Valentinians use the writings of the evangelists, the apostles, and the prophets to prove their opinions, although he disagrees vehemently with their interpretations and does not consider their opinions valid Christian exegesis.[122]

Thus, it seems to me that the western Valentinians are further along in the shift from a lodge movement to a reform movement. Irenaeus confirms this. He hints at this type of relationship when he describes the Marcosians and his concern that many women in his own district

---

[121] *Ptolemy to Flora* in Epiph., *Pan.* 33.7.9. Greek: Koll 1915, 457. Translation mine.

[122] Iren., *Adv. haer.* 1.3.6.

in the Rhône valley have left his church to attend Marcosian gatherings instead.[123]

First Apocalypse of James

The *First Apocalypse of James* contains within it some striking traditions about correspondences between the heavens and the earth. The main point of the text is to reveal, through James the brother of Jesus, a secret death liturgy, a liturgy which both Irenaeus and Epiphanius record was used by various groups of Valentinians to ensure that the soul would escape the grasp of the archons and properly ascend.[124] I understand this document to be Valentinian, mainly because the point of the text is to reveal, through a secret teaching to James, this Valentinian death liturgy. But in addition, the text assumes a Valentinian discussion of the nature of the primal Monad and its male and female polarities.[125] It also uses Valentinian terminology such as "Achamoth" when referencing the fallen Sophia, and assumes distinct Valentinian doctrines such as the view that the ignorant demiurge treated the descending Son well, like his own son.[126] Even the reference to the demiurge as "the Just God" is a Valentinian attribute.[127] The text encourages the believer to endure persecution (likely at the hands of other Christians) and even martyrdom. The one Valentinian who appears to have addressed the issue of martyrdom was Heracleon, and he writes that confession can happen either "in faith and conduct" *or* "with the mouth." Since not everyone is brought "before authorities" to confess "with the mouth," it is not a universal route to salvation like "works and action." Heracleon's teaching does not appear to me to condemn martyrdom, but to support it. So I think *James* tells us what Valentinianism looked like in the third century as it became more eclectic while still retaining distinctive Valentinian features.

---

[123] Iren., *Adv. haer.* 1.5, 7.

[124] *1 Apoc. James* NHC V,3 33.15–35.19; TC 20.10–22.16; Iren., *Adv. haer.* 1.21.5; Epiph., *Pan.* 36.3.1–3.

[125] *1 Apoc. James* NHC V,3 24.26–30; TC 10.19–27.

[126] *1 Apoc. James* NHC V,3 34.3; TC 21.4; *1 Apoc. James* NHC V 39.8–18; TC 26.11–18.

[127] *1 Apoc. James* NHC V,3 31.31; TC 18.17; cf. *Ptolemy to Flora* in Epiph., *Pan.* 33.3.6–7, 33.7.5.

The good news is that these third-century Valentinians believed that they had the liturgy which would vanquish the cosmic powers and gain the soul its freedom. The bad news is that things on earth are not what they seem to be, and suffering is around every corner. In order to endure the suffering and overcome the powers, there are heaven-earth correspondences that need to be learned, in addition to the liturgy itself. The adage "know thy enemy" is *apropos* for these Gnostics. So surrounding the revelation of the liturgy are teachings about the archons—who they are and what to expect from them. This information is revealed to embolden James, and other Gnostic Christians who face persecution and martyrdom, so that they will know that their real enemies are not the human beings who arrest them but the celestial powers who seek to destroy them. In fact, Jesus tells James not to worry about the human enemies and the suffering he will face. What he must save himself from are not these, but the archons who will pursue him mightily. He must learn exactly who they are and how many there are.[128]

The Twelve and Seventy-Two

So *James* makes it immediately clear that the issues of astrological correspondences are of particular relevance to the Gnostic Christian. In the opening pages of the text, we learn that Jesus is going to be arrested very soon, and that James' arrest and stoning will follow this. Jesus warns him away from Jerusalem. Why? Because Jerusalem is the dwelling place of numerous archons.[129] The archons that Jesus wants him to be most familiar with are the twelve archons who rule the twelve heavens, each consisting of a hebdomad. So Jesus tells James that he wants him to concentrate "not all of them, but the twelve Archons (ⲛ̄ⲧⲟⲟⲩ [ⲧⲏⲣⲩ] ⲁⲛ ⲁⲗⲗⲁ ϩⲉⲛⲁⲣ[ⲭⲱⲛ] ⲡⲓⲙⲛ̄ⲧⲥ̣[ⲛ]ⲟ̣ⲟⲩⲥ)."[130]

The beginning of his revelation teaches James that there are twelve heavens of hebdomads rather than seven as scripture purports. Jesus explains that whoever wrote the scriptures only understood so much, and not this mystery. Thankfully, Jesus has come to reveal the truth.[131]

---

[128] *1 Apoc. James* NHC V,3 25.20–23; TC 12.3–6.
[129] *1 Apoc. James* NHC V,3 25.7–19; TC 11.9–12.3.
[130] *1 Apoc. James* NHC V,3 25.24–25. Reconstruction of Coptic is mine, based on the TC 12.7.
[131] *1 Apoc. James* NHC V,3 26.2–9; TC 12.13–24.

The twelve hebdomads, he says, correlate with seventy-two "twin part-ners (ⲥⲟⲉⲓⲥ)."[132] Later both versions of *James* employ ⲥⲟⲉⲓϣ when Jesus gives a quick review of his teaching.[133] It should be noted that the lacuna in the Nag Hammadi version was wrongly reconstructed to read "twelve (ⲡⲓⲙⲛ̄ⲧ)" when in fact the Tchacos Codex version now shows us the correct reading is "seventy-two (ⲡⲓϣⲃⲉ)."[134]

NHC V 35.28–36.6		TC 22.23–23.4	
35.28	[...]	22.23	ⲉⲓⲥϩⲏⲏⲧⲉ ⲓ̈ⲁⲕⲕⲱ Look James,
35.29	[...]	22.24	ⲕⲉ ⲁⲉⲓϭⲱⲗⲡ̄ ⲛⲁⲕ ⲉⲃⲟⲗ ϫⲉ I have revealed to you
36.1	ⲡⲉⲧⲣ̄ ϣ[ⲟⲣⲡ̄ ⲛ̄ϣⲟⲟ]ⲡ [ⲁⲩⲱ][135] He-Who-[Is-Preexistent], [and]	22.25	ⲁⲛⲟⲕ ⲟⲩⲉⲩ ⲁⲩⲱ ⲡⲉⲧϣⲟ who I am, and He-Who-Is-
36.2	[ⲛ̄ⲧ]ⲩⲡⲟⲥ [ⲛ̄ⲡⲓ]ⲙⲛ̄[ⲧⲥ]ⲛⲟⲟⲩ[ⲥ] [the] type of [the] twelve	22.26	ⲟⲛ ϫⲛ̄ ⲛ̄ϣⲟⲣⲡ ⲁⲩⲱ ⲡⲧⲩ Preexistent, and the type
36.3	ⲙ̄ⲙⲁⲑⲏⲧⲏⲥ ⲙⲛ̄ [ⲡⲓϣⲃⲉ] disciples with [the]	23.1	ⲡⲟⲥ ⲙ̄ⲡⲙⲛ̄ⲧⲥⲛⲁⲟⲩⲥ ⲙ̄ⲙⲁⲑⲏ of the twelve disciples,
36.4	ⲥⲛⲟⲟⲩⲥ ⲛ̄ⲥⲟⲉⲓϣ [...ⲧⲉⲥϩⲓⲙ]ⲉ[136] seventy-two twin pairs, [the female]	23.2	ⲧⲏⲥ ⲁⲩⲱ ⲡϣⲟⲃ̄ ⲛ̄ⲥⲟⲉⲓϣ ⲁⲩ and the seventy-two twin pairs,
36.5	ⲁⲕⲭⲁⲙⲱⲑ ⲧⲉ̣[ⲧⲟⲩ]ⲣ̄ϩⲉⲣ Achamoth, which is	23.3	ⲱ ⲁ̄ⲭⲁⲙⲱⲑ ⲧⲉ̣ⲥϩ̄ⲓ̣ⲙⲉ ⲧⲁ̣ⲓ ⲉϣⲁⲩ and Achamoth the female, being
36.6	ⲙⲏⲛⲉⲩⲉ ⲙ̄ⲙⲟⲥ ϫⲉ ⲥⲟⲫⲓⲁ translated, "Sophia".	23.4	ⲣ̄ ϩⲉⲣⲙⲏⲛⲉⲩⲉ̣ ⲙ̣ⲙⲁⲥ ϫⲉ ⲧⲥⲟⲫⲓⲁ translated, "Sophia".

---

[132] *1 Apoc. James* TC 13.4. Kasser et al. 2007, 127. I read this as a variant of ⲥⲟⲉⲓϣ: The Nag Hammadi version uses ϣⲟϣⲟⲩ: NHC V,3 26.15. I am dependent on the thorough discussion of these words found in Funk's contribution to this volume.

[133] *1 Apoc. James* NHC V,3 36.4; TC 23.2.

[134] This case is made by Funk in his contribution to this volume. Coptic: Schoedel in Parrott 1979, 90; Kasser et al. 2007, 145.

[135] A possible reconstruction based on TC manuscript.

[136] A possible reconstruction based on TC manuscript.

The meaning of Jesus' esoteric teaching is clear. The twelve disciples are "types" of the twelve archons and their heavens, while the seventy-two twin partners refer to the seventy(-two) lesser disciples sent out two-by-two according to Luke 10:1.[137] These lesser disciples of the church correspond astrologically to the seventy-two lesser heavens.

So in the end, the secret teaching of *James* is that there are twelve archons who correspond to the twelve Zodical signs of the Zodiac, in which seventy-two powers—the ruling decans and horoscopes—reside. These powers are armed forces, who pursue Jesus and fight against him.[138] This multitude of powers is further aligned with the people in Jerusalem who plot against Jesus and arrest him, a fate and enemy that James also will face.[139] Among them are the twelve archons who correspond with the twelve disciples, whose forgetfulness and ignorance Jesus came to rebuke, and the seventy-two lesser disciples who were sent out to preach.[140] For the salvation of the faithful, Jesus came to rebuke the archons and to overpower each of them.[141] And this is exactly what Jesus does. After he has revealed his full teaching to James, Jesus immediately rebukes the twelve disciples who are with him.[142]

James as Addon(aios)

James' own relationship with the archons is difficult to determine. The Tchacos Codex version allows us to reconstruct a damaged portion of the Nag Hammadi Codex where Jesus tells James that he has been a "servant" of the demiurge, the "just god (ⲡⲛⲟⲩⲧⲉ ⲛ̄ⲇⲓⲕⲁⲓⲟⲥ)." This is why James has received the name, "James the Just (ⲓ̈ⲁⲕⲕⲱⲃⲟⲥ ⲡⲇⲓⲕⲁⲓⲟⲥ)."[143] Does this correlation suggest that James the Just, the leader of the twelve disciples after Jesus' death, is the earthly corre-

---

[137] Manuscript of Luke and patristic literature show a widespread variant that read "seventy-two" instead of "seventy." On this, see Funk's article in this volume.

[138] *1 Apoc. James* NHC V,3 27.18–24.

[139] *1 Apoc. James* NHC V,3 25.10–19; TC 11.11–12.3; *1 Apoc. James* NHC V,3 32.28–33.14; TC 19.24–28.

[140] *1 Apoc. James* NHC V,3 28.8–10; TC 14.22–25.

[141] *1 Apoc. James* NHC V,3 30.2; TC 16.17; *1 Apoc. James* NHC V,3 30.5–6.

[142] *1 Apoc. James* NHC V,3 42.21–22.

[143] *1 Apoc. James* NHC V,3 31.31–32.3; TC 18.16–20. Coptic: Schoedel in Parrott 1979, 82; Kasser et al. 2007, 137; translation mine.

spondence of the Just God, the leader of the twelve archons?[144] James is reported in the Tchacos Codex version only to ask Jesus who the seventy-two powers correspond to now that James has "removed" himself "from the archons' number" (ⲧⲛⲁⲥⲁϩⲱⲓ ⲉⲃⲁⲗ ⲛ̄ⲧⲏⲡⲥ ⲛ̄ⲛ̄ⲁⲣⲭⲱⲛ).[145] This apocalypse goes on to report that once James receives Jesus' revelation, James chooses to cease his worship of the Just God, stopping his prayers to him. Jesus tells James that this has stirred up the Demiurge's wrath and anger, which soon will be waged against James.[146] James is warned not to allow the archons to become jealous of the fact that he now knows more than they.[147] Nevertheless, James' defection will result in James' arrest orchestrated by the archons, and a face off with the Demiurge's army of powers. Ultimately, James will die at their hand, just as Jesus did.

Seven Women as Sophia's Pillars

The final heaven-earth correspondence to examine is the doctrine of the seven wise women, the prophetesses. The names of these women are Salome, Mariam, the other Mary (?), Arsinoe, Sapphira, Susanna, and Joanna.[148] The presence of these women among Jesus' disciples is not unique to this apocalypse. References to them appear also in the Sophia of Jesus Christ and the Manichaean literature.[149] Individual revelations to several of these named women are too numerous in the literature to list here. These references allude to an alternative tradition of the transmission of Jesus' teaching, albeit a transmission of esoteric teaching that existed alongside the exoteric teaching.

James wants to know what correspondences exist between the heavens and Jesus' seven female disciples. Jesus tells him that they correlate with the seven spirits who live in the Demiurge's heavens. These are

---

[144] The apocalypse actually refers to the twelve disciples as belonging to James: "his disciples" (1 Apoc. James NHC V,3 30.21; TC 17.11).

[145] 1 Apoc. James TC 13.1–4. Coptic: Kasser et al. 2007, 127; translation mine.

[146] 1 Apoc. James NHC V,3 31.23–32.11; TC 18.12–19.5.

[147] 1 Apoc. James NHC V,3 40.12–13; TC 27.21–23.

[148] The lacunae in the 1 Apoc. James NHC V,3 40.25–26 has traditionally been filled with the name "Martha" based on the list of the women's names in the Manichaean Psalms. The TC version, however, only has three women's names preserved. Brankaer-Bethge (2007, 242–244) have suggested a viable solution. Originally there were four names, including "the other Mary" (ⲧⲕⲉⲙⲁⲣⲓⲁ), as NHC suggests. This name dropped out of the TC version, probably due to scribal error.

[149] Soph. Jes. Chr. BG,3 77.9–15; NHC III,4 90.15–18). Veilleux 1986, 94–95.

prophetic spirits who resided in these spheres long before Jesus himself descended through them to earth. What prophets did they inspire?
The Jewish prophets recorded in the scriptures. They were the spirits
who spoke through the mouths of the prophets, proclaiming the little
that they knew about Jesus' advent, whatever they were capable to tell
since they did not know about the supreme God.[150]

Although the apocalypse links these seven women to the "spirits" mentioned in Isaiah 11:2, the spirits of wisdom, insight, counsel, strength, understanding, knowledge, and fear, this interpretation
of the seven women must be dependent on a well-known verse from
Proverbs: "Sophia has built her house. She has hewn her seven pillars."[151] It is quite possible, as Ulrich Wilckens argued long ago, that
Sophia's seven-pillared house is dependent upon Ishtar's seven-pillared house, which was thought to be the cosmos with its seven planets encircling the earth.[152] The concept takes root in both Judaism
and Christianity that the world, in fact, depends on these pillars who
were made to correspond to certain ideal figures, righteous men or
prophets.[153]

The number of the pillars varies between seven and twelve, a variation that should not be surprising given the planetary and Zodiacal
systems. In Christian literature, the most developed usage of the seven
pillars is found in the *Pseudo-Clementine* corpus where a cycle of
male prophets and ideal men who are called "the seven pillars of the
world...who were superior to everyone deemed worthy to know him
(God)."[154] The seven are listed with slight variations as Adam, Enoch,
Noah, Abraham, Isaac, Jacob, and Moses.[155] They are righteous men
and prophets who are inspired by God to teach the truth about the
Law and the scriptures and to reveal God's will.[156] Irenaeus, however,
knows of the pattern of the twelve, suggesting that the twelve apostles
are the pillars. He says that the twelve tribes of Israel were replaced
with the twelve-pillared foundation of the Church.[157]

---

[150] *1 Apoc. James* TC 26.19–27.2.
[151] Prov 9:1.
[152] Wilckens 1971, 733–734.
[153] Wilckens 1971, 732–736; Gieschen 1994, 47–82.
[154] *Ps.-Clem. Hom.* 18.13–14.
[155] *Ps.-Clem. Hom.* 2.16–17, 2.52, 17.4, 18.13; *Rec.* 2.47, 3.61.
[156] Gieschen 1994, 47–82.
[157] Iren., *Adv. haer.* 4.21.3.

The correlation of the prophets with realms of the archons is a popular Gnostic doctrine, although whether or not the correlation is positive or negative varies across the Gnostic systems. Irenaeus, for instance, tells of the Sethians who had a negative correspondence. He correlates twenty-two prophets with specific archons. Each archon had for himself several prophets whose sole purpose was to be a herald for that particular archon. Each prophet was supposed to extol the Archon and proclaim him god. The purpose of this was to convince humans that they should worship the Archons. But Sophia worked behind the scenes, whispering to the prophets about the imperishable Aeon and Christ. So when the archons hear their prophets teaching about these things, they are utterly terrified and wonder what is going on.[158]

Hippolytus knows of Valentinians who teach similarly about the prophets. These Valentinians think that the Demiurge is not just ignorant but a silly god whose prophets were foolish and knew nothing. To support this position, they quote John 10:18, "All who have come before me are thieves and robbers" and Ephesians 3:4, "The mystery which was not made known to former generations." None of his prophets spoke about the Gnostic teachings, because these were unknown to the Demiurge.[159]

But this teaching was not universal among the Valentinians. According to Irenaeus, the Valentinians he knows declare that those souls which contain a spiritual seed that is better than all others are destined to be prophets, kings and priests. Thus they are able to reveal higher knowledge to the rest of humankind. In fact, the Demiurge loves these souls more than all others, although he does not know why.[160] Similarly, Clement of Alexandria tells us that the Valentinians thought that the prophets were inspired by the spirit, even though they did not know that it was the same "paraclete" which was later poured out on the Christian Church.[161] In fact, when Jesus descends into the Demiurge's realm, he finds there Christ "whom it was foretold that he would put on, whom the Prophets and the Law announced as an

---

[158] Iren., *Adv. haer.* 1.30.10–11.
[159] Hipp., *Ref.* 6.35.1.
[160] Iren., *Adv. haer.* 1.7.3.
[161] Clem. Alex., *Exc.* 24.1–2.

image of the Savior.[162] The belief that certain truths were revealed by the Prophets also is assumed by Marcus and his scriptural exegesis.[163]

A Separatist Movement

What might these correspondences tell us about the Valentinians who authored the *First Apocalypse of James*? The pattern of *James* is a *counterpart* pattern very similar to the Sethian one developed in the *Gospel of Judas*. Unlike other Valentinian traditions discussed previously, the apostles in *James* are ignorant and are mapped directly onto the twelve dominant Archons in the heavens. In the Tchacos Codex at least, James himself appears to be correlated with their leader, the Demiurge Addon(aios). James is able to break this correlation when he receives esoteric teaching from Jesus, and on this basis, stops worshiping Addon(aios). Since we are in a Valentinian context, this should not be surprising because the Demiurge is a psychic figure who is saved by Jesus' direct teaching after the resurrection.

These correspondences suggest to me that the Valentinians who wrote this text are no longer considering themselves to be part of the Apostolic Church. Like the Sethians who made this break earlier, the Valentinians begin to turn against the teaching of the apostolic twelve, understanding it to be ignorant, so much so that Jesus rebukes it. In place of the "rebuked" apostolic tradition, these Valentinians have cornered a non-apostle as the recipient of the truth, James the brother of Jesus. They develop a lengthy chain of transmission for this tradition from James to Addai to Manael-Masphel to Levi to Levi's seventeen year old son, who may be the author of this text.[164] This suggests to me that *James* is a text reflecting Valentinian experience in Syria in the mid-third century, when they were less and less welcome in Apostolic churches, even actively persecuted by the Apostolic Christians, and likely had begun to worship separately outside those doors. The selection of Addai as a tradent suggests that these Valentinians at one time had been part of the mainline church in Syria, and were claiming as their own a piece of a well- known mission story about how Christianity first came to this part of the world.[165]

---

[162] Clem. Alex., *Exc.* 59.2.
[163] Cf. Iren., *Adv. haer.* 1.19.1–2.
[164] *1 Apoc. James* NHC V,3 36.13–38.11; TC 23.10–25.14.
[165] Eus., *Eccl. Hist.* 1.13.1–5.

It is also fascinating to find in the same text, seven female prophet-esses who inspire the biblical prophets. The seven male pillars have become female. This is a *counterpart* correspondence, and a negative one at that because the female has replaced the male. Such a cor-respondence certainly provides a critique of Christian systems that uphold the traditional male pillars of the Jewish scripture as "right-eous." I think the substitution is intended to point out that the Jewish prophets, the righteous pillars, were not male spirits or male prophets as tradition says, but deficient female ones, who did not understand completely what was going on. Since the Apostolic Church was put-ting so much emphasis on the "truth" of their doctrines because they had been foreshadowed or predicted by the Jewish prophets, I think we are again seeing a strong critique of that Apostolic teaching.

What is even more amazing, though, is the turn in the text to then say that Jesus' seven female disciples are *counterpoints* to the seven deficient female spirits who inspired the prophets. In other words, once the seven female disciples heard Jesus' message when he preached on earth, they immediately recognized who he was. Because of this, Sapphira, Susanna and Joanna have been "set apart for a place of faith (ⲧϣⲟⲙ̣ⲛ̣ⲧⲉ ⲉⲧⲉ ⲛⲉ̈ⲓ ⲛⲉ [ⲥ]ⲉⲡⲟⲣ[ⲭ̅ ⲉ]ⲃⲟⲗ ⲉⲩⲙⲁ ⲛ̅ⲡⲓⲥⲧⲓⲥ)."[166] Salome, Mary, the other Mary(?), and Arsinoe are "worthy of He-Who-Is."[167] They have been saved from "the blindness that was in their hearts" because they "recognized (ⲣ̅-ⲛⲟⲓ̈)" who Jesus was.[168] The Valentinian redemptive process, which is imagined as a transformation from the deficient female state to the perfect male state, coincides with the fact that these "historical" women recognized Jesus as the one whom the prophets forecasted.[169] In Valentinian lingo, the text says, "the female has attained the male."[170]

So here is a *counterpoint* correspondence that is developed to sup-port the Valentinian need for a transmission of tradition separate

---

[166] *1 Apoc. James* TC 29.1–6. Based on the Coptic parallel with Rom 1:1, the verbal unit ⲡⲟⲣⲭ̅ ⲉⲃⲟⲗ ⲉ- can have the meaning "to set apart for," which must be the mean-ing here given the context, rather than "separate from" which the *Critical Edition* has. See Kasser, et al. 2007, 159.

[167] *1 Apoc. James* NHC V,3 40.2–6; TC 27.25–2. Coptic: Schoedel in Parrott 1979, 96; Kasser et al. 2007, 155.

[168] *1 Apoc. James* TC 28.2–5. Kasser et al. 2007, 157.

[169] *1 Apoc. James* NHC V,3 41.15–18; TC 28.14–21.

[170] *1 Apoc. James* NHC V,3 41.15–18; TC 28.18–21. Coptic: Schoedel in Parrott 1979, 98; Kasser et al. 2007, 157.

from the Apostolic tradition, seven women disciples who are blessed with esoteric teaching become the new seven pillars of Sophia's house. This provides yet more evidence for a later dating of this important Valentinian document, a date that reflects a time in Christian relations when the Valentinians were no longer considered members of the Apostolic church and had to worship as a completely separate group. The pattern that they develop by this time in history is that of separatists—religionists who under persecution, leave a church they once loved, taking along many of its traditions, while, at the same time, criticizing it severely.

Pistis Sophia

A fourth century text, the *Pistis Sophia*, represents the height of Gnostic speculation about cosmic correspondences. The text is dependent on the late third century *Books of Jeu*, and together they appear to comprise a formulaic compendium of Gnosis. The cosmology assumed by these books is not that of a single school of Gnosis, but rather an eclectic blend of Sethian, Valentinian, and Manichaean teachings. The result is a homogenized Gnosis, bland and technical, that appears to represent a sort of standardization of Gnostic thought in the fourth century.

The Thirteenth Aeon

The God-world in *Pistis Sophia* is called the "Treasury of Light." Below this is the thirteenth Aeon, a divine world of twenty-four invisible emanations, with Authades, a disobedient Aeon, in charge. Pistis Sophia is one of these emanations. At some point, she decides to cease performing the "mystery of the thirteenth Aeon," and instead turns to worship the light shining from the Treasury above the thirteenth Aeon. Authades and all of his Archons in the thirteenth Aeon hate her for ceasing to honor him, since he is the Lord over this particular divine realm.

In order to stop Pistis Sophia, Authades decides on a plan to steal her power and shut her down. First, he emanates a great lion-faced archon whom he sends out of the thirteenth realm into Chaos. Second, he persecutes Pistis Sophia so that she will want to leave his kingdom. In this way he tricks her into running away from his kingdom and taking shelter in Chaos. But once she does this, the lion-faced archon,

Ialdabaoth-Adamas, captures her, assaults her, and steals her power. This archon, son of Authades, is called the Tyrant and great demon ruler over Chaos.[171]

With this, Pistis Sophia finds herself trapped in the twelfth realm of the cosmos. With no power, she cannot reenter her realm of origin, a place of "correction (Ⲇⲓⲕⲁⲓⲟⲥⲩⲛⲏ)," nor can she ascend to the Treasury of Light.[172] Devoid of the light she once had, she is now said to be like a "demon." She exclaims in her misery, "I have become like a distinct demon who lives in matter and in whom there is no light (ⲁⲓ̈ϣⲱⲡⲉ ⲛ̄ⲑⲉ ⲛ̄ⲟⲩϩⲓⲆⲓⲟⲥ ⲛ̄Ⲇⲁⲓⲙⲱⲛ ⲉϥⲟⲩⲏϩ ϩⲛ̄ ⲟⲩϩⲩⲗⲏ ⲉⲙ̄ⲛ̄ⲟⲩⲟⲓ̈ⲛ ⲛ̄ϩⲏⲧϥ̄). And I have become like a counterpart of the spirit who is in a material body in which there is no power of light (ⲁⲩⲱ ⲁⲓ̈ϣⲱⲡⲉ ⲛ̄ⲑⲉ ⲛ̄ⲟⲩⲁⲛⲧⲓⲙⲓⲙⲟⲛ ⲙ̄ⲡ̄ⲡ̄ⲛ̄ⲁ ⲉϥϩⲛ̄ ⲟⲩⲥⲱⲙⲁ ⲛ̄ϩⲩⲗⲓⲕⲟⲛ ⲉⲙ̄ⲛ̄ϭⲟⲙ ⲛ̄ⲟⲩⲟⲉⲓⲛ ⲛ̄ϩⲏⲧϥ̄). And I have become like a decan, which is alone upon the air (ⲁⲩⲱ ⲁⲓ̈ϣⲱⲡⲉ ⲛ̄ⲑⲉ ⲛ̄ⲟⲩⲆⲉⲕⲁⲛⲟⲥ ⲉϥϩⲓϫⲙ̄ ⲡⲁⲏⲣ ⲙⲁⲩⲁⲁϥ)."[173] Below her are the eleven other realms of the cosmos with forty-nine Archons ruling the total twelve. This is the sphere of *heimarmene*.[174]

Pistis Sophia directs a series of repentant prayers to the Treasury of Light, and eventually Jesus emerges to save her and other souls trapped in Ialdabaoth-Adamas' cosmic system. He does this by physically moving Pistis Sophia to a place at the top of the twelfth cosmic realm, but below the thirteenth middle or in-between aeon. This upper edge of the twelfth realm is identified as the place where the decans are located. She is safe here from further assault by the archons who reside spatially below her. Jesus leaves her in this upper region until he can take her to her place in the height at the end of time.[175]

Twelve Powers as Souls of the Apostles

Jesus' own movement down into Chaos, and his subsequent death and resurrection, completely restructure the cosmos. As he descends, he brings with him twelve powers that he took from the twelve Saviors in the Treasury of Light. Jesus, as the angel Gabriel, cast these powers into the wombs of the apostles' mothers. This means that his twelve

---

[171] *PS* 2.66.
[172] *PS* 1.50. Coptic: Schmidt-MacDermot 1978b, 94; translation mine.
[173] *PS* 1.39. Coptic: Schmidt-MacDermot 1978b, 63; translation mine.
[174] *PS* 1.10.
[175] *PS* 2.75.

286 APRIL D. DECONICK

apostles do not have souls created by the archons, but instead have
powers from the Light Treasury.[176] He claims to have done this so
that the twelve can serve the entire world and are able to withstand
the threat of the Archons, the sufferings and dangers of the world, and
the persecutions which the Archons will bring upon them.[177] As part
of the cosmic restructuring, Jesus says that the twelve disciples will be
installed as the new Zodiac. He explains that they will sit on twelve
powers of light until all the ranks of the twelve saviors have been set
up at their places of inheritance.[178] This Zodiac installation appears to
be temporary, until the end of time when Jesus will take the apostles to
the place of their inheritance, where they will be set up as rulers over
their own emanations in Jesus' Kingdom.[179] James is singled out. He
corresponds with the "first" in this new Kingdom. Because he will be
called "first" among all the invisible ones and gods in the twelfth and
thirteenth realms, he appears to correlate with the evil Authades, but
as his positive replacement, or *counterpoint* correspondence.[180]

Jesus' death is understood as the moment when the old *axis mundi*
was replaced. Jesus is installed as the new cosmic pole, a great beam of
light that reaches from the very depth of the earth up through the heavens. As he was dying on the cross, he ascends the pole and shakes up
all the Powers, shaking even the earth.[181] Then Jesus turns the Zodiac
and the planets into new positions so that the Archons are disoriented
and the astrologers cannot read the skies.[182] The Archons become confused, wandering around the skies in error, unable to understand the
new cosmic orientation or their own paths in the sphere.[183] Why has
Jesus done this? "I have turned their paths," he says, "for the salvation
of all souls. Really truly I say to you, unless I had turned their paths,
a multitude of souls would have been destroyed…Because of this, I
have turned their paths so that they are confused and agitated, and
give up the power which is in cosmic matter, which they make into
souls, so that those who will be saved with all the power are purified

---

[176] *PS* 1.8.
[177] *PS* 1.7.
[178] *PS* 1.50.
[179] *PS* 2.86.
[180] *PS* 1.52.
[181] *PS* 1.3.
[182] *PS* 1.18.
[183] *PS* 1.21.

quickly and ascend, and those who will not be saved are quickly dissolved."[184]

A New Religious Movement

In *Pistis Sophia* and the *Books of Jeu* upon which *Pistis Sophia* is dependent, we are witnessing the twelve apostles become transmitters of the *esoteric* tradition. The Gnostics, according to *Pistis Sophia*, are saved through the replacement of the Zodiac Archons with the twelve disciples whose souls were powers from the Treasury of Light. Eventually they would be exalted to their places of inheritance as "Saviors" in the Treasury of Light.

Why are the twelve apostles reappropriated in this fashion by these Gnostics? This shift seems to be part of a broader agenda of the author of *Pistis Sophia* who similarly reappropriates Jewish scripture through a programmatic reinterpretation of the prophets to forecast the Gnostic story and confirm esoteric truths about Sophia and Jesus. These Gnostics are adopting the basic teachings of the Apostolic Church—the authority of the twelve apostles and the prophetic significance of the Jewish scripture—for their own agenda.

Can we discern what this agenda might have been? From the evidence in *Pistis Sophia*, the *Books of Jeu*, and other late third and early fourth century Gnostic texts, it appears to me that the earlier distinct varieties of Gnosis, such as Sethianism and Valentinianism, are in the process of consolidation, harmonization, and standardization. This process parallels what is happening within the Apostolic Church. At this time the Apostolic Church is consolidating its power, choosing its scriptures, shoring up its hierarchy and clergy, and creating homogeneous creeds, theology, and practices. All this the Apostolic Church claims has been handed to them along a direct line that it can trace back to the twelve apostles.

When it comes to late third and early fourth century Gnosticism, to a large extent we are dealing with mimicry. Some of the Gnostics are imitating the success of the Apostolic Church in order to compete successfully with it. As the earlier Gnostic movements consolidate into a new eclectic religious movement that we can call "Gnosticism," some of the Gnostic communities imitate apostolic scriptures with their own

---

[184] *PS* 1.23. Translation: MacDermot in Schmidt-MacDermot 1978b, 65, 67.

Gnostic versions of them. They focus on simplifications of their complex myths into condensed formulaic formats, such as can be seen in the *Letter of Peter to Philip,* which subverts the apostolic kergyma. As independent Gnostic fellowships emerge on the scene, so does a need for handbooks such as the *Books of Jeu* and *Pistis Sophia.* Some of the Gnostic communities go so far as to legitimize their teachings by reappropriating the Twelve as their own authorities on all things esoteric.

This program of mimicry combined with a bold eclecticism, to a certain extent was successful, producing powerful synthetic Gnostic religions like Manichaeism and Mandaeism. But the success of Gnosticism beyond the fourth century runs amok of the newly-fledged Orthodoxy backed by imperial Rome. From the Apostolic traditions, Orthodoxy emerged as the establishment religion. As such, it took legal actions against the Gnostics, excommunicating, exiling and defrocking them, burning their books and churches, forbidding them to meet as churches, hold services, or perform their own liturgies.[185] Under such heavy persecution, Gnosticism had a very difficult time surviving. As so many of our later sources tell us, the Gnostics were forced to hide within the Church again or meet clandestinely without.

---

[185] Layton 1995, 345–347.

FATE AND THE WANDERING STARS

The Jewish Apocalyptic Roots of the *Gospel of Judas*

Nicola Denzey Lewis

"Judas, your star has led you astray." So says Jesus to his disciple Judas in the *Gospel of Judas*.[1] The words seem to be a clear rebuke. Yet what is meant? The word 'star' or 'stars' is used on numerous occasions within the extant manuscript of the *Gospel of Judas*. Central to my investigation of this passage will be Jesus' claim in 42:7–9 that each person follows his astral destiny. Is this a general statement, or does Jesus simply mean that each *disciple* has his own star? Given that the twelve disciples are probably types of the twelve signs of the zodiac, how do we contend with Judas' role as the 'thirteenth,' and his connection to astral destiny? Does Jesus have an astral destiny? Finally, is there a seminal relationship between the cosmological sections of the text and the dialogical sections in which Jesus teaches Judas about the "error of the stars"?

To approach these questions, I will compare the *Gospel of Judas'* cosmological scheme and its system of fate with Jewish apocalyptic writings from the late Second Temple Period. I will argue that this gospel reflects a Jewish cosmological system, which is deeply concerned with apocalyptic speculation reminiscent of other Jewish apocalyptic texts. I will endeavor to uncover the cosmological system alluded to in the *Gospel of Judas* by placing it within the intellectual horizons of Jewish teachings on the nature and influence of the stars—particularly on the confluence between cosmology and systems of astral fatalism.

STARS IN THE *GOSPEL OF JUDAS*

The word 'star' (ⲥⲓⲟⲩ) appears fifteen times in our extant manuscript—more often than in any other Christian text from this period of

---

[1] *Gos. Jud.* 45,13–14.

antiquity.[2] The word is confined to specific portions of the narrative—in dialogic material between Jesus and Judas—which strongly suggests to me that the other cosmological portion of the narrative from 47:2 to 54:12 derives from a separate and independent source. There, we find no stars, but 'luminaries' (ⲫⲱⲥⲧⲏⲣ), which (as I shall discuss below) are somewhat different. They derive from Jewish sources that, harkening back to passages like Ex 3:2 and Deut 4:15, equate light with divine epiphanies. Nevertheless, the two sections are related through their cosmic imagery.

As to *Gospel of Judas*'s theory of the stars, there are a few other initial basic observations to be made. First, the stars in this text are not signifiers or luminaries merely adorning the heavenly realms as in Philo's writings or in later Christian theology, but they apparently exert force; they lead Judas and the disciples to 'err.'[3] There is an obvious pun here on the Greek word for planets (πλάνητες ἀστέρες or πλανήτοι) that 'wander' or 'err' (πλανάω). Thus the stars here appear at face value to be connected to a specific kind of determinism—sidereal determinism—but not necessarily planetary or zodiacal determinism. Whether or not this determinism is connected to planetary or zodiacal systems should remain, for now, an open question.

Second, each of the twelve disciples has his own star, including Judas, whose star Jesus says leads Judas 'astray.'[4] Judas's own star is mentioned on four separate occasions: 45:13–14, after Judas's Temple vision; 55:10–11, where Jesus tells Judas "your star will ru[le] over the [thir]teenth aeon." The third usage in 56:21–24 comes in the midst of a set of four verses in Septuagintal style:

> Already your horn has been raised,
> And your wrath has been kindled,
> And your star has passed by,
> And your heart has [become strong].

The final usage occurs at the end of the gospel in 57:16–20, as Jesus issues his final instructions to Judas: "Lift up your eyes and look at the

---

[2] Of all early Christian literature, perhaps only the *Ps.-Clem. Recog.* comes close to disclosing an elaborate theory of sidereal influence and astrology. Following that, one relationship of Jesus to astrology is most fully laid out in *PS*. On this, see Van der Vliet 2005, 519–536 and earlier, Hodges 1997, 359–73.

[3] *Gos. Jud.* 45,13. To cite here only one later Christian articulation of the same idea, see Clem. Alex., *Ecl.* 55 (3. 152. 15–19).

[4] *Gos. Jud.* 42,7–8.

cloud and the light within it and the stars surrounding it. And the star that leads the way is your star."

So what are we to make of this? Initially, commentators such as Marvin Meyer explained the ancient theory that each person has his or her own star, appearing first in Plato's *Timaeus* and still present in, for example, Clement of Alexandria's writings.[5] But I am led here immediately to two questions. First, does Judas's being led astray function positively or negatively within the narrative itself? Second, should the assertion that Judas and the other disciples all have their own star be interpreted as a more general theory of sidereal determinism: that *everyone* has a guiding star? I am not prepared to say that this is the best interpretation of the passages in *Gospel of Judas*; it is not clear to me that the experiences of Judas and the disciples are meant to stand for the experience of ordinary Christians. It could be that the correspondence is particular and specific.

Third, stars work in concert with angels or spirits.[6] This idea is very common in antiquity, appearing in both Jewish and pagan sources. According to *Corpus Hermeticum* XVI, for instance, each star is assigned its own daimon. "Thus deployed," Hermes observes, "[the daimones] follow the orders of a particular star, and they are good and evil according to their natures, that is to say, their energies."[7] The third-century Platonist Porphyry, too, equates stars and daimones,[8] as does Nag Hammadi's *Paraphrase of Shem*, which states that the star-*daimones* control life on earth.[9] The *Testimony of Truth* calls the old leaven [of the law] the "errant (πλάνη) desire of the daimones and stars."[10]

However, the word *daimôn* never appears in *Gospel of Judas* as a synonym for 'star'—only for Judas. Instead we find an equation of 'star' with 'angel.'[11] This pairing appears to derive from Jewish traditions, starting as early as Deut 4:19 where the stars form part of the angelic 'host of heaven.' In *1 Enoch* angels are as numerous as the stars.[12] They

---

[5] Plato, *Tim.* 41d–42b; Clem. Alex., *Ecl.* 55.1 (3. 152. 14f).
[6] *Gos. Jud.* 37,4–5; 40,16–17; 41,4–5.
[7] *CH* XVI, 13.
[8] Porphyry, *De Regressu Animae* 34.10–12 (Bidez 1964).
[9] *Paraph. Shem* VII,1, 27,25 ff; see also 34,7.
[10] *Testim. Truth* IX,3, 29,15–18.
[11] The same identification occurs in the Greek Magical Papyri; see *PGM* I. 74–6.
[12] *1 En.* 43:2.

regulate the stars' courses and thus the seasons of the year.[13] *2 Enoch* 4 alludes to the angels who govern the stars. From Jewish apocalyptic literature also derives the language of stars governed by "archons" and "authorities."[14]

Fourth, it is difficult to assign any location to the stars in *Gospel of Judas*, because the text's cosmological sections appear unrelated to the dialogic passages in which Jesus speaks of the stars.[15] The text's cosmology accounts for the creation through emanation of various luminaries (ⲫⲱⲥⲧⲏⲣ), but these do not appear to be stars. We cannot tell, therefore, if the author of *Gospel of Judas* thought that the stars were all located in one sphere, or in concentric spheres, or if, in fact, he thought of them as contained in spheres at all. Where the stars are located, however, presumably has ramifications for helping us determine whether or not they are understood to be *causal* (ruling *heimarmene* in a general sense) or merely *locative*, corresponding to the souls of Judas and the twelve on earth as their celestial counterparts in the aeons.

Plenty of ancient sources, both Jewish and 'Gnostic,' feature stars in the heavens that function metaphorically rather than causally; not every text featuring powerful stars necessarily points to an espousal of Greek astrology. For example, Philo follows Plato's *Phaedrus* in holding that the fixed sphere of the stars surrounds the seven planets and marks the boundary between the cosmos and the purely intelligible world of divinity.[16] But he does not equate this fixed sphere with the zodiac (which, at any rate, is not fixed), nor does he maintain that the stars have any function beyond acting as signs.[17] In other words, we must be careful not to assume that the stars in *Gospel of Judas* are located in, for example, the *heimarmene* realm (as in the *Pistis Sophia*) unless the text makes that clear, or that they necessarily are connected with astral destiny in a general sense.

A second example is the appearance of the Star of Bethlehem in the Gospel of Matthew's infancy narrative in chapter 2. There, the star appears to the Magi, but also to Herod who, as we may recall, is deeply

---

[13] *1 En.* 75:3.
[14] *2 En.* 4; *T. Adam* 4:4.
[15] *Gos. Jud.* 47,2–54,12.
[16] On Philo's cosmology: *Mos.* 1.12; *Conf.* 5; *Cher.* 22.
[17] Stars as merely signs in Philo: *Spec.* 1.87–90; *Opif.* 19.16.

troubled by it.[18] In a sense, the star 'leads' Herod to Jesus in a similar way that Judas's star leads him to the Heavenly Temple, or to complete his 'destiny' at the end of the *Gospel of Judas*. The star 'leads' while simultaneously signifying something like the birth of the Messiah, but it is not connected to anyone's astral destiny. It is not part of a theory of astral fatalism or astrology. As Alan Scott observes, "it would appear that in this era astronomical language is often used for purposes which are not astronomical."[19] In the case of the Gospel of Matthew, the conceptual background for the Star of Bethlehem derives from Jewish prophecy, such as Balaam's proclamation that "a star has marched forth from Jacob" (Num 24:17). My suspicion is that we find a similar Jewish worldview behind the *Gospel of Judas*.

Fifth, every single instance of the word 'star' in the *Gospel of Judas* indicates a negative evaluation of them and their power. They are equated with "error."[20] Their activity causes Jesus to laugh. They either 'lead' Judas and the disciples, or else they are said to bring things to "completion" (ϫⲱⲕ).[21] Their power is limited to lower beings, however, and does not affect Jesus, the primary beings Autogenes and Adamas, the Great Invisible Spirit, or those of the holy generation (ⲧⲅⲉⲛⲉⲁ ⲉⲧⲟⲩⲁⲁⲃ).

These five observations about the "stars" in the *Gospel of Judas* give us a preliminary "map" to further explore significant issues of interpretation pertaining to star language and imagery in the *Gospel of Judas*. Although the assumption has been that the text's astrology owes itself to Greek influence, it is important to note that there is nothing particularly Platonic or Ptolemaic about the cosmology of the *Gospel of Judas*—nothing beyond what most educated people in the second century held about the influence of the stars, at any rate—and any overt astrological references remain undeveloped in the text.[22] Missing are any technical astrological terms that we find in texts such as the *Pistis Sophia* and the *Books of Jeu*. We should be careful not to make the assumption that there stands a full-blown Greek astrological or astronomical system behind the gospel, unless the text itself leads us in that direction.

---

[18] Matt 2:3.
[19] Scott 1991, 100.
[20] *Gos. Jud.* 46,1–2; 55,16–17.
[21] *Gos. Jud.* 40,17–18; 54,17–18.
[22] On a presumed Greek astrological system, see, for instance, DeConick 2007, 25 ff.

I suggest that the 'astrology' in *Gospel of Judas* derives from sectarian Jewish apocalyptic teachings. Since Judaism was deeply Hellenized throughout the Second Temple Period and post-Second Temple Period, I understand any protestations to this component of my argument. To a certain degree, a delineation of "Jewish" from "Greek" leads us in the wrong direction. Nevertheless, basic characteristic features of both cosmology and star-language in the Gospel of Judas can be usefully illuminated solely by drawing comparisons with Jewish apocryphal literature. In its so-called 'astrology,' therefore, the *Gospel of Judas* strikes me as drawing clearly on Jewish literary traditions.

The Cosmology of the *Gospel of Judas*

My contention in this paper is that the *Gospel of Judas*, as we have it, weaves together at least two sources, and that the 'frame narrative' in which Jesus invokes star-language in 33:22–47:1 and 54:13–58.26 is a separate composition from his explanation of cosmology in 47:2–54:12. Both the language and the imagery differ in the two sections. A brief overview of the text's cosmogony and uranography is in order at this point.

The Great Invisible Spirit dominates the cosmic structure, from which emanates Autogenes with four unnamed attendants from two separate luminous clouds.[23] Next, Autogenes calls Adamas into being by a speech-act.[24] Adamas, hidden in a cloud of light is surrounded by myriads of angels who serve him.[25] So far, the structure here is typically Sethian, mirroring the *GosEg*'s primary Triad Logos-Autogenes-Adamas. At this point, the physical cosmos is laid out. Twelve aeons of the twelve luminaries shine in the heavens.[26] Each luminary (ϕⲱⲥⲧⲏⲣ; the word 'star' is absent from these passages) governs six heavens (ⲟⲩⲡⲁⲛⲟⲥ) to equal seventy-two luminaries/heavens.[27] Each of these seventy-two luminaries in turn governs five firmaments (ⲥⲧⲉⲣⲉⲱⲙⲁ) producing a total of 360

---

[23] *Gos. Jud.* 47,5–26.
[24] *Gos. Jud.* 48,1–2.
[25] *Gos. Jud.* 48,21–25. Note the similarity to Jewish *merkavah* traditions; the Adamas is like a throne vision of the angel Metatron in the heavens. On these traditions, see Fossum 1985; Segal 1977.
[26] *Gos. Jud.* 49,18–19.
[27] *Gos. Jud.* 49,23.

luminaries/firmaments.[28] This cosmos, we learn, is called 'corruption' or 'perdition' (ⲫⲑⲟⲣⲁ), perhaps because of the fracturing of the cosmos into lower, contingent forms.[29]

The governing conceptual paradigm here is not drawn from Ptolemaic cosmology, but is a Sethian-style cosmos based on Jewish or even Babylonian astrological traditions. The numbers 12, 72, and 360 indicate a preoccupation with cosmology not for the purpose of mapping physical space, but the division of time: 12 months, 72 weeks in the Babylonian calendar, and 360 days in a year (= 72 weeks × 5 days or 12 months × 30 days). It seems here, then, that the author's prevailing metaphysical occupation was with the construction of *time*, rather than Ptolemaically-ordered *space*. This is not to say that we have tapped into a developed philosophy of time; my point is merely to point out that Greek conceptual models of planets and other luminaries encased in concentric zones around the earth nowhere appear here; instead, the cosmos are emanationist and perhaps calendrical, but not easy to map out spatially.[30]

The problem is heightened in *Gospel of Judas*'s next passages: it then appears that Autogenes has with him 72 luminaries and 72 aeons: "In that place the first human appeared with his incorruptible powers."[31] Is this a whole separate realm? The name of this aeon is "El."[32] Was this meant to be, Eleleth, one of the four chief luminaries of Sethian cosmologies, or is it a sort of incipient and inverted Jewish mysticism that locates the Jewish God (here, 'El') in the chief heaven surrounded by a host of celestial beings? We also find, in this aeon, the first human, his incorruptible powers, and the "cloud of knowing."[33]

---

[28] *Gos. Jud.* 50,2–4. For seventy-two firmaments, see also the *1 Apoc. Jas.* NHC V,3, 26,16. Here, there seems to be a clear tension between systems of seven and systems of twelve. There are twelve times seven which equal seventy-two; of course, 12 × 7 is 84 not 72—an error the *Gospel of Judas* avoids. For an explanation of the error, see Schoedel 1970, 118–29.

[29] *Gos. Jud.* 50,14.

[30] The problem is actually a typical one. The seven planetary archons of Sethian texts such as *Ap. John* are associated not with the Ptolemaic concentric spheres, but with conceptions of a planetary week (Pétrement 1984, 100). There is a similar lack of spatial correlation between the planetary Mithraic grades and the Ptolemaic order; again, the grades seem connected to time rather than space (see Beck 1988). For Ophite planetary archons connected to time rather than space, see Denzey 2005, 89–122.

[31] *Gos. Jud.* 50,18–22.

[32] *Gos. Jud.* 51,1.

[33] *Gos. Jud.* 50,18–51,1.

Next, twelve angels are called into being to rule chaos and the underworld.[34] First, from a cloud issues forth from the "rebel" Nebro/Ialdabaoth "whose face flashed with fire and whose appearance was defiled with blood."[35] Nebro creates seven angels, including Saklas who is here a separate being from Ialdabaoth, another angel who comes from the cloud.[36]

The twelve rulers make twelve angels, although the text names only five:

1) [Se]th (?), "who is called the Christ (?)"
2) Harmathoth
3) Galila
4) Yobel
5) Adonaios

The text concludes, "These are the five who ruled the underworld, and first over chaos" (52:11–13). There are significant parallels here with other Sethian lists, most notably those found in the *ApJn* and the *GosEg*.[37] Let me work through this list backwards, starting with the least controversial. Of Adonaios, I have nothing illuminating to say. Yobel, the Hebrew for Ram and thus the Jewish name for the zodiacal sign of Aries, offers the only clear association with the signs of the Zodiac. Galila corresponds to the *Apocryphon of John*'s Kalila[38] or Kalila-Oumbri[39] and the *Gospel of the Egyptians*' Galila. The second angel, Harmathoth, is clearly a conflation of the first two rulers in the *ApJn*'s three recensions, Harmas and Athoth. I surmise that the combination was probably a scribal error. That leaves us with the troubling name of the first archon. To match with our extant lists, he should be

---

[34] *Gos. Jud.* 51,5–7.

[35] *Gos. Jud.* 51,8–15. There is a wicked archon named Nebruel in the *Holy Book of the Great Invisible Spirit*. Hippolytus also notes that the Peretae—who, interestingly, say the stars are powers of destruction—have an archon named Nebro in their cosmology (*Haer.* 6.15.6 [Marcovich 1986, 183]).

[36] *Gos. Jud.* 51,16.

[37] Compare *Gos. Eg.* NHC III,2, 58,5–22: "The first angel is Athoth. He is the one whom the great generations of men call [...]. The second is Harmas, who is the eye of the fire. The third is Galila. The fourth is Yobel. The fifth is Adonaios, who is called 'Sabaoth'. The sixth is Cain, whom the great generations of men call the sun. The seventh is Abel; the eighth Akiressina; the ninth Yubel. The tenth is Harmupiael. The eleventh is Archir-Adonin. The twelfth is Belias. These are the ones who preside over Hades and the chaos."

[38] Cf. *Ap. John* NHC III,1, 16,20–17,5; BG,2, 40,5–18.

[39] Cf. *Ap. John* NHC II,1, 10,29–11,3.

Athoth or Iaoth, but the lacunate manuscript gives no hint that the missing letter was an ⲱ̅; the name had to have ended in -ⲉⲑ. Atheth is a possibility, and there is some merit to DeConick's proposed reading for our symposium: "[Ath]eth, who is called the Good (kh(rēsto)s)" rather than "Seth, who is called the Christ." I find it more plausible than krios, "Seth who is called the Ram" [i.e. Aries].[40]

Yet I am not entirely convinced, given the proclivities of the *Gospel of Judas*, that "Seth, who is called the Christ" is incorrect. The gospel—which I think we can agree is unrelentingly dark and which (despite some points of contact with Sethian cosmology) does not emphasize Seth or salvation through Seth—may well be anti-Sethian rather than Sethian. Since the Savior here is identified as 'Jesus' rather than 'Christ' throughout the gospel, it is possible that the author thought that those who equated Jesus with Christ—or who equated Seth with the Christ—were terribly in error, actually calling upon an archon without realizing it.

The twelve angels presumably correspond to the twelve signs of the zodiac, but it is frankly difficult to determine a precise correspondence.[41] Thinking on the list of the twelve names as it more generally appears in a variety of sources, A.J. Welburn demonstrates fairly convincingly that the twelve do correspond to the zodiac, as well as to specific planets through astrological systems of planet-sign correlations standard in antiquity.[42] Starting with the only two clear planetary associations (Harmas as Mercury, Iobel as Aries), Welburn reconstructs the list from the *Apocryphon of John* with its correlations as follows:[43]

---

[40] See Van der Vliet 2006a, 137–52.

[41] Compare the attempts of Giversen (1963, 205), who essentially gives up on determining any correspondence between archons, planets and constellations in *Ap. John*.

[42] For these systems, see Giversen 1963, 211–212; T. Barton 1994, 96; Boll et al. 1966, 58–59. Each of the signs corresponds to a certain planet which 'rules' over it. The signs of the zodiac commence either at Leo and run in progression through to Cancer, or at Aries and run through to Pisces. The corresponding planets run in a progression from the Sun to Saturn and back inward to the moon. The first system of planet-sign correlations was evidently known by certain early Christians other than the author or redactor of *Ap. John*. In *PS*, the evil planetary archons are even described as being 'bound' or 'crucified' in their corresponding sign.

[43] Welburn 1978, 250. Welburn notes that *Ap. John* NHC II,1 takes Adonaios and Sabaoth as one entity (a mistake repeated by the redactor of *Gos. Eg.*), then moves Kain up a spot and adds his brother Abel erroneously, perhaps seeking to complete the pair by word-association (see also Giversen 1963, 210 who reaches the same conclusion). Care seems to have been taken by the ancient redactor, despite his evident

Iaoth	Leo	(ruled by)	Sun
Hermas	Virgo		Mercury
Galila	Libra		Venus
Iobel	Scorpio		Mars
Adonaios	Sagittarius		Jupiter
Kain/Sabaoth	Capricorn		Saturn
Abel/Kainan	Aquarius		Saturn
Abiressine	Pisces		Jupiter
Iobel	Aries		Mars
Armupiael	Taurus		Venus
Melcheiradonin	Gemini		Mercury
Belias	Cancer		Moon

The redactors of *Apocryphon of John* divided this list of twelve into seven archons who rule the firmaments plus five archons who rule the abyss. As Welburn notes, this is a traditional division in astrology: seven 'day' signs lie above the intersection of the celestial ecliptic and equator, the remaining 'night' signs below.[44] The *Gospel of Judas* preserves only the names of the five who rule the abyss—fitting for a cosmos shrouded in darkness. Still, there is no real 'smoking gun' to connect the five named angels of the *Gospel of Judas* to these zodiacal signs or planetary associations.

It seems that the five angels listed in *Gospel of Judas* comprise a cosmology based on a (zodiacal? calendrical?) system of twelve rather than a (planetary) system of seven.[45] It would be sloppy to introduce or presuppose a system of seven here. In this way, the *Gospel of Judas* departs from most Sethian cosmogonic texts that emphasize a Hebdomad, including the *Apocryphon of John* and the *Gospel of the Egyptians*. According to Irenaeus, *Adversus Haereses*, the Sethian system presupposes a Hebdomad composed of the seven stars/planets. So the lack of emphasis on the seven strikes me as significant. In my opinion, it is suppressed or ignored because the author's emphasis is

---

confusion at points in the list to keep separate the first seven rulers from the five who rule over the abyss.

[44] Welburn 1978, 253–254. Unfortunately, the division of signs in astrology (from Aries to Libra above the ecliptic, and from Scorpio to Pisces below) do not correspond with the divisions in the *Ap. John*. Welburn's proposed solution, that *Ap. John*'s list reveals a "solar mystery," cannot be properly substantiated. It should be added that if Van der Vliet 2006a, 137–52 is correct in his restoration of the text "Seth, who is called the Ram," then we have two signs of the five corresponding to the constellation Aries.

[45] Welburn 1978, 253–254. For a survey of sources that develop sevenfold planetary systems, see A. Collins 1995, 83–84. Also helpful is Flamant 1982, 223–42.

on the twelve disciples. The emphasis is on the pattern of twelve that is disrupted by Judas's departure from the twelve and Matthias's addition, so as to "complete" the Dodecad once more, and focus on the hidden cosmic significance of this shift.

This means that so-called 'astrological' language enters the text because it is a way to articulate the cosmic dimensions of this shift, not because there stands behind the *Gospel of Judas* a fully developed Ptolemaic uranography. Not incidentally, we find that some Jewish *literary* sources frequently adopt zodiacal symbolism or language, not because their authors were convinced of the veracity of astrology, but because the twelve signs of the zodiac and the twelve months could so conveniently represent the twelve tribes of Israel.[46] We find a similar emphasis on the number twelve associated with the Heavenly Jerusalem in the Book of Revelation: it has twelve gates, each one guarded by an angel.[47] On the twelve foundations of the city walls are the twelve names of the twelve apostles.[48] Twelve jewels adorn the city walls.[49] Here, the imagery is 'zodiacal' without being determinative; that is, the appearance of an incipient zodiac here does not indicate that that zodiac is connected to a belief in astrological fatalism.

VISIONS OF THE TEMPLE

It is useful at this point to look more closely at the points of contact between elements in this gospel and Jewish sources and imagery. I will focus on one main element here: the text's Temple visions.

We find in the *Gospel of Judas* incipient *hekhalot* traditions, particularly in the fact that we have not one, but two visions of a Temple. According to 44.24–45.9, Judas has a Temple vision. It is described as a vision of a great 'house' [ογηει, restored]. Jesus responds to Judas' recounting of this vision,

---

[46] The *locus classicus* for this type of identification remains Philo's description of the symbols of the sun, moon, *stoicheia* and zodiac on the vestments of the High Priest in *Mos.* 2.125. Similarly, the fifth Sibylline Oracle, likely of second-century Jewish authorship, gives an extended passage on the 'battle of the stars' utilizing zodiacal language, yet cannot be considered an attestation of Jewish astrology (*Sib. Orac.* 5.512–31). For more examples, see also Philo, *Migr.* 32; *QG* 4.164; Jos., *B.J.* 5.5.4; 6.5.3.

[47] Rev 21:12.
[48] Rev 21:14.
[49] Rev 21:19.

your star has led you astray (ⲁⲡⲉⲕⲥⲓⲟⲩ ⲡⲗⲁ[ⲛⲁ] ⲙⲙⲟⲕ)...No person of
mortal birth is worthy to enter the house you have seen, for that place
is reserved for the holy. Neither the son nor the moon will rule there,
nor the day, but the holy will bide always in the aeon with the holy
angels.[50]

Remarkably, the disciples also have a Temple vision, but they see a
very different Temple than Judas sees.[51] Theirs is a great house with
a great altar served by twelve priests. God's "name," the Tetragrammaton, lives in the Temple; a crowd throngs outside. Jesus asks for a
description of the priests, so the disciples outline various egregious
activities they are committing: they are sacrificing their wives and children, committing sodomy and murder, "and the men who stand over
the altar are invoking your name."[52] Jesus then interprets the vision:
the priests are the disciples, the disciples correspond to twelve generations, and the cattle are the people they have led astray.[53]

Elaine Pagels and Karen King have read the disciples' Temple vision
allegorically as a reference to the Church and the perceived corruption
of apostolic authority; they see the monstrous activities of the priests—
namely human sacrifice—connected to the exhortations to martyrdom
by some Christians following in apostolic tradition.[54] Given the parallel here with the *Testimony of Truth* where the Christians who boast
of their salvation through martyrdom do so through the "agency of
the wandering stars," this way of reading the text is compelling.[55] It
seems to me, however, that we should place these Temple visions back
within Jewish sectarian literature—much of which is rife with images
of the Temple, both in its earthly, degraded form and as the Heavenly
Temple.

My initial impression upon first reading the *Gospel of Judas* was
that while Judas sees the uncorrupted Heavenly Temple in his vision,
the disciples see the corrupt earthly Temple. This dichotomized vision
falls right in line with a number of Jewish apocalyptic texts from
the Second Temple Period. In these, a seer is granted a vision of the
Heavenly Temple, which is then contrasted with the shockingly corrupt

---

[50] *Gos. Jud.* 45,14–19.
[51] *Gos. Jud.* 38,2–3.
[52] *Gos. Jud.* 38,24–26.
[53] *Gos. Jud.* 39,28.
[54] Pagels-King 2007, 44ff.
[55] *Testim. Truth* IX,3, 34,7–10.

Temple on earth. Certainly there were numbers of disaffected Jews in the Second Temple Period who believed that the Jerusalem Temple had been hopelessly defiled; the perspective is reflected in Qumranic texts such as the *Songs of the Sabbath Sacrifice* and the *Temple Scroll*. In the *Testament of Levi*—where, incidentally, we find our earliest Jewish reference to a seven-heavened cosmos—Levi tours the heavens including the heavenly Temple, where he receives the garments of a high priest. He then returns to the earthly Temple, which is profoundly corrupted. In one passage, he speaks of the corruption during the seventh jubilee (presumably corresponding to the Hellenistic Hasmonean priesthood):

> There shall be such pollution as I am unable to declare in the presence of human beings, because only the ones who do these things understand such matters. Therefore they shall be in captivity and preyed upon; both their land and their substance shall be stolen. And in the fifth week they shall return to the land of their desolation, and shall restore anew the house of the Lord. In the seventh week there shall come priests: idolators, adulterers, money lovers, arrogant, lawless, voluptuaries, pederasts, those who practice bestiality.[56]

Interestingly, following this seventh jubilee, God places a new priest in the Temple at the "completion" of the days. This priest, furthermore, is likened to a star: "And his star shall rise in heaven like a king.... This one will shine forth like the sun at his ascension."[57] Receiving further sanctification from the celestial "Temple of Glory," this new priest will open the gates to Paradise, reinstate Adam, give Adam and Eve the fruit to eat, and conquer Belial—giving the new blessed race the ability to conquer all evil spirits. I see striking parallels here between *Gospel of Judas* and *Testament of Levi*. The *Gospel of Judas* likewise speaks of a succession of wicked priests preceding the good priest who will take over at the 'completion' of the time of the twelve.[58] "On the last day they [i.e. the twelve disciple/priests] will be put to shame."[59]

The trope of the corruption of the earthly Temple is fairly standard fare in Jewish apocalyptic, and should not particularly shock us when we find it here. In the case of the Second Temple Period literature, condemnations of the earthly Temple were, of course, connected to

---

[56] *Test. Levi* 17 (Charlesworth 1985, 2:794).
[57] *Test. Levi* 18.
[58] *Gos. Jud.* 40,7ff.
[59] *Gos. Jud.* 40,25–26.

the Hellenization of the priesthood and the influence of foreign (i.e. Greek) modes of behavior. The situation was no different in the second century, as sectarian Jews and 'Gnostics' looked upon the fate of the Temple and the influence of Roman or Graeco-Roman culture on an earlier set of ideals.

Upon reviewing the literature, however, I was struck by those Jewish apocalyptic texts that state unequivocally that even the Heavenly Temple was defiled. In *1 Enoch*, the seer Enoch has a Temple vision and finds that fornicating angels are defiling it. The sexual sins of the fallen angels in *1 Enoch*'s ancient core, the *Book of the Watchers*, are associated with the sexual sins of Temple priests; in fact, the point is made that the fallen angels *are* the priests. But they are also stars.[60] The angels/priests/stars are also guilty of other transgressions, including murder. In *1 Enoch* 18:13–16, in fact, the star/priests are punished for their transgression.[61] Again, the points of contact with *Gospel of Judas* are striking: the point is made explicitly there that the temple priests are the twelve disciples, but they are also star-angels: "those who say 'we are like angels'; they are the stars that bring everything to completion."[62]

Already in Second Temple Period, Jewish apocalyptic authors could conflate Temple priests with errant stars. I think this is significant, because we find a clear equation of the activities of the defiled Temple with the error of the star-angels. In fact, the use of cosmic imagery to describe the Temple permeates a number of Jewish writings.[63] Both Philo and Josephus note the astrological symbolism of the Jerusalem Temple. Philo states in *De Specialibus Legibus* that the stars are the offerings made in the temple that is the cosmos, while the angels are the priests in this temple.[64] Philo speaks here of the Heavenly Temple. He was part of a class of writers who conceptualized the heavens *as* a Temple, as opposed to a Temple *in* the heavens, as in *Gospel of Judas*, *1 Enoch* and *Testament of Levi*.

---

[60] *1 En.* 75:3.

[61] Compare *Ps-Clem. Hom.* 8.12ff.

[62] *Gos. Jud.* 40,16–18; cf. 41,4–5. The sacrifice is received from a "minister of error" (ⲡⲇⲓⲁⲕⲟⲛⲟⲥ ⲛ̄ⲧⲉⲡⲗⲁⲛⲏ) (40,22–23); note we have here a virtual pun with a "planetary minister."

[63] Klawans 2006, 12.

[64] Philo, *Spec.* 1.66.

But the earthly Temple also employed cosmic imagery. In a significant passage in the *Jewish War*, Josephus describes the Temple's outer veil in place since the time of Herod: eighty feet high, it is wrought in blue and fine linen, in scarlet and purple, featuring an image of the cosmos.[65] Pictured on it "was a panorama of the entire heavens," reports Josephus.[66] Within the Temple itself, the twelve loaves of bread on the table represent the signs of the zodiac, and the seven branches of the menorah represent the seven planets.[67]

The *Gospel of Judas*'s description of two celestial "houses" ought to be placed within the context of Jewish writings on the nature of the Heavenly Temple. The move to 'demonize' the Temple and its priests is not the shocking innovation of *Gospel of Judas*'s author. To charge its priests with sexual sins was already commonplace, and to transpose the offenders from "priests" to "disciples" makes sense in a post-Second Temple Period world. It was not new to associate priests with errant or sinful angels or stars. Cosmic imagery for the Temple was common, and disaffected Jews had no difficulty with demonizing even a Heavenly Temple. Other texts such as the *Testament of Levi*, like the *Gospel of Judas*, contrast a heavenly undefiled Temple with an earthly defiled one.

Visions of the Temple do not come from earthly dreams; they derive from Jewish mystical ascent traditions in which the seer is given access to the realities of the cosmos. Thus I see no reason not to think that both Judas and the other disciples actually "see" their Temple visions in the heavens. While this idea troubles us less, I suspect, with Judas's vision of the Spiritual Temple, it works less well for the disciples' vision of the corrupt Temple. I argue here that the corrupt Temple, however, is also located in the heavens and is not meant to be the earthly Jerusalem Temple at all, but the demonic 'mirror' in the lower aeons of the inaccessible, incorrupt Temple beyond, where dwell the immortal generation. The *Gospel of Judas*'s choice to contrast a heavenly undefiled Temple in the upper realms with a heavenly defiled Temple in the lower realms is innovative but consistent with the author's worldview.

---

[65] Jos., *B.J.* 5.5.4.
[66] Ulansey 1991, 123–25; See also Pelletier 1958, 168–79.
[67] Jos., *B.J.* 5.5.5; cf. *A.J.* 3.146, 182; cf. Philo. *QE* 2.78; *Her.* 221; *Mos* 2.102; also *Spec.* 1.172.

A Scathing Indictment

I do not believe that there stands behind the *Gospel of Judas* a coherent Ptolemaic cosmology. Significantly absent are the planets and their spheres, and the twelve aeons and their luminaries are not said to be located in any particular sphere. The word *heimarmene* is never used. Even if this material were in the *Gospel of Judas*'s missing passages, it would likely belong to the cosmological revelation section that stands distinct from the dialogical material in which Jesus reveals the nature of the errant stars to Judas. I find that the employment of star language derives from Jewish sources, which often speak of stars but rarely bother to locate them consistently in a particular cosmos. Jewish texts show no consistency in this regard.[68] To give a provocative comperandum from Nag Hammadi, in the *Apoc. Paul*, the apostle on his heavenly tour is greeted by the twelve apostles (!), who rise with him to the ninth and tenth heavens. These twelve apostles reside in the Ogdoad, where they appear to be associated with the signs of the zodiac.[69]

The language of the stars and the ostensible astral fatalism of the *Gospel of Judas* appears to derive from earlier Jewish apocalyptic ways of thinking about the stars as a) associated with the angels; and b) connected somehow with the functioning of the corrupt Heavenly Temple. Judas and the disciples are identical to the stars; perhaps we might say that they stand in some syzygetic relationship to them. When, then, Jesus laughs at the error of the stars, he laughs at the witlessness of the disciples. And when Jesus points out that Judas and the disciples all have stars that lead them astray, this should not be taken as a general theory of sidereal causality that governs all people. Rather, it is the most scathing indictment of Judaism, the early Jesus movement, and the Christianity that grows from a tradition the author of the *Gospel of Judas* could only see as wholly corrupt.

---

[68] Compare *Treat. Seth* NHC VII,2, 58,18–21.
[69] See Scott 1991, 99.

FATE INDELIBLE

The *Gospel of Judas* and Horoscopic Astrology

Grant Adamson

In a 1940 article, folklorist Wayland Hand showed that as late as the mid 1800s it was not uncommon for Europeans to speculate about the birthday of Judas. The date, most often given as April 1 or April 7, was of course generally inauspicious, and it was believed that whoever happened to be born on the same day as Judas would die as he did. Hand argues that such speculation was more than a matter of "mere idle curiosity." Rather it "represents an attempt...to view the dire deed of Judas in terms of a predetermined fate, of which the birthday itself becomes, consciously or unconsciously, the outward symbol." While doubting the attribution of his earliest source to the thirteenth-century Catholic sage Albertus Magnus, Hand is confident that the speculation goes back at least to the 1500s, arising "[o]ut of the great wealth of magic and superstition and out of the maze of religious, astrological, and hermetic lore that circulated in all levels of society from the time of the humanistic revival, orally as well as in divers almanacs, peasants' weather forecasts, dream and fortune books, medical prescriptions, herbals, horoscopes, chiromantic handbooks, etc., etc."[1] These same types of lore (if not much of the very lore itself that Hand mentions here) circulated in all levels of society and among all peoples throughout the Roman Empire, Hellenistic astrology being virtually inseparable from Hermetism and magic. So it should come as no surprise that the long lost *Gospel of Judas*, reportedly discovered in the 1970s and first published by the National Geographic Society in April (!) 2006, incorporates astrological teaching on nearly every page.

One of the most obvious astrological references in the *Gospel of Judas* is found on the penultimate page of the manuscript. After telling Judas that he will exceed all others in wickedness by sacrificing Jesus to Saklas, the Savior's final words to his betrayer are as follows:[2]

---

[1] Hand 1940, 1–4.
[2] *Gos. Jud.* TC 57,15–20 (Kasser et al. 2007, 232–3); translation mine.

57,15	ⲉⲓⲥ ϩⲏⲏⲧⲉ ⲁⲩⲭⲉ ϩⲱ[ⲃ] ⲛⲓⲙ ⲉⲣⲟⲕ	Behold, everything has been told to you.
57,16	ϥⲓ ⲉⲓⲁⲧⲕ ⲉϩⲣⲁⲉⲓ ⲛⲕ̄[ⲛ]ⲁⲩ ⲉⲧϭⲏ-	Look up and see the
57,17	ⲡⲓ ⲁⲩⲱ ⲡⲟⲩⲟ<ï>ⲛ ⲉⲧ<ⲛ̄>ϩⲏⲧⲥ̄	cloud and the light in it
57,18	ⲁⲩⲱ ⲛ̄ⲥⲓⲟⲩ ⲉⲧⲕⲱⲧⲉ ⲉⲣⲟⲥ	and the stars surrounding it.
57,19	ⲁⲩⲱ ⲡⲥⲓⲟⲩ ⲉⲧⲟ ⲛ̄ⲡⲣⲟⲏⲅⲟⲩ-	The leading star
57,20	ⲙⲉⲛⲟⲥ ⲛ̄ⲧⲟϥ ⲡⲉ ⲡⲉⲕⲥⲓⲟⲩ	is your star.

Featuring prominently on the cover of the original publication of the *Gospel of Judas*, these lines have been badly misinterpreted, along with those that come after them, in which it is said that Judas looked up and "he" entered the cloud.[3] For scholars who see Judas in this second-century Sethian text as a positive figure, either wholly or in part, 57,15–26 is a key passage. In their view, it is the moment of his transfiguration, enlightenment, liberation, or redemption.[4]

A recently published example of this view appears in Seonyoung Kim's article from the volume of proceedings of the 2006 Sorbonne conference. In the first section of the article, Kim rightly distinguishes "the negative function of the stars" in the *Gospel of Judas* from both the role of the young gods in the *Timaeus* and the system of beneficent and maleficent planets in Ptolemy's *Tetrabiblos*.[5] Yet, discussing 57,15–26 in the third section of the article, Kim seems to forget this distinction. In an attempt to deal with the apparent disconnect between the star that "leads the way" for Judas at the end of the text and the star in a previous passage that deceives Judas into thinking he could join the holy generation in the divine realm beyond the visible cosmos, Kim writes:

> [T]he character of the Judas's star [sic] is not the same as in an earlier part of the text. Clearly, while interpreting Judas's own vision, Jesus said, 'Your star has led you astray (45,13–14).' Judas was deceived by his star and misunderstood his vision. However, in the latter part of the text, preceding the scene of Judas's entering into the luminous cloud (57,22–23), Jesus said, 'It is your star that leads the way (57,19–20). [Kim's footnote here reads: Literally, he is his star.] A sudden change in the characteristic

---

[3] *Gos. Jud.* TC 57,21–26.

[4] Refer to Kasser et al. 2006a, 10, 44 n. 143, 100–1, 164–5, 169; Ehrman 2006b, 96, 180; Pagels-King 2007, 90, 98, 164; also Gathercole 2007a, 107–8, 111–13; and now the somewhat less assertive statements, that is, excepting Ehrman's, in Kasser et al. 2008, 16, 52 n. 156, 87–88, 145, 154.

[5] Kim 2008, 295–6.

of Judas's star stands out, and there is no bridge which explains or connects the two different characteristics.[6]

Kim offers two "possible explanations" for the apparent disconnect: first, that on the penultimate page of the manuscript Judas "is no longer led astray by stars. Rather, he himself is his star;" and second, that "it might be thought that he is freed from the evil one, and a more positive star takes its place." After some recapitulation, Kim concludes the article thus:

> In our text, the stars are depicted as influencing Judas and the other disciples, and seeking to lead them astray. While Judas was also led astray by his star in the first part of the text, by the end, he seems to be freed from its influence. If we can identify salvation in the *Gospel of Judas* with liberation from the domination of the stars, it may be that in the end Judas is finally freed from his star, and so is redeemed.[7]

There are several problems with this interpretation, none of them minor. For one, Kim's first explanation of the apparent disconnect between the characteristics of Judas' star mistakes ⲛ̄ⲧⲟϥ in the phrase ⲛ̄ⲧⲟϥ ⲡⲉ ⲡⲉⲕⲥⲓⲟⲩ to be referring to Judas. And Kim apparently fails to recognize that ⲡⲉⲕ- is not third person.[8] The phrase cannot be understood to mean that Judas is his star. Moreover, it is far from clear how Judas would escape astral influence by becoming so. As for the second explanation, namely that Judas' star is "more positive" by the end of the text, this contradicts the valid distinction Kim makes in the first section of the article. Unlike in the *Timaeus* and the *Tetrabiblos*, with very few exceptions there are no positive stars in Sethian literature.[9] Rather, the astral rulers of Sethian myth do such things as rape Eve and have Jesus killed in their efforts to prevent the transcendent Savior from accomplishing redemption during repeated descents to earth. If the leading star in 57, 19–20 were positive, it would be quite unusual. And the apparent disconnect between this allegedly beneficent star and all the other stars in the *Gospel of Judas*, including the one that distinctly deceives Judas into thinking he could escape his fate, would remain inexplicable.

---

[6] Kim 2008, 308.

[7] Kim 2008, 308–9.

[8] The problem apparently stems from the pun on 57,19–20 in Kasser et al. 2006a, 44 n. 142: "Judas is literally the star of the text;" cf. Kim 2008, 308 n. 52.

[9] For the exceptions, refer to the enthronement of Sabaoth in *Hyp. Arch.* NHC II,4 and *Orig. World* NHC II,5, and to the procosmism in *Marsanes* NHC X.

In short, Kim's explanations are not explanations at all but attempts to maintain the assumption that there is "a sudden change in the characteristic of Judas's star" marked by Jesus telling him it is the one that "leads the way," as if this were somehow a good thing. Kim is not alone in this assumption or in the corollary assumption that it is Judas who enters the cloud and is therein transfigured, liberated, redeemed, etc. Unfortunately, due to the poor condition of the Tchacos Codex, the question of who enters the cloud, Judas or the Savior, cannot be resolved to everyone's satisfaction. This is no matter, I submit, since even a basic understanding of the astrological context of the *Gospel of Judas* is alone sufficient to establish that the only place Judas' star can lead is around the ecliptic. It does not lead him or anyone else to salvation.

Horoscopic Astrology

During the opening centuries of the Common Era, astrologers across the Mediterranean region made prognostications based on the position of the stars both at the time of a person's birth and thereafter.[10] These prognostications concerned all facets of life, ranging from such questions as what kind of disposition, vices, and physical characteristics the native would have, to whether he or she would marry, raise children, become wealthy, or not. One of the oldest extant handbooks of horoscopic astrology, though hardly the first or last, was written by Claudius Ptolemy in the second century, most likely within a few decades of the composition of the *Gospel of Judas*. In the *Tetrabiblos*, Ptolemy discusses, for instance, the quality of the soul (ποιότης ψυχῆς) and states that given the position of Saturn in relation to Mercury and the Moon at the time of birth, the astrologer can predict that the native will be treacherous. What Ptolemy literally says, among other things, is that the star of Kronos actually 'makes' people who devise plots against their friends, go about at night, lay ambushes, and are betrayers (ποιεῖ...ἐπιβουλευτικοὺς οἰκείων...νυκτερέμβους, ἐνεδρευτάς, προδότας).[11] Part of the rationale behind such prognostications was the division of the planets into subgroups of maleficent (κακοποιοί:

---

[10] A useful introduction is Barton 1994.
[11] *Tetrabiblos* 3.13 (Robbins 1956, 338–47); cf. Thomassen 2008, 167 n. 26, where the passage was first cited in connection with *Gos. Jud.*

Saturn, Mars), beneficent (ἀγαθοποιοί: Jupiter, Venus, Moon), and mixed or common (κοινοί: Mercury, Sun), according to whether they were understood to be predominantly cold and dry, hot and moist, or a combination of both.[12] In this case, the maleficent planet Saturn makes individuals with treacherous souls.

Besides the nature of the planets, it was also important for the astrologer to know where the planets were located against the back-drop of the fixed stars of the zodiac. These were said to be fixed (ἀπλανές), not because they stand still, but because they proceed consistently in their circular path around the earth, as opposed to the planets (πλανῆται), which seem to wander (πλανᾶσθαι) as they make their way through the sky. Technically five in number, the planets were each thought to have two of the twelve zodiacal signs as their own houses (οἶκοι), one solar the other lunar.[13] Thus, it was held that the five planets and two luminaries exert more or less influence depending on the sign they happen to be in.

The stars of the zodiac were also thought to be influential in and of themselves. For instance, Ptolemy states that the stars "in the shoulders" and "in the left arm and the cloak" of Aquarius "exert an influence like that of Saturn and Mercury; those in the thighs, like that of Mercury in a greater degree and like that of Saturn in a lesser degree; those in the stream of water, like that of Saturn and, in some degree, like that of Jupiter."[14] Altogether, Ptolemy says that Aquarius is "cold and wintry," and its aspect "disharmonious with beneficence (ἀσύμφωνον πρὸς ἀγαθοποιίαν)" because it opposes Leo, the house of the sun, on the zodiacal wheel.[15] Diametrical aspect or opposition was one of the basic angular relationships of the zodiacal signs. It and quartile, namely, when the signs aspect each other in the shape of a square, were considered disharmonious (ἀσύμφωνοι); trine and sextile, that is, when the signs aspect each other in the shape of an equilateral triangle and hexagon respectively, were considered harmonious (σύμφωνοι).[16] Because the planets appear to move through the signs when viewed from the earth, they were thought to aspect each other

---

[12] Refer to *Tetrabiblos* 1.4–5.
[13] *Tetrabiblos* 1.17 (Robbins 1956, 78–79); cf. 1.12.
[14] *Tetrabiblos* 1.9 (Robbins 1956, 53).
[15] *Tetrabiblos* 1.17 (Robbins 1956, 81); translation slightly modified.
[16] *Tetrabiblos* 1.13.

in the same way, which accordingly affected the influence they were
believed to exercise.[17]

Some astrologers went even further in determining the location of
the planets, wanting to know where they were against the backdrop of
yet another group of stars called decans (δεκανοί). These were originally constellations marking ten day divisions within the Egyptian calendar, as seen, among other places, on star charts painted inside of
sarcophagi. Later, they were incorporated into Hellenistic astrology.
Circling the earth at or just beyond the sphere of the zodiac, the thirty
six decans were apportioned to the zodiacal signs, three to a sign, just
as each sign occupies thirty degrees in the wheel of the zodiac for a
total of three hundred sixty degrees.[18] The decans could also be halved,
yielding six per sign, with five instead of ten degrees in each of the seventy two.[19] It is precisely this type of elaborate zodiacal-decanal system
that seems to underlie the *Gospel of Judas*, with its twelve aeons, seventy two heavens, and three hundred sixty firmaments.[20] The cosmological structure of a zodiacal-decanal system comprised of the usual
thirty six decans can be seen on a set of astrological boards found
in 1967 in the village of Grand, France, approximately two hundred
miles north of Lyon.[21] The boards are made of ivory and gold and
date on archaeological grounds to no later than the last half of the
second century CE. Carved inside a ring at the center of the boards
are the busts of a man and woman representing the all powerful sun
and moon. Around them in the next ring are depicted the figures of
the zodiac. And standing in a circle above the zodiacal signs are the
Egyptian decans in hieratic poses, many of them with theriomorphic
features.[22]

The astrological tablets from Grand and other boards like them were
used in the actual practice of casting and interpreting horoscopes.[23]
After learning where the stars were when the native was born, by

---

[17] See Barton 1994, 99–102, with figures of the different aspects.

[18] On the thirty six decans, see e.g. Firmicus Maternus, *Mathesis* 2.4, 4.22; Stobaeus,
Excerpt 6.

[19] On the seventy two pentads, i.e., thirty six 'decans' and thirty six 'horoscopes,'
refer especially to P. Oxy. 465 in Grenfell-Hunt 1903, 126–37 and the sources cited
there.

[20] *Gos. Jud.* TC 49,7–50,19. I intend to make a complete study of the Greco-Egyptian
astrological system of *Gos. Jud.* in my dissertation.

[21] See Evans 2004, 1–44.

[22] There are color images of both boards in Abry 1993, plates 1–6.

[23] Sources and discussion in Evans 2004.

consulting reference works and through calculation rather than direct observation, the astrologer would then place eight small stone markers in the appropriate spots on the board to represent the five planets, two luminaries, and the horoscopic point (ὡροσκόπος) or ascendant.[24] The latter refers to the sign or more precisely the degree of the zodiac rising above the eastern horizon at any given moment, such as at a person's birth.[25] It was thought to be one of the single most influential positions that a star could occupy and served as the starting point for the entire birth chart.[26] Starting from the ascendant, the nativity was divided into four quadrants. Opposite the horoscopic point is the descendant, and perpendicular to them are midheaven above and the lower midheaven below. Also starting from the ascendant, the birth chart was further divided into eight or twelve equal places (τόποι), each pertaining to particular facets of life, from livelihood and property to death.[27]

With all the information for the nativity plotted on a board in front of him, the astrologer could readily see where the planets had been in relation to each other, the zodiac, and decans, as well as which stars were in the ascendant, the other quadrants, and places. Such an apparatus allowed the astrologer to make prognostications more easily and efficiently without attempting to visualize the configuration of the stars solely from a list of coordinates or exhausting time and materials in order to draw the birth chart on a sheet of papyrus. It was no doubt also more impressive to clients to see their nativity displayed in semi-precious stones on a board of ivory and gold elaborately carved with the images and names of the astral deities determining their fate from above.

The foremost prognostication astrologers made was how long the native would live. As Ptolemy writes, "The consideration of the length of life (ὁ περὶ χρόνων ζωῆς λόγος) takes the leading place among inquiries about the events following birth, for, as the ancient says [Ptolemy is likely referring to Petosiris or Nechepso], it is ridiculous to attach particular predictions to one who, by the constitution of the years of his life, will never attain at all to the predicted events."[28] There were

---

[24] Refer to *PGM* CX and *Historia Alexandri Magni* 1.4.5–6, both cited in Evans 2004, 4–5.
[25] See e.g. *Tetrabiblos* 1.12.
[26] See e.g. Dorotheus of Sidon, *Carmen astrologicum* 1.5.
[27] See e.g. Firmicus Maternus, *Mathesis* 2.19–20.
[28] *Tetrabiblos* 3.10 (Robbins 1956, 271).

different methods among astrologers for calculating the length of life, some more sophisticated than others. Ptolemy's preferred method, one of the most complex, has been summarized by Auguste Bouché-Leclercq as follows:

> His theory rests essentially upon the likening of the zodiac to a wheel upon which the life of the individual is cast with a greater or lesser force from a certain place of departure (τόπος ἀφετικός) and finds itself arrested, or in danger of being arrested, by barriers or destructive places (τόποι ἀναιρετικοί), without being able in any case to go beyond a quarter of the circle. The number of degrees traversed, converted into degrees of right ascension, gives the number of the years of life.[29]

The method described and demonstrated by Ptolemy's predecessor Dorotheus of Sidon, also known as Dorotheus the Egyptian, who incidentally was said to have addressed his handbook of horoscopic astrology to his son 'Hermes,' is also complex.[30] Whereas, writing in the fourth century, Firmicus Maternus has a much simpler approach.[31] Whatever the method, astrologers believed that a person's lifespan was determined by the stars at birth and that the time of death, like all other facets of life, could be ascertained from the nativity, even down to the month and day, as in the *Book of Hermes Trismegistus, On the Thirty Six Decans*.[32]

Not only did the astrologers occupy themselves with predicting when the native would die but also how, and cases of violent death were of special interest. Methods varied in complexity, following directly from the consideration of the length of life. Thus Ptolemy explains that a violent death can be predicted for the native "whenever both the evil planets dominate the destructive places (ὅταν ἢ ἀμφότεροι κυριεύσωσιν οἱ κακωποιοὶ τῶν ἀναιρετικῶν τόπων), either in conjunction, or in quartile, or in opposition, or also if one of the two, or both seize upon the sun, or the moon, or both luminaries."[33] For instance,

---

[29] Bouché-Leclercq 1899, 411, as cited in Robbins 1956, 271 n. 4.

[30] Dorotheus of Sidon, *Carmen astrologicum* 3.1–2.

[31] Firmicus Maternus, *Mathesis* 3.25.

[32] *Liber Hermetis Trismegisti de triginta sex decanis* 8–9. As with many astrological handbooks, this is a conglomerate work. It is extant only in Latin, the Greek original of which may have been written in the seventh century CE or later, though it appears to contain material that is significantly earlier. See the introduction in Zoller 1998, i–iv, especially x–xi, which, however, is not entirely reliable (e.g. 82 n. 25, where it is wrongly stated that Dorotheus wrote in Arabic). The most recent edition of the Latin text of *Liber Hermetis* is that of Feraboli 1994, for whom "Difficile dire quando il florilegio fu composto" (xxi).

[33] *Tetrabiblos* 4.9 (Robbins 1956, 430–1).

if Saturn is in conjunction with the sun at midheaven, the astrologer can predict that the native will die by falling headlong from a height (ἀπὸ ὕψους κατακρημνιζομένους), and if Mars is in quartile or diametrical aspect to the sun or moon, the astrologer can predict that the native will kill himself (αὐτόχειρας ἑαυτῶν γινομένους).[34] Underlying this and all prognostications was the fundamental astrological doctrine that the stars are not just celestial indicators of mundane events but in fact the very cause of many if not all things that happen on the earth.[35]

CASTING JUDAS' HOROSCOPE

Though he is not said to use a board like the ones found at Grand nor does he enter into the methodological details of prognostication, the Savior speaks as an astrologer in the *Gospel of Judas*, teaching astrological doctrine and employing technical astrological terms as he predicts the fate of the disciples from the stars. When he appears to the disciples for the first time in the text, Judas is the only one able to stand in his presence and correctly identify him as having come from the immortal aeon of Barbelo. So the Savior offers to disclose to Judas the mysteries of the kingdom of the stars and he begins to reveal to him his fate:[36]

35,21	ⲓ̄ⲏ̄ⲥ ⲇⲉ ⲉϥⲥⲟⲟⲩⲛⲉ	And Jesus, knowing
35,22	ϫⲉ ϥⲙⲉⲟⲩⲉ ⲉⲡⲕⲉⲥⲉⲉⲡⲉ ⲉⲧ-	that he was thinking about the rest
35,23	ϫⲟⲥⲉ ⲡⲉϫⲁϥ ⲛⲁϥ ϫⲉ ⲡⲱⲣⲝ̄	that is exalted, said to him, 'Part
35,24	ⲉⲃⲟⲗ ⲙ̄ⲙⲟⲟⲩ ⲧⲁϫⲱ ⲉⲣⲟⲕ ⲛ̄-	from them, and I shall tell you the
35,25	ⲙ̄ⲙⲩⲥⲧⲏⲣⲓⲟⲛ ⲛ̄ⲧⲙⲛ̄ⲧⲉⲣⲟ	mysteries of the kingdom (i.e. of the stars),
35,26	ⲟⲩⲭ ϩⲓⲛⲁ ϫⲉ ⲉⲕⲉⲃⲱⲕ ⲉⲙⲁⲩ	not in order that you may go there (i.e. the
35,27	ⲁⲗⲗⲁ ϫⲉ ⲉⲕⲉⲁϣ ⲁϩⲟⲙ ⲛ̄ϩⲟⲩⲟ	aeon of Barbelo) but so that you will grieve
36,1	ϫⲉ ⲟⲩⲛ̄ⲕⲁⲓⲟⲩ[ⲁ] ⲅⲁⲣ [ⲛ]ⲁϣⲱⲡⲉ	greatly. For someone else will take
36,2	ⲉⲡⲉⲕⲙⲁ ϩⲓⲛⲁ ϫⲉ ⲉ̄[ⲣⲉⲡ]ⲙⲛ̄ⲧ-	your place in order that
36,3	ⲥⲛⲟⲟⲩⲥ ⲛ̄ⲥ[ⲃⲟⲩ̈ⲓ] ⲟⲛ ⲉⲩⲉ-	the twelve disciples again may
36,4	ϫⲱⲕ' ⲉⲃⲟⲗ ϩⲛ̄ ⲡⲉⲩⲛⲟⲩⲧⲉ	be completed by their god.'

---

[34] *Tetrabiblos* 4.9 (Robbins 1956, 432–4).

[35] See e.g. Ptolemy, *Tetrabiblos* 1.1–3 and Firmicus Maternus, *Mathesis* 1.5–9.

[36] *Gos. Jud.* TC 35,21–36,4 (Kasser et al. 2007, 188–91); translation mine.

For readers and auditors of Luke-Acts, already implicit in this prognostication are Judas' betrayal of Jesus and his own violent death, where-
upon he is replaced by Matthias, thereby becoming the thirteenth.[37]
While the fate of the other disciples is also discussed in subsequent
pages of the *Gospel of Judas* and is intertwined with his, the text is
largely concerned with the fate of Judas. In that sense, it can, and I
think should, be read as his horoscope more so than as his gospel.
Each time the Savior refers to Judas and the number thirteen, among
other things, he effectually reiterates his prediction of the betrayal and
of the replacement of Judas after the ill-fated disciple's own death. The
length of life is something Judas and the Savior twice discuss in fact.

Their first discussion of the length of life occurs on page 43 of the
manuscript. Speaking of himself in the third person and referring to
the act of salvation metaphorically as 'giving to drink' or 'watering,'
the Savior says that he has come "to water the paradise of God and the
[fruit] that will endure, because the conduct of that generation will
not [be] corrupted."[38] Judas wonders "what kind of fruit this generation has."[39] And the Savior explains that "the souls of every human
generation will die." As for members of the holy generation, however,
after they have "completed the time of the kingdom," that is, after
their lifespan determined by the archontic rulers comes to an end,
their bodies will die but their souls will be resurrected.[40] Judas then
asks, "What then will the rest of the human generations do?"[41] And
the Savior replies that their situation is "impossible (ⲁⲧϭⲟⲙ):" their
souls cannot be resurrected any more than fruits can be harvested
from seeds that have been sown on rock.[42] Judas goes on, nonetheless,
to ask the Savior to hear him recount a dream he has had. The Savior
laughs, calls Judas the thirteenth daemon, in effect reiterating his previous prognostication of the betrayal and of Judas' death and replacement, and condescendingly agrees. Judas relates how in the dream
he saw himself as "the twelve disciples," namely Matthias included,

---

[37] See Acts 1:15–26.
[38] *Gos. Jud.* TC 43,6–10 (Kasser et al. 2007, 204–5); translation mine, reading
ⲡ[ⲕⲁⲣ]ⲡⲟⲥ in 43,7 and [ⲛ̄ⲥⲉⲛ]ⲁ- in 43,8, with Turner 2008, 232. Cf. John 4:7–15;
7:37–39.
[39] *Gos. Jud.* TC 43,13–14 (Kasser et al. 2007, 204–5); translation mine.
[40] *Gos. Jud.* TC 43,15–23 (Kasser et al. 2007, 204–5); translation mine.
[41] *Gos. Jud.* TC 43,24–25 (Kasser et al. 2007, 204–5); translation mine.
[42] *Gos. Jud.* TC 43,26–44,7 (Kasser et al. 2007, 204–7); reading ⲟⲩⲁ[ⲧϭⲟⲙ in 44,3
with Turner 2008, 232.

were stoning him. Fleeing from the twelve, Judas comes to a large house surrounded by great people and implores the Savior to let him in. But the Savior refuses, telling Judas that his star has deceived him (ⲁⲡⲉⲕⲥⲓⲟⲩ ⲡⲗⲁ[ⲛⲁ] ⲙ̄ⲙⲟⲕ) into thinking he could escape his fate and join the holy generation. "I have told you the mysteries of the kingdom," the Savior says, "and I have taught you about the deception of the stars (ⲧⲉⲡ[ⲗ]ⲁⲛⲏ ⲛ̄ⲛ̄ⲥ[ⲓ]ⲟⲩ)."[43]

Judas and the Savior discuss the length of life for a second time on page 53 of the manuscript after the Savior describes the creation of Adam and Eve. This time the Savior explains that although Adam with his generation received "his measured lifespan in the place where he received his measured kingdom and ruler," that is, although the occasion of their death was determined by the stars, the true God "caused knowledge to be given to Adam and those with him, in order that the kings of Chaos and Hades might not rule over them."[44] As before, Judas then asks what those who are not of the holy generation will do. And the Savior replies that they remain subject to the stars which cause them to commit all sorts of atrocities in his name, such as fornication and infanticide. In connection with them, he mentions Judas' star again and the number thirteen, then laughs. Naturally, Judas wants to know why the Savior is laughing "[at us]," and the Savior's suspiciously disingenuous reply is that he is laughing at "the deception of the stars (ⲧⲉⲡⲗⲁⲛⲏ ⲛⲛⲥⲓⲟⲩ)," not necessarily at those like Judas who are unfortunate enough to be controlled by them.[45]

From their discussions about the length of life, it is clear that the Savior is not teaching Judas a form of astral determinism that is universally irrevocable or everywhere effective. Through knowledge (ⲅⲛⲱⲥⲓⲥ), members of the holy generation are free from the rule of the stars, except as it concerns their bodies.[46] They will still die under the circumstances determined by the stars. But in the meantime, their souls are not subject to the astral influences that cause the rest of the human generations to sin. This appears to have been a relatively common position on fate in antiquity, one with which Firmicus

---

[43] *Gos. Jud.* TC 44,15–46,2 (Kasser et al. 2007, 206–11); translation mine.
[44] *Gos. Jud.* TC 53,5–54,12 (Kasser et al. 2007, 224–7); translation mine. Cf. the astrally determined lifespan of Adam and Eve in *Orig. World* NHC II,5, 121,13–18.
[45] *Gos. Jud.* TC 54,13–55,17 (Kasser et al. 2007, 226–9); translation mine.
[46] Cf. *Ap. John* BG,2, 65,16–66,12.

Maternus takes issue. After cataloguing just a few of the horrors and injustices of the past, he writes:

> All these events are caused by the movements of the stars (*stellarum cursibus*) and by these various patterns Fortune destroys us.... But there are some who agree with us to a certain extent and admit that Fate and Fortune have a certain power, which they call *himarmene*.... They claim that this thing which they call *himarmene* is connected to humankind and all living things by a certain relationship. We are so created that after a certain time, the course of our life is finished (*completo vitae cursu*). We are brought back to the divine spirit which sustains us (*ad divinum illum spiritum, qui nos sustentat*), after the dissolution of the body. They claim that we are subject to Fate, this is, to Chance, for attaining the end of life.... But all the things that pertain to our daily lives they say are in our power. What we do while we are alive belongs to us; only our death belongs to Chance or Fate.[47]

This nuanced position, which Firmicus considers nonsensical, fits well with what the Savior teaches Judas about the limited influence of the stars over members of the holy generation. They are only ruled by fate when it comes to their death. This is why the man Jesus, a paradigmatic member of the holy generation, still ends up dying when and how he does. As for the rest of the human generations, they are subject to the stars in both body and soul, from birth to death and everything in between. Their situation is more in line with Firmicus' own position on astral determinism, which is that "nothing is placed in our power, but the whole is in the power of Fate. Whatever we do or suffer, the whole thing happens to us by this same judgment of Fortune."[48]

The difference between the holy generation and the rest of the human generations amounts to more than just knowledge. As the Savior explains to Judas, there is a difference in their spirits and souls as well. Members of the kingless generation have their spirits and souls from the Great One through the divine angel Gabriel. All other people are animated by Saklas through the archontic angel Michael, and only temporarily at that, for the duration of their servitude to the chief astral ruler.[49] When disembodied, as the Savior tells Judas in their first discussion about the length of life, the souls of those who do not

---

[47] *Mathesis* 1.8.1–3 (ed. Monat 1992, 81–82; trans. Bram 1975, 26–27); translation slightly modified.

[48] *Mathesis* 1.9.3 (Bram 1975, 28).

[49] *Gos. Jud.* TC 53,18–25 (Kasser et al. 2007, 224–5). Cf. the role of the serpent/Michael as the source of spirit, soul, and all things worldly, in Irenaeus, *Haer.* 1.30.5.

belong to the holy generation will die and cannot possibly be resurrected. Whether these different spirits and souls are received at birth
or later in life through a process of initiation, the Savior repeatedly
tells Judas that he cannot join the holy generation. After his dream, the
Savior tells him the he has been deceived by his star into thinking that
he could, a star to which, as April DeConick puts it, Judas "remains
indelibly connected" throughout the text, despite the revelation he
obtains from the Savior.[50]

On the question of fate, not all astrologers were of the same opinion
as Firmicus Maternus. Ptolemy's claims, for instance, are not so broad.[51]
And according to other astrologers more inclined towards magic (or
were they first and foremost Egyptian priests and theurgists?), a person's fate could be changed and even erased through the proper rites
and invocations. Of course, Christians, including Valentinians, held
similar beliefs about the possibility of canceling fate and had their own
rituals for escaping the rule of the stars. Thus, after the Savior rather
unconvincingly assures Judas that he is not laughing directly at him
and the rest of the human generations subject to astral influence in
both body and soul, Judas asks the Savior about the efficacy of baptism: "What will those who have been baptized in your name do?"[52]
But the non-Christian rituals for escaping fate are also quite relevant
for understanding what is going on in the *Gospel of Judas*. The most
detailed account of such practices comes from the three versions of the
Eighth Book of Moses preserved in *PLeid*. J 395, commonly known as
PGM XIII. The papyrus was copied in the mid fourth century, but the
practices described in *VIII Moses*, if not some form of the text itself,
probably go back as far as the first.[53]

Instead of consulting a fallible, mortal astrologer, the practitioner
of *VIII Moses* would summon a deity to come down and cast his
horoscope. If the rite was done correctly, the deity would appear,
though not necessarily well disposed, and would tell the practitioner
about such things as his native star, his accompanying daimon, and the
circumstances of his death. If the practitioner behaved appropriately

---

[50] DeConick 2008, 264.

[51] *Tetrabiblos* 1.1–3.

[52] *Gos. Jud.* TC 55,21–23 (Kasser et al. 2007, 228–9).

[53] On the redaction history of the three versions, see Smith 1984, 683–93, who
concludes that "*PLeid*. J 395 is *at least* the fifth generation of a literary family" (688
n. 1; original emphasis).

in the divine presence by not looking the deity in the face and not crying out or weeping while his horoscope was being cast, he could further succeed in getting the evils of his fate erased and perhaps even cheat death for a time. For example, in one of the versions of *VIII Moses*, the instructions for meeting with the deity are as follows:

> Now when the god comes in do not stare at his face, but look at his feet (μὴ ἐνατένιζε τῇ ὄψει, ἀλλὰ τοῖς ποσὶ βλέπε) while beseeching him, as written above, and giving thanks that he did not treat you contemptuously, but you were thought worthy of the things about to be said to you for correction of your life. You, then, ask, 'Master, what is fated for me?' And he will tell you even about your star, and what kind of daimon you have, and your horoscope and where you may live and where you will die (καὶ ἐρεῖ σοι καὶ περὶ ἄστρου καὶ ποῖός ἐστιν ὁ σὸς δαίμων καὶ ὁ ὡροσκόπος, καὶ ποῦ ζήσῃ καὶ ποῦ ἀποθανεῖσαι). And if you hear something bad, do not cry out or weep, but ask that he may wash it off or circumvent it, for this god can do everything (ἐὰν δέ τι φαῦλον ἀκούσῃς, μὴ κράξῃς, μὴ κλαύσῃς, ἀλλὰ ἐρώτα, ἵνα αὐτὸς ἀπαλείψῃ ἢ μεθοδεύσῃ. δύναται γὰρ πάντα ὁ θεὸς οὗτος). Therefore, when you begin questioning, thank him for having heard you and not overlooked you. Always sacrifice to this [god] in this way and offer your pious devotions, for thus he will hear you.[54]

There is no explicit warning in any of the versions of *VIII Moses* as to what would happen if the practitioner were to look up at the deity or to cry out or weep over his impending misfortune. But it is said in two of the versions that without a knowledge of astrology, above all the ability to determine the rulers of the hour and day, "the god will not listen, but, thinking you uninitiated, will refuse to receive [you] (ὁ θεὸς οὐκ ἐπακούσεται, ἀλλ᾽ ὡς ἀμυστηρίαστον οὐ παραδέξεται)."[55]

On several counts, the exchange between the Savior and his betrayer in the *Gospel of Judas* can be read as a meeting between the practitioner of *VIII Moses* and the deity he invokes to cast his horoscope and erase his foul fate. What is most instructive about reading the *Gospel of Judas* alongside *VIII Moses* is not the similarities between them but in fact the differences. Compared to the practitioner of *VIII Moses*, Judas is ultimately incompetent. When the Savior first appears during the disciples' celebration of the Eucharist and challenges them to stand before him, Judas begins to behave appropriately in the divine

---

[54] *PGM* XIII. 704–18 (ed. Preisendanz 1972, 2:119; trans. Betz 1992, 189); translation slightly modified.
[55] *PGM* XIII. 427–8 (ed. Preisendanz 1972, 2:108; trans. Betz 1992, 184); see also *PGM* XIII. 56–57.

presence by not looking the Savior in the eyes, as the practitioner of *VIII Moses* is instructed to do:[56]

35,2	ⲡⲉⲧ[ⲧ]ⲁ̣[ⲭⲣ]ⲏ̣ⲩ ⲛ̄ϩ[ⲏ]ⲧⲧⲏⲩⲧⲛ̄ ⲛ̄ⲛ̄-	Let he who is strong among you
35,3	ⲣⲱⲙⲉ *vac* ⲙ̣ⲁ[ⲣⲉϥⲣ̄] ⲡⲁⲣ̣ⲁ̣ⲅⲉ ⲙ̄ⲡⲣⲱ-	bring forward the
35,4	[ⲙⲉ] ⲛ̣ⲧⲉⲗⲉⲓⲟⲥ ⲁⲩⲱ ⲛϥⲱϩⲉⲣⲁⲧϥ̄	perfect man and stand
35,5	ⲙ̄ⲡⲉⲛ̄ⲧⲟ ⲉⲃⲟⲗ ⲙ̄ⲡⲁⲡⲣⲟⲥⲱ-	before my
35,6	ⲡⲟⲛ ⲁⲩⲱ ⲁⲩⲭⲟⲟⲥ ⲧⲏⲣⲟⲩ ϫⲉ	face. And they all said,
35,7	ⲧⲛ̄ϫⲟⲟⲣ ⲁⲩⲱ ⲙ̄ⲡⲉϣ ⲡⲉⲩⲡⲛⲁ̅	'We are strong.' But their spirits
35,8	ⲧⲟⲗⲙⲁ ⲉⲱϩⲉⲣⲁⲧϥ̄ ⲙ̄[ⲡⲉϥ]ⲙ̄-	could not find the courage to stand
35,9	ⲧⲟ ⲉⲃⲟⲗ ⲉⲓⲙⲏ ⲓ̈ⲟⲩⲇⲁⲥ [ⲡⲓⲥ]ⲕⲁ-	before him except Judas
35,10	ⲣⲓⲱⲧⲏⲥ ⲁϥϭⲙ̄ ϭⲟⲙ ⲙⲉⲛ̣ [ⲉ]ϣ̄-	Iscariot. While he found the strength to
35,11	ϩⲉⲣⲁⲧϥ̄ ⲙ̄ⲡⲉϥⲙ̄ⲧⲟ ⲉⲃ[ⲟⲗ] ⲛ̄-	stand before him,
35,12	ⲡⲉϥϭⲙ̄ ϭⲟⲙ ⲇⲉ ⲉϭⲱϣ̄ⲧ̄ [ⲉϩ]ⲟⲩⲛ	he could not look him
35,13	ⲉϩ̄ⲣⲁϥ ⲛ̄ⲛⲉϥⲃⲁⲗ ⲁⲗ[ⲗⲁ ⲛ̄]ⲧⲁϥ-	in the eyes but
35,14	ⲕⲧⲉ ϩ̄ⲣⲁϥ ⲉⲡⲁϩ̄ⲟⲩ	turned his face away.

However, the Savior quickly informs Judas that he is going to tell him the mysteries of the kingdom, not in order that he may go to the aeon of Barbelo, but so that he will grieve greatly, something the Savior repeats later on in the manuscript. On page 46, Judas loudly objects when the Savior tells him that he has been deceived by his star into thinking he could join the holy generation. As he begins to realize that the things he is learning from the Savior about the mysteries of the kingdom and the deception of the stars will not enable him to escape his fate, Judas emphatically protests:[57]

46,5	ⲡⲉϫⲁ[ϥ] ⲛ̄ϭⲓ ⲓ̈ⲟⲩⲇⲁⲥ ϫⲉ ⲡⲥⲁ̅ϩ̅ ⲙⲛ̄-	Judas said, 'Teacher,
46,6	ⲡⲟⲧⲉ ϩ̅ⲱ̅ ⲡⲁⲥⲡⲉⲣⲙⲁ ϩⲩⲡⲟⲧⲁⲥ-	my seed will never (be) subject
46,7	ⲥ̣[ⲉ] ⲛ̄ⲛⲁⲣⲭⲱⲛ ⲁϥⲟⲩⲱϣⲃ̄ ⲛ̄ϭⲓ	(to) the archons!' Jesus
46,8	ⲓ̅ⲥ̅ [ⲡⲉ]ϫ̣ⲁϥ ⲛⲁϥ ϫⲉ ⲁⲙⲟⲩ ⲛ̄ⲧⲁ	answered and said to him, 'Come and
46,9	ϣ [±...] ⲙ̄ⲙⲟ̣[ⲕ] ⲭ̣[ⲉ ± ....]	I will [...] you [...]
46,10	[± ....]	[...]
46,11	ⲉⲣ [...ⲁ]ⲗ̣ⲗⲁ ϫⲉ ⲉⲕⲉϣⲱⲡⲉ ⲉ-	[...] but so that you will
46,12	ⲕⲁϣ [ⲁϩⲟ]ⲙ ⲛ̄ϩ̄ⲟⲩⲟ ⲉⲕⲛⲁⲩ ⲉ-	grieve greatly when you see
46,13	ⲧⲙⲛ̄[ⲧⲉ]ⲣⲟ ⲙⲛ̄ ⲧⲉⲥⲅⲉⲛⲉⲁ	the (archontic) kingdom and all its
46,14	ⲧⲏⲣⲥ̄	generation.'

---

[56] *Gos. Jud.* TC 35,2–14 (Kasser et al. 2007, 188–9); translation mine.
[57] *Gos. Jud.* TC 46,5–14 (Kasser et al. 2007, 210–11); translation mine. On 46,5–7, refer to DeConick 2007, 52–53; 2008 242–3; also Turner 2008, 188–9.

This behavior and the grieving that Judas will do are the exact opposite of the instruction for meeting the god in *VIII Moses*, where the
practitioner is told not to cry out or weep if the god says anything
undesirable during the casting of his horoscope.

Furthermore, unlike the practitioner of *VIII Moses*, Judas is completely ignorant of astrology. He is able to identify the Savior as having
come from the immortal aeon of Barbelo; he knows the invocation, as
it were. But he knows nothing of the stars, let alone which ones are
ruling the hour and day. In this regard, it may seem that by telling
Judas about the archons, where they come from, and how they determine human action, the Savior takes pity on Judas instead of ignor-
ing him and refusing to receive him as uninitiated, as the god of *VIII
Moses* would. Yet it is precisely so that he will grieve greatly that the
Savior teaches Judas the mysteries of the kingdom.[58]

THE ASCENDANCY OF JUDAS' STAR

Whether due to Judas' incompetence and misbehavior vis-a-vis the
practitioner of *VIII Moses* or for other reasons more inborn, halfway
through the *Gospel of Judas* he fails in calling upon the Savior to rescue
him from his fate at the hands of the twelve disciples.[59] And towards
end of the manuscript, the Savior makes it clear that Judas' baptism
cannot erase the misfortune that awaits him.[60] The initial lines of the
Savior's response to Judas' final question regarding the efficacy of baptism are for the most part missing. But it should be remembered that
in response to his prior questions as to what the rest of the human
generations will do, the Savior does not give Judas any hope.[61] The way
Judas asks the question, "What will those who have been baptized in
your name do?" signals that this ritual, like the Eucharist and all other
forms of worship practiced by Apostolic Christians in the name of
Jesus, is actually service to Saklas rather than to the true God.[62] When

---

[58] The purpose clause introduced by ϩⲓⲛⲁ in *Gos. Jud.* TC 35,26 includes not only
the verb in that line but also the one in 35,27, both being third future/optative. They
should be translated accordingly, as both DeConick 2007, 68 and Turner 2008, 230
do. For the grammar, see Layton 2004 § 338.

[59] *Gos. Jud.* TC 45,11–14; discussed above.

[60] *Gos. Jud.* TC 55,21–56,20; refer to DeConick 2007, 121–4; 2008, 262–4.

[61] *Gos. Jud.* TC 43,24–44,7; 54,14–55,11; discussed above.

[62] Refer to *Gos. Jud.* TC 34,8–11; 39,18–22.

the text picks up again in the middle of page 56, this is in fact what the Savior is talking about.

After alluding to the betrayal with multiple references to Judas' replacement among the twelve, the Savior now openly informs Judas that he will exceed all others in wickedness by sacrificing Jesus to the chief astral ruler.[63] In support of this prognostication, the Savior tells Judas that his star has already passed by (ⲡⲉⲕⲥⲓⲟⲩ ⲁϥϫⲱⲃⲉ).[64] As April DeConick observes, this "is astrological language indicating that Judas' actions are determined."[65] What Judas' star has passed by is the eastern horizon. The seven planets pass it by with varying frequency, while the twelve signs of the zodiac pass by the eastern horizon roughly once every twenty four hours. In ancient astrology, the degree of the zodiac found to be rising above the eastern horizon at any given moment was called the horoscopic point (ὡροσκόπος) or ascendant. And it was one of the single most influential positions that a planet or other star could occupy.[66] The immediate effect of the ascendancy of Judas' star is to incite him emotionally to betray Jesus. As his star appears, Judas' wrath flares (ⲡⲉⲕϭⲱⲛⲧ̄ ⲁϥⲙⲟⲩϩ̄).[67] That is, Judas is not about to hand Jesus over out of any sense of loyalty or friendship.

Addressing his betrayer for the last time, in a fragmentary passage the Savior seems to mention once more the grief that Judas will soon experience.[68] He speaks of the eschaton, and says:

57,15	ⲉⲓⲥ ϩⲏⲏⲧⲉ ⲁⲩϫⲉ ϩⲱ[ⲃ] ⲛⲓⲙ ⲉⲣⲟⲕ	Behold, everything has been told to you.
57,16	ϥⲓ ⲉⲓⲁⲧⲕ ⲉϩⲣⲁⲉⲓ ⲛⲣ̄[ⲛ]ⲁⲩ ⲉⲧϭⲏ-	Look up and see the
57,17	ⲡⲓ ⲁⲩⲱ ⲡⲟⲩⲟⲓ̈ⲛ ⲉⲧⲛ̄ϩ̄ⲏⲧⲥ̄	cloud and the light in it
57,18	ⲁⲩⲱ ⲛ̄ⲥⲓⲟⲩ ⲉⲧⲕⲱⲧⲉ ⲉⲣⲟⲥ	and the stars surrounding it.
57,19	ⲁⲩⲱ ⲡⲥⲓⲟⲩ ⲉⲧⲟ ⲙ̄ⲡⲣⲟⲏⲅⲟⲩ-	The leading star
57,20	ⲙⲉⲛⲟⲥ ⲛ̄ⲧⲟϥ ⲡⲉ ⲡⲉⲕⲥⲓⲟⲩ	is your star.[69]

It has been suggested by Bart Ehrman that "the soul of Judas is the guiding star for all those who will be saved once they transcend this

---

[63] *Gos. Jud.* TC 56, 17–2; refer to Painchaud 2008, 183–4; DeConick 2007, 57–59; 2008, 245–6.

[64] *Gos. Jud.* TC 56,23 (Kasser, et al. 2007, 230–1).

[65] DeConick 2007, 126.

[66] Refer to Barton 1994, 86–113; Neugebauer-van Hoesen 1959, 200; Jones 1999, 2:460; Dorotheus of Sidon, *Carmen astrologicum* 1.5.

[67] *Gos. Jud.* TC 56,22 (Kasser et al. 2007, 230–1).

[68] *Gos. Jud.* TC 57,6 (Kasser et al. 2007, 232–3).

[69] *Gos. Jud.* TC 57,15–20 (Kasser et al. 2007, 232–3); translation mine.

life;" by Elaine Pagels and Karen King that "Judas is but the first-fruits of those who follow Jesus. His star leads the way;" and by Simon Gathercole that whereas "[p]reviously, Judas was not complete…, [n]ow, however, he has the *gnōsis*, the true revelation about the generation of the cosmos and of the generation of Adamas and Seth. His personal star is ahead of all the rest, whether the others here are the rest of the disciples in particular or the whole of the human race in general."[70] Part and parcel of this interpretation of the Savior's final words to his betrayer is an understanding of the stars in the *Gospel of Judas* that is based on the *Timaeus*, a text of unquestionable importance in Sethian literature, but one that is parodied therein alongside the opening chapters of Genesis. The chief ruler of Sethian myth is almost as much a mockery of the *Timaeus*' demiurge as he is of the god of Hebrew scripture.[71] And unlike the young gods and other stars in the *Timaeus*, his subordinates are not destinations of eternal bliss to which only righteous souls will be privileged to return. They are brigands, prison guards, kings of Chaos and Hades, from whom the spirit or soul must endeavor to escape. In Sethian texts such as the *Gospel of Judas*, it is to the aeons and transcendent luminaries (ⲫⲱⲥⲧⲏⲣ) of the divine realm that the righteous return, not to the stars (ⲥⲓⲟⲩ) within the visible cosmos.

Besides Sethian parody of the *Timaeus*, this interpretation also ignores the astrological context. In his *Tetrabiblos*, Ptolemy uses προηγεῖσθαι repeatedly in participial form. As F. E. Robbins notes in his edition, "Ptolemy characterizes three parts of each sign, leading, middle, and following.… The 'leading' portion is so-called because it is the part which first rises above the horizon."[72] For instance, Ptolemy writes of Aries that "its leading portion (τὰ μὲν προηγούμενα) is rainy and windy, its middle (τὰ δὲ μέσα) temperate, and the following part (τὰ δ' ἑπόμενα) hot and pestilential."[73] The participle is also used of entire zodiacal signs, planets, etc. It is a technical term that refers to one or more astral phenomena leading another in their circuit through the sky. The term occurs repeatedly, not only in the *Tetrabiblos* but also in the works of other astrologers such as Vettius Valens and

---

[70] Ehrman 2006b, 96; Pagels-King 2007, 98; Gathercole 2007a, 107.
[71] See e.g. Turner 2001, 49.
[72] Robbins 1956, 201 n. 4.
[73] *Tetrabiblos* 2.11 (Robbins 1956, 200–1).

Hephaestio of Thebes.[74] Accordingly, when the Savior tells Judas that the leading star (ⲡⲥⲓⲟⲩ ⲉⲧⲟ ⲛ̄ⲡⲣⲟⲏⲅⲟⲩⲙⲉⲛⲟⲥ) is his star, it is not going to lead him or anyone else to salvation. Rather, having passed the eastern horizon, it leads the other archontic stars, particularly those surrounding the cloud, in their perpetual circular path around the earth. If Judas is the one who then enters the cloud, he is in no way liberated from astral domination. Simply put, if he were finally freed from the influence of his star at the close of the text, Judas would not betray Jesus.

Thus the Savior speaks as an astrologer in the *Gospel of Judas*, predicting Judas' fate, teaching astrological doctrine and using technical astrological terms, including ⲡⲣⲟⲏⲅⲟⲩⲙⲉⲛⲟⲥ at 57,19.[75] If there is anyone asking for help to escape from the cosmic realm and its astral rulers, it is Judas who asks the Savior, not vice versa. Like the deity invoked in *VIII Moses*, the Savior surely has the power to cancel fate. But he does not to do so for his betrayer or the rest of those who do not belong to the holy generation. The influence of Judas' native star, the same star that earlier in the text deceives him into thinking that he could join the holy generation, only intensifies as it passes by the eastern horizon and becomes visible on the eve of the betrayal. It now leads the other archontic stars in their circuit through the night sky, just as Judas leads (προήρχετο) those who arrest Jesus in Luke 22:47, as Birger Pearson has pointed out.[76] Reading the *Gospel of Judas* as a horoscope explains why Judas is the central figure in the text without being a 'gnostic hero.' He is indeed the recipient of a private revelation, but not all horoscopes are good news. Such a reading also explains why the text ends where it does, with the betrayal, that is, with the fulfillment of the first half of the Savior's initial prognostication that someone else would replace the deceased Judas among the twelve. As readers and auditors of Luke-Acts, the readers and auditors of the *Gospel of Judas* are left to understand that following the betrayal, Judas died violently

---

[74] Refer to the indices in Pingree 1973, 437; 1974, 464; 1986, 548.

[75] As for what the author of *Gos. Jud.* is doing, i.e., explaining the fate of an infamous person ex post facto, compare the horoscope of the Roman emperor Hadrian, written in the mid to late second century by Antigonus of Nicaea and cited by Hephaestio of Thebes, *Apotelesmatica* 2.18. The fact that Luke-Acts is rather amenable to astrological interpretation no doubt facilitated the composition of *Gos. Jud.*: note the man bearing the jar of water (cf. Aquarius), the house, and its ruler (οἰκοδεσπότης) in Luke 22:10–11; and the lot (κλῆρος) that Judas is said to have received in Acts 1:17.

[76] See his contribution in this volume.

and, after the selection of Matthias, became the thirteenth. From the text itself, the readers and auditors of the *Gospel of Judas* are left to understand that Judas was stoned, presumably to death, by the twelve (cf. συγκατεψηφίσθη at Acts 1:26), and that he eventually died in soul as well, like the rest of those temporarily animated by the chief astral ruler through Michael, never joining the holy generation.

THE STAR OF JUDAS IN THE *GOSPEL OF JUDAS*

Niclas Förster

A special characteristic of the *Gospel of Judas* is its astronomical and astrological interest, especially traces of concerns about the influence of stars and planets. According to the *Gospel of Judas*, Jesus informed the twelve disciples: "Each of you has his own star."[1] Judas also is related to a star of his own. This star is mentioned in several passages of the Gospel and its influence can be considered to be negative because the star of Judas "led him astray."[2]

Since 2006, when the text of the Tchacos Codex was published, scholars have been discussing the astral character of these passages, presupposing that each soul is assigned to a star.[3] Ezio Albrile has examined the astral character of these passages against the background of Zoroastrianism as it may have evolved into Gnosticism.[4] Already Seonyoung Kim has compared it with contemporary astrological writings.[5] However, what celestial body should be identified as the star that influenced Judas is a question that has not yet been raised.

In this paper, I will try to answer this question by scrutinizing Judas' star, placing it against the background of Gnosticism and the religious history of antiquity. The idea that a special star is related to Judas will be explained as a symbol of his superior position, especially in comparison with the other disciples of Jesus, but also with respect to humanity as a whole.

Nevertheless the star of Judas belongs to the earthly sphere of the seven planets because it deceives Judas and does not reveal to him any knowledge about the first unknown God and the house of the holy which are both localized above the seven heavens of the planets. This deception is explicitly stressed by Jesus.[6] It is in this context that

---

[1] *Gos. Jud.* 42.7–8.
[2] *Gos. Jud.* 45.12–14.
[3] E.g. the possible connection to Plato Tim 41d–42b was discussed by Meyer 2006, 153–154.
[4] Albrile 2008.
[5] Kim 2008.
[6] *Gos. Jud.* 45.13.

Jesus declares that the sun and the moon do not influence the sphere situated above the seven heavens.[7] At the end of the Gospel a final passage describes how Judas enters a cloud of light. In this passage, Jesus reveals to him that among the stars surrounding this cloud the star of Judas "goes ahead" of the others.[8] In another passage, Jesus mentions six wandering stars. This is probably an allusion to the plants circling around the sun that stands firm in the middle.[9]

Associated with the imagery of Judas' star is the number 13. Reflecting the Sethian Gnosticism that is present in the *Gospel of Judas*, Judas is described as the thirteenth disciple and the thirteenth daemon. This numerology is associated with the creator and ruler of the earthly realm.[10] In Sethian writings, this world creator is often called Yaldabaoth. So in this Sethian Gnostic system, Judas is related to Yaldabaoth (also called Saklas), the creator and ruler of the lower and earthly realms.[11] Thus Judas' star, the thirteenth heavenly being, will preside over the archontic kingdom whose work is "everything that is evil".[12] What is this star? The star of Judas, which "goes ahead" of the others and rules over them? What is the thirteenth heavenly being in relation to the twelve, which is situated underneath the sphere of the fixed stars? As I will argue, Judas' star is the sun.

POPULAR ASTROLOGY

I will begin my observations on the sun as Judas' star by a brief overview of some essential features of astrology contemporary to the *Gospel of Judas*. Here we should keep in mind that in the second century astrology was at the peak of its theoretical development. It influenced a large part of the intellectual climate of Roman society, so much so that several emperors shared its convictions. In addition to this, many people who lived around the Mediterranean at this time regarded the

---

[7] *Gos. Jud.* 45.20–21.

[8] *Gos. Jud.* 59.19–20.

[9] *Gos. Jud.* 55.17–18.

[10] Cf. the discussion of the place of the *Gospel of Judas* in Sethian tradition by Brankaer-Bethge 2007, 431–433; Turner 2008a, 190–209 and Schenke Robinson 2008a, 75–80. The relevant passages could be secondarily inserted. However, the additions do not concern the section about the star of Judas; cf. the discussion by Schenke Robinson 2008a, 78.

[11] Brankaer-Bethge 2007, 343 and 428–433 on the cosmology of the *Gos. Jud.*

[12] *Gos. Jud.* 56.17.

sun as a male deity. Various sources describe it as the king or ruler of the universe or as the father and leader of heaven and earth. The Egyptians as well as the Mesopotamian nations venerated the sun. Thus Greek sources refer to the wide acceptance of the cult of the sun, stating that all Greeks and all barbarians venerate the sun.[13] Already in the Homeric poems, the sun occupies a special position among the Olympic gods because it brings the light to the gods. Later, this belief develops into the idea that sun god Helios should be considered the father of the world while all other deities his sons and daughters.

The same worldview also influenced hermetic writings. In theses treatises Helios is the most important deity in heaven and the king of all other divine beings. He rules over many daemons that are partly good and partly bad. All of these daemons are related to their particular stars. Late in this development in Byzantine times, the book *Hermippos* was written. Its author praises the sun god as the leader of the entire universe, the father of everything, the nourisher of all mortals, and the good driver who safely directs his carriage in the sky.[14]

According to the cult information we have about the Persian deity Mithras, the sun god commands the rotation of the celestial axis. In some reliefs found in the temples of Mithras, the sun god holds in his hand symbols representing the constellation of the great bear. This constellation is situated near the celestial pole. This configuration underscores the sun god's role in the rotation of the entire universe.[15]

Finally, the veneration of the sun shapes the astrology that informs the Greek magical papyri found in Egypt. In some of these magical spells and incantations, the magician tries to guarantee for himself the assistance of the sun because the sun is the powerful king of the earth. Therefore he calls upon the sun god using the names that are known among the people living inside and outside the borders of the Roman Empire.[16] The magician even considers himself an incarnation of this most powerful deity and transforms himself into the king of all gods and the lord of all stars.[17]

---

[13] Cf. Plato, *Leg.* 887e.

[14] Bouché-Leclercq 1963, 322–323; cf. also the material collected by Fauth 1995, xxx–xxxi.

[15] Ristow 1978, 984; Merkelbach 1984, 141–142, 336; Fauth 1995, 20.

[16] Gundel 1968, 9.

[17] PGM XIII. 334–340 (Betz 1986, 181); cf. on this text Fauth 1995, 96–97. The magician stresses in this spell that he is "in the middle of the cosmos, between heaven and earth"; cf. also Gundel 1968, 10.

CAIN, JUDAS, AND THE SUN

The connection of Judas to the sun can be confirmed by Irenaeus'
report about the Gnostic group that in his words "brought forth"
the "fabricated" *Gospel of Judas*.[18] In *Against the Heresies,* Irenaeus
summarizes the doctrine of those Gnostics who regard the biblical
figure of Cain as a superior being. According to the church father,
these Gnostics associated Cain with other biblical figures and groups
that are looked upon in a negative light (like the tribe of Korah or
the Sodomites). Judas is also connected to these biblical "antiheroes."[19]
He achieved the true gnosis: "And furthermore Judas the betrayer was
thoroughly acquainted with these things."[20] Irenaeus does not explain
how he received his knowledge.[21] Nor does he explain why Judas was
connected with Cain, the tribe of Korah or the Sodomites.[22]

Crucial for understanding this connection between Judas and Cain
is the astrological background behind it discussed in the *Apocryphon
of John.* This is probably the most widely known of all treatises on
Sethian Gnosticism. It is similar to the *Gospel of Judas* in several
respects.[23] During a post-resurrection appearance, Jesus reveals secret
teachings to the apostle John, the son of Zebedee in the *Apocryphon of
John.* In the first part, Jesus describes to John the realm of the supreme
deity and explains to him how the creation with all its shortcomings
originated with the fall of Sophia. The *Apocryphon of John* also provides an account of the creation of the lower world by the ill-begotten
son of Sophia, Yaldabaoth. He brings into being subordinate archons
to help him control and rule the cosmic realm below the divine world.
Among many others, these are the twelve powers of the zodiac and the
seven archons of the seven planets. However, Yaldabaoth's knowledge
is limited: he is aware of his mother Sophia but unaware of the divine
realm above her. Alluding to biblical texts such as Isa 45:5, he even
dares to declare himself the only God with no other besides him.

---

[18] Iren., *Adv. Haer.* 1,31,1: "Et confinctionem adferunt huismodi…" (Rousseau-
Doutreleau 1979, 386).
[19] Pearson 2007, 49.
[20] Iren., *Adv. Haer* 1,31,1: "Et haec Iudam proditorem diligenter cognovisse
dicunt…" (Rousseau-Doutreleau 1979, 386).
[21] Nagel 2007, 222.
[22] Pearson 1990, 97.
[23] Cf. Lüdemann 2006, 45; Pearson 2007b, 50, 96; Nagel 2007, 222.

In the *Apocryphon of John*, the twelve "authorities" or "powers" that were created by Yaldabaoth and can be interpreted as signs of the zodiac are also listed and their names are explicitly mentioned.[24] Furthermore it is presupposed that certain planets rule the constellations of the zodiac. This theory can be found in astrological writings of antiquity.[25] It explains why the zodiacal signs are connected with planetary spirits in the list of the *Apocryphon of John*. This connection is of importance for interpreting the star of Judas mentioned in the *Gospel of Judas* because "Cain" is the name given to one of the zodiac signs and this sign is explicitly connected with the sun.[26] The *Apocryphon of John* even declares that Cain is the one "whom the generations of men call the sun."[27] This equation is repeated almost verbatim in the *Gospel of the Egyptians*, another treatise which is influenced by Sethian Gnosticism.[28]

This teaching corresponds to Irenaeus' description of the Gnostics who produced the *Gospel of Judas* and held Cain in high esteem. Given the fact that Cain is related to the sun (which, as we have seen, is explicitly stated in the *Apocryphon of John* and the *Gospel of the Egyptians*), and Judas is connected with him according to Irenaeus, we can assume that Judas is related to the same star. This connection to the sun can explain why both Cain and Judas are thought to have outstanding knowledge. This knowledge was due to their connections with the most powerful star of the sky: the sun.

But above this sphere the star had no influence so Judas' access to this higher realm was limited according to the *Gospel of Judas*.[29] It can be said that his star leads him astray because he has no knowledge of the divine realm. Jesus explicitly stresses that this upper divine sphere is free of the influence of the sun and the moon.[30] So the star that determines Judas fate will not protect him from final destruction.[31]

---

[24] Pearson 1990, 99.

[25] Gundel 1972, 553; cf. also Gundel-Gundel 1950, 2122–2124.

[26] In the version of the *Apoc. John* in NHC II,1 10,34 it is the sixth sign, in other versions (BG 40,14) it is the seventh.

[27] NHC II 1, 10,35–36 (Waldstein-Wisse 1995, 67): "ⲡⲁⲓ̈...ⲉⲧⲟⲩⲙⲟⲩⲧⲉ ⲉⲣⲟϥ̅ⲛ̅ϭⲓ ⲛ̅ⲅⲉⲛⲉⲁ ⲛ̅ⲣⲣⲱⲙⲉ ⲭⲉ ⲡⲣⲏ".

[28] NHC III 2, 58,15–17.

[29] Schenke Robinson 2008a, 71.

[30] *Gos. Jud.* 45.20–21.

[31] *Gos. Jud.* 54.16–18.21–24; Cf. Schenke Robinson 2008a, 68.

THE SUN AND THE NUMBER THIRTEEN

Judas rules over the other disciples because he himself is related to the sun; he is related to the ruler of the universe. Since Judas is related to the sun, he of course also is related to the demon connected with the sun. The idea that Judas as the thirteenth disciple has powerful influence over the twelve aeons and their daemons is immediately explainable within this astrological context. What are the most important passages in the *Gospel of Judas* related to this doctrine? Beginning with the *Gospel of Judas* 44.20, Judas is connected to the number thirteen several times. Jesus calls him the thirteenth daemon. As the "thirteenth" Judas is also connected to the number twelve, which is of great astrological importance because of the twelve signs of the zodiac. Of course, Judas is also the thirteenth of Jesus' disciples after the election of the new Apostle Matthias. In the *Gospel of Judas* 55.10–11 (a passage that has unfortunately only been preserved as a fragment) Jesus also reveals to Judas that his star will rule over the thirteen aeons. This rule of Judas is also mentioned in the *Gospel of Judas* 46.20–23.

As the thirteenth, Judas is positioned above the number twelve, which is as a symbol for both the Zodiac and the twelve disciples of Jesus. In the *Gospel of Judas,* however, the number twelve has strong negative connotations and is related to the lower world of fate.[32] Thus Judas as the thirteenth is bound to the influence of the creator-god Yaldabaoth and will not escape the final dissolution when "the stars come to an end."[33] This observation can be substantiated by other Gnostic writings. In the Sethian *Gospel of the Egyptians* the two angels Saklas and Nebruel rule Chaos and Hades and occupy the thirteenth heaven together with Yaldabaoth as the "god of the thirteen aeons."[34] Twelve are below them.

The conviction that the sun as the thirteenth celestial body is related to the twelve constellations of the zodiac as well as to the six moving planets (while it itself stands firm in the center) is illustrated by Jewish sources. Important is a passage from the *Questions and Answers*

---

[32] Cf. Van der Vliet 2006a, 141; Brankaer-Bethge 2007, 364–365.
[33] *Gos. Jud.* 54.17–18. Schenke Robinson 2008a, 69.
[34] NHC III 2, 63.19 and *Zost.* NHC VIII, 1, 4, 25–28 cf. also DeConick 2008, 252 with further references and Brankaer-Bethge 2007, 324, 343, 365; Kim 2008, 307. Thus Judas' inferior position is marked by the influence of Yaldabaoth.

in Exodus by Philo of Alexandria. Philo shared the astronomical and astrological convictions of his times and used them in his allegorical exegesis of several biblical passages. In his interpretation of the book Exodus, Philo discusses the meaning of the menorah that stood in the temple of Jerusalem. He interprets this lamp stand as a symbol of the things which are in heaven.[35] He explains Exodus 26:32 and the menorah with its six arms extending from the middle, writing "that the zodiac lies over and glancingly comes near the summer and winter solstices". Philo also explains about the middle arm of the candelabrum and to the six arms on both sides: "the approach to them is from the side, (and) the middle place is that of the sun. But to the other (planets) he distributed three positions on the two sides; in the superior (group) are Saturn, Jupiter and Mars, while in the inner (group) are Mercury, Venus and the moon."[36] This allegorical explanation of the shape of the Jewish menorah makes clear that the sun is in the central position of the Zodiac as well as of the planets. Philo also refers to the obliquity of the ecliptic and the summer and winter solstices.

Furthermore the allegorical exegesis of Philo and also the Gnostic teachings of the *Gospel of Judas* can be illustrated by the artistic tradition of Roman times. Many pagan sculptures and painters picture the sun god in the middle of the twelve signs of the zodiac while driving in his carriage.[37] Because of its central position, the sun god can be regarded as the thirteenth deity connected with the other twelve divine beings associated with the signs of the zodiac. The central position also symbolizes that the sun god rules the entire zodiac.

In the Gnostic *Gospel of Judas*, the cosmology is different, so it is important to realize that this lower realm has to be distinguished from the higher sphere. Judas' relation to his special star therefore does not give him access to the world above.[38] According to the *Gospel of Judas*, all human beings (including Judas) are destined by the erroneous stars and they will be destroyed together with their respective celestial bodies.[39]

---

[35] QE 2, 74.
[36] QE 2, 75 (Marcus 1987, 124).
[37] Gundel 1978, 441–442; Gundel 1992, 115, 127, 129–130.
[38] Cf. Turner 2008a, 190; DeConick 2008.
[39] *Gos. Jud.* 55.15–17.19–20; cf. Brankaer-Bethge 2007, 324–325; Schenke Robinson 2008a, 67–68.

SUN VENERATION AND THE JEWISH GOD

In late antiquity, the pagan image of the sun god driving a carriage with four horses was adapted by Jews and used for decorating the mosaics on the floors of several synagogues. In spite of its obvious pagan character, the Jewish community did not reject it. A well-known example can be found in the synagogue of Beth Alpha, which was built in the sixth century CE and was excavated in Israel.[40] The fact that this pagan image of the sun and the zodiac was adapted by Jews for decorating their synagogues may be explained by rabbinic texts that hand down the idea that the sun rides on a chariot that lights up the world.[41]

The same religious syncretism that combined Jewish and pagan ideas also influenced the magical papyri. Some of these texts show traces of the idea that the Jewish god as the creator of the entire universe is situated above the sun and the angel of the sun and that he therefore could command this star. In many respects, this superior position resembles the role of Yaldabaoth as described in the *Apocryphon of John*. Because the magicians who used these spells tried to take advantage of the superior position of the Jewish god, it may be helpful to take a brief look at the views of the Jews about their God's relationship to the sun and their views about pagan veneration of the sun.

It must be stressed that many biblical passages condemn the veneration of the sun and the moon.[42] However, it is also presupposed that under certain circumstances this cult was attractive to Jews and therefore could have been perceived as a potential danger to Jewish beliefs. It is probably for this reason that biblical authors were reluctant to use solar imagery. Yet in some passages God's splendor is compared to the sun.[43] In the *Wisdom of Solomon* wisdom is expressly put above the sun and its light: the splendor of wisdom is seen to surpass all the stars; wisdom even is described as the true ruler of the world.[44] This comparison suggests that the divine sphere of heavenly light is different from the sun.

Many biblical passages associate God's appearance with the splendor of light. Some passages distinguish the divine light from the light

---

[40] Avigad 1993, esp. 192.
[41] *Num. Rab.* 12:4.
[42] E.g. Deut 17:3.
[43] Sir 42:16.
[44] Wis 7:28–8,1.

of the celestial bodies. This distinction is based on the Pentateuchal narrative that confronted its interpreters with the problem of the relationship between the light, which was created on the first day according to Gen 1:3, and the luminaries, which were created on the fourth day according to Gen 1:16.

Rabbinic sources try to manage this Biblical distinction hermeneutically, some even regarding it as esoteric teaching.[45] According to *Genesis Rabbah*, a collection of Midrashic comments to Genesis, Rabbi Samuel ben Rabbi Nahman interpreted the creation of the light on the first day as allusion to the divine appearance. He says that, after the creation of light, God wrapped himself in the light as in a garment and its splendor shone from one end of the world to the other.[46] The Babylonian Talmud hands down a teaching about the light of the first day of creation according to Rabbi Eleazar ben Pedat who lived in the third century. According to this rabbi, the light was hidden away for the righteous human beings who would come: "When the Holy One, blessed be he, looked at the generation of the Flood and the generation of the Tower of Babel and saw that their deeds were corrupt, he arose and concealed it from them, as it is said 'From the evil-doers their light is withheld' (Job 38,15). And for whom did he hide it away? For the righteous in the time to come..."[47]

These speculations about the first light of creation are connected with the speculations about an eschatological light that will appear at the end of the world to replace the light of the sun and the moon. The book of Isaiah even hands down the belief that in the time of the messiah there will be no need of any earthly light because God's brightness will shine.[48] In rabbinic texts, this eschatological light also can be interpreted as a fiery cloud related to the divine cloud that protected Israel after the Exodus from Egypt.[49] This cloud brought light upon Israel in the past and will reappear in the eschatological future.[50]

---

[45] Cf. Urbach 1987, 208–209.
[46] *Gen. Rab.* 3, 4.
[47] *bHag* 12a (Goldschmidt 1899, 818):

שנסתכל הקד וש ברוך הוא בדור המבול ובדור הפלגה וראה
שמעשיהם מקול קל ים עמד וגנזו מהן שנאמר וימנע מרשעים
אורם ולמי גנזו לצדיקים לעתיד לבא:

[48] Isa 60:19–20.
[49] Exod 14:20.
[50] Cf. *Mek. Tractate Beshallah* 5 (Lauterbach 1976, 226).

The author of the *Gospel of Judas* also mentions the difference between the divine light and the sun. In the last part of the gospel, he even describes somebody ascending into a cloud of light. The identity of the entering person is unclear. It could be Judas.[51] After entering this cloud, this person leaves the sphere that is influenced by this star because this star is situated outside the splendor of the superior light. In its basic features, this passage corresponds to the biblical description of the eschatological light. The idea that certain human beings will enter the divine light resembles rabbinic speculations about the light concealed for the righteous in the last days.

In order to understand the relation of Judas to the sun, it may be important to consider Jewish messianism.[52] The prophecy of Balaam in the book of *Numbers* is of immediate relevance.[53] Many Jews interpreted Balaams predication that "a star has marched forth from Jacob" as a prophecy about the coming messiah. This interpretation also influenced the translation in the Targums.[54] According to Matthew 2:2, there was a star that announced the birth of Jesus. In antiquity this was understood to be a special astrological constellation that reflected the birth of the messiah. This idea of a man linked to a star emerges again during the Jewish uprising during the reign of Hadrian, when the nickname of its leader Bar Kokhba, "son of the star", was used as an allusion to the patronymic of Simeon ben Koseba.[55]

Therefore, connecting Judas to a special star, and especially the sun which "goes ahead" of the other stars, may be understood as a political statement. It may hint at Jewish messianism. Because of the Gnostic syncretism that combined Jewish and pagan influences one should also bear in mind the possible pagan implications of the star. The sun can play an especially important role in legitimizing pagan rulers who make claims to power. A number of pagan rulers identified themselves with the sun god and this identification had close ties to pagan ruler cults. A well-known example from Greek history is the petitionary prayer directed to King Demetrius Poliorcetes when he entered Athens in the years 291 or 290 B.C.E. While entering Athens, he is said to have been

---

[51] Cf. Turner 2008a, 221; DeConick 2008, 255.

[52] Horbury 1998a, 93.

[53] Num 24:17.

[54] Cf. e.g. Tg. Ps. J. on Num 24:17: "…and the Messiah and the strong rod from Israel shall be anointed (ויגדל המשיח ושבט תקיף מישדאל)" (Clarke-Magder 1995, 261).

[55] Von Stuckrad 2000a, 151–152.

outrageously acclaimed and greeted by Athenians. A choir was trained specially for singing a cultic song that expressly identified Demetrius with the sun god and his friends and advisors with the surrounding stars.[56] This identification was supposed to introduce the king to the public as a deity appearing in Athens. In this connection, the sun symbolized the display of royal magnificence.

This example of the pagan use of the star as a symbol of the royal power can be paralleled with a strategy that some Jewish kings choose for their appearance in public. It is not accidental that the star was the symbol of the Jewish kings and that it can be found on the coins of the rulers of the Hasmonean dynasty.[57] In one exceptional case, the Jewish king Herod Agrippa even allowed the pagan population of his kingdom and pagans from the cities of Tyros and Sidon to acclaim him as a divine being. The Jewish king dressed himself in a special royal robe since the robe was made entirely out of silver.[58] When the silver began to reflect the sunlight, the crowed interpreted this as the appearance of a deity.[59] We can assume that king Herod Agrippa intentionally chose his dress as a strategy to link himself with a divine being. This historic event is reported by Luke in his book of Acts as well as by Josephus in the Jewish Antiquities.[60] Both authors write that the crowd assembled in the theatre of Caesarea hailed the king as a divine being. Since Herod Agrippa did not rebuke the crowd or stop the blasphemous flattering, God punished him by a sudden death.

Thus the association of Judas with the sun and divine light may have more than marginal political implications.[61] This symbolism was widely spread in antiquity and was adapted by pagan kings as well as by Jewish rulers.[62] It is also connected with Jewish messianic expectations. Thus the star as a sign of superior power was influenced by contemporary political symbolism. This symbolism was transferred into the special Gnostic doctrine of the *Gospel of Judas* where Jesus reveals that Judas will rule over the other twelve aeons. Here the symbol of

---

[56] Athenaeus, *Deipn* 6. 253 d-f; Cf. on this hymn, Förster 2007, 44–50.
[57] Von Stuckrad 2000a, 112–119; Von Stuckrad 2000b, 29.
[58] Acts 12:21.
[59] *Ant.* 19:344.
[60] Acts 12:20–23; *Ant.* 19.344–345. Cf. on the self-deification of Herod Agrippa, Förster 2007, 35–44.
[61] Cf. the material collected by Fauth 1995, 189–202; esp. 200–201; Förster 2007, 42–44.
[62] On this symbolism cf. also Mastrocinque 2005, 199–200.

the star was reinterpreted in this Gnostic sense. The Gnostic concept of Judas' star was the result of a highly syncretistic combination of ideas taken from popular astrology, Jewish and Christian speculations about the sun as divine light, and concepts of divinity promulgated by pagan ruler cults.

THE GOD OF JERUSALEM AS THE POLE DRAGON

The Conceptual Background of the Cosmic Axis in *James*

Franklin Trammell

With the discovery of the Tchacos Codex, we now have another version of the *1 Apocalypse of James* which, unlike the extant Nag Hammadi text, makes mention of the πόλος, or cosmic axis.[1] The reference occurs during a discussion of James and Jesus with regard to the number of the rulers of the cosmos and the seventy-two inferior heavens. The passage reads:

> ⲛⲉⲧⲛⲁⲁⲩ [ⲇⲉ] ⲉⲣⲟⲟⲩ ⲛⲉ ⲛ̅ϭⲟⲙ ⲉⲧⲏ̅ⲡ[ϣ]ⲱ̈ï ⲛⲁï ⲉⲧⲉⲣⲉ ⲡ̅ⲡⲟⲗⲟⲥ ⲧⲏⲣ[ϥ̅≫]> [ⲱ₂]ⲉ̅ⲣ̣ⲁⲧ̅ϥ̅ ϩ̅ⲓⲧⲟⲟⲧⲟⲩ: "[But] those who are greater than they [the seventy-two lower heavens] are the powers who are above, those through which the whole axis (of the universe) stands."[2]

These superior ruling powers that are over the seventy-two inferior heavens are the twelve archons, as the Nag Hammadi version makes clear:

> ⲁⲩ ⲱ₂ⲉ ⲉⲣⲁⲧⲟⲩ ⲉⲃⲟⲗ ϩ̅ⲓⲧⲟⲟⲧⲟⲩ ⲁⲩⲱ ⲛⲁï ⲛⲉ ⲛⲏ ⲉⲧⲁⲩⲡⲱϣ ϩ̅ⲛ ⲙⲁ ⲛⲓⲙ ⲉⲩϣⲟⲟⲡ ϩⲁ ⲧⲉ[ⲝⲟⲩⲥⲓ]ⲁ ⲙ̅ⲡⲙⲛ̅ⲧⲥⲛⲟⲟⲩⲥ ⲛ̅ⲁⲣⲭⲱⲛ: "They [the seventy-two] were established by them [the twelve], and they have been divided in every place, existing under the authority of the twelve archons."[3]

According to this new passage on the *polos* found in the Tchacos Codex, then, the central axis around which the sphere of the cosmos revolves is established by the twelve archons.

Upon inspection of the text, it is apparent that the author of the Tchacos version of *James* utilizes a perceived astrological relationship between the *polos* and the twelve constellations of the zodiac and negatively identifies the twelve apostles with the twelve zodiacal powers. Additionally, Wolf-Peter Funk has noted that the reference to the seventy-two 'twin partners' in *James* connects them with the

---

[1] TC 13:6–9.
[2] Coptic text: Kasser et al. 2007, 127; my translation.
[3] NHC V, 26:19–23. Coptic text: Parrott 1979, 72; my translation.

seventy (two) 'lesser disciples' who are sent out in Luke 10:1 two by two.[4] In this way the seventy-two represent an extension of the twelve.[5] This correspondence, however, is part of a larger structure underlying *James*. Implicit to this structure is the equation of the "God who dwells in Jerusalem" with a dragon or serpent whose powers make up the cosmos. This dragon is crucified to the *polos* by Jesus and his archons are restrained through the affliction of the sons of light.

The Numbers Twelve, Seven, and Seventy-Two

That the author of the Tchacos version of the *1 Apocalypse of James* can associate the twelve archons with the establishment of the axis is due to his assumption that the pole of the universe lies at the center of the zodiacal circle. The author, following popular imagination, does not distinguish between the ecliptic pole, the position of which is in the center of the zodiacal wheel, and the equatorial pole, the point at which the cosmic axis intersects the celestial sphere.[6] The twelve "greater powers" of the *polos* in the *1 Apocalypse of James* are accordingly the twelve signs of the zodiac. The number seventy-two is arrived at in *James* by multiplying these twelve archons by the lower six heavens. Each of the twelve is understood to contain the totality of the lower six spheres and is "over his hebdomad" as a seventh power. The combined powers of each of the sixfold-twelve total seventy-two and form the lower heavens. Factoring the twelve rulers separately, the complete structure of the cosmos is expressed by the author of *James* as being "twelve realms of seven."[7] The following diagram illustrates this structure.

Particularly relevant for understanding the system in *James* are those traditions which identify the seventh power as the mediator and ruler over the others. Yaldabaoth, for example, functions as the

---

[4] Funk's article in this volume notes that the number varies between seventy and seventy-two in manuscripts of Luke and patristic literature.

[5] The number seventy-two as a designation for apostles is also found in Syriac tradition and some Manichaean psalms. On this see Murray 2006, 133, 172 n. 11, 173 n. 1.

[6] See Beck 2006, 109; Richer 1994, 63–71; Scholem 1962, 76 n. 47.

[7] NHC V, 26:2–5; TC 12:14–17

THE TWELVE HEBDOMADS

The twelve zodiacal powers are in the seventh heaven, rather than in the usual eighth sphere of the fixed stars, with the seventy-two lower heavens beneath them. The central point marks the *polos*.

ruling seventh power according to some "gnostic" sources.[8] In other instances, the seventh power is understood to contain the full potency of the other six. An example of this arrangement is preserved in the medieval *Sefer ha-Bahir*, a text which includes an interesting complex of motifs that bear a striking resemblance to the structure employed in *James*.

---

[8] See Pearson 2007, 53, 57.

The *Bahir* speaks of a cosmic tree which is identified with *Tsaddiq*, the Sabbath, and the seventh potency which comprises within itself the lower six powers.[9] This tree also has twelve aspects or branches.[10] The *Bahir* further associates the numbers twelve and seventy-two with the Name or names of God.[11] In one passage, the number seventy-two is understood to derive from the number twelve, since each of God's twelve leaders or directors has six powers.[12] The number seven also is prominent and linked to the divine image comprised of seven holy forms or hypostases deriving from the feminine *Binah*. These seven elsewhere are depicted symbolically as seven sons.[13] God's forms are thus represented as both sons and powers.[14] So too in the *Bahir* the numbers twelve and seventy-two correspond to the powers of God. The All-Tree itself, linked with the seventh potency or the Sabbath, is said to have twelve aspects and to be comprised of the powers of God.[15]

Comparably, the author of *James* emphasizes that the structure of the heavens consists of twelve realms of seven.[16] It is assumed in *James* that the twelve and seventy-two are the powers of the "God who dwells in Jerusalem," since he is the "figure (τύπος) of the archons" and Jerusalem is a "dwelling place of many archons."[17] The Hebrew God,

---

[9] *Sefer ha Bahir* § 71 (Abrams 1994, 161). See Wolfson 1995, 71–72.

[10] *Sefer ha Bahir* § 64 (Abrams 1994, 155–56). See Wolfson 1995, 207 n. 74. Wolfson has put forth substantial evidence which suggests that lying behind some of the Bahiric passages on the All-Tree is a Jewish-Christian tradition which identified Jesus as the All-Tree or *axis mundi*. On this and other traditions of the mediating or ruling seventh potency see Wolfson 1995, 63–88 and corresponding notes. Cf. the twelve arms of the universe in *Sefer Yetsira* § 47 (Hayman 2004, 149–50).

[11] *Sefer ha-Bahir* §§ 63, 64, 70, 76, 79, 80, 81, 112, 113 (Abrams 1994, 155–57, 161, 163–69, 197). See also Urbach 1994, 130–31, and the remarks of Idel 1988a, 123–24. The divine Name is elsewhere identified with the cosmic pillar or axis. See, for instance, Herm. *Sim.* IX, 14:5; PGM 1: 196–222; PGM IV:1167–1226; Wolfson 2005, 124–25, 291, cf. 213

[12] *Sefer ha-Bahir* § 63 (Abrams 1994, 155).

[13] See Wolfson 2005, 147–49.

[14] Idel 1988a, 126.

[15] Idel 1988a, 126.

[16] TC 12:14–17. On the twelve hebdomads in the *1 Apoc. Jas.*, see the discussion of Wolf-Peter Funk's article in this volume.

[17] TC 12: 2–3; 18:12–17; 23:16–18. These seventy-two are those which are divided over the seventy-two nations of the world in Jewish and Christian tradition, as noted by Schoedel 1970, 123. See Ginzberg 1925, 194–95 n. 72 and the discussion of Séd 1979, 156–84. Cf. also Scott 2002, 51–55. In rabbinic sources the number is usually seventy. The Bahir §§ 112–13 (Abrams 1994, 197) connects the numbers seventy, seventy-one, and seventy-two as being different ways of counting the same structure.

the God of the seventh day, belongs in the seventh heaven, in connection with the seventh planet, Saturn.[18] That Jesus says he "went in
by" the Great Ruler Addon during his descent into the cosmic realms
confirms the Just God's position at the highest point in the universe.[19]
He is therefore the first power that Jesus encounters upon entering
the cosmos. Similar to the function and position of *Tsaddiq* or the
Sabbath in the *Bahir*, the Just God, ruling the axis of powers from
the seventh heaven in the form of the twelve archons, encompasses
the totality of the lower six spheres within himself. Since the twelve
are set over the seventy-two and each of the twelve contain the entire
lower six heavens, they function as individual seventh powers.[20] The
twelve, then, operate as the God of Jerusalem's twelve 'overseers.' This
structure explains how the *1 Apocalypse of James* can speak of each of
the twelve archons as being "over his hebdomad."[21]

Based on the evidence within *James*, especially in light of the comparable complex of motifs preserved in the *Bahir*, the author of *James*
is identifying the archons who establish the axis with the twelve powers of the Hebrew God who rule the cosmos from the seventh heaven.
As the figure of the archons, he is the totality of them and by extension, the seventy-two of the lower six heavens who are the "powers of
all their might."[22]

The Dragon and the Figure of the Archons

The exact form of the figure of the archons is not stated explicitly in
James. Yet it appears from several internal clues that the "God of Jerusalem" is understood to be a zodiac bearing dragon existing in both
the highest sphere of the cosmos and at the center of the universe.

---

[18] See Welburn 1978, 244–45. Yaldabaoth is identified with the planet Saturn
according to Celsus. Tacitus, *Hist. 5, 4* associates the Jewish God with that planet. See
also Jackson 1985a, 105–6 n. 86; Cf. Welburn 1978, 254.

[19] TC 26:11–14.

[20] On the twelve as the seventh power over the hebdomad see Wolf-Peter Funk's
article in this volume. Cf. Wolfson 2005, 157.

[21] NHC V, 25:26–26:1; TC 12:10–12

[22] NHC V, 26:18–19. The description of the twelve aeons and the seventy-two luminaries in *Gos. Jud.* 49:1–50:18 attests to a pleromic model of this structure, wherein
the Father consists of the twelve aeons. Cf. *A Manichaean psalm book* (Allberry 1938,
1:10–15; 9: 13–14; 136: 14; 198: 25–26).

This concept of a cosmic dragon has an astrological basis in the position of Draco, a constellation that has stars in all the signs of the zodiac and surrounds the north ecliptic pole. The additional close position of Draco's tail relative to the north equatorial pole allows for the ancient perception that a cosmic pole dragon dwells at the top of the celestial sphere ruling over the twelve gods of chaos, or the zodiacal signs which hang from its body, being both above them and at their center. The dragon is accordingly noted in a number of ancient sources to be the ultimate power at the center or highest point of the universe.[23]

Elsewhere, the *polos* is closely associated with the mythological sea dragon Leviathan. For instance, a midrash in *Pirqe de Rabbi Eliezer* mentions this serpent "between whose two fins stands the middle pole of the earth."[24] Another midrashic source states that the "world rotates around the fin of the Leviathan."[25] In addition, some later Jewish sources relate the *Teli* dragon mentioned in *Sefer Yetsira* with the axis of the universe and with the "pole serpent" mentioned in Isa 27:1 and Job 26:13.[26] That the *Teli* is described in *Sefer Yetsira* as being "in the universe like a king on his throne"[27] recalls the constellation Draco dwelling over the houses of the zodiac.

The *Teli* is consistently identified with another celestial dragon widely known in ancient and medieval astronomy and astrology as the cause of eclipses. The lunar nodes—the two points where the ecliptic, the path of the Sun, intersects the orbit of the moon—are specified as the head and tail of the *Teli* dragon in a number of astrological systems, including those of the Manichaeans and the Mandaeans. The

---

[23] See Hipp., *Ref.* IV, 47; MacKenzie 1964, 512; Epiphanius, *Panarion haer.* 26, 10:8; Mastrocinque 2005, 160–72; Rasimus 2006, 76–77, and the discussion below.

[24] *Pirqe de Rabbi Eliezer*, § 9 (Luria 1852, 23a–b). Fishbane 2003, 279 n. 18.

[25] *Midrash Aseret HaDibrot* (Jellinek 1967, 1:63); See also *Midrash Konen* (Jellinek 1967, 2:26). See also Ginzberg 1925, 45, who notes the antiquity of these statements based on the passage in Apoc. Ab. 21:4.

[26] Scholem, 1962, 77 n. 48; Sharf 1976, 36. The noun *bariah* in the Isaiah and Job texts denotes a bar or pole. Reeves 1995, notes that Ibn Ezra on Job and Radaq on Isaiah both connect the *nahash bariah* to a celestial serpent column. See also Fishbane 2003, 291–92. For sources on the *Teli* see Sharf 1976, 33–51, esp. 40–41.

[27] Sefer Yetsira § 59 (Hayman 2004, 176): תלי בעולם כמלך על כסאו. In *Sefer Raziel*, the twelve zodiacal signs hang from Leviathan, as noted by Karppe 1901, 157 n. 1.

former refer to this dragon as *Athalya* and the latter *Talia*.[28] The lunar nodes are those points where eclipses occur so this dragon is imagined as swallowing the sun and moon.

The lunar dragon, in its most precise form, bears the zodiacal signs on its body, spanning a hundred and eighty degree arc in the sky and carrying at all times six signs on its back.[29] In some sources, the distinctive characteristics of Draco and the lunar dragon become blurred and the two are identified. This is the case in the Ponza Zodiac, for instance, where a large serpent is represented within the zodiacal circle spanning the same arc as the lunar dragon but situated relative to the center of the universe in a way that also suggests a conflation with Draco.[30] This central point lies in the middle of the zodiacal circle. The Mandaeans also explicitly identify the lunar dragon (*Talia*) with Draco.[31] As we will see below, one particular Manichaean tradition of the lunar dragon informs the thought world behind Jesus' crucifixion in *James*.

Another noteworthy way in which the cosmic dragon or serpent is conceived in antiquity is as the boundary of material existence. The *ouroboros* snake, for example, is variously associated in ancient sources with the Dragon constellation, the band of the zodiac, the god of the cosmic pole or the cosmos itself, Leviathan, and Iao. It may also function as a symbol of the primordial waters surrounding the world or of the outermost sphere of the cosmos.[32] This encompassing sphere

---

[28] The 'lunar dragon' is attested in a wide variety of ancient and medieval sources and is sometimes identified with Draco as well as the sea dragon Leviathan. See, for example, Beck 2004, 157 ff., esp. 159 ff., 171, 177–90; Sharf 1976, 38–51; Leisegang 1955, 217; Mackenzie 1964, 512–15, 521–22, 525; Drower 1949, 62 n. 2, 95–96, 111–12, 115–16; Mastrocinque 2005, 162–63; Starr 1939, 56, 157–59; Hartner 2008; Azarpay 1978, 363–74; Powels-Niami 1995, 79–81, 86; Goldstein-Pingree 1977, 121–22; Holden 1988, 75. Cf. Beaulieu, 1999.

[29] See, for instance, Beck 2004, 159, 162–63; MacKenzie 1964, 515, 525.

[30] Beck 2004, 152 ff.

[31] In the system of the medieval Jewish astronomer Shabbetai Donnolo, the constellations, the planets, the sun, and the moon are all joined to the *Teli* dragon. According to him it functions as both the axis mundi and the eclipse dragon. See Sharf 1976, 34f. In the *Bahir*, the *Teli* is identified as "the likeness which is before the Blessed Holy One," whose "locks are hanging." *Sefer ha Bahir* § 75 (Abrams 1994, 163). Abrams 1994, 274, cites a variant text which adds that the Teli 'contains the spheres.' Cf. Zohar III, 48b; Wolfson 1988, 81 n. 29, 86 n. 46. Cf. Idel, 1988b, 77–78.

[32] On the *ouroboros*, or the circular snake who 'eats the tip of its tail,' see Mastrocinque 2005, 12, 16, 48, 95–96, 148–53, 160–68, 175, cf. 117–18; Liesegang 1955, 221; Jackson 1985b, 22–23, 39 n. 18, n. 22; Rasimus 2006, 62. On the association of

is intimately related to the *axis mundi* according to the philosophical concept of the universal soul. According to this system two circles, one of which encompasses the world and the other being the center of the earth, are connected by the ladder of ascent.[33] This concept is present in the Ophite diagram mentioned by Origen wherein Leviathan is drawn on a circle and in its center. It asserts that Leviathan is the soul which travels through all things.[34] Within the larger circle of Leviathan are the seven circles of the archons.

In the *Pistis Sophia*, the outer darkness is a great dragon surrounding the whole world and containing twelve dungeons of punishment which correspond to the zodiacal powers.[35] An archon dwells in each of the twelve chambers. While all of the chambers are within the *ouroboros* dragon, each of the twelve functions as an individual gate leading to the world of light. Ascending souls enter through the tail of this dragon, but are trapped when it returns its tail into its mouth. Here the dragon is explicitly understood to be the passageway of souls as well as the barrier surrounding the material realm.

In several other 'gnostic' sources, the figure of the zodiacal and planetary powers is depicted by combining solar imagery with the icon of the dragon.[36] The Sun is often understood to be the leader or ruler of the planetary powers, having seven forms because it contains the powers of the planets within it.[37] The path of the Sun, whose symbol

---

the serpent with the waters encircling the earth that form a barrier between the human realm and the divine, see Mastrocinque 2005, 25–30, 160; Beck 2004, 221–22 n. 42. See also Jonas 1958, 116–18. According to Rashi on Isa 27:1, Leviathan encircles the earth. See Grünbaum, 1877, 275; West 1971, 42 n. 9; Fishbane 2003, 278. Cf. Epstein 1996, 363; Wakeman, 1973: 19. On the chaos waters as forming the boundary between the material realm and the celestial realm see the discussion of Morray-Jones 2002.

[33] On this philosophical understanding of the Universal Soul see Altmann 1967, 1–32.

[34] Origen, *Contra Celsum* VI, 25: 12–14 (Marcovich 2001, 402). See Mastrocinque, 2005, 106 n. 480; Rasimus 2006, 60.

[35] *PS*, III, 126, (Schmidt-Macdermot 1978b, 317 ff.). Cf. Rasimus 2006, 87.

[36] On the connection between the serpent and the Sun see Leisegang 1955, 216–32; Beck 2004, 190–200, 225 n. 72; Rasimus 2006: 87; PGM I. 144–145; PGM IV. 1637–1640. In magical texts and some Hellenistic Jewish milieus the Jewish God becomes identified with the sun or conflated with a sun god who rules the pole. See sources cited in Mastrocinque 2005, 56, 153 and corresponding notes; Leisegang 1955, 222–23; Smith 1990, 29–39. In the Jewish magical text *Sefer ha-Razim* 4:61–63 (Margalioth 1966, 99, cf. 12; Morgan 1983, 71), the solar deity Helios, as in PGM 1, 222, is invoked as ruler of the axis or *polokrator*. Cf. *Sefer ha-Razim* 4:47–57 (Margalioth 1966, 98–99; Morgan 1983, 70–1); Stuckrad 2000b, 20. In the *Pistis Sophia* IV, 136, (Schmidt-Macdermot 1978b, 354), the *ouroboros* and disk of the Sun are considered as the same.

[37] Welburn 1978, 246–47.

is sometimes an *ouroboros*, makes up the line known as the ecliptic which runs through the middle of the zodiacal band. According to the reconstruction of A.J. Welburn, Iaoth, the head of the twelve archons in the *Apocryphon of John*, is ruled by the Sun. The Sun corresponds to Iao, whose form is a seven-headed dragon.[38] Whatever way these are configured, the twelve archons together are the powers of Yaldabaoth, whose τύπος is a lion faced-dragon.[39] This form is given to the King of Darkness in some Manichaean and Mandaean sources.[40] A very similar image is associated with the Egyptian god Chnoubis, whose serpentine body has a lion's head emanating rays.[41] Interestingly, a number of magical gems and amulets equate Chnoubis with the Hebrew God.[42] In certain astrological contexts the snake and the lion may serve to symbolize "complementary aspects of the sun." The snake in this sense functions as a "symbol of the sun as the great agent of *Time*," while the lion represents "the *power* of the sun."[43] In another astrological sense the combination of lion and dragon signifies the totality of the planetary and zodiacal powers and the "figure" that comprises them.

Also relevant to this discussion is the 'gnostic' tradition of the redeemer figure taking on the form of a serpent in order to elude the cosmic ruler and his archons. In the *Trimorphic Protennoia*, during the descent through the realm of the archons, Protennoia eludes them by taking on the form of the son of the chief creator. This son is the serpent Nous in the Sethian system.[44] In Sethian Gnosis, according

---

[38] Welburn 1978, 250.

[39] According to the long recension of the *Apoc. John* NHC II 10, 8–9.

[40] See Jackon 1985a, 40–43. Cf. Ps. 91:11–13; 11Q11 Col. V, 11–13. Mandaean tradition frequently identifies the King of Darkness with Leviathan.

[41] Incidentally, Chnoubis' position as decan is linked with Saturn and the number thirteen. See Gundel, 1936, 77, 79; Jackson 1985a, 82, 105–7. The Sun and Saturn are intimately related in ancient astronomy/astrology. See, for instance, Brown 2000, 68–70; Koch-Westenholz 1995, 85, 122–25; Jackson 1985, 22; Jackson 1985a, 146–49, 156.

[42] On the identification of Chnoubis and the Hebrew God see Mastrocinque 2005, 64–9. On Chnoubis see also Spier 1993, 39–41 and corresponding notes. Jackson 1985a, 78, notes that "some Chnoumis gems are simply radiate serpents with normal serpent heads." Various magical gems associate the Hebrew God with a dragon. See, for example, Bonner 1950, Plate II, 24, which has the name Iao accompanied by the picture of a dragon. Another important example (King 1887, 103) depicts an ouroboros along with the name Iao, identified with Abrasax, the numerical value of which is 365, containing all the powers of the cosmos.

[43] Beck 2004, 196ff, emphasis original. See also Jackson 1985a, 131–49, esp. 139, 145–46.

[44] *Trim. Prot.* (NHC XIII,1) 48:25–49:22. Cf. Hipp. *Ref.* V, 14.

to Hippolytus, the perfect Word of supernal light, during his descent from the pleroma, temporarily assumes the form of a serpent.[45] This disguise allows for safe passage through the realms of the serpentine *kosmokrator*.

This very broad astrological thought world related to the idea of a cosmic dragon or serpent demonstrates the appropriateness of ascribing such a form to the 'figure' of the archons in *James*. As the τύπος of the zodiacal powers he embodies them. It is implied that he is brought forth from the deficient female Achamoth, just as the lion-faced dragon Yaldabaoth is birthed from Sophia.[46] Even though his position is in the highest realm of the cosmos, he is at the same time "the God who dwells in Jerusalem," at the perceived center of the world.[47] Further, the Great Ruler Addon(aios) thinks that Jesus is his son when he passes through his realm, potentially implying that he has taken the form of a serpent during his descent.[48] The insinuation in *James* that the God of Jerusalem is a dragon or serpent becomes even more apparent, however, when the fate of this 'figure of the archons' is examined.

CRUCIFYING THE DRAGON

In *James* it is said that Jesus' crucifixion is inflicted upon the "figure of the archons."[49] It is thus through the seizing of a son of light by the cosmic powers that their ruler and figure is pierced. This tradition of dark powers consuming light and being fixed or bound as a result is a prominent theme in Manichaean tradition. A few examples of this motif within Manichaeism are particularly illuminating for the conceptual background of *James*.

In one of the Manichaean psalms, for instance, the *Athalya* (Heb. *Teli*) dragon swallowing the sun is an image directly connected with

---

[45] Hipp. *Ref.* V, 14. See Mastrocinque 2005, 194, 36; Rasimus 2006, 27, 80–81. Cf. Liebes 1993, 16–17.

[46] TC 10:20–24; 21:2–26; 22:1–14.

[47] Ezek 5:5; 38:12; Midr. Tanh., *Qedoshim* 10 (Buber 1885, 39b); Scott 2002, 19–20; 56–58. Clement of Alexandria's *Stromata* V, 6 mentions the opinion of some that the two cherubim on either side of the mercy seat, whose wings correspond to the twelve signs of the zodiac, are identified with the two bears. These bears are the constellations of Ursa major and Ursa minor, between which the celestial pole is situated.

[48] TC 26:11–19; NHC V, 39

[49] TC 18:8–16

Jesus' crucifixion. Afterwards follows the fettering and binding of the powers.[50] This theme is expressed elsewhere in Manichean mythology wherein the five sons of the King of Darkness, whose likeness is Leviathan, are poisoned when Primal Man gives himself and his sons to them for food.[51] In one Manichaean text, two dragons, representing the lunar nodes,[52] are hung and bound along with the seven planets at the time of Creation.[53] In the *Kephalaia* these nodes replace the sun and moon to fill out the traditional seven powers and they are said to be the father and mother of all the planets.[54] In another text, primordial monsters that have swallowed elements of light are attached to the sphere.[55] The link between the *Athalya* swallowing the sun and Jesus' crucifixion in the Manichaean psalm book may therefore be viewed as a recapitulation of the primordial binding and crucifixion of the powers of chaos.[56]

These sources reflect the mythological thought world that is drawn upon by the author of *James*. The correlation between monsters or dragons who are defeated through the sacrifice of a divine representative is one which is expressed in *James* through the idea that Jesus' crucifixion has effectively crucified the "figure of the archons." This

---

[50] "Psalms of Heraceides" (Allberry 1938, 196: 1–13). Cf. Jer. 51:34–44.

[51] See Reeves 1992, 192–97, 206 n. 67. Cf. *A Manichaean Psalm Book* (Allberry 1938, 76: 6–15; 83: 25–28; 201: 25–29.

[52] Boyce 1977, 21; cited in Reeves 1995. See also Beck 2004: 177–79.

[53] Boyce 1975, 60 § 1; translated in Klimkeit 1993, 225–26; cited in Reeves 1995. See also *Acta Archelai* 8:1 (Beeson 1906, 11) where at the time of creation, the archons are fixed to the sphere of the firmament. Cf. also a Manichaean pslam book (ed. Allberry, 201:11–32). The word *polos* may be used to denote this sphere or the vault of heaven. See also *Keph.* 85.26–27; 114; 115.1–34; 122.24; 123.19–21; 136.23–25. Cf. 118.13–120.20. A very fragmentary Manichaean astrological text contains a reference to the cosmic dragon, using the Syriac cognate of the Hebrew *Teli*. See Burkitt, 1925, 114, A. col. v 1 line 1 (end); cited in Reeves 1995. See the remarks of Scholem 1962, 77 n. 48.

[54] *Keph.* 85.26–27.

[55] *Škand-Gumānāk-Vičār* 16:18–19 (Menasce 1945, 253); cited in Reeves 1995. In assembling and analyzing some of these Manichaean sources and others of considerable interest, Reeves notes a remarkably similar complex of motifs relating to the threefold hierarchizing of the cosmos in Manichaean tradition, Sefer Yetsira, the Bahir and Dayṣānite cosmology. In this tripartite system, as expressed in Sefer Yetsira and the Bahir, the Teli or cosmic serpent corresponds to the macrocosmic level, followed by the planetary spheres or the realm of the zodiacal powers, with the microcosmic level corresponding to the heart or mind. I would like to thank Prof. Reeves for kindly sharing this study with me and for drawing my attention to these texts.

[56] Another important example of this theme is found in Mandaean tradition. In one myth the savior-god Hibil allows himself to be devoured by Karkûm, who then spews venom and is cut in pieces. See Jonas 1958, 116–22. Cf. also Eliade 1959, 33.

crucified 'figure' of the zodiacal powers, born of deficient Wisdom, pierced through the sacrifice of a 'son of light,' dwelling at the center of the world and in the highest sphere of the cosmic realm, the form of whose son Jesus takes during his descent, fits the picture of a dragon or serpent based on the parallel traditions noted above.[57]

The mention by Jesus of the one who, "when he is seized" by the archons, "seizes (them)," as well as the suffering of Levi's son as restraining the archons, suggests that, in addition to Jesus' death, it is the repeated seizing and affliction of various 'sons of light' which keep the powers of the cosmic realms under submission.[58] Within the *1 Apocalypse of James*, then, is an expression of the tradition found in the aforementioned sources in which the capture of the light is required in order to overcome the serpentine forces of darkness. The crucifixion of the dragon by Jesus may be viewed as recapitulating the primordial binding or piercing of the chaos dragon.[59] In *James* this process is further repeated by other sons of light.

THE AXIS AND THE TWELVE SIGNS OF THE ZODIAC

The tradition of the crucified pole dragon is not explicated fully by the author of *James* due to his more prominent agenda which is to identify the twelve zodiacal powers who establish the axis with the twelve disciples. This correspondence between the apostles and the zodiacal powers has been emphasized over the underlying structure of the Hebrew God as the pole dragon. The author's negative correlation between the apostles and the zodiacal powers serves to attack the representatives of apostolic Christianity by making them the type

---

[57] Cf. Zohar I:47a, wherein Leviathan and his mate are equated with the seventy princes who rule the earth.

[58] TC 16:20–21; TC 25:9–14

[59] Cf. Job 26:13: "By his spirit, the sky became fair. His hand has pierced the pole serpent." On different versions of the primordial sea monster myth see Gunkel 1895; Wakeman 1973. On the recapitulation of this myth in later Judaism see Fishbane 2003, 282; Liebes 1993, 16–17. The recapitulation of the primordial conquering of volatile chaos is expressed in the alchemical tradition of "Abraham Eleazar the Jew," in the image of the crucified serpent, represented by Moses' staff. For the self-proclaimed astrologer the nailing or fixing of the serpent to a cross and the alchemical practices related to the 'spirit of Python' have the power to subdue the whole world. See Patai 1994, 238–57, esp. 246, cf. 573 n. 17.

of the twelve divinities of chaos.[60] In so doing, the author is able to identify his contemporary apostolic opponents with the ruling powers who killed Jesus and James.[61]

This correlation functions to reverse any positive associations being made between the twelve apostles and the signs of the zodiac in other Christian traditions. In the Tchacos version of *James*, it is the twelve archons, corresponding to the apostles, through which the axis of powers blocking the soul's ascension is established. The author's employment of the number seventy-two as a designation for the lesser apostles identifies them as subordinates of the twelve overseers of the serpentine Hebrew God, the ruler of the cosmos. This doctrine of vertical correspondence evinced in *James* is an essential component of astrological imagination.[62]

---

[60] On this identification in the *Gos. Jud.* and on positive associations between the twelve apostles and the zodiacal signs see DeConick's article in this volume.
[61] TC 16:16–18; TC 18:14–15
[62] See Von Stuckrad, 2000b, 5.

SALVATION AND PRAXIS

BAPTISM IN THE *GOSPEL OF JUDAS*

A Preliminary Inquiry

Elaine Pagels

Now that we are moving beyond the polarized controversies that characterized the earliest reception history of the *Gospel of Judas*, the theme of baptism offers a promising line of inquiry.[1] As we shall see, the *Gospel of Judas* invokes traditional Christian metaphors of "rebirth" into a new *genos* to warn that only those ritually "reborn" through baptism, and not those of mere human birth, "will…be able to see" the divine realm.[2] Comparison with other Sethian (and Christian) texts shows that Jesus' teaching in the *Gospel of Judas* follows a traditional catechetical pattern that begins with *warning*, proceeds to *instruction*, and then *exhortation*, preparing the disciple for the baptism of which Jesus speaks toward the climax of the text. For although ritual is seldom mentioned explicitly in this text, or, for that matter, in Sethian and Christian texts in general, John Turner has shown in a major article that "beneath the mythical map there lies ritual territory."[3] Once we recognize that anticipation of this transformative ritual underlies the entire text, we can account for both the negative and positive statements that led to earlier, deadlocked discussions. Thus, as we shall see, comparing the *Gospel of Judas* with a wide range of correlated texts not only helps us move beyond the earlier extreme—and opposite—assessments of the text, but also helps place it into the context of a cluster of well-known Sethian traditions (for discussion, see 362 ff.).

I am grateful to Karen King and Lance Jenott for their helpful comments as I prepared a draft for the Codex Judas Congress, hosted by April DeConick, and to members of the meeting for further comments and criticism.

[1] For some of these earliest assessments, see Pearson 2007a; Painchaud 2007. See also his interesting and incisive 2006b and 2006a, 553–568; DeConick 2009; compare Kasser et al. 2007.

[2] Cf. *Jn* 3:5. See, for example, Williams 1996, esp. 198–199; Buell 2005; Turner 2006, 941–992; Townsend 2007. For a more persuasive interpretation of the text in the context of social history, see Iricinschi et al. 2006, 32–37; see also the incisive article by Marjanen forthcoming.

[3] Turner 2006, 942.

For as we all know, the initial editors of this text, noting with some surprise certain unique features that highlight Judas and his role, tended to emphasize ways in which this text depicts this most despised disciple as one entrusted with a special mission and favored with special revelation, while other colleagues responded to their interpretation (and, no doubt, to the way National Geographic handled the whole matter) by sharply criticizing them for having overlooked negative aspects of the text's portrait of Judas. Some, indeed, went so far as to interpret the *Gospel of Judas* as an unrelentingly dark, even bitter and ironic, narrative that characterizes Judas simply as an "evil demon"—unrepentant, unsalvageable, damned, and doomed.[4]

I am grateful to have learned from the work of colleagues who take the latter view that what we read in that first edition, including some of the more nuanced views that Karen King and I later published,[5] can only be part of the story. Yet the same is true of one-sidedly negative readings of the *Gospel of Judas*. Clearly, scholars who read it that way meant to challenge what they saw as a facile first-read by the initial editors, whose motto, they might have said, was to "accentuate the positive, eliminate the negative, and don't mess with Mister In-Between." But when scholars do the opposite—"accentuate the negative, elimi-

---

[4] Turner has suggested that although its author obviously uses terminology that is both Christian and Sethian, leading us to expect to find soteriological content in the vision he presents, this author has, in his words, squeezed out all soteriological significance from his own reformulation of these theologies, offering "no soteriological narrative at all" (see Turner's contribution to this volume). Pearson (2007a) has gone further, characterizing the *Gospel of Judas* as a text that can only be read *sui generis*, a text that cannot be in any sense a gospel, since, on his interpretation, it proclaims only "bad news." Painchaud, after having extended and developed suggestions about polemical aspects of the text, recently said that he agrees with Pearson that the *Gospel of Judas* is completely unique in the sense that it uses religious language in an ironic way. In one article, Painchaud offers a complex interpretation which suggests that the author, when depicting Jesus promising to reveal "the mysteries of the kingdom," uses such terminology not to express but to undermine its ordinary meaning, thus hinting at what Painchaud regards as the clue to the discriminating reader that any "revelation" Judas receives actually reveals little more than his inevitable doom (Painchaud 2007, 12: "*Tout le texte apparaît donc comme une vaste mise en scène ironique*, ponctuée par le rire de Jésus...consistant à renverser l'interprétation, à première view obvie, des 'mystères du Royaume' pour reveler ceux du 'Règne' de la mort et de Royauté de Saklas...").

For a more persuasive interpretation of the text in the context of social history, see Jenott 2006; see also the incisive article by Marjanen forthcoming.

[5] Pagels-King 2007.

nate the positive"—the results are no more adequate to interpreting the text as a whole.[6]

Where, after all, do one-sided interpretations leave us? Those on both sides of such debates may seem to help make sense of certain passages; but what then do we make of the *Gospel of Judas* as a whole? Is the *Gospel of Judas* really only "bad news," only an ironic *mise en scène*, in which Jesus offers Judas secret teaching in order to raise his hopes for salvation, only to mock them later? How, then, can we understand this text in the context of the history of Christianity during the second century, and, for that matter, during the third and fourth centuries, when this text, among so many others, was still being

---

[6] The most obvious way to accentuate either the positive or negative—and to persuade—(or, one might say, to coerce) readers unfamiliar with Greek or Coptic to agree with us, is to translate key terms in ways that render them unambiguously positive or negative. And so many scholars who have put forth the various interpretations offered so far have attempted to bolster either an overly dismal—or an overly optimistic—reading of the text by translating certain key terms—terms well known to be multivalent—with terms that overspecify their meaning, in order to drive the interpretation in either a positive or negative direction. Perhaps the most obvious example occurs in 44,20, where Jesus laughingly calls Judas "*thirteenth daimon.*" While some colleagues insist that in this text the term can bear only *one* possible connotation—that of the English term "demon"—the very heat of these arguments demonstrates what we all know: that the multivalence of this term is almost too obvious to mention. While we understand those who cite New Testament and Nag Hammadi parallels to argue for an unambiguously negative translation, we can hardly ignore the wide range of associations we find in sources ranging from the Septuagint to Greek philosophical writers ranging from Philo to Apuleius and Plutarch (see the discussion in Dillon 1977, 31, 90, 171, 216, 287, 317, 378, for example, offering sections on demonology of the various philosophers. Note, too, John Turner's influential work (Turner 2001), in which he investigates philosophic background of Sethian texts, as the work of Bentley Layton and Harold Attridge does for other Nag Hammadi texts. The range of associations of the term has led more than five of our colleagues to variously translate the term as it appears in the *Gospel of Judas* as *demon, god,* or *spirit,* and I am among those who think that their work deserves more than dismissal, or, worse, ridicule.

The article that Louis Painchaud has prepared for this meeting reminds us, indeed, that the author of the *Gospel of Judas* may not be bound by any single meaning of each term (Painchaud 2007). Painchaud's article also offers us a salutary warning to be wary of interpretations of the text that depend insisting that there can be *only one, single, unambiguous reading* of certain key terms, encouraging us to hope that he will put aside the suggestion made at the close of his article—that the twenty-first century translator "must" do what, as he notes, the Coptic translator wisely refrained from doing—translating the term "kingdom" in two distinctly different ways, i.e. in certain passages the "Royaume en haut" and, in others, the "Règne en bas". We hope that our colleagues will put aside any thought of deliberately mistranslating—or, at least, over translating—the text, since to do so not only would impose a complicated interpretation upon the text and its readers, but would also destroy the effect of what Painchaud sees as the author's intentional use of ambiguity.

translated and treasured? One of our colleagues has raised an important question: who would write such a deeply ironic anti-gospel, and
why?[7] Even more difficult to answer: why would someone else, more
than a hundred years later, bother to translate it into Coptic, copy it
in an elegant script, and carefully bind it into a codex together with
such religious revelation texts as the *Letter of Peter to Philip*, the *James*
text, and *Allogenes*?

Besides characterizing this text as a kind of bizarre fable for which
we clearly have no precedent, and for which we find no plausible historical context, such interpretations fail to account for all the passages
that do *not* fit such a reading, except to suggest that what they say is
not what they mean (hence the suggestion about "irony"). What are
we to make of all those positive statements—for example, with the
statement that opens this gospel—that Jesus came to earth "for the
salvation of humanity." Are we to read this statement, too, as ironic?
And what about all those passages that seem to speak positively of
Judas—that say, for example, that he alone, of the twelve, is able to
stand before Jesus; that he alone recognizes Jesus' spiritual origin, so
that Jesus then invites him to come apart from the others to reveal
"mysteries" not known to the others—the latter a trope familiar from
many other texts, which signals the opening of revelation? What about
the passages that tell how the "twelve" have a nightmare that Jesus
uses to indict them, while Judas receives a vision of the place of the
heavenly race, even while telling him that he may not enter that place?
How are we to understand the subsequent passages in which Jesus tells
him that he shall rule over those who curse him, and then instructs
him about baptism—virtually all these predicting what awaits Judas in
the future; are all these statements to be taken as "ironic" as well?[8] I
confess that I, for one, have difficulty recognizing which terms, if any,
are to be taken as ironic in a Coptic translation of a second century
Greek text—especially when the text is bound into a volume, copied
and treated like the religious texts that surround it, with no hint that
this one alone is meant as an ironic, Kafkaest fable—or as a joke.

Such questions lead us to the question before us now: How can we
move beyond discussions characterized initially by such clashing and

---

[7] Pearson 2007a.

[8] Louis Painchaud has aptly noted these texts in one of his incisive early articles,
Painchaud 2008.

polarized interpretations, and incorporate what we have learned from each other into a more capacious and more adequate understanding of this difficult text? The primary problem, then, is this: *How can we take account—and make sense of—both the positive and negative features of this difficult text that have given rise to such diametrically opposed interpretations?*

The work of Jean Sevrin and John Turner points us toward the missing piece in our discussion of this text—a text that came to us like an impossible puzzle, with countless fragments to be pieced together, and no picture on the box. What's missing from much of our interpretation is the underlying theme of *the transformative power of baptism.* For as both Sevrin and Turner have shown, the theme of baptism is utterly central to Sethian theology and practice—as of Christian life in general.[9] This underlying theme is what accounts for the striking contrast we find as well in the *Gospel of Judas*—contrast between negative and positive statements, between dire warnings of the fate of those who lack it, and the glorious hopes promised to those who receive it. For baptism offers, above all, the promise that a person may be utterly *changed*, rescued from certain damnation to receive the promises of salvation, raised out of darkness into light, *reborn* from death to new—and eternal—life. And its practitioners understand that this ritual "makes a difference"[10]—indeed, makes *all* the difference—between *before* and *after.*

The anticipation of this performative ritual (along with a polemical concern with mistaken understanding of ritual)[11] underlies the entire text of the *Gospel of Judas*, from the *apophasis* that opens the text through the various stages of catechistical instruction intended to prepare the initiate for baptism, to that climactic moment in which Judas asks about baptism and Jesus responds and speaks directly of it. Once we see this, we understand not only how apparently contrasting positive and negative statements fit into the message of this gospel, but shows how essential *both* kinds of statements are to the teaching it offers.

One might ask, however, if this is so, why do we not find more frequent direct mention of baptism throughout the text, instead of only

---

[9] Sevrin 1986; Turner 2006.
[10] With appreciation of J.Z. Smith's classic article, Smith 1985.
[11] See Os (forthcoming).

at its climax? John Turner's recent and important study of "the Sethian baptismal rite" opens with the reminder that such reserve is characteristic of ancient religious texts, even when their authors take for granted that, in his words, "religion *is* cult, or, to use the word we use when we approve of a particular cult, *religion is liturgy.*"[12] Turner goes on to point out that "while liturgical texts from late antiquity"—whether Christian, Sethian, or neo-Platonic—"are few and terse, surviving texts are verbose about doctrine, but close-mouthed about ritual." Although he wrote the article shortly before the publication of the *Gospel of Judas*, these comments, as well as his analysis throughout the entire article, apply remarkably well to the *Gospel of Judas*. In this text, however, the difficulty is increased by breaks in the papyrus—for here, to our frustration, just as Jesus begins to speak about baptism, the text is broken, and what he teaches is lost to us. Yet, as noted above, Turner reminds us that even when texts are relatively silent about ritual process, "beneath the mythical map there lies ritual territory."[13]

From this point Turner goes on to discuss seven Sethian treatises, showing that every one of them attests to developed baptismal ritual—texts that include the *Apocalypse of Adam*, the *Gospel of the Egyptians*, *Melchizedek*, the Pronoia hymn from the *Apocryphon of John*, and *Trimorphic Protennoia*, as well as texts such as *Zostrianos* and *Marsanes* in which, as he points out, the dominant baptismal imagery serves as the paradigm for transcending the limitations of the present cosmos. And as we might expect, such texts often include traces of polemic against what their authors regard as inadequate forms of baptism and also of eucharist, as does the *Gospel of Judas* as well. So before we turn back to our primary text, let's quickly glance at some of these sources, which offer considerable help in setting a context for what we find there.

We begin with the *Apocalypse of Adam*, which speaks of "the hidden *gnosis* of Adam which he gave to Seth, which is the holy baptism of those who know the eternal *gnosis*, through those born of the *logos*."[14] The text opens as Adam speaks to Seth, explaining to his son that he has named him for the progenitor of "the great generation," even though Adam laments that now, having lost the primordial *gnosis*, he and all his progeny have come to live "in fear and slavery" under the

---

[12] Turner 2006, 941, italics mine.
[13] Turner 2006, 942.
[14] *Apoc. Adam* 85, 22–29.

power of the creator, and so under "the authority of death."[15] In this text, as we shall see in the *Gospel of Judas*, much of the baptismal instruction involves teaching about the different "races" of humankind (here designated as *genea* or *sperma*, "seed," "progeny"; similarly designated in the *Gospel of Judas*, where *genea* appears throughout, and *sperma* occasionally, as in 46,6)—first those generated from Adam, then from Noah through his sons, all of these placed in contrast with the "seed of the great race" that is born from above, "born of the logos and the imperishable illuminators who come from the holy seed" for which Seth was named.[16]

After the flood episode, the creator, alarmed at the presence of that "great race," accuses Noah of having disobeyed him: "you have created another race so that you might scorn my power!" Protesting this false accusation, Noah loyally orders his three sons and all their progeny to serve the creator "in fear and slavery all the days of your life." But the illuminator, seeing the servile bondage in which humankind is being held, comes into the world to "redeem...souls from the day of death."[17] The author of the *Apocalypse* reveals how each of the thirteen kingdoms of the world, in turn, testifies to the illuminator, praising above all his miraculous and heavenly birth. Each of these "kingdoms" apparently marks a level of the initiation process, and each conveys an increasingly greater level of *gnosis*, culminating in the "thirteenth kingdom" which confers "glory and power" upon the initiate, and finally brings him "to the water." The text indicates that one who comes to this point in the ritual attains to the level in which the "kingless race.... shines forth," and prepares to receive the baptism that transfers one to that "kingless race."[18] Those initiates who "receive (the illuminator's) name" invoked "upon the water" then move beyond the power of death, coming to be celebrated as "those who have known God," and so "shall live forever."[19] Thus, as Turner notes, the final stage of Sethian baptismal ritual delivers initiates from slavery to the creator and from bondage to death, which rule as if "all-powerful" in the world below, and incorporates them ritually "into an

---

[15] *Apoc. Adam* 76, 20.
[16] *Apoc. Adam* 85, 27–29.
[17] *Apoc. Adam* 76, 16–18; cf. also 19–20.
[18] *Apoc. Adam* 82, 19–83, 4.
[19] *Apoc. Adam* 82, 5–6; 83, 14.

elect group, the 'seed of Seth,' and into a new state of awareness," and into "a new cosmic situation."[20]

Next let's consider the *Gospel of the Egyptians*, which similarly attests to the power of "holy baptism" to transform the situation of the "holy ones." This gospel reveals that since the devil was working to deceive and persecute those who were subjected to "the judgment of the archons and the powers and the authorities," the "great Seth....established holy baptism" in order "to save her (that is, the *genea*) that went astray."[21] Because of this gift of baptism, those who renounce "the world and the god of the thirteen *aeons*" now may become transformed, or, to use the conventional Christian metaphor, born again, "born from above."[22] For the great Seth prepared this baptism "through a logos-begotten body...prepared secretly through the virgin"—that is, through a divine and heavenly birth—"*so that the holy ones may be born through the holy spirit, through invisible, secret symbols.*"[23] Hans Martin Schenke has characterized this "gospel" as a catechetical or initiatory text intended to prepare candidates to receive this baptism.[24] Rather than referring to a single form of baptismal ritual, those various texts offer, as Turner notes, variations on the them of baptism and its interpretation.

The tractate *Marsanes*, too, as Birger Pearson, its editor, notes, apparently was written by—and addressed to—members of a community that practiced liturgy, and especially baptism. This tractate, too, refers to thirteen "seals," each associated with progressively higher levels of reality. Beginning from the material (*hylikos*) and cosmic (*kosmikos*) level, the initiate is to progress from the visible world through the eighth level, which concerns the noetic world, toward the ninth and tenth, which concern the divine world, and finally toward the realm of the eleventh and twelfth, the "invisible one," before attaining to the "thirteenth seal" which , the revealer says, "I have established together with the summit of *gnosis*, and the certainty of rest."[25] Pearson writes that the "thirteenth seal" here "corresponds to the highest heavenly

---

[20] Turner 2006, 944.
[21] *Gos. Eg.* 63, 7–8.
[22] *Gos. Eg.* 63, 17–18.
[23] *Gos. Eg.* 63, 10–14.
[24] Schenke 1980, 2, 588–616.
[25] *Mars.* 1,13–16.

realm, which in *Pistis Sophia* is called the 'thirteenth *aeon*.'"[26] Since Marsanes reveals that this final seal "speaks concerning the Silent One who is Unknown, He who truly exists." Pearson comments that one who attains to this level "has achieved the very apex of *gnosis*, and is assured of eschatological 'rest'."[27] Although much of the text is broken, we see fragments that refer to the fountain, apparently of baptism, in which one is sealed "with the seal of heaven."[28] Thus the initiate has progressed from the material world to the spiritual one, transported from the realm of change and death to become a participant in what is divine and eternal. Characterizing what he sees as a basic scheme of Sethian baptismal ritual, Turner describes how those reborn into "the seed of Seth" are thus transferred onto a "new cosmic situation."[29] Those who previously were born mortal, subject to the cosmic powers and bound to die, now, through baptism, are released from these tyrannical powers. According to the *Gospel to the Egyptians*, the baptized initiate now may rejoice that he will "not taste death," for, being "raised up," as the initiate exclaims in the ritual, "I have become light," that is, have become an eternal being.[30]

Before turning finally to the *Gospel of Judas*, let's glance at the text called *Zostrianos*, for since the discovery of the former, we can hardly help noting intertextual resonances. This text, similarly, tells how Zostrianos, whom we meet first as a doomed man, finds release through baptism and finally comes upon a luminous cloud, where he receives illumination, and is transformed into the image of a being of light. As the text opens, we hear how this paradigmatic initiate, Zostrianos, having been torn by doubt, ignorance, confusion and driven by despair into suicidal depression, comes to receive revelation from "the angel of the *gnosis* of eternal light," so that, the text continues, "I very eagerly and very gladly embarked with him upon a great luminous cloud, and left my body behind...*we eluded the entire world and the thirteen aeons in it...but their chief was disturbed at our passage, for our luminous cloud, being an essence superior to everything cosmic, was ineffable....*Then I knew that the power in me was greater than the darkness, because it contained the entire light. *I was baptized*

---

[26] Pearson 1981, 254.
[27] Pearson 1981, 254.
[28] *Mars.* 66, 3–5.
[29] Turner 2006, 944.
[30] *Mars.* 67, 5.

there, and I received the image of the glories there, and I became like one of them."[31]

When we turn to the *Gospel of Judas*, we find a gospel that opens declaring that Jesus, like the illuminator in the *Apocalypse of Adam*, appeared on earth "for the salvation of humanity."[32] Yet as the narrative begins, even after Jesus has called twelve disciples, he finds that even they do not know who he is. Thus at first Jesus speaks as if human salvation is impossible, declaring that "no race of the people among you will know me."[33] Not even one of his disciples can meet his challenge to "bring forth the perfect human." But when Judas, unlike the others, stands forth and recognizes who Jesus is, Jesus offers him secret instruction. When Judas asks his first question—as we shall see, the most relevant question, since it implicitly concerns baptism (36, 6–8; when "the great day of light will dawn" for "that great race"), Jesus initially departs without answering. The next day, after he reveals that he has gone to "another great and holy race," the other disciples join in asking about "that great...and holy race." Jesus tells them that "no one born of this *aeon* will see that race...no person of moral birth will able to go with it."[34] As Jesus' instruction proceeds, Judas repeatedly questions him about the human "races," and comes increasingly to realize, to his deep distress, how separate he is from the "holy race."[35] What Jesus teaches *first*, then, to Judas as to all his disciples, is that every one of them, like Judas—*like all of us, for that matter*—are "of human birth"—and so cannot enter into the divine realm which belongs only to "the great race."

Yet some scholars have taken such passages to reveal the "bad news" that Judas in particular, being born human, and thus destined for destruction, is wholly unredeemable. Those who agree that Judas is doomed, damned from start to finish, insist that the text has made this very clear: after all, hasn't Jesus begun his instruction telling Judas that he, along with all the disciples, are "of mortal birth"? And hasn't Jesus told his disciples that "no one of mortal birth" can even see, much less go with (or to) that "holy *genea*," since belonging to the latter requires spiritual, not fleshly, birth? Hasn't Jesus specifically told Judas that

---

[31] *Zost.* 4,20–5, 16.
[32] *Gos. Jud.* 33, 9.
[33] *Gos. Jud.* 34, 16–17.
[34] *Gos. Jud.* 37, 1–8.
[35] *Gos. Jud.* 43, 12, 24–25; 46, 16–18.

"no one of mortal birth is worthy to enter" the divine region that Judas glimpses in his vision?

Had Jesus' instruction ended here instead of *beginning* at this point, the message of this gospel might, indeed, be "bad news"—not just for Judas, but for every human being who ever lived. In that case, "the salvation of humanity" which Jesus came to effect would be an impossibility.[36] But does such teaching mean what one scholar interprets it to mean—not only that one born "of mortal birth" *initially* cannot enter the divine realm, but also that such a person *can never* do so?[37] As we noted, those who interpret the text this way are, in effect, placing Jesus in the unprecedented role of one of ironically—and quite maliciously—taunts a doomed and hopeless man. Yet *not only does the author not say this; the language he uses implies the opposite*—unless we take the term *genos* literally, in the sense it acquired during the nineteenth century, as if *race* constituted a fixed biological category.

What then, has led some scholars to assume that Judas' character is fixed? Has he no capacity to change? Has no one born "of the races of humankind" any possibility of receiving salvation? Those who interpret the term this way see Judas' character as immutable because, as they keep insisting, he belongs to the "mortal race." Yet as Denise Buell and others recently have demonstrated, Christian writers of the second to fourth centuries, when using such terms as *genos* and *genea* to discuss who is included and excluded from "God's people," characteristically use these terms as metaphors for those who belong to God.[38] We recall how second century Christian apologists speak of those who have come forth from the "races" that formed the identity of their birth to accept *rebirth* into what the anonymous author of the *Epistle to Diognetus* called "this new *genos*," and which certain believers, intending to distinguish themselves from Jews, on the one hand, and Greeks, on the other, sometimes called "the third *genos*." So common was this metaphor among Christians from the second century on that the fourth century bishop Eusebius of Caesarea actually decided to write the history of "the race of Christians" as if they actually constituted a new "*ethnos*" like Greeks or Jews.[39] Philippa Townsend has discussed the use of the term *genea* as it occurs specifically in the *Gospel*

---

[36] *Gos. Jud.* 33, 9.
[37] Painchaud 2007; Pearson 2007a.
[38] Buell 2005.
[39] Iricinschi 2009 (forthcoming).

of Judas.[40] Yet all these authors use the term metaphorically, not to indicate a fixed category into which one is born, but a mutable group that its members have voluntarily decided to *join.*[41]

How, then, can a person of mortal birth—how can anyone—become part of that holy "race"? Our brief survey of other Sethian texts demonstrates that the *Gospel of Judas* offers an answer that recalls Jesus' warning to Nicodemus (*John* 3:5, a saying that may have circulated independently in Christian baptismal liturgy): anyone born in a merely human way "*cannot enter into the kingdom of God.*" Louis Painchaud's intuition that certain passages in *Judas* bear affinities with the teaching of John 3, then, is right on target.[42] For when Jesus tells Nicodemus that "what is born of flesh is flesh, and what is born of spirit is spirit" we do not take him to mean that no one born human—like Nicodemus, or like ourselves—can ever "see the kingdom of God"; were that the case, the *Gospel of John*, too, would be entirely "bad news." But the teaching of Jn 3:5 is meant first to warn of the consequences of neglecting baptism, and thus urge the hearer to receive, and thus be "born from above" ritually, by means of "water and the spirit."

For the author of the *Gospel of Judas* knows as well as any other Christian evangelist that *before he can persuade people to accept baptism, first he has to persuade them that they desperately need it; that without it they are—and may remain forever—utterly lost.* Thus the Jesus of John's gospel first tells Nicodemus the "bad news" ("unless a person is born from above, he cannot enter the kingdom of God"), just as the Jesus of the *Gospel of Judas* first warns his hearers that they face certain death, before he offers the course of instruction that opens the promise of salvation. As we follow the progression of that instruction, we can see that, like any catechesis, it includes *warning,* followed by *instruction,* proceeding to *exhortation.* First, as we have seen, Jesus warns his disciples that, being "of mortal birth," they face destruction. Next, Judas, although himself "born human" glimpses Jesus' spiritual origin, and so Jesus instructs him about the "holy, immortal *genea,*"

---

[40] Townsend 2007.

[41] See also Williams 1996, 193–99. Note, too, the prominent theme of mortals undergoing transformation into an angelic state in the afterlife, in order to ascend into the divine realm, as Paul apparently assumes in I Cor 15:50, and in his admission that when "taken up" into the third heaven, he was apparently not "in the body" I Cor 12:3; see also Himmelfarb 1993, 47–71 and Collins 1997, 23.

[42] Painchaud 2007, 1 n. 3.

even though he himself still remains apart from it.[43] Although much of this instruction is lost because of breaks in the text, the context indicates is that it contrasts the fate of the "human races" over which Jesus promises that Judas eventually shall rule, with that of the "great, holy race" that is "kingless," existing in the "great and infinite *aeon*" beyond all the regions of the cosmos.[44]

Only when he comes toward the conclusion of his teaching does Jesus finally reveal the "good news"—that God has caused *gnosis* to be given "to Adam and those with him"—*gnosis* that frees those who receive it from domination by the lower powers, which "will be destroyed, along with their creatures."[45] Right at this point, Judas asks Jesus about "those who have been baptized in your name"—and Jesus begins to speak about "this baptism"—but, of course, at this point the text is broken, and the response obliterated.

Yet, Judas certainly knew the right question to ask: for the text resumes with Jesus' final promise about what is to come, effected, apparently, through baptism: "then the (image)[46] of the great gen-eration of Adam"—that eternal generation, which exists from the aeons—will be exalted."[47] Jesus concludes his teaching with this prom-ise ("Look, you have been told everything" 57,15), and then proceeds to invite the disciple to "lift up your eyes and look at the cloud and the light within it."[48] At that point the disciple accepts Jesus' invita-tion, lifts up his eyes, and enters[49] into "the luminous cloud" from which a voice—perhaps spoken to those gathered for the ritual—is

---

[43] *Gos. Jud.* 35, 2–3; 46, 18.

[44] *Gos. Jud.* 43, 25; 47, 5–6.

[45] *Gos. Jud.* 55, 19–20.

[46] Note the discussion of Jenott suggesting that the damaged word should be recon-structed with *karpos* instead of *typos*, as in the first critical edition—a suggestion that fits better the terminological context, Jenott 2008.

[47] *Gos. Jud.* 57, 16.

[48] *Gos. Jud.* 57, 16.

[49] Here we pause to consider the recent flurry of discussion about the implied sub-ject of 57,23. Since this sentence previously names Judas as the one who "lifted up his eyes and saw the luminous cloud," the clearest and most accurate translation would show that the same subject "entered into it." Yet several scholars have argued that the obvious translation cannot be correct, since, as they interpret the broken line in 46, 25, Jesus has told Judas that he will not ascend. As we have seen, these arguments are neither necessary nor persuasive, since here, as in other analogous texts, the process of baptismal initiation leads naturally into the transformative ascent.

heard making a proclamation about the "great generation" into which the baptizand is being incorporated.[50]

We note in closing that while this paper cannot possibly solve all the difficulties we find in this text, much less explore all possible parallels between the *Gospel of Judas* and our other extant sources, it is meant to offer an invitation to consider such correspondences while including this missing piece—the transformative power of baptism. Doing so not only will help illuminate the relationship between both the negative and positive aspects of the portrayal of Judas we find there, but also give clues about the religious significance of this text—not a joke, but an esoteric—and remarkably challenging—gospel.

---

[50] Turner 2006, 944ff.

STOP SACRIFICING!

The metaphor of sacrifice in the *Gospel of Judas*

Bas van Os

The *Gospel of Judas* describes itself as follows:

> The hidden word of pronouncement
> about which Jesus spoke with Judas Iscariot,
> in the eight days
> before (the) three days
> before he celebrated Passover.

This incipit tells the reader up front that the work contains esoteric information that cannot be found in the public accounts of Jesus' life. The essence of that hidden information is '*apophasis*', or 'pronouncement' as Karen King translates.[1] This translation is well chosen, for the *Gospel of Judas* is as much a verdict pronounced over 'apostolic' Christianity and its sacrifices, as a declaration of an alternative gnostic Christian view of reality.[2]

The temporal indications, which locate the discourse before Jesus' arrest and crucifixion, are clear from a grammatical point of view. The problem, however, is that Jesus does not celebrate a Passover meal in the *Gospel of Judas*. At the end of the work, Jesus does go into a guest room, but only to pray. In fact, the author shows a Jesus who does not want to participate in the eucharistic meal of his disciples and who opposes sacrificing. Both are denounced as worship of Saklas. It seems impossible that this Jesus would ever celebrate the Jewish Passover.

Perhaps the original Greek played on the resemblance between *pascha* and *paschein* (suffering).[3] It is also possible that the temporal

---

[1] Pagels-King 2007.

[2] As both groups would primarily designate themselves as Christian, I have only capitalized this term. I add the adjective *gnostic* for Christians who denounce the biblical demiurge (the defining concept in Williams 1996). I use the adjective *apostolic* for those Christians whom the author of the *Gospel of Judas* describes as followers of the apostles (34.14–16).

[3] Cf. Melito of Sardis *On Pascha* 46.

indications in the incipit have a symbolic and rhetorical function: the eight days may point to the Octave of Easter in early Christianity[4] and the three days to Jesus' death and resurrection. Jesus, according to the author, revealed everything *before* Judas had Jesus arrested and before Jesus suffered as the Passover lamb of apostolic Christianity. This would fit well with what Jesus tells Judas at the end of the revelation: "you will sacrifice the man who bears me."[5]

The metaphor of human sacrifice is not only applied to the crucifixion of Jesus. It also appears in the third scene, where the apostles describe their dream to Jesus.[6] Twelve priests sacrifice people, even women and children, on an altar in a great house. Although these priests invoke Jesus' name over their sacrifices, they commit all kinds of abominable acts. Jesus then explains that the apostles themselves are these twelve priests and calls out to them: "Stop sacrificing!"[7]

But what is meant with this metaphor of human sacrifice? Elaine Pagels and Karen King argue that it refers to martyrdom.[8] They see the incitement to martyrdom by church leaders as a central concern of the author of the *Gospel of Judas*, which would explain the anger and polemics of the author towards apostolic Christian leaders.[9] Accordingly, the women and children sacrificed in the apostles' dream "*no doubt* represent the martyrs of the author's own day whom church leaders encouraged to die for their faith."[10]

The purpose of this article is to cast some doubt on this interpretation, which I call the *martyrdom hypothesis*. I will argue that there are better grounds to interpret the *Gospel of Judas* as a polemic against apostolic Christian sacramental practices, with baptism as a re-enactment of Jesus' own "passover." I will conclude this article with the implications of this alternative interpretation for our understanding of the text's narrative.

---

[4] Cf. *Barn.* 15.8,9, Justin Martyr *Dial.* 24.1, 41.4, and 138.1.
[5] *Gos. Jud.* 56.19–20.
[6] *Gos. Jud.* 38.1–41.8.
[7] *Gos. Jud.* 41.1–2.
[8] Possibly the first publication in which the martyrdom hypothesis appeared was by Iricinschi-Jenott-Townsend 2006. The possibility was also suggested as a secondary meaning (in addition to the eucharist) by Kerchove 2008, 311–330.
[9] Pagels-King 2006, 59.
[10] Pagels-King 2006, 65–66, emphasis added.

The Case Against the Martyrdom Hypothesis

Perhaps the biggest problem with the martyrdom hypothesis is that the *Gospel of Judas* nowhere speaks of persecution by Roman authorities. The only type of persecution mentioned is the stoning of Judas in 44.24–45.1, but this is not done by Roman authorities, but by the apostles. In order to prove that sacrifice is a metaphor for martyrdom, Pagels and King need to refer to other texts. A clear instance is Ignatius of Antioch (107 CE), who sees his impending execution as a sacrifice to God.[11] In her 2008 article, Kerchove adds other early Christian texts.[12] Pagels and King, however, are interested in the views of gnostic Christians. They focus on two texts from Nag Hammadi: the *Apocalypse of Peter* and the *Testimony of Truth* to reconstruct gnostic Christian response to martyrdom. Their reconstruction rests mainly on four references to martyrdom in the *Testimony of Truth*.[13] From the earliest editions of the Nag Hammadi Library, translators and commentators have read the *Testimony of Truth* as if it spoke of martyrdom. This has, of course, influenced the choices that these translators have made. A good example is 34.1–6, where the 1981 translation from Giversen and Pearson reads: "But when they are 'perfected' with a (martyr's) death,…"[14]

The question is, however, whether translators have gone too far in their interpretation. In *The Nag Hammadi Scriptures* (2007), Pearson now translates the same phrase as: "But when they are full of passion,…"[15] Is it possible that the *Testimony of Truth* is not about martyrdom after all? In that case, the textual support for the reconstruction by Pagels and King is extremely limited, as no other gnostic Christian sources are cited to support their view. Before proceeding with the *Gospel of Judas*, therefore, I will first offer a close reading of the four passages in the *Testimony of Truth* that are supposed to refer to martyrdom.

---

[11] E.g. Rom 4,1 and 7,2–3.
[12] Kerchove (2008, 326) adds Rev. 6:9, the *Mart. Poly.* 14,1–2, Iren., *Adv. Haer.* 5.28,4, Orig., *Mart.* 30 and Cyprian, *Letter* 76,3.
[13] *Apoc. Peter* NHC VII,79.11–16 (referred to by Pagels-King 2006, 73) does not speak of martyrdom or persecution. For a discussion of the possible meanings of this text, see Havelaar 1999, 98.
[14] In Pearson 1981b, 133.
[15] In Meyer 2007a, 618.

Testimony of Truth (NHC IX,3)

Although the text is badly damaged, especially toward the end, it is useful to first give an overview of its contents before embarking on the interpretation of the passages that may refer to martyrdom. The author, or speaker, starts with contrasting those who listen with physical ears and those who have spiritual ears. The first group lives under the error of the angels, demons and stars. Theirs souls are controlled by passion so they will fulfil the law of the creator that commands them to marry and procreate. In the next section, he explains the meaning of Jesus' baptism by John in the river Jordan. This water stands for sensual pleasures and intercourse. He then discusses the futility of the testimony of his opponents (the texts that would refer to martyrdom), only to come back to condemn sexuality and return to the scene at the River Jordan. He goes on to explain the need the renounce the world and its creator and to know the true testimony. He also condemns gnostic Christians who 'enter into death, in the waters' and thus observe the 'baptism of death'.[16] Finally, he discusses the futility of baptism and explains that true baptism lies in the renunciation of the world.

For our discussion it is important to note that confession or testimony was an essential part of the baptism ritual. It is therefore interesting to see how the author says approximately the same things about the futility of both the testimony and the baptism of his opponents:

Testimony	Baptism
32.8–13: For (if) only words which bear testimony were effecting salvation, the whole world would endure this thing [and] would be saved.	69.17–20: But [. . .], if those who are baptized were headed for life, the world would become empty.
44.30–45.6: This, therefore, is the testimony of truth (*martyria*). When man knows himself and the God who is over truth he will be saved. And this one will be crowned with the unfading crown.	69.22–28: But the baptism of truth is something else; it is by renunciation of the world that it is found. But those who say only with the tongue that they are renouncing it are lying, and they are coming to the place of fear.

---

[16] *Test. Truth* NHC IX,3 55.4–9.

The *Testimony of Truth* is referred to by Pagels and King as follows:

> This author declares that "foolish people, thinking in their heart that if they only confess in words, 'We are Christians,'…while giving themselves over to a human death," they will gain eternal life. These "empty martyrs…testify only to themselves." What their actions really testify to, the author says, is their ignorance: "they do not know…who Christ is," and they foolishly believe that "if we deliver ourselves over to death for the sake of the name"—the name of Christ—"we will be saved." The author of the *Testimony of Truth*, like the author of Judas, suggests that such people do not know the true God. Those who imagine that human sacrifice pleases God have no understanding of the Father; instead, they have fallen under the influence of wandering stars that lead them astray (*Testimony of Truth* 34:1–11)…The true testimony, this author declares, is "to know oneself, and the God who is over the truth." Only one who testifies to this message of deliverance wins the "crown" that others mistakenly say that martyrs earn by dying (*Testimony of Truth* 44:23–45:6).[17]

In this section, Pagels and King refer to four passages from the *Testimony of Truth*.[18]

The first passage is 31.22–30. After the author stated that the water of Jordan stands for sensual passions, he explains that the word of truth can give the knowledge to combat the passions. In contrast to this there are those who do not understand:

> The foolish,
> - thinking in their heart that if they confess 'We are Christians' (in word only, not in power),
> - giving themselves over to ignorance, to a human death (not knowing where they are going, nor knowing who Christ is),
> - thinking that they will live (when they are erring),
> hasten towards the powers and the authorities.
>   And they fall into their clutches because of the ignorance that is in them.

> For (if) only words which bear testimony were effecting salvation, the whole world would endure this thing [and] would be saved.

The 'foolish' do not trust that a martyr's death will save them, but rather their confession, their testimony. According to the author this

---

[17] Pagels-King 2006, 72.

[18] Pagels and King rightly do not refer to the passage about Isaiah in 40.21–22,30. The subject of that passage is the allegorical interpretation of his separation (he was sawed in two), not his death or martyrdom.

testimony is such a trivial thing that, if it were true, the whole world would confess. It is hard to imagine the confession in the face of life-threatening persecution as something that all the world would gladly copy.

But the text goes on. In a damaged passage, the author says that in their ignorance the foolish 'will destroy themselves,' whereas 'if [God would] wish a [human] sacrifice, he would become [vainglorious].' Although we do not have enough context to decide with certainty what the human sacrifice is that the foolish are thinking of, it seems connected to Jesus, as the author proceeds to contrast this false idea of human sacrifice with what Jesus really came to do.

The second passage referred to by King and Pagels is 33.20–27. In this passage the word *martyr* is used, which—when used in an English translation—immediately gives the interpretation of the passage by the translators.

> How numerous they are.
> They are blind guides, like the disciples. (They boarded the ship. At some thirty stades, they saw Jesus walking on the sea).
> These are empty witnesses (*martyrs*), testifying to themselves alone.
> In fact, they are sick and cannot get themselves up.

But the word *martyr* only became a technical term for Christian martyrs in the late second and third century. In most instances it is best translated by its general meaning, 'witness'. In this instance this applies as well. The author does not criticize the death of his opponents at the hands of Roman authorities, but their witness about Christ. They are the same people as the blind guides who do not understand who Jesus is. They cannot witness about the true Christ, because they are spiritually blind and have never seen the true Christ. They testify to who they are themselves, not to who Christ truly is. Their sickness is ignorance, not the Roman arena. In the context of this passage, therefore, the translation 'martyr' is not correct.

The third passage used by King and Pagels is 34.1–11. Here the author comes back to his key point in the opening of his discourse: "the passion, which is their delight, controls the soul." Those who live their life in passion should not expect to live when they die, even when they entrust their soul to 'the name'.

> But when they are filling up (*or*: finished) in passion, this is the thought that is within them: 'When we deliver ourselves up to death in (*or*: for) the name we will be saved. But this is not how matters stand.

Rather, through the stars they say they have "completed" their [futile] "course",...

The interpretation that people can live passionately because they will get salvation anyway if they seek martyrdom does not seem logical, given the low number of martyrdoms. I would rather see here either a more general expression for dying as a believer or perhaps the idea that one dies in baptism.

The expression 'to deliver oneself' comes back a little further. There the author speaks of those 'who do not have the word that gives life in their heart,' and who 'will die' for that reason.[19] Their situation is described in a badly damaged passage.[20] It is contrasted with those who received "him" with gnosis:[21]

> But [when they have come] up to [...] sacrifice, they die [in a] human [way], and they [deliver] themselves [...] (...) But [those who receive him to themselves [with uprightness] and [power] and every knowledge [are the ones whom] he will transfer [to the] heights, unto life eternal. [But] those who receive [him] to themselves with [ignorance,] the defiling pleasures prevail over them.

It seems that the author does not speak about martyrdom, but about those who do and those who do not receive Christ. This is not at the end of their lives, as those who do not receive him continue to live a life of defiling pleasures. The second part of our passage seems to have a parallel in § 67 of the *Gospel of Philip* where it is said that it is necessary that the initiand "not only receives the name of Father, Son and Holy Spirit, but they themselves are acquired by you. If one does not acquire them, even the name shall be taken from him."

The remark of the author concerning sacrifice is comparable to the criticism of mainstream Christian baptism in the *Gospel of Philip*: "they sacrificed them alive, but when they were sacrificed, they died. As for Man, he was sacrificed dead to God, and he came alive."[22] The author of the *Gospel of Philip* sees the sacrifice of living people to the creator (in mainstream Christian baptism)

---

[19] *Gos. Jud.* 37.23–25.
[20] *Gos. Jud.* 38–6–9.
[21] *Gos. Jud.* 38.22–39.1.
[22] *Gos. Phil.* § 14.

as deceptive: these hopefuls die because they are sacrificed to the powers that devour them. The sacrifice of Jesus, however, is different. His
death on the cross marks his escape from these powers. The contrast
between vain sacrifices of living people and the sacrifice of the true
Man, Christ, seems to be present also on page 72 of the *Testimony
of Truth*, but this page is too damaged to follow the argument of the
author.

The last passage cited from the *Testimony of Truth* is 44.23–45.6.
It speaks about the crown, that, according to Pagels and King, "others mistakenly say that martyrs earn by dying." The last lines read as
follows:

> This, then, is the testimony of truth: When man knows himself and
> the God who is over the truth. This one will be saved, and he will be
> crowned with the unfading crown.

I note that the passage itself does not make the comparison with martyrdom. The unfading crown is a prize promised to all believers in for
instance I Corinthians 9:25 and I Peter 5:14. In eastern Christianity,
all those who were baptized received a crown, probably as a symbol
of the nuptial union between the believer and Christ and prefiguring
their future bliss. There is no need to read in this passage a reference
to martyrs only.

Due to the damages in the document, it is not possible to determine with certainty the meaning of expressions like 'a human death',
'delivering oneself' and 'sacrifice' in the *Testimony of Truth*. We can
say, however, that the overall purpose of the author is to convince
his audience that they should not trust to be saved by the ritual of
baptism and the words of their confession. The author sees baptism
in water as a descent into death and sensual pleasure. It is possible,
therefore, that the *Testimony of Truth* does not oppose the confession in martyrdom, but the testimony in baptism. We cannot use
this text as a basis to reconstruct gnostic Christian opposition against
martyrdom.

Details of the Metaphor in the Gospel of Judas

My doubts increase when I take into account some of the details of the
metaphor in the *Gospel of Judas*, which do not seem to fit very well

with the martyrdom hypothesis. When Jesus explains the dream of his disciples, he says:[23]

> It is you who are bringing the offerings at the altar you have seen. That one is the god you serve, and you are those twelve men you have seen. And the cattle that you saw brought in for sacrifice are the *multitude* you lead astray. At the altar there, [the ruler of chaos][24] will establish himself and make use of my name in this way, and *the race of the pious* will remain loyal to him.

The altar here does not seem to be the altar of the Roman emperor, but rather the altar of the apostles or the church. The "race of the pious" seems to consist of the apostolic Christians who are made loyal to the deceptive lower god to whom they sacrifice, as the pious disciples did in their eucharistic meal.[25]

Furthermore, the author speaks of a "multitude" that are sacrificed. But most scholars regard second century Roman persecutions as sporadic and the number of martyrs as relatively small (the only martyrdom of a 'multitude' of believers in that period happened in Lyons and Vienne in 177 CE).[26] The emperors Trajan and Hadrian both urged moderation in the persecution of Christians.[27] Only if other citizens brought charges, the authorities would react. Pagels and King are aware of this problem, but try to overcome it as follows:[28]

> Although not many people, numerically speaking, were arrested in the first and second centuries, *every believer* was no doubt acutely aware of the danger and had to consider what to do if caught and accused.

Another problem is the fact that the priests are not sacrificed in the dream of the apostles, only their followers are slaughtered. Pagels and King believe that church leaders incited their followers to martyrdom and point to Tertullianus' *On Fleeing in Times of Persecution* as evidence.[29] But isn't Tertullian's position the exact opposite of what we see in the *Gospel of Judas*? Tertullian advises the people to come together in groups of three instead of large church assemblies, or by

---

[23] *Gos. Jud.* 39.18–40.6 (emphasis added).
[24] Reconstruction suggested by Karen King.
[25] *Gos. Jud.* 33.22–34.11.
[26] Cf. *The Martyrs of Lyons*, in: Eus., *Eccl. Hist.* V § 1.13.
[27] *Eccl. Hist.* III § 33 and IV § 9.
[28] Pagels-King 2006, 44–45, emphasis added.
[29] Pagels-King 2006, 46–47.

night instead of by daylight, all in order to avoid arrest. Like others,[30] Tertullian believes that ordinary Christians should flee, as Jesus commanded, but—and that is his main point—their shepherds should not flee if that meant that they would leave their sheep behind.[31] Prior to the Decian persecution around 250 CE, Roman authorities had no desire to arrest all potential believers. Around 202 CE in Alexandria, when Origenes' father was arrested (and his property confiscated) in Alexandria, his wife and children were not arrested.[32] Often the authorities tried to persuade Christians with friendly words to pay homage to the emperor and walk free. If believers persisted, not all would be executed. Some would be given alternative punishments or could be bought free by the Christian community. Lucian of Samosata describes how a Christian community around 167 CE would do everything to ransom their leader Peregrinus.[33] Roman persecutors would often try to arrest the leaders, so that if they could be persuaded to sacrifice to the emperor, the others would follow without further bloodshed. Even in the "large-scale" arrests in Lyon and Vienne, the immediate goal was to arrest the leading figures.[34]

It is rather strange, therefore, that the church leaders in the *Gospel of Judas* can stand completely at ease at the altar of the supposed persecution. Only the cattle, that they lead astray, are sacrificed in large numbers. It gets even stranger when we note that these Christian leaders actually kill the cattle at the altar themselves. If the metaphor would accurately refer to Roman persecutions, we would expect that *Roman* priests would kill the victims. But in the *Gospel of Judas*, the twelve apostles are the ones who do the slaughtering. Indeed, the name of Jesus is not invoked by the "martyrs," but by the officiating priests.[35] This pivotal role of the priests seems to be an important point for the author:

> For to the human races it has been said, 'Look, God has received your sacrifice from the hands of priests'—that is, a minister of error.[36]

---

[30] See for instance the explicit remarks in the *Martyrdom of Polycarp* 4–6 (†125 CE), as well as in the later *Martyrdom of Agape, Irene and Chione* 1.2 (†304 CE).

[31] *On Fleeing* 6 and 11.

[32] *Eccl. Hist.* VI, § 2.

[33] *Peregrinus* 11–13.

[34] Cf. *The Martyrs of Lyons*, in: Eus., *Eccl. Hist.* V § 1.13.

[35] *Gos. Jud.* 39.7–11. It is stated several times that their acts are performed in the name of Jesus (*Gos. Jud.* 38.5, 38.26, 39.11, 39.12, 39.16, 40.4, 54.25 and 55.9).

[36] *Gos. Jud.* 40.18–23.

A final observation regards the presence of children among those who are sacrificed.[37] Infants were not involved in official Roman persecutions.[38] Even if only older children would have been meant here,[39] it is unlikely that second century Roman authorities would execute such children for being Christians. In Roman eyes, childhood started at about 7 years of age and ended with the advent of adolescence. From that point onward girls and boys were seen as young men and women, and eligible to marry. Although the exact ages for this transition were fluent at first, later Roman law codified this as 12 years for girls and 14 years for boys.[40] Under Roman law, as in modern legislation, children were not held responsible in the same way as adults: they were *doli incapax* (incapable of criminal intent), unless proven otherwise.[41] For adolescents, their age could count as a mitigating circumstance. Pliny the Younger asked emperor Trajan whether this distinction between adolescents and adults applied also with respect to the charge of Christianity.[42] The youngest person in the persecutions in Lyon and Vienna was Ponticus, an adolescent of about 15 years. A contemporary account expresses amazement that the crowd did not show mercy for his tender age.[43] During the Decian persecution (around 250 CE), which was the largest and most systematic

---

[37] *Gos. Jud.* 38.16–17.

[38] Cf the treatment of the newborn children of imprisoned martyrs in *The Martyrdom of Saints Perpetua and Felicitas.*

[39] I believe it is more likely that infants were meant. In their dream, the apostles see the twelve priests committing all kinds of abominable acts. In his explanation, both to the twelve and later again to Judas alone, Jesus places these acts in an eschatological framework. The antichrist will appear and mislead the pious, the followers of the apostles. He will be surrounded by leaders that perform all kinds of vices, while sacrificing the faithful on the altar in the name of Jesus (cf. 2 Thess 2:3–4, 7–12). There are three instances in the *Gospel of Judas* where the vices are listed (38.14–23, 40.7–16 and 54.24–55.9). In the first list, the 'sacrifice of children' has replaced the traditional infanticide. It seems that the change of the word to 'sacrifice' is deliberate, probably to link the list to the sacrifice scene in the temple. These lists seem to be typical vice lists that Jews and Christians used to distinguish themselves from others. The combination of idolatry, adultery, sodomy and infanticide can also be found in the *Sib. Or.* III.763–765. Infanticide in such lists seems to refer to the practice of abortion and exposure of new-borns in Graeco-Roman society (cf. *Barn.* 14.5, *Did.* 2.2; see also Tacitus, *Germania* 19).

[40] Cf. Rawson 2003, 142.

[41] Rawson 2003, 138.

[42] *The Letters of the Younger Pliny*, nr 93.

[43] *The Martyrs of Lyons*, in Eus., *Eccl. Hist.* V § 1.53. For a later example of a lenient treatment of a young adult, see the *Martyrdom of Maximilianus*, a conscript who refused to serve in the army († 295 CE).

campaign against Christianity by Roman authorities, an adolescent of about 15 years old was released on account of his age.[44]

THE SACRAMENTAL HYPOTHESIS AS A BETTER ALTERNATIVE

An alternative interpretation is what I call the sacramental hypothesis.[45] In this hypothesis, the *Gospel of Judas* opposes apostolic sacramental practices as sacrifices to a lower god. The textual basis for this interpretation is strong. From the New Testament writings onward, the eucharist (and even baptism as we will see below) has been described as the re-enactment of the sacrifice of Jesus.

The *Gospel of Judas* contains several references to eucharist and baptism. Already in the first scene of the *Gospel of Judas* Jesus condemns the apostolic eucharist. He laughs when his disciples offer a eucharistic prayer over the bread. He tells them that they are trapped into this service by "their god." When they protest and say that he is the son of their god, Jesus answers that neither they nor their followers will ever know him. It seems that this opening scene effectively replaces the last Supper of the synoptic gospels. At the end of the *Gospel of Judas*, Jesus only uses the guest room to pray. Indeed, Jesus does not eat at all in the *Gospel of Judas*, and he does not give thanks to the creator. The implication is that Jesus never instituted the eucharist of the apostles. Instead, as we learn in the second scene, he leaves them behind and ascends to the other race, which can be seen as an alternative and spiritual form of "communion."

I also note that that the problems with respect to the martyrdom hypothesis do not apply to the sacramental hypothesis. Church leaders encouraged their followers to enlist for baptism and thus be admitted to the eucharist. The multitude of believers followed their advice. Some of them even had their families baptized, including children.[46] The sacramental hypothesis also sheds some light on the remark,

---

[44] Eus., *Eccl. Hist.* VI § 41.

[45] Van der Vliet 2006b, 155–158, argues that the metaphor of sacrifice refers to the eucharist. Kerchove 2008, 326, believes the metaphor refers primarily to the eucharist, but does not 'exclude' the hypothesis that the author may also refer to martyrdom.

[46] See for example *Apost. Trad.* xxi.4. The dating of this document is complex, but Bradshaw et al. 2002, 124, believe that the passage in which infant baptism is found belongs to the oldest 'layer' of the text, which they suggest could date from the mid-second century. The objections of Tert., *Bapt.* 18.4 also point to a second century practice of baptizing (some) children.

quoted above, that the sacrifices are offered up by priests.[47] From the end of the first century onward, church leaders argued that the sacraments should be administered by the clergy and not by lay believers.[48] But it is not merely the fact that the priests claim a position at the altar as mediators of salvation that angers the author. In the eyes of the author, the apostolic priests are ministers of error, because they serve the creator god Saklas instead of the highest Father. In the same passage, therefore, Jesus goes on to denounce the practice altogether, when he says: "Stop sacrificing."[49]

We can understand the anger of the author towards the error of apostolic Christianity, if we appreciate his deep conviction that a believer who sacrifices to a false god is under the power of that god and is not saved by the highest Father. Such an anger is comparable to the anger that Cyprian of Carthage felt when a significant number of Christians gave in to the demand of the Roman emperor Decius (around 250 CE), and offered sacrifice in worship of the emperor. He too felt that they lost their salvation when they—and their children—participated in these pagan 'sacraments':

> Why do you bring a sacrifice with you, o wretched man? Why do you immolate a victim? You yourself have come to the altar as an offering. You yourself have come as a victim...And that nothing might be left to aggravate the crime, infants too, either carried in the arms of their parents or conducted (by them), lost (the salvation) that they had gained (through baptism) in the very first of their nativity.[50]

Human sacrifice as a metaphor for baptism

I will now focus on the meaning of *human* sacrifice in the *Gospel of Judas*. There are several reasons why this particular metaphor should not be identified with the eucharist but rather with baptism. A general point concerns the metaphor itself. Whereas sacrificial language is often found in relation to the eucharist, it always refers to a re-enactment of Jesus' sacrifice, not to sacrificing the believer. This is different for baptism. Already in the Pauline corpus, baptism is described as a re-enactment of the death of Christ, such as in Romans 6:3–5 and

---

[47] *Gos. Jud.* 40.18–23.
[48] Cf. 1 *Clem.* 41, Ign., *Smyrn.* 8 and *Apost. Const.* 6.15.
[49] *Gos. Jud.* 41.2.
[50] *Laps.* 8–9, translation ANF, words between brackets added.

Colossians 2:12. Tertullian calls it "the symbol of death,"[51] and uses
Romans 6 in his conflict with gnostic Christians over the resurrection
of the flesh. According to Tertullian, the bodies of the believers figura-
tively "die in our baptism" in order to rise again in reality. Only thus
can the bodies be presented "as a living sacrifice, holy and acceptable
unto God."[52] In this way, early Christian sources maintain that baptism made animal sacrifices redundant.[53]

The *Gospel of Judas* itself speaks about baptism in various places.
Towards the end of the document, Judas asks about the apostolic followers who have been baptized in Jesus' name.[54] The expression 'baptized *in Jesus' name*' in 55.23 and 56.1 recalls the dream of the apostles
where their followers were sacrificed in Jesus name. Unfortunately this
section is too damaged for definite conclusions, but I note that there
are two utterances of Jesus that start with the phrase 'Truly I say,' one
about baptism and one about sacrifices. It may well be that the author
here denounces baptism as the worship of Saklas, just like he did with
the apostles' eucharist in the opening scene.

This suggestion gains strength when we look at a part of Jesus'
explanation in the *Gospel of Judas* that we have not yet discussed.
There seems to be a relationship between sacrificing in Jesus' name
and the planting of trees in Jesus' name: the priests at the altar
"planted trees without fruit, in my name, in a shameful manner."[55] I
have never seen the metaphor of planting trees used in the context of
martyrdom or the eucharist. But we do see it in the context of baptism, for instance in the words of John the Baptist to the Pharisees
who came to be baptized.[56] In Romans 6:4–5, Paul explains that those
who have been 'entombed' with Christ (*synetaphèmen*) in baptism
are 'planted together' (*symfytoi*)[57] with Christ. They are to "bear fruit
for God."[58]

---

[51] *On Repentance* vi.
[52] Rom. 12:1; *Res.* xlvii.
[53] Cf. Heb. 10: 5–10, *Ps.-Clem. Rec.* 1.39.1 and 1.54.1, and *Sib. Or.* 7.64–70, 76–88.
[54] *Gos. Jud.* 55.21–56.20.
[55] *Gos. Jud.* 39.5–17.
[56] Matt 3:7–10.
[57] The Vulgate reads here: *complantati*.
[58] Rom 7:4.

Passover and Baptism

The *Gospel of Judas* is not the only early Christian work that connects the Passover with the baptism. Tertullian calls the Passover a fitting day for baptism, as the believer is baptized in the Lord's passion.[59] There are two main lines of exegesis in early Christian exegesis of the Passover. The first one is to explore the relationship between the Passover lamb and Christ, as is done extensively in the homily *On the Passover* by Melito of Sardis. The second line is to connect the experiences of the Israelites with those of the newly baptized. The crossing through the Red Sea is both a type of baptism in 1 Corinthians 10:1–2, as well as in Jewish proselyte baptism.[60] A more extensive treatment of this idea is found in Origen's *On the Passover*.[61] For Origen, the true Passover takes place when people are baptized: "they come up out of Egypt, cross the Red Sea and will see Pharao (Satan) engulfed." The newly baptized sacrifice Christ as their Passover lamb. They are sacrificed themselves, as they are anointed with his blood, just like the Israelites anointed their houses in Egypt with the blood of the lamb in order to escape the angel of death.[62] The believers are crucified and resurrected in Christ. As the Israelites ate the Passover lamb in which they were "typified," so Christians are typified in Christ, whose body they eat in the eucharist.

In the second century CE, then, apostolic Christian leaders called Christians to be baptized, especially so as Easter was approaching. They used Passover imagery to explain their sacrificial theology to their followers. The *Gospel of Judas* may have been written to counteract the Passover/Easter-narrative of apostolic Christianity. It urges those gnostic Christians who are still inclined to participate in apostolic Christian worship, to stop sacrificing to Saklas. It defines the identity of the own gnostic Christian group in contrast to the group it is most close to.

---

[59] Tert., *Bapt.* 19.

[60] Skarsaune 2002, 356–357.

[61] Sections referred to in particular: 1.5–20, 3.10–25, 4.15–35, 6.14–23, 25.15–3 from below, 37.37–38.4, 42.1–6. Numbering follows Orig., *Pasch.* and *Dial.* (Daly 1992).

[62] Cf. Melito, *On the Passover* 16; Justin Martyr, *Dial.* 39–40.

Sacrifice and Baptism in Other Gnostic Christian Sources

The *Gospel of Philip* belongs to another stream of gnostic Christianity than the *Gospel of Judas*. It stands in the Valentinian tradition and accepts mainstream Christian sacraments and (proto-canonical) scriptures, but interprets these in a gnostic way. In my dissertation, I argue that its teaching functioned in the context of Valentinian baptismal instruction.[63] The teacher ensures his baptism candidates that gnostic Christian baptism is superior to mainstream Christian baptism.[64] There are several passages in *the Gospel of Philip* that resemble the concept of "sacrificing to Saklas" in the *Gospel of Judas*: § 14, 15 and 50. The link between sacrifice and the sacraments becomes explicit in the temple metaphor in § 76 of the *Gospel of Philip*, where baptism is equated to one of the parts of the Jerusalem temple "where to offer sacrifice."[65] Baptism is, in fact, a sacrifice to the Demiurge. Without gnosis, this is lethal. That is why such sacrifice needs to be salted with the spiritual element of Sophia, as § 35 explains. The *Gospel of Philip* therefore holds on to mainstream Christian sacraments, but sees a great difference in fate between mainstream and gnostic Christians who participate in these rituals: whereas the first go down into death, the latter will live.[66]

In *Melchizedek*, it seems that "cattle" should not be "offered up for sins," but that people should receive true baptism. The text may refer to the baptism of Jesus when it says that "he included himself in the living offering together with your (Melchizedek's) offspring."[67] For the author of *Melchizedek*, animal sacrifice was designed from the start to bind humanity to cosmic powers and death.[68]

---

[63] Van Os 2007.

[64] I use "mainstream" because the adjective "apostolic" does not apply here, as the *Gos.Phil.* sees its own sacramental practice as part of the apostolic tradition (§ 95).

[65] The temple contains the throne of the Demiurge, which believers have to pass on their way to the Father (just like the souls need to ascend through the heavens, and pass the heaven of the Creator god, to reach the divine *plerôma*). The only one who can secure their passage is Jesus, the High Priest. Cf. Stöckl Ben Ezra 2003, 243.

[66] See for instance *Gos. Phil.* NHC II, 3 § 109: 'As Jesus fulfilled the water of baptism, so he has poured out death. Therefore, we indeed go down into the water, but we do not go down into death, so that we are not emptied in the spirit of the cosmos. When he blows, it becomes winter. When the Holy Spirit blows, it becomes summer.'

[67] *Melch.* NHC IX,1 6.24–8.9.

[68] Cf. *Orig. World* NHC II,5 123.4–12.

Many gnostic Christian authors attack mainstream Christian baptism as a baptism of death. The author of the *Testimony of Truth* argues that both mainstream and gnostic Christians who submit to physical baptism, are baptized into death. The argument against mainstream Christians is found in 69.8–31. Elsewhere, in a badly damaged passage, a certain teacher and his followers are accused of Valentinian misconceptions, as they observe "the baptism of death."[69] The *Paraphrase of Shem* pictures John the Baptist as an eschatological demon, who uses baptism to bind people, from which gnostic Christians should refrain.[70] Mainstream Christian baptism, according to the author in 40.27–29 is a baptism "of the seed of darkness in severity, so that it may mix with unchastity," and he exclaims: "Blessed are they who guard themselves against the heritage of death, which is the burdensome water of darkness."[71] We can also find this expression in the *Book of Thomas the Contender*, which contains a series of "woes" against mainstream Christians: "You baptized your souls in the water of darkness."[72] Against those who "labor at preaching": "you kill them daily in order that they might rise from death."[73] In *Zostrianos*, we see how mainstream Christian baptism is denounced: "Do not baptize yourselves with death, nor entrust yourselves to those lower than you instead of to those who are better."[74] The author of the *Second Treatise of the Great Seth* seems to say that the mainstream Christian emphasis on baptism as dying with Christ is wrong: "it is slavery that we should die with Christ."[75]

The opinions that gnostic Christian writers hold with respect to a positive or negative understanding of baptism and eucharist are often related to their understanding of the nature of salvation and the role of Jesus. For the author of the *Gospel of Philip*, for instance, Jesus had to separate from his earthly body at the cross. The re-enactment of the crucifixion in the apostolic practice of baptism and eucharist symbolizes the salvation of the believer. Some other Valentinians, however, are reported to believe that the divine Savior left the earthly Jesus

---

[69] *Gos. Jud.* 55.1–57.6.
[70] *Para. Shem* NHC VII,1 30.24–27, 31.14–19, 36.23–29, 37.19–38.18. Cf. 30.1–21.
[71] *Para. Shem* NHC VII,1 48.8–11.
[72] *Thom. Cont.* NHC II,7 144.1.
[73] *Thom. Cont.* NHC II,7 144.42–145.1.
[74] *Zostr.* NHC VIII, 1 130.26–131.2.
[75] *Sec. Treat. Seth* NHC VII, 2 49.26–27.

before all of his suffering, including the abuses of his arrest, because the divine Savior *could not* suffer.[76] This idea is similar to the statement ascribed to Basilides, that anyone who "confesses the crucified is still a slave, (…) but he who denies him has been freed."[77] For Basilides, Jesus was never crucified. Salvation belongs to the soul and is attained by gnosis. I suggest that for those who see Jesus' role primarily as a spiritual being who reveals saving knowledge, the crucifixion and its sacramental re-enactment in this world are not required for salvation. This may explain why some authors seem to denounce a *physical* baptismal ritual altogether.

IMPLICATIONS FOR OUR UNDERSTANDING OF THE *GOSPEL OF JUDAS*

The range of opinions among gnostic Christians raises the question what the position of the author of the *Gospel of Judas* is with respect to the sacraments. Does he side with those gnostic Christians who had only a different understanding of baptism, or with those who combined a different understanding with a different practice, or with those who completely spiritualized the concepts of eucharist and baptism?[78]

Although some doubts remain as a result of the lacunae in our text, I tend to place the author in the third group. This is best observed in the opening scene: Jesus has not instituted the eucharist and he does not partake of it. I also note that the crucifixion is not necessary for Jesus in the *Gospel of Judas*: he could assume different bodily forms and did not need to be crucified in order to ascend to the other race.[79] Finally, the dream of the apostles is followed by an explanation of Jesus, contrasting the apostles and their followers with the lasting race that is "watered" in God's paradise.[80] This section is too damaged to draw a firm conclusion, but it is possible that the first lines refer to the type of baptism in this *aeon* that Jesus did not come to institute,[81]

---

[76] Iren., *Adv. Haer.* 1.7.2 on certain Valentinians. Cf. *1 Apoc. Jas.* NHC V,3 and *Apoc. Peter* NHC VII, 3.
[77] Iren., *Adv. Haer.* 1.24.4.
[78] Cf. Iren., *Adv. Haer.* 1.21. Elsewhere Irenaeus accuses of inconsistency those gnostic Christians who retain traditional formulae of the eucharist, in which thanks is given to the very creator whom they denounce (*Adv. Haer.* 4.18.5).
[79] *Gos. Jud.* 33.18–21; 36.11–17.
[80] *Gos. Jud.* 43.1–11.
[81] This is reminiscent of the statement against physical baptism in the *Test. Truth* IX, 69.15–17: 'For the Son of Man did not baptize any of his disciples' (cf. John 4:2).

"but (*alla*) he has come to water God's paradise and the race that will last."

Finally, I would like to indicate how the findings presented above may be of relevance for some of the issues in interpretation that are currently debated among scholars: (1) the act of Judas, (2) the identity of the one who enters the cloud, and (3) the role of Judas.

"You will outdo all of them, for you will sacrifice the man who bears me" (56.18–20)

Seeing that the *Gospel of Judas* urges its readers to 'stop sacrificing', it seems wrong to see the final act of Judas as positive. If Judas sacrifices to Saklas the "man that bears" Jesus, he will "outdo" all worshippers of Saklas in a negative sense. For the author of this gospel, then, Judas did not set in motion the wheel of salvation. He started the error of the apostles who worship the crucified in their baptism and eucharist.

"And he entered it" (57.23)

Scholars are divided over the question whether Jesus or Judas ascends into the cloud. If it is Judas, the question is whether the cloud represents the *plerôma* of the highest Father or Saklas' cloud. If we would only look at the grammar of the present text, it seems more likely that Judas entered the cloud, as he is the subject of the preceding verb.[82] But from a narrative perspective we have the prediction that Judas will sacrifice the man who bears Jesus. This is what follows in the next scene. It would fit the narrative of the gospel very well, if the "ascension" of Jesus is placed here, prior to the arrest and crucifixion. The inner Jesus would then leave Judas behind, who then sacrifices the outer man to Saklas.

"You thirteenth demon" (44.20)

What, finally, does this tell us about the role of Judas? Judas is an ambiguous figure in the gospel that carries his name. On the one hand, he knows Jesus and receives a revelation of the cosmos and the *eschaton*. He also has a predictive dream of his persecution by the apostles (the

---

[82] I note an interesting parallel in the story of the transfiguration in Luke 9:34. Here too the Greek text is ambiguous and the variant readings in early manuscripts show that some early copyists understood that the disciples entered the cloud, whereas others believed that Moses, Elijah and Jesus entered the cloud. See Fitzmyer 1981, 802.

stoning of Judas in 44.24–45.1).[83] But Judas cannot look Jesus in the
eye and Jesus repeatedly tells him that he will not be part of the other
race. There is no soteriology in the revelation to Judas. Elsewhere, in
a narrative analysis of the *Gospel of Judas*,[84] I argue that Jesus is the
only person with whom a gnostic Christian audience can fully identify.
The twelve apostles represent quite clearly the "others'", the apostolic
church whose sacraments are rejected. Through his polemics against
the apostles and the parody of their sacramental practices, the author
marks the identity of his own group and guards its boundaries. The
ambiguous figure of Judas, in this analysis, stands for those gnostic
Christians who cross these boundaries. Gnostic Christians who continue to sacrifice while knowing the truth, are not following Jesus but
Judas.

The *Gospel of Judas* sets out an alternative version to counteract the
"apostolic" narrative and its Easter call to baptism. According to the
author, crucifixion and resurrection are not part of the scheme of salvation. Their re-enactment in baptism and eucharist are nothing but the
continuation of the Jewish sacrificial cult. Participation in these rituals
is denounced as worship of Saklas. The main message of the *Gospel of
Judas*, therefore, can be summarized in two words: 'Stop sacrificing!'

---

[83] This is reminiscent of saying 13 of the *Gos. Thom.*, which many scholars interpret as a statement about the persecution of gnostic Christians by proto-orthodox
Christians.
[84] Van Os 2008.

WHOSE SAVIOR?

Salvation, Damnation and the Race of Adam in the *Gospel of Judas*

Johanna Brankaer

One of the striking characteristics of the *Gospel of Judas* is that it lacks an elaborate soteriological perspective. With the sole exception of the race of Adam, no one seems to be the object of salvation. On the one hand, the human race is heading for eternal condemnation, together with the entire demiurgic reality. On the other hand, the great and holy race does not seem to need salvation. Although Jesus' death is the goal of the narrative, the soteriological value of his death is barely explored. The main point of the *Gospel of Judas* is the denial of a specific soteriological interpretation of Jesus' death. So no alternative understanding is offered. The lack of interest in a systematic soteriology is also reflected in the representation of protology, the creation of the world, and human beings. There is no mention of a 'fall' that needs restoration. There are no interventions of divine entities to prepare the human beings for future salvation.

The *Gospel of Judas* is a highly polemical text whose main concern it is to feature negatively the Eucharist as it is practised in the main church, and perhaps baptism too. The fact that baptism is connected with Jesus' name might indicate that it is similar to the Eucharist, since it also is understood as a human sacrifice. The priests in the disciples' dream vision invoke Jesus' name, which is also used to mislead the races of the pious.[1] The 'apostolic' character of the church is mocked and its sacrificial understanding of the cross is dismantled with the argument that it is a mere continuation of the Jewish Temple cult. The *Gospel of Judas* is a writing that fights against certain ideas and practices known to its author and readers. So it often adopts a tone of mockery, harsh criticism, and perhaps even parody.

Some specialists are convinced that there are no literary precedents to see the *Gospel of Judas* as a parody. If parody is defined as "the

---

[1] *Gos. Jud.* 38,25–26; 40,4–7. For a discussion of critical stance of the author of the *Gos. Jud.* to baptism, see the contribution of Bas van Os in this volume.

mocking imitation by one author of another author's style," this may not apply to our text.[2] The text, however, does stand in relation to a subtext that the reader is supposed to recognise, which is one of the most important markers of parody.[3] This relation between text and subtext is not a novelty at the time when the *Gospel of Judas* was written.[4] The Gnostic myth, especially the creation narratives, parody the creation stories found in the book of Genesis. It is not as much the subtext's style as its contents that are mimicked with a touch of irony. The *Gospel of Judas* can only be understood in relation to the subtext, a subtext identified with a tradition that is associated with Apostolic Christianity rather than a specific writing. This relation to the subtext has an allure of parody.

So the *Gospel of Judas* contains a touch of irony and satire, even what we might call parody. In spite of its title, the *Gospel of Judas* does not seem to communicate any 'good news'. On the contrary, it talks extensively about the structure of the archontic world and the condemnation of everything that is a part of it.

JESUS' DEATH AND ITS SIGNIFICANCE

Even if Jesus' death falls outside the chronology of the frame narrative of the *Gospel of Judas*, its interpretation and its implications are proleptically interwoven into the actual narration, as well as the disciples' discourse and Jesus' revelations. The setting of the narrative is a period of eight days preceding Jesus' passion and death.[5] The story effectively ends with Judas handing over Jesus to the scribes.[6] What will happen after this act is common knowledge to the reader. Jesus has predicted his own death by referring to the sacrifice of the man

---

[2] Booth 1974, 71s.

[3] Booth 1974, 123–134.

[4] On irony in the New Testament, see Camery-Hoggatt 1992, 90–177.

[5] I take that the eight days refer to the events contained in the text and that the three days are beyond the narrative and refer to the actual passion, death and resurrection. This does not mean however, that the eight days function as temporal markers in the text.

[6] The role of the High priests remains unclear. Their grumbling at the fact that Jesus went in to pray is mentioned. From then on it seems to be the scribes who take upon them the actual arrest, following Jesus inside and negotiating with Judas.

who bears him.[7] Nevertheless, it remains remarkable that Jesus' death is not once *explicitly* mentioned in the *Gospel of Judas*.

The narration of Jesus' arrest

Although Jesus' actual death is beyond the narrative of the *Gospel of Judas*, the last moments before his arrest are described in some detail. The author has made an uncommon selection of narrative elements, some of which correspond to the different canonical gospels. In just a few strokes he pictures the scene.

We first hear about the high priests. They are discontent about the fact that Jesus went praying in the κατάλυμα.[8] Their actual role in the arrest of Jesus remains unclear unless we understand that the scribes are at their service. The fact that they are mentioned at the beginning of this section associates these officiants of the Temple cult with what happens next. The scribes observe Jesus carefully in order to apprehend him during his prayer.[9] They are afraid of the people who regard Jesus as a prophet.[10] The people are not responsible for Jesus' death. Only the representatives of the religious authorities and Judas are guilty. The scribes appear to be afraid, so they seem to be planning to seize him in the private setting of prayer rather than in public, although the text does not articulate this. The contact between the scribes and Judas seems to be initiated by the high priests, perhaps finding in him an unexpected opportunity to lay their hands on Jesus.[11] The communication between Judas and the scribes remains opaque to the reader. The scribes, who are waiting for their chance, seem surprised to find Judas where they are. They recognize Judas as one of Jesus' disciples.

---

[7] *Gos. Jud.* 56,19–21.

[8] *Gos. Jud.* 58,9–12.

[9] *Gos. Jud.* 58,12–16.

[10] *Gos. Jud.* 58,16–19. In Matt 26:5 the authorities find it better not to kill Jesus in the middle of the Passover feast in order not to trouble the people. In the process before Pilate, the people, who are under the influence of the authorities, are found to be more willing to shed Jesus' blood than the Roman governor himself (Mark 15:11–14/Matt 27:20–25/Luke 23:18–23). Certain versions of Luke 23:13 only mention the high priests and the leaders of the people instead of the high priests, the leaders and the people. In the Fourth Gospel, Pilate is alternatively in dialogue with the 'Jews' and the Jewish authorities (19:1–16).

[11] *Gos. Jud.* 58,19–20. The Coptic expression † ογοϊ can render the Greek ζητεῖν as well as ἔρχεσθαι πρός (see Crum 1939, 472ab), even if the latter expression seems to occur more often with the possessive article, as it is the case in our text. In both cases there seems to be a connotation of intentionality.

Judas answers them "according to their wish."[12] That this wish would be Jesus' imprisonment and death is not stated, although this might again be considered common knowledge of the audience or readers. The next thing we hear is that Judas receives money and hands Jesus over to them.

In this elliptic presentation of Jesus' imprisonment there is no explicit nor implicit reference to his death or the plan to kill him. Although this might be considered common knowledge and thus superfluous in the narrative, the fact that the author chooses only these elements of the picture and leaves out others is no mere coincidence. The silence about Jesus' death is deafening. With the exception of the mention of Jesus when he enters the κατάλυμα to pray, a striking feature of this section is the virtual absence of Jesus. While the canonical and many other gospels picture Jesus as the protagonist of his passion and death, he does not seem to have any part in what is happening in the *Gospel of Judas*. Jesus' passion and death are not the primary focus of this text.

The emphasis lies entirely on the role of his opponents and especially of Judas, even though the role of Judas in the narrative of the arrest remains unclear. There is no need to identify Jesus. Since the scribes are already inside the κατάλυμα, they do not have to fear the people, so it is not clear what prevents them from apprehending Jesus themselves.

The position of Judas makes more sense at the symbolical level than at the level of narrative economy. The traditional παραδίδοναι at the hand of Judas corresponds to the ⲀⲘⲀϨⲦⲈ by the scribes. It is significant that this Coptic verb can express the way in which the archons get a hold of the world, human beings and eventually Jesus. ⲀⲘⲀϨⲦⲈ occurs once in the *Gospel of Judas* as a transitive verb. It is possible that the verb is being used intransitively in another passage where it may refer to Judas' heart.[13] In the other texts of the Tchacos Codex, however, as well the verb as the substantive are frequently used to refer to the power of the archons and the way they held the world imprisoned.[14] So one could say that Judas, by handing over Jesus, is leading the scribes to him in order to seize him. This appears to correspond

---

[12] *Gos. Jud.* 58,23–24.
[13] *Gos. Jud.* 58,15; 56,24.
[14] *Ep. Pet. Phil.* 3,4.25; *1Apoc. James* 11,9s.18.21; 15,15; 19,24; 20,1; 25,4s.14; 29,26, 30,6.20.21).

with the Gospel's statement that Judas' star would be the leading star.[15] The scribes would be the stars following him. Perhaps we should, from this perspective, take seriously the association between the name Judas and Judaism.[16]

The interpretation of Jesus' death

The *Gospel of Judas* clearly depicts Jesus' death as a sacrifice. When Jesus predicts his death, he tells Judas, "But you will exceed (or: be worse) than all the others, for the man who carries me, you will sacrifice him."[17]

Unfortunately, the context of this saying is very poorly preserved, but some significant elements allow us to understand the reasoning behind it. Jesus speaks about those who bring offerings to Saklas, whom they think is their God.[18] After a lacuna, something is being said about "everything that is bad."[19] In this context, it is said that Judas will "do more" than all of them. As it is shown in the disciples' dream and its interpretation, those who sacrifice to Saklas do evil things. Judas does even more *because* he will *sacrifice* the man who bears Jesus.[20]

Attention has been drawn to the fact that Jesus is distinguished from the man who bears him. This 'human substrate', the earthly or bodily Jesus, has been seen as his 'lesser' part. It has been seen as the part from which he needed to be separated so he could ascend to the pleroma.[21] This interpretation is based on similar texts that express a clearly dualistic Christology.[22] Even though this passage in the *Gospel*

---

[15] *Gos. Jud.* 56,17–20.

[16] For the modern reluctance to see Judas in a negative daylight because of the association between Judas and Judaism, see DeConick 2007, 148–154.

[17] *Gos. Jud.* 56,17–21. I take that the ⲣ̄ ϩⲟⲩⲟ refers to the ϩⲱⲃ ⲛⲓⲙ ⲉⲧϩⲟⲟⲩ in the preceding sentence and takes its negative connotation from this context.

[18] *Gos. Jud.* 56,11–13. For the reconstruction of 56,13, cf. Brankaer-Bethge 2007, 368.

[19] *Gos. Jud.* 56,17.

[20] The enclitic γάρ or "because" points to a causal connection in this context.

[21] The expression "the man who bears me" is uncommon to express this kind of dualism. In such a context, we are more likely to find expressions about something Jesus put on (and can get eventually rid of). Cf. the extensive evaluation of similar material in Nagel 2007, 257, 265–270.

[22] *Treat. Seth* NHC VII,2 and the *Apoc. Peter* NHC VII,3 come here to mind. Both writings deal with Jesus' death as a ruse against the demiurgic powers that are deceived by the death of his body. In *Treat. Seth*, Jesus has evicted the previous occupant of the body he takes on at incarnation (51,20–52,10). The archons have only killed an image of Jesus that they counterfeited themselves. It is Simon of Cyrene who is

of Judas presents Jesus and the man who bears him as distinct elements, stating that only the latter will be sacrificed, there is no trace of a negative representation of this element and far less even of Jesus' need to be separated or liberated from it. Interestingly, Jesus refers to the human that bears him and not to the body or flesh. The term 'human' in itself has no negative connotation in our text except when used in the expression 'the human race'. The man who bears Jesus does not withhold him from visiting the great and holy race, from appearing and disappearing when and how he wants.[23] The killing of Jesus' bodily substrate is a sacrifice—and therefore an act that corroborates the archontic world order. Even worse, it is not just a human sacrifice, which in itself is bad enough in the imagination of the disciples.[24] It is the sacrifice of the 'perfect human' if 35,3 identifies Jesus with the 'perfect human'. This identification is found in other texts.[25]

Jesus' death—or rather sacrifice—is not presented as a salutary event, wanted by God or by Jesus himself. It brings no profit to his disciples, even if they think so when they remember and re-enact this sacrifice in the context of the Eucharist, which is proleptically situated before Jesus' actual death in the *Gospel of Judas*. The only one who profits from this sacrifice is the archontic deity the disciples take for the real God.[26] Jesus laughs at the Eucharistic practice of the disciples, because it reveals their fundamental misunderstanding not only of his identity ('the son of their God'), but also of the significance of his death.

If Jesus' death has any positive consequence, this remains basically unexplored in the *Gospel of Judas*. As a sacrifice, it is the continuation of Jewish ritual practice. As the founding event of the Eucharist, it is seen as an act that only serves the Demiurge. It is easy to see how in a polemical text like the *Gospel of Judas*, that explicitly attacks the Eucharist, Jesus' death can only be interpreted in an utterly negative

---

actually crucified (55,9–56,20). In *Apoc. Peter* only the bodily likeness of Jesus is crucified while Peter sees the real Jesus laughing above the cross (81,3–82,3).

[23] *Gos. Jud.* 36,15–17; 36,10.12; 44,14.15.

[24] The sacrificial dream vision has them startled and frightened (39,4–7). This might explain why they went into hiding before telling their dream-vision to Jesus (37,25–26).

[25] Eph 4:13; Col 1:8; Matt 5:48; *Apoc. John* BG,2 22,9.15s.; 30,14–18; 35,4; 71,12; *Hyp. Arch* NHC II,1] 91,2. In 35,3, the disciples are challenged to bring out or to pass by the perfect human. It is not because they fail to do so, that every human being is unable to become perfect. The expression teaches us that not all of humanity is rejected, even though the so-called human races are.

[26] *Gos. Jud.* 40,18–23.

way: it has been perpetrated by those whom the text accuses of false believes and practices.

Jesus as a Saviour figure

The sole explicit representation of Jesus as the Saviour is not to be found in the context of his death. On the contrary, it is found in the context of his earthly activity. There is just a brief reference to his salutary role at the very beginning of the text, in the retrospective description following the title:

> 33,6–9: When he had appeared on the earth, he accomplished signs and great wonders for the salvation of humanity.

In a very general way, Jesus' earthly ministry is presented here as salutary. Through signs and miracles the salvation of humanity has become possible. The verb ⲟⲩⲱⲛϩ ⲉⲃⲟⲗ refers to Jesus' appearance without explicitly connecting it with a previous non-earthly existence. There is no allusion to a 'descent' into the cosmos or to 'incarnation'.[27] In fact, it is only Judas who makes a statement about Jesus' extra-cosmic origin, telling him that he has come from the immortal Barbelo aeon and that Jesus has been sent by the one whose name Judas is not worthy to utter.[28] There is no real 'uptake' of this information in the following narrative or dialogue. At this point of the story, we do not have any reason to doubt these declarations either. Even if Jesus has descended from a superior level of reality, the author has chosen not to draw too much attention to this material. Surely it is a part of the canvas on which the *Gospel of Judas* has been written, but it is not highlighted at all.

---

[27] As we find them in other texts, e.g. *Apoc. John* NHC II,1 and BG,2, *Treat. Seth* NHC VII,3, *Trim. Prot.* NHC XIII,1.

[28] There is a similar situation in *Gos. Thom.* NHC II,2, saying 13. Just like Judas in *Gos. Jud.*, Thomas has knowledge about Jesus he doesn't share with the other disciples. This sets them apart from the others. Both Thomas and Judas refer to the unspeakable when speaking about Jesus' identity and origin. The differences between both scenes are however hard to dismiss. In *Gos. Thom.* 13 Jesus asks the disciples to what he can be compared. On the one hand, Thomas refuses to answer this question. Read together with saying 14.5 Thomas' answer might refer to the esoteric nature of the knowledge he possesses. Judas, on the other hand, answers a question Jesus has not asked. Knowing this things makes him special, but not in the same way as Thomas, who is virtually equated to Jesus as he transcends the condition of the disciple. Judas is set apart to learn about the kingdom (unlike Thomas he does not have perfect γνῶσις), without the hope of entering it and with the sole promise of future suffering.

The signs and wonders belong to the fund of messianic eschatological terminology. In the NT there is some ambiguity associated with this
kind of thaumaturgy. Mark and Matthew attribute σημεῖα (μεγάλα)
καὶ τέρατα to the ψευδόχριστοι καὶ ψευδοπροφῆται.[29] The expression
occurs in a similar context in some writings from Nag Hammadi.[30] In
Acts, the expression is used in a positive way to describe the divine
power at work in the signs and wonders performed by Jesus and to
describe the power in the signs and wonders made by the disciples
in the process of evangelization.[31] In the *Gospel of Judas* the signs
and wonders belong unambiguously to Jesus' saving activity. The
Apocalypse of Adam offers an interesting parallel to this usage. In this
writing it is the φωστήρ, the Illuminator of knowledge, who performs
signs and miracles in order to "to bring contempt upon their powers
and their archon."[32]

The salvation of humanity is the goal of Jesus' earthly activity, without
any implication of this goal being already achieved.[33] It is remarkable
that humanity is presented as the beneficiary of Jesus' saving activity,
since the human race is usually presented as the race excluded from
salvation. So the abstract term ⲙⲛ̄ⲧⲣⲱⲙⲉ and the expression ⲧⲅⲉⲛⲉⲁ
(ⲛ̄)ⲣⲱⲙⲉ should not be considered as synonyms. Maybe the last group

---

[29] Mark 13:22//Matt 24:24. The expression σημεῖα καὶ τέρατα also occurs in John
4:48 in a hermeneutical context. Even if these terms imply some ambiguity, the correlation between signs and wonders and faith is undeniable.

[30] In *Great Pow.* NHC VI,4 45,14–24, it is the Imitator sent by the archons who
will perform signs and miracles in order to convert Jesus' followers to Jewish Law and
especially circumcision. In *Interp. Know.* NHC XI,1 1,14s., the poorly preserved text
seems to refer to the erroneous signs and wonders of the one who comes after Jesus.

[31] Cf. Acts 2:22, 43; 4:30; 5:12; 6:8; 7:36 (about Moses); 15:12. It is explicitly stated
that God is eventually the one who performs the signs and miracles in 2:22 and
15:12.

[32] *Apoc. Adam* NHC V,5 76,28–77,3. The appearance of this saviour figure confuses
the God of the forces (77,4s.). Morard 1985, 98, connects this theme in *Apoc. Adam*
with its negative interpretation in *Great Pow.*, implying that the Saviour beats the
Archon in its own league (thaumaturgy).

[33] The Illuminator in the above mentioned parallel in *Apoc. Adam* inaugurates
eschatological times. He will save those who have γνωσις from death and judge the
archons. Before attaining final salvation, the humans will have to suffer from the wrath
of the archons. The salvation of humanity in *Gos. Jud.* also seems to occur in an
eschatological context: the τύπος of the race of Adam will be elevated and the ruler
will be destroyed. Before salvation the world will however suffer under the archontic
domination. Another interesting parallel between *Gos. Jud.* and *Apoc. Adam* consists
in the fact that both texts talk about the erroneous usage of the Saviour's name (e.g.
Apoc. Adam NHC V 77 18–22; *Gos. Jud.* 39,8–17).

should be only considered as a sub-category from the first.[34] We will deal more extensively with this in the next section.

The opening phrase of the *Gospel of Judas* actually presents this writing as a 'Gospel' talking about Jesus' salutary activity during his lifetime. Even if this opening does not seem to set the tone for the rest of the text,[35] it is significant that Jesus' earthly ministry is presented as salutary, whereas his death does not seem to have any soteriological implications, at least not for humankind. Jesus' death implies the (precipitated?) end of his salutary activity on earth.

Other passages on salvation are remarkably vague about who makes it happen. Neither Jesus nor any other saviour figure is mentioned. Instead, salvation appears as an impersonal process, wanted by God, but executed by no one in particular.[36]

SOTERIOLOGICAL ELEMENTS IN *GOSPEL OF JUDAS*

In this section I'd like to explore some further soteriological elements in the *Gospel of Judas*. After assessing Jesus' role as a savior, we should now turn our attention to the possible beneficiaries of salvation, if indeed there are any.

Soteriological determinism in the Gospel of Judas?

On several occasions, the *Gospel of Judas* opposes the human race and another race, described as great and holy, a race without a king. The first race seems destined to destruction; the other race, out of reach of the archons, already existing in a superior aeon. The terms 'human race' (ⲧⲅⲉⲛⲉⲁ ⲛ̄(ⲛ) ⲣⲱⲙⲉ) and the 'other great and holy race' (ⲕⲁⲓⲛⲟⳓ ⲛ̄ⲅⲉⲛⲉⲁ ⲉⲥⲟⲩⲁⲁⲃ) seem to function as technical terms expressing the sharp dualism between the inner-cosmic and the pleromic spheres of reality.

---

[34] *Gos. Jud.* 37,12 f. might corroborate this theory. Unfortunately, this passage is not well preserved.

[35] Some have suggested that the frame narrative was not originally part of the text of *Gos. Jud.*, but relates it to 'traditional material'. See e.g. Schenke Robinson and Turner in this volume. It might of course also be a way to integrate traditional material in way that it is shown to be coherent with the rest of the text.

[36] *Gos. Jud.* 54,8–12.

When the disciples ask Jesus where he went after leaving them on
the previous day, he tells them about the great and holy race, which
he opposes to the human race.

> 36,15–21: Jesus said to them: "I have gone to another great race, that is
> holy." His disciples said to him: "Lord, What (or how) is the great race,
> that is loftier than us (?) and that is holy, not being in these aeons—
> now?"

The fact that Jesus presents the holy race as "*another* race" excludes
the disciples from this reality. Thus the group of disciples is pictured
as representative of a race that is not holy. The contrast between both
groups appears in Jesus' words and in the disciples' words. The great
race is loftier than that of the disciples. It is holy. It is not "in these
aeons", in the corruptible aeons where the disciples are. The disciples
seem to think of a possible future connection between both races, for
it is only *now* that the great race and the disciples are not in the same
aeons. Jesus however mocks the very idea of any relation between the
disciples and the holy race. This idea is another misconception of the
disciples concerning Jesus' identity and their own role and destiny.
The disciples should not even be thinking about this other race that
is so fundamentally different from them.[37] The context establishes a
direct connection between the disciples and the human race.[38]

The separation of the great and holy race is categorical and extends
from eternity to eternity.

> 37,1–10: "Truly, I say to you that everything begotten of these aeons will
> not see that race, neither will any of the angelic hosts of the stars reign
> over that race, neither will anything begotten human, and mortal come
> together with it, because that race does not come forth from this cosmos,
> that has come into being."

The origin of both races is different: the holy race did not come forth
from this cosmos or these aeons.[39] Therefore no one of the human race

---

[37] *Gos. Jud.* 36,22–26.

[38] Cf. the question starting with ⲁϩⲣⲱⲧⲛ̄ p. 36,24–26. Something similar will be
said about Judas when he has told his vision about the great house that is reserved for
the holy. Judas has no access to this reality for he is of mortal human birth (ⲡⲉⲭⲡⲟ
ⲛ̄ⲣⲱ[ⲙ]ⲉ ⲛⲓⲙ ⲛ̄ⲑⲛⲏⲧⲟⲛ). The Coptic noun ⲭⲡⲟ renders different Greek words derived
from γεννάω. It might refer to a reality similar to γενεά or γένος in other passages.

[39] I take that the lacuna in 37,2 has [ⲛ̄ⲧⲉ ⲛ]ⲉⲉⲓⲁⲱⲛ instead of [ⲛ̄ⲧⲉ ⲡ]ⲉⲉⲓⲁⲱⲛ as
suggested in the editio princeps. The disciples refer to "these aeons" in their question
(36,21).

(which obviously belongs to the reality of the cosmos) can ever join it. There will be no eschatological *Aufhebung* of the difference that separates both groups. Both races are ontologically separated by another origin and final fate. They never get mixed between these chronological extremes. There is no moment in the history of the holy race, where it gets mixed up with the cosmic reality, where it is historically subjected to the astrological reign of the archons.

The great and holy race does not play a role in the narrative. Its main function in the *Gospel of Judas* consists in representing attributes that are denied the human race. While the human race is characterized in opposition to the great and holy race, it is described in more specific ways. This may allow us to get a better grasp of this category.

It is clear from page 36 of the *Gospel of Judas* that the disciples belong to the race which is opposed to the great and holy one. When Jesus laughs at their Eucharist, he has already identified them with the human race.[40] Jesus makes it clear in this scene that the disciples' theological premises must be wrong because they rely on a false knowledge about him. Their ignorance derives from their misconception about the real God, whom they are not able to distinguish from the Biblical Creator God.

> 34,13–18: Jesus said to them: "In what (way) do you know me? Truly, I say to you, no race will know me among the humans that are among you."

Jesus is directly addressing the disciples in these words and he is doing so as a reaction against the cult they practice. It is specified that from "the humans that are among you" (meaning the disciples) no race will know Jesus. Thus, J. van der Vliet translates "the race of your followers" ("het geslacht van jullie volgelingen"), making clear that the human race is connected to the disciples and their religious convictions.[41] From this, one could imagine, that Jesus is only talking about a restricted part of humanity, one that is identified as the human race in other passages. It is the races of humans associated with the disciples that are unable to attain to any correct knowledge about Jesus. They

---

[40] *Gos. Jud.* 34,15–18.
[41] Van der Vliet 2006b, 74.

are misled. Mistaken that they serve Jesus' Father, they unwillingly
serve 'their' God.[42]

It is again in a cultic setting that we encounter the human races
(ⲛ̄ⲅⲉⲛⲉⲁ ⲛ̄ⲛⲣⲱⲙⲉ). The context is the disciples' dream about a sacrificial service at the Temple. Jesus explains that the priests who bring
the offerings invoke his name and he adds:

> And I also say to you that my name has been written on this temple of
> the races of the stars by the races of man.

The human races seem to be responsible for the association of the
name of Jesus with the Temple, and thus with the Jewish sacrificial
cult, which is interpreted from the perspective of astral fatalism.[43]
Although the disciples distinguish between themselves and the officiants of the cult they witness, Jesus identifies both groups.[44] This has
to be taken in a metaphorical way: in the same way that the Temple
priests lead the animals to the sacrificial altar, so the disciples mislead
the masses in their own sacrificial cult.[45] They are like the priests of
a deceptive religion that serves an inferior God in criminal ways.[46] It
seems reasonable to identify the disciples in this context not only with
the priests, but also with the representatives of the human races, since
they are the ones who have connected Jesus' name to this illegitimate
sacrificial cult. Under a new name the human races—unknowingly—
continue the cult of the races of stars, that is, the archons venerated in
the Jewish Temple cult.

The identification between the 'human race(s)' and the disciples
becomes all the more convincing in the light of the following passage:

> 40,18–23: It has been said to the races of man: "See! God has accepted
> your sacrifices from priestly hands—that is the servant of error."[47]

---

[42] We can probably connect a still unplaced fragment that refers to the "servants
of Saklas" (ϩⲛ̄ϩⲁⲗ ⲛ̄ⲥⲁⲕⲗⲁⲥ) with this kind of context. This fragment is made up
from the fragm. I 2 + C 29 + H 34 + C 4, put together by Wurst and presented at the
Houston Codex Judas Conference.

[43] I would now suggest the reading ⲉⲡⲉ[ⲉⲓⲣ̄ⲡⲏ]ⲓ̈ ⲛ̄ⲛⲅⲉⲛⲉⲁ for the end of 39,13
(instead of ⲉⲡⲉⲣⲡⲏⲓ̈ ⲛ̄ⲛⲅⲉⲛⲉⲁ in Brankaer-Bethge 2007, 268).

[44] In their dream-vision the disciples stand by while the twelve priests perform their
sacrifices (38,10s.).

[45] *Gos. Jud.* 39,18–40,2. This might be a reference to the Apostolic Church's call for
martyrs. Cf. E. Pagels-King 2006, 73.

[46] *Gos. Jud.* 38,14–39,3.

[47] Even if the Coptic text as it is preserved has no grammatically corresponding
antecedent for the relative phrase (unless we correct the text with Nagel 2007, 245

The human races are the ones that have brought sacrifices to their archontic divinity. Although Jesus has compared the disciples to the priests in the interpretation of the dream-vision, they are again differentiated in this passage. The priests appear here as the intermediate between the disciples and their God. The disciples do not appear as independent actors, but are led astray by the priests, by the stars, by the angels. This makes them ultimately a laughing stock. Thus, the human race again is associated with the sacrificial Temple cult, the reign of the stars and the leadership of the disciples.[48] Moreover, and in contrast to the other race, the human race is mortal.[49] One can assume they belong to the creations of the stars that will be destroyed at the end of times.[50] Their souls will die and their flesh comes from the race of angels.[51]

From the preceding examples, we can conclude that the category of the human race(s) designates especially the disciples and the Apostolic Church they represent. In contrast, the great and holy race represents the pleromic reality the disciples will never have access to. Of the characters of the frame narrative, only Jesus is able to move between the two levels of reality.[52] The character of Judas undergoes a transformation in the text. He has some knowledge about the superior race, but the access to this reality is twice explicitly denied to him.[53] He is dissociated from the other disciples, but only to become the thirteenth demon, to move to the archontic level, where his star leads the others. He is not elevated to the level of the holy race, but rather to the level of the race of the stars that govern the human races. The sacrifice of Jesus' body is the ultimate deceit that will allow the disciples to continue unconsciously the Jewish Temple cult.

---

n. 94. and read ⲛ̄‹ⲚⲞⲨ›ⲞⲨⲎⲎⲂ), it is clear that the servant of error is the priest(s). It is unlikely that the relative sentence refers to God (cf. Plisch 2006, 5–14).

[48] *Gos. Jud.* 40,17–18.

[49] *Gos. Jud.* 43,15–16.

[50] *Gos. Jud.* 55,19–20. For the association of the human race and the stars, see also 54,21–22. It is likely that this is a reference to the human race—that possibly exists among others, such as the races of the stars.

[51] *Gos. Jud.* 43,15s.; 54,7s.

[52] Interestingly, Jesus is not presented as belonging to the holy race either. In 36, 16s. Jesus only tells he *went* to this race. Jesus—as the Autogenes—is probably ontologically prior to the holy race. This might indicate that the holy race refers to beings that are already saved (maybe by nature, but the text does not draw on this possibility).

[53] Cf. *Gos. Jud.* 35,26; 46,25–47,1.

The Race of Adam

The entire spectrum of reality is not covered by the holy race which is beyond any need for salvation, and the human race which will never access salvation. There is a middle group living under the archons and still awaiting salvation. This middle group is referred to as the "race of Adam". In what seems to be an eschatological prediction, it is said that the great Archon will be destroyed. This does not appear to be advantageous to either the disciples or Judas, who will suffer greatly.[54] In this context, the race of Adam is mentioned in a positive way.

> 57,9–14: Then the τύπος of the great race of Adam will be exalted, for that race existed before heaven and earth and the angels through the aeons.

Unlike the holy race, the race of Adam needs salvation. Unlike the human race, the race of Adam will obtain salvation in the end. This exaltation at the end of times is mirrored in the pre-existence of this race. The figure of Adamas may be the celestial prototype of this race, a point which I will discuss later in this chapter.

There seems to be some middle ground between the completely pleromic holy race and the human race heading for eternal condemnation. When Jesus talks about "the race that will last, for they will not defile the way of that race, but it will come to be from eternity to eternity", Judas asks what kind of fruit "this race" has.[55] Because the "race that will last" is situated in Paradise, it is unlikely that the holy race is meant here.[56] Paradise is not usually situated in the Pleroma. Normally it is the Demiurge who places the human being in paradise and expels him later.[57] Some texts associate Paradise with the psychic sphere.[58] Even when Paradise reproduces all the good things from the

---

[54] *Gos. Jud.* 35,26; 46,11s. and possibly 57,6.

[55] *Gos. Jud.* 43,7–14.

[56] This is maybe comparable to the immovable race in other Gnostic Texts. Cf. the analysis of this terminology by Williams 1985, 160–179. The author does not refer to the expression "the race that lasts", but his conclusions about the absence of soteriological determinism connected with this notion seem also to apply for the understanding of this expression in *Gos. Jud.*

[57] E.g. *Apoc. John* BG 55,18–56,2; *Hyp. Arch.* NHC II,4 88,24–32; *Orig. World* NHC II,5 115,27–30; *Apoc. John* BG 61,18–62,1; *Hyp. Arch* NHC II,4 91,3–5; 121,4s.; *Test. Truth* NHC IX,3 47,10–14.23–27.

[58] *Tri. Tract.* NHC I,5 101,29–31; 102,19–21; *Hyp. Arch* NHC II,4 90,13–15.

Pleroma and is the dwelling place of the pneumatics, it is but an image of the Pleroma for the sake of those created by the Logos.[59]

Moreover, the holy race is usually referred to in a more or less technical sense as "*that* race" (ⲧⲅⲉⲛⲉⲁ ⲉⲧⲙ̄ⲙⲁⲩ). In this passage, however, we have "*this* race" (ⲧⲉⲉⲓⲅⲉⲛⲉⲁ). The fact that it will last indicates that this race will somehow be saved instead of disappearing with the stars and their creations.[60] The section referring to the "fruit of this race" develops the idea that the human race(s) are not opposed to the holy race, but rather to another category of humans.

> 43,14–23: Jesus said: "(As to) every human race, their souls will die. These, on the other hand, when the time of the Kingdom comes to an end, the spirit is separated from them, their bodies will die, but their souls will be made alive and they will be elevated."

The ⲛⲁⲓ in l. 16 could refer to those belonging to ⲧⲉⲉⲓⲅⲉⲛⲉⲁ in Judas' question.[61] In this case, this race is clearly distinct from the holy race, which is never under the rule of the archons. The humans Jesus is talking about seem to live in the cosmos, for it is only when the time of the archons' kingdom is fulfilled that their souls will be made alive and elevated, just as the τύπος of the race of Adam will be elevated in the last days.[62] For now they live in the body, but apparently this is not living in the full sense, since they will not be made alive until they are separated from the body. So the beneficiaries of salvation are human beings with body and soul—and it is their souls that will be saved.

Judas asks subsequently what will happen to the "rest of the human race".[63] This question reveals that the ones who will be saved are also human and distinct from "the rest of the human race". The latter category might be the group normally referred to by Jesus as "the human race(s)". From Jesus' answer it is clear that this group cannot expect any form of salvation. Jesus takes up the theme of the fruit from Judas' question, only to declare that

> 43,26–44,2: It is impossible to sow (seed) on a rock and receive its fruits.

---

[59] *Tri. Tract.* NHC I,5 96,27–34. For references to the trees of paradise, see *Tri. Tract.* NHC I,5 106, 25–31; *Gos. Phil.* NHC II,3 15, 84, 92; *Orig. World* NHC II,5 110, 8–13. In *Orig. World*, Egypt is compared to paradise (122,33–123,2).

[60] *Gos. Jud.* 55,19–20.

[61] *Gos. Jud.* 43,14.

[62] *Gos. Jud.* 43,23–25.

[63] *Gos. Jud.* 43,23–25.

Still,

> 44,3–7: Some will [curse⁶⁴] the [defiled] race and the corruptible Sophia and the hand that has created mortal humans—their souls go up to the aeons on high.

Again, there seems to be an exception within the category of humanity: there is some place left for remorse or conversion that allows the soul to receive redemption.[65] If the place they go to is identified as [ⲉⲡⲙⲁ ⲉⲧ]ⲙ̄ⲙⲁⲩ, reconstructed in the next sentence, then it seems that these souls will finally attain to the reality of the holy race. About this place Jesus expressly says to Judas that "every begotten mortal human" (ⲛⲉⲭⲛⲟ ⲛ̄ⲣⲱⲙⲉ ⲛⲓⲙ ⲛ̄ⲑⲛⲏⲧⲟⲛ) is unworthy to enter it.

PROTOLOGY IN *GOSPEL OF JUDAS*

The absence of a 'Fall' and 'Restoration'

Although the *Gospel of Judas* contains an important cosmological section, it does not relate the existence of the archons, cosmogony or anthropogony to a 'fallen principle'. The description of the unfolding of the Pleroma continues into the description of cosmic realities, without any clear 'break' between either sphere. This unfolding is presented in an arithmetical way which recalls a passage from *Eugnostos*.[66] At the end of this cosmological section, there is a reference in *Gospel of Judas* to seventy-two heavens and 360 firmaments:

> 50,11–18: The multitude of those immortals is called 'cosmos', that is perdition, (coming) from the Father and the 72 luminaries that are with the Autogenes and his 72 aeons.

After a similar mathematical description, *Eugnostos* has:

> NHC III,3 85,3–9: When the (360) firmaments were completed, they were called the 360 heavens after the name of the heavens before them. And (although) all of these are perfect and good, the defect of femaleness appeared.

---

[64] It is clear that the verb in the lacuna should indicate some negative attitude with regard to the realities mentioned. For the reconstruction of ⲟⲩⲛ[ϩⲟⲓⲛ]ⲉ ⲛⲁ[ⲥⲁϩⲟⲩ], cf. Brankaer-Bethge 2007, 342.

[65] Comparable to the remorse of Sabaoth, who curses his father and mother, in other texts, e.g. *Hyp. Arch.* NHC II,4 95,13–17.

[66] *Eugn.* NHC III p. 84,12–85,9. Cp. *Gos. Jud.* 49,9–50,14.

If we can compare both texts, the limit between the Pleroma and cosmos might be situated between the seventy-two heavens and their luminaries and the 360 firmaments—with the latter belonging to the cosmos. In *Eugnostos*, a breach in the system is indicated by the appearance of the deficiency or defect of femaleness. There is no trace of anything similar in the corresponding part of *Gospel of Judas*. There is no female entity in the description of the appearance of the highest aeons that causes the first duality and allows indirectly for a later deterioration of reality. Nor is there a female entity that appears at the 'limit' of the Pleroma, an entity who is more directly responsible for the existence of the cosmos.

Barbelo, who has been mentioned by Judas in another context, is not integrated in the cosmological description of reality.[67] Autogenes follows immediately after the Invisible Spirit who utters the wish that "a great angel may come into being for my assistance."[68] A female entity does not appear chronologically or logically between the Spirit and Autogenes, unless we take the luminous cloud from which Autogenes appears as a description of Barbelo, who has been identified by Judas as the aeon Jesus comes from.[69]

This discrepancy between the implicit cosmology in Judas' statement about Jesus' identity and the explicit cosmology in Jesus' discourse could, on the one hand, be explained by a diachronic redaction theory stating that the redactor or compiler of the *Gospel of Judas* used different sources for both sections.[70] On the other hand, from a synchronic point of view, we should try to explain how both representations can stand next to each other in the text as a whole. Are they understood to be complementary? Is it the same reality, described in different sets of terminology, belonging each to its own tradition? Are there two conflicting visions in the text, and if so, which one is to be taken seriously?

---

[67] *Gos. Jud.* 35,17–19.

[68] *Gos. Jud.* 47,16–18.

[69] *Gos. Jud.* 47,14–16. The association between Jesus and the Autogenes appears frequently in Gnostic texts. Cf. e.g. *Apoc. John* BG 31,16–18. Van der Vliet, 2006, 103, suggests that the cloud Nebro and Saklas come from is the hylic Sophia. In that perspective it could be possible that the other important female entity is also presented as a cloud of light. If this is the case here, the reader should infer this from known traditions, like we find in *Apoc. John* NHC III 9,10–17, that the Autogenes comes forth from Barbelo (and the invisible Spirit).

[70] Cf. the contributions of Schenke Robinson and Turner in this volume.

I think it is important to point out that one version is attributed to
Judas, while the other to Jesus. Jesus' discourse is addressed to Judas
whom he wants to teach "about the [light-aeons that] no human has
seen" including Judas himself.[71] What does Jesus add with regard to the
things Judas already knew? Does he explain those things in a way that
Judas did not previously understand? Is he implicitly criticizing Judas'
statement about the divine triad? Or does he just leave out information that Judas obviously is aware of already? The fact that the author
of the text was familiar with Barbelo traditions and does not draw on
them in Jesus' cosmological discourse is certainly significant. This does
not necessarily imply a critique of these traditions. The articulation
of this discourse is at the service of its function. By obliterating the
'female component,' the cosmogony is dissociated from salvation history. Just as there is no uptake of Judas' statement about the Barbelo-
Aeon, neither is it repeated that Jesus comes from this reality. When
talking about Autogenes, Jesus gives us no reason to assume that he
is talking about himself. This is another characteristic that isolates the
story of the beginnings from a global salvation history.

Another passage from the *Gospel of Judas* evokes a 'parallel' passage
from the *Gospel of the Egyptians,* but it distinguishes itself from the
'parallel' by the absence of the reference to a female principle found in
the *Gospel of the Egyptians.* The cloud from which Nebro and Saklas
come is called the "hylic Sophia" in *Gospel of the Egyptians.*[72] She is
not mentioned in the 'parallel' passage of *Gospel of Judas.*[73] Sophia
is only once referred to in the *Gospel of Judas,* in an anthropological
context:

> 43,25–44,7: Jesus said: "It is impossible to sow on a rock and receive
> their fruits. It is like that. Some will [curse] the [defiled] race, the cor-
> ruptible Sophia, and the hand that has created humans mortal, and their
> souls go up to the aeons above."

Unfortunately, the first verb of the sentence is lost in a lacuna. Since
the realities that are enumerated in the following lines are negative,
one can expect a verb that indicates a distancing from them. The
corruptible Sophia is associated with the defiled race and the hand

---

[71] *Gos. Jud.* 47,2–5; 45, 13–17.
[72] *Gos. Egy.* NHC III pp. 56,26–57,1.
[73] *Gos. Jud.* 51,4–9.

that made mortal humans.[74] This statement points to a version of the cosmogony and anthropogony that is different from what we find in Jesus' cosmological discourse.

These two examples show that the author of the *Gospel of Judas* is apparently aware of traditions with a primeval triad, with Barbelo as its second member, and traditions about the fall of Sophia associated with the demiurgical creation of human beings. By not describing a fall, the *Gospel of Judas* has no ground to describe salvation in terms of restoration of this fall. The 'Savior' has no deficient counterpart he needs to save. The description of cosmogony does not call for a Saviour that corrects a deficiency.

The anthropogony in *Gospel of Judas* has also some particularities in comparison with similar texts. Saklas and his angels create Adam and Eve "after the image and the likeness", although we don't know of what or whom.[75] These terms normally occur in a paradigm of double creation, so that the created has something from a higher realm and something from the lower. The lack of precision at this point contributes, just as the absence of a fallen principle, to the overall impression of a continuity between the Pleroma and the cosmos. This impression is corroborated by the fact that Eleleth, one of the luminaries normally associated with Barbelo, is the one who calls the rulers of Chaos and Hades into existence.

The race of Adam and Anthropogony

Compared to the cosmological developments, anthropogony is treated rather marginally in a short section at the end of Jesus' cosmological discourse. After the creation of Chaos and Hades, Saklas says to his angels "Let us create a human being according to the likeness and the image."[76] Then it is briefly reported that they moulded (πλάσσειν) Adam and his wife Eve.[77] After some kind of conflict that we cannot make out in the extant passage, the archon shortens the human life span. The *Gospel of Judas* does not seem to mention any other entities or beings involved in this. The disobedience (?) of the first humans

---

[74] This could be a reference to the archons (Nebro is defiled with blood in 51,11) or to the non-Gnostic humans (43,9).

[75] *Gos. Jud.* 52,16s.

[76] *Gos. Jud.* 52,14–17.

[77] *Gos. Jud.* 52,18–19.

does not seem to be connected to the interference of some pleromic being who prepares them for future salvation.

That Eve is called Zoe "in the cloud" might be an implicit reference to the cloud of Adamas.[78] Zoe and Adam(as) would then be the pleromic equivalents of the first humans. It is their pre-existence that accounts for the latter's later salvation. Those who seek and find these pre-existing prototypes of humanity might be linked to salvation.[79] At the end of times, the τύπος of the race of Adam will be exalted. Could the pre-existing Adamas be this τύπος, even if it is not explicitly said that the first humans were created by the archons after *Adamas'* image?

A sign of future salvation is the fact that the first humans received some knowledge in order not to be completely dominated by the archons. However, this is not mentioned in the short anthropogonic story. It is only mentioned at the end of the following dialogue with Judas about the mortality of the human spirit.[80] Jesus discourages Judas and the other disciples from seeking the spirit in themselves.[81] Rather he talks about Adam and those who are with him: they will not be dominated by the kings of Chaos and Hades, because they have received γνῶσις.[82]

It is said that God is the one who caused them to receive knowledge. But the use of a causative infinitive hides the actual subject of this giving where one would expect to find a mention of a savior figure or an adjuvant savior. I use the expression 'adjuvant savior' for entities that play a role in the preparation of salvation but who are not actual saviors whose advents initiate the era of completion. The adjuvant saviors are often female figures implied in the primeval 'fall'. Of course, the silence on this point in the *Gospel of Judas* could be connected with the absence of references to a female principle in the cosmological

---

[78] *Gos. Jud.* 52,19–21; 48,21–23. This is the original cloud out of which the Autogenes came into being (47,18–20).

[79] The fact that 'all the races' seek them under their pleromic names (52,21–25) might imply that not all of them find them. It does not say anything about the salutary outcome of this search.

[80] *Gos. Jud.* 54,8–12.

[81] *Gos. Jud.* 54,4–8.

[82] This section might express some kind of opposition between the human race (the disciples, including Judas) and the race of Adam.

section.[83] This section does not provide for any savior figure that prepares future salvation.

Adamas and the incorruptible race of Seth appear in the cosmogony, but they have no part in the anthropogony.[84] It is not clear what the connection between Adamas, Seth and humanity actually is. Did Adamas exist in the luminous cloud from the twelve luminaries and twenty-four powers? In this context, he makes a race appear, the incorruptible race of Seth.[85] The text continues with the appearance of the seventy-two luminaries and 360 luminaries. It is probably not Adamas who makes these appear, but rather Autogenes who supervises the appearance of a multitude of other entities in the preceding and possibly in the following section. Adamas is situated at the highest level of reality, but his integration in the overall system and his precise function(s) remain unclear. The most striking feature is that he is not implicated in any way in the anthropogony, not even in a passive way as celestial prototype. Due to the place in the narrative where he is mentioned, he seems completely detached from the human sphere of being. Thus the soteriological relevance of Adamas and the race of Seth remain implicit at best.

The cosmological discourse as a whole is *not* meant to answer the 'unde malum?' and to explain the persistence of something good in a bad cosmos. This section seems to serve the global goal of the *Gospel of Judas* of depicting the variety of archontic realities that constitute the reference frame of the beliefs of the disciples and of the reality in which Judas will eventually find his place. The articulation of the cosmogonic and anthropogonic discourse shows that these beliefs have no common ground with the reality of salvation.

The disciples, Judas and the Stars

The implied reader of the text is able to decipher the main characters of the text as representative of realities known by him. The disciples stand for the Apostolic Church, the stars for the Jewish authorities and the archontic deities they represent. Judas, by sacrificing Jesus, in a way becomes the leader of the Jews who are associated with the archontic

---

[83] In some texts, it are female entities that bestow salutary knowledge to humans in order to restore their previous error, e.g. *Apoc. John, Orig. World, Trim. Prot.*

[84] *Gos. Jud.* 48,21–49,7.

[85] *Gos. Jud.* 49,5–6.

deities. By instituting the Eucharist, ironically he also becomes the founder of Apostolic Christianity. The targeted Christians in this text would be appalled by the idea that they are no real Christians, but in fact still Jews. This is expressed in the reaction of the disciples to their dream-vision and its interpretation by Jesus.

The stars in the *Gospel of Judas* have two functions: they bring things to completion, and they are a (mis-)guiding principle. Little attention is given to the fact that the stars themselves are governed by fate or εἱμαρμένη, that they are restrained to the fixed courses of their orbits.[86] The fact that they bring things to an end points toward their temporality. From a human point of view, they could be seen as *producing* time. From an eternal point of view, they are temporal markers subjected to time and to eschatology. They do not belong to eternity, for they will not only bring external things to completion, they will themselves come to an end. Just like the archons, they seem unaware of the higher reality that transcends them and ultimately determines their destiny. This is part of the overall ironic dimension of the text. The most startling illustration of this is the image of a laughing Jesus, mocking the disciples' ignorance and the error of the stars.

If we want to understand which reality corresponds to the stars, we have to take seriously their (mis-)guiding function. In our text, this function mainly is exercised with regard to all of the disciples, Judas included. They are all led astray by the stars. Even though in one instance we are told that each of the disciples has his star, only Judas' star appears in the other instances in Jesus' discourses.[87] This does not necessarily imply any identification or equation between the disciples and the stars. The relation between both realities is asymmetrical. The stars influence the disciples, who have themselves no influence on the stars. The disciples *follow* the stars, because of their misconceptions about the divine. Theoretically, they could *stop* following the stars, which means that they could stop struggling with Jesus, and they could stop sacrificing.[88]

---

[86] This dimension is not explored in the text. The stars are subjected to the power of a higher reality in that they will be brought to completion themselves, cf. 54,17–18. It is also said about the "six stars and the five warriors" that they will be destroyed, cf. 55,17–20.

[87] The context of this saying is unfortunately not very well preserved (42,7s.). Cf. 45, 13; 55,10; 56,23; 57,19s.

[88] *Gos. Jud.* 42,6–7; 41,1–2.

The stars appear at several occasions as the object of the beliefs and worship of the human races or the disciples. They are connected with the sacrificial cult and possibly with the Temple.[89] This evidence suggests a possible identification between the stars and the archons, both of which are closely connected with the angels. Just like the archons the stars have a limited sphere of action; they have no hold on the pleromic holy race.[90] Like the archons, the stars have their own creations or races.[91] Representing the archontic sphere of reality, the stars are associated with the biblical creator God and Jewish cultic practice. The disciples are accused of continuing these Jewish beliefs and practices under a thin layer of Christian varnish, which is the (ab)use of Jesus' name. The stars represent this 'error' of the disciples. They stand for the beliefs and rites the disciples are not aware of practicing. This unawareness is expressed in their confusion, anger, and their wrong conviction that Jesus is the son of their God, and that the God they believe in is Jesus' Father!

The case of Judas seems to be slightly different. Whereas initially just like the other disciples, he also is led astray by his star, his star will play an eminent role later on. It will dominate the thirteenth eon, it will ascend and eventually it will lead the other stars.[92] Unlike the other characters, Judas evolves throughout the story. At the end, Judas and his star seem to coincide with one another. In 55, 10s., the kingship of Judas' star is presented as a thing of the future. This future is characterized by the appearance of different kinds of vicious men. This presentation of all sorts of wickedness has strong eschatological overtones.

From 56, 21 onward, Judas seems to be transformed. This is at first expressed in a hymn-like section that mentions that Judas' star has ascended. ϫⲱ(ⲱ)ⲃⲉ can also mean "pass by", but in an astronomical or astrological context the meaning "ascend" seems more appropriate.[93] Since the stars function as temporal markers, the ascent of Judas' star could symbolize the beginning of a new era, inaugurated by Jesus' death. At the end of Jesus' last discourse, Judas is able to see that his

---

[89] *Gos. Jud.* 40,17–22; 41,4–6; 39,12–15.
[90] *Gos. Jud.* 37,4–6; 44,9–11?.
[91] *Gos. Jud.* 55,17–20; 39,13–14; 54,21–22.
[92] *Gos. Jud.* 55,10s.; 56,23; 57,19s.
[93] Crum 1939, 759b.

star has become the guiding star.[94] This could be a reference to the scene where Judas leads the representatives of the Jewish authorities to Jesus at the moment of his arrest, given Birger Pearson's understanding that the stars surrounding the cloud are the people who imprison Jesus.[95] Thus Judas is not leading the twelve disciples, but the (twelve?) stars of the Jewish authorities. Judas becomes the one who leads the stars; these are the Jewish scribes (and high priests?), not the twelve disciples, who are not in any direct way 'guilty' of Jesus' imprisonment and death. The use of the number twelve with regard to the stars does not necessarily imply an association with the twelve apostles. It could just as well be a reference to the twelve tribes of Israel and other Jewish' traditions.[96] Then it is only in a secondary way that this number is applied to the group of disciples. They have to be twelve, because the system they adhere to and come to represent demands that they are twelve.

Clearly Judas is a leader of the Jewish authorities. It is only in a secondary sense that Judas (mis-)leads the disciples.[97] This is mainly the consequence of their salutary interpretation of Jesus' death. The disciples re-enact in the Eucharist the sacrifice of Jesus, and thus Judas' central action.[98] It is interesting that Judas is the one who will sacrifice Jesus while he actually only hands him over within the narrative of the *Gospel of Judas*. Since the action of handing over can symbolise the gesture of sacrificing, this might be one of the reasons that the actual death of Jesus and its perpetrators are omitted from the narrative. In a way, by delivering Jesus to his murderers, Judas has become one of the erring stars the disciples follow. It is Judas, the Jew, who makes it possible for Christians to hold on to Jewish sacrificial practice and so the worship of the creator God.

READING GOSPEL OF JUDAS AS A WHOLE

Even if the *Gospel of Judas* might contain materials from different sources and strata, the text has been transmitted and read in its present

---

[94] *Gos. Jud.* 57,19–20.
[95] Cf. the contribution of B. Pearson in this volume.
[96] See the contributions of Denzey Lewis and Förster in this volume.
[97] For the disciples do not accept Judas as an authority. He is taken from their group and replaced by another (35,24–36,4).
[98] *Gos. Jud.* 56,17–21.

form. In this form it must have conveyed meaning to its public. This does not mean that the text is consistent and systematic in every detail. It is after all not a systematic treatise. But the different parts are in some way connected. They have not been arbitrarily put together. We should assume that the text is coherent in its entirety.

The frame narrative makes sense from the perspective of the rest of the text, even when it expresses things that are not placed in the forefront in the rest of the writing. It is complementary in that it provides the background on which the rest can be understood. It conveys information about the thinking that is woven in the canvas of the text, but not treated explicitly. From the frame narrative, we learn that the goal of incarnation is salutary, that Jesus' death is not.

In order to polarize the wickedness of the opponents, the harsh polemic of the *Gospel of Judas* obscures some positive elements it provides concerning salvation. The "dualistic" representation of two races serves this goal. It stresses that the human race, associated with Apostolic Christianity, is different from the holy race which belongs to a completely separate reality. This is done in order to accentuate the fallacious teaching and the final condemnation of the opponent. However this does not imply the impossibility of salvation for all human beings. This is clear from the more discrete allusions to the race of Adam and some elements of the frame narrative.

The lack of concern for soteriology is shown in the absence of any fall or restoration in the cosmological section. There is no explicit link established between anthropogony and the capacity to be saved inherent to the general category of humanity. From this perspective, it is not surprising that Jesus is only marginally pictured as a savior figure in the *Gospel of Judas*. The "Savior" remains in a way anonymous. So the *Gospel of Judas* uses impersonal expressions when talking about salvation. These impersonal grammatical constructions hide somewhat the actor of salvation.

In order to criticize the Eucharist practised by the Apostolic Church, Jesus' death is presented as something utterly negative. It is a sacrifice that surpasses the Temple sacrifices, because a human being is slaughtered, and this human being is the "perfect human". This is remembered and re-enacted in the Eucharist, showing that the Apostolic Church is ignorant about its own practises and the very God it honors.

Because of this polemical setting, the *Gospel of Judas* treats marginally the possibility of salvation. This is reflected by the fact that the race of Adam does not correspond to any of the characters of the frame narrative. The human races are represented by the disciples and their followers. Jesus is the only one with access to the holy race. In the end, Judas is exalted to the level of the archons that mislead the human races by astral fatality. Jesus does not bring salvation to any of these characters. Thus the saved remain 'virtual' in the narrative setting and have to be found beyond the story, in the world of its implied reader who condemns with the author a form of Christianity that represents for him a travesty of the sacrificial Temple cult.

FROM PERPLEXITY TO SALVATION:
THE *GOSPEL OF JUDAS* READ IN LIGHT OF PLATONIC DIDACTIC STRATEGIES

Tage Petersen

Blessed will they be who understand (νοεῖν) what is discussed (ⲉⲧⲟⲩϣⲁⲝⲉ) with them and will be revealed to them (ⲥⲉⲛⲁⲟⲩⲟⲛϩⲟⲩ ⲉⲃⲟⲗ). Blessed will they be, for they will come to understand (νοεῖν) truth: you (pl.) have found rest in the heavens.[1]

These few lines conclude the section in *The Concept of Our Great Power* that until the discovery of the *Gospel of Judas* was the only extant primary testimony among the Gnostic texts mentioning Judas' delivering of Jesus. The passage is of interest both for the light it sheds on the general understanding of Gnostic texts, but also specifically for the understanding of the *Gospel of Judas*, suggesting a clue to one of the challenges confronting the modern reader of Gnostic texts, namely the question of the text's *Sitz im Leben*.

It has been stated that the *Gospel of Judas* is no gospel in the usual sense of the word, since it does not carry a message from which the reader can gain salvation. However, this can be contested by approaching the Gospel from the perspective of the ancient philosophical dialogue. In an attempt to do so the paper draws attention to the strategies of philosophical dialogue as well as to the fact that literary tropes are often tied to genre, keeping in mind that the work that takes place in literary texts takes place both in its literary figures and is at least intended by the writer to take place also in the reader. Based on this reading strategy, the *Gospel of Judas* (given the fragmentary state of the text) does appear to carry a message of salvation to the reader even though several scholars have said otherwise. But first a brief note on the general character and context of Gnostic texts. The reason why Gnostic texts are difficult to comprehend it not only that they are loaded with concepts and mythemes unfamiliar to modern readers, but also very little is known about their intended use and the way

---

[1] *Great Pow.* NHC VI,4, 42,23–31 (Meyer 2007a).

they were read. We often know little about the texts the author had in mind when writing his own tract, texts that he would have expected the more or less competent reader to recognize.[2] Neither do we have much explicit knowledge of the context(s) of the texts in antiquity, what kind of impact the author hoped to have on the reader, or who the intended reader was. Was the main concern of the texts to make theological statements or were the texts intended as part of a religious practice? Of course no single answer can cover the host of texts now in our possession, but assumptions can be made as to the overall context in which the texts are to be understood, and for this the few lines from *The Concept of Our Great Power* are important.

Thus, what the passage seems to suggest is that the path to the understanding (*noein*) of the truth consist of two levels: understanding (*noein*) that which is *discussed* and that which is *revealed*.[3] Given that we are entitled to see this as a distinction between discursive knowledge and revelation (i.e. noetic knowledge) and the first as a precondition for the last, we may assume the text at hand is at least part of the salvific instruction necessary for bringing about the understanding of the truth. This is quite in line with the saying of Sallustius: "the mind sees all things, words express some first other thereafter."[4] Consequently the text could be intended as instrumental in the transformation that leads to salvation. This function is particularly clear in the case of the hermetic texts, but it is testified as well in other Gnostic texts.[5] Further these texts can be seen as belonging to the *religio mentis* prevalent in Hellenistic and Roman time, that made the "inner man" (often called the soul or spirit) the battleground for a soteriology that aimed at

---

[2] For instance, the initial words "eight days three days before he celebrated Passover" (*Gos. Jud.* TC 33,3 ff.). These obscure words are unparalleled in the NT, but rather than assuming a mistake on behalf of the copyist, it seems that *Gos. Jud.* shares a mytheme also known from the apocryphal *Narrative of Joseph of Arimathaea* §1, namely that Jesus was taken twice. The first took place "on the third day before the Passover". This reminds us that although "Christianity" is by far the best documented religion of late antiquity, only a fraction of the texts produced has been handed down.

[3] The text is perhaps playing on the two different levels of understanding covered by *noein*, namely that which is perceived by the eyes and that which is perceived by mind, observed respectively apprehended, placing the latter on top.

[4] Sallustius, *On the Gods and the World*, §4.

[5] CH 4.10; CH 16.2; *Disc. 8–9* VI, 6, 54, 6 ff.; 54, 13 ff.; *Gos. Thom.* NHC II,2, log. 1; *Jas.* TC,2, 29,9; *Apoc. Jas.* NHC V,3, 41,9–10 1; *Eugnostos* NHC III,3, 90,4; 74,19–20 ("This is a beginning to gnosis", ⲟⲩⲁⲣⲭⲏ ⲛ̄ⲥⲟⲟⲩⲛ ⲧⲉ ⲧⲁⲓ); 76,13–14. *1 Jeu* 1.

bringing him into congruence with god.[6] In order to make the person fulfil his human potential these movements developed different kinds of rituals, meditations and hierarchical structures both with regard to mythological and social structures.[7] And of course texts.

In the following the *Gospel of Judas* will be approached from the perspective of the *religio mentis*. I will examine the use of rhetorical and didactical strategies in the Gospel known from contemporary texts such as the platonic dialogue *Meno* and the hermetic text Corpus Hermeticum 13. The first section of the paper draws attention to the importance of the platonic tripartite epistemology (*doxa, aporia, episteme*) for understanding the course of argument in the dialogue, i.e. the notion that in order for the interlocutor to be able to gain true knowledge he must first get rid of false assumptions (*doxa*); this manifests itself in the mental collapse (*aporia*) of the interlocutor, which is the epistemological point of zero. Reaching this point is the decisive condition for the spiritual breakthrough to take place.

Further by distinguishing between "the text internal level" and "the reader response level," attention is drawn to the impact of the dialogue on the reader. In turn these results are applied in the analysis of the hermetic text CH 13 and followed by a summary of the results. In the light of the results, the Gospel is approached in the last section of the paper, suggesting that the results may elucidate what kind of work the Gospel does for the reader, and how. The results will also illuminate the way in which the text can be regarded as instrumental in bringing about salvation. As an additional benefit we may also be able to further qualify the discussion of the fate of Judas.

Initially the problem of the intended reader of the text needs to be addressed. Several different groupings can be imagined as intended audiences for the text. If we follow the different soteriological groupings outlined by *The Apocryphon of John* (NHC II, 1,25,16–27,30) we are left with four possibilities: 1) the spiritual athletes, 2) "ordinary" spirituals 3) those in need of additional reincarnation in order to be saved, and 4) the apostates whom eternal punishment awaits. With regard to 1–3 the text may serve to confirm their belief. If this is so, it is likewise clear with regards to 4), the apostates, that the text does

---

[6] This interest in the transformation of man, by putting aside the delusions of the senses in order to bring forth the inner man, was not a novelty of Late Antiquity, as the numerous studies of Pierre Hadot has shown.
[7] Sørensen 1999, 111.

not seem to reveal anything else except what was probably common knowledge for an insider as well as for an apostate (a former-insider). Thus, a fifth category needs to be added.

Since the text addresses and dismisses central doctrine of mainstream Christianity and subsequently replaces them by new ones, it seems very likely that the intended reader was not a person adhering to the core of the group, but rather either remotely attached to it or an outsider. Thus, the text may be considered "a call to conversion" and as such it is enrolled among the protreptic writings known from church fathers and philosophers alike.

THE DIALOGUE AS A MODEL

Although the *Gospel of Judas* must be considered formally a gospel because of its title, it meets the specifications for a dialogue as well.[8] As noticed by Pheme Perkins, the Gnostic dialogues seem to have drawn on a variety of models. The dialogues, she argues, do not "aim at an exchange of ideas and an examination of philosophical positions" but "merely provide the revealer with an opportunity *to discharge his mission*" i.e. to set *"off statements of Gnostic myth and teaching"* (my emphasis). Thus the philosophical dialogue tradition is not likely to have been a source for the Gnostic composition.[9] Instead she suggests that more proximate models are represented by Jewish apocalypses with their heavenly journeys and the hermetic teacher-student dialogues, which she considers to be interested primarily in a philosophical description of reality and the soul's divinization.[10]

Two things should be noticed. Despite Perkins' reluctance to derive Gnostic dialogues from the philosophical dialogue, reading the Gospel against the background of the didactic strategy as known from the early dialogues of Plato might shed light on both the line of argument of the dialogue and its significance to the reader. Likewise it should be noticed that Perkins' implicit understanding presupposes that the aim of the philosophical dialogue is to exchange ideas and examine posi-

---

[8] See Rudolph 1996, Perkins 1980.

[9] Perkins 1980, 19.

[10] Likewise Perkins notices that the *erotapokriseis* has been suggested as the model followed by the Gnostics, but rejects, as does also Rudolph, that the Gnostic dialogues can be reduced to the model of Q&A of this genre since it lacks the introductory "setting" characteristic of both philosophical and Gnostic dialogues (Perkins 1980, 20).

tions and as well her assumption that the Gnostic dialogues provide opportunity to set off statements of myth and teaching seems to imply a too narrow understanding of the dialogue genre. The point of both is less that of setting forth theoretical systems, than to provide methods for transforming the "reader's" perception of being as well as himself. As Pierre Hadot has pointed out, ancient philosophy proposed to mankind an art of living."[11]

Plato and the Dialogue

It is often said that it is in Plato's early works that the dialogue is most authentic, centered around Socrates' questioning of his interlocutor who considers himself to pose knowledge on a given subject. In the course of the dialogue, however, it is revealed that the knowledge of the interlocutor is not knowledge proper, but *doxa*, i.e. false or only apparent knowledge, opinion.[12] As a consequence of this disclosure the interlocutor is carried to the point of perplexity (*aporia*), and this is in fact the point of the dialogue. Thus, the point of the dialogue is not to *teach* knowledge, since the knowledge coveted is of such a nature that cannot be gained from others; one needs to *acquire* it by oneself. In order for this to take place the interlocutor must rid himself of all false assumptions—the consequence of which is aporia, i.e. to be placed in a condition from which there is no escape. Only then is it possible to locate the true path to knowledge.[13] This is what is expressed through the metaphor of *maieusis*, midwifery. The role of Socrates is not to give birth to, but to deliver the thought of the interlocutor. Or from a different perspective, discourses (or texts) are deliverers of the mind.

A good example of this is found in the dialogue *Meno*. For the present purpose, there is no need to go into details as to the philosophical arguments of the dialogue, since the suggestion of this paper has less to do with these arguments than with the epistemology imbedded in the discourse. Thus, it suffices to note that Socrates' interlocutor Meno is said to be a distinguished man from Thessaly, well-educated by the sophist Gorgias, from whom he had learned the nature of *aretê*—to such a degree that he even considered himself capable of teaching others. However, entering into conversation with Socrates brings about a

---

[11] Hadot 1995, 272.
[12] On true and false opinion (doxa), see Desjardins 1990, 3 ff.
[13] See Sløk 1992, 33; Desjardins 1990, 4 ff.; Sayre 1995.

dramatic change in his self esteem, because he realizes that what he
thought he knew, he does in fact not know. None of the three definitions on the nature of the nature of *aretê* that he is able to put forward
can survive the scrupulous investigation of Socrates. This leads to an
increasing degree of resignation and perplexity. Thus, although Meno
in the beginning of the conversation shows great confidence in his
own knowledge concerning the nature of *arête*,—as the good student
he believes to have done his homework,—he realizes during the questioning of Socrates that this is not the case. Having realized that his
third and last definition is guilty of the elementary logical error circu-
larism, he simply gives up and declares that Socrates is comparable to
the electrical ray paralysing whoever gets near him.

In other words, Meno is left in complete perplexity (*aporia*) and
appears to have lost all hope of ever getting to know the nature of
aretê. But as is well-known this is not the end of the dialogue. Meno's
perplexity is rather the necessary precondition for the possibility of
acquiring true knowledge. Only by reaching the epistemological point
of absolute zero is this possible. Thus Socrates and Meno set out on
a joint quest for the nature of *aretê*. Unfortunately, for Meno as well
as the reader, the dialogue ends without reaching a conclusion to the
discussion. But the reason why the dialogue ends without coming to
fruition is that *episteme* is a non-discursive knowledge. It cannot be
taught, only experienced. That the dialogue can be said to be *aporetic*
in a twofold sense has important bearings on the understanding of the
other texts under consideration here. But before leaving the Platonic
dialogue a quick word on the nature of the genre is needed.

The Dialogue as a Two Level Discourse

In order to understand how the dialogue works as a genre one has to
distinguish between two levels of discourse. The first level—we may
call it *the text internal level*—consists of the conversation in which the
interlocutors address each other in a discussion of a certain topic, e.g.
on the nature of *aretê*. It is on this level that the central figure of the
dialogue (i.e. Socrates) is conceived as addressing the other interlocutors, not the reader. This takes place on the second level.

This second level—*the reader response level*—consists of the dialogue
as text or book written by Plato. As a text, the written dialogue is a
fiction. Yet, it is with this fiction that the reader must engage. He must
disregard Plato and instead seek to take part in the debate by engaging

in the discussion not as reader, but as interlocutor, and to do it in such a way that he takes a stand on the arguments put forward in the text.[14] In other words the dialogue is intended to act upon the mind of the interlocutor-reader by offering a point of identification to which he can relate in his quest for knowledge. This point we may either locate in the literary representations of the text (*in casu* Meno) or alternatively in the *doxae* confronted and substituted by true knowledge.

Paying attention to these two levels of discourse as well as to the platonic tripartite epistemology (*doxa, aporia, episteme*) which are in play on both levels of discourse could prove useful for the understanding of the line of argument in both the *Gospel of Judas* and CH 13 to which we will turn first. In fact, a Platonic reading of the hermetic text comes close to what Reitzenstein termed "Lesemysterium," viz. a *Lehrschrift* simultaneously performing a ritual on the reader.[15]

The Hermetic Dialogue "On Rebirth"

Among the fragments of Codex Tchacos a few pieces suggest that the codex in addition to the four preserved texts originally contained a hermetic text known from Corpus Hermeticum as "On Rebirth" (CH 13). These hermetic texts were previously understood within the framework of various diverting philosophical doctrines and systems, but thanks to Garth Fowden's groundbreaking work, hermetism it is now generally regarded as a spiritual way—a teaching and initiation process—aimed at guiding the student-reader towards the mystical experience of god.[16]

"On Rebirth" starts by Tat reminding his teacher Hermes that the teaching on rebirth had been held out as a prospect for him, when he had begun to make himself a stranger to the world.[17] This teaching, we are told, is of the utmost importance, since it is emphasized that rebirth is a precondition for salvation, that results in man's deification.[18] Thus, CH 13 is located on the final step on the "Way of Immortality." This rebirth, however, is not pointed to as a distant soteriological goal, but as a mental state that is the result of a *praxis*.

---

[14] Sløk 1992, 28.
[15] Reitzenstein 1927, 51 ff.
[16] Fowden 1986; see also Mahé 1991; Petersen 2003.
[17] For various views regarding the origin of the concept of rebirth in the history of ideas, see Copenhaver 1992, 181 and Dodd 1953, 48.
[18] CH 13.1.10.

In order to account for the text's significance for the reader, Reitzenstein described it as a *Lesemysterium*. The term was not intended to designate the text as a mystery in the "narrow sense" of the word, but rather as a description of a mystery, set forth in a discourse and mixed with a doctrinal writing (*Lehrschrift*). Reitzenstein assumed that the author's intention was to play the role of a mystagogue hoping that his presentation would exert the same effect upon the reader as that of an actual mystery.[19] "In der Phantasie soll der Leser ein solches (Mysterium) erleben. Dem Wort, auch dem geschriebenen, kann die Wunderkraft anhaften, die mit der Handlung sich verbindet."[20]

It was presumably the mixture of teaching and performance that led Reitzenstein to hold that the words of the text were in one way or another efficacious or instrumental in assisting the reader to spiritual enlightenment.[21] Although his idea was never worked out in full detail, the concept of the *Lesemysterium* does have the merit of drawing attention to the impact of a text on the reader.

However, it appears that the Platonic dialogue may have been closer to the mind of the author of CH 13 than the ancient mystery cults, since the rhetorical strategy applied in the attempt to bring about the spiritual enlightenment of Tat seems strikingly similar to the Platonic didactical strategy applied in *Meno*. It is a strategy that fits well with Reitzenstein's close focus on the efficaciousness of the text on the reader. From the outset Tat, just as Meno, holds preliminary knowledge, setting him apart from the multitude. But despite his preparation, the lecture does not develop quite as imagined.

Throughout the text, Tat's lack of understanding is what moves the instruction forward. Thus Tat replies when he is unable to follow the

---

[19] Reitzenstein thus assumed that by reading the text, the reader would be able to experience the same as Tat when he heard the instruction: "Wer sie als Bücher veröffentlichte, erwartete zwar, dass der Leser, wenn Gott ihn begnaden will dieselbe Wirkung beim Lesen empfinden werde, wie Tat angeblich beim hören; die Wunderkraft der Gottesbotschaft wirkt auch in dem geschriebenen Wort," (1927, 64).

[20] Reitzenstein 1927, 51 f.

[21] This was noticed also by Festugière (1954, 210; 203 n. 1). Utilizing Reitzenstein's concept of *Lesemysterium* in analysing other Gnostic and hermetic texts, Sørensen remarks that these texts "refer to their own purpose in a way which at least resembles Reitzenstein's notion of the *Lesemysterium*. Beyond *Eugnostos* and CH 16, Sørensen refers to CH 4.11 as an example of a text which clearly instructs the student not merely to read the text, which is referred to as an image of God, but to behold it with the eyes of his heart, i.e. meditate upon it—a meditation that is said to prepare the way for spiritual understanding (1989, 55 f.).

instructions of his teacher: "I am entirely at a loss" (13.2), "You tell me a riddle; you do not speak as a father to a son" (13.2), "I have been borne a son strange to his father's race..." (13.3), "You have driven me quite mad..." (13.4), "...you have made me speechless, bereft of (my) wits..." (13.5), "I have really gone mad..." "I expected that I would have become wise through you, but the senses (αἴσθησις) of my mind (νόημα) have been blocked (13.6)." When Hermes subsequently declares regarding rebirth, "How can you understand it through the senses—something understood only through its power and energy yet requiring one empowered to understand the birth in god?" this makes Tat cry out, "Then, I am incapable, O Father (Ἀδύνατος οὖν εἰμι, ὦ πάτερ)."[22]

This however, does not imply that Tat suddenly realizes that what he had previously been promised will in fact never be fulfilled. On the contrary, just as we saw with regard to Meno, reaching the point of absolute zero is not the end but in fact the beginning of Tat's quest for novel insights into the true coherence of the world. Read in context, Tat's aporetic outburst signifies that although he thought that he had done his homework properly and thus was well prepared before the final lecture, the state of perplexity is needed in order to gain true knowledge. Thus it is significant that exactly at this point where Tat has reached the state of aporia the text initiates the decisive instruction on "the irrational torments of matter" intended to lead Tat towards rebirth.[23] Compared to Meno, which continues to follow the line of dialogue, the dialogue between Hermes and Tat, which in the first part is characterized by rapid questions and answers, changes into an instruction proper in which Hermes so to speak is "filling the empty vessel" that Tat has become. As the result of the rebirth, Tat has become what other hermetic texts designate as the perfect human (τέλειος ἄνθρωπος).[24]

---

[22] CH 13.7 (Nock-Festugière 1946); trans: mine.

[23] CH 13.7, 11 ff.

[24] CH 4.4. This, however, does not prevent him from posing questions that do not exactly seem too bright, but which nevertheless lead to further instructions from his teacher (§14). A comparable example involving preliminary knowledge, perplexity and redemption although in a mythological clothing is found in a short passage in Hyp. Arch. in which Norea, the heroine of the story, is met by the foul rulers, who attempt to rape her, demanding that she serves them as they claim her mother did. Norea's preliminary knowledge tells her that this was not the case, since she knows that she is "from above". This knowledge, however, is not sufficiently for her to escape their grasp, leading her to call upon "the holy one, the god of the entirety". As reply

Common to *Meno* and CH 13 at *the text internal level* is that the interlocutors of both Socrates and Hermes believe themselves to hold true knowledge, and that this misconception is confronted in the course of the dialogue. The confrontation of the false or insufficient knowledge, which prevents the interlocutor from gaining true knowledge, takes place in such a way that it leads the interlocutors to perplexity (*aporia*). Reaching the state of *aporia*, which according to Plato is indeed a very painful process, is the necessary precondition or state for gaining true knowledge.

From this follows that a reading of the texts on *the reader response level* should pay attention to the fact that the statements of the interlocutors of Socrates and Hermes express false or at best insufficient knowledge and as such are not intended to be received and adopted by the interlocutor-reader. On the contrary. They reflect a spiritual process and are either to be regarded as *doxa* (which must be abandoned and disregarded if the interlocutor-reader is to gain true knowledge), or they are to be seen as outbursts of *aporia*. In no way are we to understand them as doctrines that the author wishes to convey to the reader. The important point to notice is that the purpose of the character delineation of Meno and Tat is not to (re)present them as having fixed characters, but on the contrary to delineate their development. As a consequence, when assessing the statements regarding the status of the interlocutors, the preferable reading strategy is to give precedence to this dynamic rather than to see the statements as conveying static doctrines.

The dialogues under consideration represent a genre that puts forward arguments or statements to which the interlocutor-reader must actively relate, that is, to make them his own. Some are to be abandoned, while others are to be accepted, in order for the transformation to take place. The effect which the reader-response level of the text has on the reader is well-captured by Reitzenstein's *"Lesemysterium"*.

Eleleth arrives with the task of saving and telling her about her origin: "Do you think these rulers have any power over you?... These authorities cannot defile you and that generation; for your abode is in incorruptibility, where the virgin spirit dwells..." (*Hyp. Arch.* NHC II,4, 92,20 ff. [Layton 1978]). This is followed by an instruction on cosmology that professes to have soteriological significance not only for Norea but for future generations as well. Thus, expressing the consequences of the instruction it is said at the end of the text that "all who have become acquainted with this way exist deathless in the midst of dying mankind" (96,25).

The *Gospel of Judas* as dialogue

In the following, the *Gospel of Judas* will be read from the point of view of *religio mentis*. For the sake of clarity, the text will be approached first from the text-internal perspective, focusing on the aporetic epistemological rhetoric of the text, second from the reader-response perspective investigating the content of the *doxae* confronted. In the last section, the inevitable question of the nature of the fate of Judas foreseen by the text will be discussed briefly.

One of the intriguing aspects of the *Gospel of Judas* is the apparent absent of a figure capable of serving as a role model for the reader, in so far that Judas gains nothing from his instruction. Thus, it has been suggested that the message of the gospel depends on the reader's perspective—that the story is about tragedy if you are Judas, about ridicule if you are an apostolic Christian, and if you are a Sethian, it is a story of humour.[25] Of course different readers respond differently to a text; some Christians might find the *Gospel of Judas* ridiculous, and some would most probably be offended, but I hesitate to believe that Sethians would have considered the gospel a story of humour and laughter. To the author, I believe, the message of the gospel was indeed seriously meant.

But why did the author choose to write a text in the dialogue genre instead of a hymn, sermon, prayer, or some other genre to convey his message?[26] And why did he not explain explicitly the status of Judas and the salvation of humankind for whose sake Jesus appeared on earth according to the gospel?[27] One reason to choose the dialogue genre could be that it was well-known from other gospels that Jesus engaged in conversations with his disciples, just a Socrates was known to do. Since neither the dialogues of Plato nor CH 13 are to be considered recordings of conversations which took place in the past, but literary works that engage the reader in the quest for knowledge as interlocutor, I suggest that we approach the Gospel in like manner.

By approaching the Gospel as a "*Lesemysterium,*" employing the Platonic didactic and reading the gospel from what was previously termed the *reader-response level*, we realize that the gospel actually

---

[25] DeConick 2007, 140.
[26] See Sayre 1995.
[27] *Gos. Jud.* TC 33,6 ff.

does offer points of identification for the reader, namely the disciples *and* Judas, or, to be more exact, the *positions* of both.[28] By means of the Platonic didactic strategy, the author sets up a scenario easily recognizable by the reader and invites him to engage in the dialogue as interlocutor by meeting him in his *doxa*, that is, not to confirm, but to confront and to reject his *doxa*.

The Aporetic Epistemological Rhetoric of the Text

Approached from *the text-internal level*, it is immediately clear that the dialogue of the *Gospel of Judas* is somewhat more complicated than *Meno* and CH 13, since the conversation in the Gospel is not restricted to two interlocutors. It involves Jesus as well as the disciples and Judas. It even places them, at least at the outset, in opposition to each other, although in the end, they appear to be equally wrong according to most commentators.

Thus, if we for a moment restrict ourselves to Judas' part of the dialogue since he is the only one among the disciples able to respond as a competent student to Jesus' initial challenge to bring forth the perfect human (ⲡⲣⲱ[ⲙ]ⲉ ⲛ̅ⲧⲉⲗⲓⲟⲥ) and to stand before him,[29] and if we also disregard the fact that the text twice explicitly seems to state that Judas will gain nothing from the instruction received, the structure of the rather short dialogue between Jesus and Judas quite closely follows the didactical rhetorical pattern: preliminary knowledge; perplexity; instruction regarding the true nature of the universe.

The rather short dialogue between Jesus and Judas in the first half of the Gospel consist of just three scenes.[30] As is well known from the very first (explicit) appearance of Judas in the dialogue, it is evident that he does hold a preliminary knowledge: "I know who you are and from what place you have come. You have come from the immortal aeon of Barbelo. And I am not worthy to utter the name of the one who has sent you."[31] This statement appears to qualify him in a special way since Jesus encourages him to separate himself from the other disciples.[32] But contrary to what one might expect, this does

---

[28] See Brankaer-Bethge 2007, 258.
[29] *Gos. Jud.* TC 35,2–5.
[30] *Gos. Jud.* TC through 47,1.
[31] *Gos. Jud.* TC 35,15–20 (trans. Kasser et al. 2007).
[32] *Gos. Jud.* TC 35,24.

not become the starting point for a straightforward instruction but rather for an increasing perplexity. Instead of replying to Judas' question about when Jesus will tell him "these things," the scene ends by Jesus leaving him.[33] In the second scene following Jesus' interpretation of the dream of the disciples, Judas is told about the different generations and their destinies.

The peek of perplexity in the text is reached in the third scene, when Judas in response to Jesus' interpretation of his dream concludes that he in fact will never join the holy men in the house: "At no time may my seed control the Archons!" and asks "What is the advantage I received, since you have separated me from that generation?[34] This has been taken as proving that Judas will never join the holy generation and that he is even well aware of this.[35] However, we should bear in mind that although Tat's outburst "Then, I am incapable!?" in CH 13.7 signifies that he takes the preceding words of his teacher to mean that an insurmountable barrier has been set up, preventing him from reaching the desired rebirth, the subsequent text proves him wrong. Instead, his total *aporia* becomes the starting point of the instruction proper. And this is exactly what appears to happen in the gospel.

Similar to the rhetoric followed by the hermetic text, Judas' statements do not end the dialogue, but rather marks the beginning of the instruction of the second half of the gospel on cosmogony and

---

[33] *Gos. Jud.* TC 36,6, 9–10. The passage in which Judas asks about the destiny of the generation (43,12 ff.) seems to serve as transition from the instruction of the disciples to that of Judas since the author looses interest in the disciples after the reference to parable of the Sower. In passing we may notice that since stone and Peter are synonymous in Greek the reader would most probably see the reference to the parable as an attempt to reject the apostolic church's claim to authority.

[34] *Gos. Jud.* TC 46,6 (trans. DeConick 2007); 46,16 ff. (trans. DeConick 2007). The nature of this generation is not quite clear. In this volume, Gathercole sees the generation as related to the kingdom, but if that is the case, it is puzzling that Judas is made to react in two different ways to what appears to be two similar statements of Jesus. In the first place it seems to leave him unaffected that he is to be separated from the disciples and the kingdom (*Gos. Jud.* TC 35,23–36, 10) while he is affected when he concludes that he has been separated from the generation (46,16). This suggests to me that the reason why is because he appears to be stuck in the middle—betwixt and between the two alternatives disciples or generation. Thus, he seems to be aware that the kingdom is not a desirable place. The ideal reader on the other hand knowing the kingdom as the ultimate goal and Judas as *the* evil *par excellence* would quite happily accept Jesus statement as meaning that Judas is excluded from something attractive.

[35] DeConick 2007, 52.

anthropogony concerning things no one had seen before.[36] Reaching the end of the instruction Jesus declares: "Look, you have been told everything. Lift up your eyes and look at the cloud and the light within it..."[37] Thus, as a result of receiving the instruction Judas appears to be able to see what no one has seen before. The structural similarities between the two texts should warn us against drawing too hasty conclusions regarding the fate of Judas on the basis of his aporetic outburst.

While the part of the text devoted exclusively to the dialogue between Jesus and Judas consists of less than half of the first section of the gospel, the aporetic character of the text becomes more distinct if we include the dialogue between Jesus and all the disciples. On three occasions, as a consequence of having their alleged knowledge exposed as *doxa*, the reaction of the disciples is characterised by the word ϣⲧⲟⲣⲧⲣ.[38] The first time is as a reaction to Jesus' rejection of their Eucharist, their understanding of who he is and their lack of ability to know him.[39] The second time comes after realizing that they do not belong to the great and holy generation.[40] The third time follows after the disciples tell Jesus about their dream.[41]

If these similarities between the *Gospel of Judas* and CH 13 indeed suggest that the author works within the framework of the Platonic didactic dialogue, we may next ask what *doxae* the dialogue confronts.

The level of reader-response interpretation confronting the doxae

What are the *doxae* that prevent the interlocutor-reader from being saved? In short, the text presents an argument for re-evaluating what other Christians (who are known, for example, from Irenaeus) adhered to as central Christian doctrines. Apart from the Eucharist, the main

---

[36] Before reaching the end of the instruction Judas asks as to the life expectancy of humans and the fate of the soul "[what] is the longest that a person will live?", "does the human spirit die" (*Gos. Jud.* TC 53, 17), and concerning the fate of those baptised in the name of Jesus (55,21 ff.). This seems to be paralleled in Tat's question to Hermes, "does the (spiritual) body constituted of powers ever succumb to dissolution?" §14 (Copenhaver 1992).

[37] *Gos. Jud.* TC 57,15 (Kasser et al. 2007).

[38] ϣⲧⲟⲣⲧⲣ can be a translation of a variety of Greek words, one of which is aporia, Crum 1939, 597b.

[39] *Gos. Jud.* TC 34,18.

[40] *Gos. Jud.* TC 37,18.

[41] *Gos. Jud.* TC 39,5.

points of these doctrines concern the nature of Jesus, the authority and status of the disciples, the "perfect man" (ⲡⲣⲱⲙⲉ ⲛ̅ⲧⲉⲗⲓⲟⲥ), the question of "membership" of the elect or holy generation, eschatology, and perhaps the role of Judas. Basically, they all go back to the question of knowing who Jesus is.

As one would expect, the refutation of the reader's *doxae* mainly takes place in the first section of the text. The prologue of the text sets off on neutral as well as common ground, hinting at matters well-known by all kinds of contemporary Christians. Thus it is stated that Jesus came for the salvation of humankind and that some walked the way of righteousness and some in their transgressions.[42] But provided that the ideal reader belongs to mainstream Christianity, his *doxae* will soon be challenged as he realizes that, according to this secret discourse, he does not walk the path of righteousness, but rather in his transgressions. The prologue ends by addressing the interlocutor-reader directly, assigning him a privileged position at the expense of the disciples.[43]

Thus, in the first scene new and disturbing insights are presented to the reader. To perform the Eucharist is not to do what is right. It is not to give praise to the Father of Jesus, but to the god of the disciples. Thus, the Eucharist is not a valid soteriological tool which is why Jesus laughs instead of approving the disciples' action.[44] Neither the disciples nor any generation from them shall know Jesus.[45]

The *doxa* that salvation can be gained from imitating the disciples is rejected twice. First it is rejected in the scene in which Jesus challenges them to lead forward the perfect man, ⲡⲣⲱⲙⲉ ⲛ̅ⲧⲉⲗⲓⲟⲥ. Contrary to what our ideal reader would expect, none of the other disciples are able to pass the test, but only Judas who gives the highly surprising answer that he knows who Jesus is and that he comes from Barbelo. Since to be ⲡⲣⲱⲙⲉ ⲛ̅ⲧⲉⲗⲓⲟⲥ is linked to knowing Jesus, it is reasonable to suspect that the intertext which would be called to mind of

---

[42] For righteous, see Matt 21:32; 2Pet 2:21; Prov 8:20, 12:28, 16:17, 16:31. For transgressors, see 2 Cor 11:3; Eph 4:14; Titus 3:3, 3:11; Heb 13:9.

[43] Jesus revealed himself only occasionally to the disciples, whereas "you (singular) would find him among them…" (*Gos. Jud.* TC 33,20–21).

[44] It should be noticed that Jesus explicitly states that he is not laughing at the disciples. The nature of this laughter is debated, but note that ⲥⲱⲃⲉ is a neutral term, see *Der Erste Setna-Roman* (P. Kairo 30646); 3,4; 6,2; in particular 3,10–12 (cp. TC 34,2ff. and 55,12); "*Warum lachst du über mich? Er sagte: Ich lachte nicht über dich, ich habe gelacht, weil du Schriften liest, di nicht haben* (?) […]".

[45] *Gos. Jud.* TC 34,4 ff. In addition to this the reader learns that anger and perplexion are from the god of the disciples (= Rom 4:15 "For the law brings wrath").

the ideal reader would be Eph. 4:13.[46] Thus: "until we all reach unity in the faith and in knowledge of the son of God and become perfect man (ἀνήρ τέλειος) (sahidic: ⲉⲩⲣⲱⲙⲉ ⲛⲧⲉⲗⲓⲟⲥ)."[47] In fact we may consider the whole section 34,4–35,9 in the *Gospel of Judas* an exegesis on this passage intended to confront the assumption that the true Christians should be those of mainstream Christianity. The disciples and their followers are presented as having neither oneness in faith since they are disputing divinity.[48] Nor do they have knowledge of the son of God since they neither know Jesus nor his father. From this it follows that none of them are a perfect man.

In the second rejection of the disciples as role models, the reason is given for their impotence. Contrary to what one would expect, the reader realizes that it is not they who belong to the great and holy race, but someone quite different from them.[49] Thus, contrary to what the engaged reader might expect, it is rejected as *doxae* that the Eucharist is a soteriological tool, that the disciples (and their followers) are role models assigned a privileged position, and that Jesus is the son of the god of the disciples.

But these are not the only *doxae* confronted. The gospel makes an additional point with regard to eschatology and soteriology revealing that the eschatological expectations associated with the teaching of the disciples are anything but desirable. This takes place in the section that opens with the notorious passage in which Jesus, as a result of Judas' confession, encourages him to step away from the other disciples. He tells him this since Jesus knew that he was thinking upon something exalted and wants to tell him the mysteries of the kingdom, but "not so that you will go there, but you will grieve a great deal. For

---

[46] See also i.e. Heb 5:14; Col 1:26; 4:12.

[47] μέχρι καταντήσωμεν οἱ πάντες εἰς τὴν ἑνότητα τῆς πίστεως καὶ τῆς ἐπιγνώσεως τοῦ υἱοῦ τοῦ θεοῦ, εἰς ἄνδρα τέλειον... Eph 4:13.

[48] What the disciples actually are doing when Jesus first approaches them are somewhat unclear. According to the Coptic text they are ⲣ̄ ⲅⲩⲙⲛⲁⲍⲉ ⲉⲧⲙⲛⲧⲛⲟⲩⲧⲉ. This either mean that they are practicing divinity, thus performing some kind of spiritual exercise, or they might be disputing divinity, as suggested by Nagel 2007, 240, 260 referring to *Gos. Mary* BG,1,9,20–23. See also Eus. *Hist. eccl.* 7.7.5. Given the overall critic of the disciples' belief and practice in the text and the fact that the same construction is used in *Gos. Jud.* TC 44,20 it seems reasonable to give precedence to Nagel's suggestion (2007,260 ff.). For likely intertexts, see also 2 Tim 2:14 ff.; Heb 5.14. Either way, the ambiguity might be deliberately chosen.

[49] *Gos. Jud.* TC 36,13 ff. Cf. Matt 24:24; 24:31; Luke 6:13; Col 3:12; 2 Thess 2:13; Titus 1,1; 1 Pet 1:1; Rev 17:19.

someone else will replace you, in order that the 12 [disciples] may again come to completion in their god."[50] This marks the beginning of a rather lengthy passage that ends in Jesus' summary-statement.[51] Unfortunately, this statement is rather badly damaged, but what is left does seem to suggest that Jesus recapitulates what has been said about the kingdom, the influence of the stars and perhaps also something related to "above the twelve realms". But what happens, according to April DeConick, is that Judas is excluded from the kingdom, which she identifies with the house that he subsequently sees in the great vision, because he is not worthy of entering.[52] This, however, may not necessarily be the case. Contrary to this, Simon Gathercole argues in his contribution to this volume that the opposite might well be the case, namely that it is the *kingdom* that is not worthy of Judas, and that the kingdom is a specific reference to the twelve disciples and the apostolic church, thus making the kingdom *their* destiny. Therefore, in spatial terms the kingdom seems to be located beneath the place foreseen for Judas since he is to be above in the 13th Aeon.

To this we might add that reading the text from the reader-response perspective suggests that the author's intent is to correct *doxae* related to eschatology and soteriology. That the notion of the kingdom is closely related to eschatology is seen from Judas' reply to the promises of Jesus. He replies with a double question: "when will you tell me these things" and "when will the great day of light dawn for the [...] generation?"[53] The great day of light, as well as the kingdom, are well known notions of eschatology.

Understanding the dream of the disciples as intentional counter-teaching about traditional eschatological expectations about the manifestation of the kingdom on earth goes along with the fact that [Ath]eth, the first among the angels ruling over chaos and Hades, is called Christ

---

[50] *Gos. Jud.* TC 35,26–36,4 (Kasser et al. 2007). For "exalted", see also 57,10.

[51] *Gos. Jud.* TC 45,24–46,4.

[52] DeConick 2007, 52. Could "house" refer to "The wonderful mystery of your house," *Pr. Paul*? Likewise "vision" to "when you see the Eternal Existent, that is the great vision" *Dial. Sav.* III,5, 137,3 ff.?

[53] *Gos. Jud.* TC 36,6–9 (Kasser et al. 2007). Perhaps Judas' initial double question is not to be taken as redundant, but rather to be dealing with to different eschatologies, a mainstream Christian (the kingdom) and a Gnostic (the great day of light, as far as I know this concept is only attested in Gnostic texts).

as well.[54] This is a truly subordinate Christology![55] It also fits with what is said to take place when Saklas has finished his time, which actually seems to recapitulate the dream of the disciples.[56] Thus we may regard the interpretation of the dream of the disciples to be revealing the true nature of the kingdom that Mark 1:15 warns is approaching.

At the reader-response level at least three things happen. First, it is rejected that to belong to the tradition of the disciples is to belong to the holy generation. Second, an account is given of two different eschatological perspectives: the mysteries of the kingdom, which is the perspective foreseen for those adhering to the disciples; and a large house where mention is made of the holy generation. Third, with regard to the soteriology, the *doxa* rejected is the assumption that mortals can have access to salvation. This is most likely related to ⲡⲣⲱⲙⲉ ⲛⲧⲉⲗⲓⲟⲥ and to the section on baptism that unfortunately is missing. In short, in order to follow the way of righteousness one needs to abandon the way of the disciples, their kingdom and its god in favour of the holy generation and the house.

The Status of Judas in Light of the Didactic Rhetoric of the Text

Teacher, enough! At no time may my seed control/be controlled by the Archons! ⲡⲥⲁϩ ⲙⲏⲡⲟⲧⲉ ϩⲱ ⲡⲁⲥⲡⲉⲣⲙⲁ ϩⲩⲡⲟⲧⲁⲥⲥ[ⲉ] ⲛⲛⲁⲣⲭⲱⲛ.[57]

As April DeConick notes, Judas is not asking a question but makes an emphatic statement.[58] Together with the statement of 46,14 ("What is the advantage?") and the statements negated by ⲟⲩⲭ ϩⲓⲛⲁ (35,26) and ⲛⲉⲕⲃⲱⲕ (46,25) this has been read as declaring that Judas will gain nothing from the instruction, and that he himself is well aware of this. At this point the Gospel would seem to deviate from *Meno* and CH 13 by turning the Platonic rhetoric upside down, transposing the aporetic outburst and question of the frustrated student into prophetic statements that reveals his sad destiny making him little more than the plaything of Jesus.[59]

---

[54] *Gos. Jud.* TC 52,4 f.
[55] For Christ as one of Sabaoth's associates, see *Orig. World* NHC II,5, 114,17 "Sabaoth and his Christ" and *Tri. Prot.* NHC XIII,1, 49,7? For a different interpretation of [Ath]eth and Christ (XC), see Kasser et al. 2008, 47, DeConick 2007, 112 and the chapter by DeConick in this volume.
[56] *Gos. Jud.* TC 54,19.
[57] *Gos. Jud.* TC 46,6 (trans. DeConick 2007).
[58] DeConick 2007, 53.
[59] Likewise the negation turns the grief foreseen for Judas into his destiny, whereas in Plato knowledge is produced in pain. Concerning grieving and suffering, see also

But within this perspective one may ask what exactly is taking place in the passage on p. 46,6? According to DeConick, it deals with the fate of Judas.[60] But this seems only to be the case in an indirect manner, since the text does not state that "my fate" or "my life" is under control of the Archons!" To the contrary, it is the *seed* of Judas that is controlled by the Archons. Why does the author mention the seed of Judas? And who is this seed? If the text does depict Judas as the bad guy in charge of the apostolic church, the answer to the question would be that the seed is the Christians adhering to this group.

That, however, might not be the case, since the text sets up the dichotomy between the god of the disciples and Judas and states that Judas will be cursed by the *other* generations.[61] Instead, it might be suggested that the text has more than one polemical edge. Apart from "the apostolic church," the polemic could also be directed against Christian Gnostics known from Irenaeus and Epiphanius, Gnostics who saw a positive potential in Judas in regard to salvation.[62] Thus, the polemical point could be first the rejection of apostolic Christianity and second the rejection of the Gnostic Christian idea that Judas was instrumental in a positive way in the process of salvation.

But interpreting the Gospel from the perspective of Platonic didactic rhetoric seems to have rather interesting implications for the understanding of the four passages and thereby for the text as a whole. From this approach it appears that the passage is alluding to Judas as representative of the immortal race.[63] The dialogue-approach suggests

---

Ap. John NHC II,1, 1,20: "I grieved [greatly in my heart];" *Gos. Thom.* NHC II,2, log. 58: "Blessed is the man who has suffered, and found life;" log. 2: "Let him who seeks continue seeking until he finds. When he finds, he will become troubled. When he becomes troubled, he will be astonished, and he will rule over the all;" 2 Cor 5:1–2 (NRSV): "For we know that if the earthly tent we live in is destroyed, we have a building from God, a house not made with hands, eternal in the heavens. For in this tent we groan, longing to be clothed with our heavenly dwelling;" cf. 2 Cor 5:6; Rom 8:13. Cf. Iren., *Adv. Haer* 2.20.2 (ANF 1): "the passion (*passio*) of the twelfth Æon (i.e. Achamoth) was proved (*demonstro*) through the conduct of Judas…being an emblem (*typus*) of her;" and *Haer.* 1.3.3, 4.1, 4.5, 7.1. On Judas and Achamoth, see Petersen 2007; also Meyer 2008.

[60] DeConick 2007, 53.

[61] *Gos. Jud.* TC 36,2 ff.; 46,21 f.

[62] An example of polemic against doctrines upheld by "Gnostics" and others is found in *Melch.* NHC IX,4, 4–10.

[63] See Pagels-King 2007, 142. Wurst says that identifying Judas as a demon based on the demonology of Mark is problematic, since Gnostic demons are unable to know the divine (i.e. NHC VI, 4,41, 20ff.; TC 44, 9-13). Regarding the "Thirteenth" (TC 44,21; 46,20; 55,10f.), I do not see that it expresses the fixed character of Judas as Ialdabaoth. If this were so, why is Judas not cursed by *all* but only the *other* generations

that two of the four passages, namely Judas' statements on p. 46,6 and p. 46,14, can be regarded as expressions of the *aporia*-dynamic known from *Meno* and CH 13.[64] Concerning ⲟⲩⲭ ϩⲓⲛⲁ, we saw above that it is not to be taken for granted that it signifies that Jesus tells Judas that although he will be told "everything", he will never profit from it.[65] Rather, if this kingdom is related to *doxa* concerning eschatology as suggested above, this does not exclude the possibility that Judas will reach salvation. The rejection that it does make is related to Judas and his destiny. But the rejection seems in fact to be positive—Judas is not going to the kingdom, since this is a place no one wants to go to.

Likewise, we may notice that other explanations than exclusion from salvation can account for the grieving foreseen for Judas. It could be explained in the light of the *Exegesis on the Soul*, which stresses the importance of the relation between repentance and distress, grief, sigh and weeping for obtaining salvation.[66] It could imply that, after he is told that he now knows something better waits him in the future, he groans in longing, just as we find it in *Romans* 8:23: "We ourselves, who have the first fruits of the Spirit, groan inwardly while we wait for adoption, the redemption of our bodies" and in 2 *Corinthians* 5.[67] Since his grieving is related to seeing the (archontic) "kingdom and all

---

(TC 46:22)? If it is bad for Judas that his star will rule over the thirteenth aeon, why does Jesus subsequently state that he is not laughing at Judas but at the error of the stars (TC 55,10ff.)? The reference to the thirteenth delineates Judas' development, utilising a mythem found in *Pistis Sophia* (cf. Bousset 1907:17ff.; Meyer 2008a, 2008b). See my forthcoming article on laughter and demonology.

[64] That education can be troublesome is testified by one of Libanius' students. He questioned "the aim of all the sweat" and the result he had achieved after "countless efforts" asking: "What is the gain (*ti kerdos*)?" (*Or.* 62.12 [Cribiore 2001, 11]). Painchaud is undoubtedly right that the question is echoing Ecclesiastes, but I hesitate to think that the intention should be that of assimilating Judas with the preacher/Solomon showing him to be a demon. Since, for instance, Origen's students first read Proverbs, then Ecclesiastes, then Songs of Songs—corresponding to ethics, physics and theology—another possibility is that the intertextual associations of the ideal reader would bring him back to his initial teaching—reminding him that the teaching on the Eccl. taught him about going beyond the sensory things, that visible and corporal things are fleeting and brittle leading to the renunciation of the world, and instead to reach out for the unseen and eternal things, Origen *Comm. Cant. Prol.* 3.1–23; see also Hadot 2004, 239f; Mansfeld 1994, 13.

[65] *Gos. Jud.* TC 35,26.

[66] *Ex. Soul* NHC II,6, 135,4 ff.

[67] What is at least to be assumed from 2 Cor 5:1–2, 4 is that Paul and the author of the *Gos. Jud.* share a mythological horizon related to the building metaphor, which distinguishes between an earthly and a heavenly building, attached to an earthly respectively heavenly existence, and that the earthly existence is considered an obstacle for entering the heavenly house, leaving spiritual man to groan, in longing for god.

its generation" we may also refer to the grieving of Sophia realizing the imperfection she gave birth to.[68]

Further, in the light of the Platonic didactic and the general context of spiritual growth, Jesus' statement about Judas being led astray by his star does not mean that Judas is eternally doomed. Rather it serves to explain why Judas misunderstood the situation, namely believing that he as mortal (without further notice) could enter the house and thus join the great men. The fact that the "mortal" is to be considered as synonymous with "human beings" indicates that in order to be able to enter the house, one needs to be or to become perfect human (ⲡⲣⲱⲙⲉ ⲛⲧⲉⲗⲓⲟⲥ).[69] Neither Judas nor the disciples have yet understood that salvation is a purely spiritual matter, and it is due to this lack of understanding that his subsequent perplexity can be understood. As we saw above, the perplexity does not represent the end but the beginning of the instruction.

However, the primary obstacle to this reading is of course the passage on p. 46,24 ff.: "And in the last days, they <missing lines> to you. And you will not ascend (ⲛⲉⲕⲃⲱⲕ) to the holy [generation]."[70] This appears quite explicitly to seal the destiny of Judas, but two questions should be raised.

The first has to do with the agent of the corrupt passage. Just before the passage, Jesus is said to answer Judas, telling him about what his enemies will do to him.[71] Then immediately following the corrupt passage, the text states that "Jesus said…"[72] Since the normal construction in the text seems only to mark who is talking when a change takes place, this might suggest that what is said on p. 46, 24 ff. is not a prediction by Jesus, but rather what is said by the disciples or enemies of Judas who want to curse him as well.[73] This could perhaps make sense since they themselves believe they belong to the holy generation.[74]

---

[68] *Gos. Jud.* TC 46,11 ff.; Iren., *Adv. Haer.* 1.2.3. Cf. note 59.

[69] *Gos Jud.* TC 35,2–3; 35,4. An explicit argument for the possibility of growing from one salvation group to another, is the call to stop sacrificing (41,1 f.).

[70] See DeConick 2009. 69–71, for a discussion of the passage and the sense of ⲛⲉⲕⲃⲱⲕ. Previously I took the ⲛⲉⲕ to be a conjunctive (Layton 2004, §351), but that appears not to be the case (Petersen 2007). Otherwise the construction with a number of future forms ending in a conjunctive would match the construction found in *Great Pow.* NHC 42,23–31.

[71] *Gos. Jud.* TC 46,18.

[72] *Gos. Jud.* TC 47,1.

[73] But see *Gos. Jud.* TC 39,5, 18. This point was suggested by my colleague Jørgen Podemann Sørensen. See also the quote 40,16 ff. followed by "Jesus said" in 41, 1.

[74] *Gos. Jud.* TC 36,19 ff.

The second question has to do with the lacuna. It has been suggested that a line or two could have dropped out between pp. 46,24 and 46, 25.[75] In that case, it becomes difficult to interpret the passage and one ought not to lay too much weight on it in the overall interpretation of the text. For what it is worth, the content of the missing line(s) could have been something like "And in the last days < perilous times / the great day of light / the Saviour > shall[76] < come, but before this happens they will... > to you and you will not ascend to the holy [generation]". But of course the problem is that we have no way of knowing how the text ran and that is actually my point.[77] Thus, I am not saying that Judas is a hero or the Gnostic *par excellence*, but merely pointing to the fact that due to the fragmented text, conclusive evidence for either position does not seem to be available. Depending on how we choose to construct the "*Sitz im Leben*" of the Gospel, different interpretations become possible. One may only hope that some of the missing pages eventually turn up.

Regardless of whether Judas gains anything or not from the instruction, a reading from the reader response level indicates that the text could function as an instrument for insights leading to salvation. We may speculate as to the consequences for the reader of realizing towards the end of the text that "you have been told everything," i.e. the truth about the cosmos and the human.[78] Perhaps he would stop doing what the disciples did and instead aspire to do what none of the disciples and their followers were able to: abandon the Eucharist and instead aspire to bring forth the perfect man in order to gain access to the house, i.e. the luminous cloud. How this is brought about, the text does not tell. Perhaps because of the lacunae, especially p. 56,1 ff. or perhaps because the author, like a Socratic midwife, deliberately leaves the reader in a state of *aporia*, in labour pains, in order to bring forth that which cannot be taught—non-discursive knowledge the result of which is perfect man. Provided that the reader is able understand what is discussed with him, we might consider the *Gospel of Judas* as intended to be a beginning to gnosis.

---

[75] Kasser et al. 2007,54 ff.

[76] Taking ϭⲉ[ⲛⲁ] as a passive, cf. 2 Tim 3:1 (Coptic).

[77] Cf. *Hyp. Arch.* NHC II,4, 96,20 ff. in which there appears to be a time span between Norea's revelation and the final salvation; also the fate of Achamoth in Iren., *Adv. Haer.* 1.4.5, 7.1, 8.4.

[78] *Gos. Jud.* TC 57, 15.

TEXT AND INTERTEXT

"WHAT IS THE ADVANTAGE?" (*GOS. JUD.* 46.16)

Text, Context, Intertext

Louis Painchaud and Serge Cazelais*

ⲟⲩ ⲡⲉ ⲡⲉϩⲟⲩⲟ? It is clearly an important question for Judas in the gospel that bears his name, as shown by the fact that the Iscariot twice poses it to Jesus—first with regard to his own fate, and then secondly with regard to human life.[1] In the significance that it attaches to this question, the *Gospel of Judas* is following in venerable footsteps: the very same question resounds through the book of Ecclesiastes, appearing in the introduction and then repeatedly afterwards.[2]

In order to understand this question, and its function in the *Gospel of Judas*, we shall first need to ascertain the precise meaning of the Coptic (ⲡⲉ)ϩⲟⲩⲟ, in order to be able to analyse its use in its present context. Having done so, we will then examine the intertextual echoes that the use of this phrase arouses, and their significance for a nuanced understanding of the figure of Judas in the *Gospel of Judas*.

THE GREEK UNDERLYING ⲟⲩ ⲡⲉ ⲡⲉϩⲟⲩⲟ

Literally, ⲡⲉϩⲟⲩⲟ means "the greater part," "the most," and hence "abundance," but also, paradoxically, both "profit" or "extra," and "superfluous" or "useless"—showing that the word can take on different, even contradictory, nuances depending on its context. For example, in a mercantile context, to sell ⲉⲭⲛⲟⲩϩⲟⲩⲟ means, to make a profit.[3] In 2 Cor 9:1, on the other hand, ⲟⲩϩⲟⲩⲟ ⲉⲣⲟⲓ ⲡⲉ ⲉⲥϩⲁⲓ ⲛⲏⲧⲛ̄[4] means "it is superfluous for me to write to you." In a question, ⲟⲩ ⲡⲉ ⲡⲉϩⲟⲩⲟ can refer to surpassing expectations, as when in Matt 5:47 Jesus asks,

---

* We would like to thank Wolf-Peter Funk and Bernard Barc for their important comments and suggestions on a preliminary version of this text, as well as Michael Kaler, who translated this paper into English with his usual skill.
[1] *Gos. Jud.* 46.16–17; 53.8–9.
[2] Eccl 1:3; 3:9; 5:15; cf. also 3:19.
[3] Crum 1939, 735a.
[4] Wilmet 1959.

"If you only greet your brothers, what more are you doing (than others) (ογ πε πε2ογο ετετῆειρε ῆμοϥ)?"[5]

The expression can also mean, "What profit?" or "What good?", as we find in a letter of Shenute. Writing to a nun that was reproaching him for not visiting her, Shenute asks, "And if I had come to you without really wanting to do so, what good would that do you? (ογ πε πε2ογο ετναϣωπε νε)".[6] The question ογ πε πε2ογο is here effectively equivalent to the question ογ πε π2ηγ, "What is the profit?" or "What is the use?" The Sahidic version of Romans 3:1 provides a clear example of the link between these two phrases. In the context of a debate with an imaginary Jewish interlocutor, Paul asks, "What is the advantage of being a Jew? What is the use of circumcision?", a question rendered in Coptic as ογ πε πε2ογο ῆπιογααι η ογ πε π2ηγ ῆπcⲃⲃε.[7]

The ambiguity of the Coptic 2ογο is shared by its Greek equivalents περισσόν and περισσεία, which refer to that which exceeds, and thus potentially either profit or that which is superfluous or useless. The two Sahidic New Testament versions of the question ογ πε πε2ογο that we have seen both translate τί περισσόν;[8] in Ecclesiastes, the same Coptic phrase is used to translate τίς περισσεία or τί περισσόν.[9] There is no doubt that our *Gospel of Judas* is the Coptic version of a Greek original. Based on what we have seen, it is thus quite likely that the question ογ πε πε2ογο translates the Greek τίς περισσεία or τί περισσόν.[10] Given the ambiguity of this phrase, we must examine the context of its use if we want to determine its precise meaning.

Text and Context

The interpretation of the first occurrence of the question ογ πε πε2ογο, at 46.16, is not especially problematic:

---

[5] Wilmet 1959.

[6] Amélineau 1914, 513.9 ; Amélineau translates "Que t'arrivera-t-il de plus?"

[7] Rom 3:3. Horner 1969b, 24–25.

[8] Rom 3:1. The Coptic phrase translates the Greek Τί οὖν τὸ περισσὸν τοῦ Ἰουδαίου ἢ τίς ὠφέλεια τῆς περιτομῆς.

[9] Eccl 1:3 and Eccl 3:9; 5:15.

[10] As suggested by Brankaer-Bethge 2007, 281 n. 30. They translate both occurrences of the question in the same way: "Was ist das Besondere?" (275 and 281).

> When Judas heard these (words), he said to (Jesus), "What is the
> advantage that I have received, since you have set me apart from that
> generation?"[11]

Judas' question is explicitly presented as his reaction to information he
receives from Jesus. Jesus, in response to Judas' earlier question, has
just denied him entry to the place reserved for the holy generation.
Judas now wants to know what benefit he has gained, given that he has
lost the hope of attaining his true aspiration.[12] It is quite probable that
here the original Greek would have read τί περισσόν, as in Matt 5:47
and Rom 3:1, or perhaps τίς περισσεία. In either case, the meaning of
the phrase here is unambiguous and it has been rendered similarly by
all the translators.

It is a different story when we turn to 53.8–10, in a section where
the lacunous (53.1–7) and probably corrupted (53.11–17) nature of the
text makes interpretation problematic. Let us begin with the Coptic
text of 53.8–10:

ϊΟΥΔΑϹ ΔΕ ΠΕΧΑϥ Ν̄ῙϹ̄ [ΧΕ ΟΥ] ΠΕ ΠΕϨΟΥΟ ΕΤϥΝΑΩΝ[Ϩ] Ν̄ϬΙ
[Π]ΡΩΜ[Ε][13]

The critical edition notes that the meaning of ϨΟΥΟ is not clear here.[14]
Most translators have taken it to refer simply to duration, in this case
the duration of human life.[15] However, as we have seen, in any context
the word always refers to that which is extra, excessive, or superfluous.

---

[11] *Gos. Jud.* 46.14–18. ΝΑΪ Ν̄ΤΕΡΕϥϹΩΤΜ̄ ΕΡΟΟ[Υ] Ν̄ϬΙ ϊΟΥΔΑϹ ΠΕΧΑϥ ΝΑϥ ΧΕ ΟΥ
ΠΕ ΠΕϨΟΥΟ Ν̄ΤΑΕΙΧΙΤϥ̄ ΧΕ ΑΚΠΟΡΧΤ̄ ΕΤΓΕΝΕΑ ΕΤΜ̄ΜΑΥ (46.14–18), Kasser et al.
2007, 211.

[12] With regard to the translation of this passage, the question posed by Judas would
be meaningless if ΧΕ ΑΚΠΟΡΧΤ̄ ΕΤΓΕΝΕΑ ΕΤΜ̄ΜΑΥ did not mean "since you have separated me from that generation" (46.17–18), as it was correctly translated by Rodolphe
Kasser in Kasser et al. 2006b, 45 and in Kasser et al. 2006a, 245.

[13] One would have expected ΟΥ ΠΕ ΠΕϨΟΥΟ ΕΤϥΝΑΩΝ[Ϩ Μ̄ΜΟϥ], since the extra-
posited adverbial complement of ΩΝϨ ought normally to be recalled within the clause
through the use of Μ̄ΜΟϥ. However, there does not seem to be enough space at the end
of the line for this particle, even though there might be room for something: the line
as reconstructed is only fifteen letters long, while surrounding lines contain twenty, or
nineteen with a *vacat*. Be that as it may, what Crum 1939, 525b considers a transitive
use of ΩΝϨ remains rare, and normally such usage is found with some reference to
duration (days, etc.), which is not the case for ϨΟΥΟ.

[14] Kasser et al. 2006a, 225.

[15] For example, "[What] is the extent (of time) that the human being will live";
"Jusqu'à quel point sera longue la durée de la vie de l'être humain ?" (Kasser et al.
2006b); "[Quelle] est la longueur (de la vie) dont pourra vivre l'homme" (Kasser
et al. 2007).

In no case can it refer simply to the duration of human life. If we want to understand ογ πε πεϩογο and its probable Greek antecedent τί περισσόν or τίς περισσεία, we must examine it in context.

Unfortunately, the immediate context has several significant problems. First, the text of the first four lines of page 53 is incompletely preserved. These four lines conclude Jesus' discussion of creation of Adam and Eve by Saklas, followed, first, by reflections on their names, then by details about one of Saklas' commandments, and finally the prediction of the Archon with regard to the lifespan (ογοειϣ) of Adam and, most likely, his children.[16] This latter section is unfortunately disrupted by a lacuna, and the sense of the entire passage cannot be ascertained without the reconstruction of its missing contents. The passage reads, ϫε ερεπεκωνϩ ϣωπ[ε ....] ῆογοειϣ μῆ νεκϣη[ρε.[17] If we leave to one side Nagel's suggestion of νακ, there are only two logical possibilities to fill the lacuna in line 5, namely ῆνοϭ or ῆκογϊ. In other words, the Archon is either promising Adam a long life, or a short one,[18] and Judas' question, ογ πε πεϩογο, is in response to this declaration.

The following section, which is materially in better shape, provides us with Jesus' response. The beginning is clear, except as regards the interpretation of the phrase ϩῆογηπε: "Why are you astonished that Adam and his descendents have received his lifespan (πεϥογοειϣ) ϩῆογηπε?"

Literally, the phrase ϩῆογηπε means "in a number": without knowing its precise sense here, we cannot understand the exact meaning of Jesus response and of the whole dialogue. The note in the critical edition mentions that this expression can translate the Greek πλῆθος or μέτρον, so that the Coptic expression could mean, "greatly, in abundance," or in fact its opposite, "limited."[19] However, the only occurrence of ηπε as being equivalent to πλῆθος in Crum refers to Gen 48:16, where the Coptic text translates πλῆθος πολύ (ηπε εναϣωс). The word ηπε alone does not normally refer to a large number, but

---

[16] *Gos. Jud.* 52.14–19; 52.19–25; 52.25–53.4.

[17] *Gos. Jud.* 53.5–7.

[18] The first option, "You shall live long with your children," was taken up in the 2006 edition, although the restored Coptic text was ϫε ερεπεκωνϩ ϣωπ[ε νακ] ῆογοειϣ μῆ νεκϣη[ρε (53.5–7). A note in the critical edition (Kasser et al. 2007, 225) gives as possible restitutions ϣωπ[ε ῆνοϭ] ῆογοειϣ or, as Nagel suggests, ϣωπ[ε νακ] ῆογ(ογ)οειϣ ("Your life will last [for you] for a time").

[19] Kasser et al. 2006a, 225.

rather to that which is limited. The interpretation of this passage from the *Gospel of Judas* thus seems clear: the Archon has predicted a brief life for Adam, Judas asks Jesus ΟΥ ΠЄ ΠЄ϶ΟΥΟ, and Jesus responds by asking him why he is amazed that Adam's lifespan should be numbered, that is brief, or limited.

Judas' question—which we translate freely as "What profit is there in human life?"—and Jesus' response—namely, "Why are you amazed that the human has received life in a number," i.e. a limited lifespan—would follow logically if the Archon had predicted that Adam's life would be brief. On the other hand, if we take the Archon's prediction as promising a long life for Adam, Judas' question then becomes incomprehensible—hence the note in the critical edition concerning the lack of clarity of the meaning of ϶ΟΥΟ in this context. In fact, both here and on page 46, if the question ΟΥ ΠЄ ΠЄ϶ΟΥΟ is to make any sense at all, it would require that Judas have a negative perception of the information which precedes it. At page 46, Judas asks his question because he has been denied the realm of the holy generation; here, because of the brevity of human life.

This first argument, based on textual coherence, is supported by a second, having to do with the conception of the Archon. In gnostic myth, Ialdabaoth-Saklas is a power associated with material creation, generation, and death. It is thus far more likely in a gnostic text that he should be identified with the creator in Genesis, denying immortality to Adam than that he should promise him long life.[20] And in fact, the *Gospel of Judas* itself associates Saklas with a finite time span.[21]

Other arguments support this conclusion as well. Scripturally speaking, the declaration by the Archon of the brevity of Adam's life is supported by Gen 3:22 and 6:3. The fact that the *Gospel of Judas* ascribes this to the Archon (ΠЄΧΑϤ ΝΑϤ ̄Ν϶Ι Π[ΑΡΧШΝ], 53.5, the restitution being almost certain) points us in the direction of Gen 3:22 (καὶ εἶπεν ὁ θεός) and 6:3 (καὶ εἶπεν κύριος ὁ θεός), where the refusal of immortality to Adam or the enumeration of his years are associated with the Creator. Moreover, the theme of the abridgement of human life by the Archon is echoed as well in two other gnostic texts, namely the

---

[20] Gen 3:22. Thus it seems to us that we must reject the interpretation of this passage suggested by Kasser's translation. To assume that a prediction of a long life to Adam would be coherent with the scriptural guarantee of one hundred and twenty years (Gen 6:3) is anachronistic.

[21] *Gos. Jud.* 54.19.

Writing without Title on the origin of the world[22] and the *Apocalypse of Adam*.[23]

Thus the only real choices in terms of restitutions would be either Nagel's proposal of ⲚⲀⲔ, or ⲚⲔⲞⲨⲈⲒ—or rather, for reasons of space, ⲚⲔⲞⲨⲓ. Were we to adopt Nagel's proposal, the passage should be translated as follows: "Your life will be [yours] for a certain time with your children."[24] However, although it is possible both paleographically and grammatically, the combination of ϢⲰⲠⲈ with dative meaning possession, does not fit in with the overall theme of duration that seems to be the point here. On the other hand, a restitution of ⲚⲔⲞⲨⲓ would fit in perfectly with this theme, and is also quite acceptable from a grammatical point of view. If we suppose that this shorter spelling was used, perhaps even with the final ï written below the Ⲩ, then it would be only one letter longer than ⲚⲀⲔ. For all of these reasons, we feel that the restitution of ⲚⲔⲞⲨⲓ at the end of line 5 is the best option. This would produce a reading of ⲬⲈ ⲈⲢⲈⲠⲈⲔⲰⲚⳞ ϢⲰⲠ[Ⲉ ⲚⲔⲞⲨⲓ] ⲚⲞⲨⲞⲈⲒϢ ⲘⲚ ⲚⲈⲔϢⲎ[ⲢⲈ, and could be translated as "Your lifespan will be brief with your children."[25]

But even with this issue resolved, we are still not out of the woods, as several problems remain. The repetition of the adverbial expression ⳞⲚⲞⲨⲎⲠⲈ in 53.13.15, as well as the contrast between the masculine ⲠⲘⲀ and the feminine pronominal suffix of ⲚⳞⲎⲦⲤ suggest that we are dealing with a corrupt text. The repetition of ⳞⲚⲞⲨⲎⲠⲈ could well be due to a mistake, in which case it would be necessary to eliminate the second occurrence, as has been done in the critical edition. With regard to the phrase as a whole, although it is quite possible that something is missing from the text as it stands, or that the Coptic translation is less coherent than was the original Greek version, nonetheless the overall sense is comprehensible: On the one hand, Jesus reaffirms

[22] NHC II 121.13–27. "Après cela, les archontes jaloux voulurent réduire leur temps. Ils ne le purent pas à cause de la Fatalité établie depuis le début, car un temps avait été fixé pour chacun : mille ans d'après la course des luminaires. Les archontes, donc, ne purent pas réaliser cela et chacun de ceux qui font le mal enleva dix années, et cette durée entière passa à neuf cent trente années… Ainsi donc, depuis ce jour-là, la durée de la vie a décliné jusqu'à la fin des temps." Painchaud 1995a, 203.

[23] NHC V 67.10–14. "C'est pourquoi les jours de notre vie diminuèrent. Je compris en effet que j'étais tombé au pouvoir de la mort." Morard 1985, 27.

[24] Wolf-Peter Funk, private communication.

[25] *Gos. Jud.* 53.5–7.

the limits of human life.[26] On the other, he associates Adam and his descendents with the kingdom, or with the reign of the Archon.[27]

Even as it stands, the phrase makes sense when translated roughly literally: "Why are you astonished that Adam has received a lifespan in a number in the place where he received kingship with his Archon?" If the original Greek had been misunderstood by the Coptic translator, or if errors had crept in during the transmission of the text, as the repetition of ϩⲛ̄ⲟⲩⲏⲡⲉ would suggest, the original sense could well have been something like, "Why are you astonished that Adam has received a length of life in a number in the kingdom of the Archon," with the "kingdom" referring to the material universe over which death rules,[28] and the expression "in a number" specifying the limited nature of human life.

However we interpret the situation, clearly the issue at hand is the mortality of Archon-dominated humanity, as is indicated by the next question that Judas asks: "Does the human spirit die?"[29] Jesus responds to this new question by establishing two different categories of beings. Some have received spirit as a loan.[30] Others, the kingless ones who are not ruled by the Archon, have received spirit as a gift.[31] We can thus render the entire passage as follows:

> And the [Archon] told him, "Your life will be [short] with your children." And Judas said to Jesus: "[What] is the advantage of human life?" Jesus answered, "Why are you wondering about this, that Adam, with his generation, has received a span of life in a number in the place †where he has received his kingdom {in a number} with his Archon†?" Judas asked Jesus, "Does the human spirit die?"

The two occurrences of the question ⲟⲩ ⲡⲉ ⲡⲉϩⲟⲩⲟ thus have the same sense. In the *Gospel of Judas*, Judas poses this question twice—once having to do with his own fate, and once having to do with the duration of human life. Jesus' responses to these two questions are linked. With regard to Judas' fate, he reaffirms that Judas will be denied entry to the place reserved for the holy generation; with regard to human life, he reaffirms its limits. In both cases, as well, Jesus' response involves

---

[26] *Gos. Jud.* 53.12–13.
[27] *Gos. Jud.* 53.14–15.
[28] Cf. *Gos. Jud.* 43.16–18. Painchaud 2008, 643–645.
[29] *Gos. Jud.* 53.17. This is explicit in *Apoc. Adam* 67.10–14—see note 18 above.
[30] *Gos. Jud.* 53.21–22.
[31] *Gos. Jud.* 53.18–25.

reference to government or to kingship,[32] albeit government and king-
ship of the lower world. Thus the fate of Judas is parallel to that of
Adam, who is a representative of all humanity created by the Archon.
In both cases, stern limits are placed upon their future expectations.
Judas will not go up to the place of the holy generation, and those who
do not belong to the kingless generation will not escape death.

So we can conclude that the meaning of the question ⲟⲩ ⲡⲉ ⲡⲉϩⲟⲩⲟ,
which quite probably translates the Greek Τί περισσόν (or τίς περισσεία),
is clear, and that its two occurrences—in both cases meaning "what is
the advantage?"—are well integrated into their respective contexts.

INTERTEXT

Before we begin to explore the intertextual ramifications of the question
ⲟⲩ ⲡⲉ ⲡⲉϩⲟⲩⲟ, let us note that Judas is made to ask it twice, suggesting that the question is particularly significant. This being the case, it
follows that if the question, and its context, involve scriptural allusions,
their identification would be important not just for the understanding
of the question, but also for our understanding of the text as a whole.
Our examination of this question will not be from the diachronic perspective of source criticism, but rather from a synchronic, intertextual
perspective,[33] an approach which—to speak generally—is indispensable to the study of Jewish and Christian literature in antiquity.

Now, Judas' question certainly brings to mind a limited number of potential scriptural references. In the Septuagint, it is found
exclusively in Ecclesiastes, where it functions almost as a leitmotif,
expressed in Greek as τί περισσόν or τίς περισσεία and in Coptic as
ⲟⲩ ⲡⲉ ⲡⲉϩⲟⲩⲟ.[34] In the New Testament, it occurs at Matt 5:47 and
Rom 3:1.

Have we to do in these cases with meaningful allusions, or with
nothing more than coincidences with no bearing on our understand-

---

[32] *Gos. Jud.* 46.18–47.1; 53.11–16. This passage is doubtless to be linked to the theme
of Adam's kingship—for a survey of rabbinic and gnostic sources on this theme see Ri
2000, 149–53. In the *Apocalypse of Adam* from Nag Hammadi codex V, the Demiurge
grants kingship to Noah and his sons, but having done this, he enslaves them. That
which they receive is dependent on the creator. For commentary see Morard 1985,
85.

[33] See on this Boyarin 1990, esp. 135 n. 2.

[34] Eccl 1:3; 3:9.19; 5:15.

ing of the *Gospel of Judas*? At this point it will be helpful to remind ourselves of three criteria for identifying an allusion. The possible allusion must in some way be perceived as standing out from, or foreign to, its context; the allusion, if present, must cast new light on its context when recognised; and the possibility of a given passage being allusive is increased by the presence of other references in the same context or in the work as a whole to the source from which the allusion is drawn.[35]

As for the first of these criteria, suffice it to say that foreignness of the question ογ πε πεϩογο at 53.8–9 has been indicated by the uncertainty that has marked the efforts to translate and interpret this passage. We now turn to examine whether any of the scriptural parallels mentioned above can provide us with new illumination on the *Gospel of Judas*.

The parallel to Matt 5:47 does not seem to be significant. In this passage, Jesus simply asks his disciples in what way they distinguish themselves by greeting their brothers, since even the pagans do this. The situation is different with regard to Ecclesiastes. At Eccl 6:11b–12 LXX (Rahlfs), not only the question, but the wider context as well, is echoed in *Gos. Jud.* 53.5–17:

> Τί περισσὸν τῷ ἀνθρώπῳ ὅτι τίς οἶδεν τί ἀγαθὸν τῷ ἀνθρώπῳ ἐν τῇ ζωῇ, ἀριθμὸν ἡμερῶν ζωῆς ματαιότητος αὐτοῦ

> What advantage has a human being? For who knows what is good for a human being in his life, during the number of days of vanity of his life?

We find here the same linking of terms (human being, life, number) as we saw in the *Gospel of Judas*. Furthermore, we are now in a position to clarify the meaning of the adverbial phrase ϩⲛ̄ογηπε, which corresponds literally to the Greek adverbial accusative ἀριθμόν. Let us add that the passage from Ecclesiastes may well be a reflection on the creation of humanity,[36] and in the *Gospel of Judas* the passage in question immediately follows a discussion of the creation of humanity.[37] Clearly, we have to do here with an element that seems foreign in the context of

---

[35] Painchaud 1996, 136.

[36] As Françoise Vinel notes in Vinel 2002, 141, in Eccl 6:10, ἄνθρωπος and the Hebrew *'ādām* are used without an article, which is exceptional in Ecclesiastes, and has led some exegetes to suggest that here we have to do with a proper name, which would make of this passage a meditation on the creation.

[37] *Gos. Jud.* 52.14–53.4.

the *Gospel of Judas*, and whose meaning is clarified through reference to Ecclesiastes—in which, significantly, we find another link to this passage of the *Gospel of Judas*, with regard to its use of ϩⲛ̄ⲟⲩⲏⲡⲉ.

With regard to the interpretation of ἀριθμόν (ⲏⲡⲉ) in this context, it must refer to the limited duration of human life, as is clearly shown by the reprise of the same expression in Sir 17:2 LXX (ἡμέρας ἀριθμοῦ) and 37:25 (ζωὴ ἀνδρὸς ἐν ἀριθμῷ ἡμερῶν). It becomes even more likely that the *Gospel of Judas* is simultaneously evoking both Eccl 6:11b–12 and Sir 17:2 when we note that in Sirach, the limited duration of human life is associated with the power that humans have been granted by their creator over the things of the earth (καὶ ἔδωκεν αὐτοῖς ἐξουσίαν τῶν ἐπ' αὐτῆς Sir 17:2b LXX).[38]

The recognition of this reference to Ecclesiastes permits us to resolve two problematic aspects of the text, namely the meaning of the question ⲟⲩ ⲡⲉ ⲡⲉϩⲟⲩⲟ and the adverbial phrase ϩⲛ̄ⲟⲩⲏⲡⲉ. While it would be interesting to undertake a more thorough investigation for other references to Ecclesiastes, for the moment we shall limit ourselves to this clear and unequivocal example.[39] With regard to it, we must ask, Is this no more than a mere reminiscence, or is it an allusion intended to evoke its source in the reader's mind? And if the latter, how does this allusion work within the *Gospel of Judas* as a whole?

Let us begin by noting that the passage of Ecclesiastes to which the *Gospel of Judas* alludes is a significant one. It marks the conclusion of the first half of the book by summing up the doubts of the Preacher.[40] And also, as we have seen, its question works as a leitmotif in the text, contributing to its atmosphere from its first appearance in the intro-

---

[38] As is the case with Sirach, the *Gospel of Judas* joins together in a common context references to the authority or royalty conferred on humans by their creator, and the brevity of human life. The similarity of the two works' approaches to the same themes makes it conceivable that our text is intended to refer to Sirach, as well as Ecclesiastes.

[39] One can perhaps also hear echoes of the language of Ecclesiastes in certain phrases from the *Gospel of Judas*. For example, its description of the realm of the holy generation as a place where neither the sun nor the moon reign (*Gos. Jud.* 45.20–21) opposes this realm to our lower world in a similar way as our world is insistently referred to in Ecclesiastes as the world "under the sun" (Eccl. 1:3, etc.). Similarly, the idea evoked at 33.10–13 ("Some walked in the way of righteousness while others walked in their transgressions") is one that is frequently repeated in Ecclesiastes (for example, 2:15–16; 3:16; 7:15).

[40] Vinel 2002, 141.

duction.⁴¹ One could say that the work as a whole is summarized in this one question.

To twice put this question on Judas' lips represents the same interpretive process as the decision of the authors of the gospels of Mark and Matthew to have the crucified Jesus quote the beginning of Psalm 22.⁴² In both cases, the reader is invited to read the one text in the light of the other to which it alludes; further, he or she is invited to see the new text as being already implicit in the old—a mental leap that is fundamental to midrashic thought.⁴³ Just as the citation from Psalms serves to identify the crucified one with the speaker in the psalm, so too in our view the allusion in the *Gospel of Judas* is meant to identify Judas with Qoheleth, in other words, the son of David, the king in Jerusalem.⁴⁴ Finally, Jesus' repeated prediction that "you will grieve a great deal" (ϫⲉ ⲉⲕⲉⲁⲱⲁϩⲟⲙ ⲛ̄ϩⲟⲩⲟ 35.27; ϫⲉ ⲉⲕⲉⲱⲱⲡⲉ ⲉⲕⲁⲱ ⲁϩⲟⲙ ⲛ̄ϩⲟⲩⲟ 46.11–12), although unparalleled in Ecclesiastes, could even be another clue to the identification of Judas with Qoheleth/Solomon!

This identification is doubly significant. On the one hand, it assimilates Judas—to whom has been promised rulership, and whose star reigns—to the successor of David, and thus to Jewish royalty, which is perfectly in line with the use in the *Gospel of Judas* of the notion of βασιλεία.⁴⁵ This links up as well with the denunciation of sacrificial interpretations of Christianity as no more than the perpetuation of the Jewish sacrificial cult,⁴⁶ a perpetuation which Judas will make possible through his sacrifice of the man who bears Jesus.⁴⁷ Through assimilating Judas to Solomon, and having Solomon's words placed on his lips, the *Gospel of Judas* links its protagonist with the builder of the Temple and with its sacrificial cult.

But while the attribution of Ecclesiastes to Solomon is explained by the convention of wisdom literature that Solomon was the Sage *par excellence*, it would rather have been his association with demons, knowledge of which was widespread⁴⁸ and well-attested in gnostic

---

⁴¹ Eccl 1:3.
⁴² Mk 15:34b; Matt 27:46b.
⁴³ "What is so striking (and strange) about midrash is its claim that the new context is implied by the old one..." Boyarin 1990, 23.
⁴⁴ Eccl. 1:1.12.16.
⁴⁵ *Gos. Jud.* 46.23. See Painchaud 2008.
⁴⁶ Let us note in passing that the denunciation of sacrifice, a very important theme in the *Gospel of Judas*, could well be an echo of Eccl 4:17.
⁴⁷ *Gos. Jud.* 56.19–20.
⁴⁸ Giversen 1972, 17–18.

sources,[49] that would have tempted the gnostic author of the *Gospel of Judas*—an association which coheres perfectly with the author's description of Judas as a "demon."[50] The allusion to Ecclesiastes thus serves to identify Judas with Solomon, the son of David, the king in Jerusalem and master of demons, with regard to the Jewish cult denounced in the *Gospel of Judas*.

Have we as well an allusion to Rom 3:1, "What advantage has the Jew?" (τί οὖν τὸ περισσὸν τοῦ 'Ιουδαίου < ΟΥ ΠΕ ΠΕϨΟΥΟ ⲚⲠΙΟΥⲆⲀⲒ)?[51] There is nothing to indicate any reliance of the author of the *Gospel of Judas* on Paul here, although it is clear that in this chapter of Romans Paul himself draws on Ecclesiastes, as can be seen from the echo of Eccl 7:20 in Rom 3:10.

There is, however, another scriptural text to which Judas' question at 46.16–17 might well allude. It is possible that his question ΟΥ ΠΕ ΠΕϨΟΥΟ is meant to evoke the question posed to his brothers by our protagonist's namesake, the patriarch Judah/Judas (Gen 37:26 *mah betzah* MT; Τί χρήσιμον LXX; Τί κέρδον Symmachus).[52] True, the formulation of the question is not exactly identical, but in both cases we have to do with advantage or profit.

Ultimately it is Judas, the fourth son of Jacob, who is the favoured heir in Gen 49:8–12, despite what one might expect based on birth order.[53] In ancient Jewish exegesis, it is precisely the fact of having posed this

---

[49] See *Apoc. Adam* 79.3–7; *Testim. Truth* 69.29–70.30; the *Writing without Title* 107.1–3; see also the reference in the *Writing without Title* to the "jars of water that are in Egypt" (ϨⲨⲆⲢⲒⲀ ⲚⲘⲟⲟⲨ ⲈⲦϨⲚⲔⲎⲘⲉ, 122.18–20) and the commentary of Painchaud 1995a, 473–75. This passage does not have to do with aquatic creatures, as has been assumed by all the translators since the mistaken correction of ϨⲨⲆⲢⲒⲀ to ϨⲨⲆⲢⲀ proposed by Böhlig-Labib 1962, 94–95 and established by Tardieu 1974. Rather, it refers to the jars of water within which Solomon sealed the demons and which he sent to Egypt, as was clearly seen by Doresse 1958, 195 and note 38, 269, and as is shown by comparison with the parallel in *Testim. Truth* 69.29–70.30 [ϨⲨⲆⲢ]ⲒⲀ 70.12; see the commentary of Mahé-Mahé 1996, 211.

[50] *Gos. Jud.* 44.20. We ought to remember as well that this association of Solomon and demons is linked to the Hebrew text of Eccl. 2:8—Midrash Rabba interprets the *sidah sidoth* of Eccl 2:8 as referring to demons (Freedman-Simon 1961, 57). Likewise with the Targum of Qohelet—see Targum of Qohelet 2.5, in Manns 1992, 145–198.

[51] The question returns in Rom 3:9, but the textual tradition of this verse is complex and its interpretation is difficult; see on this Brown et al. 1990, 839. The reading τί οὖν προκατέχομεν περισσόν is well attested in the manuscript tradition and in Patristic sources.

[52] The Louvain parchment (Hamouli 1) has a lacuna running from Gen 37:22–35; as for its better preserved twin in the Pierpont Morgan collection, it contains only the three last book of the Pentateuch, see Lefort 1937, 9. The Bohairic version has ΟΥ ⲘⲠⲉⲐⲚⲀⲚⲉϤ, see Peters 1985, 100.

[53] Οὐκ ἐκλείψει ἄρχων ἐξ Ιουδα καὶ ἡγούμενος ἐκ τῶν μηρῶν αὐτοῦ Gen 49:10 LXX.

question that entitles him to receive his authority.[54] This link between the patriarch Judah's question and the authority that he receives is paralleled by the link in the *Gospel of Judas* between the question that Judas poses and the promise made to him that he will rule (ⲕⲛⲁϣⲱⲡⲉ ⲉⲕⲁⲣⲭⲓ <ἄρχειν 46.23). Just as was the case with the allusion to Ecclesiastes, the link with Gen 37:26 would serve then to assimilate Judas' promised royalty to Jewish royalty. The domination that Judas will exercise over the Christians who curse him would then be understood as perpetuating the rule of Judah over the Christian adversaries, just as the sacrificial cult seen in dreams by the disciples perpetuates the cult rendered to Saklas in the Temple of Jerusalem.

There may be another aspect of the *Gospel of Judas* that supports the idea of a rapprochement between the two Judases, for the reference to Judas' ascending star (προηγούμενος 57.19–20)[55] refers the reader to Balaam's oracle:[56] "A star shall rise out of Jacob" (ἀνατελεῖ ἄστρον ἐξ Ἰακώβ Numbers 24:17b LXX). This verse, whose rendering in the LXX differs greatly from the Hebrew text,[57] is a significant and frequently-cited passage in messianic speculation, whether Jewish (rabbinic or heterodox) or Christian.[58] It is specifically referred to the reign of the patriarch Judah in the *Testament of Judah* 14.5.[59]

It is enough for the time being to conclude that the two occurrences of the question ⲟⲩ ⲡⲉ ⲡⲉϩⲟⲩⲟ, both set on Judas' lips, have the same function, namely, to assimilate him to king Solomon. In order to fully account for the significance of this assimilation of Judas to Solomon through these allusions to Ecclesiastes, it would be necessary to consider it in the light of contemporary Jewish speculations about Solomon, of which his association with demons and magic is but one aspect. Suffice it to recall here that according to Sanhedrin 20b,[60] Solomon's

---

[54] In discussing this question, midrash Rabba on Genesis associates it with Judah's kingship. "Then Judah said to his brothers, 'What profit…' (Gen 37:26). Said R. Judah bar Ilai, 'In three passages in which Scripture speaks of Judah, Judah spoke before his brothers, and they made him king over them: 'Then Judah said to his brothers,' 'And Judah and his brothers came to Joseph's house' (Gen 44:14), 'Then Judah came near to him' (Gen 44,18)", Neusner 1985, 197; see on this Abécassis 2001.

[55] In astrological terminology, this term refers to the star in the horoscope that is in the ascendant, see Le Boeuffle 1987.

[56] See Barc 2008, 672–676.

[57] Dorival 1994, 140–41.

[58] See on this Dorival 1994, 451–52.

[59] See Philonenko 1987, 811–44.

[60] Said R. Simeon b. Lakish, "At first Solomon ruled over the creatures of the upper world, as is said, 'Then Solomon sat on the throne of the Lord as king' (1 Chr 29:23).

life was a long descent. At the beginning, his reign was over the upper world as well as over the lower world, but as time progressed he came to rule only over the beings of the lower world, and in the end, only over his own sceptre, an interpretation based on an implausible reading of Eccl 2:10, a quotation which evokes of course a much larger context in Eccl. 2:4–11, in which the conclusion is that there is no profit under the sun (ⲙ̄ⲙ̄ ⲟⲩϩⲱⲃ ⲛ̄ϩⲟⲩⲟ ϣⲟⲟⲡ ϩⲁ ⲡⲣⲏ).[61]

As for the possible connection of Judas Iscariot with Judah, the Patriarch, and the question ⲟⲩ ⲡⲉ ⲡⲉϩⲟⲩⲟ with Gn 37:26, a more detailed examination of this last hypothesis would require an unprecedented (thus far) exploration of the links between the construction of the figure of Judas Iscariot in early Christian texts, both canonical and extra canonical, and the reception of the figure of the patriarch in contemporary Jewish traditions.

Finally, one should ask whether it is a mere coincidence if Jesus asks Judas in the *Book of the Resurrection of Christ by Bartholomew the Apostle* 3[b] almost the same question as Judas asks himself to Jesus in the Gospel of Judas:[62]

ⲧⲟⲧⲉ ⲓⲥ ⲁϥⲕⲟⲧϥ ⲉⲡⲣⲱⲙⲉ ⲛⲧⲁϥⲡⲁⲣⲁⲇⲓⲇⲟⲩ ⲙⲙⲟϥ
ⲉⲧⲉ ⲓⲟⲩⲇⲁⲥ ⲡⲓⲥⲕⲁⲣⲓⲱⲧⲏⲥ ⲡⲉ
ⲡⲉϫⲁϥ ⲛⲁϥ ϫⲉ ⲛⲧⲁⲕⲧⲓϩⲏⲩ ⲛⲟⲩ ⲱ ⲓⲟⲩⲇⲁⲥ ϫⲉ ⲁⲕⲡⲁⲣⲁⲇⲓⲇⲟⲩ ⲙⲙⲟⲓ
...

ⲛⲧⲟⲕ ϩⲱⲱⲕ ⲟⲩⲟⲓ ⲛⲁⲕ ϩⲉⲛⲟⲩⲟⲓ ⲉϥⲕⲏⲃ ⲙⲉⲛ ⲟⲩⲛⲟϭ ⲛ̄ⲭⲡⲓⲟ ϩⲓ ⲥⲁϩⲟⲩ
ⲉϥϩⲟⲟⲩ

Jésus se retourna vers l'homme qui l'avait livré,
c'est-à-dire Judas Iscariote.
Il lui dit : « En quoi as-tu bénéficié, ô Judas, de m'avoir livré ?
...
Mais toi, Judas, malheur à toi ! Double anathème et malédiction sur toi. »

Then he reigned over the creatures of the lower world, as is written, 'For he had dominion over all the region on this side of the river, from Tisfah even to Gaza' (1 Kgs 5:4). (...) But in the end he ruled only over Israel, as it is said, 'I Qohelet, have been king over Israel' (Qoh 1:12). Then he ruled on Jerusalem alone, as it is written 'The words of Qohelet, son of David, king of Jerusalem' (Qoh 1:1) In the end he ruled only over his own bed, as it is written, 'Behold, it is the bed of Solomon, three score mighty men are about it' (Song 3:7). In the end he ruled only over his staff, as it is written, 'This was my portion from all my labor' (Qoh 2:10), Neusner 2005, 89–90. See for the French translation, Steinsaltz 1996, 196.

[61] Diebner-Kasser 1989, 264.
[62] Text from the ms 129/17, fol. 63 of the Bibliothèque Nationale published by Revillout 1985. The text from the British Museum MS. Oriental, No. 6804 edited by Budge 1913, 6 and 185, is lacunous.

Even if the formulation of the question (ⲚⲦⲀⲕⲦⲓⲀⲎⲨ ⲚⲞⲨ) is not the same as in the Gos. Jud 46.16–17, it is noteworthy that the Saviour asks to Judas in *Book Bar.* almost the same question as Judas asks Jesus in our Gospel: 'What is the profit, or what is the advantage?' It is also noteworthy that both texts introduce references to Judas' curse in the context of this question.

The fact that this question is very close to the one Judas asks to his brothers in Gn 37:26 is also intriguing and would require a close examination of the relationship which might exist between the construction of the Christian Judas, either canonical, apocryphal or Gnostic, and the Jewish traditions about the patriarch Juda.

WHAT IS THE ADVANTAGE?

We have established that the question ⲞⲨ ⲠⲈ ⲠⲈϨⲞⲨⲞ, posed twice by Judas (46.16 and 53.8–9) is in all probability a translation of the Greek τί περισσόν or τίς περισσεία. In both cases it has the same sense: "What is the advantage?" We have also seen that the second occurrence, as well as its immediate context in 53.5–16, are best interpreted as a subtle, allusive interplay of references to Gen 3:22 and 6:3, Eccl 6:7–12, and Sir 17:2 LXX. This procedure is characteristically midrashic, clustering and linking scriptural references in a way that effaces distinctions not only between the new text and the scriptural texts, but also between the scriptural texts themselves.[63]

We have also raised the question of the significance of this interplay, and we have suggested that its function is to assimilate Judas to the Preacher, that is, Solomon, son of David, who is a symbol both of royalty and of the demonized Jewish tradition—which in turn provides the background for the designation of Judas as a demon at 44.20.

Finally, we have suggested the possibility that Judas' question is also intended to evoke, Gen 37:26, which in turn raises the extremely complex and heretofore unexplored issue of the possible relations between the two Judases, the patriarch and the disciple. But regardless of what one might think of this last suggestions, the midrashic intertextual

---

[63] See on this Fraade 2007, 105–6.

452   LOUIS PAINCHAUD AND SERGE CAZELAIS

link with Ecclesiastes is sure, and hence must be seen as one of the inspirations of the *Gospel of Judas*.[64]

In conclusion, it is appropriate to ask how this assimilation of the apostle Judas to such figures of Jewish royalty as Solomon and perhaps also Judah coheres with the *Gospel of Judas* as a whole. Now, it is generally agreed that this text is directed against a sacrificial interpretation of Christianity that was in the process of consolidating itself in the second century. This is clearly shown by Jesus' interpretation of his disciples' dream and his injunction to cease sacrificing.[65] With regard to the symbolism employed in the description of the disciples' dream, it is likewise clear that they are being presented as the continuators of the Jewish cult—in other words, the sacrificial cult of the Temple of Jerusalem. In this construction, Judas is presented by Jesus as the one who will rule over them even while they curse him, a promise that has received insufficient attention to date.[66]

But who are "they"? Certainly not the Jews, nor the pagans, who would have no reason to curse the Iscariot, but rather the Christians themselves, or—more specifically—the Christians whose Christianity the *Gospel of Judas* considers a betrayal of Jesus name. The fact that Judas will rule over these Christians is to be expected, since as the one who sacrifices the man that bears Jesus, Judas himself becomes the initiator of the sacrificial cult in which these Christians have been ensnared by the successors of the apostles.[67] Judas is thus the initiator of a Christian sacrificial cult, the perpetuation of the cult associated with a Temple that was built by Solomon with the aid of demons. The idea that he should himself be referred to as a demon and assimilated to Solomon is thus perfectly coherent with the central message of the text.

---

[64] Speaking of midrash and the Melkita and their approach, Daniel Boyarin writes that "the texts cited (sometimes only alluded to) are *the generating force behind the elaboration of narrative or other types of textual expansion*" Boyarin, 1990, 22, italics his.

[65] *Gos. Jud.* 39.5–41.8; 41.1–2.

[66] *Gos. Jud.* 46.20–23.

[67] *Gos. Jud.* 56.19–20.

THREE DAYS AND EIGHT DAYS

Chronology in the *Gospel of Judas*

Matteo Grosso

The academic debate that emerged after the release of the original English translation of the *Gospel of Judas* and then its *Critical Edition* attests to the fact that this gospel is filled with passages that challenge interpreters.[1] Indeed, the problems start in the very first lines. Take for instance the expression found in lines 3–6. The expression reads and is translated in the *Critical Edition*:

ⲛ̄ [ϣ]ⲙⲟⲩⲛ ⲛ̄ⲥ̄ⲟⲟⲩ ϩⲁ ⲑⲏ ⲛ̄ϣⲟ[ⲙ]ⲛ̄ⲧ̄ ⲛ̄ⲥ̄ⲟⲟⲩ ⲉⲙⲡⲁⲧⲉϥⲣ̄ ⲡⲁⲥⲭⲁ

(…) during eight days, three days before he celebrated Passover.[2]

When the author defines the chronological frame of the secret revelatory discourse he is presenting, his words are enigmatic and even ambiguous, juxtaposing two combined indications of time. The first temporal indication mentions "eight days", while the second refers to "three days" before Passover.[3] Which passion's chronology lies behind this puzzling expression? What is the meaning and significance of this chronology from a literary point of view, within the context of the treatise itself, and in the light of the main issue concerning its relationship to earlier gospel narratives?

I gratefully acknowledge all the punctual comments and reactions I received at the Houston conference. My deepest gratitude goes to April DeConick, for encouraging me to undertake the uneasy task of carrying out a research on the *Gospel of Judas* and, also, for helping me to improve the language and style of this paper. While I was working on an early version of it, I had the chance to share some of the ideas here developed in a seminar chaired by Giovanni Filoramo at University of Torino: I thank the participants for their advice. Thanks also to Edoardo Bona for the technical support he provided me during the typewriting process.

[1] I refer to Kasser et al. 2006a; Kasser et al. 2007.

[2] Kasser et al. 2007, 185. Alternatively, it is possible to intend ⲣ̄ ⲡⲁⲥⲭⲁ as a translation of the Greek verb πάσχειν, so that we should read: "three days before suffering" or "three days before his passion".

[3] Gos. Jud. 33,1–2.

CHRONOLOGICAL INDICATORS IN EARLY GOSPEL NARRATIVES

The role played by numerology in the expression of fundamental aspects of early Christian thought is widely acknowledged. The richness of the symbolic meanings intrinsic to most of the numbers occurring in ancient Christian texts is drawn mainly from their biblical sources, although it is also often influenced by analogous conceptions deriving from different cultural heritages of antiquity, as François Bovon observes.[4] In Bovon's view, numbers were used by early Christians as "theological tools".[5] We should consider the chronologies recorded in ancient Christian literary works as a peculiar branch of these theological tools.[6] In gospel narratives, the chronologies have multiple functions. They play as literary devices, articulating and organizing the accounts or lending them an aura of historical authenticity. But often they carry deeper, more pregnant meanings of an ideological or theological nature. Not all the early Christian authors give an equal importance to these tools, nor are all of these tools used in an identical way.

The *Gospel of Mark*, which normally is quite vague in providing the temporal settings of the episodes it records, sets out the events of Jesus' last days—from Jesus' entrance in Jerusalem to the announcement of his resurrection—in an articulated chronological frame. It very precisely assigns Jesus' teachings and actions to different days.[7] Because of its accuracy and abundance of details, especially with respect to the previous section of the Markan gospel, it is likely that this scheme is intentional. It appears to be in harmony with Mark's focus on the concept of the time of salvation, the καιρός, which is a gracious and limited period that coincides with Jesus' coming to the world, when the possibility of obtaining salvation is given to humankind.[8] As the moment of Jesus' death is approaching, the narrator becomes more

---

[4] Bovon 2001, 267–88.

[5] Bovon 2001, 267.

[6] Naturally, the chronological setting of an episode can be indicated also without using numbers, e.g. in expressions like: "it was night", or "the same day" etc.; in most of cases, however, numbers or enumerations are involved, either explicitly or implicitly.

[7] Mark 11:1–16:1.

[8] The term καιρός has five occurrences in Mark, more than in any other NT writing. It occurs in the first sentence attributed to Jesus, a kerygmatical expression that outlines the whole message of the Gospel: πεπλήρωται ὁ καιρὸς καὶ ἤγγικεν ἡ βασιλεία τοῦ θεοῦ· μετανοεῖτε καὶ πιστεύετε ἐν τῷ εὐαγγελίῳ (1:15); the other occurrences are localized in the last part of the Gospel, when Jesus' passion is approaching, in this way

concerned and attentive in his record of the progression of the days, and even of the hours, related to that event.

There have been divergent opinions among scholars on the reckoning of days mentioned in the last chapters of *Mark*.[9] Although an historical reconstruction of the events is not my task, I want to recall the writer's effort to frame the last days of Jesus' earthly life in a 'day-by-day' scheme, alongside his interest in mentioning also the passing of hours on the day of Jesus' death.[10] The temporal organization of the Markan passion narrative is quite complex.[11] A close look allows us to distinguish a first group of three days, thematically linked to the temple, where Jesus and his disciples enter everyday, and where he delivers his teachings.[12] These first three days are pointed out by precise references to the evenings and to the mornings: ὀψίας ἤδη οὔσης τῆς ὥρας in Mark 11:11; τῇ ἐπαύριον in Mark 11:12; ὅταν ὀψὲ ἐγένετο in Mark 11:19; πρωΐ in Mark 11:20. In this way, Mark evokes the creation tale of *Genesis* 1:1–2:3.

The following three days are signaled through a sort of countdown, with reference to the Passover feast: "after two days it was Passover and the Unleavened Breads" in Mark 14:1; "on the first day of the Unleavened Breads, when the Passover was immolated" in Mark 14:12. The sixth day of the series, the day of Jesus' death, is called in Mark 15:42 by its name, the "Preparation" (παρασκευή) coinciding with our Friday. The temple is no longer the setting of Jesus' actions. The episodes assigned to this second group of three days include the conspiracy against Jesus by the high priests (14:1–2), the anointing at Bethany (14:3–9), Judas' meeting with the high priests (14:10–11) [day 4], the preparation for the last supper (14:12–16) [day 5] and the

---

parallelling the increasing interest manifested by the redactor in temporal indications: see 10:30; 11:13; 12:2; 13:33.

[9] Cf. e.g. Schreiber 1961, 154–83; Schreiber 1967; Schenke 1971.

[10] The third: 15:25; the sixth: 15:33; the ninth: 15:33–34. Also in the previous night the narrator does not fail to record the passing of the hours: cf. 14:35.37.41; 14:30.68.72.

[11] For the following observations on Markan passion's week I heavily rely on the reconstructions proposed by Corsini 1985, 241–51; and Mazzucco 2000, 105–33, esp. 112–15.

[12] The Apocalyptic discourse of Mark 13:5–37 is spoken by Jesus outside the temple (cf. 13:1), "in front of it" while he is on the Mount of the Olives (cf. 13:3); nevertheless, the content of this discourse is strictly related to the temple.

events from the last supper to Jesus' burial (14:17–15:47) [day 6].[13] After the dramatic episodes recounted in these six days, the narrative flow continues on and references two supplementary days. The first is the Sabbath. In obedience to the traditional prescription, no event is assigned to this day, but it is mentioned twice: 16:1 and 16:2. The other is the day after the Sabbath which is bound to the sixth day in a grouping that takes the Sabbath as its point of reference so that the grouping includes the "Preparation" or Sabbath Eve, the Sabbath itself and the day after the Sabbath.

The complete scheme emerging from the *Gospel of Mark* is the following:

Week day	Markan reference	Description of activity	Temporal indications
Day 1	Mark 11,1–11	Jesus' entry into Jerusalem and his first visit to the temple.	The beginning of this day is not stated. Nevertheless, the evening is mentioned: ὀψίαϛ ἤδη οὔσης τῆς ὥρας (11:11)
Day 2	Mark 11:12–19	Part 1 of the fig-tree episode and Jesus' action inside the temple.	τῇ ἐπαύριον (11:12) ὅταν ὀψὲ ἐγένετο (11:19)
Day 3	Mark 11:20–13:37	Part 2 of the fig-tree episode; teaching on faith an prayer; debate on Jesus' authority; parable of the vineyard; teaching about the tribute; debate with the Sadducees on the resurrection; teaching on the first commandment; dispute on the relationship between the Messiah and David; teaching against the scribes; episode of the widow; prediction of the temple's ruin; eschatological discourse.	προΐ (11:20)

---

[13] In accordance with the traditional Jewish use, we must place the beginning of the Passover day at the sunset of the previous day, that is punctually recorded in the text: cf. 14:17: καὶ ὀψίας γενομένης ἔρχεται μετὰ τῶν δώδεκα. In each of these three-days series it has been recognized to be a climactic structure that both quantitatively and qualitatively culminates in the last day of each series (the third and the sixth in the main enumeration). Therefore this parallel structure invites to link the third and the sixth day; this relationship supported by numerous textual correspondences on the thematic level. Cf. Mazzucco 2000, 113–114.

able (cont.)

Week day	Markan reference	Description of activity	Temporal indications
Day 4	Mark 14:1–11	Plot against Jesus; anointing at Bethany; meeting of Judas with the high priests.	ἦν δὲ τὸ πάσχα καὶ τὰ ἄζυμα μετὰ δύο ἡμέρας (14:1)
Day 5	Mark 14:12–16	Preparation for the Passover dinner.	τῇ πρώτῃ ἡμέρᾳ τῶν ἀζύμων, ὅτε τὸ πάσχα ἔθυον (14:12)
Day 6	Mark 14:17–15:47	The last supper; prediction of Peter's denial; prayer in the Gethsemani; Jesus' arrest; trial; Peter's denial; Jesus' condemnation by Pilate; Jesus' passion, death and deposition.	ὀψίας γενομένης (14:17); εὐθὺς πρωΐ (15:1); ἦν δὲ ὥρα τρίτη (15:25); γενομένης ὥρας ἕκτης (15:33) ἕως ὥρας ἐνάτης (15:33); τῇ ἐνάτῃ ὥρᾳ (15:34); ἤδη ὀψίας γενομένης (15:42); ἦν παρασκευὴ (15:42)
Day 7	Mark 15:42, 16:1–2	No events are assigned to this day.	προσάββατον (15:42); διαγενομένου τοῦ σαββάτου (16:1); τῇ μιᾷ τῶν σαββάτων (16:2)
Day 8	Mark 16:1–8	The women at the sepulcher.	διαγενομένου τοῦ σαββάτου (16:1); λίαν πρωΐ τῇ μιᾷ τῶν σαββάτων (16:2)

Such an accurately constructed and sophisticated scheme, rich in symbolic allusions and biblical overtones, establishes internal literary relationships between different days and functions as a reading key to the episodes included in the account.[14]

In the other synoptic gospels the accurate temporal arrangement of the episodes preceding Jesus' death provided by the Markan redactor is dissolved into more generic pieces of information. Whether a choice of the writer or the result of an independent use of the sources, the *Gospel of Matthew* sets into a two-day scheme the events which Mark displays in the first three days of the passion's week. The two morning-journeys from Bethany to Jerusalem are reduced to one.[15] From 26:2,

---

[14] Corsini detects in the features of the sixth days series references and allusions to the creation week of *Gen* 1:1–2:4 and the last of the seventy weeks prophecy of *Dan* 9:27. Cf. Corsini 1985. Cf. Mazzucco 2000, 112–115. See also Grosso 2005, 121–147.

[15] Cp. Mark 11:12.20 with Matt 21:18. For a presentation and critique of different scholarly opinions on sources and redaction cf. Telford 1980, 71–74.

Matthew follows the same sequence as Mark for the remaining part of the week. The result is that the overall structure, from the entry into Jerusalem to the discovery of the empty tomb, forecasts seven days instead of eight.[16] A minor difference is that Matthew omits to record the crucifixion's time.[17] Despite this, this gospel is more precise in recording the time of the discovery of the empty tomb.[18]

In accordance with his historiographical interests, Luke enriches his work with a number of temporal indications which are different, responding to distinct needs. This is especially true in his account of Jesus' infancy.[19] But, in the Lukan chronicle of Jesus' last days, the detailed scheme adopted by Mark is totally lost. In this section of the gospel the temporal indications are in fact quite vague compared with Mark's version of the passion account. In Luke 19:47 we find: "every day he was teaching in the temple." In chapter 20:1, Luke writes: "on one of those days, while he was teaching the people in the temple." In chapter 21:37, these words are used: "during the day he used to teach in the temple, during the night he used to go outside." Luke speaks of the approach of "the feast of the Unleavened Breads, which is called the Passover" in 22:1. According to 22:7, "the day of the Unleavened Breads arrived." The narrator provides us with the general chronological setting of Jesus' death—the Passover feast—but he is not interested in reporting a careful scan as Mark does. Nevertheless, he appears to give a certain importance to the theological meaning of the 'hour', in connection with Jesus' death.[20]

In the *Gospel of John*, the narrator emphasizes the theological connotations of Jesus' crucial 'hour' by aligning it with the time of his condemnation by Pilate. It happened at noon, when the ritual slaughtering of the lambs began.[21] Such a pregnant meaning is probably to be kept in mind while we read the other episodes where the hours of the day are recorded.[22] As J. Edgar Bruns noted years ago, the "pervasive symbolism" of the fourth Gospel includes the use of time indications.[23] It has also been noted by commentators how carefully the Johannine

[16] Matt 21:1–28:1.
[17] Cf. Matt 27:35.
[18] Cf. Matt 28:1: ὀψὲ δὲ σαββάτων, τῇ ἐπιφωσκούσῃ εἰς μίαν σαββάτων.
[19] Cf. Luke 1:5.10.24.26.39.56.59; 2:1.22.42.43; 9:28.
[20] Luke 22:14.53; 23:44.
[21] John 19:14; Brown 1970, 883.
[22] John 1:39; 4:6.52; Cf. Grech 2003, 777–85.
[23] Bruns 1966–67, 285–90.

writer provides a chronological structure to the first events of Jesus' life he recounts. The passing of the days is progressively marked by τῇ ἐπαύριον in 1:29.35.43 and implied by τῇ ἡμέρᾳ τρίτῃ in 2:1, which introduces the account of the wedding at Cana. There are divergent opinions in scholarship on the effective reckoning the days in this section of the gospel.[24] Nevertheless the significance of a week scheme remains clear as it parallels the creation's week of *Genesis*, a book recalled also in the Johannine prologue.

About Jesus' last week, John does not point out a clear sequence of single days. John adopts, however, a chronology distinct from the Markan one. He records that the anointing at Bethany took place "six days before Passover" and that "the following day" Jesus entered triumphantly into Jerusalem.[25] Jesus' last supper is introduced by the imprecise indication "before the feast of Passover" (13:1). The day of Jesus' death is indicated by its name, the "Preparation" (παρασκευή, 19:31).

The *Gospel of Peter* is very careful in providing the temporal frame of the passion events, both in terms of days and of hours.[26] Substantial attention to the chronological data is a fundamental feature of this gospel. The fragmentary conditions of the text, though, do not allow us to prove that the recorded events were framed in a developed hebdomadal construction similar to the Markan one.

PRIOR UNDERSTANDINGS OF THE CHRONOLOGY IN THE *GOSPEL OF JUDAS*

It is remarkable that the *Gospel of Judas*, even if it does not consist in a narration of actions, is quite scrupulous in providing the temporal context of the revelations it includes. In terms of eschatology, this text manifests a broad interest in the chronological aspects of Gnostic salvation.[27] There are several places where this is apparent. In 36,7–8 Judas

---

[24] For a summary of scholarly solutions cf. Brown 1966, 105–7.

[25] John 12:1; 12:12.

[26] See *Gos. Pet.* 5 (σάββατον ἐπιφώσκει; πρὸ μιᾶς τῶν ἀζύμων); 15 (ἦν δὲ μεσημβρία); 22 (τότε ἥλιος ἔλαμψε καὶ εὑρέθη ὥρα ἐνάτη); 27 (ἐνηστεύομεν καὶ ἐκαθεζόμεθα πενθοῦντες καὶ κλαίοντες νυκτὸς καὶ ἡμέρας ἕως τοῦ σαββάτου); 34 (πρωΐας δὲ ἐπιφώσκοντος τοῦ σαββάτου); 35 (τῇ δὲ νυκτὶ ᾗ ἐπέφωσκεν ἡ κυριακή); 45 (νυκτὸς); 50 (ὄρθρου δὲ τῆς κυριακῆς); 58 (ἦν δὲ τελευταία ἡμέρα τῶν ἀζύμων).

[27] See the references to Sethian numerology at pages 49–51 of the *Gospel of Judas*.

questions Jesus about the "great day of light." According to 40,25–26, when Jesus interprets the disciples' nightmare, he declares that "on the last day they (i.e. the priests who sacrifice) will be guilty." In 53,11–16, we are told that "Adam and his generation received numbered days." In 46,24 a reference to the "last days" occurs, although the subsequent lacuna makes it difficult to develop further reflections on this point.

With the exception of 33,3–6, the temporal indications related to the dialogues reported in the text are:

> 33,23–24: ⲛⲟⲩϩⲟ[ⲟ]ⲩ, "one day"
> 36,11: ϣⲱ[ⲣ]ⲡ ⲇⲉ ⲛⲧⲉⲣⲉϥϣⲱⲡⲉ, "now, the next morning"
> 37,20–21: ⲕⲁⲓϩⲟⲟⲩ, "another day"

We are instinctively brought to consider these literary elements as linked to the expression "during eight days, three days before he celebrated Passover." But the comparison does not lead to an immediate or plain solution. On the contrary it raises further questions of a different order. Which days are the mentioned days? Which passion chronology is implied by the text? What is the meaning and nature of the reference to the "eight days"?

In his introduction to the *Gospel of Judas* in the *Critical Edition* of Codex Tchacos, Gregor Wurst rightly points out how the expression "three days before he celebrated Passover" "could be the key to the structure and the composition of the *Gospel of Judas*."[28] He remarks that this indication is mirrored in the registration of three different days, marked by the indications found at 36,11 and 37,20–21. He left open the possibility that a fourth day could be supposed in the text.[29] Wurst is aware that the abrupt transition to a new sequence between lines 14 and 15 of page 44 could imply a temporal break (as a passage to a new day), but he warns that a scribal error can be identified at 44,14: ⲁϥⲃⲱⲕ, "he departed," in spite of ⲁ⟨ⲩ⟩ⲃⲱⲕ, "⟨they⟩ departed," implying that originally the text intended Jesus and the disciples to move away together.[30] While subscribing to these observations, I would like to add that the subsequent phrase ascribed to Judas suggests a strict continuity with what happens before. Judas says: "As you have listened to all of them, now also listen to me. For I have seen a great vision."[31] This

---

[28] Gregor Wurst in Kasser et al. 2007, 179.
[29] Kasser et al. 2007, 180.
[30] Kasser et al. 2007, 180; cf. 207 n. 13–15.
[31] Gos. Jud. 44,16–18.

recollection of the disciple's questions about their own earlier vision calls for the unity of the narrative flow. Thus there is no need to imply a temporal break at this point.

According to Professor Wurst, the *Gospel of Judas* gives an account of the dialogues that occurred in the last three (or four) days of Jesus' life. He supports this statement by observing that the occurrence of the noun ⲕⲁⲧⲁⲗⲩⲙⲁ in the last part of the treatise alludes to the setting provided by the Gospels of Mark and Luke to Jesus' last supper.[32] After this Jesus' arrest takes place and the betrayal is accomplished with the handing of Jesus to his opponents. Although this account of Jesus' arrest departs significantly from the canonical ones, omitting mention of the garden of Gethsemane scene, at the same time it assumes the identical basic sequence of the events: the arrest takes place after Jesus has left the ⲕⲁⲧⲁⲗⲩⲙⲁ.[33]

Alongside Wurst's analysis, other proposals have been put forward by scholars on this specific topic. Gesine Schenke Robinson offers a very detailed configuration of what would have been the subdivision of the days originally intended by the writer. Her reconstruction, however, departs significantly from the one proposed by Gregor Wurst.[34] Her comprehensive inquiry is compelling for many reasons. Nevertheless it raises questions that I would like to address. Based on her reading of 33,3–6, she thinks that Jesus delivers his revelations on eight consecutive days, which terminate three days before he would have suffered. She thinks that the formula ⲣ̄ ⲡⲁⲥⲭⲁ derives from the Greek verb πάσχειν. This possibility, admitted also by the editors of Codex Tchacos,[35] seems to me remote, the alternative one being supported by the Coptic translations of the Greek phrase ποιεῖν τὴν πάσχα in Matthew 26:18 and Hebrews 11:28. Moreover, I find the use of πάσχειν problematic, if not misplaced, in a text that, as Professor Schenke Robinson herself observes, assumes a Docetist understanding of Jesus' crucifixion. This problem, by the way, is not insurmountable, given that Jesus' Passover and Jesus' passion, as we will see, may easily

---

[32] Cp. Gos. Jud. 58,11 with Mark 14:14; Luke 22:11.

[33] The *Gospel of Judas* does not mention the last supper; according to the text, Jesus went to the ⲕⲁⲧⲁⲗⲩⲙⲁ for his prayer (ⲡⲣⲟⲥⲉⲩⲭⲏ cf. 58:12.16); this term is compatible, in my opinion, with a ritual context. It would sound odd, by the way, to find Jesus celebrating the last supper, given the sharp critique expressed in this text against the eucharist.

[34] Cf. Schenke Robinson 2008a, 63–98.

[35] Cf. Kasser et al. 2007, 185 n. 5–6.

coincide. More questionable is the fact that this translation choice is supported with her remark that "there is no reason for him [i.e. Jesus] to stop talking to his disciples three days *before* a Passover if *he* were to celebrate."[36]

Nevertheless, if we look at the Synoptic Gospels, we see that the last supper is likely to be held as a Passover meal.[37] According to the Synoptic accounts, then, Jesus and his disciples did actually celebrate the core of the Passover feast: the communal dinner held on the evening before the Passover day, when liturgically that day has already begun. If we look at the *Gospel of John*, on the other hand, the identification of Jesus' last supper with a Passover meal is less probable (although not impossible),[38] but the effort sustained by the writer to make Jesus' passion and crucifixion coincide with the time when the lambs were slain in the temple produces the result that Jesus celebrated Passover in a very special way, as a victim of the sacrifice. In both cases, we can affirm that Jesus actually celebrated Passover.

According to Professor Schenke Robinson's hypothesis, the "three days" mentioned at *Gospel of Judas* 33,4–5 (consisting in three days before Jesus' suffering) "could count from the day of his ascent in the cloud via (1) the day of the arrest, and (2) the day of the trial, (3) the day of the crucifixion."[39] Now, so far as I could ascertain, none of the extant early Christian sources assigns those dramatic events (the arrest, the trial, the crucifixion) to three different days. Rather, according to both the Synoptics and John, they are assigned to *two* different days, perhaps to only *one*, if we think according to the Jewish liturgical use, which fixes the beginning of the new day at the sunset of the previous one. According to our accounts, the trial takes place the very same night of Jesus' arrest. Then, without a substantial breaking of the temporal line, it is followed by his condemnation by Pilate—early in the morning according to Mark 15:25, who locates the crucifixion at 9:00 a.m., at twelve o'clock according to John 19:14—and then by his passion and death. All these events belong to the same liturgical day,

---

[36] Schenke Robinson 2008a, 73.
[37] Mark 14:12; Matt 26:17; Luke 22:7–8. This is the most natural reading of the synoptic accounts, given the question posed by the disciples: "Where do you want that we go to prepare, so that you can eat the Passover?" (Cf. Mark 14:12 and parallels; see also Mark 14:14). The issue, though, is much more intricated: for a comprehensive discussion see: Morris 1995, 684–95.
[38] Morris 1995, 684–95.
[39] Schenke Robinson 2008a, 73.

a very long and dramatic one beginning with the last supper, when it was evening (καὶ ὀψίας γενομένης) according to Mark 14:17 and it was night (ἦν δὲ νύξ) according to John 13:30. Consequently, the Gnostic ascent of Jesus' soul, placed before his arrest, must be located on the same day of his passion, according to the Jewish reckoning, or, at least on the day before, according to our modern method of counting days. In any case, it is not three days before the passion.

Professor Schenke Robinson then observes that in the *Gospel of Judas* "the beginning and/or the end of the first four days are clearly indicated."[40] The phrase "after Jesus said this he departed" in 44,13–14 (which does not contain any explicit temporal indication), she thinks indicates "the end of the fourth day," even though it would logically indicate the end of the third day which started in 37,20–21: "another day Jesus came to [them]."[41] Such a reconstruction implies a chronological change on the base of a variation of scene and characters, involving different grammatical subjects and topics, where the text is silent on any temporal data.[42] According to this hypothesis the eight different days (a number that would be coherent with the indication found in the incipit) are distinguished as follows: Day 1: 33,22–36,10; Day 2: 36,11–37,20; Day 3: 37,20–42,?; Day 4: 42,?-44,14; Day 5: 44,15–47,1; Day 6: 47,1–53,4; Day 7: 53,5–54,2; Day 8: 54,3?-58,?.[43]

Although this attempt is intriguing, because it takes into serious account the importance of the temporal indication of 33,3–6 in structuring the text, it remains quite speculative, mainly because it forces us to locate the presence of chronological marks in the lacunae (on page 42 and at the first lines of page 54), and to assume a temporal shift where the text does not clearly state it as in the *Gospel of Judas* 44,14–15, 47,1, and 53,5. A similar hypothesis has been presented by Rodolphe Kasser, who, in a footnote of his French translation in the critical edition, put forward a possible subdivision in eight chapters, corresponding to eight days, structured in this way: Day 1: 33,22–36,10; Day 2: 36,11–37,20; Day 3: 37,20–44,14; Day 4: 44,15–47,1; Day 5: 47,1–50,19; Day 6: 50,19–53,7; Day 7: 53,8–56,9; Day 8:

---

[40] Schenke Robinson 2008a, 73.

[41] Schenke Robinson 2008a, 73 n. 58.

[42] We already recalled that even the change of scene is dubious, given the possibility of a scribal error (ⲁϥⲃⲱⲕ [he departed] in spite of ⲁ⟨ⲩ⟩ⲃⲱⲕ [⟨they⟩ departed]) that would have marked a breaking of the narrative flow, where actually the characters involved remain the same. Cf. Kasser et al. 2007, 180.

[43] Schenke Robinson 2008a, 73 n. 58; 74.

56,10–58,5(?).[44] Again 44,14, 17,1, 50,19, and 53,7–8 do not provide any temporal marks; 56,9–10 and 58,5 are fragmentary.

Although these two eight-day hypotheses are based on circumstantiated reflections on the internal organization of our dialogue, the discrepancies between them demonstrate that a subdivision into eight days is not clear at all. Interpreters like Schenke Robinson and Kasser must struggle to recognize in the narrative flow eight coherent thematic unities that correspond to as many days. In my view, a strict correspondence between the chronological organization of the accounts and the thematic subdivision of a text is an assumption. The two levels may not overlap, given the possibility of multiple reprises of a single theme in different days, or of a development of different themes inside a single temporal unity.

A BETTER SOLUTION

We cannot exclude that one or more temporal indications were originally standing in the lacunose parts of the manuscript. But the only chronological markers which are extant are those located at 33,23–24, "one day," 36,11, "the next morning," and 37,21, "another day."[45] This evidence compels me to conclude that the temporal structure objectively emerging from the text is one that contemplates a three-day structure, as first recognized by Gregor Wurst.[46] After the introduction in 33,1–21, we have a first day mentioned in 33,22–36,10, which includes Jesus' reproof of the eucharist offered by the disciples and the confession scene, when Judas comes to stage. On the second day, in 36,11–37,20, Jesus speaks to the disciples about the great holy generation. The third day, according to 37,20–58,26, addresses the disciples' nightmare, its explanation by Jesus, Jesus' instruction on the error of the disciples, the account of Judas' dream with its interpretation by Jesus, the instruction to Judas about the Sethian world, the dialogue between Jesus and Judas on the fate of human being, the prediction of Judas' fate and the account of the betrayal. The extraordinary extension of the third day in respect to the first two is not surprising, since

---

[44] Kasser et al. 2007, 237.

[45] At 37,23–24 we find a complementary reference to the previous night: "…for we have had great [dreams] [during] this night (ⲛ̄ⲧⲉⲉⲓⲟⲩϣⲏ) that has passed".

[46] Cf. Kasser et al. 2007, 180–81.

it is a feature common to other texts.[47] It is the climax of the narrative progression of the revelation.

Once it is established that the revelation to Judas is displayed in a three-day scheme, we must try to solve two further problems. First, how can we interpret the reference in the incipit to a period of eight days? Second, where should we locate the three-day revelation in the main frame of the passion chronology?

If we look to the Gnostic texts, we hardly find a parallel to the expression ⲛ̄ [ϣ]ⲙⲟⲩⲛ ⲛ̄ϩⲟⲟⲩ, "during eight days."[48] Although the number eight is frequently mentioned in Nag Hammadi treatises, it is never, to my knowledge, associated with an extended period of time nor with a group of days. Rather it is used to indicate different cosmological elements, such as the eighth aeon, the eight heavens, or the eight forms of the Cherubim chariot.[49] The speculations about the Ogdoad during the second century, both in Christian and Gnostic environments, should also be taken into consideration.[50] But the mystical reflection on the Ogdoad, as it emerges from the ancient sources, focuses on the 'eighth' day, that, as the day of the resurrection, transmits its significance to the preceding ones. In the incipit of the *Gospel of Judas*, on the contrary, we deal with an extended and continuous period of eight days, without any particular focus on the last one. It is notable that the number eight occurs six times in the New Testament, and in five of those six occurrences it is used with the purpose of counting time, once referring to years, four times referring to days.[51]

---

[47] See for instance the previous observations on the structure of the passion's week in the Gospel of Mark, where the third and the sixth day of the series embrace an amount of material more extended in respect to the previous ones.

[48] Gos. Jud. 33,3.

[49] Cf. *Hyp. Arch.* (NHC II,4) 95,33; *Orig. World* (II,5) 104,31; 105,5.11; 23.28; 106,8; 108,4; 112,12.20; 125,5; *Ap. John* (III,1) 17,2; *Eugnostos* (III,3) 85,19; 87,1; *Gos. Eg.* (IV,2) 70,3; *Apoc. Adam* (V,5) 80,21; *Disc. 8–9* (VI,6) 52,4; 53,25; 55,16; 62,4; *Zost.* (VIII,1) 127,4; *Testim. Truth* (IX,3) 55,2; *Marsanes* (X,1) 4,2; 32,25; *Soph. Jes. Chr* (BG,3) 123,10; 124,9.

[50] Cf. *Gos. Eg.* (NHC IV,2) 51,17.22; 53,3.15.26; 63,23.24.29; 64,9; 65,3; *Disc. 8–9* (VI,6) 58,17; *Treat. Of Seth* (VII,2) 65,37; 62,30; *Testim. Truth* (IX,3) 55,1; 56,3; *Soph. Jes. Chr.* (BG,3) 95,13; 114,6. For the patristic witnesses cf. Irenaeus, *Adv. Haer.* I, 1,1; 4,1; 5,2–3; 11,1; Hipp. *Ref.* VI, 31–34.38.47; VII, 23.25.27; Clement of Alexandria, *Exc. ex Theod.* 63,1; *Strom.* IV,152,2; V,36,3; VI,108,1.140,3; VII,57,5. For the Barbelo-Gnostics, according to Epiphanius, the Ogdoad is the eighth heaven, in which Barbelo resides (cf. Epiph., *Pan.* 40,2).

[51] Cf. Luke 2:21 ("and when the eight days of the circumcision were accomplished, he was named Jesus…"); 9:28 ("About eight days after these speeches…" [introducing the Transfiguration episode]); John 20:26 ("After eight days his disciples were

None of these occurrences thematically fits with the temporal setting of the revelation contained in the *Gospel of Judas*. Nevertheless, in the light of the biblical symbolism, we can recognize in the use of the number eight a general allusion to completion, a reference to a fulfilled and well-defined period of time.[52] Yet the expression ⲛ̄ [ϣ]ⲙⲟⲩⲛ ⲛ̄ϩⲟⲟⲩ does not simply indicate a week. The author is aware of the difference between these eight days and a week, since elsewhere he uses the term ϩⲉⲃⲇⲟⲙⲁⲥ.[53] The 'eight days' mentioned at 33,3–6 are something different from a week, and not only quantitatively.

The combination of the phrases "during eight days" and "three days before he celebrated Passover" suggests that the author intended to locate the revelation contained in the gospel in a precise moment of the salvation history. As John D. Turner has pointed out, in early Sethian treatises that manifest adherence to a "descent pattern," the periodic revelatory descents of the divine envoys occur in coincidence with topical moments in human history, such as the time of the flood, the judgment upon Sodom and Gomorrah, and the "eschatological nullification of the anti-divine forces", which appears to be the case in the *Gospel of Judas*.[54] In fact, the temporal setting of the revelation is connected with the final attack of the demonic forces against Jesus, a battle that takes place in a special, unrepeatable moment. This combat directly involves Jesus during his last week, when, according to the canonical accounts, after he enters Jerusalem, he faces the increasing opposition of the high priests and the Jewish leaders (characters mentioned also in the *Gospel of Judas*). This is a clear symptom of the final attack that the antagonistic forces launch against him. This ultimate assault materially realized through Judas, who is called "demon" in our text.[55] The demonic forces seem to succeed in their task for a while, but, according to the Gnostic view, Jesus escapes the crucifixion by abandoning his body. At the end, his victory will be manifested with his resurrection. By mentioning a period of eight days, the author

inside again and also Thomas was with them"); Acts 9:33 ("There he [Peter] found a man named Eneas, who has been on a bed for eight years and that was paralytic"); 25:6 ("After being remained among them no more than eight or ten days [Festus] came down to Caesarea…"); 1 Pet 3:20 ("a few, eight people, were saved through the water").

[52] On the number eight as symbol of plenitude see Bovon 2001, 283.
[53] Gos. Jud. 38,15.
[54] Cf. Turner 2002, 203–11.
[55] Luke 22:3; John 13:27; Gos. Jud. 44,20.

of the *Gospel of Judas* intended to refer to this specific, significant moment in the salvation history. It is probable, in my view, that when he wrote these words he had in mind the passion account of the *Gospel of Mark*, the only one that, as I outlined in the first part of this paper, with precision arranges in eight days (3+3+2) the events embraced by Jesus' entry into Jerusalem and his resurrection.[56]

By referring to this traditional reckoning of the passion's days, the writer of the *Gospel of Judas* provides a fundamental chronological frame to the revelation he presents, locating it in that crucial period of salvation history. Secondarily he specifies that, within the ambit of that period of eight days, the revelatory discourses addressed to Judas occurred specifically in three days. A three-day revelation, as we saw, is exactly what we can detect in the text according to the temporal indications provided by the author at 33,23–24; 36,11; 37,20–21.

How can we better locate these three days? A possibility is that the author intended the revelation to end three days before Passover, as some scholars have already suggested.[57] According to the Markan scheme, that would mean that the revelation ended on the fourth day of the series, since Passover is the sixth day. But a better solution is to understand that the dialogues occur over the three days which lead up to the Passover feast. These three days would correspond to the fourth, the fifth and the sixth of the Markan series.[58]

Although this is not explicit in 33,3–6, I think that it is sufficiently clear in the light of other textual hints. In the first place, the preposition ϩⲁⲑⲏ probably translates an original Greek πρὸ, as it does in the parallel expression found at John 12:1: "Jesus therefore before six days to the Paskha came to Bethania."[59] Thus, this preposition refers to a starting point rather than an ending one. The natural reading would suggest that the revelation starts three days before Passover.

Second, as underscored by Gregor Wurst, the word ⲕⲁⲧⲁⲗⲩⲙⲁ occurring at 58,11 provides a patent reference to the setting of the last supper according to Mark 14:14 and Luke 22:11, after which the betrayal is accomplished and Jesus is arrested. As I already pointed

---

[56] See above.

[57] See i.a. Gathercole 2007, 63; Pagels-King 2007, 124.

[58] According to the ancient way of counting, the Passover day must be included in our reckoning, like in Mark 14:1 the expression "after two days was the Passover and the Unleavened Breads" actually states that the following day was Passover.

[59] Cf. Nagel 2007, 238 n. 65. For the text of John cf. Horner 1969, 200.

out, despite the omission of the Gethsemane scene, the basic traditional sequence of the events is not altered in the *Gospel of Judas.*

Third, the final scene of the *Gospel of Judas* more likely refers to the handing over of Jesus to the people who were sent by the high priests than to the plot between Judas and the high priests found in Mark 14:10–11, since the incident took place after the last supper. According to Mark 14:10–11, the priests only promised to give Judas some money: ἐπηγγείλαντο αὐτῷ ἀργύριον δοῦναι. They did not actually give him the money. The *Gospel of Judas*, however, is clear in affirming: "Then Judas received some money. He handed him over to them."[60]

In the *Gospel of Mark*, aside from the mention of Judas as a member of the twelve disciples (3:16–19), Judas comes to the stage as a character on the fourth day of the passion week. This is after the episode of the anointing at Bethany, when he visits the high priests (14,10–11).[61] Hence Judas carries out his role in the brief space of three days: the fourth, the fifth and the sixth of the passion week. These three days can easily be understood to correspond with the three days recounted in the *Gospel of Judas*. In fact, in the light of the textual hints I have presented in this paper, the concluding story of the *Gospel of Judas* is the delivery of Jesus' body in the hands of his opponents. In other words, the three days mentioned in the *Gospel of Judas* correspond with the fourth, the fifth and the sixth of the Markan series. This parallelism is strengthened by the fact that the prediction of Judas' betrayal in Mark is pronounced by Jesus during the last supper (Mark 14:18–21), on the sixth day of the Markan series, on the third day after Judas's first appearance in the Markan passion story. Analogously, in the *Gospel of Judas*, the prediction of Judas' betrayal (56,17–20: "the man who bears me you will sacrifice him") is located on its third day.[62]

It is noteworthy that a close parallel to this temporal setting can be found in *James*, the second treatise of Codex Tchacos. It follows an analogous pattern, where the revelation addressed to the apostle

---

[60] *Gos. Jud.* 58:24–26.

[61] This day begins at 14:1 with the indication ἦν δὲ τὸ πάσχα καὶ τὰ ἄζυμα μετὰ δύο ἡμέρας. For the complete scheme of the Markan passion week, see above.

[62] One may object that on sixth day of the Markan series, beginning at 14:17 (ὀψίας γενομένης), there would be no room for so extended a revelation as the one contained in the third day of *the Gospel of Judas*, that would hence overlap with the traditional recount of the last supper. Nonetheless we must keep in mind that the author was far less concerned of giving a realistic account than of providing its work with meaningful theological links with the passion narrative.

begins the very same day that it begins in the *Gospel of Judas*. In *James* 11,9–10, Jesus even says: "They will [arrest me] after three days".

How should the opening reference to three days and eight days finally be understood? The preposition ⲛ̄ at 33,3 of *Gospel of Judas* likely translates the Greek ἐν, which, in temporal locutions, indicates something occurring for an extended period of time. Therefore the clearest translation choice appears to be the English preposition "during," as has been done by the editors of the *Critical Edition*. Nevertheless, I find it urgent to make more specific in my translation that the narrator intended the reader to understand that the secret revelation was taking place at a particular point *in the course of eight days*, namely that it started three days before Jesus celebrated Passover. These eight days are not a vague period. Rather they coincide with the temporal setting given by Mark to Jesus' ministry in Jerusalem and to his passion, death and resurrection, which is a meaningful and crucial moment for Christian and Gnostic believers.

Such a subtle reference to the *Gospel of Mark* supports the writer's inspiration to parody the canonical gospels, an inspiration detected in the *Gospel of Judas* by April DeConick. She says, "Whoever wrote this Gospel operated from a perspective informed by highly literal interpretations of biblical stories about the twelve disciples and grounded in an apocalyptic cosmology in which Archons created and ruled the universe as opponents of the supreme God, Jesus' Father".[63] Moreover, she has been demonstrating that the author of this treatise was a "careful reader" of the *Gospel of Mark* and founded much of his critique of the apostolic stream of Christianity by developing ideological concepts found *in nuce* in that Gospel.[64] It is probable, in my view, that alongside Mark's basic storyline and the other traces of Markan literary elements, our author also inherited from Mark a particular interest in the temporal data, and the arrangement in eight days of the passion week. This became the general chronological setting in which he located the secret revelation addressed to Judas.

---

[63] DeConick 2007, 103.
[64] DeConick 2007, 100–8.

THE *GOSPEL OF JUDAS* 45,6–7 AND ENOCH'S HEAVENLY TEMPLE

Lance Jenott

In a scene from the *Gospel of Judas*, Judas Iscariot describes his enigmatic vision of a magnificent house to Jesus:[1]

3 ⲁⲉⲓⲛⲁⲩ ⲉ[ⲩⲏⲉⲓ ⲁⲗⲗⲁ ⲧⲉϥⲁϊ̈ⲏ]ⲥ ⲁⲩ
4 ⲱ ⲡⲉϥϣⲓ ⲛⲁⲃⲁⲗ ⲛⲁϣ [ϣⲓⲧ⳥] ⲁⲛ
5 ⲛⲉⲣⲉ ϩⲛ̅ⲛⲟϭ ⲇⲉ ⲛ̅ⲣⲱⲙⲉ ⲕ[ⲱ]ⲧⲉ
6 ⲉⲣⲟϥ ⲡⲉ ⲁⲩⲱ ⲛⲉⲟⲩ‹ⲛ̅ⲧ⳥ ⲟⲩ›ⲥⲧⲉⲅⲏ ⲛ̣ⲟⲩ
7 ⲟ̣ⲧⲉ ⲡⲉ ⲛ̅ϭⲓ ⲡⲏⲉⲓ ⲉⲧⲛ̅ⲙ̣[ⲁⲩ] ⸳ ⲁⲩ
8 ⲱ ϩⲛ̅ ⲧⲙⲏⲧⲉ ⲙ̅ⲡⲏⲓ̈ ⲉⲣ[ⲉ ⲟⲩ]ⲙ̣ⲏ
9 [ⲛϣⲉ   ].̣ [   ] ⲕ̇

Translation:
I saw [a house, but its size] and
expanse my eyes were not able to [measure].
There were some great people surrounding
it, and that house had a *roof of greenery* (?).
And in the middle of the house there was a
[crowd] […]

Since the publication of the first English translation of the *Gospel of Judas* (National Geographic Society, 2006), the meaning of the ⲥⲧⲉⲅⲏ ⲛ̣ⲟⲩⲟⲧⲉ witnessed by Judas has continued to mystify readers and researchers alike. Indeed, the editors of the critical edition note that the "complement ⲛ̣ⲟⲩⲟⲧⲉ may be regarded, if the reading is correct, as a *crux*, because a 'roof of greenery (or, herbs)' remains difficult."[2] Among other translations one finds "roofed with greenery," "roof of herbs," "a grass roof," and even "a thatched roof."[3] Interpretations of its

---

[1] *Gos. Jud.* 45,3–9, following the transcript of Kasser et al. 2007, with additional reconstructions according to an unpublished transcript generously shared with me by Wolf-Peter Funk. The translation is my own.

[2] Kasser et al. 2007, 209 (*loc. cit.*). They continue, "One may speculate whether ⲟⲩⲟⲧⲉ is a scribal error for ⲟⲩⲟⲥⲧⲛ̅, so that the original text would have read: 'And that house had a broad roof.'"

[3] Pagels-King 2007; Gathercole, 2007; DeConick 2007; Meyer 2007b.

significance have ranged from images of the bountiful foliage of paradise to the greenery of the hanging gardens of Babylon.[4]

Alternatively, Jacques van der Vliet has suggested reading the phrase simply as "one single room."[5] According to his rendition, ⲟⲩⲟⲧⲉ should be understood as a variant of the rare feminine form of ⲟⲩⲱⲧ, ⲟⲩⲱⲧⲉ ("single, alone"), and the Greek noun ἡ στέγη in its sense of "roofed space, room, chamber." While van der Vliet's reading is certainly feasible, and has the virtue of simplicity, the description of the house as consisting of "a single room" would still lack any apparent significance.[6]

A ROOF OF LIGHTNING

Rather than "greenery" or "single," I suggest that we read ⲟⲩⲟⲧⲉ as a variant or corrupted spelling of the feminine noun ⲟⲩⲏⲧⲉ, "lightning" or "fire."[7] Indeed, the noun's third letter, currently reconstructed in the NGS edition as ⲟ (ⲟⲩⲟⲧⲉ), may in fact be an epsilon (ⲉ) whose center stroke has faded. The round shape of the letter, like an uncial sigma, is clearly visible on photographs of the manuscript, and there are numerous examples of epsilons with faded center strokes elsewhere in the codex.[8] If the character is an epsilon, then ⲟⲩⲉⲧⲉ would simply be a phonetic variant of ⲟⲩⲏⲧⲉ.[9]

---

[4] See, for example, Gathercole 2007a, 84.

[5] Van der Vliet 2006a, 144–145.

[6] In comparison with 1 Enoch's vision of the heavenly temple—which I will pursue below—one could imagine that, under van der Vliet's hypothesis, the author of *Judas* meant to differentiate his depiction of the great house from that of Enoch's, which consists of an inner and outer building. But if that is the case, then it would be difficult to explain why the author of *Judas* has taken over Enoch's clear use of στέγη as "roof" and used it in the sense of "room."

[7] See the lexical entries in Černý 1976, 218: "lightning"; Westendorf 1965, 278: "Donnerwetter, Blitz und Donner" from Demotic *wt*, "Feuer, Blitz"; Crum 1939, 495a: "lightning (?), calamity"; Spiegelberg 1921, 172: "Blitz"; Bishop Bsciai, "Novem auctarium lexici sahidico-coptici," *Zeitschrift für ägyptische Sprache* 24 (1886), p. 102: "κεραυνός, *fulmen*."

[8] See for example TC 1,4 ⲛⲉⲥⲛⲏⲩ; 19,19 ⲉⲥⲉ; 40,19 ⲅⲉⲛⲉⲁ; 43,2 ⲉⲧ; 44,2 ⲛⲉⲩ[ⲕⲁⲣ]ⲡⲟⲥ; 44,26 ⲥⲉ; 51,22 ⲉⲡⲟⲩⲁ; 54,25 ⲡⲟⲣⲛⲉⲩⲉ. Only faint or partial ink traces of a center stroke appear in other cases: 23,11 ⲛⲧⲁⲉⲓ; 27,22 ⲛⲥⲉⲕⲱϩ; 40,20 ϩⲏⲏⲧⲉ; 45,24 ⲉⲧⲟⲩⲁⲁⲃ; 46,16 ⲟⲩ ⲡⲉ; 47,7 ⲗⲁⲟⲩⲉ; 47,23 ⲁⲅⲅⲉⲗⲟⲥ; 48,13 ⲉⲭⲱϥ; 50,24 ϭⲏⲡⲉ; 52,21 ϩⲣⲁⲉⲓ; 53,26 ⲛⲉⲧⲯⲩⲭⲏ. An examination of the character under ultraviolet light may conclusively determine whether it is an omicron or epsilon, but I have not yet been able to arrange such an analysis.

[9] On vocalic interchange see, for example, Crum 1939, 49–50; 66a.

Though rare in Coptic literature, ογητε translates κεραυνόω—"to strike with lightning bolts"—in the Sahidic Coptic of Isaiah 30:30 (where the Boharic version simply preserves the cognate noun κεραγνος).[10] Admittedly, in later writings the word does appear to carry the more general sense of "calamity," as seen in a letter of Shenoute referring to God's punishment on the house of Eli the priest.[11] Yet its more specific meaning "lightning," captured by the Sahidic translation of Isaiah's κεραυνόω, finds confirmation in its Demotic root *wt*, "fire, lightning."[12]

ENOCHIC INTERTEXTUALITIES

The reading cτεγη ηογετε, "a roof of lightning" or even "fire," would have a clear precedent with descriptions of the heavenly house found in *The Book of the Watchers*, which describes its roof as consisting of shooting stars, lightning and fire.[13] In 1 Enoch 14, Enoch describes the ceilings (στέγαι) of the first "great house" (οἶκον μέγαν) that he encounters as "shooting stars and lightning flashes" (διαδρομαὶ ἀστέρων καὶ ἀστραπαί).[14] After he enters the first house, Enoch sees "a house greater than the former one, and it was all built of tongues of fire…Its floor was of fire, and its uppermost part (ἀνώτερον) was flashes of lightning and shooting stars (ἀστραπαὶ καὶ διαδρομαὶ ἀστέρων), and its roof was a flaming fire" (ἡ στέγη αὐτοῦ ἦν πῦρ φλέγον).[15] Among the much later traditions developed in the *Sefer Hekhalot* (or 3 Enoch), this roof

---

[10] Isa 30:30 (LXX): "God shall make the glory of his voice heard, and he shall show the anger of his arm with anger and wrath and devouring fire. And he shall cast lightning bolts (κεραυνώσει) violently, like rain and mightily hurled hailstones." Compare Jerome's more literal translation *adlidet in turbine et in lapide grandinis* of MT ברד ואבן זרם נפץ. Coptic translations of the three other instances of κεραυνός in the LXX (Job 38:35, Wis 19:13, 2 Macc 10:30) are unfortunately not preserved in any of the editions of Coptic biblical texts that I have been able to locate.

[11] Cf. 1 Sam 2–3. ηταιει ηος ηογητε εϊ εχη πηϊ η2ελι πογααβ χε αчαμελει ετcβω πεчωηρε ("Because he was negligent to instruct his sons, this great calamity came upon the house of Eli the priest.") For the complete text see Wessely 1909, 87. The general sense of "calamity," especially from a divine source, may be related to the way Greek authors frequently used κεραυνός to describe a punitive lightning bolt of Zeus (see, for example, Hesiod, *Theogony* 141, 690, 854; Herodotus, 7.10e).

[12] Erichsen 1954, 105. Cf. Westendorf 1965, 278; Černý 1976, 218.

[13] *1 En.* 1–36.

[14] *1 En.* 14:10–11. Translations of 1 Enoch are modified from Nickelsburg-Vanderkam 2004. I follow the Greek text of Black 1985.

[15] *1 En.* 14:15–17.

of lightning in God's heavenly throne room has become "walls of light-ning" (ברקים—a word which translates into Greek as both ἀστραπή and κεραυνός).[16]

That the *Gospel of Judas* intends to invoke images of the heavenly temple by recalling Enoch's "roof of lightning (or 'fire')" can be cor-roborated by a number of other suggestive parallels between Judas's vision and descriptions of the heavenly house in 1 Enoch:

(1) Both Enoch and Judas witness a large house (ⲡⲏⲉⲓ; οἶκον μέγαν) whose glory and majesty Enoch is not able to describe (μὴ δύνασθαί με ἐξειπεῖν ὑμῖν περὶ τῆς δόξης καὶ περὶ τῆς μεγαλωσύνης αὐτοῦ), and whose great size and expanse (ⲱⲓ) Judas's eyes "were not able to [mea-sure]" (ⲛ ⲁϣ[ϣⲓⲧϥ] ⲁⲛ).[17]

(2) 1 Enoch 14 and the *Gospel of Judas* are the only descriptions of the heavenly house that refer to its στέγη.[18]

(3) The *Gospel of Judas* refers to this heavenly house as "the aeon" (ⲡⲁⲓⲱⲛ), while 1 Enoch calls it "the high, holy heaven of the aeon" (τὸν οὐρανὸν τὸν ὑψηλὸν τὸν ἅγιον τοῦ αἰῶνος).[19]

(4) Both Enoch and Judas describe their experience as a "vision" (ϩⲟⲣⲟⲙⲁ; ὅρασις), which occurred within a "dream" (ⲣⲁ[ⲥⲟⲩ]; ὕπνος).[20]

(5) Judas's enigmatic vision of "great people surrounding" the house (ϩⲛ̄ⲛⲟϭ ⲇⲉ ⲛ̄ⲣⲱⲙⲉ ⲕ[ⲱ]ⲧⲉ ⲉⲣⲟϥ) closely resembles Enoch's descrip-tion of the "myriads of myriads" who "stood encircling" (κύκλῳ μυρίαι μυριάδες ἑστήκασιν) the outside of the heavenly throne room.[21]

---

[16] *3 En.* 33:3 (Charlesworth 1983). For the Hebrew text, see Schäfer 1981, §50. For translation into Greek, e.g., Job 38:35.

[17] *Gos. Jud.* 45,3–5, 6, 8, 16; *1 En.* 14:10, 15.

[18] Compare with the descriptions of heaven found in other ancient Jewish and Christian revelation literature: Dan 7; Rev 4; *2 En.* 20–22; *3 En.* 30–33; *Apoc. Zeph.* 5; *Apoc. Ab.* 15–19; *T. Levi* 3, 5; *Gk. Apoc. Ezra* 1; *Rev. Ezra* 59–60; *Apoc. Sedr.* 2:3–5; *3 Bar.* 11; *T. Isaac* 6:1–6, 7:1–2; *T. Adam* 4:8; *Ascen. Isa.* 9; *Apoc. Paul* (NHC V) 22,23–30. Other than the *Testament of Adam*'s passing reference to "the inner cham-ber of our Lord" (extant only in Syriac), none of these accounts explicitly speak of a "house," let alone refer to its "roof" (στέγη or equivalent). The *Songs of the Sabbath Sacrifice* from Qumran (4Q403) may imply a magnificent roof-top when it refers to the "chief expanse of the heights" (מרומים רוש רקיע) in its description of the heav-enly temple's architecture (its foundations, columns, corners, beams, walls, structure, construction).

[19] *Gos. Jud.* 45,23; *1 En.* 15:3.

[20] *Gos. Jud.* 37,22–24; 44,15–18, 24; *1 En.* 13:7–8; 14:2, 8, 14. Note that in the *Gospel of Judas*, the Twelve disciples and Judas relate their respective dream-visions to Jesus on the same day, indicating that both visions occurred during the previous night.

[21] *Gos. Jud.* 45,5; *1 En.* 14:22.

(6) In both 1 Enoch and the *Gospel of Judas*, mortals are denied entry to the house. According to Enoch, "no angel could enter into this house and look at his (God's) face because of the splendor and glory; and no flesh was able to see him (οὐκ ἐδύνατο πᾶσα σάρξ ἰδεῖν αὐτοῦ)."[22] The guiding angel leads mortal Enoch only to the house's threshold, where he remains with his head lowered so as not to see the face of God's glory, and "hears" (but does not see) God's pronouncement.[23] In what appears to be a later development of this scene found in the *Book of Parables*, Enoch is permitted to see God, but not before his flesh melts from his body and his spirit is transformed.[24] In the *Gospel of Judas*, Jesus similarly tells Judas that "no one born of mortal man" can enter the house because it is "the place reserved for the holy ones" (apparently the holy, kingless race) who "will stand for all time in the aeon with the holy angels."[25] Though the *Gospel of Judas* is somewhat less restrictive than 1 Enoch by permitting both angels and the holy race into the aeon, both visions clearly restrict mortals, or "the flesh," from entering.

(7) Both 1 Enoch and *Judas* permit "the holy ones" to enter the house. Enoch uses the metonym "holy ones" (οἱ ἅγιοι) to refer to the special angels who are allowed to draw near God's presence.[26] Intriguingly, the *Gospel of Judas* applies the metonym to the kingless, holy race itself. In the *Gospel of Judas*, the "holy ones" (ⲛⲉⲧⲟⲩⲁⲁⲃ) are not the special angels of Enoch, but are those who "will stand (ⲱⲡⲉⲣⲁⲧⲟⲩ) with the angels" in the house forever in the eschatological time.[27] The full soteriological significance of this scene comes into further relief when we translate ⲱⲡⲉⲣⲁⲧⲟⲩ literally as "stand" (rather than the smoother "abide" of the NGS translation) since, as Michael Williams has demonstrated, language of standing and stability possessed strong salvific connotations in late antiquity.[28] Nor should we forget that the idea of becoming angels, or at least like them, was a popular soteriological theme in Jewish apocalypses, and for the community who owned the Dead Sea scrolls.[29]

These intertextualities with 1 Enoch 14 corroborate the reading of 45,6–7 as ⲥⲧⲉⲅⲏ ⲛ̅ⲟⲩⲉⲧⲉ ("a roof of lightning" or "fire"), rather than

---

[22] *1 En.* 14:21–22.

[23] *1 En.* 14:24–25. Cf. this scene with Judas's ability to stand before Jesus, but not look him in the eyes (*Gos. Jud.* 35,10–14). That the mortal Enoch is restricted from entering the throne room may have important implications for how we understand Judas's own restriction from the heavenly house, and therefore the character of Judas in this text as a whole. But I restrict myself from further analysis of this important question here.

[24] *1 En.* 71:11.

[25] *Gos. Jud.* 45,22–24.

[26] *1 En.* 14:23.

[27] Cf. *1 En.* 62:8: "all the chosen will stand in his presence on that day."

[28] Williams 1985.

[29] Himmelfarb 1993, 47–71. See also Matt 22:30; *2 En.* 22:10.

ⲞⲨⲞⲦⲈ ("greenery," or "a single room"). Thus we can see that the author of the *Gospel of Judas* invoked traditional Jewish imagery to describe the cosmic splendor of the heavenly house's ceiling, and that Jewish apocalyptic literature contributed to his conception of the heavens.[30] He may have had access to some version of the *Book of the Watchers* in Greek, or otherwise knew about the στέγη from a tradition derived from 1 Enoch.[31]

CONTRASTING TEMPLES

The author's invocation of the heavenly temple in Judas' vision should be understood as a deliberate contrast with his depiction of the earthly temple administered by the Twelve disciples—a literary device that the author of 1 Enoch himself pioneered. Martha Himmelfarb has analyzed how the author of the *Book of the Watchers* depicts the heavenly house and angelic host as a temple and priests in order to create an implicit contrast with, and criticism of, the earthly temple in Jerusalem.[32] By invoking similar imagery, the *Gospel of Judas* establishes its own criticism and contrast, between the transcendent heavenly temple seen by Judas, and the sinful, misguided ritual activity in the house of sacrifices (the earthly temple) witnessed by the Twelve disciples. The multitude whom the Twelve disciples sacrifice upon the altar are "led astray" (ⲡⲗⲁⲛⲁ: literally "wander"), whereas those in the heavenly temple "stand" with the holy angels for all time.[33] Of course the *Gospel of Judas* uses the symbolic language of priests, altar, offerings and sacrifice not to criticize the Jewish temple cult (which by the author's time was long destroyed), but rather to criticize the "sacrifices" of the Christian eucharist rituals—and I would argue the glorification of martyrdom as a eucharist "sacrifice"—taught by some leaders in the apostolic churches who derived their authority from the Twelve disciples.[34]

---

[30] Researchers have noted that other Christian demiurgical writings, especially the *Apoc. John*, seem indebted to Enochic traditions: see, for example, Pearson 1984; Stroumsa 1984, 37–70; Perkins 1993, 24–25.

[31] On the use of 1 Enoch among early Christians in general see Reed 2005; for its circulation in Egypt see Pearson 2000, 216–231.

[32] Himmelfarb 1993, 9–28.

[33] *Gos. Jud.* 39,28; 45,22.

[34] See Iricinschi et al. 2006, 32–37; and elaboration in Pagels-King 2007. Using the imagery of temples, priests and sacrifices for polemical purposes against other Christians was probably a strategy that the author of *Judas* adopted from the rhetorical

Like many early Christian writings, the *Gospel of Judas* employs symbolic language of birth and race in order to demarcate one moral and ritual community from another (whether real or imagined).[35] Yet despite his strong differentiation between the immortal, holy race, and those who belong to mortal humanity, the author nevertheless proclaims that Jesus "appeared on earth... for the salvation of humanity."[36] Therefore instead of reading the *Gospel of Judas* as an example of soteriological determinism, I assert that we can understand it as yet another advocate of an "inclusive theory of conversion."[37] That is, the *Gospel of Judas*, not unlike the Gospel of John, would have allowed for rebirth into the kingless race, whereby one obtained immortality and admission into that holy aeon.[38] Like Enoch's immortal elect who shall stand in God's presence under a roof of fire and lightning, the members of the *Gospel of Judas*'s holy race shall stand in that aeon "for all time" (ⲛ ⲟⲩⲟⲉⲓⲱ ⲛⲓⲙ)—or beyond time to be exact, "where neither the sun, nor moon, nor day will rule."[39]

---

ploys of other second-century Christian authors who were indeed criticizing Jewish sacrificial practices (e.g., the author of Hebrews and Melito of Sardis, *Passover Homily*). However, we must be careful to distinguish between *criticism* of ritual practices and wholesale *rejection* of them (cf. Himmelfarb 1993, 27). The author of *Judas* may have endorsed a Eucharist ritual, while at the same time criticized others in the apostolic churches for not understanding its "true" meaning.

[35] See Williams 1985; Buell 2005.

[36] *Gos. Jud.* 33,6–9.

[37] See Williams 1996, 189–212.

[38] John 3:1–8.

[39] *Gos. Jud.* 45,20–21. As Turner and other researchers have asserted, exactly *how* the author imagines the process (or "mechanism") of salvation remains unclear. The reception of *gnôsis* does seem to have some importance (e.g., God gave it to Adam and those with him so that the kings of chaos would not rule over him [54,8–12]). Based on the *Gospel of Judas*'s apparent interest in and discussion of baptism in the name of Jesus (55,21ff., now unfortunately heavily damaged by lacunae), both Pagels and Townsend have suggested that the transformative power of ritual baptism—a major redemptive feature of so-called "Sethian" texts—also plays a role in the *Gospel of Judas*'s process of salvation. Although debate continues over the degree to which the *Gospel of Judas* should be considered "Sethian," baptism was nevertheless a central initiating rite in most early Christian communities, and it remains an intriguing suggestion for the *Gospel of Judas*'s understanding of the potential for human transformation. For a current discussion of the centrality of baptism in Sethian writings see Turner 2006, 941–992.

PARADISE, KINGDOM AND THE THIRTEENTH AEON IN THE *GOSPEL OF JUDAS*

Simon Gathercole

Although there are only three references to *pardesim* in the Old Testament and three to *paradeisos* in the New Testament, there is a veritable explosion of attention to paradise in early Christian literature after the NT.[1] With this came a corresponding abundance of debates. As Augustine put it: "I am not unaware that many have said many things about paradise, but there are three general positions on this matter. The first belongs to those who want to understand paradise only in physical terms; the second to those who understand it merely spiritually; and the third view belongs to those who take paradise in both senses—physical and spiritual."[2] Or again, is paradise to be thought of as the place of ultimate salvation and the location of God's dwelling? Many take this for granted, but the apostle Paul only regarded it as located in the third heaven and Origen regarded it as a holding place for the saints before their entry into the kingdom.[3] On a more pernickety level, how many trees are there? Some thought there were a great many; the *Gospel of Thomas*, along with the *Pistis Sophia* and the Manichaeans, counted five; in one place the *Gospel of Philip* says there are only two of significance.[4] And are there nut-trees there?[5]

The topic of paradise in the *Gospel of Judas* is important in its own right, not merely as a way into the *Judasfrage*. In many ways, the figure of Judas is not as central to the *Gospel of Judas* as some of the current discussion might suggest. What is central is saving knowledge, the holy generation and the eschatological destiny of that generation—the latter in particular being the topic to be discussed here. In the end,

---

[1] Neh 2.8; Eccl 2.5; Song 4.13; Luke 23.43; 2 Cor 12.4; Rev 2.7.
[2] *Gen. litt.* 8.1.
[3] 2 Cor 12; Orig., *Princ.* 2.11.6. I am grateful to Markus Bockmuehl for the Aug. and the Orig. references.
[4] For the five trees, see *Gos. Thom.* NHC II,2, log. 19; *PS* I,1; I, 10; II, 86; II, 93; II, 96; for *1–2 Jeu* and the *Untitled Text*, see Schmidt-MacDermot 1978a, 96, 100, 103, 104, 119, 231; *Keph.* VI, p. 30: for trans. see Gardner-Lieu 2004, 200; cf. *Gos. Phil.* II,3, 71,22: 'There are two trees growing in Paradise...'.
[5] Tert., *Val.* 20, suggests that Ptolemy imagines nut-trees in paradise.

however, it is nigh on impossible completely to set aside the problem of the status of Judas in the work! Nevertheless, this chapter will attempt to explore the motif of paradise as far as possible without directing attention to Judas in the first instance. It will first examine in detail the passages about paradise as (1) a garden, and (2) a great house. It will then explore whether paradise is to be equated with (3) the kingdom, (4) the thirteenth aeon, or (5) the boundless aeon, with some remarks on other possibilities. One corollary of drawing attention to the topic of paradise in the *Gospel of Judas* is that it may well bring some clarity to the current debate as to whether the *Gospel of Judas* really has any soteriological interest at all, or whether it is merely a δυσαγγέλιον.

THE GARDEN IN THE *GOSPEL OF JUDAS*

The Spring of/for the Tree in the Gospel of Judas *43,2–4*

[π]ηгн мпѡнн ... ...o... [ка]їрос мпееіаіѡн...

the [sp]ring (?) of the tree of *(most of line missing)* [ti]me of this aeon... *(most of line missing).*[6]

We begin with the rather unpromising looking opening of p. 43, which is unfortunately full of gaps in the manuscript. Though not complete, the reading [π]ηгн seems very plausible on the basis of the ink and the abundant Genesis imagery in this section. A spring is already mentioned in Genesis 2.6 (πηγὴ δὲ ἀνέβαινεν ἐκ τῆς γῆς καὶ ἐπότιζεν πᾶν τὸ πρόσωπον τῆς γῆς), and *Gospel of Judas* 43 will shortly proceed to allude to Genesis 2.9, as we shall see. Not much can be deduced from "the spring of/for the tree": springs[7] and trees[8] are both regular features of paradise, following on from their presence in Genesis 1–2. What is not clear is the relationship between the spring and the tree. The most logical relationship is probably that noted in the *Critical Edition*: it is 'the spring *for* the tree', with the spring nourishing the tree. However, there are other options.

1QH has an extensive interpretation of Genesis 2 in which the description of paradise occupies some twenty lines of text. The speaker

---

[6] *Gos. Jud.* TC 43,2–4.
[7] See e.g. Song 4.12; Rev 21.6.
[8] See above.

gives praise to God for setting him in abundant waters despite the spiritual drought around him, and talks in reasonable horticultural terms about various trees growing in a well-irrigated garden:

> I give [you] thanks, [Lord], because you have set me at the source of streams in a dry land, at the spring of water in a parched land, in a garden watered by channels [...]...a plantation of cypresses and elms, together with cedars, for your glory. (1QH 16,4–5; tr. García Martínez)

Next, however, the tree (or trees—the text is unclear) of life itself becomes a spring:

> Trees of life in the secret source, hidden among all the trees at the water, which shall make a shoot grow in the everlasting plantation, to take root before they grow. Their roots extend to the gul[ly], *and its trunk opens to the living waters to be an everlasting spring.* (1QH 16,5–8)

This is simply to make the point that although one would expect the spring to be nourishing the tree in *Gospel of Judas* 43, the [ⲡ]ⲏⲅⲏ ⲙⲡϢⲏⲛ may actually be a spring flowing from the tree. The life-giving property of the tree may be in view, a theme also present in the *Gospel of Philip*, where life comes through the tree's liquid: 'it is from the olive tree that we get the chrism, and from the chrism, the resurrection' (*G. Phil.* 73, 15–19).[9] If the trees were plural, they could be the holy ones themselves, as in Ps. 1, *Pss. Sol.* 14, 1QH and, e.g. the *Gospel of Truth*.[10] However, the tree here in the *Gospel of Judas* appears to be singular, so it is probably a singular life-giving tree in view. The point of the rest of lines 3–4, one might speculate, is that these paradisal realities do not belong to the time of this aeon ([ⲡⲕⲁ]ⲓ̈ⲣⲟⲥ ⲙⲡⲉⲉⲓⲁⲓⲱⲛ).[11]

Watering the paradise of God in the Gospel of Judas 43, 6–7

ⲁⲗⲗⲁ ⲛ̅ⲧⲁϥⲉⲓ ⲉⲧϭⲟ ⲙ̅ⲡⲡⲁ[ⲣⲁ]ⲇⲉⲓⲥⲟⲥ ⲙ̅ⲡⲛⲟⲩⲧⲉ

But it came to water the pa[ra]dise of God...[12]

---

[9] There is a similar point made in *Orig. World*, where the olive tree is again the source of the chrism (NHC II,5, 111,2–8).

[10] 'He is good. He knows his plantings, because it is he who planted them in his paradise. Now his paradise is his place of rest' (*Gos. Truth* NHC I,3, 36, 35–39).

[11] Cf. *Gos. Jud.* TC 36,17–21.

[12] *Gos. Jud.* TC 43,6–7.

Here we have a clear allusion to Genesis 2.9: ποταμὸς δὲ ἐκπορεύεται ἐξ Εδεμ ποτίζειν τὸν παράδεισον.[13] The spring is not what waters the paradise of God in the next section: ⲡⲏⲅⲏ is feminine, and a masculine subject is doing the watering. The translation in the *Critical Edition* suggests a person doing it ('but he has come to water…'),[14] but what we most probably have in the missing sections here is a reference to a river. Now we have moved from Gen. 2.6 and the spring, to Gen. 2.9 in which a river comes to water the garden of Eden.[15]

Here, then, we have a clearer allusion to the Garden of Eden, which is interesting for the *positive* use it makes of Genesis 1–3. The most striking use of Genesis in the *Gospel of Judas* comes in the account of Saklas's creation of Adam and Eve—something of a reading of Gen. 1–2 against the grain.[16] On the other hand, there is constructive use of Genesis in the theogony/cosmogony. The constant refrain of ⲙⲁⲣⲉϥϣⲱⲡⲉ/ⲙⲁⲣⲟⲩϣⲱⲡⲉ (47, 16–17; 48, 1–2 etc.—cf. Gen. 1.3, 5, 6, etc.), the generation of the luminaries (ⲛ̅ⲫⲱⲥⲧⲏⲣ—cf. Gen. 1.14, 16) and firmaments (ⲛ̅ⲥⲧⲉⲣⲉⲱⲙⲁ—cf. Gen. 1.6, 7, 8, etc.) suggest considerable indebtedness to Gen. 1–2.

What we have in the *Gospel of Judas*, then, is a bifurcating interpretation of Gen. 1–2 in which the non-human elements are drawn out positively, and the human component given a negative nuance. This "misanthropic" interpretation of Gen. 1–2 offers further proof (if proof were needed) of the *Gospel of Judas*'s rather gloomy stance toward humanity. On the other hand, the non-human elements in Genesis are retrieved and used to express the order of the heavenly aeons (in the case of the material in pp. 47–50) and the lush wonder of heavenly paradise here in p. 43.

The Denizens of Paradise in the Gospel of Judas 43, 7–11, 13–14

ⲁⲩⲱ ⲡ[ⲡⲉ]ⲛⲟⲥ ⲉⲧⲛⲁⲙⲟⲩⲛ ⲉ[ⲃ[ⲟ]ⲗ ⲭⲉ [ⲛ̅ⲥⲉⲛ]ⲁⲭⲱϩⲙ ⲁⲛ ⲛⲧϭⲓⲛⲏⲙ[ⲟⲟϣⲉ
ⲛ̅]ⲧ̅ⲅⲉⲛⲉⲁ ⲉⲧⲙ̅ⲙⲁⲩ *vac* ⲁⲗ[ⲗⲁ …] ⲡⲉ ⲭⲛ ⲉⲛⲉϩ ⲛϣⲁ ⲉ[ⲛⲉϩ]

---

[13] The phrase "paradise of God" is also biblical, first occurring in Gen 13.10, and thereafter in Ezek 28:13; 31:8–9, and Rev 2.7.

[14] Kasser et al. 2007, 205.

[15] ⲉⲓⲉⲣⲟ, the most common Coptic word for river, is also masculine and so would fit grammatically here.

[16] *Gos. Jud.* TC 52,14–19.

...and the [gene]ration/race which will endure, because the walk of that generation will never be defiled. Ra[ther], it is...forever.[17]

A brief note on the text of the 'non-defilement'.[18] Although there is no major problem with the *Critical Edition*'s reconstruction as it stands ([ⲛ̄ϥⲛ]ⲁⲭⲱ̄ϩⲙ ⲁⲛ), it is perhaps a little odd that the text would then be clarifying the point that the gardener or river watering the garden will not defile the holy generation. Why would such a clarification be note-worthy? It may be slightly better to take the verb as a 3rd person plural with passive meaning ([ⲛ̄ⲥⲉⲛ]ⲁⲭⲱ̄ϩⲙ ⲁⲛ) for which there is plenty of room in the gap in the manuscript.[19]

As far as the end of line 10 is concerned, ⲁⲗ[ⲗⲁ...] is a reasonable enough reconstruction, although it requires a fairly short adjective to fit in the end of the line. Perhaps the *vacat* + ⲁⲗ[...] marks the beginning of a new sentence altogether, a sentence like ⲁⲗ[ⲏⲑⲏⲥ] ⲡⲉ ⲭⲛ ⲉⲛⲉϩ ⲛⲱⲁ ⲉ[ⲛⲉϩ]. Other possible adjectives might include ⲁⲗ[ⲏⲑⲓⲛⲟⲥ], or "stranger" terminology (ⲁⲗ[ⲗⲟⲅⲉⲛⲏⲥ], ⲁⲗ[ⲗⲟⲫⲩⲗⲟⲥ] etc.). Förster's *Lexicon* does not suggest any other likely options,[20] although Liddell-Scott suggests a number of possible, but not necessarily probable, epi-thets beginning with ἀλ-.

Be that as it may, lines 7–11 appear to introduce the inhabitants of this paradise. They are 'the generation/race which will endure' (ⲡ[ⲅⲉ]ⲛⲟⲥ ⲉⲧⲛⲁⲙⲟⲩⲛ), as per the descriptions of them further down where they will apparently exist for eternity (very probable in the albeit highly lacunose 43,10–11) and their bodies will die but their souls will be alive and will be taken up.[21] They will not be defiled: contrast the apostolic representatives of the *magna ecclesia*, one of whose charac-teristics, in Jesus' interpretation of the temple vision, is ⲁⲕⲁⲑⲁⲣⲥⲓⲁ.[22]

ⲁⲱ ⲛ̄ⲕⲁⲣⲡⲟⲥ ⲡⲉ̣[ⲧⲉ] ⲟⲩⲛⲧⲁⲥϥ ⲛ̄ϭⲓ ⲧⲉⲉⲓⲅⲉⲛⲉⲁ

What fruit does this generation produce/have?[23]

---

[17] *Gos. Jud.* TC 43,7–11.
[18] I.e. *Gos. Jud.* TC 43,8–9.
[19] In fact, the lines do not quite seem to be aligned in the photograph, and so there is perhaps more space available than is suggested.
[20] Förster 2002.
[21] *Gos. Jud.* TC 43,20–23.
[22] *Gos. Jud.* TC 40,13–14.
[23] *Gos. Jud.* TC 43,13–14.

The horticultural imagery continues in Judas's question: in the *Critical Edition's* translation, 'what kind of fruit does this generation produce?'.[24] This question is perhaps influenced by Paul's discussion in Romans 6.21–22:

> Rom. 6:21 (NA[27]) τίνα οὖν καρπὸν εἴχετε τότε;
> *Gospel of Judas* 43,13–14 ⲁⲱ ⲛ̄ⲕⲁⲣⲡⲟⲥ ⲡⲉ[ⲧⲉ]ⲟⲩⲛⲧⲁⲥϥ ⲛ̄ϭⲓ
> Rom. 6:21 sah ⲁⲱ ϭⲉ ⲡⲉ ⲡⲕⲁⲣⲡⲟⲥ ⲉⲛⲉ ⲟⲩⲛ̄ⲧⲏⲧ̄ⲛⲉϥ

So the question in the *Gospel of Judas* here almost certainly goes back to a Greek original resembling the question in Rom. 6.21. It is unclear whether the reference is to spiritual fruit they will produce, or to benefit they will receive.[25] The latter is more probable, especially in the Coptic as it stands. The question partly hinges on whether one supposes a reference in the Greek original to agricultural imagery (assuming the presence of ἔχειν καρπόν in the Greek *Vorlage*), and whether this can also be read into the Coptic.[26]

The glimpses of the garden that we have in *Gospel of Judas* 43 are tantalisingly fleeting. Yet this paradise, corresponding perhaps to the place to which Jesus escaped at the end of the first day, is not completely hidden.[27] It is developed further, in different (though somewhat overlapping) imagery, on p. 45 of our codex.

The House in the *Gospel of Judas*

Judas' Vision of the House in the Gospel of Judas 45,3–8 and 14–24

> ⲁⲉⲓⲛⲁⲩ ⲉ[ⲟⲩⲏⲉⲓ...]ⲥ ⲁⲱ ⲡⲉϥϣ! ⲛⲁⲃⲁⲗ ⲛⲁϣ[ϣⲓⲧϥ] ⲁⲛ ⲛⲉⲣⲉ ϩⲛ̄ⲛⲟϭ
> ⲇⲉ ⲛ̄ⲣⲱⲙⲉ ⲕ[ⲱ]ⲧⲉ ⲉⲣⲟϥ ⲡⲉ ⲁⲱ ⲛⲉⲟⲩ<ⲛ̄ⲧϥ̄ ⲟⲩ>ⲥⲧⲉⲅⲏ ⲛ̄ⲟⲩⲟ̣ⲧⲉ ⲡⲉ
> ⲛ̄ϭⲓ ⲡⲏⲉⲓ ⲉⲧⲙ̄ⲙ[ⲁⲩ] ⲁⲩⲱ ϩⲛ̄ ⲧⲙⲏⲧⲉ ⲙ̄ⲡⲏⲓ̈ ⲉⲣ[ⲉ ⲟⲩ]ⲙⲏ[ⲏⲩⲉ]

I saw [a house]...and its measure my eyes would not be able [to measure]. And some great men were a[ro]und it and the house had a roof of herbs. And in the middle of the house was a cr[owd].[28]

---

[24] *Gos. Jud.* TC 13–14.

[25] Cf. Dunn's (1988, 32) comment about the idiom referring to general return or benefit.

[26] The usage in the second century tends to be agricultural: 1 Clem. 43.5, and frequently in Herm. It appears in Wis. 3.13 in connection with a woman having children.

[27] *Gos. Jud.* TC 36,9–17.

[28] *Gos. Jud.* TC 45,3–8.

To go through this passage briefly, Judas sees a house (line 3): ⲉ[ⲟⲩⲏⲉⲓ] is a very sensible restoration given that ⲏⲉⲓ comes up twice later in the passage (ll. 7, 8) and the reference to 'its measurements' (ⲡⲉϥⲱⲓ) requires a masculine antecedent. Line 4 obviously emphasises the house's massive extent, and immeasurability given the limitations of the human senses, even if the restorations are more uncertain here.[29]

What about the "great men around it"? I wondered in my first comment on this passage whether these characters might be angelic figures of massive dimensions,[30] such as one encounters for example in *Gospel of Peter* 9–10: in the description of the resurrection there, two angels descend from heaven, go into the tomb, emerge with Jesus (and, famously, the talking cross), and are described as stretching up to heaven (τῶν μὲν δύο τὴν κεφαλὴν χωροῦσαν μέχρι τοῦ οὐρανοῦ). Resembling the imagery in the *Gospel of Judas* even more closely is the *Shepherd of Hermas*, where one encounters both in the opening section and again later in a section that dominates the book as a whole a massive building representing the church.[31] At a number of points, Hermas sees figures 'surrouding the tower'—the phrase κύκλῳ τοῦ πύργου appears nine times in *Hermas*. Initially the stones lie around the tower.[32] Later, in the Parables, the men responsible for and involved in the building work are evidently of gigantic size:

> I saw that six men had come, lofty (ἄνδρας...ὑψηλούς) and glorious and alike in appearance, and they called a multitude of men. And those who came were also lofty men, handsome and powerful. And the six men ordered them to build a tower above the rock...[33]

In the end, all the saints will stand around the tower and rejoice.[34] The vision reveals "seven women around the tower."[35] Later in the Parables, we see the virgins walking around the tower and so on.[36] But the men of great height resemble the men in the *Gospel of Judas* most closely, and are interpreted in *Hermas* as glorious angels.[37]

---

[29] There is an obvious contrast with the 'great house' which the disciples see in their temple vision (*Gos. Jud.* TC 38,1–2).
[30] Gathercole 2007a, 84.
[31] Herm. 9–18; 78–110.
[32] Herm. 10.8.
[33] Herm. 80.1.
[34] Herm. 12.2.
[35] Herm. 16.2.
[36] Herm. 83.2.
[37] The six men: Herm. 89.8; the others: Herm. 89.6.

Rather than angels, however, Pagels and King suggest "elders"[38]—ΝΟϬ
in the sense of being a leader or possessing greatness of wisdom rather
than of physical stature.[39] Elders may be a good suggestion here, especially as it recalls the book of Revelation in which the elders are seated
on twenty-four thrones which *surround* the magnificent throne of the
Lord.[40] They are κυκλόθεν τοῦ θρόνου, and ⲘⲠⲔⲰⲦⲈ ⲘⲠⲈⲐⲢⲞⲚⲞⳠ in
the Sahidic NT. Pagels/King note Isa. 24.23 as another parallel, with its
statement: "the Lord of hosts reigns on Mount Zion and in Jerusalem,
and his glory will be before his elders (Gk: ἐνώπιον τῶν πρεσβυτέρων)".
Interestingly, Gregory Beale mentions this passage as perhaps standing
behind Rev. 4.4 as well.[41] The *Gospel of Judas* has neither Revelation's
thrones, nor Isaiah's Lord reigning, because paradise in the *Gospel of
Judas* is kingless, a theme to which we will turn later.

On the other hand, whether these elders are in any sense human
figures remains questionable. It is more likely that the "elder" interpretation and the angelic interpretation should be combined. This is
particularly likely if the restoration of lines 8–9 is correct, in which the
editors suggest [ⲞⲨ]ⲘⲎ[ⲎϢⲈ]; in this case, these gigantic figures surrounding the house are distinguished in some way from the "crowd"
of others. This scenario (whether or not this particular restoration is
correct) is reinforced by the subsequent statement by Jesus that "that
place is kept for the holy ones…they will stand for all time in the aeon
with the holy angels." This presupposes a distinction, though probably not a distinction which should be pressed, between the angels
on the one hand and the "perfect human" spirits of those who have
been imprisoned in human flesh.[42] It might also be the case that the
"surrounding" here suggests that these angel-elders have a kind of cus-
todial role, guarding the house and ensuring that "no progeny of mortal flesh" will enter this house, and that certain cosmic powers (Sun,
Moon, Day) will not have dominion over it.[43]

---

[38] Pagels-King 2007, 141.

[39] In addition to their references, one might also note Sahidic Heb 13.7, 17
(ⲚⲈⲦⲚ̄ⲚⲞϬ, "your leaders"); cf. ⲈⲒⲢⲈ ⲚⲞϬ in *Gos. Thom.* NHC II,2, log. 12.

[40] Rev 4.4.

[41] Beale 1999, 324.

[42] I use the phrase 'perfect human' here because of its human, though positive connotations in *Gos. Jud.* TC 35,3–4.

[43] *Gos. Jud.* TC 45,14–22.

The next lines are perhaps more difficult, as the reference to the "roof of herbs" has been described as a "crux" by the editors.[44] On the other hand, it is uncertain whether things are quite so desperate. Despite some problems both in the language[45] and in the text itself,[46] it seems plausible to understand the house to have a roof of herbs. The suggestion by the editors that the herbs are a problem requiring emendation is unnecessary.[47] Crum's dictionary provides a parallel to the word ογο(ο)τε being used in a paradisal setting. In Isaiah 1.30, the unrighteous of Jerusalem are likened to a terebinth stripped of its leaves, 'and a garden which has no water' (καὶ ὡς παράδεισος ὕδωρ μὴ ἔχων). In one Sahidic text of Isaiah, παράδεισος is translated by μα ῆογοτε,[48] a point which supports the idea of a reference to paradisal imagery in the *Gospel of Judas* here. The image of a verdant roof resonates with the river that we have just seen watering the paradise of God.[49]

The Inhabitants of the House in the Gospel of Judas *45,14–24*

ῆϥῆπωλ λν ῆϭι πεχπο ῆρω[μ]ε νιμ ῆθνητον εβωκ ε2ογν επηει
ῆτλκνλγ εροϥ χε πτοπος γλρ ετῆμλγ ῆτοϥ πετογλρε2 εροϥ
ῆνετογλλβ πμλ ετε ῆπρη μῆ ποο2 νλῬ εϙο ῆμλγ λν ογλε
πε2οογ λλλλ εγνλωϩερλτογ ῆογοειω νιμ 2ῆ πλιων μῆ ῆνλγγελος
ετογλλβ

No progeny of any mortal man is worthy to enter into the house which you saw, for that place is kept for the holy ones, the place where the Sun and the Moon will not have dominion, nor will the Day. But they will stand for all time in the aeon with the holy angels.[50]

---

[44] Kasser et al. 2007, 209 n. 6–7.

[45] Although probably a feminine singular, ϲτεγη might be a Coptic borrowing of the Greek neuter plural of στέγος. The editors have suggested ογϲτεϲη (Kasser et al. 2007, 209).

[46] There is almost certainly a scribal omission here as well as damage to the manuscript.

[47] The suggestion of replacing νογοοτε with νογοϲτῆ (Kasser et al. 2007, 209 n. 6–7) is not particularly convincing. More plausible is another proposal, made by Jacques van der Vliet that the text reads ϲτεγη νογοτε in the sense of "one room" (or perhaps, one storey). The fem. form of ογωτ, however, is rare, and is in any case usually ογωτε. See Layton 2004, 122–123 (§158); Crum 1939, 494a supplies no instances of the spelling ογοτε for the feminine of ογωτ.

[48] Crum 1939, 493b.

[49] *Gos. Jud.* TC 43,6–7.

[50] *Gos. Jud.* TC 45,14–24.

Picking up on the subsequent statement by Jesus again, the inhabitants of this house are—as elsewhere in the *Gospel of Judas*—not regarded as a subset of humanity but distinguished absolutely from (mere) mortals. In the opening scene on Day 1 of the *Gospel of Judas*, Jesus had announced: "Truly, [I] say to you, no generation among the men who are in your midst will know me."[51] Then again on the second day, the disciples were told:

> Truly [I] say to you, [no-]one born [of] this aeon will see that [generation]. No army of star-angels will rule over that generation. Nor will anyone born of mortal man be able to accompany it. For that generation does not come forth... ... which has come into being... ... The generation of men in your midst is from the generation of humanity (almost one line missing) power... ... other powers... ... as you are kings among [them].[52]

The holy ones who will reside in this house ('that place') will not be subject to the dominion of 'Sun', 'Moon', and 'Day' (ΠΡΗ ΜΝ ΠΟΟϩ...ΟΥΛΕ ΠΕϨΟΟΥ). These terms have superlinear strokes in the text, though not all are in the same form. The first, ΠΡΗ, has a stroke fully covering both letters, suggesting a name. It would, then, be an archontic figure rather than merely a calendrical item,[53] and—moreover—an evil divine power (given the sun's potential here as a ruling force). In the case of the following terms, however, the matter is not so straightforward: the stroke above ΠΟΟϩ does not cover the entirety of the letters, and the stroke above ΠΕϨΟ | ΟΥ covers the first two letters of the noun, up to the end of the line in 45,21, but the stroke does not resume at the beginning of the next.[54] Does this perhaps mean that the strokes over these three words are not intended to identify them as *nomina*?[55]

In any case, there is resemblance here to the account of paradise in *On the Origin of the World*: "Then Justice created Paradise, being beautiful and being outside the orbit of the moon and the orbit of the

---

[51] *Gos. Jud.* TC 34,15–17.

[52] *Gos. Jud.* TC 37,1–16.

[53] I suggested previously that ΠΕϩΟΟΥ may have been a scribal error for ΠΕϴΟΟΥ, i.e. 'Evil one' (Gathercole 2007a, 83, 181 n. 26). Indeed, from the published photographs in the Critical Edition and the high resolution online images it is possible that the word may be read ΠΕϴΟΟΥ. Since I have not seen the originals, however, I defer to the editors on this point.

[54] Cf. *Gos. Jud.* TC 46,24.

[55] I am grateful to Gesine Schenke Robinson for this suggestion.

sun in the land of wantonness…"[56] There is an interesting connection here with *Jubilees*, to which *Origin* is indebted here and elsewhere. In *Jubilees*, it is clear that paradise is created on the third day, before the luminaries which are created on the fourth day: for this reason, paradise can be envisaged as outside of time, a theme also found elsewhere in the Nag Hammadi corpus and the Syrian tradition.[57] This theme thus further cements the connection between the paradise explicitly mentioned in *Gospel of Judas* 43 and the house here in *Gospel of Judas* 45: they are clearly two different images for the same thing.

THE KINGDOM

After these statements about the "place" reserved for the holy ones, and the aeon where they will reside with the angels, Jesus tells Judas:

ⲉⲓⲥ ϩⲏⲏⲧⲉ ⲁⲉⲓϫⲱ ⲉⲣⲟⲕ ⲛ̄ⲙⲙⲩⲥⲧⲏⲣⲓⲟⲛ ⲛ̄ⲧⲙⲛ̄ⲧⲉⲣⲟ

Behold, I have spoken to you the mysteries of the kingdom.[58]

The language here echoes and combines 1 Corinthians 15:51 (ἰδοὺ μυστήριον ὑμῖν λέγω) and Matthew 13.11/Luke 8.20 (ὑμῖν δέδοται γνῶναι τὰ μυστήρια τῆς βασιλείας…). First impressions might suggest that Jesus has thus been talking of the kingdom in his depiction of the paradisal house. Indeed, this was the interpretation followed by the earliest literature on the *Gospel of Judas*.[59] Louis Painchaud, however, proposed a very different understanding of the kingdom language in which it is rather "a designation of the domination of the archons over the lower world, merely a synonym for the error of the stars".[60] This interpretation has a number of merits, and will be developed here.

Principally, this reading takes account of the co-existence in the *Gospel of Judas* of the language of the kingdom and of the "kingless generation."[61] In other texts where this pairing is found, a strong con-

---

[56] *Orig. World* NHC II,5, 110,2–6.

[57] On the connection between Jubilees and *Origin*, see Wintermute's note in Charlesworth 1985, 2:56 n. "m." The theme is also implied in *Gos. Thom.* NHC II,2, log. 19, where the trees in paradise are not subject to the seasons. I am grateful for Dr David Taylor's mention that the theme is present in Syriac literature, though I have not been able yet to investigate this myself.

[58] *Gos. Jud.* TC 45,24–26.

[59] E.g. Gathercole 2007a, 85–86.

[60] Painchaud 2007.

[61] *Gos. Jud.* TC 53,24.

trast is drawn between them. The *Apocalypse of Adam* provides a useful parallel here, because, like the *Gospel of Judas*, it refers both to kingdoms, the number thirteen, and to a kingless realm. A sequence of kingdoms is listed, from one to thirteen, concluding: "And the thirteenth kingdom says of him that every birth of their ruler is a word. And this word received a mandate there. He received glory and power. And thus he came to the water, in order that the desire of those powers might be satisfied."[62] After this thirteenth, the apocalypse refers to a higher realm:

> But the generation without a king over it says that God chose him from all the aeons. He caused a knowledge of the undefiled one of truth to come to be in him. He said, "Out of a foreign air, from a great aeon, the great illuminator came forth. And he made the generation of those men whom he had chosen for himself shine, so that they could shine upon the whole aeon".[63]

One also finds the same contrast in two sections towards the end of *On the Origin of the World*:

> Then the saviour created [...] of them all—and the spirits of these [are manifestly] superior, being blessed and varying in election—and also (he created) many other beings, which have no king and are superior to everyone that was before them. Consequently, four races exist. There are three that belong to the kings of the eighth heaven. But the fourth race is kingless and perfect, being the highest of all. For these shall enter the holy place of their father. And they will gain rest in repose and eternal, unspeakable glory and unending joy. Moreover, they are kings within the mortal domain, in that they are immortal. They will condemn the gods of chaos and their forces.[64]

> When the prophecy and the account of those that are king becomes known and is fulfilled by those who are called perfect, those who—in contrast—have not become perfect in the unbegotten father will receive their glory in their realms and in the kingdoms of the immortals: but they will never enter the kingless realm.[65]

There is perhaps a similar contrast implicit in *Gospel of Judas* 53,16–25. Here one sees a distinction between Michael's allocation of spirits *temporarily* to those whose mission in life is to serve, i.e. to be subjects.

---

[62] *Apoc. Adam* NHC V,5, 82,10–19.
[63] *Apoc. Adam* NHC V,5, 82,19–83,4.
[64] *Orig. World* NHC II,6, 124,33–125, 14.
[65] *Orig. World* NHC II,6, 127,7–14.

Contrast the great generation, who are subject to no-one: they have spirits *and* souls (with the implication of the latter's immortality) and so are eternal beings. The depiction, therefore, of the great generation as 'kingless' (ⲁⲧⲣⲣⲟ) problematises an equation of paradise with the kingdom.

Secondly, there are hints elsewhere in the *Gospel of Judas* that the kingdom is negative in the work, although some of the kingdom language is difficult to evaluate as either positive or negative. To note the ambiguities first, Jesus' statement on p. 43 that an eschatological terminus comes "when the time of the kingdom is fulfilled"[66] is ambiguous. It could mean that the time *for the kingdom* is fulfilled, and thus the kingdom can now appear (the meaning of the similar phrase in Mk 1.15, for example). Or it could mean that the time *of* (i.e. the period of) the kingdom *is now over*.[67] The next two references, 45,26 and 46,13, are ambiguous as well. The final mention, however, which links the kingdom of Adam to an archon suggests that kingdom there at least is not to be taken positively.[68]

Finally, there is some evidence in the *Gospel of Judas* to suggest that the kingdom has a specific reference to the twelve disciples and the apostolic church. This understanding of the kingdom enables us to make sense of the first address of Jesus to Judas:

> Separate yourself from them. I will speak to you the mysteries of the kingdom—not so that you might enter it, but so that you will grieve greatly. For another will come to your place so that the twelve [disciples] might again be complete in their god.[69]

Judas will not enter the kingdom. This much seems clear now from the *Critical Edition* (with the new reading ⲟⲩⲭ ϩⲓⲛⲁ in 35,26), so the question is: why? Will he not enter it because *he is not worthy*? This is April DeConick's view: she identifies the kingdom with the house which Judas sees but which he is not worthy to enter.[70] There seems to me another possibility, however. That is, that Judas will not enter

---

[66] This should probably be translated as a passive, rather than understanding the subject as the souls of the human generation, reflecting the language of Mark 1.15: πεπλήρωται ὁ καιρός.

[67] My translation of ϩⲟⲧⲁⲛ ⲉⲩϣⲁⲛϫⲱⲕ ⲉⲃⲟⲗ ⲙⲡⲉⲟⲩⲟⲉⲓϣ ⲛⲧⲙⲛⲧⲉⲣⲟ (43, 17–19) here is ambiguous reflecting the ambiguity.

[68] *Gos. Jud.* TC 53,14.

[69] *Gos. Jud.* TC 35,23–36,4.

[70] DeConick 2007, 52.

the kingdom *because it is not worthy of him*. This is not to suggest necessarily that Judas is the hero and the true gnostic, but rather that the kingdom is a realm below him. This seems to me to be the most natural interpretation of *Gospel of Judas* 35,23–36,4. In this passage, Jesus says that Judas' non-entry into the kingdom is directly related to his replacement by another apostolic disciple. We have four relevant components here:

- you will not enter the kingdom
- you will grieve greatly
- because another will take your place
- in order to make up the number twelve

It seems to me that the best arrangement of these components is:

- *you will not enter the kingdom* (but will grieve greatly)
- *for (ⲅⲁⲣ) another will take your place*—in order to make up the number twelve

So Judas's replacement explains why he will not enter the kingdom. This seems the best arrangement because the alternative would be that Judas's replacement by another is the source of his grief, which does not really work: Jesus would hardly be saying that Judas would lament not being one of those "in their god". Rather, the ⲅⲁⲣ connects the replacement with Judas' non-entry. If this is correct, then it is Judas's exclusion from the twelve which means that he will not enter the kingdom—which must therefore be *their* destiny. The kingdom is the domain of the other, irredeemable disciples: there is perhaps support for this in 37,16, which states fairly clearly that the disciples do in some way rule. Judas is excluded from this realm and so will not go there because the kingdom is beneath him.

The separation of Judas from the kingdom is probably also noted in 46,14–18.[71] Jesus tells Judas that he will grieve when he sees the kingdom with all its generation (46,11–14). Judas then asks what benefit he will receive as a result of being separated from that generation (46,14–18). Here DeConick's translation is surely correct:[72] the sense of ⲡⲱⲣⲝ ⲉ- in the examples in Crum certainly indicates that, surprisingly perhaps

---

[71] Note, however, the reservation below that the phrase 'that generation' may be a technical phrase for the holy generation.

[72] With DeConick (2007, 51–52) on the translation, but not on the interpretation.

given the usual sense of ϵ-, Judas is excluded *from* the kingdom.[73] Meyer, in his response to DeConick, misreads Crum here.[74] One can add to this the evidence provided by Guillaumont in a different context about ϵ- with verbs of separation.[75] On the other hand, I would again take issue with DeConick's construal of the general thrust. She comments: "Judas is upset because he has received esoteric teaching from Jesus, teaching which he sees as useless because he has been separated from the Gnostic generation who populate the upper world."[76] Judas, however, is probably not commenting here on his separation from the Gnostic generation, but on his separation from the generation *of the kingdom.* This "*kingdom* and all *its* generation" is the topic of conversation, again probably the domain of the twelve disciples, not the place of the holy generation.[77] Jesus' reply then makes good sense. We have recently heard that Judas will not enter the kingdom because someone else will replace him to restore the number to twelve.[78] Here Jesus tells Judas that the benefit he will receive for his being separated from the kingdom is that he will be the thirteenth: as such he will rule over the others, i.e. over the twelve who will curse him.

Let us return to p. 45, and Jesus' statement, "Behold, I have spoken to you the mysteries of the kingdom."[79] If the *Gospel of Judas* is being consistent—and we do have to take this as a real "if"—then the most likely referent of kingdom is the domain of the twelve disciples (including Judas's replacement). It is slightly counterintuitive that Jesus should talk about the house which Judas has seen and then announce that he has revealed the mysteries of the kingdom which is actually something quite different. However, it might well be that Jesus' announcement that he has declared the secrets of the kingdom to Judas is a summary-statement of his teaching in the first half of the work as a whole: preparatory to the revelation of the theogony/

---

[73] A brief check of the NT examples (Sahidic Matt 10.35; Rom 8.35; 1 Cor 7.10; 2 Cor 6.17) confirms this.

[74] Meyer, 2008a, 3–4, comments that Crum gives two options for ⲡⲱⲣϫ ϵ-: (a) 'separate from', and (b) divide/be divided into. This is correct, but the citations which Crum gives indicate the sense of one thing dividing into two or more parts, i.e. "divide up into". It does not mean one thing separating itself from another.

[75] Guillaumont 1962, 15–23 (17).

[76] DeConick 2007, 52.

[77] *Gos. Jud.* TC 46,13–14.

[78] *Gos. Jud.* TC 35,23–36,4.

[79] *Gos. Jud.* TC 45,24–26.

cosmogony in the second half, he has cleared the ground by under-
mining the whole basis of the apostolic church.

This identification of the kingdom with the apostolic church must
remain tentative, however, for two reasons. The relationship between
Judas's grief, his replacement and his inability to enter the kingdom,
as I have outlined it above, is not completely certain. It is also possible
that the phrase "that generation" is a set phrase for the holy generation; in this case, the separation from "that generation" in *Gospel of
Judas* 46,17–18 would not refer to Judas's separation from the infernal
kingdom but from the holy generation, and leave open the possibility—as per Louis Painchaud's approach—that Judas ends up with the
rest of the twelve after all. Nevertheless, I am inclined to think that the
view I have suggested above is like democracy in Churchill's assessment: it is the worst view except for all the others.

PARADISE AND THE THIRTEENTH AEON

ⲁⲩⲱ {ⲁⲩⲱ} ϥⲛⲁⲣⲉ[ⲣⲟ ⲛ̄ϭⲓ] ⲡⲉⲕⲥⲓⲟⲩ ⲉⲝⲛ̄ ⲡⲙⲉ͞ⳝⲙⲛ̄ⲧ[ϣⲟⲙ]ⲧⲉ ⲛⲁⲓⲱ͞

and {and} your star will ru[le] over the [thi]rteenth aeon.[80]

So far, then, we have examined (1–2) the presentations of paradise,
and (3) perhaps seen a disjunction between the kingdom and Judas
the thirteenth, who is superior to the kingdom. Does this mean (4)
that paradise is equated with the thirteenth aeon which is to be ruled
over by Judas's star?

Nag Hammadi and other Parallels to the Thirteenth Aeon

Various parallels might be drawn to support either a positive or a negative understanding of the thirteenth aeon. DeConick, for example,
argues that passages such as the rescue in *Zostrianus* from the world
and its thirteen aeons makes it clear that the thirteenth is just as bad
as the other twelve.[81] Meyer, on the other hand, has argued strongly for
a positive interpretation on the basis of the character of the thirteenth
aeon in *Pistis Sophia* 1.50, where it is described as 'the thirteenth aeon,
the place of righteousness'.

---

[80] *Gos. Jud.* TC 55,10–11.
[81] DeConick 2007, 111.

Pistis Sophia clearly has a positive sense of the thirteenth aeon. The same is also found in *1 Jeu*.[82] In *1 Jeu*, there are two treatments: in the fragment of the hymn, the formula departs from the usual formula of referring to the first, second, third, etc. up to the twelfth aeon, and describes this thirteenth aeon as the place of the twenty-four emanations (as per PS).[83] In the other description, it is the place where the First Mystery "has set up the three gods and the invisible one".[84] On the other hand, the parallel from *Zostrianus* mentioned above, and an equally negative verdict in the *G. Egy.* III 64,3–4 (//IV 75,17–19), both go in the opposite direction. In sum, we are probably forced to rely on internal evidence from the *Gospel of Judas* itself.

The Thirteenth Aeon in the Gospel of Judas: *Internal Evidence*

Judas's star is said to rule over this thirteenth aeon. Paradise is certainly pictured as an aeon in the work.[85] However, despite the fact that certain parts of the *Gospel of Judas* seem to present Judas in a high position in the heavenly hierarchy, it is very unlikely that the thirteenth aeon can be identified with paradise.

First, even if one were to take a positive view of Judas in his eponymous Gospel, it would be assigning an amazingly high status to him to describe him as, effectively, the one who reigns over the realm of paradise. Secondly, if the *Gospel of Judas* is consistent here, it is rather odd to suppose that Judas would reign over what is elsewhere described as a "kingless" generation.[86] Third, Judas's request to be received in with the inhabitants of the paradisal realm is apparently rejected by Jesus.[87] In sum, paradise should not be identified with the thirteenth aeon. Rather, as we shall see, the thirteenth aeon is more likely to be a region/divinity between paradise and the twelve.

---

[82] In *2 Jeu*, the thirteenth aeon is not so important, since there are 14 aeons and then another realm above.

[83] Schmidt-MacDermot 1978a 82.

[84] Schmidt-MacDermot 1978a, 134.

[85] *Gos. Jud.* TC 45,20–24; cf. 44,7.

[86] *Gos. Jud.* TC 53,24.

[87] *Gos. Jud.* TC 45,11–19.

The thirteenth aeon between paradise and the kingdom

To recap, the place of Judas and his realm between paradise and on the one hand and the kingdom on the other rests on two sets of inferences:

- First, Judas is probably not to enter paradise. His request to Jesus that he be admitted is not granted (45,11–19), and his non-ascent to the holy generation is probably reinforced by the problematic passage 46,24—47,1.
- Second, there is his probable separation from the kingdom of the twelve. He is to depart from the twelve, and another will replace him (35,23–36,4). He is separated from the kingdom and its generation, and will rule over them (46,13–23).

Given these points, assigning a position to the thirteenth aeon would be very difficult in a system that was based on a simple duality of righteous vs wicked, such as one finds in apocalyptic Judaism, Qumran and the NT. On the other hand, the idea of a "middling group" between the righteous and the wicked goes back, according to the Tosefta, to the school of Shammai.[88] A similar idea, though not genetically related, is a feature of Valentinian theology—usually based around the *hulikos—psuchikos—pneumatikos* distinction. A bifurcation in the redeemed is also a feature of works conventionally classified as Sethian.[89] As such, there is no problem in principle with imagining Judas in a middle position.[90]

The reference to the holy generation as "kingless" might actually encourage the idea that there is a *tertium quid*. Bergmeier, in his discussion of "kinglessness" in 1982, treated many of the passages which have now been used as parallels to the *Gospel of Judas*, and—probably particularly on the basis of *On the Origin of the World*—wrote as follows:

---

[88] *t. Sanh.* 13.3. See Avemarie 1996, 39; Gathercole 2002, 153.

[89] E.g. *Paraph. Shem*, where the two classes are the pneumatics, whose destiny is the place of the unbegotten Spirit and the noetics, who ascend to the hymen, the place of faith.

[90] It is possible that this is suggested, too, by the narrative movement of *Gos. Jud.* TC 44,24–45,19. Here, Judas is separated from the twelve who are pursuing him, but when he sees the paradisal house, he cannot go in there either. So he is excluded both from paradise, but also from the domain of the twelve over whom he will reign (46,22–24; cf. 56,21), and whom he will perhaps also judge (56,22).

Auffällig an einer Reihe gnostischer Zeugnisse war nur dies: ἀβασίλευτος bezeichnete nicht nur allgemein die Zugehörigkeit zur transmundanen Unvergänglichkeit, sondern speziell die Teilhabe am vollkommenen Heil, und zwar in zum Teil betonter Abhebung von einer *Heilsstufe minderen Rangs*. [emphasis original][91]

If this is right, then the designation of the holy generation as "kingless", encourages further the idea that there is a realm in between paradise and the region of the damned. The thirteenth aeon seems to fit this intermediate position well.

PARADISE AND THE BOUNDLESS AEON

There remain several other features of the *Gospel of Judas*'s cosmogony which might be candidates for identification with paradise. The first aeon mentioned in the *Gospel of Judas* is the aeon of Barbelo. This is mentioned by Judas as the provenance of Jesus.[92] However, this reference occurs outside of the discourse of the theogony, and is not integrated with it. It is not mentioned again after *Gospel of Judas* 35, and so any conclusions about its location in the grand scheme of things will be mere guess-work.

Another difficulty concerns the cloud of light on page 57. This is something of a *crux*, because the cloud of light appears in the first instance in 47,15–16, and at that point in the theogony we appear to be in the realms of pure light. The cloud of light there may well actually be identified with the Great Invisible Spirit him(?)self. It is possible that Judas enters this cloud at the conclusion of his revelation, such that he acquires knowledge of the true Cloud of Light.[93] Another possibility is that Judas is leaping into the cloud that is properly in his domain, i.e. in the thirteenth aeon. On this model, the cloud of light on the top ontological level is replicated (in an inferior manner) at the middle level of being—that of Judas. Either way, there is little reason to identify the cloud of light with the paradisal aeon. On the other hand, if it is Jesus who is leaping into the cloud, the identification is more plausible, though by no means certain. Overall, a positive view

---

[91] Bergmeier 1982, 316–339, 327. On the theme, see also Fallon 1979, 271–288.
[92] *Gos. Jud.* TC 35,17–19.
[93] There have been serious objections made to the idea of Judas doing the leaping into the cloud: Gesine Schenke Robinson and others have proposed Jesus as the figure in question.

of the cloud of light is supported by the fact that the cloud of light appears so in Tchacos *Allogenes* 62,11, though the *Allogenes* parallel would not support an identification with paradise.[94]

To go to what is apparently the top, there is the "great, boundless aeon" which could not be measured by any angel, and indeed has not been seen by any angel.[95] It would probably be over-pedantic to conclude that this aeon is not co-extensive with paradise simply because the latter is populated by both the holy *and* the holy angels.[96] It seems, however, that there is a correspondence between the house "whose measurement", Judas says, "my eyes could not [measure]" and the "boundless" aeon of which "no generation of angels can see its measurement".[97] An identification, while likely, cannot be deemed certain; one might also imagine that the aeon of the holy generation is *within* this boundless invisible aeon described by Judas.

Where is Paradise?

We are probably left assuming that paradise is neither associated with the thirteenth aeon, nor with the negative kingdom of the twelve. This paradise, described in the *Gospel of Judas* both with the language of Genesis as well as with Temple imagery, is inhabited by angelic figures, as well as by "another great generation, which is holy", "the great generation which is more exalted than us [sc. the twelve] and which is holy and not in these aeons". There is, however, overlap between the Eden imagery of *Gospel of Judas* 43 and the more solid picture in *Gospel of Judas* 45: both have lush, horticultural imagery because of the great house's roof-garden, and the association of this great house with Eden is strengthened by the traditional characterisation of Eden's creation before the luminaries which ties in nicely with the house being outside of the dominion of any astrological forces or calendrical rhythm, existing in timeless permanence. The composite paradise of the *Gospel of Judas* 43 and 45 is probably to be identified with, or included within, the boundless aeon mentioned at the beginning of Jesus' theogony. There is no suggestion that the *Gospel of Judas* regards paradise as anything

---

[94] Contra DeConick 2007, 118.
[95] *Gos. Jud.* TC 44,8–13?; 47,5–13; 48,23–26.
[96] *Gos. Jud.* TC 45,22–24; cf. also the "great men" in 45,5.
[97] *Gos. Jud.* TC 45,4; 47,6–8.

like an intermediate position on the way to a higher realm. In terms of Augustine's three-fold schema, it is fairly clear that, given the *Gospel of Judas*'s views of material creation (ⲕⲟⲥⲙⲟⲥ is paraphrased as ⲫⲑⲟⲣⲁ in *Gospel of Judas* 50,13–14) and the body (the spirits of the holy generation leave their bodies in 43,14–23), the *Gospel of Judas* would follow the second option, in which paradise is envisaged as entirely spiritual. The presence of nut trees remains an open question.

As noted at the beginning, highlighting the theme of paradise in the *Gospel of Judas* draws attention to the positive, optimistic dimensions of the work amid the undeniable gloom. The attention in the work to paradise, the great house, and other soteriological imagery shows, I would suggest, that the work is not merely a bitter parody of the Gospel genre, but an account intended to communicate saving gnosis, as indeed the *incipit* implies.[98]

---

[98] I must extend my gratitude not only to the participants in the Codex Judas Congress at Rice University, but also to the members of the SNTS Christian Apocrypha Seminar present at the Lund Meeting in July-August 2008. Their comments have proven invaluable.

MANUSCRIPT MATTERS

ADDENDA ET *CORRIGENDA* TO THE CRITICAL EDITION OF THE *GOSPEL OF JUDAS*

Gregor Wurst

Two years after the publication of the critical edition of the *Gospel of Judas* it may be useful to publish a list of corrections and new readings that are based on the identification of new fragments from plates A–I and on suggestions made by different colleagues.[1]

CORRECTIONS

With regard to printing errors, two corrections within the text of the *Gospel of Judas* should be made. A minor error is printed on page 43 of the codex, where the end of line 11 actually reads ⲡ]ⲉ, not ⲡⲉ].[2] More important is a mistake at the top of page 57 where unfortunately one line (the line after line 4) has dropped off during the preparation of the camera-ready manuscript.[3] The corrected text reads:

```
1   ⲁⲗⲏⲑ[ⲱⲥ ϯⲭⲱ ⲙⲙⲟⲥ ⲛⲁⲕ ϫⲉ] ⲛⲉⲕ
2   ϩⲁⲉⲟ[ⲩ                    ]ⲱ
3   ⲡ[.] . [              ⲱ]ϣⲱⲡⲉ
4   [                        ] . . ⲟ
5   [                    ] ⲱ (omitted line)
6   [                    ] ⲙⲉ :
```

So page 57 actually counts 27, not 26 lines.

There are also five places in the text where our reading of traces of letters or our restoration of a *lacuna* is certainly not correct. First, at page 42, lines 2–5 the text should read:[4]

```
2   ⲛ[ⲁⲓ ⲛⲧⲉⲣⲟⲩⲥⲱⲧ]ⲙ ⲉⲣⲟⲟⲩ
3   ⲛ̅[ϭⲓ ⲛ̅ⲙⲁⲑⲏⲧⲏⲥ ⲡⲉ]ϫⲁⲩ ⲛⲁ[ϥ]
4   ϫ[ⲉ ⲡ]ⲭ̅ⲥ̅ ⲃⲟⲏⲑⲓ ⲉⲣⲟⲛ ⲁⲩⲱ
5   ⲛ̅[ⲕⲧ]ⲟⲩϫⲟⲛ : . . .
```

---

[1] Kasser et al. 2007.
[2] Kasser et al. 2007, 205.
[3] Kasser et al. 2007, 233.
[4] Kasser et al. 2007, 203.

This restoration of lines 2–3, printed only in the *apparatus* in the critical edition, has recently been corroborated by Gesine Schenke Robinson, too.[5] For lines 4–5, I follow a suggestion made by Wolf-Peter Funk.

Second, at page 44,[6] line 9 our reading ϫ[ε ⲙⲛ̄ ⲁⲣⲭⲏ] ⲟⲩ[ⲗⲉ is certainly not correct, as Wolf-Peter Funk pointed out to me, because there are traces of the upper parts of some letters, that do not fit with the proposed restoration ⲁⲣⲭⲏ. Tentatively, I would now propose to restore to read ϫ[ε ⲙⲛ̄ ⲁⲣ]ϫⲱⲛ ⲟⲩ[ⲗⲉ, but to confirm this reading certainly needs further examination of the papyrus.

Third, as a result of a discussion by email with Wolf-Peter Funk, the printed text of page 47, line 4 is not only problematic, as indicated in the *apparatus* of the critical edition, but grammatically incorrect.[7] It is impossible to translate ⲗⲁⲟ[*vac* ⲅⲉ] ⲛ̄ⲣⲱⲙⲉ here with "[no] human", because in that case a negation would be required. After reexamining the infrared photograph of this page, my present opinion is that the correct reading is ⲧⲅⲉ[*vac* ⲛⲉⲁ] ⲛ̄ⲣⲱⲙⲉ, so that the phrase means "(that ?) the human gene[ration] will see". Of course, this does not resolve the problem, because the reader expects a negative phrase here, but maybe we should not introduce a conjecture into the text too quickly.

Fourth, at page 48, lines 2–3 ⲁⲩⲱ ⲁⲥϣⲱⲡⲉ [ⲛ̄ϭⲓ ⲧⲉⲡⲣⲟⲟⲗ]ⲟⲥ "and [the emanation] occurred", we accepted John Turner's restoration of this *lacuna*. However, as Peter Nagel has convincingly shown, there is no attestation for πρόοδος in the sense of "emanation" before Plotinus. Furthermore, the standard expression for "emanation" in Coptic gnostic literature is προβολή. As a consequence, Nagel proposes to abandon the idea that some kind of "emanation" was mentioned here, and he restores the *lacuna* to read ⲁⲩⲱ ⲁⲥϣⲱⲡⲉ [ⲛ̄ⲑⲉ ⲛ̄ⲧⲁϥϫⲟ]ⲟⲥ "and it happened, [as he did say]", which makes good sense and is certainly correct.[8]

Fifth, at page 56, line 24 the *lacuna* is too small for the proposed restoration ⲁ[ϥⲁⲙⲁϩ]ⲧⲉ, as rightly pointed out by Peter Nagel and Gesine Schenke Robinson.[9]

---

[5] Schenke Robinson 2008, 90 n. 43.
[6] Kasser et al. 2007, 207.
[7] Kasser et al. 2007, 213.
[8] Nagel 2009, 133–134.
[9] Cf. Schenke Robinson 2008, 96 n. 83; Nagel 2009, 135.

ADDITIONS

Since the publication of the critical edition, it was possible to place some further fragments. Most of these new placements do only confirm the restorations of small *lacunae* that have been proposed in the critical edition, as is shown by the following list:

p. 35:13–14 frag. C 27 ↑	ⲉϩⲣⲁϥ ⲛ̄ⲛⲉϥⲃⲁⲗ : ⲁⲗⲗⲁ ⲛ̄ⲧⲁϥ ⲕⲧⲉ ϩ̄ⲣⲁϥ ⲉⲡⲁϩⲟⲩ : ⲡⲉⲭ[ⲁ]ϥ ⲛⲁϥ
p. 36:12–14 frag. C 27 →	ⲁϥⲟⲩ[ⲱ]ⲛϩ ⲉⲃⲟⲗ ⲛ̄ⲛⲉϥⲙⲁⲑⲏ ⲧⲏⲥ : ⲁⲩⲱ ⲡⲉⲭⲁⲩ ⲛⲁϥ ⲭⲉ ⲡϭⲁ[ϩ] ⲛ̄ⲧⲁⲕⲃⲱⲕ ⲉⲧⲱⲛ ⲉⲕⲣ ⲟⲩ ⲉ
p. 47: 9–10 frag. E 21 ↑	ⲛ̄ⲡⲛⲁ ⲛⲁϩⲟ̄ⲣⲁ[ⲧ]ⲟⲛ [ⲛ̄ϩⲏⲧ]ϥ̄ ⲡⲁⲓ̈ ⲉⲧⲉ ⲙ̄ⲡⲉⲃⲁⲗ ⲛⲁ[ⲅⲅⲉⲗⲟⲥ]
p. 48:9 frag. E 21 →	ⲧ̣[ⲃⲁ ⲛ̄]ⲁⲧⲏ̣ⲡ̣ⲉ : ⲁⲩⲱ ⲡⲉⲭⲁϥ
p. 49:6–7 frag. I 5 ↑	ⲛⲁ ⲫⲑⲁⲣⲧⲟⲥ ⲛ̄ⲥⲧⲏⲑ̄ ⲉⲃ[ⲟⲗ] ⲙ̄ⲡⲙ̄ⲛ̄ⲧⲥⲛⲟⲟⲩⲥ ⲛ̄ⲫ[ⲱⲥⲧⲏⲣ]
p. 50:6–7 frag. I 5 →	[ⲁ]ⲧⲏⲡⲉ ⲉⲩⲉⲟⲟⲩ ⲙⲛ̄ ⲟⲩⲱⲙ [ⲱⲉ] ⲉⲧⲓ ⲁⲉ ϩⲛ̄ⲡⲁⲣⲑⲉⲛⲟⲥ >>
p. 53:4 frag. E 20→	ⲧⲁⲉⲓ (beginning of line)
p. 54:3 frag. E 20 ↑	ⲡ]ⲉ̣ⲭⲁⲟⲥ (end of line)
p. 53:10 frag. E 10 →	ⲓ̈ⲏⲥ (end of line)
p. 54:10 frag. E 10 ↑	ⲧ̣[ⲛⲉ]ⲙ̣ⲁ̣ϥ (beginning of line)

In one case, however, it was possible to reconstruct a larger new fragment on the basis of four smaller ones, i.e. fragments I 2 / C 29 / H 34 / C 4 (see Figures 1 and 2). During a visit to the Bodmer Library, Geneva, in March 2009 it was also possible to locate this big new fragment on pages 55–56 of the Tchacos Codex.[10] I first give the transcription of the Coptic text, and afterwards I will discuss a possible restoration of the *lacunae*:

---

[10] Kasser et al. 2007, 229–231.

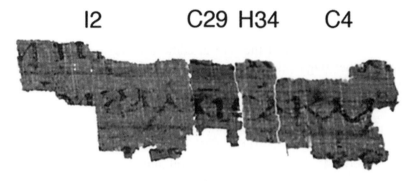

Figure 1

p. 55: 9	[. .] ⲙⲡ . [. .] ⲉⲃⲟ[ⲗ ϩ]ⲛ . [. . .]	[ ] out of
		[ ]
10	[. . .] ϩⲙ̄ϩⲁⲗ ⲛ̄ⲥⲁⲕⲗⲁⲥ̣ [. . . . . .]	[ ] servants[11] of Saklas [ ]
11	ⲧⲏⲣⲟⲩ ⲉⲩⲣ[12] ⲛⲟⲃⲉ [ⲟⲛ ϩ]ⲛ̣ ⲡⲁⲣⲁⲛ	all, sinning [also] in my name.
12	ⲁⲩⲱ {ⲁⲩⲱ} ϥⲛⲁⲣ ⲉ[ⲣⲟ ⲛ̄ϭⲓ] ⲡⲉⲕⲥⲓⲟⲩ	And your star will rule…

In line 11, there is direct contact between the new fragment and the large island-fragment of page 55, the letters ⲩ ⲉⲩ being legible partly on the new fragment, partly on the island-fragment. On this basis it was possible to reconstruct the reading of line 11.

The verso page 56 then reads as follows:

p. 56: 8	[ ] . . . [ ]
9	[†ϫⲱ ⲙ̄]ⲙⲟⲥ ⲛⲏⲧⲛ̄ ϫⲉ [. . .]
10	. . ⲟ . [. .] ϭⲓⲝ ⲛ̣[ⲡ]ⲱⲙⲉ ⲉϣ [. . .]
11	ⲙⲟⲩ [. . . .] . ⲃⲉ ⲉⲣⲟⲓ̈ : *vacat*

It is obvious that at the end of line 9 a saying of Jesus begins, and that this saying ends with ⲉⲣⲟⲓ̈ in line 11. Comparing page 43:15–16 ⲅⲉⲛⲉⲁ ⲛⲓⲙ ⲛ̄ⲣⲱⲙⲉ ⲥⲉⲛⲁⲙⲟⲩ ⲛ̄ϭⲓ ⲛⲉⲩ†ⲩ[ⲭⲏ] or page 53:17 ϣⲁⲛ̄ⲧⲛ̄ⲁ ⲛ̄ⲣⲱⲙⲉ ⲙⲟⲩ, one may here restore to read ⲛ̣[ⲡ]ⲱⲙⲉ ⲉϣ[ⲁϥ] ⲙⲟⲩ, and the traces at the beginning of line 10 can be read as ⲁ̣[ⲁ]ⲟⲩ[ⲉ. So I suggest this saying to be restored to read:

---

[11] Or: "serving" (?).

[12] We missed to note in the *apparatus* that the ⲡ is clearly legible in older photographic evidence.

p. 56: 9   [†ⲭⲱ ⲙ̄]ⲙⲟⲥ ⲛⲏⲧⲛ̄ ⲭⲉ [ⲙⲛ̄]   [I say] to you: '[No]
        10   ⲗ[ⲁ]ⲟⲩ[ⲉ ⲛ̄]ϭⲓⲭ ⲛ[ⲣ]ⲱⲙⲉ ⲉϣ[ⲁϥ]   hand of (a) mortal
        11   ⲙⲟⲩ [ⲛⲁ . .] . ⲃ̣ⲉ ⲉⲡⲟⲓ̈ :   man [will …] against me.'

Unfortunately, the reading of the main verb in line 11 is not clear to me. The first letter after the *lacuna* may be read as ⲟ̣ or ⲱ̣, so that the reading [ⲛⲁⲣ̄ ⲛ̄]ⲟ̣ⲃ̣ⲉ ⲉⲡⲟⲓ̈ "[will sin] against me" seems possible. But maybe there are other solutions.

Figure 2

THE SIGNIFICANCE OF THE TCHACOS CODEX
FOR UNDERSTANDING
THE *FIRST APOCALYPSE OF JAMES*

Wolf-Peter Funk

The discovery of a manuscript that provides us with another Coptic version of a literary work that has already been known for some time usually fascinates mainly scholars whose special interest lies in the fields of Coptic translation practice and phraseology, and these are few. For the great majority of readers of Coptic sources, such a second version is of rather limited value: interesting only to the extent that it sheds light on passages that were obscure in the older version or, if the first known manuscript had lacunas, to the extent that it helps to fill these. In both these respects, the version of the *Apocalypse of James* provided by the Tchacos codex is of great usefulness. Though it is not preserved in perfect shape either, the proportion of extant text to the original whole text is much greater here than in Nag Hammadi Codex V. And as a fortunate circumstance, in a great many sections of the text, the imperfections and uncertainties on one side are well compensated for by clear and clarifying elements on the other side. Given the unequal state of preservation of the two manuscripts, it is clear that more can be learned from the Tchacos text for the restoration of the NH text than vice versa (and most of what can be learned from NH for the constitution of the Tchacos text has already been taken into account in the Tchacos edition).

SOME NEW RESTORATIONS IN CODEX V

New Restorations Supported by the Parallel Version

New insights for appropriate restorations of lacunas with support from the parallel version are of course numerous, and they are best dealt with in an informed re-edition of the entire text. I will here only mention a few cases.

Starting on page 29 of Codex V, the two (or more) lines at the bottom of pages, of which only small remainders survive, can now be restored with confidence. One of these is line 26 of page 30, where we had only an omega after a long lacuna, followed by an attributive element meaning "second." Seeing that the Tchacos text reads "This one is the second teacher" (James as a kind of Paraclete), albeit with the word ⲥⲁϩ for 'teacher', we can be reasonably sure that the lacuna plus omega in Codex V is to be restored with the other word for 'teacher', which is long enough for the lacuna and happens to end in omega: ⲡⲣⲉϥϯⲥⲃⲱ. If anyone had proposed this reading before we had the parallel text, it would have been discounted as too speculative, but now it can be regarded as a restoration that is fully justified.[1] Even more important, especially in the interest of textual integrity, is the information that Codex Tchacos provides for the restitution of the preceding sentence. The fragmentary elements extant in Codex V around the small lacuna at the beginning of line 24 were so hard to interpret that the first editor felt justified to assume two omissions—one before and one after the lacuna—and to "emend" the text accordingly, so as to suit the letters to what he thought had to go into the lacuna.[2] The two subsequent editors of *1ApocJas*, William R. Schoedel (1979) and Armand Veilleux (1986), wisely refused to adopt these illegitimate emendations; but apart from presenting a more faithful reading of the manuscript in terms of word-division,[3] they were unable to improve the understanding of the passage: the lacuna remained unrestored. Now the Tchacos Codex comes to our rescue and fully confirms those later editors' doubt. The sentence one reads in the other manuscript says, "And they had him as a comforter" (17:12f.).[4] Again, it would

---

[1] Note that for the entire (rather intriguing) section about James and his pre-Easter disciples (V 30:13–31:1 par. Tchacos 16:27–17:19), we can only now begin to understand what is narrated.

[2] This practice—recasting the text according to one's idea of a restoration, instead of restoring the lacuna in such a way that it suits the extant letters—was not uncommon among the first generation of Nag Hammadi scholarship. It was recognized as unacceptable only with the more rigorous philological approach that characterized the advanced stages of research starting in the 1970's. The practice became more and more obsolete, but a few passages in Nag Hammadi writings had to suffer from it until very recently.

[3] In both these editions, one reads correctly] . ⲙ̄ⲙⲉⲟⲩ ⲛ̄ⲛⲟⲩ- after the lacuna (instead of Böhlig's -ⲙⲙⲉ ⲟⲩⲛⲛⲟⲩ-). The stroke above the mu is in fact a single-letter (and thus word-initial) stroke, recognizable by its roundedness, not a syllable-binding one as would be expected for Böhlig's ⲁⲧⲙ̄ⲙⲉ (cf. 28:12; 35:3.15). Also, the traces preceding the stroked mu (ignored by Böhlig) do not easily lend themselves to being read as a tau (upsilon seems more likely).

[4] Just to mark the contrast, it may be allowed to quote the result of Böhlig's (now obsolete) manipulation in my own reckless rendering (Funk 1991: 322): "He <was ignorant that> there is a comforter."

have been too much speculation before we had the parallel text, if anyone had claimed the form ⲙ̄ⲙⲉⲟⲩ readable in V 30:24 as a dialectal variant spelling⁵ of ⲙ̄ⲙⲁⲩ 'there' and made good use of it by restoring an expression that means 'have'. In order to do so, furthermore, one needs to recognize here another instance of the non-Sahidic personal construction with ⲛ̄ⲧⲁ⸗ in the Bipartite Pattern (without existential), which is common in the Middle Egyptian and Bohairic dialects⁶ and also found in other "northern" texts of the Nag Hammadi library,⁷ but altogether relatively rare. To be sure, if three successive editors could not fathom a Coptic clause around those two and a half letters missing, it had to be one of a less common nature! The irresistible result is not only that NHC V 30:22–25 now can be seen to make sense without any emendation, but also to say precisely what Tchacos says: "…those who listened to him willingly. And they had him as a comforter, saying…"⁸

In the last lines of page 31 there is now a reasonable possibility of restoration which is of some importance, since it has to do with James' role and relationship to the old and new faiths. With a little help from Tchacos (whose text is not exactly the same), NHC V can be restored to read: "But [you are concerned that the] just [God] became angry with [you, since you used to be a] servant to him,"⁹ before we read what has always been readable: "That is why you have this name,

---

⁵ Not found in this form elsewhere in Codex V, but cf., e.g., ⲛ̄ϩⲁⲟⲩ 63:7 and ⲛ̄ϩⲉⲟⲩ 81:29 (both for ⲛ̄ϩⲁⲁⲩ 'tomb').

⁶ All of the *loci classici* can be found in the northern gospel versions; cf., for "fa," Jn 4:11 ⲁϥⲛ̄ⲧⲉⲕ ⲉⲃⲁⲗ ⲧⲱⲛ "whence have you got it?" (ed. Crum, dialect *F4*); for "mae," Matt 13:12; 25:29 ϥⲛ̄ⲧⲉϥ "he has it" (ed. Schenke, dialect *M*); for "pbo," John 9:21.23 ⲧⲉϥⲙⲁⲓ̈ⲏ ⲛ̄ⲧⲁϥ "he has his age"; John 17:5 ⲉⲛⲁϥⲉⲛⲧⲏⲓ "(glory) which I had" (ed. Kasser, dialect *B4*). But note that in none of these cases ⲙⲙⲁⲩ (or ⲙⲙⲉⲩ) is used. The only case so far, in the corpus of Early Bohairic, where a similar construction can be found with the accompanying adverb is the cleft sentence of John 8:41 ⲟⲩⲓ̈ⲱⲧ ⲉⲧⲉⲛⲧⲁⲛ ⲙⲙⲁ "it is one father that we have."

⁷ Cf. VII 122:18 ⲥⲉⲛ̄ⲧⲉ ⲙ̄ⲙⲁⲩ "you (*fem.*) have them," 125:27 ⲛ̄ϥ̄ⲛ̄ⲧⲁⲛ ⲙ̄ⲙⲁⲩ ⲁⲛ "we do not have it," and VIII 77:20 ⲉⲥⲛ̄ⲧⲁⲥ ⲙ̄ⲙⲁⲩ ⲛ̄ⲟⲩϣⲟⲣⲡ̄ ⲛ̄ϭⲟⲙ "she having it (i.e., that which derives from His ineffable power) as a pre-potency." These other NH occurrences are noteworthy (1) for the fact that the adverb ⲙ̄ⲙⲁⲩ is regularly used in this construction (for Bohairic, cf., e.g., CSCO 43, 131:7 ϥⲉⲛⲧⲏⲓ ⲙ̄ⲙⲁⲩ "he is there with me" or "I have him") and (2) that, in the case of VIII 77:20, the construction even occurs with an "ⲛ̄- of identity," to signify 'have (something/somebody) as a…'—just as it does in our text. A very similar formula is found, e.g., in the Bohairic of Heb 12:9 ⲛⲁⲩⲛ̄ⲧⲁⲛ ⲙ̄ⲙⲁⲩ ⲛ̄ⲣⲉϥⲧⲥⲃⲱ, literally, "we had them as instructors/correctors."

⁸ NHC V 30:22–25 ⲛⲉⲧⲉⲛⲉⲩⲥⲱⲧⲙ̄ ⲉⲣⲟϥ²³ [ϩⲛ̄ⲟⲩ]ϣⲱ ⲛ̄ϩⲏⲧ⸱ ⲁⲩⲱ ⲛⲁϥⲛ̄²⁴[ⲧⲁ]ⲩ ⲙ̄ⲙⲉⲟⲩ ⲛ̄ⲛⲟⲩⲣⲉϥ†ⲛⲁⲙ²⁵[ⲧⲉ

⁹ NHC V 31:28–32:1 [ⲛ̄ⲧⲟⲕ]²⁹ ⲇⲉ ⲉⲥⲣ̄ⲙ̄[ⲉⲗ ⲛⲁⲕ ϫⲉ ⲁϥ]³⁰ ϭⲱⲛⲧ⸱ ⲉⲣ[ⲟⲕ ⲛ̄ϭⲓⲡⲛⲟⲩⲧⲉ]³¹ ⲛ̄ⲇⲓⲕ[ⲁⲓⲟⲥ ⲉⲡⲓⲗⲏ(?) ⲛⲉⲕⲉ (**p. 32**) [ⲛ̄]ϩⲙ̄ϩⲁⲗ ⲛⲁϥ ⲛⲉ·

'James the Just'." Similar unmitigated gains of readable text can be obtained for the last few lines of pages 32–34. After p. 34, however, Codex V is more heavily damaged and an ever growing number of lines at the bottom of pages is completely lost; the parallel text, therefore, can no longer be used as a basis for restoration, it can only be read in lieu of what is lost in Codex V.

Starting on page 35 and continuing through the end of the text, it is the top lines of each page that are partially extant with a considerable number of fragmentary remains and are therefore in need of some help for restoration. In many of these cases, the Tchacos parallel is sufficiently clear to make a full restoration of the lines in Codex V possible. Thus, for example, in lines 3–5 of page 38, one only needs to substitute two different expressions of "many" for what Tchacos has (ones that are more current in Codex V) and the small but telling remains fit perfectly into a restored reading that says exactly what Tchacos says: "[and he will be powerful in] many provinces, [and many will be] saved through [him]."[10] Since the preceding context is extant in Codex Tchacos without interruption (where NHC V, at bottom of p. 38 and top of p. 39, has a huge gap), we now also know that the subject ("he") of this sentence and the one that follows still is the same as before the gap: the younger son of Levi, the third member in the chain of transmission after Addai.[11] But this section can also serve to demonstrate the imperfections of our understanding. The next statement concerning the same person (Tchacos 25:7f. "and he will make this teaching become a *dogma* in many provinces") is missing from the Codex V text; in the sentence following after that both manuscripts have a regrettable lacuna for "his fellow-[…]," the instigators

---

[10] NHC V 38:2–5 [ⲛ̄ϥ̄ⲁⲙⲁϩ²ⲧⲉ ϩⲛ̄ⲟⲩⲙ]ⲏⲏ[ϣⲉ ⲛ̄ⲉⲡⲁ]ⲣ⁴ⲭⲓ[ⲁ ⲁⲩⲱ ⲟ]ⲩ̄ⲛ̄ⲟ[ⲩⲁⲧⲟ ⲛ]ⲁ [ⲛ]ⲟⲩⲟϩ̅ ⲉⲃⲟ[ⲗ ϩ]ⲓ̈ⲧⲟⲟ[ⲧ̄ϥ̄·]

[11] It may be worth noting that the claim of *1 Apoc. Jas.* to a Syrian (and Jewish-Christian) Addai tradition, already apparent in the Codex V version, is fully confirmed by the Tchacos Codex. In his sweeping dismissal of the Addai traditions wide-spread in Eastern Syria and Mesopotamia as late and post-Manichaean, Han Drijvers chose to ignore the evidence of this writing, which is certainly not to be dated later than the middle of the third century. But Drijvers' derivation (cf. most recently, Drijvers 1996, 164f.) of the Addai traditions from the Manichaean apostle Adda/Addas (not Addai/Addaios), the emissary to the Roman Empire in the West, has never been really convincing. The entire complex needs thorough rethinking, even though our sources of information remain scanty.

of persecution,[12] and following this, they plainly contradict each other. That the right teaching is "proclaimed" or "preached" by those persecutors, as NHC V has it, is of course much less plausible than its being "despised" (Codex Tchacos)—just before the section is summed up in both manuscripts by ascribing this adverse turn of events to the influence[13] of the archons (Tchacos 25:14 par. V 38:11, but with lac.).

In another case—concerning the leaf inscribed with pages 39 and 40—full restoration of some upper lines has even made it possible to place a fragment of Codex V that had not hitherto been placed (frg. 8). These lines can now be restored with much more confidence than before. On the vertical fibre side, with the quotation from Isaiah 11:2, one can now read (39:4–8) "a spirit of [wisdom], a spi[rit of] thought, [a] spirit of counsel und a power, a spirit [of mind, a] spirit of know[ledge, a spirit] of fear."[14] Note that the Coptic wording of this passage in Codex V, with its six spirits plus one power, comes much closer to the notion of "seven spirits" than that of the Tchacos Codex, where the seven mental states are assigned to only four spirits, three of which carry double properties. On the horizontal side of this leaf, the combined insight gained from the parallel version and the newly placed fragment allows us to make some real sense of the extant portions to read (40:5–8): "[You] have [satis]fied me [about] these things. These [seven (women)] who have been [presented] as a group—which one among them is more [honoured than the others]?"[15] It may be noted in passing that the parallel passage in the Tchacos Codex, which is slightly obfuscated by the unwarranted introduction of a third person singular, must have been intended to convey the same sense, approximately (Tchacos 27:6–9): "Rabbi, since (so far) he took these seven

---

[12] The lacuna in "his fellow-[…]" must be felt as particularly painful since it deprives us of the precise term for the relationship with the persecuting party, who apparently are to be sought among the apostolic church. If this could be taken more seriously, it might even help revalue the largely legendary traditions about Abgar IX and his initiatives to make Christianity the official religion in the state of Edessa as early as the third century.

[13] In my opinion, the alternative interpretation of 25:14 which the first editors offer in their note ("in the rulers' power" or, more precisely, "according to the power of the rulers") is much more likely than the one found in the continuous translation.

[14] NHC V 39:4–8 o]ⲩⲡⲛ̅ⲁ̅ [ⲛ̅ⲥⲟⲫⲓⲁ] ⁴ⲟⲩⲡⲛ̅[ⲁ̅ ⲛ̅ⲧⲉ]ⲩⲙⲉⲩ[ⲉ ⲟⲩ]ⲡⲛ̅ⲁ̅ ⁵ ⲛ̅ϣⲟϫ[ⲛⲉ ⲙ]ⲛ̅ⲛⲟⲩϭⲟⲙ ⁶ⲟⲩⲡⲛ̅ⲁ̅ [ⲛ̅ⲛⲟⲩⲥ ⲟⲩ]ⲡⲛ̅ⲁ̅ ⁷ ⲛ̅ⲅⲛⲱ[ⲥⲓⲥ] ⲟ[ⲩⲡⲛ̅ⲁ̅] ⲛ̅ⲧⲉⲩ⁸ϩⲟⲧ[ⲉ·

[15] NHC V 40:5–8 ⲁ[ⲕⲧ]ⲱ[ⲧ'] ⲙ̅ⲡⲁϩⲏⲧ' [ⲉⲧⲃ]ⲉⲛⲁⲓ̈ ⁶ϯ[ⲥⲁ]ϣϥⲉ 'ⲉ'ⲧ[ⲁ]ⲩ[ⲕⲁⲁ]ⲩ ϩⲓⲟⲩⲥⲟⲡ' ⁷ⲛⲓⲙ ⲛ[ⲉⲧ'ⲧⲁⲓ̈ⲏⲟⲩ]ⲧ' ⲛ̅ϩⲏⲧⲟⲩ ⁸ⲛ̅ϩⲟⲩ[ⲟ ⲉⲛⲓⲕ]ⲉ[ⲕⲟⲟ]ⲩⲉ·

(women) to be presented (only) as a group[16]—do you have (= can you indicate to me) some who are more honoured than the others?" In both versions this is the basic question that triggers the exemplary distinction of good and bad women disciples.

Restorations Confirmed or Disconfirmed by the Parallel Text

Restorations of smaller lacunas which had already become commonly accepted (and also quite a few that translators had assumed additionally), were in most cases confirmed by the parallel text in Codex Tchacos (where extent). Very rarely, an established restoration in Codex V was disconfirmed and had to be changed; the most spectacular case of this kind—with far-reaching implications—is probably the passage where we find "the twelve disciples and the seventy-two twin partners" (that is, the ones sent out two by two, cf. Luke 10:1) mentioned together: Tchacos 23:1–2 (ⲡⲙⲛⲧⲥⲛⲁⲟⲩⲥ ⲛ̄ⲙⲁⲑⲏⲧⲏⲥ ⲁⲩⲱ ⲡϣⲟ̄ⲃ ⲛ̄ⲥⲟⲉⲓϣ). A small lacuna on the side of Codex V (p. 36:3) had invited the first editor to restore not "seventy-two" but "twelve" for a second time: "twelve disciples and twelve partners"—and this second "twelve" had never been challenged in later editions of the text.[17] Given the crucial importance of these numbers for the doctrine and conceptual makeup of this tractate, this meant a gross misunderstanding with serious implications. The imperfect text of the manuscript of Codex V can now with confidence be restored to read the same "seventy-two partners"[18] as it is found in Codex Tchacos. Not only can the lacuna at

---

[16] For prepositional syntagms based on ⲙⲛ- and using a form of ⲉⲣⲏⲩ, yet denoting *togetherness* (just as ⲟⲓⲟⲩⲥⲟⲛ) instead of *reciprocity* see Crum 59a (in the lower part). By the way, ⲟⲓⲟⲩⲥⲟⲛ and ⲟⲓⲛⲉⲩⲉⲣⲏⲩ are frequently used after ⲧⲏⲣⲟⲩ as interchangeable variant expressions for "(all) together" in parts of the Askew Codex (*Pistis Sophia*); cf., e.g., 32:22; 35:4; 40:13 (Schmidt-MacDermot 1978b) in the vicinity of 39:24; 40:14,16; 41:7.

[17] Böhlig-Labib 1963: 46; Schoedel 1979: 90; Veilleux 1986: 46.

[18] It should be pointed out that the interpretation of this ⲥⲟⲉⲓϣ as "pairs" (Schoedel, Veilleux) has always been rather unlikely in view of the post-Crum evidence of lexical usage. The first editor Böhlig had correctly understood "Paargenossen" (that is, the plural of 'one of a pair', thus 'partners', 'consorts', or 'twins'), but it seems that Funk (1991: 324 "the twelve consorts," from the German of 1987/90) and Schletterer-Plisch (2003) were the only translators who followed his example. I am not sure what these restored "zwölf Paargenossen" in Böhlig's opinion were precisely to refer to—he probably followed the rule-of-thumb, often neglected by editors, that for any ⲥⲟⲉⲓϣ of unclear reference in a Gnostic text, the meaning 'one of a pair' is *a priori* the more likely one.

The later misconceptions are probably due to an uncritical application of what can be found in Crum (374b), where the unfortunate split of the lemma into two separate

V 36:3 easily be filled with [ⲡⲓϣⲃⲉ][19] instead of the former [ⲡⲓⲙⲛ̄ⲧ], but the new reading can in fact be given as [ⲡⲓϣⲃ]ⲉ by taking into account the extant end of the elongated middle stroke[20] of the ⲉ, a horizontal line on the papyrus for which there had been no explanation so far.

Emendations of the Manuscript Suggested by the Parallel Text

Apart from issues of restoration, there are also a few cases where the parallel text invites to suggest an emendation of the manuscript reading. The Codex Tchacos edition already contains a few such cases where the text was to be emended on the basis of NHC V, the most obvious being perhaps the insertion of negative ⲁⲛ in the last sentence of *James*, to read the famous prayer formula known from Hegesippus, in the mouth of James martyr,[21] "My Father…, forgive them, for they do not know what they are doing." Only the first half of the "framing negation" ⲛ̄-…ⲁⲛ, the prefixed element ⲛ̄, is readable in the manuscript. Inversely and more surprisingly, we need to assume such a half-realized negation of a clause in Codex V p. 28:10 when comparing it with Tchacos 15:1, "I am not worried about you." In Codex V, there has always been a form of the nexus with the same ⲛ- prefixed to the Second Present ⲉⲓ̈-ϭⲓ-ⲣⲟⲟⲩϣ, but this spelling had formerly been understood by all editors and translators as the Imperfect, even though a preterite sentence "I was worried about you" sounds awkward in the context. The presence on the papyrus of at least half the negation is now, with the parallel text in hand, reason enough to suggest a negative

---

entries ⲥⲁⲓϣ and ⲥⲟⲉⲓϣ and the lack of the meaning 'one of a pair' in the latter case prevents proper understanding. These two entries in the dictionary have been outdated for a long time, both through the safe attestation of the 'double' (or 'twin', 'consort', = σύζυγος) for ⲥⲁⲓϣ in several Manichaean codices and the occurrence of Sahidic ⲥⲟⲉⲓϣ with the meanings 'mate, consort' or 'twin' in Nag Hammadi Codices, cf. II 29:27; 138:8; ⲥⲁⲉⲓϣ *L6* at XI 22:27, also in the broader sense of "(having no) equal" in a negative expression at VII 39:2.

[19] ϣⲃⲉ is the habitual spelling for ϣϥⲉ in Codex V (cf. 26:15, 17), unless it is given as a cipher (12:27).

[20] The typical equivalent of a line filler in Codex V when the last letter of a line is ⲉ.—With hindsight, one might even say that "[seventy]-two" instead of "tw[elve]" would always have been the only legitimate restoration at the end of line 3 of page 36 in Codex V, because only with this restoration the end of the horizontal line visible after the lacuna near the margin finds its proper paleographical explanation.

[21] Note that the safe identification and restoration of these words in Codex V was only possible on the basis of the Tchacos version. From now on, NHC V 44:5–8 is to be read: ⲡⲁⲓ̈ⲱⲧ' ⁶ ⲉ[ⲧ'ϩⲛ̄ⲙⲡⲏⲟⲩⲉ ⲕⲱ] ⲛⲁⲩ ⁷ ⲉⲃ[ⲟⲗ· ⲛ̄ⲥⲉⲥⲟⲟⲩⲛ] ⲅⲁⲣ ⁸ ⲁⲛ ⲛ̄[ⲡⲉⲧⲟⲩⲉⲓⲣⲉ] ⲙ̄ⲙⲟϥ:

sentence here too: ⲛⲉⲓϭⲓⲣⲟⲟⲩϣ <ⲁⲛ> ⲉⲧⲃⲏⲏⲧⲕ (and no Imperfect), "It is not about you that I am worried."

Concerning emendation, however, I would like to stress that certain criteria must be fulfilled to make it work and to justify this sort of critical handling of the text. There is no point in simply trying to harmonize the two versions when they do not agree. Rather, when a passage appears to be coherent in itself—both syntactically and semantically—it needs to be left standing as is, no matter what the other version says or how much more convincing it may be.[22] But there are a number of cases where a passage has always posed a serious problem—whether at the morphological, lexical, syntactic, or semantic levels—and in these cases the parallel version can be very helpful to clarify the issue (which does not mean that going in the same direction is always warranted).

FOUR LONG-TIME ITEMS OF *CRUX INTERPRETATIONIS*

Nag Hammadi Codex V 24:16–19

The first real syntactic problem that the NH version always presented was right on the first page, at 24:16–19, which apparently offers something like: "and I know you quite well so that when I give you a sign, comprehend and listen", with a purpose clause introduced by ⲭⲉⲕⲁⲁⲥ, but apparently interrupted by an embedded Conditional, and never resumed except for the following imperatives (whose occurrence, as it seems, in a clause introduced by ⲭⲉⲕⲁⲁⲥ does not conform to any known syntactic pattern of Coptic). This had given rise to a number of preliminary suggestions, which were all more or less dubious philologically. One cherished by the *Berliner Arbeitskreis* for some time was to suppose haplography of the kappa (suffix in ⲛⲁⲕ, which is followed by the naked infinitive/imperative ⲉⲓⲙⲉ), so as to read a dialectal Conjunctive ⲕⲉⲓⲙⲉ, "so that, when I give you a signal, you

---

[22] In certain cases one may of course hesitate and feel tempted to suggest an emendation, even though the transmitted text appears flawless. Seeing, for instance, that ἀπαρχή is a much favoured term (and concept) in this tractate (cf. Tchacos 12:7; 28:9.11.14; NHC V 25:25; 41:[3].[7].11; [42:9]) but that the Tchacos Codex only writes ἀρχή in the last of those passages, at 29:9, for what should be "the firstfruits of *gnosis*" (instead of its "beginning") one may assume that this is due to a slight corruption. What is perhaps most significant is the use of this term to describe the preliminary or abridged character of the revelation given in this text and its discourse: "not everything, but ἀπαρχαί" (NHC V 25:24f. = Tchacos 12:7f).

may comprehend." In my opinion none of these suggestions can be uphold any longer. For one thing, "give a sign/signal" is only a deceptive resolution of the verbal compound †-ⲙⲁⲉⲓⲛ into its constituent parts, whereas it normally rather signifies 'designate' in a large sense, thus also 'explain, instruct'. Next, the Tchacos text shows that there was indeed a simple purpose clause and that the verb of instruction was the one directly predicated in that clause, "so that I may instruct you." The easiest way to remedy the slightly corrupt passage seems to emend the text of NHC V simply to read the same form as in Codex Tchacos, that is, a Second Future ⲉⲓ̈ⲛⲁ- (or, since there is also the letter ⲱ present in the corrupt form, possibly ⲉⲓ̈ⲛⲁⲱ- "so that I may be able to explain to you"), instead of the Conditional ⲉⲓ̈ⲱⲁⲛ.[23] I think this is fairly plausible, but I am not fully convinced. When we look carefully at the two parallel texts, there is another problem. Immediately preceding this clause ("so that I may instruct you"), the two versions have different statements that actually somehow complement each other. While NHC V says, "nor am I ignorant about you" (or, less literally, "and I know you quite well"), which fits in very well with the preceding clause ("though you are not my brother in the flesh") but is a poor base for the above-mentioned purpose clause, which follows, Tchacos says affirmatively, as an entirely new sentence: "You are ignorant about –?–", apparently "you(rself)", but which clearly needs to be corrected into "me" to make sense, because it is immediately followed by "so that I should inform you who I am" (note that "who I am" is absent from NHC V). One may easily get the impression that the two kinds of messages—one to conclude the quest for James' identity, the other to open the new quest for Jesus' identity and role—are both needed here and were perhaps originally found side by side in the text;[24] the disappearance of one or the other in either version may have been due to homoioteleuton: the occurrence of a predication of ignorance in both clauses. But is this really likely? The original text may as well have had only one of these intentions expressed, though it would not be easy to say which one.

---

[23] The inverse situation, that is, a Conditional in Tchacos which warrants emending into either a Second or Third ("Absolute") Future, can be found at p. 21:24 (where NHC V 34:25 has an Absolute Future).

[24] It is conceivable that the obvious error of "ignorant about you(rself)" in Codex Tchacos is the result of fusing two complementary sentences into one. A similar confusion of two separate messages into one is probably found at NH V 26:15f. par. T 13:3f.

Nag Hammadi Codex V 26:15f.

A long-time lexical *crux* was the occurrence of a noun ϣⲁϣⲟⲩ, hard to identify in the Coptic lexicon, in NHC V 26:15f. (par. T 13:3f.). Here again, we can read a single sentence on both sides with quite a different message in each case. NHC V (26:15f.) has a responsive clause: after "I have received (= found out?) their number," it adds: "they are seven-two ϣⲁϣⲟⲩ", and the problem has always been, what is ϣⲁϣⲟⲩ? One such lexeme is known to the dictionary, designating a certain kind of ceramic or earthenware container, usually understood as 'pot, jar' (like the Greek lexemes it translates: κεράμιον or κεραμός); but it does not mean 'vessel' in general (nor 'measure', as Schoedel prefers). Nevertheless, most translators have used this lexicon entry to understand "seventy-two vessels," which hardly makes a lucid statement and operates with a generalized meaning of the word that is not actually attested.

Looking at Codex Tchacos (13:3f.), we find a sentence that is very clear in itself, though not in the context, "These seventy-two twins (or partners)—what are they?" The demonstrative article seems out of place since no such thing or number have been mentioned before. What the preceding sentence says is only, "So then, Rabbi, I shall withdraw from the number of the archons," and it remains unclear whether this is perhaps to be understood as an interrogative or conditional clause.[25] Whether this preceding sentence fits the context or not, two things can definitely be learned from the Tchacos text here. (1) Our obscure lexeme may be a crumbled remainder of something that was to mean 'twin' or 'partner', and (2) these seventy-two are subject to a question (the question for their identity: ⲛⲓⲙ ⲛⲉ). With this in mind, our mysterious ϣⲁϣⲟⲩ (followed by the subject pronoun ⲛⲉ) takes on a wholly different aspect. Its last part ⲟⲩ may well originally have been the interrogative ⲟⲩ 'what?' (here used instead of Tchacos' ⲛⲓⲙ), and the remaining ϣⲁϣ may be either a true or a modified, corrupt form of any noun of the root ϣ—ϣ, which could easily mean something

---

[25] Understood as a conditional clause in the *editio princeps* ("then if I shall withdraw"), although the function of ⲉϣⲭⲛⲉ, which must have a very unusual conditional meaning at its first occurrence (11:18), is far from clear here (followed by ⲟⲩⲛ ϭⲉ). Be that as it may, any talk of withdrawal appears less fitting in this context than the simple affirmation of the number found in NHC V, especially when this is followed by the question for the identity of the numbered items.

like 'equal', 'one of a pair'.²⁶ The scribe of Codex V probably did not understand it in this way, or else he would not have applied a syllabic line break ϣⲁ | ϣⲟⲩ,²⁷ and the attributive construction of the word in an indefinite noun phrase "seventy-two ϣⲁϣⲟⲩ" shows that this was a declarative (nominal) sentence for him. But this does not mean that it could not have been a long-time copying corruption, whose point of departure was something closer to the Tchacos text, e.g., "I have found out their number: seventy-two. These ϣ—ϣ ("twins, consorts," or similar)—what are they?" And such an assumption has far more in its favour than assuming any talk of ceramics in this context.

Nag Hammadi Codex V 30:11

The expression ⲁϥϣⲛ̄ⲧϥ̄ is found in NHC V 30:11, followed by ⲭⲉ ⲡⲭⲟⲉⲓⲥ. Following the first editor, Alexander Böhlig, every translator tried to understand this as "The Lord greeted him" (= said good-bye to him). There are at least two problems here. For one thing, ⲭⲉ needs to be taken as a "variant" of ⲛ̄ϭⲓ-, the preposition introducing a post-poned subject. This is not impossible, especially since the same form occurs elsewhere in the manuscript (NHC V 67:18) and may, though highly unusual even here, be considered a survival of the Bohairic ⲛ̄ϫⲉ- (left without full Sahidicization). The other problem is the verb itself.

---

²⁶ See the various noun entries ϣⲁϣ in Crum (604a), especially the first one ('door-post' or any part of a building that is arranged in twins); seemingly an unlimited deri-vation pattern based on the verb ϣⲱϣ 'be equal'. Note also that the northern Coptic forms of the normal 'twin, consort' word ⲥⲟⲉⲓϣ are spelled with these two consonant letters ϣ—ϣ (ϣⲱⲓϣ B, ϣⲁⲓϣ F).

²⁷ As in most other manuscripts, occasional misinterpretation of his exemplar's *lectio continua* by the scribe (through momentary distraction or whatever other fac-tors) can also be observed in Codex V. One of the simplest cases is found in *1ApocJas* itself, at 31:16. Ever since the *editio princeps*, the letters of that line have been con-vincingly divided into ⲉⲧⲃⲏⲏⲧ followed by ⲟⲩⲁⲉ ("do not be concerned for me or for this people"), a reading now also confirmed by Codex Tchacos, which only has the complements in reverse order ("for the people or for me," 18:5f.). But this is not what the scribe had in mind when he copied this line—or else he would not have spelled it exactly the way he did. Following his normal practice, he would have written ⲉⲧⲃⲏⲏⲧ' with a flagged tau, and ⲟⲩⲧⲉ instead of ⲟⲩⲁⲉ. (The scribe of Codex V always spells ⲟⲩⲧⲉ [at least 17 safe occurrences, in four different tractates] for the Coptic sync-ratism of loaned οὐδέ / οὔτε, just as some other scribes always spell ⲟⲩⲁⲉ.) What the scribe here actually spelled out unequivocally reflects a word-division into ⲉⲧⲃⲏⲏⲧⲟⲩ plus ⲁⲉ and thus the beginning of a new clause. If we really wanted our translation to be faithful to the scribe's work (and nothing else), we would have to translate: "do not be concerned. And as for them, for this people, I am…" etc. But of course, no transla-tor wishes to produce nonsense even if it means only a *re*production of the scribe's.

To be sure, the infinitive ϣⲓⲛⲉ can be used to express the meaning 'greet' (even 'bid farewell'), but not as a transitive verb with direct object construction. The expression as it stands has inevitably to be taken to mean "he asked him," which does not make sense in this context. Now, seeing that the parallel sentence in the Tchacos version (16:26) says ⲁϥⲃⲱⲕ ⲛ̅ϭⲓ ⲓ̅ⲥ̅ "Jesus went away" one may easily seek a solution in the way of assuming a corruption on the part of NHC V. If, as I think it can be argued quite strongly, all Codex V texts received their peculiar dialectal colour through imperfect Sahidicization of original Bohairic texts,[28] there may just have occurred one or the other mishap in this gradual process of transfer. The normal Bohairic equivalent of what we read in the Sahidic of the Tchacos Codex would have been ⲁϥϣⲉⲛⲁϥ ⲛ̅ϫⲉ-, and this looks too much like our obscure ⲁϥϣ̅ⲛ̅ⲧ̅ϥ̅ ϫⲉ- to be disregarded as a likely point of departure in the first Coptic wording of this version, which may or may not have been retouched on the way but eventually ended up in a nonsense corruption.

Nag Hammadi Codex 32:26

Finally, as another *crux* now resolved, I need to mention what is doubtless the most brilliant contribution of the Tchacos editors Kasser and Wurst in terms of "collateral benefit" for Codex V. For the text of p. 32:26, they identified a new reading ⲁϥⲉⲥⲓ in Codex V (parallel to Tchacos 19:19). Even though this new reading involves a poorly known verbal infinitive (ⲉⲥⲓ NH = ⲉⲥⲉ T, and cf. ⲉⲥⲓⲉ *L4* Mani), probably meaning 'be relieved', it must be considered a substantial improvement. The old reading *ϣⲉⲥⲓ, taken to be the stative of ϣⲓⲥⲉ 'be bitter' (Schoedel, Veilleux), was never really satisfactory. Not only had it the wrong letter for the stressed vowel (ⲉ instead of ⲁ) but, more importantly, there was no syntactic environment (conjugation) as required for the use of a stative here, immediately following ⲁⲩⲱ. In the new reading of 32:26, whatever the precise nature and origin of the verb may be,[29] it has at least proper syntax when the Perfect con-

---

[28] See Funk 1995, 139–142).

[29] Etymologically, it is no doubt related to ⲁⲥⲁⲓ 'be light, relieved'; therefore, the apparent lack of a iota in the Tchacos spelling makes it less recognizable than the spelling ⲉⲥⲓ in NHC V 32:26.—Under the standard form ⲉⲥⲓⲉ, the infinitive of this verb is safely attested in dialect *L4* if one adds to the known occurrence at *PsB* II 100:24 (Allberry) another verbal occurrence in the unpublished *Synaxeis* codex (in the 1st synaxis of the 3rd Discourse); in that manuscript it is also found at least five

jugation ⲁϥ- is read instead of ϣ- (which should not have been given as a safe reading in the first place). And the rest of page 32 can easily be restored to say the same things as Codex Tchacos.[30]

The opposition τὰ ἴδια *vs.* τὰ ἀλλότρια

To the unprepared reader of translations—if he goes to the trouble to read both versions in parallel—some passages must be puzzling for the contradictory usage of possessive pronouns. Why does one version say "mine" and the other "ours"[31]? Or, more importantly, why should it be "mine" on one side and "theirs" on the other[32]? In the first-mentioned case, the diversity occurs in the "redemption discourse" (or dialogue of passwords); and this has already provided the key to the enigma if one bothered to compare the Greek version.[33] Seeing that the Greek source text has τὰ ἴδια (in opposition to τὰ ἀλλότρια) and no personal possessive at all,[34] one may conclude that this probably was the case in all occurrences of those possessive pronoun expressions throughout the writing. The contradictory evidence that the new version provides also in another case can only confirm this conclusion.

The conceptual opposition expressed with the plural neuter terms τὰ ἴδια vs. τὰ ἀλλότρια, with all their extremely reduced, scanty semantics—is

times used as a nominal infinitive (all probably signifying 'lightness', not 'relief'). If Allberry's reading (ⲉϥ)ⲁ̣ⲥ̣ⲓ̣ⲉ in *PsB* II 142:19 was correct, then the form ⲁⲥⲓⲉ may function as a stative of this verb (similar to the opposition ϩⲙⲉⲥⲧ vs. ϩⲙⲁⲥⲧ), but this remains uncertain, for the time being.

30 NHC V 32:26–28 ⲁ]ⲩⲱ ⲁ̣ϥⲉⲥⲓ ⲉⲙⲁⲧⲉ 27 [ⲉⲃⲟⲗ ϩⲙ̄ⲡⲓϣⲛ̄ϩ]ⲏ̣ⲧ' ⲉⲧ'ϣⲟ28[ⲟⲡ' ⲛ̄ϩⲏⲧϥ̄· "And he felt great relief [from the sad]ness that had been [within him]." Instead of ϣⲛ̄ϩⲏⲧ 'grief', the lacuna in line 27, which has a little more space, might also contain a nominalized infinitive ϥⲓ-ϣⲛ̄ϩⲏⲧ 'grieve, be sad' (for which cf. NHC V 21:16f.; 32:19). In his time, Crum (715a) only knew the constituent noun, not the verbal compound with ϥⲓ-. If our present-day documentation is not too much biased by chance, this usage of the verbal compound may be another Middle Egyptian trait of the language of Codex V since the only other document known to use it is a personal letter written in standard *M* (cf. *ZÄS* 119:47 [line 34], 58).

31 Tchacos 21:9 (*bis*) par. NHC V 34:8f. (*bis*).

32 Tchacos 15:11 par. NHC V 28:24.

33 In the corpus of Irenaeus' works, the excerpts in question can only be read in the Latin translation (*Haer.* I, 21:5), where the oppositional pair was likewise expressed in personal terms: *mea et aliena*, but Epiphanius preserves the Greek (*Pan.* 36,3). A convenient synoptic presentation of the two (along with the Coptic text of Codex V) can be found in Veilleux 1986: 87f.

34 Cf. also the *locus classicus* for the translation of τὰ ἴδια in all Coptic versions: John 1:11.

one of the typical ontological notions used to designate the spheres and persons who/which are akin to those "from the One Who Is" and those who/which are not. There is no reason to assume that besides τὰ ἴδια the Greek text of *James* had also sometimes οἱ ἴδιοι as is the case in John 1:11b for the more personal reference in the second clause of the same verse. The two opposite expressions were probably used throughout the Greek text of *James* in the same form as they are found in the "redemption discourse", that is, in the neuter plural form of most generic meaning. Nevertheless, to judge by the semantic context, some occurrences can be seen to uphold a certain ambiguity between the abstract "property" meaning and the personal designation of "kin, relatives" while others may be solely personal. Or in other words, the ontological opposition was expressed as if talking about things ("goods" or "matter"), to distinguish the sphere of "one's own property" from the sphere of "what belongs to others," even where the actual reference is to persons.

In order to translate a statement containing τὰ ἴδια from Greek into Coptic, any translator had to make a choice of his own, with little help from his Greek source text except the general contextual situation of the passage in question (supposed to be present in the translator's mind). While he had a simple word to render ἀλλότρια (ϣⲙⲙⲟ), there was no such word for ἴδια. Similar to the Latin translator, he had to use a possessive pronoun and thus had to choose among the members of the grammatical category of "person", which in Coptic are eight. Not every translator was likely to make the most appropriate choice in a given case, and two different translators are not likely to make always, or even mostly, the same choice. Therefore, the apparent contradictions we find in the parallel versions are by no means surprising. Even that puzzling passage with "theirs" on one side and "mine" on the other (i.e., Tchacos 15:10f. par. NHC V 28:22–24) can, upon rethinking, be seen to convey the same message on both sides: "I have no memory—the ἴδια are ignorant [= inactive?] within me" (Tchacos) is not very different from "There is oblivion within me, and the memory of the ἴδια I do not have" (NHC V).[35]

---

[35] The most important detail here to be learned from the comparison is the range of the negation in NHC V 28:24, which was hitherto understood as applying to the short relative, "which are not theirs," whereas it can now be seen much more likely to apply to the sentence as a whole, "I do not remember." In the following *gnosis* sentence (two clauses in NHC V but only one in Tchacos), which concludes the entire "hymn" section, both manuscripts are so heavily mutilated that they can hardly be used to help each other.

However, this situation may also be taken into account for our own translation practice in modern languages, although the conclusion we might like to draw from such an insight may not always and everywhere be the same. Similar to Coptic and Latin, there is not much of a problem in most modern languages for "what does *not* belong (to one)," what is "alien" or "foreign," the ἀλλότρια, but there can be a problem in the case of ἴδια. In those languages that, like Greek, have non-personal words of common usage for what is "one's own," easily to be used as nouns—as is the case, for example, in German: "das Eigene" (or even "das Eigentliche") as opposed to "das Fremde"—it will be advisable to give preference to such neutral words and drop any reference to grammatical/possessive person. But in other languages, such as English or French, comparable abstract expressions either do not exist or would be too unidiomatic if used without any personal reference, so that the possessive person may still be inevitable ("my own" etc.).[36] The paradox lies in the fact that even then, in using a personal possessor, we could legitimately make our own choice of preference for what we understand to be the most appropriate person in the context of a given text passage, no matter which possessor we find expressed in the Coptic translation. What matters here is not *who* owns but whether it is "own" or not.

FEMININITY, FEMALE PROPHECY, AND PARTICULAR WOMEN

That the theme of "femininity" (or "femaleness") plays an important part in the Apocalypse of James has always been recognized; it marks indeed a kind of thematic "trajectory" that can be traced all along the tractate. It is introduced right on the first page, in the middle of Jesus' brief discourse on his own identity and origin in "the Being One" (or "Him Who Is"), as a fictitious occasion for the entire dialogue when he says to James (rather abruptly): "Since you have inquired about femaleness, I tell you" etc. etc.—with the ensuing explanations about the inferior ontological status of the Female ("not preexistent") being not exactly the same in the two versions but more or less compatible with one another. This theme can be seen briefly to pop up again in the central part of the writing, the redemption discourse, in the passage

---

[36] In some contexts, the neutral "one's own" may be a way out of the dilemma.

dedicated to Achamoth, but it becomes an issue of greater literary
weight only on the last pages of the tractate, after the chain of succession and transmission (starting NHC V on p. 38, in Tchacos on
p. 25). James' initial question of this chapter, inquiring about the seven
women disciples,[37] uttered along with his amazement at the fact that
such great blessing and power can be found in "powerless vessels," is
first answered by Jesus with a hint at the decisive difference his own
coming has made: now that the Son of Man has come and revealed
the hidden things, it has become possible for the "children of Light"
(apparently including women) to take possession of these hidden
things. This first part of Jesus' reply can only be read thanks to the
Tchacos Codex, since NHC V is rather fragmentary in this part of the
manuscript. Because of its huge lacunas we did not know anything
about the contextual embedding of what follows (already discernible
as such and partly restorable in Codex V): the quote of the "seven spirits" in an adapted version of Isaiah 11:2; now we can see that the text
actually identifies these two sets of Seven, the female disciples and the
seven spirits of the prophecy (Tchacos 26:4–7). In a hidden way, the
seven women disciples had already been announced by the prophet.

In a sense, therefore, "femaleness" appears not only as an ontological category but also as a hermeneutic principle of preliminary, imperfect revelation. Instead of simply rejecting Old Testament prophecies,
Jesus assigns to it a positive value in carrying hidden messages. This
line of thought culminates, after a brief deviation into narrative about
Jesus' encounter with Adonaios during his descent to the earth, in the
explicit appropriation of the prophecy, stating that these seven spirits
were already there when he himself came down, among the people
where "no prophet spoke without these seven spirits, and those are
the seven spirits who proclaimed about me through the mouth of
humans" (Tchacos 26:21–27). One may suspect a certain link here to
the typically Jewish-Christian motif of "female prophecy" (as it occurs
in the Pseudo-Clementines).

While this important dimension of the female spirits is completely
lost in the manuscript of Codex V—due to the large gap between what
remains of pages 39 and 40—the ensuing reply and question of James

---

[37] A piece of ancient tradition which among the Nag Hammadi tractates finds its
clearest expression in the *Sophia of Jesus Christ* (cf. III 90:17 par. BG 77:13, in the
opening sentence).

can be fully restored among small lacunas (see above, note 15), with the help of the parallel text. By this restoration, one obtains more or less automatically a question that is slightly better comprehensible than the clumsy Tchacos text, cf. (NHC V 40:6–8): "Concerning these seven (females) that were represented (as a group) together—which ones among them are more [honorable] than the others?"[38] James wants names, specific individuals, and he gets them: three on the good side and, somewhat later, three on the bad side. (Apparently these are given as examples on each side, with no necessity to add up to the traditional number of seven.) But when Jesus' discourse goes somewhat astray—from the blessed three women to his own role as a new, spiritual kind of priest, who receives from all sides "firstfruits and firstborns" within the sphere of corruption, impure offerings, and has the mysterious power to send them up in purified form—James does not give in, he insists on hearing about the other side of the story, those three women who "wasted their labour" (Tchacos 28:21f.). They are then named and explanations are given, but unfortunately the unique Tchacos text is far from clear in this paragraph. Yet, in spite of the numerous difficulties that the text still presents for an appropriate understanding, it must be noted that for the entire complex chapter about females—both generic and individual—it is only the new manuscript that gives us any real clues about what is going on.

THE SWITCH FROM SEVEN TO TWELVE AND ITS IMPLICATIONS

The switch from Seven to Twelve—as an ideological correction in the count of archontic heavens—must be a point of greatest weight in the teaching of the *First Apocalypse of James* and probably related to its *raison d'être*. This has always been in evidence, since the author makes his James interrupt Jesus' revelation discourse by asking very explicitly (V 26:2–5 = T 12:14–17): "So then, Rabbi, there are (now) twelve hebdomads and no longer seven, as they are[39] in the Scripture?" This question, together with the discourse immediately following it, is also the only topic (apart from James' martyrdom) that received some scholarly attention in the past[40]—attention which was only partly successful,

---

[38] For a brief discussion of the textual relationship see above, around notes 15 and 16.
[39] Tchacos: "as we have it in the Scripture."
[40] See Schoedel 1970; Séd 1979.

however. Before the text of Codex Tchacos became known, it was
not entirely clear what the author may have hoped to achieve by this
switch, let alone its meaning and implications for the world and community view expressed in this writing. It was not possible to grasp
the hermeneutic significance of this numerical reorientation and to
unravel its meaning more clearly, because the only passage where
twelve and seventy-two could be seen to occur together was the context of the question quoted above, that is, the entire section V 25:24–
26:19, which is heavily mutilated in its first part and which apparently
talks only about archons and heavens, not disciples. From the studies
dedicated to this subject early on (in particular, Schoedel 1970 and Séd
1979) one gets the impression that an interest in numerical speculation itself may have been what prompted the author to put forward the
change from seven to twelve. Such speculations evolving in a zodiacal
context, where twelve can be made to function as the thirtieth part of
360 and seventy-two as the double of thirty-six (the number of decans
that make it multiply by ten so as to add up to 360) are indeed fairly
wide-spread and can be found to describe the universe in other writings, one of which was even included in the volume of Nag Hammadi
Codex V itself: the *Letter of Eugnostos*.[41] But the dialogue set forth
in the *First Apocalypse of James* does not dwell any further on these
numbers in their potential universal relationship and symbolism. They
are simply presented as givens and serve mainly one purpose: a "typological" assignment of the conventional groups of disciples[42] and, by
extension, the church that relies on their authority, to the world of
the archons.[43]

---

[41] In *Eugnostos*, cf. especially the two pages of NHC V 11f. (par. III 83f.) where a
numerical structure very similar to that of *1 Apoc. Jas.* is achieved when the twelve
chief rulers are said to put forth six subordinate powers each so that the group of
twelve, as a result, is found side by side and connected with a group of seventy-two.
In *Eugnostos*, the implicit "twin" character of these seventy-two is given by their being
males and females, with $6 \times 6 =$ thirty-six on each side, so that "la formule classique
36×2" (Séd 1979, 169) becomes more apparent than in *1 Apoc. Jas.*

[42] The term "apostle" is not found to occur in this tractate.

[43] Nicolas Séd (1979) may have implied something along these lines when he discussed the numerical problems of the tractate with regard to both the archons and
the disciples, but he did not make it explicit. John Painter came very close to such
a conclusion when he found (2004, 171f.) that "the twelve are to be distinguished
from the archons and identified as the children of Achamoth, the lesser Sophia."
Furthermore, he found there was "a conflict between James and the twelve because
in the first Apocalypse of James the twelve form no part in the chain of revelation

The crucial passage for our newly gained understanding is NHC V 36:2–4 where, prior to reading Codex Tchacos, no editor or translator (myself included) had seen any reason to challenge the first editor's restoration of another "twelve" in the phrase "twelve disciples and [twelve] consorts." But the parallel passage found in Codex Tchacos (23:1–2) has disconfirmed this restoration: the correct reading[44] in both codexes is "twelve disciples and seventy-two consorts" or "twin partners." Chained together in this way with the great Twelve, the phrase "the seventy-two twin partners" can only refer to the group of "lesser disciples" sent out by Jesus according to Luke 10:1, where "seventy-two" was a wide-spread textual variant besides "seventy," both in the transmission of the Luke text and in Patristic literature.[45] Since these "lesser disciples" are said to be sent out "two by two" in the gospel text,[46] they can aptly be designated as "twins" or "consorts." Both groups together can be seen to symbolize the entirety of the Christian mission effort as authorized by the pre-Easter Jesus in the canonical literature. And "mission" easily translates into "transmission" of the revelation—right or wrong—in the context of a writing where this gradually unfolds as one of the central issues.

The two-fold numerical item is here framed in the sense of a typology: "the (proto-)type of the twelve disciples and the seventy-two (twin) consorts," which in turn is listed in its proper place in a general résumé of the various items that Jesus has revealed to James thus far.[47] In this list of items, the topic of "prototype" of the two groups of disciples

---

that is passed on from the Lord through James to Addai and Addai's younger son" (Painter 2004, 172).

[44] For textual details see above, with notes 18 and 20.

[45] Already Nicolas Séd (1979, 169) had the lucidity to draw attention to Luke 10:1 and the mission of the seven-two in his discussion of the numerical connections and associations of *1 Apoc. Jas.* (mainly focussing on the archons). Reading this number only at 26:15/17 and not at 36:3f., however, he could not know at that time that the connection with the lesser disciples was in fact found in the James text. Séd's article is a broad and fascinating presentation of the various aspects of universal symbolism inherent in the number "seventy-two" (countries, nations, languages, etc.), in which connection he also points out the role of this number in the Aristeas letter and one branch of the later tradition about the Septuagint (1979, 167f., 169 with n. 43).

[46] Séd (1979, 169 with n. 44) draws attention to the Christological augmentation of this passage as it was probably found in the *Diatessaron* (in Leloir's translation: "Il les envoya deux par deux à sa ressemblance").

[47] Already the first editor Böhlig saw that V 36:2–4 contained a summary of the items of the revelation hitherto received [cf. Böhlig-Labib 1963: 33, "eine (jetzt zerstörte) Zusammenfassung der Erkenntnisse"], although he does not make this apparent in his translation (1963, 46).

is sandwiched between the issues of Jesus' own identity with reference to Him Who Is, discussed at the beginning of the dialogue, and the essential items of the redemption discourse, especially Achamoth's and James' own identity, found in the central part. Thus there can be no doubt that the revealed "prototypes" of the Twelve and Seventy-Two, who are here explicitly identified as the groups of disciples, are meant to be the twelve great and seventy-two smaller archontic heavens of the earlier passage, on page 26 of Codex V. This is the world the canonical disciples are said to belong to: the inferior, material world of the rulers—in contrast to James, who alone is adopted by Jesus as a spiritual brother and son of "Him Who Is." But to make this disciple typology possible, James' view of the archontic world had first to be corrected from Seven to Twelve.[48]

What further seems to complicate the understanding of this whole complex is the fact that James' original question (V 26:2–5 = T 12:14–17) is worded in terms of "hebdomads" (instead of "archons"), of which there are now to be twelve instead of seven. Given the style of scanty allusion and abrupt progression which is so characteristic of this writing, it is not immediately clear in what sense the term "hebdomad" is used. Two different kinds of questions need to be distinguished here.

One is related to the "seven hebdomads" of James' question. Since this is the notion to be abandoned—and no further comments are made about it—the only matter at issue is its location "in the scripture," where James claims to have picked it up. William R. Schoedel thought that this had to be Leviticus 25:8, where the expression "seven hebdomads" refers to (seven) seven-*year* periods, which add up to the period of forty-nine between two years of Jubilee.[49] While this is not entirely excluded, it would seem that the connection is much more likely to be sought in those scripture passages where "seven hebdomads" refers to

---

[48] There is no reference made to disciples in connection with the point-of-departure number, the Seven. The only reference given for this is "hebdomads" in the context of talk about archons and heavens. Thus there is no point in evoking groups of Seven among Jesus' followers, such as the group of disciples assembled in Jn 21 or the seven appointed ministers of Acts 6:3–5, as a switch in the number of disciples (as far as males are concerned). The only further use made of the number "seven" is in respect of the seven spirits operating in prophecy and the seven women disciples (see above, in the chapter on "femininity"), so that the switch from Seven to Twelve may at best be said to imply also an allusion or parallel to the change from the "female" to the "male" stage of revelation.

[49] Schoedel 1970, 122.

(seven) seven-*day* periods,[50] in particular, Leviticus 23:5 and Deutero-
nomy 16:9. Not only is the reference to seven-*day* hebdomads closer to
the other image doubtless present in the use of the term "hebdomad,"
that is, the seven days of creation, it also implicitly leads us to the
Jewish Pentecost or "Festival of Weeks." This festival and the prescriptions and customs around it, most notably, the provision of offerings
in terms of ἀπαρχαί and πρωτογενήματα,[51] presumably was still very
much present in the mind of the author's ("Jewish-Christian") community and thus could be used, as a background pattern in antithesis,
to describe the role of spiritual High Priest that the Jesus of this writing claims for himself—as made explicit at Tchacos 28:13–16 "I am
not like this. Rather, what I receive is the firstfruits of what is defiled
and I send them (up) undefiled." Not only is ἀπαρχή, towards the end
of the tractate, almost certainly used in the commonplace metaphor
of "the firstfruits of *gnosis*" (NHC V 42:[9], to summarize what James
has received), but more surprisingly, it already appears in a programmatic manner in the beginning, to describe the fragmentary, abridged
character of the revelation to be given in this text and discourse: "not
everything, but ἀπαρχαί" (NHC V 25:24f. = Tchacos 12:7f), thus constituting a kind of key-term *inclusio* for the composition of the work.
The scriptural reference to the "Festival of Weeks,"[52] therefore, is not
entirely without interest, but it has no further bearing on the progression of the text in the section we are concerned with.

---

[50] Schoedel (1970, 122) mistakenly claimed that "only here [*i.e.*, Lev 25:8] does the
expression 'seven hebdomads' occur in 'Scripture'." As can be gathered from any LXX
concordance, the expression also occurs at Lev 23:15 and Deut 16:9 [*bis*], without
counting more marginal places such as Tob 2:1 and Theodotion's version of Dan 9:25.
Apart from Daniel (messianic usage), all these passages refer to the seven weeks leading up to the "Festival of Weeks," with the Pentateuch verses representing its foundation in the Law and the Tobit occurrence a more fictional application of it.

[51] Cf. Exod. 23:19. The close connection of ἀπαρχή (a key metaphor of *1 Apoc. Jas.*)
and πρωτογένημα (both terms occur together at Tchacos 28:9) to the Festival of Weeks
is evident in works of literature where this festival is discussed and commented upon,
e.g., Philo, *Spec.* II 176–187.

[52] As it is this Festival of Weeks (or Jewish Pentecost) which, following Acts 2:1,
was the calendar fix-point of the pouring out of the Holy Spirit on the Twelve and
thus became the Christian Pentecost, it is conceivable that the abandonment of the
count of "seven hebdomads" in itself also contains a polemical note, directed against
the Apostolic Church. If such a subtle association was intended, however, this would
appear to be all but obliterated by the more powerful association of the Twelve with
the archons.

Quite another question is that of the actual usage of the term "hebdomad" in the context of this writing and its progression of thought,
which is entirely focussed on twelve, not seven. That this usage somehow relates to the seven days of creation was already suggested in
earlier studies.[53] This seems to be confirmed by the remainders of
Jesus' first declaration, introductory to the entire "firstfruits" revelation (V 25:26–26:1 par. T 12:8–12) and immediately preceding James'
"switch" question. Of this largely destroyed section (with lacunas in
both codices) at least the end can now be restored to make some sort
of sense. Concerning the "twelve" ("those whom I brought along": precise reference unclear, but apparently archons according to Tchacos
12:10f.) Jesus says that they are "[sitting or resting...], each one upon
his own hebdomad" (V 25:26–26:1 par. T 12:8–12). The use of the
term "hebdomad" to designate an archontic dwelling-place, however,
can hardly be based on its meaning 'seven' (as a whole) or 'week'. No
matter whether the verbal expression used for this predication (which
in both manuscripts is lost in lacunas) is actually "rest upon," "rule
over," or simply "be sitting"—the sense of "hebdomad" in this particular statement hints at what makes the week complete, the Sabbath.
Here we have to take into account the semantic ambiguity of terms
such as "hebdomad" and "sabbath,"[54] due to the metonymic power
inherent in them. Just as σάββατον, the precise term for the "day of
rest," the seventh day as the *completion* of the week, came to designate
the presupposed *duration*, the week as a whole, the reverse is also true:
ἑβδομάς, the precise term for the *duration* of the week, could be used
metonymically for its *completion*, the day of rest, thus being virtually synonymous with "Sabbath."[55] There can be little doubt that this
particular meaning is intended in the sentence which sees each one
of the archons sitting "upon his own hebdomad." Himself resting on
the seventh day, each creator god leaves behind the six working days,
which here appear in the form of the "smaller heavens" (presumably
each one's creations). The question that so much vexed W. R. Schoedel
("unfortunately twelve times seven makes 84—not 72" or, how come

---

[53] Cf. Schoedel 1970, 122f.; Séd 1979, 158.
[54] The term "sabbath" is not found to occur in this tractate.
[55] Bauer's dictionary attests this usage for Josephus; Lampe's for a whole range of
Patristic authors.

"a Gnostic could have said Hebdomad and meant six")[56] did not really do justice to the text. The "twelve" (both in terms of chief rulers and greater heavens) stand in their own right, each one of them being a "seventh" and looking down upon six others,[57] who are correctly summed up as "seventy-two."

At the crucial point where the focus abruptly switches from the "twelve" to the "seventy-two" (V 26:13–16 par. T 13:1–4), the Tchacos version is of greatest value because it helps clarify the otherwise hope-less *crux* of ⲱⲁⲱⲟⲩ in Codex V (see above, about NHC V 26:15f.), not only with its use of a word that must be a variant[58] of ⲥⲟⲉⲓⲱ but also with its clearly interrogative mode, being formulated as a question of identity. Nevertheless, even the Tchacos version of this passage involves one little element that is less than coherent: the demonstrative article in front of the numeral. "These[59] seventy-two twin partners," as the subject of the question, is odd when in fact neither this number nor any twin partners have ever before been mentioned in the text. If we take this circumstance seriously, we will have to say: if it is not a given

---

[56] Schoedel 1970, 123–124. To be sure, Schoedel saw very well that "the seventh day of rest is distinct from the six active days," but he went on to speculate "that James in speaking of the Hebdomad was thinking only of the active six" (which James does *not* do when he says Hebdomad) "and hence was multiplying twelve by six rather than by seven" (which James does do), all of which leads Schoedel to the mistaken conclusion that "the seventh heaven is outside the authority of the archons. Hebdomad, then, means for some purposes six instead of seven." What Schoedel failed to see was that the group of Twelve existed in addition to the Seventy-Two (no matter whether heavens, archons, or disciples) and not only as a factor of multiplication.

[57] This much might have been gathered already previously from the text we had in Codex V, cf. 26:16–18 (par. T 13:5–6) "These are the seventy-two smaller heavens belonging to them" and 26:23–24 [lac. in T] "they being under the authority of the twelve archons." What Tchacos, apart from the intriguing cosmic "axis" (13:8), has to offer in this section (before it goes silent in a large lacuna) is a much more compre-hensible version of the somewhat obscure clause of V (26:18f.) "These are the powers of all their ruling" (or "of all their might"), nicely resolved by Tchacos into something like "Greater than they" (equivalent to "Ruling over them") "are the powers above." Adding this to the list of "hints," we now have at least three relatively clear statements about the relationship of the two groups.

[58] See Kasser et al., *ad loc.* The manuscript reading is somewhat uncertain but hardly permits anything other than ⲥⲟⲉⲓⲥ, which in its turn hardly permits any other identification than being a variant spelling, however unusual, of ⲥⲟⲉⲓⲱ.

[59] In contrast to Codex V, where the system of determiners is largely shaped by a transparent Bohairic *substratum*, the use of the ⲡⲓ- type forms in Codex Tchacos agrees with more southern varieties of Coptic and thus normally has deictic value (correctly rendered already in the *editio princeps*). However, in usage with a numeral, where ⲡⲓ- and ϯ- are normal in the Middle Egyptian dialects, this deictic value may be considerably weakened.

in the text, it can only be a given in general background knowledge. The point of reference that justifies this deictic element, therefore, is most likely the one that is made somewhat more explicit later on in the text: the given fact that there are seventy-two "lesser disciples." Whether or not the Tchacos version of this passage can be considered complete (and true to the original), in all its abruptness it certainly needs a little bit of further interpretation so as to make the textual progression more transparent. To clarify this point, I would hazard an exegetical paraphrase[60] for James' combined response and new question (13:1–4), as follows: "So then, Rabbi, I shall withdraw from the number of the archons—which is twelve and no longer seven—and will not have anything to do with 'twelve' anymore. But then, there is also talk of 'seventy-two twin partners'! Now tell me: Who are these seventy-two twin partners?" In Jesus' answer, then, these latter ones are being related to the $(6 \times 12 =)$ seventy-two "smaller" or inferior heavens, which belong to "them," that is, to the twelve greater or upper powers who were earlier seen to be each sitting on their respective "seventh" (day, floor, or heaven), the "hebdomad" of V 26:1 par. T 12:12.

If the text can be read in this manner, we will no longer be trapped in the all but unintelligible account that Codex V gives of this section of the text. Nor will we have to conclude that, surprisingly, the number of "seventy-two" should be the direct result of the "twelve hebdomads" mentioned earlier in the text. Since the difference between the two quantities is precisely twelve, the reading in which the twelve and the seventy-two exist side by side—which is the only reading supported by

---

[60] See my similar attempt regarding the Codex V version (above, at the end of the section on NHC V 26:5f.), which in that case has more of a tentative remedy for the supposed corruption. Given that the divergent phrasings found in the two versions of this passage both have a clear communicative function in the context and are needed for a coherent understanding, it is in my opinion not unlikely that in this passage both versions are corrupt in the sense that they simplified what was originally a sequence of two clauses (under the influence of some sort of homoioteleuton) into a single clause; that is to say, either one in a different way, with one preserving the declarative and the other the interrogative mode. Such an assumption may appear to stretch the concept of corruption critique a little too far and thus be methodologically difficult to accept. It should be pointed out, therefore, that the overall interpretation does not depend on such a hypothesis. If the original text did *not* contain both clauses but was more or less identical with one of the versions we have, it would just have been a "poor" way of expressing what must have been essentially the same message.

the Tchacos version but is likewise applicable to the version of Codex V—provides a painless and smooth solution to these problems.

It may be left open, for the time being, in how far the switch from Seven to Twelve can also be seen as influenced by Valentinian doctrine. For the understanding of the text itself, this hardly matters at all. There is no indication in the text that the switch has any such connection: the passage where it happens does not show any of the particular Valentinian borrowings found elsewhere in this writing. The text as we have it in both versions makes only one use of this new, "archontic," value of the number Twelve found here: "*the* Twelve," that is, the conventional twelve disciples. The implications of such a typological *rapprochement* in a writing which presents the brother of Jesus as the one true disciple and receiver of revelation must be far-reaching. And it is not only the Twelve, the ultimate "pillars" of the Apostolic Church, but also the larger circle of the Seventy(-Two) that is implicated in the archontic equation,[61] thus leaving no doubt about its general application to the Great Church. The two writings named *Apocalypse of James* in Nag Hammadi Codex V both refuse to accept any other authority than that of the Brother of the Lord. In the *Second Apocalypse* the Twelve simply do not exist. As it now turns out, the *First Apocalypse* is much more explicit in its polemical delimitation.

---

[61] On the disciples side of the typology, the supposed details of the arithmetic deduction of there being a group of Seventy-Two because $12 \times 6 = 72$, as each of the twelve "resting" rulers is accompanied by a group of six lesser powers derived from the six work days of the creation week, has no further impact. The only point of this construction is the resulting number of Seventy-Two, which subsequently can be applied to the lesser disciples. There is no talk about smaller groups of these, assigned to each of the great Twelve.

THE SEVEN WOMEN DISCIPLES

In the Two Versions of the *First Apocalypse of James*

Antti Marjanen

When the Tchacos Codex was subjected to the first superficial scholarly investigation in a hotel room in Geneva in 1983, more than twenty years before its publication, scholars realized that the codex contained a manuscript which very much resembled the *First Apocalypse of James* of the Nag Hammadi Codices (NHC V,3).[1] Nevertheless, it was only after the publication of the Tchacos Codex that it was possible to confirm beyond any doubt that its second tractate was really a version of the *First Apocalypse of James*,[2] even though the text in the Tchacos Codex does not bear the same title but is simply called "James" (*iakkōbos*).

A new version of the *First Apocalypse of James* provides the opportunity to reexamine the conclusions previously drawn from the text on the basis of the Nag Hammadi version alone. In connection with my own work on Mary Magdalene in the Nag Hammadi and related documents, I studied the passages in the *First Apocalypse of James* which dealt with seven women disciples.[3] With a new and in many places better preserved version of the text at hand, I hope to shed some new light on the role of these seven women mentioned in both manuscripts.[4]

While both versions of the *First Apocalypse of James* refer to the seven women as disciples of Jesus, the texts do not fully agree in their descriptions of the women. The purpose of this paper is to discuss similarities and differences with regard to the role and function of the

---

[1] For the first description of the TC by Stephen Emmel, see Kasser et al. 2007, 10.

[2] For practical reasons I use this conventional title given by scholars to the NH version of the text for both versions, although the NH version is entitled the *Apocalypse of James* in the actual manuscript of the text (NHC V,3 24.10; 44.9–10) and the TC version bears the name *James* (TC 30.28). That the NH version of the text is called *First* is only due to the fact that there is another *Apocalypse of James*, conventionally called *Second* (NHC V,4), in the collection of the NH writings.

[3] Marjanen 1996, 122–146, esp. 129–137.

[4] *1 Apoc. Jas.* NHC V,3 38.12–42.21; TC 25.15–29.17.

women in the two versions of the *First Apocalypse of James*. I do it
under the following headings: 1) the relationship of the seven women
disciples to the seven female spirits with whom Jesus identifies them;
2) the make-up of the group of seven women disciples; 3) the attitude of James to the seven women. In connection with the detailed
treatment of these topics, I also make some observations concerning
the literary relationship of the two versions of the *First Apocalypse of
James*. These are very tentative suggestions and by no means resolve
the complex problem. In connection with the concluding remarks and
questions, I ask what function the description of the seven women
disciples in the *First Apocalypse of James* was intended to serve in the
textual strategy of the document.

THE SEVEN WOMEN DISCIPLES AND THE SEVEN FEMALE SPIRITS

The protagonist of the *First Apocalypse of James*, James the Just, is surprisingly concerned with women and matters related to femaleness. In
fact, in the very first comment of Jesus that starts the dialogue between
him and James, Jesus refers to James' prior interest in femaleness.
Therefore, Jesus takes up this subject.[5] In this passage the discussion
about femaleness seems to have to do with a female creator figure that
comes close to the idea of the lower Wisdom, Achamoth.[6] Thus it links
with a later post-resurrection scene in the text where Jesus instructs
James as to how he should answer toll collectors, who were created by
Achamoth and who try to prevent James from reaching his deliverance
after his death.[7]

There is another passage in which the risen Jesus and James deal
with the question of women. After Jesus has informed James of the
way the revelation he has imparted to James is to be passed on to later
generations of witnesses, James wants to know how Jesus himself characterizes his seven female disciples.[8] James' question suggests that the
women do not belong to the chain of transmitters of Jesus' revelation
but rather they are James' own contemporaries. Nevertheless, James

---

[5] *1 Apoc. Jas.* NHC V,3 24.26–30; TC 10.19–23.
[6] Similarly Veilleux 1986, 68–69. Cf. also *1 Apoc. Jas.* NHC V,3 34.20–35.9; TC
21.20–22.7.
[7] *1 Apoc. Jas.* NHC V,3 32.23–36.13; TC 19.21–23.14.
[8] *1 Apoc. Jas.* NHC 36.15–38.11; *1 Apoc. Jas.* TC 23.13–25.14; *1 Apoc. Jas.* NHC
38.12–23; *1 Apoc. Jas.* TC 25.15–25.

does not seem to have a clear idea about these women and, therefore, he now wants to hear what Jesus himself thinks of them.

Only the Tchacos Codex version of the text has preserved Jesus' answer in its entirety. Jesus identifies the seven women with the seven spirits, which are introduced, according to him, in a passage of the Scriptures. The catalogue of the spirits which follows and which is also found in the Nag Hammadi version of the text, albeit in a fragmentary state, resembles the characterization of the spirit of God in Isa. 11:2 (LXX).

TC 26.7–10[9]

ΟΥΠΝ︦Α︦ ΝⲤΟΦΙⲀ Ϩ[Ι] Μ[Ν︦Τ]ⲤⲀⲂⲈ ΟΥΠΝ︦Α︦ ΝⲤΟΧΗ[Ⲉ Ϩ|] Ϭ[Ο]Μ [ΟΥ]ΠΝ︦Α︦
[Ν]ⲚΟΥⳞ Ϩ| ⳞΟΟ[ΥΝⲈ] ΟΥΠΝ︦Α︦ ΝϨΟΤⲈ

NHC 39.3–8[10]

Ο]ΥΠΝ︦[Α︦ ΝⲤⲀⲂⲈ] ΟΥⲠ[ΠΝ︦Α︦ Μ̄]ⲠⲘⲈΥ[Ⲉ ΟΥⲠⲚ︦]Ⲁ̄ Ⲛ̄ⲰΟΧ[ⲚⲈ Μ̄Ⲛ̄ ⲚΟ[ΥϬΟⲘ]
ΟΥⲠⲚ︦Ⲁ︦ [ⲘⲠⲚΟΥⳞ ΟΥ]ⲠⲚ︦Ⲁ︦ Ⲛ̄ⲅⲚⲰ[Ⳟ|Ⳟ] Ο[ΥⲠⲚ︦Ⲁ︦] Ⲛ̄ⲦⲈΥϨΟⲦ[Ⲉ

Isa. 11:2–3 (LXX)[11]

πνεῦμα σοφίας καὶ συνέσεως πνεῦμα βουλῆς καὶ ἰσχύος πνεῦμα γνώσεως καὶ εὐσεβείας ἐμπλήσει αὐτὸν πνεῦμα φόβου θεοῦ

Although the fragmentary state of the Nag Hammadi version of the text prevents us from drawing firm conclusions from the similarities and differences between the versions, it is clear that both versions of the *First Apocalypse of James* are dependent on the text in Isaiah. In two respects both of them disagree with their source, however. First, the passage in the Book of Isaiah describes various characteristics of one divine Spirit, while the Coptic versions of the *First Apocalypse of James* speak of several spirits having one particular characteristic each. Second, whereas the description of the Spirit in Isa. 11:2 is six-partite, consisting of three pairs of characteristics with a seventh summary statement (Isa. 11:3), both versions of the *First Apocalypse of James* refer to seven spirits.

---

[9] The reconstruction of the TC text follows that of Kasser et al. 2007, 153.
[10] The reconstruction of the NHC text follows here that of Brankaer-Bethge 2007, 120, with slight changes.
[11] The Septuagint text of the passage in the Book of Isaiah derives from Rahlfs 1935, 581.

The interpretation of the Spirit in Isa. 11 as a seven-dimensional entity does not affect only the description of the spirits in the two Coptic versions of the *First Apocalypse of James* but also the depiction of the Spirit in Latin and Greek Christian writers of the late 2nd and early 3rd century, such as Irenaeus, Tertullian, Methodius and Victorinus of Pettau.[12] Therefore, it is very likely that the redactional change over against Isa. 11 did not take place in a Coptic translation of the *First Apocalypse of James* but in its Greek original. The structural and terminological differences between the two lists in the two versions of the *First Apocalypse of James* even suggest that the Greek prototypes behind the two extant Coptic versions were not identical.

The reason why the author increases the six dimensions of the Spirit in Isa. 11 into seven spirits is not the same as the seven-fold characterization of the Spirit in Irenaeus, Tertullian, Methodius or Victorinus of Pettau. Although their characterization of the Spirit as a seven-dimensional entity varies in detail, in each case it has to do with the emphasis of its divine origin and its relation to God and his Son, whereas the author of the *First Apocalypse of James* equates the number of the characteristics of the Spirit with the number of women disciples, known from an early Christian tradition.[13] The seven women disciples of Jesus also occur in the *Sophia of Jesus Christ*.[14]

What then does it mean that the seven women disciples of Jesus are identified by the author with the seven spirits, derived from the characterization of the Spirit in the Book of Isaiah? When Jesus explains more specifically to James how the seven spirits have functioned in salvation history, he emphasizes that although the great ruler, Addon, has been in charge of the visible world, the influence of the seven spirits has been observable through various prophets in the time preceding the appearance of Jesus.[15] Although their proclamation was only provisional and imperfect they, in part, prepared the way for Jesus to come. This statement is important because it shows that parts of the Israelite

---

[12] Iren., *Adv. haer.* 3.17.3 (*ANF* 1:445), Tert., *Marc.* 5.17 (*ANF* 3:465), Meth., *Symp.* 8 (*ANF* 6:320), Victorinus of Pettau, *Comm. Ap. 1:4* (*ANF* 7:344).

[13] Another early Christian author, who interprets the passage of Isa as a reference to the seven spirits of God, is Hipp., *Fr. Prov. 9:1* (*ANF* 5:175). In Hippolytus' case, the seven spirits do not stand for seven early Christian women, however. They refer to "the prophets, the apostles, the martyrs, the hierarchs, the hermits, the saints, and the righteous."

[14] *Sophia Jes. Chr.* NHC III,4 90.17–18; BG 77.13–14.

[15] *1 Apoc. Jas.* TC 26.11–15; TC 26.19–27.2.

prophetic tradition are regarded as positive, even though Addon is clearly a negative figure, the name given to the Israelite god.[16]

The identification of the seven women disciples with the seven spirits seems to suggest that the women disciples of Jesus have assumed a similar role to the prophets of the old times. The text may even intimate that the seven women are now seen as the mouthpieces of the prophetic spirit. In light of this it is not surprising that James is exhorted by Jesus to "be persuaded by"[17] these women or their word,[18] or at least to get to know them as fellow-Christians with prophetic understanding.[19] They are "worthy of the One Who Is" and "they have become sober and have been saved from the blindness that was in their hearts," and they have recognized who Jesus is.[20] Whereas the prototype of the twelve (apostolic) disciples who dwell in Jerusalem seems to be the twelve archontic powers mentioned at the beginning of the text,[21] Jesus' way of describing his women disciples indicates that, together with James, they belong to those followers of Jesus, who

---

[16] So also Brankaer-Bethge 2007, 237, and Funk in his contribution to this volume.

[17] 1 Apoc. Jas. TC 27.24: it is possible that the TC version of the text is corrupt and the text should read: ⲣ̄ⲡⲓⲑⲉⲥⲑⲁⲓ ⲟⲛ ⲙ̄ⲡⲉⲉⲓⲕⲉⲟⲩⲁ ⲉⲧⲉ ⲥⲁⲗⲱⲙⲏ <ⲧⲉ> ⲙ̄ⲛ̄ ⲙⲁⲣⲓϩⲁⲙⲙⲏⲛ ⲁⲩⲱ ⲁⲣⲥⲓⲛⲟⲏ ⲛⲁⲓ ⲉ†ⲛⲁⲣ̄ⲥⲩⲛ̄ϩⲓⲥⲧⲁ ⲙ̄ⲙⲁⲩ ⲛⲉⲕ; "Be persuaded also by this one (circumstance), namely by Salome together with Mary and Arsinoe, those whom I shall introduce to you." For the explanatory relative clause, see Layton 2000, 331–332. NHC V,3 40.24–25: For this meaning of ⲧⲱⲧ ⲛ̄ϩⲏⲧ ⲛ̄ in NHC V,3 40.24–25, see Marjanen 1996, 133.

[18] Some earlier interpreters, working on the basis of the NH version of the 1 Apoc. Jas. alone (Böhlig-Labib 1963, 50; Veilleux 1986, 94–95) have suggested that the seven women, who are identified as seven spirits, are not identical with the seven disciples of Jesus, mentioned by name. I do not find this argument plausible. Especially, in light of the TC version, which has better preserved the text in the passage dealing with the women disciples, it seems obvious that Salome, Mary, (another Mary/Martha), Arsinoe, Sappira, Susanna, and Johanna are the same women as the ones introduced in connection with the seven spirits.

[19] I find the first reading more likely both in the TC (for the TC version, similarly Brankaer-Bethge 2007, 123) and the NH version (for the NH version, see Marjanen 1996, 133), but the latter alternative reading is also possible, especially in view of the TC version. Even in the case of the latter interpretation, James and the women are seen as allies in the battle against archontic powers and their earthly representatives.

[20] 1 Apoc. Jas. TC 28.1–5.

[21] 1 Apoc. Jas. TC 12.8–17; 22.23–23.10; 29.18–25; NHC V,3 25.24–26.5; 36.1–13; 42.21–24. For various difficulties in evaluating the role of the twelve apostles in the NH version of the 1 Apoc. Jas., see Marjanen 1996, 137–143. If the twelve disciples are interpreted as negative figures, the seventy-two disciples have to be perceived in the same way in the text. As the seventy-two heavens are subjected to the power of the twelve archons (NHC V,3 26.21–27), so also the seventy-two disciples are subjected to the twelve (apostolic) disciples (TC 22.23–23.10; NHC V,3 36.1–13).

have understood both Jesus' and their own real identity. But is this
true with all the seven women or only with some of them? This question is dealt with in the next section of the paper.

THE MAKE-UP OF THE GROUP OF SEVEN WOMEN DISCIPLES

Before the question of the specific character of the seven women disciples is discussed something needs to be said about the composition
of the group. Who were the seven women disciples? When only the
Nag Hammadi version of the *First Apocalypse of James* was known,
two of the seven women were identified with certainty: Salome and
Mary (probably Magdalene).[22] The name of the third woman is placed
in a lacuna in the Nag Hammadi version of the text but its four last
letters can be seen and they are ιΝΟΗ. Therefore, the name was usually
restored to read Arsinoe. The discovery of the Tchacos Codex version
confirmed this conclusion.[23] The fourth woman, who was apparently
mentioned in the lacuna of the Nag Hammadi version before Arsinoe,
has been variously reconstructed. The editor of the first critical edition
of the text suggested that the name was Martha, since the same quar-
tet—Salome, Mary Magdalene, Martha, and Arsinoe—appears in the
two catalogues of women disciples in the *Manichaean Psalm-Book*.[24]
The Tchacos Codex version did not help corroborate this assumption.
The Tchacos Codex version of the text contains only three women:
Salome, Mary (ΜΑΡΙϨΑΜΜΗΝ) and Arsinoe.[25] For this reason, Brankaer
and Bethge have suggested that the third woman of the text was not
Martha but "another Mary" which was accidentally left out by the
copyist of the Tchacos Codex version because of a haplography. This
ingenious solution also explains why in the Tchacos Codex version of
the text there are only six women mentioned by name (Salome, Mary,
Arsinoe [TC 27.26–27], Sapphira, Susanna, and Joanna [29.5–6]),
although the text clearly speaks of seven women.

If Brankaer's and Bethge's proposal is accepted, it probably also
lends support to my earlier impression that the Coptic versions of the

---

[22] *1 Apoc. Jas.* NHC V,3 40.25.

[23] *1 Apoc. Jas.* TC 27.27.

[24] This was first observed by Böhlig-Labib 1963; cf. also Schoedel 1979, 99; Marjanen
1996, 129–131.

[25] These three women are also introduced as myrrhophores of Jesus' body in a
Manichaean Turfan-fragment; cf. Puech-Blatz 1987, 321.

First Apocalypse of James have no direct literary connection with each other. Since the name of Mary is spelled differently in the two versions (TC: ⲙⲁⲣⲓⲋⲁⲙⲙⲏⲛ; NHC: ⲙⲁⲣⲓⲁⲙ) the possible haplography in the Tchacos Codex version can only be accounted for, if its antecedent—whether it was a Greek or Coptic manuscript—did not use the name ⲙⲁⲣⲓⲁⲙ or μαριάμ but had its longer form, i.e., ⲙⲁⲣⲓⲋⲁⲙⲙⲏⲛ or μαριάμμην.

If the first four women of the group, Salome, Mary, another Mary, and Arsinoe, were women whom Jesus exhorted James to accept as his models, or whom he is encouraged to get to know better as prophetic fellow-Christians, what is the exact role of the three other women? Is it the same? Or are they the "bad guys" of the group as has been suggested?[26]

The description of the three women, Sapphira, Susanna, and Joanna,[27] in the two versions of the *First Apocalypse of James*, slightly disagrees with each other. When James takes up the question of the role of the three women[28] in the Nag Hammadi version, he seems to imply that the women have been despised and persecuted.[29] Whether or not this information suggests a positive picture of the women remains undecided, because a lacuna breaks the description. Although the Tchacos Codex version of James' comment is less fragmentary, it is at least equally ambiguous. First of all it is not clear whether James is making

---

[26] So Funk in his contribution to this volume.

[27] All three names are well-known in early Christian literature. Sapphira, however, who is mentioned in Acts 5:1, probably does not serve as a model for the woman of the *1 Apoc. Jas.*, since the latter is clearly an exemplary Christian (see below) whereas Sapphira of Acts is a prototype of a treacherous woman not to be followed. Susanna and Joanna are ladies mentioned by Luke in 8:3 while he introduces women who accompanied Jesus and his male disciples. Joanna is identified as the wife of Herod's steward Chuza. Joanna also appears in Lukan Easter stories as one of the witnesses to the empty tomb (Luke 24:10).

[28] Schoedel (1979, 101) and Veilleux (1986, 57) translate "these three (things)" and "ces trois choses." In light of the TC version of the text, it has become obvious that the feminine expression ⲧⲱⲟⲙⲧⲉ in the NH version must refer to three women. In fact, the three last letters of the name [ⲥⲟⲩⲥⲁ]ⲛⲛⲁ appears in the text a little later (*1 Apoc. Jas.* NHC V,3 42.4)

[29] *1 Apoc. Jas.* NHC V,3 41.20–23. It is difficult to identify the object of the verb "to cast" in *1 Apoc. Jas.* NHC V,3 41.21. Brankaer-Bethge (2007, 125) restore the word ⲙ̄ⲡⲉⲩⲟ[ⲩⲱϣϥ] "their destruction." This reconstruction is far from being certain, however, since even the letter ⲟ at the beginnning of the noun is uncertain and could very well be a ⲥ. It is furthermore unclear what the subject of the sentence is. In other words, does James ask whether the women have thrown away something or whether something they possessed has been cast away.

a statement or presenting a question.[30] An additional difficulty is to decide how the strange grammatical combination of ⲕⲁⲓ ⲙⲏⲛ with a conditional is to be understood.[31]

Depending on what one wants to emphasize in the comment of James, his attitude toward the women can be regarded either as positive or as critical of them. If one underlines the fact that the women did not suffer it probably makes them positive figures since Jesus himself escaped suffering in the *First Apocalypse of James*.[32] If one wants to stress the beginning of James' comment, the picture of women may actually be negative since James' statement or question could imply that the women have experienced a destruction which may be spiritual. The negative impression could shift again if one took the ⲕⲁⲓ ⲙⲏⲛ-clauses to indicate that the three women did not suffer, even if, according to their opponents, they deserved it, were persecuted, and instructed in things that did not exist. But even this positive interpretation finds difficulties in light of the beginning of James' statement: "The three women...have perished..." or "Have the three women...perished?"

Yet James' view of the three women is not the most decisive issue when their position among the seven women is assessed. If James' characterization is seen in negative or critical terms, Jesus' reply changes that impression. Jesus states: "James, it is not at all fitting to cause anybody to perish." With that answer, the text also emphasizes that it is the idea of destruction which was the crucial thing in James' comment or question. Nevertheless, the continuation of Jesus' answer is somewhat surprising. According to a plausible restoration by Brankaer and Bethge the text reads: ⲧϣⲟⲙⲛⲧⲉ ⲉⲧⲉ ⲛⲉⲓ ⲛⲉ ⲥⲉⲡⲟⲣⲝ̅ ⲉⲃⲟⲗ ⲉⲩⲙⲁ ⲛ̅ⲡⲓⲥⲧⲓⲥ [ⲁⲩⲭⲓ ⲅ]ⲁⲣ ⲛ̅[ⲡⲥ]ⲟⲟⲩⲛⲉ ⲉⲑⲏⲡ.[33] The end of the text emphasizes that the three women have not perished for they have received the hidden knowledge, probably the same or similar to what Jesus has imparted to James in the *First Apocalypse of James*. But what should one think about the first part of Jesus' statement? Does it create a contrast between the first and the second part of the text, between

---

[30] *1 Apoc. Jas.* TC 28.21–26. Kasser et al. 2007, 157 offers an odd solution. Their translation of James' statement has a direct word order, as if it were a comment on the destiny of the three women, but it also concludes with a question mark, as if it were a question.

[31] ⲕⲁⲓ ⲙⲏⲛ is a rare phrase in Coptic literature. Based on its Greek use, the phrase together with a conditional most likely stands for "if indeed."

[32] *1 Apoc. Jas.* TC 18.8–11.

[33] *1 Apoc. Jas.* TC 29.1–3. Brankaer-Bethge 2007, 124.

faith and the hidden knowledge, one which is not in harmony with the way faith is described elsewhere in the *First Apocalypse of James*, especially in TC 16.7–15 where faith is characterized as a pathway to knowledge?[34] Not necessarily. Rather, "becoming separated from a ⲙⲁ of faith" and "having received the hidden knowledge" describe the two phases of a progression of growth one is supposed to go through in order to become a real "gnostic," as is also suggested in TC 16.7–15 and NHC 29.19–28. So TC 28.1–3 can thus be paraphrased: "These three women have left the state of faith, for they have received the hidden knowledge."[35] This means that although faith is regarded as a positive religious concept in the *First Apocalypse of James*, it is still an inferior form of religiosity compared to gnosis.

Thus, I argue that despite the fact that the seven women are divided in two groups in the text, all of them are to be seen as close and loyal adherents of Jesus. This is in accord with the characterization of the women when they appear in the text for the first time. When James asks Jesus' opinion about his seven women disciples he does not make any distinction between various women in the group. According to the Nag Hammadi version all the women, without reservations, have become Jesus' disciples and bless him.[36] In the Tchacos Codex version the text reads somewhat differently; not only is the discipleship of women confirmed but their spiritual status is also emphasized. According to the Tchacos Codex version the women do not praise Jesus but, as James has come to know, they themselves "are praised by all the generations."[37]

If the two groups of women basically have the same spiritual status why are they then treated separately? Because of its fragmentary state, the extant version of the Nag Hammadi text does not deal with the question but the Tchacos Codex version does. In the passage which follows the introduction of Salome, Mary, (another Mary/Martha), and Arsinoe, Jesus seems to attribute the role of being "first fruits" to these four.[38] By implication, the text assumes that the other three women most probably joined the band of women disciples only later.

---

[34] Cf. *1 Apoc. Jas.* NHC V,3 29.19–28.

[35] As Brankaer-Bethge (2007, 247) have also pointed out, ⲙⲁ "ist hier nicht räumlich zu verstehen." Rather it is to be seen as a mental state.

[36] *1 Apoc. Jas.* NHC V,3 42.18–20.

[37] *1 Apoc. Jas.* TC 25.20–22.

[38] *1 Apoc. Jas.* TC 28.8–9. This conclusion is most likely, although it is not exactly clear how the phrase ⲁⲩⲱ [ⲉ]ⲛ̄ ⲙⲁ ⲛⲓⲙ ⲥⲉⲏⲡ ⲛ̄ⲧⲉ ⲛⲁⲓ is to be understood.

James and the Seven Women Disciples

When James' relationship to the seven women is assessed two observations are of interest. First, James' questions concerning the seven
women disciples in both versions of the text seem to suggest that in
the literary world of the *First Apocalypse of James* he is not personally
acquainted with these women. What he knows about them is rather
hearsay. Therefore, he also wants to get more information about these
women from Jesus who appears to know the women personally. In
the Tchacos Codex version of the *First Apocalypse of James*, James'
unfamiliarity with the women is made explicit by the fact that Jesus
promises to introduce some of the women to James.[39]

Second, James' questions concerning the women reveal a kind of
mistrusting attitude toward them although he ostensibly seems to
respect the women. While James acknowledges that all generations
praise the seven women and that the women have proved to be surprisingly powerful, he cannot but wonder how this can be true since
the women are "in weak vessels" or are themselves "weak vessels."[40] In
this way, James resorts to normal terminology of his day to describe
women, reflected also in 1 Pet. 3:7. In itself, this is not surprising, since
in the ancient Mediterranean culture the male represents what is perfect, powerful, and transcendent, whereas the female stands for what is
incomplete, weak, and mundane. James becomes thus a representative
for the normal understanding of women. It is interesting that even the
Jesus of the *First Apocalypse of James* can use similar pejorative feminine terminology when he describes the contrast between the perishable and imperishable in the Nag Hammadi version and between the
defiled and undefiled in the Tchacos Codex version. The perishable or
defiled is the work of femaleness and the imperishable or undefiled is
the work of maleness.[41]

At the same time, Jesus wants to bring James and the women—or
at least three or four of them—together. Whether the purpose of this
encounter is to let James be persuaded by something the women have

---

Brankaer-Bethge (2007, 125) translate: "Und [am] (sic!) jedem Ort sind sie zu diesen
gerechnet..." and Kasser et al. (2007, 28) render the phrase as follows: "And everywhere one has to give me..."

[39] *1 Apoc. Jas.* TC 27.27–28.1.
[40] *1 Apoc. Jas.* TC 25.23; NHC V,3 38.21–22.
[41] *1 Apoc. Jas.* NHC V,3 41.17; TC 28.19–20 "the <feminine> work".

to offer, in terms of prophetic teachings, for example, as I at least used to think, or simply to make James believe that the women are good fellow-Christians, is hard to tell. In any case, it is clear that the Jesus of the text wants to teach the protagonist, James, that these women are not only "normal" women in the ordinary Mediterranean sense of the word. They are also good allies about whom one should not be so suspicious, but one should learn to know them. If the twelve (apostolic) disciples are described in negative terms in the text, as it is very possible,[42] the positive role the women receive in the document is even more significant.

Concluding Remarks and Questions

First, even if the literary relationship of the two versions of the *First Apocalypse of James* was not my main concern, some concrete observations, such as the form and structure of the Isaiah quote and the list of the four (three) female names, suggest that there has not been direct literary contact between the versions. It is even unlikely that their Greek *Vorlage* would have been the same. On the contrary, despite the general common outline of the versions, many differences in the details between them seem to presuppose a rather complicated connection between them already in the Greek text tradition.

Second, in both versions of the *First Apocalypse of James*, the seven women disciples of Jesus, all of them, Salome, Mary, (another Mary or Martha), Arsinoe, Sappira, Susanna, and Joanna, are regarded as positive figures, who seem to function as the mouthpieces of the prophetic spirit. James is exhorted by Jesus either to follow their proclamation or at least to regard them as acceptable fellow-Christians.

Third, it is of course impossible to know even the approximate situation in which the *First Apocalypse of James* was composed. Nevertheless, it is possible to ponder what kind of impact the text was supposed

---

[42] It is possible, although not completely certain, that the twelve are portrayed as unbelieving ones in the *1 Apoc. Jas.* (TC 29.12–24; NHC V,3 42.21–24). For the negative characterization of the twelve disciples also supports the idea that in both versions of the *1 Apoc. Jas.* the number twelve reflects a negative connotation (*1 Apoc. Jas.* TC 12.8–17; NHC V,3 25.24–26.1; TC 22.23.10; NHC V,3 36.1–13). It is also conpicuous that in both versions of the *First Apocalypse of James* the twelve disciples have nothing to do with the transmission process through which Jesus' secret revelation to James is handed on (TC 23.10–25.14; NHC V,3 36.15–38.11).

to have. If the *First Apocalypse of James* is critical of the Twelve who stand for an apostolic Christianity which is taken to be a threat by the Christianity James himself represents, how should one understand that the Jesus of the text exhorts James to look for instruction from or at least allegiance to the seven strong women? Does that mean that the text tries to say that in the battle against the apostolic Christianity the James Christians should rely on those forms of Christianity where women possibly had a more visible role? Or did the text intend to create a platform for prophetic women by employing Jesus to point out their value?

Fourth, any affirmative responses to the questions presented above must still face the fact that the speech about strong women has not altered the fact that "femaleness" even in the *First Apocalypse of James* reflects the standard way of describing perishable life and defilement. Even if the text does invite its Christian readers to give more room for early Christian women, in one way or another, it nevertheless does not go so far as to eliminate completely the pejorative feminine terminology. One can of course say that in a text in which a female divinity is at least indirectly operative in the creation of the perishable, it may be natural to call the result of her activity "the work of femaleness." On the other hand, in many so-called Gnostic texts the Demiurge is mainly responsible for the creation of the perishable universe. In none of them, it is called "the work of maleness."

Fifth, is it possible that the gender of the seven women disciples is not the main issue in the description of the seven women in the *First Apocalypse of James*? Perhaps the women simply represent a prophetic type of Christianity in which women in fact happened to have a relatively visible role. In other words, does the text encourage an alliance between a contra-Twelve and a pro-woman Christianity or between a contra-Twelve and a prophetic Christianity?

QUESTIONS ABOUT THE TCHACOS CODEX

James M. Robinson

Any ancient manuscript has two dimensions, one physical and one intellectual. A manuscript is an artifact, like a potsherd, a Roman coin, or excavated archeological ruins. But it is also an intellectual thing, a text, with ideas. This is a decisive trait not shared with other kinds of artifacts. Almost all of the discussion of Tchacos Codex has been on this intellectual side of the texts, since few have had experience, much less interest, in the physical side. After all, Judas is more interesting than are codices, at least to most people. Besides, the artifact was not available for study to those outside the inner circle of editors.

I have worked a great deal on papyrus codices as artifacts and have published what I learned about their codicology.[1] To begin with, I led the team restoring the Nag Hammadi codices in the Coptic Museum. On the basis of what I learned there, I conjectured what the codicological situation might be in the case P. Berol. 8502, and asked Hans-Martin Schenke to confirm my hypothesis on the papyrus itself in Berlin, which he did. My conjecture proved indeed to be the case.[2] I also helped in the codicological analysis of a papyrus manuscript in the Chester Beatty Library that was unusual, in that sheets were not cut from the roll and stacked in the usual fashion to make the quire, but sometimes folded back and forth in accordion style.[3] And I worked in Berlin to arrange a tentative sequence of leaves in the so-called "Coptic Book," though the obscurity of the fibers made any final solution impossible.[4] On the basis of my background and interest in this rare dimension of scholarship, I thought I should address some basic questions about the Tchacos Codex and its codicology, even though it is an artifact that I have never seen.

---

[1] Robinson 1975a, 170–90; Robinson 1975b, 15–31; Robinson et al. 1984, 1–102, 103–33.
[2] Robinson 1978, 23–70.
[3] Wouters-Robinson 1987, 297–306.
[4] Schenke Robinson 2004.

Where is the Tchacos Codex?
It was in Nyon, Switzerland, near Geneva. This is where the leaves of
the Tchacos Codex were conserved and the fragments placed by Flor-
ence Darbre, conservator for the Bibliothèque Bodmer at Celigny (also
near Geneva), who was aided by Rodolphe Kasser and Gregor Wurst.
Some leaves have been on display at the Bibliothèque Bodmer and in
Washington, D.C. Gregor Wurst reported at the Judas Codex Congress that the Tchacos Codex now is all in Celigny, and that the glass
panes are no longer opened to place physically new placements, since
the risk of damaging the fragile papyrus is too great. He also reported
that the leaves are accessible to scholars at the Bibliothèque Bodmer if
one makes an appointment in advance.

*Have the efforts to attach fragments physically to the leaves to which
they belong been discontinued?*
There were reports that when the definitive edition was published,
further efforts would be discontinued. There would then be no legitimate reason not to return Tchacos Codex promptly to Egypt. Hence
the temptation might be strong to say one still had hopes of further
placements, as an excuse for keeping it from Cairo, and thus from
the rest of the academic community. In any case, this motivation was
involved in Rodolphe Kasser's successful efforts to delay the return of
the Jung Codex from Zürich to the Coptic Museum in Cairo until the
editio princeps he edited had finally appeared.[5] But since Gregor Wurst
reported at the Codex Judas Congress that newly placed fragments
are no longer actually placed physically inside the glass containers,
this need to retain the leaves in Switzerland is less applicable. But the
original is needed in identifying fragment placements, even if the fragments are not then put physically inside the glass containers.

When will Tchacos Codex be returned to Egypt?
It was to be returned to Egypt after publication, an agreement reached
with the understanding that Mrs. Tchacos would hence not be prose-
cuted in Egypt for infringement of its export laws. But when? "Eventually," "ultimately," "several years after its first publication in the West,"
according to Roberty. Gregor Wurst told me there is a deadline of

---

[5] Robinson 1977, 17–30.

around 2010 C.E.[6] At the Coptic Congress in Cairo he had no further information.

Of course it would have been ideal for it to be returned promptly to Egypt, now that the *editio princeps* has appeared.[7] It would have been a symbolic gesture restoring considerable good will, if it could have been given to the Coptic Museum in time for it to be on display there at the Ninth International Congress of Coptic Studies in Cairo on Sept. 14–20, 2008. But it has not been returned, and hence was not on display for the Congress.

In fact it would probably not have been put on display, even if it had been returned to the Coptic Museum in time. For at the opening ceremonies of the Congress at the Coptic Patriarchate in Cairo, a Coptic Bishop explained that the *Gospel of Judas* is not a Coptic Gospel. Instead, the oldest Gospel manuscripts, P[66] and P[75], both discovered in Egypt, are the Coptic Gospels (although in Greek), as demonstrated by a handout of a photograph of a page of each. Indeed, at the Coptic Museum itself, only one sheet of all the Nag Hammadi texts is on display, showing the beginning of the *Gospel of Thomas*.

What happened to the full-size color reproductions?
The Critical Edition is in some regards disappointing. The dimensions of the Tchacos Codex, as estimated by Emmel, are 30 cm. tall and 15 cm. broad.[8] Kasser had promised: "The edition will contain top-quality full-sized color photographs of all the pages of this codex."[9] Yet *The Critical Edition* contains color reproductions measuring 16 by 9 cm. Hence these are hardly more than half-size, rather than full-size as promised. Perhaps the higher cost of a volume large enough for full size reproductions would have been prohibitive (as it was in the case of the Jung Codex, whose elegant massive volumes graced the coffee tables of the wealthy in Zürich more than the bookshelves of practicing coptologists). In any case, the photographs were made available in January 2008 on the Web at ftp://ftp10.nationalgeographic.com/.

---

[6] For details see Robinson 2006, 9; Robinson 2007, 9.
[7] Kasser et al. 2007.
[8] For details see Robinson 2007, 90.
[9] For details see Robinson 2007, 9.

What is to be learned from the leather cover and cartonnage?
The Critical Edition also contains a "Preliminary Codicological Analysis of Codex Tchacos" by Gregor Wurst.[10] He reports: "First, the process of conservation and restoration of the manuscript is not yet complete with regard to the leather cover and the cartonnage pasted into it."[11] The leather cover and cartonnage are of vital importance in locating the codex in time and space,[12] as was the case with the cartonnage of the Nag Hammadi codices.[13] Apparently that conservation process is continuing. Does the return to Cairo of the whole Codex Tchacos depend on completing that last segment of conservation?

What was the original length of the codex and the number of tractates?
The original length of the codex in number of leaves is of some importance. Emmel had reported: "The absence of half of the binding and the fact that page numbers run only into the 50's lead me to suppose that the back half of the codex may be missing; only closer study can prove or disprove this supposition."[14] The closer study is now in hand, proving his supposition.

Wurst reports that there are photographs of some 50 fragments at a bank in Ohio, which provide additional information, although the papyrus fragments themselves remain inaccessible. The information on these photographs of fragments is important: There is a page number, "108." And there is a reference to Allogenes, which indicates that the fourth tractate continued beyond the extant leaves.[15] A fragment with two lines of *diplai* used to decorate a title suggests the conclusion of that tractate.[16] Furthermore, Jean-Pierre Mahé identified three fragments of *Corpus Hermeticum XIII*.[17] This suggests that there was a fifth tractate that is completely lost, except for such fragments. So these photographs of inaccessible fragments teach us more than might be expected about the last "half" of the codex.

---

[10] Wurst 2007, 27–33.
[11] Wurst 2007, 27.
[12] Stephen Emmel made this point when he first saw the codex. He is quoted in Robinson 2007, 55–56.
[13] Robinson et al. 1979. Barnes et al. 1981.
[14] Emmel, quoted in Robinson 2007, 55.
[15] Wurst 2007, 29.
[16] Wurst 2007, 29.
[17] Wurst 2007, 29–30. At the Codex Judas Congress Wurst showed photographs of the three fragments.

What can be learned from analyzing codicologically the extant quires and kollemata?

There is a further consideration to bring into focus regarding the lost last "half" of the codex. Wurst reports that what is extant consists of two quires, each consisting of two *kollemata*, 105 and 146 cm. long in the case of the first papyrus roll used to construct the first quire, and 107 and 183.5 cm. long in the case of the second papyrus roll used to construct the second quire.[18] Such long *kollemata* were unknown and their existence initially denied when we began working on the Nag Hammadi codices in the Coptic Museum, until I demonstrated their existence by publishing the measurements of the many *kollemata* in the Nag Hammadi codices that measure more than 50 cm.[19] This is incidentally a shared trait between Codex Tchacos and the Nag Hammadi codices that has not previously been noted in comparing the Nag Hammadi codices with Codex Tchacos.

This discovery of long *kollemata* facilitates considerably the placement of fragments: If the *kollemata* are long, they stretch not only across a whole sheet (a leaf and its conjugate leaf in the other half of the quire), but then onto the next sheets above or below (or both). If a leaf is some 15 cm. wide, two conjugate leaves comprising a sheet would be 30 cm. wide, whereas continuity of horizontal fibres can be traced across up to six sheets (twelve leaves) in the longest instance of 183.5 cm. Thus fragments can be associated with each other as belonging to the same *kollema*, where horizontal fibre continuity can be established, even if they do not touch, indeed even if one cannot determine to which leaf of which sheet they belong. But rather than having a total of 293 fragments of no relation to each other, one should have the possibility of bringing some fragments together as "island" placements, that is to say, as standing on a line with each other even though not touching. With persistence (and good fortune), some meaningful text comparable to what was located on the photographs from Ohio might emerge among the 293 unidentified fragments.

Why are there so many unidentified fragments?

There are nine plates of unidentified fragments, containing a total of 293 unidentified fragments. This is a very much larger number of unidentified fragments from a single codex than was the case with any

---

[18] Wurst 2007, 31.
[19] Robinson et al. 1979, 67–70.

Nag Hammadi codex. Why so many, especially given that the conservation team worked with advanced technological equipment and enjoyed better working conditions in Switzerland? Hence the large number of unplaced fragments points to another unusual trait that can be inferred from *The Critical Edition*. The large quantity is due to their coming from no-longer-extant leaves on which they could be placed. Furthermore, any leaves following the last extant leaf (pp. 63/64) would belong to a third (or more) quire(s). The unusually large quantity of unplaced fragments would alone require the postulate of a lost last "half" of the codex consisting of different quires than the two extant quires in the first "half" of the codex.

Have joins and island placements been systematically sought between unidentified fragments?
A further question with regard to the mass of unplaced fragments is whether the work of placing fragments has consisted largely in the effort to place these fragments in the lacunae of the extant pages, or whether a comparably exhaustive effort has been undertaken to make joins among these unidentified fragments themselves. If the photographs of inaccessible fragments have proven so productive as to turn up the page number 108, a reference to Allogenes, and parts of *Corpus Hermeticum XIII*, it is odd that there are no comparable references concerning such relevant information located on the 293 extant fragments, published on nine plates recto and verso. The first two plates (a and b) have relatively large fragments, five and ten fragments respectively. Although many of these consist of uninscribed margins, one should recall that placements are based ultimately on fiber continuity, which is of course present on uninscribed fragments as well as on inscribed fragments. Whereas the other fragments (on plates c to i) are small, they are no smaller than many we were able to place in Cairo on the Nag Hammadi codices. And one should recall that the actual fragments are almost twice as large as the published photographs of them.

Has this task of placing fragments among the 293 unplaced fragments been carried on to such a thorough extent that we have as little hope of making further joins or island placements among them as we apparently have of making joins between them and the leaves of the first two quires? At the Codex Judas Congress Gregor Wurst handed out a photograph of four small fragments joined to each other, but not actually identified as to the page to which they belonged. More such "identifications" should be possible. At the Codex Judas Congress, Gregor Wurst did provide some answers to these questions, including transcriptions of 27 small newly placed fragments.

What should we name Tchacos Codex?
The naming of the Rice University Congress in Houston as the "Codex Judas Congress" raised in my mind a question: Does the naming of the Congress as the Codex Judas Congress amount to a proposal to replace the name of the first European owner with a more neutral name, now that Frau Tchacos has been exposed for her rather underhanded practices? One may recall another codex with an apocryphal Gospel also purchased by Zürich and named after its owner, C.G. Jung (who in all modesty did not favor it being named in his honor, whereas Frau Tchacos apparently had no such scruples).[20] When Kasser, the leader of the editorial team publishing the "Jung Codex," finally released it to be returned to Egypt, it was renamed there Nag Hammadi Codex I, which has become its standard designation ever since. The renaming of Codex Tchacos, once it is no longer in Switzerland but is back in Egypt, would seem equally appropriate. Of course the Bruce and Askew Codices were named after the person who brought them to the British Isles.

Yet to name the whole codex after the third tractate as Codex Judas does not seem quite appropriate either. (It would be like renaming the Jung Codex the Truth Codex, because it contains *The Gospel of Truth*). Of course "Judas" gives the codex its fame or notoriety, but probably should not be its official name once it is in the Coptic Museum. Yet it would be appropriate for it to have some designation more memorable than its inventory number in the Coptic Museum (although the Berlin Gnostic codex is still only referred to as Papyrus Berolinensis 8502).

Our hostess April DeConick informs me she thinks the codex should be named neither for Tchacos nor for Judas, but for the presumed location of the discovery (on the model of naming the Nag Hammadi Codices after the nearest city to the site of the discovery). Various names have been associated with the place of the discovery, which has not been actually located by academics, and the antiquities dealer Riyad Jirjis Fam of Heliopolis, who bought it from the peasant

---

[20] For details see Robinson 2007, 16.

middlemen, has subsequently died. The site of the discovery would in any case be a relatively unknown designation, even if somehow it could be firmed up.

But the naming of discoveries after the location near which they were discovered has in other instances proven problematic. Father Pierre DeVaux complained about the title "Dead Sea Scrolls," by pointing out that they were not discovered in the water. Qumran has become the more academic designation, once the monastery and several of the caves have been located near the Wadi Qumran. But others of the caves were not near the Wadi Qumran.

The place of discovery of the Nag Hammadi Codices was first referred to as Daba, in a letter from the head of Egypt's Department of Antiquities, Abbot Étienne Drioton, to Jean Doresse, dated February 13, 1948. Daba, i.e. al-Dabba, is a whistle-stop train station a few miles upstream from Nag Hammadi. It has subsequently been renamed Rachmaniya Kibli. The jar in which the codices were kept was buried nearby, on the talus of the cliff of the Jebel et-Tarif, under the flank of a huge boulder that had fallen from the cliff. The discoverer, Muhammad Ali, pointed out to me the precise location, which agreed with a photograph Doresse had published. Hence this would be a more precise designation than is Nag Hammadi, which won out since it is the better-known city, due to the British building there the bridge where the railroad crosses the Nile. But midway between the railroad tracks and the talus there is a hamlet named Hamra Dom, which lays claim to the talus at the site of the discovery (which is marked by the many holes they dug in the talus looking for more). But Doresse himself preferred to refer to the site of the discovery as Khenoboskion, since this was the ancient name of the location midway between Nag Hammadi and the talus, where there is still a monastery going back to the Fourth Century monastic order created by Saint Pachomius.

The Bodmer Papyri are given this name because the bulk of the discovery was acquired by Martin Bodmer for his library at Celigny near Geneva. But this is not a fully satisfactory designation, not only because the most valuable of the Bodmer papyri, P^{75}, was sold at auction in 2006 and given to the Vatican Library, where it is now located.[21] For papyri from the same discovery ended up also at the Chester Beatty Library in Dublin, the University of Cologne, the University of Mississippi, and

---

[21] Robinson 2008, 172–73.

Barcelona.[22] Thus "Bodmer Papyri" is hardly an appropriate designation for this discovery. In Upper Egypt it is referred to as the Dishna papers, since Dishna, like Nag Hammadi, is the larger town down on the shore of the Nile, where the local middlemen traded the material to larger dealers who sold the material in Cairo (in the case of the Nag Hammadi Codices) or Alexandria (in the case of some of the Dishna papers, the others in Cairo). The discoverer was from the hamlet Abu Mana, and reported to me that the discovery was from the foot of the Jabal Abu Mana at al-Qurnah.

From these somewhat confusing naming and renaming of papyrus discoveries it becomes evident that renaming the Tchacos Codex with a satisfactory name is still unfinished business.

Will the Tchacos Codex be useful in improving the text and translation of the Nag Hammadi Codices?
The Nag Hammadi Scriptures, edited by Marvin Meyer, was published in May of 2007.[23] It did include improvements in the two duplicates from the Codex Tchacos. In the case of *The Letter of Peter to Philip*, edited by Meyer himself, the somewhat shorter title that I introduced on purely practical grounds a generation ago (in spite of the Nag Hammadi copy having a longer title, "The Letter of Peter Which He Sent to Philip"), has now been validated as no longer just a conjecture, but the actual title found in Codex Tchacos. And Meyer has listed in the footnotes about a dozen instances of variant readings from the Codex Tchacos, as he states at the end of his "Introduction":[24]

> Within the translation that follows, the most significant variant readings from the version of the text in Codex Tchacos are given in the notes.

And in the case of *The First Revelation of James*, introduced and translated by Wolf-Peter Funk, he comments at the conclusion of his introduction:[25]

> In the translation that follows, the conclusion of the Codex Tchacos version, which provides valuable new readings, and considerably more text is included in the notes.
>
> The study of this other version has far-reaching consequences for the establishment of a more reliable and readable text of the *First Revelation*

---

[22] Robinson 1990c; enlarged reprint in Robinson 1990–1991, 26–40; Robinson 1990b, 3–32.
[23] Meyer 2007a.
[24] Meyer 2007a, 588.
[25] Meyer 2007a, 323.

of James, but most of the work remains to be done. Since the new text has become accessible only recently, it is not possible to take the newly available information fully into account here. Updating is possible in a limited number of cases, where a more reliable reading becomes immediately evident through an examination of the parallel text.

Funk reported further on the use of *James* in the Tchacos Codex to improve the reading of *First Revelation of James* from Nag Hammadi Codex V in his paper "The Significance of the Tchacos Codex for Understanding the *First Apocalypse of James*" included in this volume of papers.

I received on August 30, 2007 the exciting news from Wolf-Peter Funk that, on the basis of studying the Tchacos Codex, he had placed an unplaced Nag Hammadi fragment, number 8 in Codex V, on page 39, lines 4+5 and on page 40, lines 5+6. It is to be hoped that such serious detailed scholarship will make up for the more popularizing beginnings of the news about Tchacos Codex.

BIBLIOGRAPHY

Abécassis, Armand. 2001. *Judas et Jésus, une liaison dangereuse*. Paris: Éditions 1.

Abrams, Daniel. 1994. *The Book Bahir: An Edition Based on the Earliest Manuscripts*. Los Angeles: Cherub Press.

Abry, J.H., ed. 1993. *Les tablettes astrologiques de Grand (Vosges) et l'astrologie en Gaule romaine*. Lyon and Paris: De Boccard.

Adkin, N. 1985. The Fathers on Laughter. *Orpheus* 6: 149–52.

Albrile, Ezio. 2008. Shining Like a Star Man. Iranian Elements in the Gospel of Judas. Pages 277–91 in *The Gospel of Judas in Context: Proceedings of the First International Conference on the Gospel of Judas*. Edited by Madeleine Scopello. NHMS 62. Leiden and Boston: E.J. Brill.

Aland, Barbara, Ugo Bianchi, and Martin Krause, eds. 1978. *Gnosis: Festschrift für Hans Jonas*. Göttingen: Vandenhoeck & Ruprecht.

Allberry, C.R.C., ed. 1938. *A Manichaean Psalm-Book Part II*. Stuttgart: W. Kohlhammer.

Altmann, Alexander. 1967. The Ladder of Ascension. Pages 1–32 in *Studies in Mysticism and Religion presented to Gershom G. Scholem on his Seventieth Birthday by Pupils, Colleagues, and Friends*. Edited by R.J.Z. Werblowsky, E.E. Urbach, and C. Wirszubski. Jerusalem: Magnes Press.

Amélineau, Émile. 1914. *Oeuvres de Shenoudi, texte copte et traduction française*. Paris: Ernest Leroux.

Argall, Randal A., ed. 2000. *For a Later Generation: The Transformation of Tradition in Israel, Early Judaism and Early Christianity*. Harrisburg: Trinity.

Avemarie, F. 1996. *Tora und Leben: Untersuchungen zur Heilsbedeutung der Tora in der frühen rabbinischen Literatur*. TSAJ 55. Tübingen: Mohr.

Avigad, Nahman. 1993. Beth Alpha. Pages 190–92 in *NEAEHL*. Vol. 1. Edited by E. Stern. Jerusalem: Israel Exploration Society.

Azarpay, G. 1978. The Eclipse Dragon on an Arabic Frontispiece-Miniature. *JAOS* 98: 363–74.

Babbitt, Frank Cole, ed. 1927. *Plutarch, Moralia I*. LCL 197. Cambridge: Harvard University Press.

Bammel, Ernst. 1968. Origen *Contra Celsum* i.41 and the Jewish Tradition. *JTS* 19(1): 211–13.

——, ed. 1970. *The Trial of Jesus: Cambridge Studies in Honour of C.F.D. Moule*. London: SCM Press.

——. 1986. Origen *Contra Celsum* i. 41 and the Jewish Tradition. Pages 194–5 in *Judaica: Kleine Schriften*. Edited by E. Bammel.Tübingen: Mohr-Siebeck.

——. 1997. *Judaica et Paulina. Kleine Schriften II*. WUNT 1.91. Tübingen: Mohr Siebeck.

——. 1997a. Der Jude des Celsus. Pages 265–83 in *Judaica et Paulina. Kleine Schriften I*. Edited by E. Bammel. Tübingen: Mohr-Siebeck.

Bammel, Ernst and Moule, C.F.D. eds. 1984. *Jesus and the Politics of His Day*. Cambridge: Cambridge University Press.

Barc, Bernard (2008). "À propos de deux thèmes de l'*Évangile de Judas*: Nébrô et les étoiles". Pages 655–681 in *Gnosis and Revelation. Ten Studies on Codex Tchacos*. Edited by Madeleine Scopello. *Rivista di Storia e Letteratura Religiosa* 44,3. Firenze: Olschki.

Barns, J.W.B., G.M. Browne, and J.C. Shelton. 1981. *Nag Hammadi Codices: Greek and Coptic Papyri from the Cartonnage of the Covers, The Coptic Gnostic Library.* NHS16. Leiden: E.J. Brill.

Barton, Carlin. 1994. Savage Miracles: The Redemption of Lost Honor in Roman Society and the Sacrament of the Gladiator and the Martyr. *Representations* 45: 41–71.

Barton, Tamsyn. 1994. *Ancient Astrology.* London: Routledge.

Beale, G.K. 1999. *The Book of Revelation.* NIGTC. Grand Rapids and Carlisle: Eerdmans, Paternoster.

Beaulieu, Paul-Alain. 1999. The Babylonian Man in the Moon. *Journal of Cuneiform Studies* 51: 91–99.

Beck, Roger. 1988. *Planetary Gods and Planetary Orders in the Mysteries of Mithras* Leiden: E.J. Brill.

———. 2004. *Beck on Mithraism: Collected Works with New Essays.* Trowbridge, Wiltshire: The Cromwell Press.

———. 2006. *The Religion of the Mithras Cult in the Roman Empire: Mysteries of the Unconquered Sun.* Oxford, New York: Oxford University Press.

Becker, Adrian H. and Annette Y. Reed, eds. 2003. *The Ways That Never Parted: Jews and Christians in Late Antiquity and the Early Middle Ages.* TSAJ 95. Tübingen: Mohr Siebeck.

Beeson, Charles Henry, ed. 1906. *Acta Archelai.* Leipzig: J.C. Hinrichs.

Bergmeier, R. 1982. Königlosigkeit als nachvalentinianisches Heilsprädikat. *NovT* 24: 316–39.

Bergson, H. 1969. *Le rire. Essai sur la signification du comique.* Paris: P.U.F.

Bermejo Rubio, F. 1998. *La escisión imposible. Lectura del gnosticismo valentiniano.* Salamanca: Publicaciones de la Universidad Pontificia.

———. 2007. La imagen de la risa en los textos gnósticos y sus modelos bíblicos. *Estudios Bíblicos* 65: 177–202.

———. 2008. L'ambigüité du rire dans l'Évangile de Judas: les limites d'une Umwertung gnostique. Pages 331–59 in *The Gospel of Judas in Context. Proceedings of the First International Conference on the Gospel of Judas (Paris, Sorbonne, October 27th–28th 2006).* Edited by M. Scopello. NHMS 62. Leiden: E.J. Brill.

Bethge, Hans-Gebhard. 1978. Der sogenannte 'Brief des Petrus an Philippus'. *TLZ* 103: 161–70.

———. 1991. The Letter of Peter to Philip. Pages 342–53 in *New Testament Apocrypha Vol. 1: Gospels and Related Writings.* Edited by Wilhelm Schneemelcher. Louisville and Westminster: John Knox Press.

———. 1997. *Der Brief des Petrus an Philippus. Ein neutestamentliches Apokryphon aus dem Fund von Nag Hammadi (NHC VIII,2).* TU 141. Berlin: Akademia Verlag.

———, ed. 2002. *For the Children Perfect Instruction: Studies in Honor of Hans-Martin Schenke.* NHMS 54. Leiden: E.J. Brill.

Betz, Hans Dieter, ed. 1986. *The Greek Magical Papyri in Translation, Including the Demotic Spells.* Chicago: University of Chicago Press.

———, ed. 1992. *The Greek Magical Papyri in Translation including the Demotic Spells.* 2nd ed. Chicago: University of Chicago.

Bianchi, Ugo, ed. 1967. *Le origini dello gnosticismo. Colloquio di Messina 13–18 Aprile 1966. Testi e Discussioni.* Studies in the History of Religions. *Numen Supplement* 12. Leiden: E.J. Brill.

———, ed. 1994. *The Notion of "Religion" in Comparative Research: Selected Proceedings of the XVIth Congress of the International Association for the History of Religions, Rome, 3–8 September 1990.* Storia delle Religionie 8. Rome: L'Erma di Bretschneider.

Bianchi, Ugo and Vermaseren, M.J., eds. 1982. *La soteriologia dei culti orientali nell'impero romano. atti del Colloquio internazionale su la soteriologia dei culti orientali nell'Impero romano, Roma, 24–28 settembre 1979.* Etudes préliminaires aux religions orientales dans l'Empire romain 92. Leiden: E.J. Brill.

Bidez, J. 1964. *Vie de Porphyre*. Hildesheim: Georg Olms.

Bienert, Wolfgang A. 1992. The Picture of the Apostle in Early Christian Tradition. Pages 5–27 in *New Testament Apocrypha vol. 2: Writings Relating to the Apostles: Apocalypses and Related Subjects*. Edited by W. Schneemelcher. Cambridge: James Clarke & Co.

Bilde, P. and Rothstein, M. eds. 1999. *Nye Religioner i hellenistisk-romersk tid og i dag*. Religionsvidenskablige skrifter 3. Aarhus: Aarhus Universitetsforlag.

Black, Matthew. 1985. *The Book of Enoch or 1 Enoch*. Studia in Veteris Testamenti Pseudepigrapha 7. Leiden: E.J. Brill.

Boer, M.B. de and T.A. Edridge. 1978. *Hommages à Maarten J. Vermaseren*. Vol. 1–3. Leiden: E.J. Brill.

Böhlig, Alexander. 1967. Der jüdische und judenchristliche Hintergrund in gnostischen Texten von Nag Hammadi. Pages 109–40 in *Le origini dello gnosticismo. Colloquio di Messina 13–18 Aprile 1966. Testi e Discussioni*. Edited by U. Bianchi. Studies in the History of Religions. *Numen Supplement* 12. Leiden: E.J. Brill.

Böhlig, Alexander and Pahor Labib. 1962. *Die koptisch-gnostische Schrift ohne Titel aus Codex II von Nag Hammadi im Koptischen Museum zu Alt-Kairo*. Deutsche Akademie der Wissenschaften zu Berlin. Institut für Orientforschung 58. Berlin: Akademie Verlag.

———. 1963. *Koptisch-gnostische Apokalypsen aus Codex V von Nag Hammadi im Koptischen Museum zu Alt-Kairo*. Wissenschaftliche Zeitschrift der Martin-Luther-Universität Halle-Wittenberg: Sonderband.

Böhlig, Alexander and Frederik Wisse, eds. 1975. *Nag Hammadi Codices III,2 and IV,2: The Gospel of the Egyptians (The Holy Book of the Great Invisible Spirit)*. NHS 4. Leiden: E.J. Brill.

Boll, F., C. Bezold and W. Gundel. 1966. *Sternglaube und Sterndeutung. Die Geschichte und das Wesen der Astrologie*. 5 ed. Darmstadt: Wissenschaftliche Buchgesellschaft.

Bonner, Campbell. 1950. *Studies in Magical Amulets, chiefly Graeco-Egyptian*. Ann Arbor: University of Michigan.

Booth, W.C. 1974. *A Rhetoric of Irony*. Chicago: University of Chicago Press.

Borret, Marcel. 1967–76. *Origène: Contre Celse. Introduction, texte critique, traduction et notes*. 5 vols, SC 132, 136, 147, 150, 227. Paris: Cerf.

Bouché-Leclercq, Auguste. 1899; 1963. *L'Astrologie Grecque*. Paris: Ernest Leroux.

Bovon, François. 2001. Names and Numbers in Early Christianity. *NTS* 47: 267–88.

Bovon, François and Geoltrain, Pierre, eds. 1997 and 2005. *Écrits apocryphes chrétiens*. Vols. 1–2. Paris: Gallimard.

Bowersock, G.W. 1995. *Martyrdom and Rome*. Cambridge: Cambridge University Press.

Boyarin, Daniel. 1990. *Intertextuality and the Reading of Midrash*. Bloomington & Indianapolis: Indiana University Press.

———. 1999. *Dying for God. Martyrdom and the Making of Christianity and Judaism*. Stanford: Stanford University Press.

———. 2004. *Border Lines: The Partition of Judaeo-Christianity*. Divinations. Philadelphia: University of Pennsylvania Press.

Boyce, Mary. 1975. *A Reader in Manichaean Middle Persian and Parthian*. Acta Iranica 9. Leiden: E.J. Brill.

———. 1977. *A Word-List of Manichaean Middle Persian and Parthian*. Acta Iranica 9a. Leiden: E.J. Brill.

Bradshaw, Paul F., Maxwell E. Johnson, and L. Edward Philips. 2002. *The Apostolic Tradition: A Commentary*: Hermeneia Fortress.

Bram, Jean Rhys, trans. 1975. *Ancient Astrology, Theory and Practice*. Matheseos Libri VIII. Park Ridge: Noyes.

Brankaer, Johanna, Hans-G. Bethge. 2007. *Codex Tchacos. Texte und Analysen*. Texte und Untersuchungen zur Geschichte der altchristliche Literatur 161. Berlin: Walter de Gruyter.

Bröker, G. 1979. Lachen als religiöses Motiv in gnostischen Texten. Pages 111–25 in *Studien zum Menschenbild in Gnosis und Manichäismus*. Edited by P. Nagel. Halle: Abteilung Wissenschaftspublizistik der Martin-Luther-Universität.

Brown, David. 2000. *Mesopotamian Planetary Astronomy-Astrology*. Groningen: Styx.

Brown, Raymond E. 1966. *The Gospel according to John, vol. 1*. Garden City, New York: Doubleday.

——. 1970. *Gospel according to John, vol. 2*. Garden City, New York: Doubleday.

Brown, Raymond E., Joseph A. Fitzmyer, Roland Edmund Murphy, eds. 1990. *The New Jerome Biblical Commentary: Student Edition*. London: Geoffrey Chapman.

Brun, J. Le. 1997. Jésus-Christ n'a jamais ri'. Analyse d'un raisonnement théologique. Pages 431–37 in *Homo religiosus: Autour de Jean Delumeau*. Paris: Fayard.

Bruns, J. Edgar. 1966–67. The Use of Time in the Fourth Gospel. *NTS* 13: 285–90.

Bsciai, Bishop. 1886. Novem auctarium exici sahidico-coptici. *Zeitschrift für agyptische Sprache* 24.

Buber, Solomon, ed. 1885. *Midrash Tanhuma*. 2 vols. Vilna: Romm.

Buch-Hansen, Gitte. 2007. *It is the Spirit that Makes Alive ([John] 6:63): A stoic Understanding of pneûma in John*. Ph.D. dissertation: University of Copenhagen.

Budge, E.A. Wallis. 1913. *Coptic Apocrypha in the Dialect of Upper Egypt*. Coptic Texts 3. London: The British Museum.

Buell, Denise Kimber. 1999. *Making Christians: Clement of Alexandria and the Rhetoric of Legitimacy*. Princeton: Princeton University Press.

——. 2005. *Why this New Race: Ethnic Reasoning in Early Christianity*. New York: Columbia University.

Burkert, W. 1996. Zum Umgang der Religionen mit Gewalt: Das Experiment des Manichäismus. *Berliner Theologische Zeitschrift* 13: 184–99.

Burkitt, F.C. 1925. *The Religion of the Manichees*. Cambridge: Cambridge University Press.

——. 1932. *Church and Gnosis: A study of Christian thought and speculation in the Second Century*. Cambridge: Cambridge University Press.

Burrus, Virginia. 1995. *The Making of a Heretic: Gender, Authority, and the Priscillianist Controversy*. Berkeley: University of California Press.

Burrus, V., R. Kalmin, et al. 2006. Border Lines: The Partition of Judaeo-Christianity: A Conversation with Daniel Boyarin. *Henoch* 28: 7–45.

Camery-Hoggatt, J. 1992. *Irony in Mark's Gospel*. Cambridge: Cambridge University Press.

Campbell, Joseph, ed. 1955. *The Mysteries*. Princeton: Princeton University Press.

Cane, A. 2005. *The Place of Judas Iscariot in Christology*. Aldershot: Ashgate.

Carroll, R.P. 1990. Is Humour also among the Prophets? Pages 169–89 in *On Humour and the Comic in he Hebrew Bible*. Edited by Y.T. Radday and A. Brenner. Sheffield: Almond Press.

Casey, Robert Pierce. 1934. *The Excerpta ex Theodoto of Clement of Alexandria*. Studies and Documents 1. London: Christophers.

Castelli, Elizabeth. 2004. *Martyrdom and Memory: Early Christian Culture Making*. New York: Columbia University Press.

Černý, Jaroslav. 1976. *Coptic Etymological Dictionary*. New York: Cambridge University Press.

Chadwick, Henry. 1953. *Origen: Contra Celsum*. Cambridge: Cambridge University Press.

——. 1976. *Priscillian of Avila: The Occult and the Charismatic in the Early Church*. Oxford: Claredon.

Chaîne, Marius. 1905. Le Livre du Coq ('Matzhafa Dorho'). *RSém* 13: 276–81.

Charlesworth, James H. 1977. Jewish Astrology in the Talmud, Pseudepigrapha, the Dead Sea Scrolls, and Early Palestinian Synagogues. *HTR* 70: 183–200.

——. 1983. *The Old Testament Pseudepigrapha*. Vol. 1. Garden City: Double Day.

——. 1985. *The Old Testament Pseudepigrapha*. Vol. 2. Garden City: Doubleday.

Clarke, Ernest G. and Shirley Magder. 1995. *Targum Pseudo-Jonathan: Numbers translated, with Notes*. The Aramaic Bible 4. Collegeville: The Liturgical Press.

Cohen, Jeremy. 2007. *Christ Killers: The Jews and the Passion from the Bible to the Big Screen*. Oxford and New York: Oxford University Press.

Coleman, Kathleen. 1990. Fatal Charades: Roman Executions Stages as Mythological Enactments. *The Journal of Roman Studies* 80: 44–73.

Collins, Adela Yarbro. 1984. Numerical Symbolism in Jewish and Early Christian Apocalyptic Literature. Pages 1222–87 in *Aufstieg und Niedergang der römischen Welt*. Edited by Hildegard Temporini and Wolfgang Haase. New York: Walter de Gruyter.

——. 1989. Persecution and Vengeance in the Book of Revelation. Pages 729–49 in *Apocalypticism in the Mediterranean World and the Near East. Proceedings of the International Colloquium on Apocalypticism, Uppsala, August 12–17, 1979*. Edited by D. Hellholm. Tübingen: Mohr.

——. 1995. The Seven Heavens in Jewish and Christian Apocalypses. In *Death, Ecstasy and Other Worldly Journeys*. Edited by John J. Collins and Michael Fishbane. Albany: State University of New York Press.

Collins, John J. 1997. *Apocalypticism in the Dead Sea Scrolls*. London and New York: Routledge.

Collins, John J. and Fishbane, Michael, eds. 1995. *Death, Ecstasy and Other Worldly Journeys*. Albany: State University of New York Press.

——. 2003. The Zeal of Phinehas: the Bible and the Legitimation of Violence. *JBL* 122: 3–21.

Colson, F.H. and G.H. Whitaker, eds. 1929a. *Philo I*. LCL 226. Cambridge: Harvard University Press.

——, eds. 1929b. *Philo II*. LCL 227. Cambridge: Harvard University Press.

Cooper, John and D. Hutchinson. 1997. *Plato: Complete Works*. Indianapolis and Cambridge: Hackett Publishing Company.

Copenhaver, B.P. 1992. *Hermetica, The Greek Corpus Hermeticum and the Latin Asclepius in a new English translation with notes and introduction*. New York: Cambridge University Press.

Corsini, Eugenio. 1985. La settimana della passione nel Vangelo di Marco. *Civiltà classica e cristiana* 6: 241–51.

Cowley, Roger W. 1985. The So-Called 'Ethiopic Book of the Cock'—Part of an Apocryphal Passion Gospel, The Homily and Teaching of Our Fathers the Holy Apostles. *JRAS*: 16–22.

Cribiore, R. 2001. *Gymnastics of the Mind*. Princeton: Princeton University Press.

Crum, Walter. 1939. *A Coptic Dictionary*. Oxford: Clarendon.

Daly, Robert J. 1992. *Ancient Christian Writers: The Works of the Fathers in Translation, No. 54*. New York: Paulist Press.

Daniélou, Jean. 1959. Les douze apôtres et le zodiaque. *VC* 13: 14–21.

Dart, J. 1976. *The Laughing Savior. The Discovery and Significance of the Nag Hammadi Gnostic Library*. New York: Harper & Row.

——. 1988. *The Jesus of Heresy and History. The Discovery and Meaning of the Nag Hammadi Gnostic Library*. San Francisco: Harper.

Dauzat, Pierre-Emmanuel. 2006. *Judas. De l'Évangile à l'Holocauste*. Paris: Bayard.

DeConick, April D. 2007. *The Thirteenth Apostle: What the Gospel of Judas Really Says*. New York: Continuum.

——. 2008. The Mystery of Betrayal. What does the Gospel of Judas Really Say? Pages 239–64 in *The Gospel of Judas in Context: Proceedings of the First International Conference on the Gospel of Judas*. Edited by M. Scopello. NHMS 62. Leiden and Boston: E.J. Brill.

———. 2009. Transgressive Gnosis: Radical Thinking about the Gospel of Judas. In *Gnosis and Revelation. Ten Studies on Codex Tchacos. Rivista di Storia e Letterature Religiosa* 44.3. Edited by Madeleine Scopello. Firenze Olschki.

Denzey, Nicola. 1998. *Under A Pitiless Sky.* Ph.D Dissertation: Princeton University.

———. 2003. A New Star on the Horizon: Astral Christologies and Stellar Debates in Early Christian Discourse. In *Prayer, Magic and the Stars.* Edited by Joel Thomas Walker and Brannon Wheeler Scott Noegel. Pittsburg: Pennsylvania State Press.

———. 2005. Stalking Those Elusive Ophites: The Ophite Diagrams Reconsidered. Pages 89–122 in *Essays in Honour of Frederik Wisse, Scholar, Churchman, Mentor.* Edited by Warren Kappeler. ARC 33. Montréal: McGill University.

Deonna, Waldemar. 1920. Notes d'archéologie Suisse VIII: Lampe chrétienne du Musée de Genève. *Anzeiger für schweizerische Altertumskunde* 22: 176–79.

Déroche, François, Adam Gacek, and Jan J. Witkam, eds. 1990/91. *Manuscripts of the Middle East vol. 5: The Role of the Book in the Civilisations of the Near East.* Leiden: Ter Lugt Press.

Desjardins, R. 1990. *The Rational Enterprise: Logos in Plato's Theaetetus.* SUNY series in Ancient Greek Philosophy. New York: State University of New York Press.

Diebner, Berndt J. and Rodolphe Kasser. 1989. *Hamburger Papyrus Bil. 1. Die Alttestament ichen Texte des Papyrus Bilinguis 1 der Staats- und Universitätsbibliothek Hamburg. Canticum Canticorum (Coptice). Lamentationes Ieremiae (Coptice). Ecclesiastes (Graece et Coptice).* Geneva: Patrick Cramer.

Dillon, J. 1977. *The Middle Platonist, 80 B.C. to 220 A.D.* Ithaca: Cornell University Press.

Dinkler, E. 1971. Peter's Confession and the 'Satan' Saying: The Problem of Jesus' Messiahship. Pages 169–85 in *The Future of Our Religious Past: Essays in Honor of Rudolf Bultmann.* Edited by James M. Robinson. San Francisco: Harper & Row.

Dirkse, P.A., J. Brashler and Douglas M. Parrott. 1979. Discourse on the Eighth and Ninth. Pages 341–73 in *Nag Hammadi Codices V,2–5 and VI with Papyrus Berolinensis 8502, 1 and 4.* Edited by D.M. Parrott. NHS 11. Leiden: E.J. Brill.

DiTommaso, Lorenzo and Turcescu, Lucian, eds. 2008. *The Reception and Interpretation of the Bible in Late Antiquity: Proceedings of the Montréal Colloquium in Honour of Charles Kannengiesser, 11–13 October 2006.* The Bible in Ancient Christianity 3. Leiden: E.J. Brill.

Dodd, C.H. 1953. *The Interpretation of the Fourth Gospel.* Cambridge: Cambridge University Press.

Doresse, Jean. 1958. *Les livres secrets des gnostiques d'Égypte. Introduction aux écrits gnostiques coptes découverts à Khénoboskion.* Paris: Plon.

———. 1960. *The Secret Books of the Egyptian Gnostics: An Introduction to the Gnostic Coptic Manuscripts Discovered at Chenoboskion.* London: Hollis & Carter.

Dorival, Gilles. 1994. *La Bible d'Alexandrie, 4. Les Nombres.* Paris: Les Éditions du Cerf.

Dothan, M. 1962. Hammath-Tiberias. *Israel Exploration Journal* 12: 153–54.

Drijvers, Han J.W. 1996. Early Syriac Christianity: some recent publications. *VC* 50: 159–77.

Drower, E.S., trans. 1949, 1964. *The Book of the Zodiac.* London: The Royal Asiatic Society.

Dunderberg, Ismo. 2008. *Beyond Gnosticism: Myth, Lifestyle, and Society in the School of Valentinus.* New York: Columbia University Press.

Dunn, J.D.G. 1988. *Romans 1–8.* WBC. Waco: Word.

Dupont-Sommer, A. and Philonenko, M., eds. 1987. *La Bible. Écrits intertestamentaires.* Bibliothèque de la Pléiade. Paris: Gallimard.

Edsman, Carl-Martin, Widengren, Geo and Puech, Henri-Charles, eds. 1974. *Mélanges d'histoire des religions: offerts à Henri-Charles Puech.* Paris: Presses Universitaires de France.

Edwards, Catherine. 2007. *Death in Ancient Rome*. New Haven: Yale University Press.

Ehrman, Bart D., ed. 2003. Ignatius: To the Ephesians. Pages 218–41 in *The Apostolic Fathers*. Vol. 1. LCL 24. Cambridge: Harvard University Press.

——. 2006a. Christianity Turned on Its Head: The Alternative Vision of the Gospel of Judas. Pages 77–120 in *The Gospel of Judas from Codex Tchacos*. Edited by Rodolphe Kasser et al. Washington, D.C.: National Geographic.

——. 2006b. *The Lost Gospel of Judas Iscariot: A New look at Betrayer and Betrayed*. Oxford: Oxford University Press.

Eliade, Mircea. 1959. *The Sacred and the Profane: The Nature of Religion*. New York: Harcourt, Brace & World, Inc.

Engberg-Pedersen, Troels. 2000. *Paul and the Stoics*. Edinburgh and Louisville: T & T Clark, John Knox.

——. 2004. The Concept of Paraenesis. Pages 47–52 in *Early Christian Paraenesis in Context*. Edited by James M. Starr and Troels Engberg-Pedersen. BZNW 125. Berlin: de Gruyter.

Englund G. ed. 1989. *The Religion of the Ancient Egyptians, Cognitive Structures and Popular Expressions, Proceedings of Symposia in Uppsala and Bergen 1987 and 1988*. Acta Universitatis Uppsaliensis Boreas, Uppsala Studies in Ancient Mediterranean and Near Eastern Civilizations 20. Stockholm.

Epstein, Marc Michael. 1996. Harnessing the Dragon: A Mythos Transformed in Medieval Jewish Literature and Art. Pages 352–89 in *Myth and Method: New Perspectives on Sacred Narrative*. Edited by Laurie L. Patton and Wendy Doniger. Charlottesville: University of Virginia Press.

Erichsen, Wolja. 1954. *Demotisches Glossar*. Copenhagen: E. Munksgaard.

Evans, Marc. 2004. The Astrologer's Apparatus: A Picture of Professional Practice in Greco-Roman Egypt. *Journal for the History of Astronomy* 35: 1–44.

Faivre, A. 1994. *Access to Western Esotericism*. Albany: State University of New York.

Falkenberg, René. 2008. Kongerigets Hemmeligheder: et forsøg på en fortolkning af *Judasevangeliet*. Pages 119–42 in *Mellem venner og fjender: En folgebog om Judasevangeliet, tidlig kristendom og gnosis*. Edited by Anders Klostergaard Petersen et al. Antiken og Kristendommen 6. Copenhagen: Anis.

Fallon, F.T. 1979. The Gnostics: The Undominated Race. *NovT* 21: 271–88.

Fauth, Wolfgang. 1995. *Helios Megistos: Zur synkretistischen Theologie der Spätantike*. Religions in the Graeco-Roman World 125. Leiden, New York, and Köln: E.J. Brill.

Feraboli, Simonetta, ed. 1994. *Hermetis Trismegisti, De Triginta Sex Decanis*. Corpus Christianorum Continuatio Mediaevalis 144. Turnhout: Brepols.

Festugière, A.J. 1954a. *Corpus Hermeticum. Fragments: Extraits de Stobée*. Vol. 3. Paris: Les Belles Lettres.

——. 1954b. *La Révélation d'Hermès Trismégiste*. Vol. 4. Paris: Librarie Lecoffre.

Fishbane, Michael. 2003. *Biblical Myth and Rabbinic Mythmaking*. Oxford and New York: Oxford University Press.

Fitzmyer, Joseph A. 1981. *The Gospel According to Luke I–IX*. *The Anchor Bible*, Vol. 28. New York: Doubleday.

Flamant, Jacques. 1982. Soteriologie et systemes planetaires. Pages 223–42 in *La soteriologia dei culti orientali nell'impero romano. La soteriologia dei culti orientali nell'impero romano. atti del Colloquio internazionale su la soteriologia dei culti orientali nell'Impero romano, Roma, 24–28 settembre 1979*. Edited by Ugo Bianchi and M.J. Vermaseren. Etudes préliminaires aux religions orientales dans l'Empire romain 92. Leiden: E.J. Brill.

Foerster, Werner. 1964. Δαίμων, Δαιμόνιον. Pages 1–20 in *Theological Dictionary of the New Testament, vol. 2*. Edited by Gerhard Kittel. Grand Rapids: Eerdmans.

Foerster, Werner, ed., and R. McL. Wilson, trans. 1972. *Gnosis: A Selection of Gnostic Texts: Volume 1: Patristic Evidence*. Oxford: Clarendon.

Fonrobert, Charlotte E. and Jaffee, Martin S., eds. 2007. *The Cambridge Companion to Talmud and Rabbinic Literature.* Cambridge: Cambridge University Press.

Förster, H. 2002. *Wörterbuch der griechischen Wörter in den koptischen dokumentarischen Texten.* Berlin: de Gruyter.

Förster, Niclas. 2007. *Das gemeinschaftliche Gebet in der Sicht des Lukas.* Biblical tools and studies 4. Leuven and Paris: Peeters.

Fossum, Jarl. 1985. *The Name of God and the Angel of the Lord: Samaritan and Jewish Concepts of Intermediation and the Origin of Gnosticism.* WUNT 36. Tübingen: Mohr Siebeck.

Foucault, Michel, 1994. *Ethics, Subjectivity and Truth. Essential works of Foucault 1954–1984. Volume 1.* Edited by Paul Rabinow. New York: The New Press.

Foucault, Michel et al. 1988. *Technologies of the Self: A Seminar with Michel Foucault.* Amherst: University of Massachusetts Press.

Foucault, Michel, Frédéric Gros, and Alessandro Fontana. 2001. *L'herméneutique du sujet: cours au Collège de France, 1981–1982.* Paris: Seuil.

Foucault, Michel and Paul Rabinow. 1997. *Ethics: Subjectivity and Truth.* London: Allen Lane.

Fowden, Garth. 1986. *The Egyptian Hermes. A Historical Approach to the Late Pagan Mind.* Princeton: Princeton University Press.

Fraade, Steven D. 2007. Rabbinic Midrash and Ancient Jewish Biblical Interpretation. Pages 99–120 in *The Cambridge Companion to Talmud and Rabbinic Literature.* Edited by Charlotte E. Fonrobert and Martin S. Jaffee. Cambridge: Cambridge University Press.

Frazer, James George. 1900. *The Golden Bough: A Study of Magic and Religion.* London: Macmillan.

Freedman, Rabbi H. and Maurice Simon. 1961. *Midrash Rabba.* Vol. VIII: Ecclesiastes. London: The Soncino Press.

Frend, W.H.C. 1965. *Martyrdom and Persecution in the Early Church: A Study of a Conflict from the Maccabees to Donatus.* Grand Rapids: Baker Book House.

Frey, Albert and Gounelle, Rémi, eds. 2007. *Poussières de christianisme et de judaïsme antiques. Études réunies en l'honneur de Jean-Daniel Kaestli et Éric Junod.* Prahins: Zèbre.

Frey, Albert, Touati, Charlotte and Amsler, Frédéric, eds. 2008. *Actes du Colloque international sur le Roman pseudo-clémentin.* Prahins: Zèbre.

Frilingos, Christopher A. 2004. *Spectacles of Empire: Monsters, Martyrs, and the Book of Revelation.* Philadelphia: University of Pennsylvania.

Funk, Wolf-Peter. 1991. The First Apocalypse of James. Pages 313–25 in *New Testament Apocrypha, vol. I: Gospels and Related Writings.* Edited by Wilhelm Schneemelcher and R. McL. Wilson. Louisville: Westminster.

———. 1995. The linguistic aspect of classifying the Nag Hammadi Codices. Pages 107–47 in *Les textes de Nag Hammadi et le problème de leur classification.* Edited by Louis Painchaud and Anne Pasquier. BCNH 3. Québec/Louvain-Paris: Les Presses de l'Université Laval/Peeters.

———. 2007. The First Revelation of James. Pages 321–32 in *The Nag Hammadi Scriptures.* Edited by Marvin Meyer. New York: HarperCollins.

Funk, Wolf-Peter, William Brashear, James M. Robinson, and Richard Smith, eds. 1990. *The Chester Beatty Codex Ac. 1390: Mathematical School Exercises in Greek and John 10:7–13 in Subachmimic.* Chester Beatty Monographs 13. Leuven and Paris: Peeters.

Furrer, Christiane and Rémi Gounelle. 2005. Évangile de Nicodème ou Actes de Pilate. Pages 249–97 in *Écrits apocryphes chrétiens.* Vol. 2. Edited by François Bovon and Pierre Geoltrain. Paris: Gallimard.

Gacek, A., Déroche, F. and Witkam, J.J. eds. 1990/91. *Manuscripts of the Middle East vol. 5: The Role of the Book in the Civilisations of the Near East.* Leiden: Ter Lugt Press.

Gamble, Harry Y. 1995. *Books and Readers in the Early Church: A History of Early Christian Texts*. New Haven and London: Yale University Press.

Garciá, Bazán, F. 2006. *El evangelio de Judas*. Madrid: Trotta.

Gardner, I. and S.N.C. Lieu. 2004. *Manichaean Texts from the Roman Empire*. Cambridge: Cambridge University Press.

Gathercole, Simon. 2002. *Where is Boasting? Early Jewish Soteriology and Paul's Response in Romans 1–5*. Grand Rapids: Eerdmans.

——. 2007a. *The Gospel of Judas: Rewriting Early Christianity*. Oxford: Oxford University Press.

——. 2007b. The Gospel of Judas. *ExpTim* 118.5: 209–15.

Gero, Stephen. 1994. The Stern Master and His Wayward Disciple: A 'Jesus' Story in the Talmud and in Christian Hagiography. *JSJ* 25: 287–311.

Gieschen, Charles A. 1994. The Seven Pillars of the Word: Ideal Figure Lists in the Christology of the Pseudo-Clementines. *JSP* 12: 47–82.

Gilhus, I.S. 1985. *The Nature of the Archons. A Study in the Soteriology of a Gnostic Treatise from Nag Hammadi (CG II, 4)*. Wiesbaden: Otto Harrassowitz.

——. 1997. *Laughing Gods, Weeping Virgins. Laughter in the History of Religion*. London and New York: Routledge.

Ginzberg, Louis. 1925. *The Legends of the Jews, Vol. 5*. Philadelphia: The Jewish Publication Society of America.

——. 1928. *Genizah Studies in Memory of Doctor Solomon Schechter. I: Midrash and Haggadah*. New York: The Jewish Theological Seminary of America.

——. 1968. *The Legends of the Jews*. 7 vols. Philadelphia: Jewish Publication Society of America.

Giversen, Søren. 1963. *Apocryphon Johannis: the Coptic text of the Apocryphon Johannis in the Nag Hammadi codex II with Translation, Introduction, and Commentary*. Acta theologica Danica 5. Copenhagen: Munksgaard.

——. 1972. Solomon und die Dämonen. Pages 16–21 in *Essays on the Nag Hammadi Texts in Honor of Alexander Böhlig*. Edited by Martin Krause. NHS 3. Leiden: E.J. Brill.

Giversen, S., Petersen, T., Sørensen, J. Podemann, eds. 2002. *The Nag Hammadi Texts in the History of Religions, Proceedings of the International Conference at the Royal Academy of Sciences and Letters in Copenhagen, September 19–24, 1995, On the Occasion of the 50th Anniversary of the Nag Hammadi Discovery*. Historisk-filosofiske Skrifter 26. Copenhagen: The Royal Danish Academy of Sciences and Letters.

Gleason, Maud W. 1999. Truth Contests and Talking Corpses. Pages 287–313 in *Constructions of the Classical Body*. Edited by James L. Porter. Ann Arbor: University of Michigan Press.

Glover, Terrot R. ed. 1931 and 1953. *Tertullian: Apology—De spectaculis*. Latin Authors. Cambridge, Mass., Heinemann. (FN as Glover 1953)

Goldschmidt, L. 1899. *Der Babylonische Talmud mit Einschluss der vollständigen Misnah*. Berlin: Calvary.

Goldstein, Bernard R. and David Pingree. 1977. Horoscopes from the Cairo Geniza. *Journal of Near Eastern Studies* 36, no. 2: 113–44.

Gounelle, Rémi. 1992. Acta Pilati grecs B (BHG 779u-w): Traditions textuelles. *Recherches Augustiniennes* 26: 273–94.

——. 2003. À propos des volailles cuites qui ont chanté lors de la passion du Christ. *Recherches Augustiniennes* 33: 19–63.

——. 2007. L'Évangile de Judas ou comment devenir un bon gnostique. Pages 49–71 in *Le mystère apocryphe: Introduction à une littérature méconnue*. Edited by Jean-Daniel Kaestli and Daniel Marguerat. Essais Bibliques 26. Geneva: Labor et Fides.

——. 2008. *Les recensions byzantines de l'Évangile de Nicodème*. Turnhout and Prahins: Brepols.

Grant, Robert M. 1959. Gnostic Origins and the Basilidians of Irenaeus. *VC* 13: 121–25.

——. 1966. *Gnosticism & Early Christianity*. New York: Harper & Row.

Graves, Margaret, trans. 2002. *Cicero on the Emotions: Tusculan Disputations 3 and 4.* Chicago: The University of Chicago Press.

Grech, Prosper. 2003. Una giornata presso Gesù: l'orario giovanneo. *StPat* 50: 777–85.

Green, Joel B. and Turner, Max. eds. 1994. *Jesus of Nazareth: Lord and Christ. Essays on the Historical Jesus and New Testament Christology.* Grand Rapids: Eerdmans.

Grenfell, Bernard P. and Arthur S. Hunt. 1903. *The Oxyrhynchus Papyri: Part III* London: Egypt Exploration Fund, Kegan Paul, Bernard Quaritch, and Henry Frowde.

Grese, William C. 1979. *Corpus Hermeticum XIII and Early Christian Literature.* Studia ad Corpus Hellenisticum Novi Testamenti 5. Leiden: E.J. Brill.

Grosso, Matteo. 2005. L'enigma del fico senza frutti: questioni critiche e interpretative su Mc 11,12–14.20–25. *Quaderni del Dipartimento di filologia linguistica e tradizione classica "A. Rostagni" n.s. 3—2004:* 121–47.

Grünbaum, M. 1877. Beiträge zur vergleichenden Mythologie aus der Hagada. ZDMG 31.

Guillaumont, A. 1962. ΝΗΣΤΕΥΕΙΝ ΤΟΝ ΚΟΣΜΟΝ (P. Oxy. 1, verso, l. 5–6). *BIFAO* 61: 15–23.

Gundel, Hans Georg. 1968. *Weltbild und Astrologie in den griechischen Zauberpapyri.* MBPF 4. München: C.H. Beck'sche Verlagsbuchhandlung.

———. 1970. Vom Weltbild in den griechischen Zauberpapyri: Probleme und Ergebnisse. Pages 185–93 in *Proceedings of the Twelfth International Congress of Papyrology.* Edited by D.H. Samuel. American Studies in Papyrology 7. Toronto: Hakkert.

———. 1972. Zodiakos: Der Tierkreis in der Antike. Pages 462–709 in vol. 10 of *Paulys Realencyclopädie der classischen Altertumswissenschaft.* Edited by G. Wissowa et al. München: Alfred Druckenmüller.

———. 1978. Imagines Zodiaci. Zu neueren Funden und Forschungen. In *Hommages à Maarten J. Vermaseren.* Vol. 1. Edited by M.B. de Boer et al. Leiden: E.J. Brill.

———. 1992. *Zodiakos: Tierkreisbilder im Altertum. Kosmische Bezüge und Jenseitsvorstellungen im antiken Alltagsleben.* Kulturgeschichte der Antiken Welt 54. Mainz: Ph. von Zabern.

Gundel, Wilhelm. 1929. Sternbilder und Sternglaube. Pages 2412–39 in vol. 3 of *Paulys Realencyclopädie der classischen Altertumswissenschaf.* Edited by G. Wissowa. Stuttgart: Metzlersche Verlagsbuchhandlung.

———. 1936. *Dekane Und Dekansternbilder: Ein Beitrag zur Geschichte der Sternbilder der Kulturvölker.* Glückstadt and Hamburg: J.J. Augustin.

———. 1950a. Astrologie. Pages 817–31 in vol. 1 of *RAC.* Edited by Th. Klauser et al. Stuttgart: Hiersemann.

———. 1950b. Astralreligion. Pages 810–17 in vol. 1 of *RAC.* Edited by Th. Klauser et al. Stuttgart: Hiersemann.

Gundel, Wilhelm and Gundel, Hans Georg. 1950. Planeten. Pages 2017–185 in vol. 20 of *Paulys Realencyclopädie der classischen Altertumswissenschaft.* Edited by G. Wissowa. München: Alfred Druckenmüller.

Gunkel, Hermann. 1895. *Schöpfung und Chaos in Urzeit und Endzeit: Eine religiongeschichtliche Untersuchung über Gen 1 und Ap Joh 12.* Göttingen.

Haardt, R. 1971. *Gnosis: Character and Testimony.* Leiden: E.J. Brill.

Hadot, Pierre. 1995. *Philosophy as a Way of Life: Spiritual Exercises from Socrates to Foucault.* Oxford: Blackwell Publishers.

———. 2004. *What is Ancient Philosophy?* Cambridge: The Belknap Press of Harvard University Press.

Hand, Wayland D. 1940. The Birthday of Judas Iscariot: A Study in Folklore. *Modern Language Forum* 25: 1–8.

Hanegraaff, W.J. 1995. Empirical Method in the Study of Esotericism. *Method and Theory in the Study of Religion* 7:2: 1–49.

——. 1996. *New Age Religion and Western Culture: Esotericism in the Mirror of Secular Thought*. Studies in the History of Religions 72. Leiden: E.J. Brill.

Harnack, Adolf. 1905. *The Expansion of Christianity in the First Three Centuries vol. 2*. London: Williams & Norgate.

Harris, William V. 2001. *Restraining Rage: The Ideology of Anger Control in Classical Antiquity*. Cambridge: Harvard University Press.

Hartner, W. 2008. D̲j̲awzahar. In *Encyclopedia of Islam, Second Edition*. Edited by Th. Bianquis P. Bearman, C.E. Bosworth, E. van Donzel and W.P. Heinrichs. E.J. Brill Online.

Harvey, W. Wigan, ed. 1857. *Irenaeus, Libros quinque adversus haereses*. Cambridge: Academy.

Havelaar, Henriëtte. 1999. *The Coptic Apocalypse of Peter*. TU 114. Berlin.

Hayman, A. Peter. 2004. *Sefer Yesira: Edition, Translation and Text-Critical Commentary*. Tubingen: Mohr Siebeck.

Hedrick, Ch.W. and Roger Hodgson, Jr., eds. 1986. *Nag Hammadi, Gnosticism, & Early Christianity*. Peabody: Hendrickson.

Hegedus, Tim. 2000. *Attitudes to Astrology in Early Christianity: A Study Based on Selected Sources*. Ph.D Dissertation: University of Toronto.

——. 2007. *Early Christianity and Ancient Astrology*. Patristic Studies 6. New York: Peter Lang.

Hellholm, D. 1989. *Apocalypticism in the Mediterranean World and the Near East. Proceedings of the International Colloquium on Apocalypticism, Uppsala, August 12–17, 1979*. Tübingen: Mohr.

Helmbold, W.C., ed. 1939. *Plutarch, Moralia VI*. LCL 337. Cambridge: Harvard University Press.

Henderson, Ian H. and Oegema, Gerben S. eds. 2006. *The Changing Face of Judaism, Christianity and Other Greco-Roman Religions in Antiquity*. JSHRZ:2. Gütersloh: Gütersloher Verlagshaus.

Hilgenfeld, A. 1884, 1963. *Die Ketzergeschichte des Urchristentums: Urkundlich Dargestellt*. Hildesheim: G. Olms.

Hilhorst, A. and Kooten, G.H. van, eds. 2005. *The Wisdom of Egypt: Jewish, Early Christian and Gnostic Essays in Honour of Gerard P. Luttikhuizen*. Boston: E.J. Brill.

Himmelfarb, Martha. 1993. *Ascent to Heaven in Jewish and Christian Apocalypses*. New York: Oxford University Press.

Hodges, H.J. 1997. Gnostic Liberation from Astral Determinism: Hipparchan 'trepidation' and the Breaking of Fate. *VC* 51: 359–73.

Hoffmann, R. Joseph. 1987. *Celsus. On the True Doctrine: A Discourse Against the Christians*. Oxford and New York: Oxford University Press.

Holden, James H. 1988. *Abu 'Ali Al-Khayyat: The Judgments of Nativities*. Temple: American Federation of Astrologers, Inc.

Holl, Karl, ed. 1915–1933. *Epiphanius*. 4 vols. Leipzig: J.C. Hinrichs.

Horbury, William. 1970. The Trial of Jesus in Jewish Tradition. In *The Trial of Jesus: Cambridge Studies in Honour of C.F.D. Moule*. Edited by Ernst Bammel. London: SCM Press.

——. 1972. Tertullian on the Jews in the Light of de spec. xxx. 13. *Journal of Theological Studies* 23: 455–9.

——. 1984. Christ as Brigand in Ancient Anti-Christian Polemic. Pages 183–95 in *Jesus and the Politics of His Day*. Edited by E. Bammel and C.F.D. Moule. Cambridge: Cambridge University Press.

——. 1992. Jews and Christians on the Bible: Demarcation and Convergence [325–451]. Pages 72–103 in *Christliche Exegese zwischen Nicaea und Chalcedon*. Edited by J. v. Oort and U. Wickert. Kampen: Kok Pharos.

——. 1998a. *Jewish Messianism and the Cult of Christ*. London: SCM Press.

———. 1998b. *Jews and Christians in Contact and Controversy*. Edinburgh: T&T Clark.

———. 2003. The Depiction of Judaeo-Christians in the Toledot Yeshu. Pages 280–86 in *The Image of the Judaeo-Christians in Ancient Jewish and Christian Literature*. Edited by Peter J. Tomson and Doris Lambers-Petry. WUNT 1.158. Tübingen: Mohr Siebeck.

Horner, George W. 1911–1924. *The Coptic Version of the New Testament in the Southern Dialect*. Vol. 1–7. Oxford: Clarendon Press.

———. 1969a. *The Coptic Version of the New Testament in the Southern Dialect*. Vol. 3. Otto Zeller: Osnabrück.

———. 1969b. *The Coptic Version of the New Testament in the Southern Dialect*. Vol. 4. Osnabrück: Otto Zeller.

Hübner, Wolfgang. 1975. Das Horoskop der Christen. *VC* 29: 120–37.

———. 1983. *Zodiacus Christianus: Jüdisch-christliche Adaptationen des Tierkreises von der Antike bis zur Gegenwart*, Beiträge zur Klassischen. Philologie 144. Königstein: Anton Hain.

Idel, Moshe. 1988a. *Kabbalah: New Perspectives*. New Haven and London: Yale University Press.

———. 1988b. *Studies in Ecstatic Kabbalah*. Albany: State University of New York Press.

———. 2005. *Ascensions on High in Jewish Mysticism: Pillars, Lines, Ladders*. New York: Central European University Press.

Inowlocki, Sabrina and Zamagni, Claudio, eds. Fortcoming 2009. *Reconsidering Eusebius: A Fresh Look at His Life, Work, and Thought*. Leiden: E.J. Brill.

Iricinschi, Eduard, Lance Jenott, and Philippa Townsend. 2006. The Betrayer's Gospel. *The New York Review of Books* 53, no. 10: 32–37.

Iricinschi, E. Forthcoming, 2009. Good Hebrew, Bad Hebrew: Christians as Triton Genos in Eusebius' Apologetic Writings. In *Reconsidering Eusebius: A Fresh Look at His Life, Work, and Thought*. Edited by Sabrina Inowlocki and Claudio Zamagni. Leiden: E.J. Brill.

Jackson, Howard M. 1985a. *The Lion Becomes Man: The Gnostic Leontocephalic Creator and the Platonic Tradition*. Society of Biblical Literature Dissertation Series 81. Atlanta: Scholars Press.

———. 1985b. The Meaning and Function of the Leontocephaline in Roman Mithraism. *Numen* 32: 17–45.

———. 1989. The Origin in Ancient Incantatory 'Voces Magicae' of Some Names in the Sethian Gnostic System. *VC* 43: 74.

Jackson-McCabe, Matt, ed. 2007. *Jewish Christianity Reconsidered: Rethinking Ancient Groups and Texts*. Minneapolis: Fortress Press.

Janeras, Sebastia, ed. 1987. *Miscel·lània Papirològica Ramon Roca-Puig en el seu vui-tante aniversari*. Barcelona: Fundació Salvador Vives Casajuana.

Jellinek, Adolf. 1967. *Beit ha Midrash*. 6 vols. in 2 vols. Jerusalem: Sifre Vahrman.

Jenott, L. 2008. Is There Soteriology in the Gospel of Judas? Paper presented at the Nordic Nag Hammadi and Gnosticism Network. Helsinki, Finland.

Jonas, Hans. 1958. *The Gnostic Religion: The Message of the Alien God and the Beginnings of Christianity*. Boston: Beacon Press.

Jones, Alexander, ed. 1999. *Astronomical Texts from Oxyrhynchus (P. Oxy. 4133–4300a)*. Philadelphia: American Philosophical Society.

Kaestli, Jean-Daniel. 2007. L'Évangile de Judas: quelques réflexions à la suite du colloque de Paris. *Adamantius* 13: 282–86.

Kaestli, J.D. and P. Chérix, eds. 1993. *L'Évangile de Barthélemy d'après Deux Écrits Apocryphes*. Apocryphes. Turnhout: Brepols.

Kaestli, Jean-Daniel and P. Chérix. 1997. Livre de la Résurrection de Jésus-Christ par l'apôtre Barthélemy. Pages 297–356 in *Écrits apocryphes chrétiens Vol. 1*. Edited by François Bovon and Pierre Geoltrain. Paris: Gallimard.

Kaestli, Jean-Daniel and Marguerat, Daniel, eds. 2007. *Le mystère apocryphe: Introduction à une littérature méconnue.* Essais Bibliques 26. Geneva: Labor et Fides.

Kappeler, Warren. 2005. *Essays in Honour of Frederik Wisse, Scholar, Churchman, Mentor.* ARC 33. Montréal: McGill University.

Karppe, S. 1901. *Étude sur les origins et la nature du Zohar.* Paris.

Kasser, Rodolphe, and Wurst, Gregor. 2006. *The Gospel of Judas: original online provisional transcription.*

Kasser, Rodolphe, Marvin Meyer and Gregor Wurst, eds., with Gaudard, François. 2006a. *The Gospel of Judas.* Washington, D.C.: National Geographic Society.

Kasser, Rodolphe, Marvin Meyer and Gregor Wurst, eds., with Gaudard, François. 2006b. *L'évangile de Judas.* Paris: Flammarion.

Kasser, Rodolphe, Gregor Wurst, eds., with Marvin Meyer and Gaudard, François. 2007. *The Gospel of Judas together with the Letter of Peter to Philip, James, and a Book of Allogenes from Codex Tchacos. Critical Edition.* Washington: National Geographic Society.

Kasser, Rodolphe et al. 2008. *The Gospel of Judas.* 2nd ed: National Geographic.

Kee, Howard Clark. 1967. The Terminology of Mark's Exorcism Stories. *NTS* 14: 232–46.

Kelley, Nicole 2006. "Philosophy as Training for Death: Reading the Ancient Martyr Acts as Spiritual Exercises." *Church History* 75.4: 723–47.

Kerchove, Anna van den. 2008. La maison, l'autel et les sacrifices: quelques remarques sur la polémique dans l'Évangile de Judas. Pages 311–30 in *The Gospel of Judas in Context: Proceedings of the First International Conference on the Gospel of Judas.* Edited by Madeleine Scopello. NHMS 62. Leiden: E.J. Brill.

Kim, S. 2008. The Gospel of Judas and the Stars. In *The Gospel of Judas in Context: Proceedings of the First International Conference on the Gospel of Judas, Paris, Sorbonne, October 27th-28th 2006.* Edited by M. Scopello. NHMS 62. Leiden: E.J. Brill.

King, Charles William. 1887. *Gnostics and Their Remains.* New York: Putnam.

King, Karen L. 1997. Approaching the Variants of the Apocryphon of John. Pages 112–13 in *The Nag Hammadi Library after Fifty Years: Proceedings of the 1995 Society of Biblical Literature Commemoration.* Edited by John D. Turner and Anne McGuire. NHMS 44. Leiden: E.J. Brill.

——. 2003. *What is Gnosticism?* Cambridge: Harvard University Press.

——. 2006. *The Secret Revelation of John.* Cambridge: Harvard University Press.

Kirk, Alan. 2007. Tradition and Memory in the Gospel of Peter. Pages 135–58 in *Das Evangelium nach Petrus. Text, Kontexte, Intertexte.* Edited by Thomas J. Kraus and Tobias Nicklas. TU 158. Berlin and New York: de Gruyter.

Klassen, W. 1996. *Judas. Betrayer or Friend of Jesus?* Minneapolis: Fortress Press.

Klauck, Hans-Josef. 1987. *Judas—ein Jünger des Herrn.* Freiburg: Herder.

——. 2003. *Apocryphal Gospels: An Introduction.* London, New York: T. & T. Clark.

——. 2006. *Judas, un disciple de Jésus: exégèse et répercussions historiques.* Paris: Les Editions du Cerf.

Klawans, Jonathan. 2006. *Purity, Sacrifice, and the Temple: Symbolism and Supersessionism in the Study of Ancient Judaism.* New York: Oxford.

Klimkeit, Hans-Joachim. 1993. *Gnosis on the Silk Road.* San Francisco: HarperSanFrancisco.

Koch-Westenholz, Ulla. 1995. *Mesopotamian Astrology: An Introduction to Babylonian and Assyrian Celestial Divination.* Copenhagen: Carsten Niebuhr Institute of Near Eastern Studies, Museum Tusculanum Press, University of Copenhagen.

Koll, Karl. 1915. *Epiphanius: Ancoratus und Panarion Haer. 1–3.* Leipzig: J.C. Hinrich.

Koschorke, Klaus. 1977. Eine gnostische Pfingstpredigt. Zur Auseinandersetzung zwischen gnostischem und kirchlichem Christentum am Beispiel der 'Epistula Petri ad Philippum' (NHC CIII,2). *Zeitschrift für Theologie und Kirche* 74: 323–43.

———. 1978. *Die Polemik der Gnostiker gegen das kirchliche Christentum. Unter besonderer Berücksichtigung der Nag-Hammadi-Traktate "Apocalypse des Petrus" (NHC VII,3) und "Testimonium Veritatis" (NHC IX,3)*. NHS 12. Leiden: E.J. Brill.

———. 1979. Eine gnostische Paraphrase des johanneischen Prologs: zur Interpretation von "Epistula Petri ad Philippum" (NHC VIII,2) 136,16–127,4. *VC* 33, no. 4: 383–92.

Kraeling, C.H. 1956. *The Synagogue*. New Haven: Yale University Press.

Kraus, Thomas J. and Nicklas, Tobias, eds. 2007. *Das Evangelium nach Petrus. Text, Kontexte, Intertexte*. TU 158. Berlin and New York: de Gruyter.

Krause, Martin, ed. 1975. *Essays on the Nag Hammadi Texts in Honour of Pahor Labib*, NHS 6. Leiden: E.J. Brill.

Krauss, Samuel. 1902. *Das Leben Jesu nach jüdischen Quellen*. Berlin: Calvary & Co.

Krosney, Herbert. 2006. *The Lost Gospel: The Quest for the Gospel of Judas Iscariot*. Washington, D.C.: National Geographic.

Kroymann, Aem., ed. 1954. Adversus Omnes Haereses. Pages 1401–1410 in *Quinti Septimi Florentis Tertulliani Opera. Opera Montanistica*. CCL 2. Turnholti: Typographi Brepols Editores Pontificii.

Laeuchli, S. 1953. Origen's Interpretation of Judas Iscariot. *Church History* 22, 4: 253–68.

Lampe, G. W. H. 1968. *A Patristic Greek Lexicon*. Oxford: Clarendon Press.

Lauterbach, Jacob Z. 1933. *Mekilta de-Rabbi Ishmael*. Vol. 1. Philadelphia: The Jewish Publication Society.

Layton, Bentley, ed. 1980a. *The Rediscovery of Gnosticism, Volume 1: The School of Valentinus*. Studies in the History of Religions. *Numen* Supplement 41. Leiden: E.J. Brill.

———, ed. 1980b. *The Rediscovery of Gnosticism. Volume 2: Sethian Gnosticism*. Studies in the History of Religions. *Numen* Supplement 41. Leiden: E.J. Brill.

———. 1987. *The Gnostic Scriptures*. Garden City: Doubleday.

———. 1995. Prolegomena to the Study of Ancient Gnosticism. Pages 334–50 in *The Social World of the First Christians: Essays in Honor of Wayne A. Meeks*. Edited by L. Michael White and O. Larry Yarbrough. Minneapolis: Fortress.

———. 2000. *A Coptic Grammar*. Wiesbaden: Harrassowitz.

———. 2004. *A Coptic Grammar*. 2nd ed. Wiesbaden: Harrassowitz Verlag.

———. 2007. *Coptic in 20 Lessons: Introduction to Sahidic Coptic With Exercises & Vocabularies*. Leuven: Peeters.

Le Boeuffle, André. 1987. *Astronomie, Astrologie. Lexique latin*. Paris: Picard.

Leclercq, H. 1907. Astres. *DACL* 1.3014.

Lefort, Louis-Thomas. 1937. Coptica Lovaniensa. *Le Muséon* 50: 5–52.

Leisegang, Hans. 1955. The Mystery of the Serpent. Pages 194–261 in *The Mysteries*. Edited by Joseph Campbell. Princeton: Princeton University Press.

Liebes, Yehuda. 1993. *Studies in the Zohar*. Albany: State University of New York Press.

Lipsius, R. A. 1865. *Zur Quellenkritik des Epiphanios*. Wien: Braumueller.

———. 1875. *Die Quellen der aeltesten Ketzergeschichte*. Leipzig: JA Barth.

Loewe, G. 1888. *Corpus Glossarium*. Lipsiae: Goetz et Gundermann.

Logan, Alastair H. B. 1996. *Gnostic Truth and Christian Heresy*. Edinburgh: T&T Clark.

———. 1997. The Mystery of the Five Seals: Gnostic Initiation Reconsidered. *VC* 51: 188–206.

———. 2006. *The Gnostics: Identifying an Early Christian Cult*. London and New York: T & T Clark.

Loofs, Friedrich. 1890. *Die Handschriften der lateinischen Übersetzung des Irenäus und ihre Kapittelteilung*. Leipzig: Hinrichs.

Louth, Andrew. 2007. Evagrius on Anger. Paper presented at the Fifteenth International Conference of Patristic Studies. Oxford.

Lovgren, Stefan. 2007. Judas Was "Demon" After All, New Gospel Reading Claims. http://news.nationalgeographic.com/news/2007/12/071221-gospel-judas_2.html.

Lucchesi, Enzo. 1997. Feuillets coptes non identifiés du prétendu Évangile de Barthélemy. *VC* 51: 273–5.

Lüdemann, Gerd. 2006. *Das Judas-Evangelium und das Evangelium nach Maria: Zwei gnostische Schriften aus der Frühzeit des Christentums*. Stuttgart: Radius.

Lundström, Sven. 1943. *Studien zur lateinischen Irenäusübersetzung*. Lund: Gleerupska Universitetsbokhandeln.

———. 1948. *Neue Studien zur lateinischen Irenäusübersetzung*. Lund: C.W.K. Gleerup.

Luomanen, Petri and Antii Marjanen, eds. 2005. *A Companion to Second-Century Christian "Heretics"*. VC Supplement. Leiden and Boston: E.J. Brill.

Luria, David, ed. 1852. *Pirqe de Rabbi Eliezer*. Warsaw: T.Y. Bamberg.

Luttikhuizen, Gerard P. 1978. The Letter of Peter to Philip and the New Testament. Pages 96–102 in *Nag Hammadi and Gnosis: Papers Read at the First International Congress of Coptology (Cairo, December 1976)*. Edited by R. McL. Wilson. NHS 14. Leiden: E.J. Brill.

———. 2006. *Gnostic Revisions of Genesis Stories and Early Jesus Traditions*. NHMS 58. Leiden and Boston: E.J. Brill.

Maccoby, Hyam. 1992. *Judas Iscariot and the Myth of Jewish Evil*. New York: Free Press.

MacDonald, Margaret Y. 1996. *Early Christian Women and Pagan Opinion: The Power of the Hysterical Woman*. Cambridge: Cambridge University Press.

MacKenzie, D.N. 1964. Zoroastrian Astrology in the Bundahisn. *Bulletin of the School of Oriental and African Studies, University of London* 27, no. 3: 511–29.

Mahé, J.-P. 1991. La voie d'immortalité à la lumière des Hermetica de Nag Hammadi et de découverts plus récentes. *VC* 45: 347–75.

———. 2002. Mental faculties and cosmic levels in The eighth and the ninth (NH VI,6) and related hermetic writings. In *The Nag Hammadi Texts in the History of Religions, Proceedings of the International Conference at the Royal Academy of Sciences and Letters in Copenhagen, September 19–24, 1995, On the Occasion of the 50th Anniversary of the Nag Hammadi Discovery*. Edited by S. Giversen, T. Petersen, and J. Podemann Sørensen. Historisk-filosofiske Skrifter 26. Copenhagen: The Royal Danish Academy of Sciences and Letters.

Mahé, Jean-Pierre and Annie Mahé. 1996. *Le Témoignage véritable (NH IX, 3): gnose et martyre*. BCNH Textes 23. Québec/Louvain-Paris: Les Presses de l'Université Laval/Éditions Peeters.

Mahé, Jean-Pierre and Poirier, Paul-Hubert, eds. 2007. *Écrits gnostiques: La bibliothèque de Nag Hammadi*. Paris: Gallimard.

Maier, Johann. 1978. *Jesus von Nazareth in der talmudischen Überlieferung*. EdF 82. Darmstadt: Wissenschaftliche Buchgesellschaft.

———. 1979. Die Sonne im religiösen Denken des antiken Judentums. Pages 346–412 in *ANRW Part 2, Principat 19.1*. Edited by H. Temporini and W. Haase. Berlin and New York: de Gruyter.

Manns, Frédéric. 1992. Le targum de Qohelet- Manuscrit Urbaniti 1. Traduction et commentaire. *Liber Annuus* 42: 145–98.

Mansfeld, J. 1994. *Prolegomena: Questions to be Settled Before the Study of an Author, Or a Text, Philosophia Antiqua*. Leiden: E.J. Brill.

Marcovich, Miroslav. 1986. *Hippolytus Refutatio Omnium Haeresium*. Berlin: Walter De Gruyter.

———, ed. 2001. *Origen Contra Celsum*. Leiden and Boston: E.J. Brill.

Marcus, R. 1987. *Philo. Questions and Answers on Exodus. Translated from the Ancient Armenian Version of the Original Greek*. LCLSupp 2. Cambridge: Harvard University Press.

Margalioth, Mordecai. 1966. *Sefer ha Razim*. Jerusalem: Keren Yehudah leb u-Mini Epshtein she-'al yad ha-Akademyah le-Mada'e ha-Yahadut be-Artsot ha-Berit.

Marjanen, Antti. 1996. *The Woman Jesus Loved: Mary Magdalene in the Nag Hammadi Library and Related Documents*. NHMS 40. Leiden: E.J. Brill.

Marjanen, Antti and Ismo Dunderberg. 2006. *Was There a Gnostic Religion?* Finnish Exegetical Society 87. Göttingen: Vandenhoeck & Ruprecht.

———. forthcoming. Does the Gospel of Judas Rehabilitate Judas Iscariot? In *Entwicklungen von Passions- und Auferstehungstraditionen im frühen Christentum*. Edited by Andreas Merkt and Tobias Nicklas. WUNT 2. Tübingen: Mohr Siebeck.

Marjanen, Antti and Ismo Dunderberg. 2006. *Juudaksen evankeliumi: Johdanto, käännös ja tulkinta*. Helsinki: WSOY.

Marshall, I. Howard. 1978. *Luke: A Commentary on the Greek Text*. New International Greek Testament Commentary. Grand Rapids: Eerdmans.

Masqal, Mikā'ēl Berhāna. 1948–49 and1990–91. *Gebra hemāmāt*. Addis Ababa, Artistic Printing Press.

Massuet, R. 1710. *Contra Haereses Libri Quinque*. Paris: JB Coignard.

Mastrocinque, Attilio. 2005. *From Jewish Magic to Gnosticism*. Studien und Texte zu Antike und Christentum 24. Tübingen: Mohr Siebeck.

Maurer, Christian and Wilhelm Schneemelcher. 1991. The Gospel of Peter. Pages 216–22 in *New Testament Apocrypha vol. 1: Gospels and Related Writings*. Edited by W. Schneemelcher. Cambridge: James Clarke & Co.

Mazzucco, Clementina. 2000. Per una rilettura del 'discorso escatologico' di Marco: osservazioni sulla struttura e sui rapporti col contesto. *Rudiae: Ricerche sul mondo classico 12*: 105–33.

———, ed. 2007. *Riso e comicità nel cristianísimo antico. Atti del Convegno di Torino, 14–16 febbraio 2005 e altri studi*. Alessandria: Edizioni dell'Orso.

Meiser, M. 2004. *Judas Iskariot. Einer von uns*. Leipzig: Evangelische Verlagsanstalt.

Ménard, Jacques-É., ed. 1975. *Les textes de Nag Hammadi: Colloque du Centre d'histoire des religions (Strasbourg, 23–25 octobre 1974)*. NHS 7. Leiden: E.J. Brill.

———. 1977. *La Lettre de Pierre à Philippe*. BCNH 1. Quebec: Université Laval.

Menasce, Pierre Jean de, ed. and trans. 1945. *Škand-gumānīk vičār : la solution décisive des doutes: texte pazand-pehlevi*. Fribourg en Suisse Librairie de l'Université.

Merkelbach, Reinhold. 1984. *Mithras*. Meisenheim: Hain.

Merkt, Andreas and Nicklas, Tobias, eds. Forthcoming. *Entwicklungen von Passions- und Auferstehungstraditionen im frühen Christentum*. WUNT 2. Tübingen: Mohr Siebeck.

Meyer, Marvin. 1981. *The Letter of Peter to Philip: Text, Translation, and Commentary*. Society of Biblical Literature Dissertation Series 53. Chico: Scholars Press.

———. 1990. The Letter of Peter to Phillip (VIII, 2). Pages 431–33 in *The Nag Hammadi Library in English*. Edited by J.M. Robinson. New York: HarperSanFrancisco.

———. 1991. "NHC VIII, 2: The Letter of Peter to Philip." Pages 227–251 in *Nag Hammadi Codex VIII*. Nag Hammadi Studies 31. Edited by John H. Sieber. Leiden: Brill.

———. 2006. Judas und die Gnostiker. Pages 129–58 in *Das Evangelium des Judas aus dem Codex Tchacos*. Edited by M. Meyer, R. Kasser, G. Wurst, aus dem Englischen übersetzt von S. Hirsch. Washington, D.C. and Wiesbaden: National Geographic Society, White Star Verlag.

———. ed. 2007a. *The Nag Hammadi Scriptures: The International Edition*. New York: HarperOne.

———. 2007b. *Judas: The Definitive Collection of Gospels and Legends about the Infamous Apostle of Jesus*. New York: Harper.

———. 2007c. On the Waterfront with Judas. National Geographic Press Release. December 6, 2007. Available from http://press.nationalgeographic.com/pressroom.

———. 2008a. *The Thirteenth Daimon: Judas and Sophia in the Gospel of Judas*. http://www.chapman.edu/meyer.

——. 2008b. *Reflections on Judas Iscariot, Sophia, and the Apostle Peter.* http://www. chapman.edu/meyer.

Middleton, Paul. 2006. *Radical Martyrdom and Cosmic Conflict in Early Christianity,* LNTS 307. London: T&T Clark.

Mimouni, S.C. 2004. *Les Chrétiens d'Origine Juive dans l'Antiquité.* Paris: Albin Michel.

Monat, P., ed. 1992. *Firmicus Maternus, Mathesis, Tome I Livres I–III.* Paris: Les Belles Lettres.

Montserrat Torrents, J. 2006. *El evangelio de Judas.* Madrid: Edaf.

Morard, Françoise. 1985. *L'Apocalypse d'Adam (NH V, 5).* Bibliothèque copte de Nag Hammadi, section Textes, 15. Québec/Louvain: Les Presses de l'Université Laval/ Éditions Peeters.

Morgan, Michael A., trans. 1983. *Sefer ha Razim: The Book of Mysteries.* Chico: Scholars Press.

Morray-Jones, C.R.A. 2002. *A Transparent Illusion: The Dangerous Vision of Water in Hekhalot Mysticism: A Source-Critical & Tradition-Historical Inquiry.* Boston and Köln: E.J. Brill.

Morris, Leon. 1995. *The Gospel according to John.* Grand Rapids: Eerdmans.

Most, Glenn W. 2008. The Judas of the Gospels and the *Gospel of Judas.* Pages 59–68 in *The Gospel of Judas in Context: Proceedings of the First International Conference on the Gospel of Judas.* Edited by Madeleine Scopello. NHMS 62. Leiden: Brill.

Murray, Robert. 2006. *Symbols of Church and Kingdom: A Study in Early Syriac Tradition.* New York: T&T Clark.

Musurillo, Herbert. 1972. *Acts of the Christian Martyrs: Introduction, Texts, and Translations.* Oxford: Clarendon Press.

Nagel, Peter. 1979. *Studien zum Menschenbild in Gnosis und Manichäismus.* Halle: Abteilung Wissenschaftspublizistik der Martin-Luther-Universität.

——. 2007. Das Evangelium des Judas. *Zeitschrift für die Neutestamentliche Wissenschaft* 98: 213–76.

——. 2009. Das Evangelium des Judas—zwei Jahre später. *ZNW* 100: 133–134.

Nagy, Ilona. 2007. The Roasted Cock Crows: Apocryphal Writings (Acts of Peter, the Ethiopic Book of the Cock, Coptic Fragments, the Gospel of Nicodemus) and a Hungarian Origin Legend. *Folklore* 36: 7–40.

Neugebauer, O. and H. B. van Hoesen, eds. 1959. *Greek Horoscopes.* Philadelphia: American Philosophical Society.

Neusner, Jacob. 1985. *Genesis Rabbah. The Judaic Commentary to the Book of Genesis. A New American Translation.* Atlanta: Scholars Press.

——. 2005. *The Babylonian Talmud. A Translation and Commentary. Vol. 16 Tractate Sanhedrin.* Peabody: Hendrickson.

Neusner Jacob and Frerichs, E.S. eds. 1985. *To See Ourselves as Others See Us: Christians, Jews and Others in Late Antiquity.* Chico: Scholars.

Newman, H.I. 1999. The Death of Jesus in the Toledot Yeshu Literature. *Journal of Theological Studies* 50(1): 59–79.

Nickelsburg, George W.E. and James C. Vanderkam. 2004. *1 Enoch.* Minneapolis: Fortress Press.

Nock, A.D. and A.-J. Festugière, eds. 1945. *Corpus Hermeticum.* Volume 1: Traités I–XII. Paris: Société d'Édition "Les Belles Lettres."

Norelli, Enrico, Daniel Marguerat, and Jean-Michel Poffet, eds. 1998. *Jésus de Nazareth: Nouvelles approches d'une énigme.* MdB 38. Geneva: Labor et Fides.

Nussbaum, Martha. 1987. The Stoics on Extirpation of the Passions. *Apeiron* 20: 129–77.

Oldfather, W.A. ed. 1925. *Epictetus II.* LCL 218. Cambridge: Harvard University Press.

Onuki, Takashi. 1989. *Gnosis und Stoa.* NTOA 9. Freiburg: Universitätsverlag.

Oort, Johannes van, and Wickert, U., eds. 1992 *Christliche Exegese zwischen Nicaea und Chalcedon*. Kampen: Kok Pharos.

Oort, Johannes van, 2006, 2007[4]. *Het evangelie van Judas. Inleiding, vertaling, toelichting*, Kampen: Uitgeverij Ten Have.

——. 2009. The Gospel of Judas as *confin(c)tio, Studia Patristica et Byzantina*.

Orbe, A. 1976. *Cristología gnóstica*. Vol. 2. Madrid: BAC.

Os, Bas van. 2007. *Baptism in the Bridal Chamber: The Gospel of Philip as a Valentinian Baptismal Instruction*. Ph.D. dissertation: University of Groningen.

——. 2008. Leerlingen en lezers in het Evangelie van Judas. In *Verhaal als Identiteits-Code*. Edited by Becking and Merz. Utrechtse Theologische Reeks 60. University of Utrecht.

Osier, J.P. 1999. *L'Évangile du Ghetto. La Légende Juive de Jésus du IIe au Xe Siècle*. Paris: Berg International.

Paffenroth, Kim. 2001. *Judas: Images of the Lost Disciple*. Louisville and London: Westminster John Knox Press.

Pagels, Elaine. 1979. *The Gnostic Gospels*. New York: Vintage Books.

——. 1980. Gnostic and Orthodox Views of Christ's Passion: Paradigms for the Christian's Response to Persecution? Pages 262–88 in *The Rediscovery of Gnosticism: Proceedings of the International Conference on Gnosticism at Yale, New Haven, Connecticut, March 28–31, 1978*. Vol. 1. Edited by Bentley Layton. Studies in the History of Religions. *Numen* Supplement 41. Leiden: E.J. Brill.

Pagels, E. and K.L. King. 2007. *Reading Judas. The Gospel of Judas and the Shaping of Christianity*. New York: Viking.

Painchaud, Louis. 1995a. *L'Écrit sans titre: Traité sur l'origine du monde (NH II,5 et XIII,2 et Brit. Lib. Or. 4926[1])*. Avec deux contributions de W.-P. Funk. BCNH Textes 21. Québec/Louvain: Les Presses de l'Université Laval/Éditions Peeters.

——. 1995b. The Literary Contacts between the Writing without Title on the Origin of the World (CG II,5 and XIII,2) and Eugnostos the Blessed (CG III,3 and V,1). *JBL* 114: 88–89.

——. 1996. The Use of Scripture in Gnostic Literature. *Journal of Early Christian Studies* 4: 129–47.

——. 2006. À propos de la (re)découverte de l'Évangile de Judas. *Laval théologique et philosophique* 62, no. 3: 553–68.

——. 2007. A Tale of Two Kingdoms: Les mystères de la basileia dans l'Évangile de Judas. Paper presented at the SBL Annual Meeting.

——. 2008. Polemical Aspects of the Gospel of Judas. Pages 171–86 in *The Gospel of Judas in Context: Proceedings of the First International Conference on the Gospel of Judas*. Edited by M. Scopello. NHMS 62. Leiden, Boston: E.J. Brill.

——. 2009. "A Tale of Two Kingdoms: The Mysteries of the ΒΑΣΙΛΕΙΑ in the *Gospel of Judas*". Pages 637–653 in *Gnosis and Revelation. Ten Studies on Codex Tchacos*. Rivista di Storia e Letterature Religiosa 44,3. Edited by Madeleine Scopello. Firenze: Olschki.

Painchaud, Louis and Pasquier, Anne, eds. 1995. *Les textes de Nag Hammadi et le problème de leur classification*. BCNH Études 3. Québec/Louvain-Paris: Les Presses de l'Université Laval/Peeters.

Painchaud, Louis and Poirier. Paul-Hubert, eds. 2007. *Colloque international L'Évangile selon Thomas et les textes de Nag Hammadi (Québec, 29–31 mai 2003)*. BCNH 8. Québec: Presses de l'Université Laval.

Painter, John. 2004. *Just James: The Brother of Jesus in History and Tradition*. 2nd ed. Columbia: U.S.C.

Parrott, Douglas M., ed. 1979. *Nag Hammadi Codices V,2–5 and VI with Papyrus Berolinensis 8502, 1 and 4*. NHS 11. Leiden: E.J. Brill.

Patai, Raphael. 1994. *The Jewish Alchemists: A History and Source Book*. Princeton: Princeton University Press.

Patton, Laurie L. and Doniger, W. eds. 1996. *Myth and Method: New Perspectives on Sacred Narrative*. Charlottesville: University of Virginia Press.

Pearson, Birger A. 1976. 'She became a tree'—a Note to CG II, 4: 89, 25–26. *HTR* 69: 413–15.

——. 1981a. The Figure of Seth in Gnostic Literature. Pages 472–504 in *The Rediscovery of Gnosticism. Volume 2: Sethian Gnosticism*. Edited by B. Layton. Studies in the History of Religions. *Numen* Supplement 41. Leiden: E.J. Brill.

——, ed. 1981b. *Nag Hammadi Codices IX and X*. NHS 15. Leiden: E.J. Brill.

——. 1984. Jewish Sources in Gnostic Literature. Pages 443–81 in *Jewish Writings of the Second Temple Period: Apocrypha, Pseudepigrapha, Qumran Sectarian Writings, Philo, Josephus*. Edited by Michael Stone. Philadelphia: Fortress Press.

——. 1986. The Problem of Jewish Gnostic Literature. Pages 15–35 in *Nag Hammadi, Gnosticism, & Early Christianity*. Edited by Ch.W. Hedrick et al. Peabody: Hendrickson.

——. 1990. *Gnosticism, Judaism, and Egyptian Christianity*. Minneapolis: Fortress Press.

——. 1994. Is Gnosticism a Religion? Pages 105–14 in *The Notion of "Religion" in Comparative Research: Selected Proceedings of the XVIth Congress of the International Association for the History of Religions, Rome, 3–8 September 1990*. Edited by Ugo Bianchi. Storia delle Religionie 8. Rome: L'Erma di Bretschneider.

——, ed. 1996. *Nag Hammadi Codex VII*. NHMS 30. Leiden: E.J. Brill.

——. 2000. Enoch in Egypt. Pages 216–31 in *For a Later Generation: The Transformation of Tradition in Israel, Early Judaism and Early Christianity*. Edited by Randal A. Argall. Harrisburg: Trinity.

——. 2004. *Gnosticism and Christianity in Roman and Coptic Egypt*. Studies in Antiquity and Christianity. New York, London: T & T Clark International/ Continuum.

——. 2007a. The Figure of Judas in the Coptic Gospel of Judas. Paper presented at the SBL Annual Meeting.

——. 2007b. *Ancient Gnosticism: Traditions and Literature*. Minneapolis: Fortress Press.

——. 2007c. Judas Iscariot and the Gospel of Judas. Institute for Antiquity and Christianity Occasional Paper 51.

——. 2008. Judas Iscariot Among the Gnostics. What the Gospel of Judas Really Says. *Biblical Archaeology Review* 34, 3: 52–57.

Pearson, Birger A. and James E. Goehring, eds. 1986. *The Roots of Egyptian Christianity*. Studies in Antiquity and Christianity. Philadelphia: Fortress.

Pelletier, André. 1958. La tradition synoptique du 'voile dechiré' à la lumière des réalités archéologiques. *RSR* 46: 168–79.

Perkins, Judith. 1995. *The Suffering Self: Pain and Narrative Representation in Early Christianity*. New York: Routledge.

Perkins, P. 1976. Ireneus and the Gnostics. Rhetoric and Composition in Adverus Haereses Book One. *VC* 30: 193–200.

——. 1980. *The Gnostic Dialogue, The Early Church and the Crisis of Gnosticism*. New York: Paulist Press.

Perkins, Pheme. 1993. *Gnosticism and the New Testament*. Minneapolis: Fortress Press.

Peters, Melvin K.H. 1985. *LXX. A Critical Edition of the Coptic (Bohairic) Pentateuch. Vol. 1, Genesis*. Atlanta: Scholars Press.

Petersen, Anders Klostergaard, Jesper Hyldahl and Einar Thomassen, eds. 2008. *Mellem venner og fjender: En folgebog om Judasevangeliet, tidlig kristendom og gnosis*. Antiken og Kristendommen 6. Copenhagen: Anis.

Petersen, Tage. 2003. *"Alt kommer jo på øjet an, der ser," En analyse af kosmologien i de såkaldt dualistiske tekster i Corpus Hermeticum*. Ph.D. dissertation: University of Copenhagen.

———. 2007. The Gospel of Judas: Some Suggestions. Paper presented at the Nordic Nag Hammadi and Gnosticism Network Seminar. Cairo.

Pétrement, Simone. 1960. La notion de gnosticisme. *Revue de Métaphysique et de Moral* 65: 385–421.

———. 1984. *Un Dieu Séparé*. Paris: Éditions du Cerf.

Philonenko, Marc. 1987. Testaments des douze patriarches. Pages 811–44 in *La Bible. Écrits intertestamentaires*. Edited by A. Dupont-Sommer and M. Philonenko. Bibliothèque de la Pléiade. Paris: Gallimard.

Piñero, A. and S. Torallas. 2006. *El evangelio de Judas*. Madrid: Vector.

Pingree, David, ed. 1973. *Hephaestio Thebanus, Apotelesmatica, Vol. I*. Bibliotheca Scriptorum Graecorum et Romanorum Teubneriana. Leipzig: Teubner.

———, ed. 1974. *Hephaestio Thebanus, Apotelesmatica, Vol. II*. Bibliotheca Scriptorum Graecorum et Romanorum Teubneriana. Leipzig: Teubner.

———, ed. 1986. *Vettius Valens, Anthologiae*. Bibliotheca Scriptorum Graecorum et Romanorum Teubneriana. Leipzig: Teubner.

Piovanelli, Pierluigi. 1997–2005. Livre du coq. Pages 2:135–203 in *Écrits apocryphes chrétiens*. Edited by Pierre Geoltrain and Jean-Daniel Kaestli François Bovon. *Bibliothèque de la Pléiade 442 and 516*. Paris: Gallimard.

———. 2003a. Exploring the Ethiopic Book of the Cock, an Apocryphal Passion Gospel from Late Antiquity. *HTR* 96: 427–54.

———. 2003b. Marius Chaîne, Joseph Trinquet et la version éthiopienne du Livre du coq. *Transversalités* 85: 51–62.

———. 2006. The Book of the Cock and the Rediscovery of Ancient Jewish Christian Traditions in Fifth Century Palestine. In *The Changing Face of Judaism, Christianity and Other Greco-Roman Religions in Antiquity*. Edited by Ian H. Henderson and Gerben S. Oegema. JSHRZ.2. Gütersloh: Gütersloher Verlagshaus.

———. 2007a. Le recyclage des textes apocryphes à l'heure de la petite 'mondialisation' de l'Antiquité tardive (ca. 325–451). Quelques perspectives littéraires et historiques. Pages 277–95 in *Poussières de christianisme et de judaïsme antiques. Études réunies en l'honneur de Jean-Daniel Kaestli et Éric Junod*. Edited by Albert Frey and Rémi Gounelle. Prahins: Zèbre.

———. 2007b. Gospel of Judas Book Review. *Studies in Religion* 36: 174–9.

———. 2008a. The Reception of Early Christian Texts and Traditions in Late Antiquity Apocryphal Literature. Pages 429–39 in *The Reception and Interpretation of the Bible in Late Antiquity: Proceedings of the Montréal Colloquium in Honour of Charles Kannengiesser, 11–13 October 2006*. Edited by Lorenzo DiTommaso and Lucian Turcescu. The Bible in Ancient Christianity 3. Leiden: E.J. Brill.

———. 2008b. L'ennemi est parmi nous': Présences rhétoriques et narratives de Paul dans les Pseudo-clémentines et autres écrits apparentés (Lausanne, 30 août-2 septembre 2006) Pages 329–36 in *Actes du Colloque international sur le Roman pseudo-clémentin*. Edited by Albert Frey, Charlotte Touati and Frédéric Amsler. Prahins: Zèbre.

Pleše, Zlatko. 2006. *Poetics of the Gnostic Universe: Narrative and Cosmology in the Apocryphon of John*. NHMS 52. Leiden: E.J. Brill.

Plisch, Uwe-Karsten. 2006. Das Evangelium des Judas. *ZAC* 10: 5–14.

———. 2006b. Berichtigungen und Nachträge to Das Evangelium des Judas. *ZAC* 10: 5–14.

Poirier, P.-H. and Painchaud, L. eds. 2006. *Coptica, Gnostica, Manichaica: mélanges offerts à Wolf-Peter Funk*. Québec: Université Laval.

Popovic, Mladen. 2007. *Reading the Human Body: Physiognomics and Astrology in the Dead Sea Scrolls and Hellenistic-Early Roman Period Judaism.* Studies on the Texts of the Desert of Judah 67. Leiden: E.J. Brill.

Powels-Niami, Sylvia. 1995. The Samaritans and Astrology. *Abr-Nahrain* 33: 74–95.

Preisendanz, Karl. 1972. *Papyri Graecae Magicae. Die griechischen Zauberpapyri.* 2nd rev. ed. by A. Henrichs. Vol. 2. Stuttgart: Teubner.

Puech, Henri-Charles and Beate Blatz. 1987. Andere gnostische Evangelien und verwandte Literatur. Page 321 in *Neutestamentliche Apokryphen in deutscher Übersetzung.* Edited by W. Schneemelcher. Tübingen: Mohr Siebeck.

Quack, Joachim Friedrich. 1995. Dekane und Gliedervergottung. Altägyptische Traditionen im Apokryphon Johannes. *JAC* 38: 97–122.

——. forthcoming. *Beiträge zu den ägyptischen Dekanen und ihrer Rezeption in der griechisch-römischen Welt.* Orientalia Lovaniensia Analecta.

Radday, Y. T. and Brenner, A. 1990. *On Humour and the Comic in he Hebrew Bible.* Sheffield: Almond Press.

Rahlfs, Alfred, ed. 1935. *Septuaginta.* Stuttgart: Württembergische Bibelanstalt.

Rasimus, Tuomus. 2005. Ophite Gnosticism, Sethianism, and the Nag Hammadi Library. *VC* 59: 235–63.

——. 2006. *Paradise Reconsidered: A Study of the Ophite Myth and Ritual and Their Relationship to Sethianism.* Ph.D. dissertation: Helsinki University/Université Laval.

——. 2007. The Serpent in Gnostic and Related Texts. Pages 417–71 in *Colloque international L'Évangile selon Thomas et les textes de Nag Hammadi (Québec, 29–31 mai 2003).* Edited by Louis Painchaud and Paul-Hubert Poirier. BCNH 8. Québec: Presses de l'Université Laval.

Rawson, Beryl. 2003. *Children and Childhood in Roman Italy.* Oxford.

Reed, Annette Yoshiko. 2005. *Fallen Angels and the History of Judaism and Christianity: the Reception of Enochic Literature.* Cambridge: Cambridge University Press.

Reeves, John C. 1992. *Jewish Lore in Manichaean Cosmogony: Studies in the Book of Giants Traditions.* Cincinnati: Hebrew Union College.

——. 1995. Bardesanite Cosmology, A Manichaean Mythologoumenon, and Gaonic Jewish Esotericism: Reflections on Some Common Motifs. Paper presented at the Syriac Symposium II. Catholic University of America.

Rehm, B. and J. Irmscher. 1969. *Die Pseudoklementinen, I: Homilien.* CGS. Berlin: Akademie-Verlag.

Reinhartz, Adele. 2007. *Jesus of Hollywood.* Oxford and New York: Oxford University Press.

Reitzenstein, R. 1927. *Die hellenistischen Mysterienreligionen nach ihren Grundgedanken und Wirkungen.* 3rd ed. Leipzig: B.G. Teubner.

Revillout, Eugène. 1985. *Les apocryphes coptes.* Patrologia orientalis II. Fascicule 2 No 7. Turnhout: Brepols.

Reynders, B. 1935. La polémique de saint Irénée. Methode et principes. *Recherches de théologie ancienne et médiévale* 7: 5–27.

——. 1954. *Lexique comparé du texte grec et des versions latine, arménienne et syriaque de l' "Adversus haereses" de Saint Irénée.* Louvain: L. Durbecq.

Ri, Su-Min. 2000. *Commentaire de la Caverne des Trésors. Étude sur l'histoire du texte et ses sources.* Corpus Scriptorum Christianorum Orientalium, Subsidia 103. Louvain: Éditions Peeters.

Richer, Jean. 1994. *Sacred Geography of the Ancient Greeks: Astrological Symbolism in Art, Architecture, and Landscape.* Albany: State University of New York Press.

Riddle, Donald W. 1931. *The Martyrs: A Study in Social Control.* Chicago: University of Chicago Press.

Riley, Gregory. 1996. Second Treatise of the Great Seth: Text, Translation, and Notes. Pages 146–99 in *Nag Hammadi Codex VII.* Edited by Birger A. Pearson. NHMS 30. Leiden: E.J. Brill.

Ristow, Günter. 1978. Zum Kosmokrator im Zodiacus: Ein Bildvergleich. Pages 985–87 in *Hommages à Maarten J. Vermaseren*. Vol. 3. Edited by M.B. de Boer et al. Leiden: E.J. Brill.

Robbins, F.E., ed. 1956. *Ptolemy, Tetrabiblos*. LCL 350. Cambridge: Harvard University Press.

Roberts, Alexander and James Donaldson, ed. 1994. *Ante-Nicene Fathers: Volume 1, The Apostolic Fathers, Justin Martyr, Irenaeus*. Peabody: Hendrickson.

Robinson, James M., ed. 1971. *The Future of Our Religious Past: Essays in Honor of Rudolf Bultmann*. San Francisco: Harper & Row.

——. 1975a. The Construction of the Nag Hammadi Codices. Pages 170–90 in *Essays on the Nag Hammadi Texts in Honour of Pahor Labib*. Edited by Martin Krause. NHS 6. Leiden: E.J. Brill.

——. 1975b. On the Codicology of the Nag Hammadi Codices. Pages 15–31 in *Les textes de Nag Hammadi: Colloque du Centre d'histoire des religions (Strasbourg, 23-25 octobre 1974)*. Edited by Jacques-É. Ménard. NHS 7. Leiden: E.J. Brill.

——. 1977. The Jung Codex: The Rise and Fall of a Monopoly. *Religious Studies Review* 3: 17–30.

——. 1978. The Future of Papyrus Codicology. Pages 23–70 in *The Future of Coptic Studies*. Edited by R. McL. Wilson. Coptic Studies 1. Leiden: E.J. Brill.

——, et al. 1979. *The Facsimile Edition of the Nag Hammadi Codices: Cartonnage*. Leiden: E.J. Brill.

——, et al. 1984. *The Facsimile Edition of the Nag Hammadi Codices: Introduction*. Leiden: E.J. Brill.

——. 1990/91. The Pachomian Monastic Library at the Chester Beatty Library and the Bibliothèque Bodmer. Pages 26–39 in *Manuscripts of the Middle East vol. 5: The Role of the Book in the Civilisations of the Near East*. Edited by A. Gacek, F. Déroche, and J.J. Witkam. Leiden: Ter Lugt Press.

——. 1990a. *The Nag Hammadi Library in English*. 3rd ed. New York: Harper SanFrancisco.

——. 1990b. Introduction. Pages 3–32 in *The Chester Beatty Codex Ac. 1390: Mathematical School Exercises in Greek and John 10:7–13 in Subachmimic*. Edited by Wolf-Peter Funk et al. Chester Beatty Monographs 13. Leuven and Paris: Peeters.

——. 1990c. *The Pachomian Monastic Library at the Chester Beatty Library and the Bibliothèque Bodmer*. Occasional Papers 19. Claremont: The Institute for Antiquity and Christianity.

——. 2006. *The Secrets of Judas: The Story of the Misunderstood Disciple and His Lost Gospel*. San Francisco: Harper Collins.

——. 2007. *The Secrets of Judas: The Story of the Misunderstood Disciple and His Lost Gospel*. 2nd updated and enlarged ed. San Francisco: HarperSanFrancisco.

——. 2008. Fragments from the Cartonnage of P75. *HTR* 101, no. 2: 169–90.

Rousseau, Adelin and Doutreleau, Louis. 1979. *Irénée de Lyon Contre les Hérésies livre I*. Édition Critique ed, SC 264. Paris: Les éditions du Cerf.

Rudolph, K. 1996. *Gnosis und spätantike Religionsgeschichte: Gesammelte Aufsatze* Leiden: E.J. Brill.

Runesson, Anders. 2008. Rethinking Early Jewish-Christian Relations: Matthean Community History as Pharisaic Intragroup Conflict. *JBL* 127: 95–132.

Saarinen, Risto. 2008. *The Pastoral Epistles with Philemon & Jude*. Brazos Theological Commentary. Grand Rapids: Brazos Press.

Samuel, D. H. ed. 1970. *Proceedings of the Twelfth International Congress of Papyrology*. American Studies in Papyrology 7. Toronto: Hakkert.

Sarrazin, B. 1994. Jésus n'a jamais ri. Histoire d'un lieu commun. *RSR* 82/2: 217–22.

Sayre, K.M. 1995. *Plato's Literary Garden: How to read a Platonic Dialogue*. Notre Dame: University of Notre Dame Press.

Schäfer, Peter. 1981. *Synopse zur Hekhalot-Literatur*. Tübingen: J.C.B. Mohr.
——. 2007. *Jesus in the Talmud*. Princeton and Oxford: Princeton University Press.
Schenke, Hans-Martin. 1962. *Der Gott "Mensch" in der Gnosis: ein religionsgeschichtli-cher Beitrag zur Diskussion über die paulinische Anschauung von der Kirche als Leib Christi* Göttingen: Vandenhoeck & Ruprecht.
——. 1980. The Phenomenon and Significance of Gnostic Sethianism. Pages 588–616 in *The Rediscovery of Gnosticism*. Vol. 2. Edited by B. Layton. Leiden: E.J. Brill.
Schenke, Ludger. 1971. *Studien zur Passionsgeschichte des Markus: Tradition und Redaktion in Markus 14,1–42*. Würzburg: Echter.
Schenke Robinson, Gesine, ed. 2004. *Das Berliner "Koptische Buch" (P 20915). Eine wiederhergestellte frühchristlich-theologische Abhandlung*. Corpus Scriptorum Christianorum Orientalium 610, Scriptores Coptici, Tomus 49, and vol. 611, Scriptores Coptici, Tomus 50. Leuven: Peeters.
——. 2008a. The Relationship of the Gospel of Judas to the New Testament and to Sethianism, Appended by a new English Translation of the Gospel of Judas. *Journal of Coptic Studies* 10: 63–98.
——. 2008b. Judas, a Hero or a Villain? Pages 155–68 in *The Gospel of Judas (2nd ed.)*. Edited by Kasser et al. Washington, D.C.: National Geographic Society.
Schletterer, Imke, and Uwe-Karsten Plisch. 2003. Die (erste) Apokalypse des Jakobus. Pages 407–18 in *Nag Hammadi Deutsch 2*. Edited by H.-M. Schenke. GCS Koptisch-Gnostische Schriften 3. Berlin.
Schlichting, Günter. 1982. *Ein jüdisches Leben Jesu. Die verschollene Toledot-Jeschu-Fassung Tam ū-mū'ād. Einleitung, Text, Übersetzung, Kommentar, Motivsynopse, Bibliographie*. WUNT 1.24. Tübingen: Mohr Siebeck.
Schmidt, Carl, ed. and Violet MacDermot, trans. 1978a. *The Books of Jeu and the Untitled Text in the Bruce Codex*. NHS 13. Leiden: E.J. Brill.
——. 1978b. *Pistis Sophia*. NHS 9. Leiden: E.J. Brill.
Schneemelcher, Wilhelm. 1991. *New Testament Apocrypha Vol. 1: Gospels and Related Writings*. Louisville and Westminster: John Knox Press.
——. 1992a. The Kerygma Petri. Pages 34–41 in *New Testament Apocrypha vol. 2: Writings relating to the Apostles: Apocalypses and Related Subjects*. Edited by W. Schneemelcher. Cambridge: James Clarke & Co.
Schneemelcher, Wilhelm, ed and Robert McL Wilson, trans. 1992b. *New Testament Apocrypha vol. 2: Writings relating to the Apostles: Apocalypses and Related Subjects*. Revised ed. Cambridge: James Clarke & Co.
Schoedel, William, R. 1959. Philosophy and Rhetoric in the Adversus Haereses of Irenaeus. *VC* 13: 22–32.
——. 1970. Scripture and the Seventy-Two Heavens of the First Apocalypse of James. *NovT* 12: 118–29.
——. 1979. The (First) Apocalypse of James. Pages 65–103 in *Nag Hammadi Codices V, 2–5 and VI with Papyrus Berolinensis 8502, 1 and 4*. Edited by Douglas M. Parrott. NHS 11. Leiden: E.J. Brill.
——. 1985. *Ignatius of Antioch* Philadephia: Fortress Press.
Scholem, Gershom G. 1955. *Major Trends in Jewish Mysticism*. London: Thames and Hudson.
——. 1960a. *Jewish Gnosticism, Merkabah Mysticism, and Talmudic Tradition*. New York: Jewish Theological Seminary of America.
——. 1960b. *On the Kabbalah and Its Symbolism*. New York: Schocken.
——. 1962. *Origins of the Kabbalah*. Edited by R.J. Zwi Werblowsky. Translated by Allan Arkush. Princeton: Princeton University Press.
——. 1974a. Jaldabaoth Reconsidered. Page 406 in *Mélanges d'histoire des religions: offerts à Henri-Charles Puech*. Edited by Carl-Martin Edsman, Geo Widengren, and Henri-Charles Puech. Paris: Presses Universitaires de France.
——. 1974b. *Kabbalah*. New York: Plume.

Scholten, Clemens. 1987. *Martyrium und Sophiamythos im Gnostizismus nach den Texten von Nag Hammadi.* JAC 14. Münster Westfalen: Aschendorffsche Verlagsbuchhandlung.

——. 2001. Kainiten. *RAC* 19: 972–82.

Schreiber, Johannes. 1961. Die Christologie des Markusevangeliums. *ZTK* 58: 154–83.

——. 1967. *Theologie des Vertrauens. Eine redaktionsgeschichtliche Untersuchung des Markusevangeliums.* Hamburg: Furche-Verlag.

Schwarz, G. 1988. *Jesus und Judas. Aramaistische Untersuchungen zur Jesus-Judas Überlieferung der Evangelien und der Apostelgeschichte.* Beiträge zur Wissenschaft vom Alten und Neuen Testament 123. Stuttgart: Kohlhammer.

Scopello, Madeleine, ed. 2008. *Gospel of Judas in Context. Proceedings of the First International Conference on the Gospel of Judas, Paris, Sorbonne, October 27th-28th 2006.* NHMS 62. Leiden: E.J. Brill.

——, ed. 2009. *Gnosis and Revelation. Ten Studies on Codex Tchacos. Rivista di Storia e Letterature Religiosa* 44,3. Firenze: Olschki.

Scott, Alan. 1991. *Origen and the Life of the Stars* New York: Oxford University Press.

Scott, James M. 2002. *Geography in Early Judaism and Christianity: The Book of Jubilees.* Society for New Testament Studies Monograph Series 113. Cambridge: Cambridge University Press.

Séd, Nicolas. 1979. Les douze hebdomades, le char de Sabaoth et les soixantedouze langues. *NovT* 21: 156–84.

Segal, Alan. 1977. *Two Powers in Heaven: Early Rabbinic Reports about Christianity and Gnosticism.* Leiden: E.J. Brill.

Sevrin, J. 1986. *Le dossier baptismal Séthien: Études sur la sacramentaire gnostique.* BCNH 2.

Sharf, Andrew. 1976. *The Universe of Shabbetai Donnolo.* New York: Ktav.

Sieber, John H. 1991. *Nag Hammadi Codex VIII.* NHS 31. Leiden: E.J. Brill.

Skarsaune, Oskar. 2002. *In the Shadow of the Temple: Jewish Influences on Early Christianity.* Downers Grove: InterVarsity Press.

Skarsaune, Oskar and Reidar Hvalvik, eds. 2007. *Jewish Believers in Jesus: The Early Centuries.* Peabody: Hendrickson.

Sløk, J. 1992. *At læse Platon.* København: Hans Reitzels Forlag.

Smith, J.Z. 1985. What a Difference a Difference Makes. In *To See Ourselves as Others See Us: Christians, Jews and Others in Late Antiquity.* Edited by J. Neusner and E.S. Frerichs. Chico: Scholars.

Smith, Mark S. 1990. The Near Eastern Background of Solar Language for Yahweh. *JBL* 109, no. 1: 29–39.

Smith, Morton. 1984. The Eighth Book of Moses and How It Grew (PLeid J 395). Pages 683–93 in *Atti del XVII Congresso internazionale di papirologia.* Napoli: Centro Internazionale per lo studio di papiri erconlanesi.

Sørensen, J. Podemann 1989. Ancient Egyptian Religious Thought and the XVIth Hermetic Tractate. Pages 41–57 in *The Religion of the Ancient Egyptians, Cognitive Structures and Popular Expressions, Proceedings of Symposia in Uppsala and Bergen 1987 and 1988.* Edited by G. Englund. Acta Universitatis Uppsaliensis Boreas, Uppsala Studies in Ancient Mediterranean and Near Eastern Civilizations 20. Stockholm.

——. 1999. Religio Mentis, Meditativ soteriologi i hellenistiske og moderne religiøse nydannelser. Pages 109–18 in *Nye Religioner i hellenistisk-romersk tid og i dag.* Edited by P. Bilde and M. Rothstein. Religionsvidenskablige skrifter 3. Aarhus: Aarhus Universitetsforlag.

Spiegelberg, Wilhelm. 1921. *Koptisches Handwörterbuch.* Heidelberg.

Spier, Jeffrey. 1993. Medieval Byzantine Magical Amulets and Their Tradition. *Journal of the Warburg and Courtald Institutes* 56: 25–62.

Staley, Jeffrey L. and Richard Walsh. 2007. *Jesus, the Gospels, and Cinematic Imagination: A Handbook to Jesus on DVD*. Louisville and London: Westminster John Knox Press.

Stanton, Graham N. 1994. Jesus of Nazareth: A Magician and a False Prophet Who Deceived God's People? Pages 164–80 in *Jesus of Nazareth: Lord and Christ. Essays on the Historical Jesus and New Testament Christology*. Edited by Joel B. Green and Max Turner. Grand Rapids: Eerdmans.

Starr, Joshua. 1939. *The Jews in the Byzantine Empire 641–1204*. New York: Burt Franklin.

Steinsaltz, Adin. 1996. *Talmud. Sanhédrin 1*. Vol. 4. Jérusalem: Institut israélien des Publications Talmudiques and Éditions Ramsay.

Stein-Schneider, H. 1985. À la recherche du Judas historique. Une enquête exégétique à la lumière des texts de l'Ancien Testament et des Logia. *Études Théologiques et Religieuses* 60: 403–24.

Stendahl, K. 1962. Hate, Non-retaliation and Love. 1QS X, 17–20 and Rom. 12: 19–21. *HTR* 55: 343–55.

Stieren, Adolphus. 1853–1858. *Sancti Irenaei episcopi lugdunensis Quae supersunt omnia*. Lipsiae: T.O. Weigel.

Stöckl ben Ezra, Daniel. 2003. *The Impact of Yom Kippur on Early Christianity*. Wissenschaftliche Untersuchungen Zum Neuen Testament. Tübingen: Mohr Siebeck.

Stone, Michael, ed. 1984. *Jewish Writings of the Second Temple Period: Apocrypha, Pseudepigrapha, Qumran Sectarian Writings, Philo, Josephus*. Philadelphia: Fortress Press.

Stroumsa, Gedaliahu G. 1984. *Another Seed: Studies in Gnostic Mythology*. NHS 24. Leiden: E.J. Brill.

——. 1986. The Manichaean Challenge to Egyptian Christianity. Pages 307–19 in *The Roots of Egyptian Christianity*. Edited by B.A. Pearson and J.E. Goehring. Philadelphia: Fortress.

——. 2004. Christ's Laughter: Docetic Origins Reconsidered. *Journal of Early Christian Studies* 12: 267–88.

Stuckrad, Kocku von. 2000a. *Das Ringen um die Astrologie: Jüdische und christliche Beiträge zum antiken Zeitverständnis*, Religionsgeschichtliche Versuche und Vorarbeiten 49. Berlin, New York: de Gruyter.

——. 2000b. Jewish and Christian Astrology in Late Antiquity: A New Approach. *Numen* 47: 2–40.

Sukenik, E.L. 1934. *Ancient Synagogues in Palestine and Greece*. London: Oxford University Press.

Sullivan, Kevin. 2004. *Wrestling with Angels: A Study of the Relationship between Angels and Humans in Ancient Jewish Literature and the New Testament*. AGJU 55. Leiden: E.J. Brill.

Tardieu, Michel. 1974. *Trois mythes gnostiques. Adam, Éros et les animaux d'Égypte dans un écrit gnostique de Nag Hammadi (II,5)*. Paris: Études Augustiniennes.

——. 1984. *Codex de Berlin*, Ecrits Gnostiques 1. Paris: Cerf.

Telford, William. 1980. *The Barren Temple and the Withered Tree. A Redaction-Critical Analysis of the Cursing of the Fig-Tree Pericope in Mark's Gospel and Its Relation to the Cleansing of the Temple Tradition*. JSNT Supplement 1. Sheffield: Academic Press.

Thoma, Clemens. 1998. Jésus dans la polémique juive de l'Antiquité tardive et du Moyen-Âge. Pages 477–87 in *Jésus de Nazareth: Nouvelles approches d'une énigme*. Edited by Enrico Norelli et al. MdB 38. Geneva: Labor et Fides.

Thomassen, Einar. 2008. Is Judas Really the Hero of the Gospel of Judas? Pages 157–70 in *The Gospel of Judas in Context: Proceedings of the First International Conference on the Gospel of Judas*. Edited by M. Scopello. NHMS 62. Leiden, Boston: E.J. Brill.

——. 2008b. Judasevangeliet og gnosticismen. In *Mellem venner og fjender: En folgebog om Judasevangeliet, tidlig kristendom og gnosis*. Edited Anders Klostergaard Petersen et al. Antiken og Kristendommen 6. Copenhagen: Anis.

Tischendorf, Konstantin von. 1876. *Evangelia Apocrypha*. Leipzig: H. Mendelssohn.

Tomson, Peter J. and Lambers-Petry, Doris, eds. 2003. *The Image of the Judaeo-Christians in Ancient Jewish and Christian Literature*. WUNT 1.158. Tübingen: Mohr Siebeck.

Toorn, Karel van der, Bob Becking and Pieter W. van der Horst , eds. 1995. *Dictionary of Deities and Demons in the Bible*. Leiden: Brill.

Townsend, P., 2007. What is this Great Race?' The Meaning of genea in the Gospel of Judas. Paper presented at the 2007 SBL Annual Meeting.

Tsouna, Voula. 2007. Philodemus on Emotions. Pages 213–41 in *Greek and Roman Philosophy 100 BC–200 AD*. Edited by Richard Sorabji and Robert W. Sharples. London: Institute of Classical Studies, University of London.

Tuckett, Christopher M. 2007. *The Gospel of Mary*. Oxford: Oxford University Press.

Turcan, Marie. 1986. *Tertullien: Les spectacles (De spectaculis). Introduction, texte critique, traduction et commentaire*. SC 332. Paris: Cerf.

Turner, John D. 2001. *Sethian Gnosticism and the Platonic Tradition*. Bibliothèque Copte de Nag Hammadi Section Études 6. Québec, Louvan-Paris: Presses de l'Université Laval, Peeters.

——. 2002. Time and History in Sethian Gnosticism. Pages 203–14 in *For the Children Perfect Instruction: Studies in Honor of Hans-Martin Schenke*. Edited by H.G. Bethge. NHMS 54. Leiden: E.J. Brill.

——. 2006. The Sethian Baptismal Rite. Pages 941–92 in *Coptica, Gnostica, Manichaica: mélanges offerts à Wolf-Peter Funk*. Edited by P.-H. Poirier and L. Painchaud. Québec: Université Laval.

——. 2007. The Book of Thomas and the Platonic Jesus. Pages 599–633 in *Colloque International L'Évangile selon Thomas et les Textes de Nag Hammadi*. Edited by Louis Painchaud and Paul-Hubert Poirier. Québec/Louvain: Les Presses de l'Université Laval/Peeters.

——. 2008a. The Place of the Gospel of Judas in Sethian Tradition. Pages 187–237 in *The Gospel of Judas in Context Proceedings of the First International Conference on the Gospel of Judas Paris, Sorbonne, October 27th-28th 2006*. Edited by Madeleine Scopello. NHMS. Leiden: E.J. Brill.

——. 2008b. The Sethian School of Gnostic Thought. Pages 785–89 in *The Nag Hammadi Scriptures: The International Edition*. Edited by Marvin Meyer. San Francisco: HarperOne.

Turner, John D. and McGuire, Anne, eds. 1997. *The Nag Hammadi Library after Fifty Years: Proceedings of the 1995 Society of Biblical Literature Commemoration*. NHMS 44. Leiden: E.J. Brill.

Ulansey, David. 1989. *The Origins of the Mithraic Mysteries: Cosmology and Salvation in the Ancient World*. New York and Oxford: Oxford University Press.

——. 1991. The Heavenly Veil Torn: Mark's Cosmic Inclusio. *JBL* 110: 123–25.

Unger, D.J. and J.J. Dillon. 1992. *St. Irenaeus of Lyons Against the Heresies*. New York: Paulist Press.

Urbach, Ephraim E. 1987, 1994. *The Sages: Their Concepts and Beliefs*. Translated by Israel Abrahams. 3rd ed. Cambridge and London: Harvard University Press.

Vana, Liliane. 2003. La Birkat ha-minim est-elle une prière contre les judéo-chrétiens? Pages 201–41 in *Les communautés religieuses dans le monde gréco-romain: Essais de définition*. Edited by Nicole Belayche and Simon C. Mimouni. Bibliothèque de l'Ecole des hautes études. Sciences religieuses 117. Turnhout: Brepols.

Veilleux, Armand. 1986. *La première Apocalypse de Jacques (NH V,3), La seconde Apocalypse de Jacques (NH V,4)*. BCNH, Section « Textes », 17. Québec: P.U.L.

——. 1986b. *Les Deux Apocalypses de Jacques.* BCNH 17. Quebec: Presses de l'Université Laval.

Veilleux, Armand and Wolf-Peter Funk. 2007. Deux Apocalypses de Jacques (NH V,3 et 4). Pages 725–76 in *Écrits gnostiques: La bibliothèque de Nag Hammadi.* Edited by Jean-Pierre Mahé and Paul-Hubert Poirier. Paris: Gallimard.

Vinel, Françoise. 2002. *La Bible d'Alexandrie. L'Ecclésiaste.* Paris: Les Éditions du Cerf.

Vliet, J. van der. 2005. Fate, magic and astrology in Pistis Sophia, chaps 15–21. Pages 519–36 in *The Wisdom of Egypt: Jewish, Early Christian and Gnostic Essays in Honour of Gerard P. Luttikhuizen.* Edited by A. Hilhorst and G.H. van Kooten. Boston: E.J. Brill.

——. 2006a. Judas and the Stars: Philological notes on the newly published Gospel of Judas (GosJud, Codex gnosticus Maghâgha 3). *Journal of Juristic Papyrology* 36: 137–52.

——. 2006b. *Het Evangelie van Judas. Verrader of Bevrijder?* Utrecht/Antwerpen: Uitgeverij Servire.

Voeltzel, R. 1961. *Das Lachen des Herrn. Über die Ironie in der Bibel.* Hamburg-Bergstedt: Herbert Reich Evangelischer Verlag.

Voorst, Robert E. Van. 2000. *Jesus outside the New Testament: An Introduction to the Ancient Evidence* Grand Rapids: Eerdmans.

Wakeman, Mary K. 1973. *God's Battle with the Monster: A Study in Biblical Imagery.* Leiden: E.J. Brill.

Waldstein, Michael and Frederik Wisse, eds. 1995. *The Apocryphon of John: Synopsis of Nag Hammadi Codices II,1; III,1; and IV,1 with BG 8502,2.* NHMS 33. Leiden, New York, Köln: E.J. Brill.

Walker, Joel Thomas and Noegel, Brannon Wheeler Scott. 2003. *Prayer, Magic and the Stars.* Pittsburg: Pennsylvania State Press.

Welburn, Andrew J. 1978. The Identity of the Archons in the Apocryphon Johannis. *VC* 32: 241–54.

Werblowsky, R.J.Z., Gershom G. Scholem, Efraim E. Urbach, and Chaim Wirszubski, eds. 1967. *Studies in Mysticism and Religion presented to Gershom G. Scholem on his Seventieth Birthday by Pupils, Colleagues, and Friends.* Jerusalem: Magnes Press.

Wessely, Carl. 1909. *Studien zur Paläographie und Papyruskunde, vol. 9.* Leipzig: Eduard Avenarius.

West, M.L. 1971. *Early Greek Philosophy and the Orient.* Oxford: Clarendon Press.

Westendorf, Wolfhart. 1965. *Koptisches Handwörterbuch.* Heidelberg.

Westerhoff, M. 1999. *Auferstehung und Jenseits im koptischen "Buch der Auferstehung Jesu Christi, unseres Herrn."* Wiesbaden: Harrassowitz.

White, L. Michael and Yarbrough, O. Larry. *The Social World of the First Christians: Essays in Honor of Wayne A. Meeks.* Minneapolis: Fortress.

Wilckens, Ulrich. 1971. Στῦλος. TDNT. Grand Rapids: Eerdmans.

Wilken, Robert L. 1984. *The Christians as the Romans Saw Them.* New Haven and London: Yale University Press.

Williams, Michael Allen. 1985. *The Immovable Race: A Gnostic Designation and the Theme of Stability in Late Antiquity.* Leiden: E.J. Brill.

——. 1996. *Rethinking "Gnosticism": An Argument for Dismantling a Dubious Category.* Princeton: Princeton University Press.

Wilmet, Michel, René Draguet, and Louis Thomas Lefort. 1950–1960. *Concordance du Nouveau Testament sahidique 5 vol.* Corpus Scriptorum Christianorum Orientalium 124, 173, 183, 185, 196. Louvain: Secrétariat du CSCO.

Wilmet, Michel. 1959. *Concordance du Nouveau Testament sahidique II. Les mots autochtones 3.* Corpus Scriptorum Christianorum Orientalium 185. Louvain: Secrétariat du CSCO.

Wilson, R. McL., ed. 1978a. *Nag Hammadi and Gnosis: Papers Read at the First International Congress of Coptology (Cairo, December 1976).* NHS 14. Leiden: E.J. Brill.

———, ed. 1978b. *The Future of Coptic Studies.* Coptic Studies 1. Leiden: E.J. Brill.

Wisse, Frederik. 1971. The Nag Hammadi Library and the Heresiologists. *VC* 25: 205–23.

———. 1978. Gnosticism and Early Monasticism in Egypt. Pages 431–40 in *Gnosis: Festschrift für Hans Jonas.* Edited by Barbara Aland et al. Göttingen: Vandenhoeck & Ruprecht.

———. 1981. Stalking Those Elusive Sethians. In *The Rediscovery of Gnosticism. Volume 2: Sethian Gnosticism.* Edited by B. Layton. Studies in the History of Religions. *Numen* Supplement 41. Leiden: E.J. Brill.

Witetschek, Stephan. 2008. Book Review of April D. DeConick, The Thirteenth Apostle. *Review of Biblical Literature* 7.

Wolfson, Elliot R. 1988. Light Through Darkness: The Ideal of Human Perfection in the Zohar. *HTR* 81: 73–95.

———. 1995. *Along the Path: Studies in Kabbalistic Myth, Symbolism, and Hermeneutics.* Albany: State University of New York Press.

———. 2005. *Language, Eros, Being: Kabbalistic Hermeneutics and Poetic Imagination.* New York: Fordham University Press.

Wouters, Alfons and James M. Robinson. 1987. Chester Beatty Accession Number 1499: A Preliminary Codicological Analysis. Pages 297–306 in *Miscellània Papirològica Ramon Roca-Puig en el seu vuitante aniversari.* Edited by Sebastia Janeras. Barcelona: Fundació Salvador Vives Casajuana.

Wright, N.T. 2006a. *Judas and the Gospel of Jesus: Have We Missed the Truth About Christianity?* Grand Rapids: Baker Books.

———. 2006b. *Judas and the Gospel of Jesus: Understanding a Newly Discovered Ancient Text and Its Contemporary Significance.* London: SPCK.

Wurst, Gregor. 2007. Preliminary Codicological Analysis of Codex Tchacos. Pages 27–33 in *The Gospel of Judas together with the Letter of Peter to Philip, James, and a Book of Allogenes from Codex Tchacos.* Edited by Kasser et al. Washington, D. C.: National Geographic.

———. 2008. Irenaeus of Lyon and the Gospel of Judas. Pages 169–79 in *The Gospel of Judas.* Edited by Kasser et al. Washington, D.C.: National Geographic.

Zoller, Robert, trans. 1988. *Hermes Trismegistus, Liber Hermetis.* Salisbury: Spica.

AUTHOR INDEX

PRIMARY SOURCES INDEX

OLD TESTAMENT

New Testament

New Testament Apocrypha including Gnostic Literature

OTHER ANCIENT SOURCES

SUBJECT INDEX

NAG HAMMADI AND MANICHAEAN STUDIES

9. Schmidt, C. (ed.). *Pistis Sophia*. Translation and notes by V. MacDermot. 1978. ISBN 90 04 05635 1

10. Fallon, F.T. *The enthronement of Sabaoth*. Jewish elements in Gnostic creation myths. 1978. ISBN 90 04 05683 1

11. Parrott, D.M. *Nag Hammadi Codices V, 2-5 and VI with Papyrus Berolinensis 8502, 1 and 4*. 1979. ISBN 90 04 05798 6

12. Koschorke, K. *Die Polemik der Gnostiker gegen das kirchliche Christentum*. Unter besonderer Berücksichtigung der Nag Hammadi-Traktate 'Apokalypse des Petrus' (NHC VII, 3) und 'Testimonium Veritatis' (NHC IX, 3). 1978. ISBN 90 04 05709 9

13. Schmidt, C. (ed.). *The Books of Jeu and the untitled text in the Bruce Codex*. Translation and notes by V. MacDermot. 1978. ISBN 90 04 05754 4

14. McL. Wilson, R. (ed.). *Nag Hammadi and Gnosis*. Papers read at the First International Congress of Coptology (Cairo, December 1976). 1978. ISBN 90 04 05760 9

15. Pearson, B.A. (ed.). *Nag Hammadi Codices IX and X*. 1981. ISBN 90 04 06377 3

16. Barns, J.W.B., G.M. Browne, & J.C. Shelton, (eds.). *Nag Hammadi Codices*. Greek and Coptic papyri from the cartonnage of the covers. 1981. ISBN 90 04 06277 7

17. Krause, M. (ed.). *Gnosis and Gnosticism*. Papers read at the Eighth International Conference on Patristic Studies. Oxford, September 3rd-8th, 1979. 1981. ISBN 90 04 06399 4

18. Helderman, J. *Die Anapausis im Evangelium Veritatis*. Eine vergleichende Untersuchung des valentinianisch-gnostischen Heilsgutes der Ruhe im Evangelium Veritatis und in anderen Schriften der Nag-Hammadi Bibliothek. 1984. ISBN 90 04 07260 8

19. Frickel, J. *Hellenistische Erlösung in christlicher Deutung*. Die gnostische Naassenerschrift. Quellen, kritische Studien, Strukturanalyse, Schichtenscheidung, Rekonstruktion der Anthropos-Lehrschrift. 1984. ISBN 90 04 07227 6

20-21. Layton, B. (ed.). *Nag Hammadi Codex II, 2-7, together with XIII, 2* Brit. Lib. Or. 4926(1) and P. Oxy. 1, 654, 655*. I. Gospel according to Thomas, Gospel according to Philip, Hypostasis of the Archons, Indexes. II. On the origin of the world, Expository treatise on the Soul, Book of Thomas the Contender. 1989. 2 volumes. ISBN 90 04 09019 3

22. Attridge, H.W. (ed.). *Nag Hammadi Codex I* (The Jung Codex). I. Introductions, texts, translations, indices. 1985. ISBN 90 04 07677 8

23. Attridge, H.W. (ed.). *Nag Hammadi Codex I* (The Jung Codex). II. Notes. 1985. ISBN 90 04 07678 6

24. Stroumsa, G.A.G. *Another seed. Studies in Gnostic mythology*. 1984. ISBN 90 04 07419 8

25. Scopello, M. *L'exégèse de l'âme*. Nag Hammadi Codex II, 6. Introduction, traduction et commentaire. 1985. ISBN 90 04 07469 4

26. Emmel, S. (ed.). *Nag Hammadi Codex III, 5*. The Dialogue of the Savior. 1984. ISBN 90 04 07558 5

27. Parrott, D.M. (ed.) *Nag Hammadi Codices III, 3-4 and V, 1 with Papyrus Berolinensis 8502,3 and Oxyrhynchus Papyrus 1081*. Eugnostos and the Sophia of Jesus Christ. 1991. ISBN 90 04 08366 9

28. Hedrick, C.W. (ed.). *Nag Hammadi Codices XI, XII, XIII*. 1990. ISBN 90 04 07825 8

29. Williams, M.A. *The immovable race.* A gnostic designation and the theme of stability in Late Antiquity. 1985. ISBN 90 04 07597 6

30. Pearson, B.A. (ed.). *Nag Hammadi Codex VII*. 1996. ISBN 90 04 10451 8

31. Sieber, J.H. (ed.). *Nag Hammadi Codex VIII*. 1991. ISBN 90 04 09477 6

32. Scholer, D.M. *Nag Hammadi Bibliography 1970-1994*. 1997. ISBN 90 04 09473 3

33. Wisse, F. & M. Waldstein, (eds.). *The Apocryphon of John.* Synopsis of Nag Hammadi Codices II,1; III,1; and IV,1 with BG 8502,2. 1995. ISBN 90 04 10395 3

34. Lelyveld, M. *Les logia de la vie dans l'Evangile selon Thomas.* A la recherche d'une tradition et d'une rédaction. 1988. ISBN 90 04 07610 7

35. Williams, F. (Tr.). *The Panarion of Epiphanius of Salamis.* Book I (Sects 1-46). 1987. Reprint 1997. ISBN 90 04 07926 2

36. Williams, F. (Tr.). *The Panarion of Epiphanius of Salamis.* Books II and III (Sects 47-80, *De Fide*). 1994. ISBN 90 04 09898 4

37. Gardner, I. *The Kephalaia of the Teacher.* The Edited Coptic Manichaean Texts in Translation with Commentary. 1995. ISBN 90 04 10248 5

38. Turner, M.L. *The Gospel according to Philip.* The Sources and Coherence of an Early Christian Collection. 1996. ISBN 90 04 10443 7

39. van den Broek, R. *Studies in Gnosticism and Alexandrian Christianity*. 1996. ISBN 90 04 10654 5

40. Marjanen, A. *The Woman Jesus Loved.* Mary Magdalene in the Nag Hammadi Library and Related Documents. 1996. ISBN 90 04 10658 8

41. Reeves, J.C. *Heralds of that Good Realm.* Syro-Mesopotamian Gnosis and Jewish Traditions. 1996. ISBN 90 04 10459 3

42. Rudolph, K. *Gnosis & spätantike Religionsgeschichte.* Gesammelte Aufsätze. 1996. ISBN 90 04 10625 1

43. Mirecki, P. & J. BeDuhn, (eds.). *Emerging from Darkness.* Studies in the Recovery of Manichaean Sources. 1997. ISBN 90 04 10760 6

44. Turner, J.D. & A. McGuire, (eds.). *The Nag Hammadi Library after Fifty Years.* Proceedings of the 1995 Society of Biblical Literature Commemoration. 1997. ISBN 90 04 10824 6

45. Lieu, S.N.C. *Manichaeism in Central Asia and China*. 1998. ISBN 90 04 10405 4

46. Heuser, M & H.-J. Klimkeit. *Studies in Manichaean Literature and Art*. 1998. ISBN 90 04 10716 9

47. Zöckler, T. *Jesu Lehren im Thomasevangelium*. 1999. ISBN 90 04 11445 9

48. Petersen, S. *"Zerstört die Werke der Weiblichkeit!".* Maria Magdalena, Salome und andere Jüngerinnen Jesu in christlich-gnostischen Schriften. 1999. ISBN 90 04 11449 1

49. Van Oort, J., O. Wermelinger & G. Wurst (eds.). *Augustine and Manichaeism in the Latin West.* Proceedings of the Fribourg-Utrecht International Symposium of the IAMS. 2001. ISBN 90 04 11423 8

50. Mirecki, P. & J. BeDuhn (eds.). *The Light and the Darkness.* Studies in Manichaeism and its World. 2001. ISBN 90 04 11673 7

51. Williams, F.E. *Mental Perception*. A Commentary on NHC, VI,4: The Concept of Our Great Power. 2001. ISBN 90 04 11692 3

52. Pleše, Z. *Poetics of the Gnostic Universe*. Narrative and Cosmology in the *Apocryphon of John*. 2006. ISBN 90 04 11674 5

53. Scopello, M. *Femme, Gnose et manichéisme*. De l'espace mythique au territoire du réel. 2005. ISBN 90 04 11452 1

54. Bethge, H., S. Emmel, K.L. King, & I. Schletterer (eds.). *For the Children, Perfect Instruction*. Studies in Honor of Hans-Martin Schenke on the Occasion of the Berliner Arbeitskreis für koptisch-gnostische Schriften's Thirtieth Year. 2002. ISBN 90 04 12672 4

55. Van Oort, J. (ed.). *Gnostica, Judaica, Catholica. Collected Essays of Gilles Quispel*. With additional Prefaces by A. DeConick & J.-P. Mahé. 2008. ISBN 978 90 04 13945 9

56. Pedersen, N., *Demonstrative Proof in Defence of God*. A Study of Titus of Bostra's *Contra Manichaeos* – The Work's Sources, Aims and Relation to its Contemporary Theology. 2004. ISBN 90 04 13883 8

57. Gulácsi, Z. *Mediaeval Manichaean Book Art*. A Codicological Study of Iranian and Turkic Illuminated Book Fragments from 8th-11th Century East Central Asia. 2005. ISBN 90 04 13994 X

58. Luttikhuizen, G.P. *Gnostic Revisions of Genesis Stories and Early Jesus Traditions*. 2005. ISBN 90 04 14510 9

59. Asgeirsson, J.M., A.D. DeConick & R. Uro (eds.). *Thomasine Traditions in Antiquity*. The Social and Cultural World of the Gospel of Thomas. 2006. ISBN 90 04 14779 9

60. Thomassen, E., *The Spiritual Seed – The Church of the 'Valentinians'*. 2006. ISBN 90 04 14802 7

61. BeDuhn, J. & P. Mirecki (eds.). *Frontiers of Faith*. The Christian Encounter with Manichaeism in the Acts of Archelaus. 2007. ISBN 978 90 04 16180 1

62. Scopello, M. (ed.). *The Gospel of Judas in Context*. Proceedings of the First International Conference on the Gospel of Judas *Paris, Sorbonne, October 27th-28th, 2006*. 2008. ISBN 978 90 04 16721 6

63. Williams, F. (tr.). *The* Panarion *of Epiphanius of Salamis: Book I.* (Sects 1-46) Second Edition, Revised and Expanded. 2009. ISBN 978 90 04 17017 9

64. BeDuhn, J.D. (ed.). *New Light on Manichaeism*. Papers from the Sixth International Congress on Manichaeism. 2009. ISBN 978 90 04 17285 2

65. Scholer, D.M. *Nag Hammadi Bibliography 1995-2006*. 2009. ISBN 978 90 04 17240 1

66. Pettipiece, T. *Pentadic Redaction in the Manichaean Kephalaia*. 2009. ISBN 978 90 04 17436 8

67. Tite, P.L. *Valentinian Ethics and Paraenetic Discourse*. Determining the Social Function of Moral Exhortation in Valentinian Christianity. 2009. ISBN 978 90 04 17507 5

68. Rasimus, T. *Paradise Reconsidered in Gnostic Mythmaking*. Rethinking Sethianism in Light of the Ophite Evidence. 2009. ISBN 978 90 04 17323 1

69. Coyle, J.K. *Manichaeism and Its Legacy*. 2009. ISBN 978 90 04 17574 7

70. Van den Berg, J.A. *Biblical Argument in Manichaean Missionary Practice*. The Case of Adimantus and Augustine. 2009. ISBN 978 90 04 18034 5

71. DeConick, A.D. (ed.). *The Codex Judas Papers*. Proceedings of the International Congress on the Tchacos Codex Held at Rice University, Houston Texas, March 13-16, 2008. 2009. ISBN 978 90 04 18141 0